# THE SIEGE OF DELHI

# THE SIEGE OF DELHI

AMARPAL SINGH

AMBERLEY

First published 2021

Amberley Publishing
The Hill, Stroud
Gloucestershire, GL5 4EP

www.amberley-books.com



British Library Cataloguing in Publication Data.
A catalogue record for this book is available from the British Library.

ISBN 978 1 4456 8235 8 (hardback)
ISBN 978 1 4456 8236 5 (ebook)

Typeset in 10.5pt on 12.5pt Sabon.
Typesetting by Aura Technology and Software Services, India.
Printed in the UK.

# Contents

# List of Maps

# Chronology

| | |
|---|---|
| **1600** | Formation of East India Company (EIC). Charter granted by Queen Elizabeth I gives the EIC a monopoly on undertaking trading expeditions to the East Indies |
| **1611** | Mughal Emperor Jahangir agrees to allow EIC to set up factories at Surat, Ahmedabad, Cambay and Gogo |
| **1634** | Mughal Emperor Shah Jahan invites EIC to set up trading posts in Bengal |
| **1682** | EIC fails to obtain trading rights throughout the Mughal Empire |
| **1690** | EIC establishes a trading post in the Calcutta region of India |
| **1696** | Construction of Fort William at Calcutta begins |
| **1707** | Death of Emperor Aurangzeb and the beginning of the decline of the Mughal Empire |
| **1739** | Delhi is sacked by the Persian Nadir Shah |
| **1757** | Battle of Plassey takes place, establishing EIC's control over the province of Bengal |
| **1760** | Shah Alam II ascends to Mughal throne |
| **1764** | Battle of Buxar; EIC forces defeat Shah Alam's forces |
| **1765** | Shah Alam II cedes right of revenue collection in Bengal to the EIC |
| **1767** | First Anglo-Mysore war between the EIC and Hyder Ali |
| **1775** | Birth of Bahadur Shah Zafar |
| **1799** | Death of Tipu Sultan, King of Mysore, at Battle of Seringapatam |
| **1803** | Delhi falls to EIC in Second Anglo-Maratha War. Shah Alam II becomes a pensioner of the Company |
| **1806** | Death of Shah Alam II. Reign of Akbar Shah II begins |

| | |
|---|---|
| **1837** | |
| 20 Jun. | Reign of Queen Victoria begins |
| 28 Sep. | Death of Akbar Shah II. Reign of Bahadur Shah Zafar begins |
| **1849** | |
| 2 Apr. | Punjab annexed by EIC |
| **1855** | |
| Feb. | Sidi Kambar embassy sent by Zafar from Delhi to Persia to discuss a possible compact with the Persians against the British |
| **1856** | |
| 7 Feb. | State of Oudh annexed by EIC |
| 10 Jul. | Crown Prince Fakir-ud-Din dies |
| **1857** | |
| Early Jan. | Rumours about the grease used for the new Enfield rifle cartridge begin circulating at the Dum Dum musketry depot near Calcutta |
| 26 Feb. | Sepoys of the 19th NI stationed at Berhampore refuse to use the new cartridges issued despite assurances that the cartridges are un-greased |
| 29 Mar. | Sepoy Mangal Pandey of the 34th NI wounds two British officers at Barrackpore |
| 31 Mar. | 19th NI is disbanded for its mutinous behaviour at Barrackpore on 26 Feb. |
| 6 Apr. | Mangal Pandey is court-martialled at Barrackpore |
| **8 Apr.** | **Mangal Pandey is hanged** |
| 22 Apr. | Jemadar Ishwari Parsad hanged |
| 23 Apr. | Major Carmichael Smyth, Commandant of the 3rd Native Light Cavalry at Meerut, orders a parade to be held the next day |
| 24 Apr. | Eighty-five troopers of 3rd Bengal Light Cavalry at Meerut refuse to use the new cartridges |
| 25 Apr. | Court of enquiry into refusal of troopers to follow orders |
| **2 May** | 48th NI mutiny at Lucknow; incidents of arson at Ambala cantonment |
| 6 May | Sections of the 34th NI disbanded |
| 8 May | Courts-martial of the eighty-five men of the 3rd Light Cavalry |

| | |
|---|---|
| 9 May | Parade ordered in the European sector of the cantonments of the whole garrison, European and native, for the morning of 10 May |
| 10 May | Mutiny breaks out at Meerut; sepoys head towards Delhi the same day |
| 11 May | Mutinous sepoys reach Delhi and begin massacring Europeans and Indian Christians |
| 13 May | News of Meerut and Delhi reaches Commander-in-Chief at Simla; Zafar declared Emperor at Delhi |
| 16 May | Massacre of European and Christian prisoners in the palace at Delhi |
| 17 May | Collected Delhi Field Force under C-in-C General George Anson departs Ambala and reaches Karnal |
| 25 May | General Anson joins force at Karnal |
| 27 May | Troops leave Meerut to join Delhi Field Force |
| 27 May | General Anson dies of cholera at Karnal and is replaced by General Barnard |
| **30 May** | **BATTLE OF HINDUN RIVER** |
| **31 May** | **SECOND ACTION AT HINDUN RIVER** |
| 31 May | Bareilly mutiny; Bakht Khan is chosen as the commander by the mutineers |
| | |
| 2 Jun. | Advance British force reaches Rai (two marches from Delhi) |
| 4 Jun. | Main force reaches Rai |
| 5 Jun. | Main force reaches Alipur |
| 7 Jun. | Meerut force (under Brigadier General Wilson) marching via Baghpat joins main British force at Alipur |
| **8 Jun.** | **BATTLE AT BADLI-KI-SERAI** |
| 23 Jun. | Anniversary of the Battle of Plassey; large-scale fighting |
| | |
| 2 Jul. | Bakht Khan leads Bareilly brigade into Delhi |
| 3 Jul. | New chief engineer Lieutenant-Colonel Baird Smith arrives at the Delhi ridge |
| 5 Jul. | General Sir Henry Barnard dies of cholera; General Reed takes over as commanding officer |
| 17 Jul. | General Reed resigns and General Archdale Wilson takes over as commanding officer |
| 31 Jul. | Lord Canning declares clemency for any mutineers not convicted of murder |
| | |
| 1 Aug. | Muslim festival of Eid al-Adha |
| 14 Aug. | Brigadier General John Nicholson arrives at Delhi with reinforcements |

| | |
|---|---|
| 17 Aug. | Contest with rebels at Rohtak; rebels defeated by Capt. William Hodson |
| 18 Aug. | British siege train leaves Ferozepore |
| 25 Aug. | **BATTLE OF NAJAFGARH** |
| 4 Sep. | British siege train arrives at Delhi |
| **14 Sep.** | **BRITISH ASSAULT ON THE CITY BEGINS** |
| 14 Sep. | Brig. Gen. John Nicholson wounded in fighting in the city |
| 16 Sep. | Attack on the magazine |
| 20 Sep. | End of hostilities in Delhi |
| 21 Sep. | Capt. Hodson apprehends Zafar at the Mausoleum of Humayun |
| 22 Sep. | Hodson executes several unarmed Mughal princes |
| 23 Sep. | Death of Brig. Gen. John Nicholson |

**1858**

| | |
|---|---|
| 27 Jan. | Trial of Zafar begins, continues for twenty-one days |
| 9 Mar. | Zafar found guilty of rebellion, treason and murder |
| 2 Aug. | Transfer of administration of India from EIC to the Crown and effective end of EIC |
| Oct. | Zafar, Zeenat Mahal and Prince Jawan Bakht depart Delhi for exile in Rangoon, Burma |
| 1 Nov. | Royal proclamation declaring the replacement of the EIC with direct British government |

**1862**

| | |
|---|---|
| 7 Nov. | Zafar dies in Rangoon aged eighty-seven |

... the Almighty Disposer of Events, though apparently determined to humble, had not resolved to destroy us. Many thoughtful and experienced men now in India believe that it has only been by a series of miracles that we have been saved from utter ruin. It is no exaggeration to affirm that in many instances the mutineers seemed to act as if a curse rested on their cause. Had a single leader of ability arisen among them, nay had they followed any other course than that they did pursue in many instances, we must have been lost beyond redemption.[1]

John Lawrence, Commissioner of the Punjab,
21 April 1858 (later Viceroy, 1864–69)

PROLOGUE

# The New Musket

The Enfield Pattern 1853 rifle-musket (P1853) was a fine weapon. The single-shot, muzzle-loading, percussion-lock firearm with a rifled bore didn't look particularly different from the earlier smoothbore musket (P1842) it was replacing in the armies of the East India Company. The difference in performance, however, was revolutionary, and the advantages of the new Enfield rifle quickly became obvious. The old musket had an effective range of not much more than 100 yards, with a maximum range around double that distance. The new rifle, in contrast, had a range of 600 to 900 yards. Being rifled, the Enfield was inherently much more accurate. The weapon was more deadly, too. Its conical Minié ball ammunition had a higher velocity and mass, sufficient to shatter bone, unlike the round ball. It quickly became apparent that a cavalry charge against infantry manned with this new weapon would be an almost hopeless endeavour. The old tactic of forming hollow squares would become redundant as cavalry could be despatched with ease thanks to the firepower of this new rifle. The user of the new weapon naturally held a huge advantage over a rival handling an older musket.

In India, manufacture of the new cartridge for the rifle was commenced at Fort William, Calcutta, in August 1856, with quantities of the new rifle arriving in the country the same month. The cartridge used was essentially a paper container greased on the outside and which on the inside held both powder and the lead projectile. The grease acted as lubricant, allowing the bullet, still encased in the paper, to be pushed down the barrel when loading. A local Indian firm, Gangadarh Banerji & Co., was employed for the supply of tallow for the manufacture of the grease. Musketry schools were opened to teach the huge sepoy army employed by the British East India Company how to use it. Instruction was necessary, as the method of firing the weapon was different from previous muskets. The soldier was required to tear the top of the greased paper cartridge holding the gunpowder and Minié ball. The simplest and most convenient method found to accomplish this was for the soldier to bite the top of the cartridge with his teeth. The gunpowder inside the cartridge was then poured down the gun barrel, after which the Minié ball (still encased in the greased paper cartridge) was pushed in. The soldier would then ram the ball down the barrel using the ramrod held in the rifle's stock under the barrel. This done, the soldier would then place the rifle's hammer on half cock. A percussion cap was then placed on the Coen, or nipple, under the hammer. The hammer was pulled back to fullback, the rifle aimed at the target and then fired. The procedure was then repeated for subsequent firing.

Very soon after the Enfield Pattern 1853 arrived in India in January 1857, rumours began circulating. The weapon itself didn't worry the sepoys of the Bengal Army; neither did the ammunition, nor the paper. Rather it was the grease on the paper that caused consternation. News had spread that the grease was composed of a mixture of cow and pig fat. While the use of these fats may have been accepted, albeit reluctantly, the firing procedure which had been developed, with the soldier utilising his teeth to tear the cartridge open, meant some grease, albeit a nominal amount, would inevitably have contact with or enter the mouth. The consumption of pig was pure anathema to the Muslim, for the pig was seen as an unclean animal. Similarly, but for entirely different reasons, the consumption of cow was offensive to the Hindu and would mean an instant loss for caste – and most of the Hindu sepoys in the Bengal Army happened to be of high caste. The imminent introduction of the new weapon therefore created a considerable predicament for both Muslim and Hindu sepoys. They were faced with a choice. They could champion their faith and refuse to use the new cartridge, or they could follow the orders of the European officers and lose their caste and religion, becoming *persona non grata* to their family, friends, home towns and wider society.

Many speculated in hindsight that it was impossible to imagine something more provocative than the introduction of a cartridge greased with cow and pig fat; indeed, this had the power to unite Muslims and Hindus and trigger the mutiny of almost the entire Bengal Army of the East India Company in one swoop. Hinduism was a belief indigenous to India. Islam, originating in the Middle East, was of a quite different nature, philosophy and cultural orientation. A natural divide therefore prevailed between the two communities. However, with the issue of the cartridge grease being uppermost in their minds during the early months of 1857, Muslim and Hindu sepoys developed an unexpected fraternity. This would lead to what the judge advocate general, on 9 March 1858 at the trial of the last Mughal Emperor, called 'a revolt unparalleled in the annals of history, either for the savagery which has been its distinctive feature, or for the suddenness with which elements, hitherto deemed utterly discordant on the score of religion, have united themselves in a common crusade'.[1] What had begun as a complaint against ammunition of dubious manufacture had quickly evolved into an immediate and existential crisis for both the British East India Company and for Bahadur Shah Zafar, the last representative of the Timurid dynasty, who still happened to occupy the fading Mughal throne in Delhi.

# Preface

> Brethren! your King and all of us are night and day labouring for the annihilation of a small body of Christians, those infidels having from fear of their lives entrenched themselves on the top of a hill which is neither practicable for Cavalry nor assailable by the Artillery. God willing, in a short time the plain of Delhi will be cleared of the existence of these impure Nazarenes.[1]
>
> Bakht Khan, Commander-in-Chief to officers of the Neemuch brigade

Easily the most noticeable natural landmark near the old walled city of Delhi during the nineteenth century was what was termed the 'Delhi ridge' to the north of the city. This was a rocky outcrop around 2 miles long with a width of little more than half a mile and with a height of perhaps 80 to 90 feet. Around 1,500 million years ago, the Indian continental tectonic plate, floating free, had drifted by small degrees northwards and collided gently with what was termed the Eurasian plate. This slow union over the eons, with the Indian plate continuing to push north, caused a series of folds in the earth all along the collision points running from Gujarat in the south-west through Rajasthan and on to Delhi, a distance of 400 miles. A combination of these tectonic movements along with subsequent volcanic lava flows for many millions of years produced a range that is said to have thrust higher than the Himalayas of today.

As these collisions grew less frequent, the erosion of wind and rain took its toll. By modern times, the ageing mountain range, one of the oldest in the world, was much reduced. The rocky outcrop of the Delhi ridge happened to be the last hurrah of this line of folds in the earth – which became known as the Aravalli range – before it petered out entirely. Made of hard, semi-crystalline quartz rock settled in layers, erosion had meant that, on the city side at least, the ridge bore many vertical drops that made it difficult to climb except in certain places.

During the nineteenth century, the top of the ridge was a largely barren place, lightly covered with low-lying scrub. However, it formed an excellent vantage point for viewing the city. From its top, everything could easily be surveyed: the city walls, the palace, the tall minarets of the Jama Masjid and the general lay of the city, as well as the Jumna River and the road from the nearby city of Meerut on its left bank. Similarly, the road south from the Punjab and Ambala to Delhi passed by the ridge. The area of the ridge also formed a strong defensive position for any army seeking to attack the city: the rough side of the ridge faced eastwards, while to the north and further west ran a large and deep canal. Any army occupying the western slope of the ridge was very well protected on three sides.

This strategic position adjacent to the city was given away cheaply by the large but leaderless army of mutineers which had congregated at Delhi in the wake of the outbreak of mutiny at Meerut on 10 May 1857. The rebels had allowed the advancing British Delhi Field Force, sent to recapture Delhi, to take the ridge and dig in well. The strength of the position was soon recognised by both sides. The very survival of the British force, much smaller than the rebel army and without sufficient heavy guns, would depend entirely on the safety the ridge offered until sufficient reinforcements could arrive and an assault on the city could be launched.

What was termed the 'Siege of Delhi' was never a siege in the conventional sense. For large stretches of the conflict, the British force found itself in real terms to be more besieged than the rebels in the city. During the months of June, July, August and September of 1857, the issue of whether the British East India Company could retain its Indian empire in the face of the large congeries of its own mutinous sepoys largely hinged on the ownership of the ridge. It was clear that if the force was beaten back from this position there would be a British collapse all across North India. All eyes were on Delhi.

I first visited Delhi at the age of twelve with my father. However, like most tourists, our visit didn't include the defensive walls of the old city, which took a considerable battering from British guns during the hostilities. Nor, in fact, did we visit the ridge outside the city. My father and I visited the Red Fort (or palace), walked the Chandni Chowk (the commercial centre of the walled city) and visited the Jama Masjid along with several other compulsory stops on the tourist trail. Even then, what impressed me most were the walls of the fort and the barbican one passed through to reach the arcaded entrance. Little of the palace complex inside the walls of the fort remains now; much of the interior was razed by the British authorities after the rebellion in order to make way for barracks for a British garrison. This act, destroying a palace built by Emperor Shah Jahan at the height of the Mughal Empire, has subsequently been considered a travesty only paralleled by the burning of the Summer Palace in Peking by British troops a few years later in 1860 during the Second Opium War.

So little of the palace remains that it is difficult to imagine the crowded city-within-a-city of history. What little survives is poorly maintained, and the interior of the place has a somewhat sad atmosphere to this day. Perhaps, though, the palace in its present shape better represents the final years of the Mughal dynasty before the events of 1857. An unsympathetic renovation by insufficiently skilled workers – always a danger in India – might rob it of its last vestiges of faded originality.

Far more atmospheric on my subsequent visits to Delhi were the still extant walls of the old city, which seem to attract far fewer visitors. The remaining sections on the north, to the south and on the river side of the city make the siege of 1857 come alive again in a way that the palace does not. I found this to be particularly true when walking along the busy Nicholson Road adjacent to the walls of the old city in the north, or when visiting the Kashmir Gate nearby. These places are immensely instructive to the visitor interested in the mutiny, and certainly gave me the impetus to write this book several years ago.

The story of the mutiny and how the East India Company almost lost its empire in India during the summer of 1857 is one of the great cautionary tales in history. Almost all the sepoy regiments in the Bengal Army either mutinied or had ambitions to do so. The arrival of the new-fangled telegraph system, laid just a few years prior to the outbreak of the mutiny, meant many of the sepoy regiments, particularly in nearby Punjab, were pre-emptively disarmed by their British officers before they could rise up. It was almost certainly this technological advantage that saved the European regiments from sure defeat and allowed the British commander-in-chief, General Anson, to prepare a force to attack Delhi. Consequently, there have been a huge number of books published on the mutiny and the close-run nature of the affair. In the aftermath of the mutiny, numerous accounts were written by historians, soldiers, civilians and administrators alike in an attempt to pinpoint the reasons for the conflict and just how the empire was eventually retained. This flood of books on the subject did not cease for the next ninety years, and continued after India achieved its independence in 1947. The story of the mutiny is therefore perhaps one of the most well-known and well-understood periods of Anglo-Indian history.

Central to any narrative of the mutiny remains the story of Delhi – the capture of the old imperial Mughal capital, and the remarkable tug-of-war between the mutineers and the British forces during the summer months of 1857 – although the mutiny would only be fully suppressed nearly a year after the fall of Delhi.

I'm sure anyone wishing to write about the mutiny soon realises, as I certainly did, what a difficult proposition it really is. The subject is vast, with simultaneous uprisings taking place against the British over a huge area from Bengal in the far east of the country to Peshawar and the borders of Afghanistan. Many mutinies in the various cantonments up and down the country, as well as the more well-known chapters like the sieges of Lucknow and Cawnpore, can be seen as almost separate stories, deserving of books devoted to them alone. Writing on the mutiny as a whole while keeping a book to a reasonable size means only a certain level of attention can be given to each episode. It's not surprising, then, that there are few modern books that deal with the three-month siege of Delhi in the depth and detail that perhaps many readers would like. To provide such a book was my goal in writing this, and I therefore purposefully limited my ambition to covering the siege along with the various associated uprisings in the cantonments of Punjab, Meerut, Bareilly and other cities whence the army of mutineers at Delhi trekked. However, even this proved too much to cover in one book. The story of the various mutinies – both successful and unsuccessful – in the many cantonments in Punjab, for example, warrants its own work. After much deliberation, I made the decision to restrict my work in the main to the conflict at Delhi.

There is often a certain level of prejudice and bigotry evident in the opinions of people of bygone ages, and the Victorian age was no different. Indeed, it was perhaps more tainted than other periods of history. For Europeans, this was the age when their cultural and religious superiority seemed axiomatic; what else could account for such a disparity in achievement with the rest of the world since the Renaissance? There was an unbreakable sense of superiority in mind, body, discipline and civilisation. Victorian Europeans had a strong Christian zeal, and Indians were invariably seen as poor benighted heathens if Hindus or fanatical followers of the false prophet if Muslim. Much of the language used therefore had the religious tilt expected of Victorian times. Viceroy John Lawrence, for instance, saw the mutiny as a fight against barbarism – of Christianity fighting against darkness and heathenism. I have tried not to sanitise the language used by people of that time as I am sure the reader understands these voices come from a different age. Retaining the language gives the reader a better, more authentic perspective of the time. For the mutiny was not only a temporal struggle for empire but also, in many senses, a religious war.

In this book I generally use the modern spellings for place names, although if it may lead to confusion then I use the nineteenth-century version. When necessary I keep names of places as they are found in original manuscripts and documents. Europeans in mid-nineteenth-century India generally spelt place names in any number of ways with no consensus apparent. For example, the reader may find the modern spelling 'Delhi' being used as well as 'Delhy', 'Dehlee' or 'Delhee' in the narrative. 'Ambala' may be spelt 'Amballa', 'Ambalah', 'Umbalah',

'Umbalaah' and so on. The reader may also find I use the terms emperor and king interchangeably when referring to Bahadur Shah Zafar, the last Mughal Emperor. Zafar and his father before him had officially been titled Padishah (or Emperor), but during Zafar's time the British authorities, determined to bring the dynasty to an end, reduced his official title to 'King of Delhi', thus destroying the mystique and role of the Mughal Emperor. The term 'king' was increasingly used in light of this, although many European civilians continued to address him as 'Emperor' as well as 'King', the habits of two centuries being difficult to efface. Zafar's successor, it was planned, would simply be allowed to use the title of prince and would not be known as 'King of Delhi'. I always find the word 'native' rather impersonal and somewhat derogatory. In any case, in 1885 the word 'native' was dropped in its usage relating to the Indian regiments. In this book I attempt to use the term Indian rather than 'native', hoping this presents a more modern aspect to the insurrection than books of an earlier age.

This book, as with my previous works, could not have been possible without the patience and encouragement of Mandeep, my extremely tolerant life partner, and my two sons, Harmeet and Jaspal, who have been with me throughout and who have proved to be a constant source of support and inspiration.

# Introduction

> ... a great killing – done slowly.
> 'The Lost Legion', Rudyard Kipling, 1892

In 1892, *The Strand Magazine* in its May edition published a short ghost story by Rudyard Kipling called 'The Lost Legion'. The tale, it was said, was based on the fate of the 55th Native Infantry during the Great Mutiny of 1857. This regiment of the Bengal Army, like many others, had rebelled against the British power at the time. Fortune was never with them. They were pursued by a force under Brigadier General Nicholson into the mountains north of the vale of Peshawar and close to the border with Afghanistan. There, in wild and inhospitable terrain, the tribesmen 'turned against [the regiment] as wolves turn against buck. It was hunted for the sake of its arms and accoutrements from hill to hill, from ravine to ravine, up and down the dried beds of rivers and round the shoulders of bluffs, till it disappeared as water sinks in the sand – this officerless, rebel regiment.'

The massacre would stay in the minds of the tribesmen of the area, Kipling wrote. They would, in later years, narrate how these sepoys had tried to persuade the tribesmen to join them in expelling the British from the country. Now was the time to kill the English, they said, and now was the time to head south for Delhi. The tribesmen, difficult to beat in their mountain fastnesses, baulked at fighting on the plains of India. In any case, they had contempt for the sepoys, privately calling them 'down-country dogs'. Instead the tribesmen would trick the sepoys into keeping their ground while they demurred, ostensibly considering the offer; in fact, they had alerted the British authorities to the whereabouts of the regiment. When the sepoys heard a British force was approaching in pursuit they realised they had been deceived and headed deeper into the mountains. However, the tribesmen had planned an ambush and as the sepoys moved further down the passes they were assailed on all sides by the tribesmen.

'That was a great killing – done slowly,' one of the perpetrators of the massacre, now an old man, related in Kipling's story. 'Yes, we killed them because we needed their gear, and we knew that their lives had been forfeited to God on account of their sin – the sin of treachery to the salt which they had eaten. They rode up and down the valleys, stumbling and rocking in their saddles, and howling for mercy. We drove them slowly like cattle till they were all assembled in one place, the flat wide valley of Sheor Kôt. Many had died from want of water, but there still were many left, and they could not make any stand. We went among them, pulling them down with our hands two at a time, and our boys killed them who were new to the sword.'

In Kipling's tale, the ghosts of the men still haunted the valley. Thirty years later, a British column planning to attack a body of local tribesmen and moving through the same valley found itself stumbling through a graveyard of cairns – they had reached the site of the massacre. The men could hear the sound of hooves moving over stony ground and the whispers of their riders behind and around them – sounds neither emanating from their own column or the tribesmen in the distance.

Whether by accident or design, Kipling's tale of the luckless sepoys and in fact the real story of the 55th Native Infantry encompassed much of what went wrong with the Mutiny of 1857 at Peshawar, in the Punjab, in India as a whole and particularly at Delhi, the epicentre of the rebellion. Lacking a guiding mind, sufficient planning, necessary discipline and often the sympathy of the local population, the mutineers who initially held the advantage of surprise and numbers fell prey to British organisation and vigour aroused by the realisation that decisive action was required to retrieve the empire from an existential threat.

When the mutiny first broke, the odds faced by the British Government seemed insuperable – at least on paper. The sepoys of the Bengal Army, trained by British officers and with access to ammunition and guns, far outnumbered the European regiments in North India and elsewhere. Tiny collections of European bureaucrats along with solitary European regiments found themselves stranded in various locations up and down the country. Only three European regiments could be found stationed between Calcutta and Delhi – a distance of some 1,000 miles in one of the most densely populated areas of the world. Of the three great British arsenals in North India, Delhi and Phillaur were entirely in the hands of the sepoys, there being no European troops present (excepting a few officers). Only at the Ferozepore magazine were there European soldiers present, albeit outnumbered by sepoys stationed nearby. The sepoys could easily have overwhelmed the few European troops and civilians scattered about across North India while at the same time denying them access to their own ammunition and guns. Further serious problems could be expected to arise at the distant outposts of British control.

All along the porous and unstable 1,500-mile border with Afghanistan, from the mountains west of Kashmir to the shores of the Indus Ocean in Baluchistan, were Muslim tribesmen ready to cast off British authority and declare Jihad and independence. Amid the mutiny of the sepoys, the frontier could surely be expected to erupt. To the north of the Punjab sat the ruler of Kashmir, Gulab Singh, who had never been trusted by the British Government. 'No one would have been astonished at Golab Singh doing anything base or treacherous. He might even have used his name, deeply tarnished as it was, to raise the old Sikh war-cry down the five rivers. Our whole Peshawur frontier was hemmed in by those untameable hill-tribes, with whom we were almost constantly at war,'[1] mused Revd John Cave-Browne, the chaplain stationed at Nowshera, Peshawar, who would accompany John Nicholson's Moveable Column around the Punjab throughout the mutiny. Further to the west, in Kabul, sat the old enemy of the British, Dost Mohammad. Some would attribute his neutrality during the mutiny to recent treaties with the British Government of India and the closer relations these agreements generated. However, at the time there was little confidence that Dost Mohammad would not take advantage of the chaos in India. Beyond Afghanistan, the Persians were still smarting from their defeat at British hands in the recent Anglo-Persian War (1856–57). Meanwhile, the Russians harboured designs on Central Asia and possibly even India during the intense rivalry with Britain over influence in the area termed the 'Great Game' in the nineteenth century.

Even assuming no additional problems appeared, General Anson, recuperating from illness in Simla at the outbreak of the mutiny, faced difficult issues in assembling a strong enough force to retake Delhi without denuding other areas of the few European troops available. It also wasn't clear if Delhi could be safely approached by a hastily composed British force; any supplies, ammunition and siege guns from the Punjab magazines of Ferozepore and Phillaur had, by necessity, to be hauled through the Cis-Sutlej Sikh states of Patiala, Nabha and Jhind to reach Delhi. Without the goodwill of the maharajas of these states – by no means a sure thing – advancing towards Delhi would have been hazardous. British power in India was precarious, heavily dependent on the loyalty of the sepoy army and the goodwill and passivity of local rulers. It must have seemed an impossible situation.

*****

By 1857, a hundred years after the founding of British power in the subcontinent following the Battle of Plassey, there had been a sea change in the way Europeans saw themselves in India. Europeans in earlier times rarely gave up Christianity for native beliefs. Without immersing themselves entirely in local belief and culture, they had nevertheless

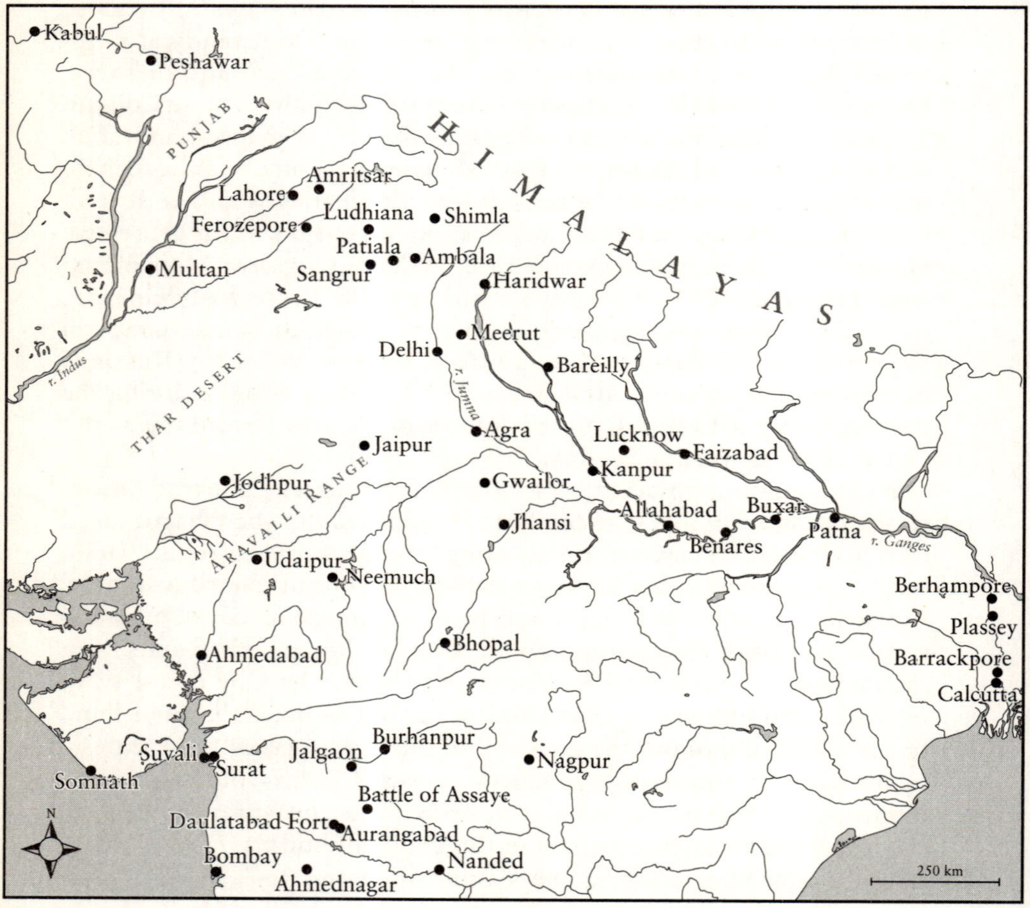
Kabul
Peshawar
PUNJAB
HIMALAYAS
Amritsar
Lahore
Ferozepore
Ludhiana
Shimla
Patiala
Ambala
Multan
Sangrur
Haridwar
Meerut
Delhi
r. Indus
THAR DESERT
Bareilly
r. Jumna
Agra
Lucknow
Faizabad
Jaipur
Kanpur
Jodhpur
ARAVALLI RANGE
Gwailor
Allahabad
Buxar
Patna
Jhansi
Benares
r. Ganges
Udaipur
Neemuch
Berhampore
Plassey
Bhopal
Barrackpore
Ahmedabad
Calcutta
Burhanpur
Jalgaon
Suvali
Surat
Nagpur
Somnath
Battle of Assaye
N
Daulatabad Fort
Aurangabad
Bombay
Nanded
Ahmednagar
250 km

North India.

successfully adopted Indian garb and oriental ways. Many had married local women and were content with the mixture, much like the Mughal or Afghan invaders before them. As time progressed, however, and supremacy over the entire subcontinent was achieved, attitudes changed and Europeans began to keep their distance. Many developed a more aloof attitude. New arrivals to the shores of India discarded the fashion of mixing with locals. Europeans were now the rulers rather than comrades in arms with the sepoy. They looked at Indian customs and attitudes with disdain or contempt. Christian missionaries had begun arriving by the turn of the nineteenth century, determined to destroy what they saw as superstition in the country and replace it with their alien beliefs. These missionaries with their predatory instincts were increasingly seen as allies of the British Government of India, whose policy was perceived by much of the general population of the country to be to push Indian society towards Christianity. New laws were brought into effect during the first half of the nineteenth century and intruded on social, cultural and religious mores, confirming these suspicions. The distance between ruler and ruled grew as the years went by. Similarly, there was a growing estrangement between sepoys and their officers.

Countless reasons for the outbreak of the mutiny were put forward by British historians, statesmen, administrators, civilians and soldiers during the mutiny and in the years and decades after. Indeed, whole books have been written on the subject. It is beyond the scope of this book to dwell in great detail on the causes of the outbreak. However, some of the more salient reasons, in particular relating to the sepoy army and to matters of religion, are covered in sufficient but by no means comprehensive detail in the earlier chapters as they are central to the narrative. Anyone interested in a detailed analysis of the origins of the outbreak of the mutiny may wish to read *The History of the Indian Mutiny* (1890) by Sir John Kaye and Colonel Malleson, which remains perhaps the best account on the subject.

In 1858, in the immediate aftermath of the mutiny, Islamic philosopher Syed Ahmad Khan wrote perhaps the first local Indian account of the reasons for the outbreak. The views he expressed in his book, *The Causes of the Indian Revolt*, were somewhat cautious and his tone was obsequious towards the British authorities. After all, the book was published at a delicate and dangerous time, when the British authorities were re-establishing their control over the country. Whatever else, his work is one of the few early Indian accounts of why the mutiny took place. He agreed with the consensus, which was that the rebellion had multifaceted origins and that the explosion was only triggered by the issue of the cartridges. Many of the reasons cited by historians were complex and beyond the cares of common villagers toiling in the fields and villages of India. Others impacted only one section of society or another. However, there is little doubt that each had a cumulative effect on the men who really mattered. These were the sepoys of the East India Company, who formed the only organised force remaining that could challenge British authority in any meaningful fashion. It is plain to see that during this time of growing dissatisfaction the British officers and administrators never understood the frustrations of the population and particularly of the sepoy army.

Many Europeans recognised that they were foreigners and that a large divide between rulers and ruled was natural. Certainly, the racial divide was a strong one, and beyond the lure of money there was little reason for the local population to help the British if matters turned against them, as Martin Richard Gubbins, financial commissioner for Oudh in 1857, elucidated:

> ... affection is a feeling which we have no right to challenge from our native subjects in India. Aliens as we are from them in blood, in feeling, in religion; nowise mingling with them in social intercourse, and interchanging few kindly offices, we have no right to expect from them love and sympathy: least of all, active assistance and support. Even supposing that our government of them were far better than it is, that it was not marked by the many faults and blemishes which undoubtedly disfigure it, still their obligation as subjects would have been discharged, if, in return for a just and equitable rule, they had rendered a faithful and regular payment of their tribute and a quiet and contented obedience...
>
> ... True our demand has been moderate, our faith has been good but what had he in connection with us that should induce him to lend us active aid, or to imperil life and property to maintain our rule?[2]

The Great Mutiny of 1857 wasn't the first show of discontent by the large sepoy army fostered by the East India Company. Perhaps the most famous confrontation came fifty years earlier at Vellore in 1806 when disgruntled sepoys had seized the fort there, killing and wounding around 200 troops. The cause, not surprisingly, had been religion. There had been a change in the recent dress code prohibiting Muslims from sporting beards and moustaches, and Hindus had been prevented from wearing religious markings on their foreheads. Hats had been introduced rather than the wearing of turbans, among other changes.

As recently as 1849, a potential problem had arisen in the Punjab, where as many as thirty sepoy regiments were stationed at the time and where it was thought that many were ready to mutiny. The issue had arisen in the aftermath of the Second Anglo-Sikh War and the annexation of the Punjab. Several cantonments were thought to be affected, with the sepoys at Wazirabad being most belligerent. The issue was that of *batta* being withdrawn after the annexation of the state. *Batta* was the name for special financial allowances granted to military personnel while in the field, and since these soldiers were no longer serving on foreign soil and therefore no longer on foreign service, no additional payment was felt to be required. This issue had begun in July 1849, at which point there had been widespread dismay among the sepoy regiments, eventually leading to the disbandment of the 66th Regiment. However, neither this nor any of the earlier mutinies was so formidable as to shake the British power in India near to collapse.

There had been prophesies of a coming trial of strength with the sepoy army. 'Mutiny with the sepoys is the *most* formidable danger menacing our Indian Empire,'[3] opined Sir Charles Napier, Commander-in-Chief in India from 1849 to 1850, a year after his service ended. Napier didn't believe the passive resistance showed by the sepoys in the Punjab in 1849 was the limit of their ambition. He believed their refusal to accept lower pay would eventually and inevitably turn to violence given that the men were armed: 'The ablest and most experienced civil and military servants of the East India Company consider mutiny as one of the greatest, if not *the* greatest danger threatening India, – a danger also that may come unexpectedly, and if the first symptoms be not carefully treated, with a power to shake Leadenhall.'[4]

Napier's reflections were published after his death in 1853. In *Defects, Civil and Military, of the Indian Government*, he elaborated on the growing remoteness between the officers and sepoys, or Indians in general: 'The younger race of Europeans keep aloof from Native officers ... How different this from the spirit which actuated the old men of Indian renown.' His advice was that officers learn the local languages and that native officers be appointed as *aides de camp* and Companions of the Bath. 'The Eastern intellect is great, and supported by amiable feelings, and the Native officers have a full share of Eastern daring, genius and ambition; but to nourish these qualities they must be placed on a par with European officers.' Napier's work was seen as somewhat prophetic after the mutiny, identifying as it did the various reasons for the troubles. Nevertheless, beyond certain circles, the possibility of such a large mutiny as eventually broke out was hardly conceivable to most Europeans at the time.

*****

Were the sepoys of the Bengal Army ever sufficiently organised and prepared for mutiny? Was there ever a conspiracy so widespread that regiments stationed as far apart as Bengal and Peshawar were plotting in concert to drive the British out of India? In retrospect, many felt so. How else could such a large rebellion have taken place? This was certainly the view of the deputy judge advocate general at the trial of Mughal Emperor Bahadur Shah, in charge of the later enquiry into how the troubles broke out. He declared at the trial that a considerable amount of subtlety, skill and wisdom had been used by the sepoys in planning such a venture, sufficient to have given so much trouble to the authorities.[5] Many Europeans present at Meerut, where the mutiny finally broke, agreed. There was evidence to show that the sepoys had agreed to rebel on 31 May, although due to circumstances the mutiny actually broke out three weeks earlier on 10 May. Also of this belief was Mr Cracroft Wilson, who would be appointed special commissioner by the Government of India to examine the events leading up to and following the outbreaks at Meerut and Delhi. Wilson felt that a vast conspiracy was forced into premature action at Meerut.

'Carefully collating oral information with facts as they occurred, I am convinced that Sunday, 31st of May, 1857, was the day fixed for mutiny to commence throughout the Bengal Army; that there were committees of about three members in each regiment which conducted the duties, if I may so speak, of the mutiny; that the Sipahis [sepoys], as a body; knew nothing of the plans arranged; and that the only compact entered into by regiments, as a body, was, that their particular regiments would do as the other regiments did,' opined Wilson. The plans, he elaborated, were for the sepoys to combine to wipe out the officers and other functionaries while they were attending church, the 31st being a Sunday three weeks hence. The treasury and magazine were to be seized and the jail opened to release their imprisoned comrades. The regiments in Delhi and its immediate vicinity were instructed to seize the magazine and fortifications:

> From this combined and simultaneous massacre on the 31st of May, 1857, we were, humanly speaking, saved by Lieutenant-Colonel Smyth commanding the 3rd Regiment of Bengal Light Cavalry…
>
> … The mine had been prepared, and the train had been laid, but it was not intended to light the slow match for another three weeks. The spark, which fell from female lips, ignited it at once, and the night of the 10th of May, 1857, saw the commencement of a tragedy never before witnessed since India passed under British sway.[6]

The only reason the mutiny broke out earlier than planned was because matters were brought to a head prematurely, principally due to the parade organised by Col Carmichael Smyth at the Meerut cantonment, in which the troopers were ordered to use the new ammunition that was suspected to be greased with animal fat. Col Smyth himself would later insist that although his action had precipitated the mutiny, paradoxically he had also saved British rule – by forcing the issue, his action had set the mutiny off prematurely, meaning planned uprisings at other cantonments elsewhere round North India failed to go off at the right time. In his defence, he would mention Sir John Packington, former Secretary of State for War, who declared that Smyth's action had saved India. Mr Vansittart of the Civil Service at Agra was another who would thank Smyth: 'It strikes me that India is not a little indebted to you; your firmness probably hurried on a catastrophe, which had it been delayed for a few weeks, would have begun with the seizure of Delhi, Agra, Allahabad, and Phillour.'[7] Another officer was heavy in his praise: 'I agree with Vansittart about your parade having brought matters to a crisis, and no doubt accelerated them, so that the whole affair, when it did break out, was not matured, and hence so much more easily managed; probably the country would have been lost otherwise.'[8] As news reached other cantonments by telegraph, more civilians and soldiers were saved by prompt action while the sepoys patiently waited for their agreed date to mutiny. Smyth alleged that he received plentiful supportive messages from elsewhere as well, both in India and from England, during the coming months.

There seems to have been some evidence from the mutineers themselves that preparations for a mutiny were under way during the early months of 1857. According to Ahsan Ulla Khan, physician of the Mughal Emperor at Delhi, who spoke with mutineers there during the siege of the city, these plans had never been fully developed with clear dates agreed on for precise synchronisation of uprisings:

> I cannot give any further information in regard to the preconcerted conspiracy of the native troops; I have said all I know. Before their defection the native troops had settled it among them to kill all Europeans, including women and children in every cantonment. I cannot explain, in detail, the arrangements which were made by the mutineers before their defection. I consider, however, that all their plans had not been yet matured when the event took place. I did not hear that any particular date had been fixed for the execution of the plans of the mutineers; but I am inclined to think that none was fixed, because if there had been, allusion would have been made to the fixed time, in the letters which were addressed by the Delhi mutineers to the other troops, which was not the case. I mean some such language as the following would have been used in those letters – viz., 'You promised to rise up on such a date, but you have not arrived yet, so that you have not kept your promise.'[9]

By 'the event', Ahsan Ulla Khan meant the mutiny at Meerut. His understanding was that if the mutiny had not taken place, plans for a general insurrection would have been perfected in the near future and would therefore have likely succeeded. The premature mutiny at Meerut, he suggested, was due to two main reasons: the severe behaviour of the Government to those who refused to use the new cartridge, and the eagerness of the troops to rescue their comrades from prison after their courts-martial for refusing. 'Gulab Shah, the officer of the 3d Cavalry, who came in from Meerut, in alluding to the severity of the Government, stated that they (Government) disarmed the troops and imprisoned the troopers in irons,' he continued.

Others had similar impressions. One of those who saw discontent but no great evidence of a maturing and far-reaching conspiracy was John Lawrence, then Commissioner of the Punjab. Lawrence perhaps had the best position from which to observe the mutiny developing in the Punjab, where there was a great preponderance of sepoy regiments. Lawrence's opinion was that the Meerut incident, premature as it was, had left the sepoys round the country in a state of unpreparedness and therefore excess caution. Beyond the reflex to mutiny on account of the new ammunition, he pointed to the almost complete lack of planning among the mutineers. There was little co-ordination, with regiment after regiment rising as and when they saw the opportunity, allowing the British authorities to take quick action and disarm large numbers of sepoys before a chance presented itself. The fact of the matter was that, of the few sepoy units that stayed loyal to the British during the uprising, none owned up to any definite plans for a mutiny or a specific date.

Neither do any papers or correspondence captured allude to a specific date for a general uprising. No attention was paid to annihilating the small pockets of European troops or civilians. In various places, sepoys simply allowed British officers to leave after withdrawing their allegiance. There was obviously a residual loyalty or respect preventing the slaughter of some superiors. At Meerut and Delhi, many British officers who approached their regiments to calm matters were shooed or warned off rather than shot dead. Sepoys of the 38th Native Infantry (NI) at Delhi, for instance, allowed many Europeans to escape and flee from the Ridge rather than kill them after the mutiny broke out. Brigadier General Graves was left unmolested, and so were the colonel and adjutants of the 38th even though they were among the last to flee the Ridge. Similarly, few regiments showed any intention to capture treasuries or magazines. Lawrence suggested that any coherent, thought-out plan – indeed, mere common sense – would have seen the mutiny succeed. Instead, the instinct for many, as at Meerut, was simply to head towards Delhi to join the rebel army, leaving any British authorities and troops to recover their poise and take the necessary actions.

As for the general Indian population, Lawrence noted that there was no popular uprising as news of the Meerut mutiny rippled across the country. This was also the case when Delhi fell. Nor was there an uprising when the Mughal Emperor openly lent his support to the rebels. Surely by this stage there should have been a popular rebellion if there had been any intention?

> The fact is that at first our enemies were not prepared to profit by such unforeseen and tremendous events. It was not till afterwards that the Mahomedans of Hindostan perceived that the re-establishment of the

> throne of Delhi, the gradual rising of the Mahomedan population, and the losses of the British at so many stations, presented an opportunity when they might again strike for empire with some prospect of success. The fact that *afterwards* in many districts the people threw off or ignored our authority, and that many individuals and some classes openly rose against us, will by no means prove a preconcerted conspiracy, but on the contrary will admit of much explanation.[10]

*****

As the mutiny progressed during the month of May and into June, flaws soon became apparent in the rebel army that had congregated at Delhi. The level of discord in the mutineers' ranks, particularly among the officers, continued without resolution. There was no clear leader acceptable to the mutineers and sufficiently able to take full advantage of the opportunities on offer. Instead, the princes of the palace, with no military experience, were raised to the status of colonels and generals. The mutineers, meanwhile, would bicker and squabble their way through the subsequent British siege of the city.

Maintaining discipline among the rebel sepoys proved difficult. Most of the rebels from Meerut lost all restraint on their arrival at Delhi, with plundering and chaos blighting the city for weeks after their appearance. This had major consequences beyond losing the goodwill of many of the local citizens, as many soldiers preferred to safeguard their ill-gotten gains and showed limited ambition in waging war against the British Delhi Field Force once it arrived in front of the city. Others, gorged with loot and with no stomach for a fight, quietly slipped off to their villages. The rebel force at Delhi was therefore in constant flux, with new arrivals and desertions all the time. Most British accounts agree that a substantial portion of the rebel army at Delhi put up little fight, content with taking potshots from a distance. Hand-to-hand combat was rare, and although the mutineers fought well behind barricades and from a distance, they invariably retreated back into the city when the British line advanced. The loyal sepoy Sitaram, whose account of life in the Bengal Army was one of the first published, was one of those whose regiments would pursue mutineers into Nepal:

> In no fight that I was in – and they were not a few – did I ever see the mutineers, be they Hindus or be they Mahommedans, ever make a good stand and fight. Usually they stood the first discharge and then took to flight – if they could not find shelter behind walls or trees. I am told it was tough work at Delhi. I was not there, but the sepoys could not have fought well to have allowed an English force of under 10,000 defeat 70,000, with the latter in possession of all the houses and fortifications.[11]

Many Europeans would also describe the general ineffectiveness of the sepoys once robbed of their British officers, their subedars not possessing the gravitas to maintain sufficient discipline. The mutineers' loyalty to the cause could not resist misfortune or lack of organisation. Morale proved difficult to maintain. Once the British Force entered the city after the first day's fighting, resistance dropped considerably as large groups of rebel troops fled the city over the following days. Fortunately for the British authorities, therefore, the rebel sepoy regiments held no significant advantage over their European counterparts apart from sheer numbers – and it became clear that this sole advantage was never fully utilised anyway.

*****

The sepoys seldom benefited from the sympathy or assistance of the local population. Nowhere was this more apparent than in the Punjab. Indeed, many historians and military men would in fact later attribute the failure of the mutiny entirely to events in the land of the five rivers. For in the Punjab was a great preponderance of sepoy regiments stationed not only to maintain order in the state annexed eight years previously but also to protect the unstable trans-Indus border region. If the bulk of the sepoy regiments in Punjab could have successfully risen up and received assistance from the local population, surely British authority over the entire north-west would have vanished instantly. But the causes of the rebellion never held much appeal for the people of the Punjab. Generally there was little belief in the rumours of polluted flour that were rampant elsewhere. The caste system had much less of a hold on the Sikh and Muslim populations that dominated Punjab society, and therefore anything that could break caste held no horror in the Punjab. For the Sikh community in particular, which had suffered significant persecution at the hands of the Mughals, there was a great aversion to the notion of helping the sepoys resurrect Mughal authority.

The sepoys, it turned out, hadn't helped their cause. During the eight years between the end of the Second Anglo-Sikh War in 1849 and the outbreak of the mutiny in 1857, the population of the Punjab had developed a special hatred for the sepoys, or *purbiahs* (easterners; specifically someone coming from the east of the Ganges) as they were called. Their appearance was quite incongruous in the Punjab. Generally of less impressive build and stature than the hardy Punjabi, they had made themselves a nuisance in the towns and cities. They were seen to swagger around in the villages and markets of the Punjab, making few if any friends and desiring none. Sepoys would boast of defeating the Sikh army, with some heard to declare one of their kind could defeat ten Punjabis such was their skill and training. Others went so far as to boast that it had been largely due to the sepoy regiments that the English had conquered the state as they formed the bulk of the East India Company's forces. There was a strong feeling around the Punjab that the sepoys had developed an unwarranted pride and that the shorter, weaker easterner could never compete with the better-built Punjabi without the assistance of European allies.

'The Punjabee soldiers disliked and despised the Hindoostanee Troops [sepoys],' John Lawrence wrote. 'They owed them a grudge for their boasting conduct, as well as for the advantages the latter enjoyed; they did not believe in their grievances, and were glad of the chance of fighting on a side which offered an opportunity of honor and profit. The Sikh had a traditional hatred against Delhi.'[12]

It wasn't only their boasts which irked the Punjab population. They were everywhere. Sepoys garrisoned the various cities of the Punjab. They stood in courtrooms in front of European magistrates dispensing justice. They were a common sight around villages and towns, with many using their position to solicit bribes. This divide between the population and the sepoys stationed in the Punjab was encouraged by the British authorities. John Cave-Browne, in his chronicle of the mutiny, stresses that the word *purbiah* was deliberately used in the Punjab by British officers and administrators to encourage a sense of difference and hatred towards the sepoy interlopers and make any union between them and the Sikh veterans impossible. This combination of a hatred for sepoys as well as the lingering Mughal dynasty meant that, in the event, a huge number of the old veterans of the Sikh Khalsa Army would instead take employment with the British as the mutiny progressed, while many Punjabi villagers were only too keen to offer up sepoy deserters, easily identified by their appearance and accent: 'All classes of the Punjab soldiers evince much zeal in our cause and an anxious desire to go against Delhy, but none more than the Seikhs, who seem to abhor the very name of the place. The decided line they have taken against the "Poorbeahs" is very remarkable,'[13] Lawrence would write to the Government of India on 30 June 1857.

Complementing this outright hostility towards the sepoys among Punjabis was the general passivity of large parts of the population around the rest of North India. Indeed, this might have been what truly killed off the mutiny. Despite their reservations about the breaking of caste, the introduction of Christian missionaries and suspicions regarding the motives of the Government, it seemed that the population largely preferred the British yoke to the uncertainties of a sepoy regime or the confusion and chaos of a prolonged interregnum. Perhaps memories of the upheavals of the eighteenth century after the decline of the Mughal empire were still too fresh; or perhaps it could be said most Indians lacked civic spirit at the time. Whatever the case, most people simply watched the mutiny unfold without taking an active part. What violence and rapine there was John Lawrence credited to general unfocussed discontent and the predatory nature of certain tribes like the Gujjars, who thrived on plunder and violence:

> ... as it appeared that the British were being swept off the face of the land, every village began to follow its own course. In most districts there was of course more or less of misconduct. But through the whole time the people even in the worst districts never embarrassed us half as much as they would have done had they been rebels at heart. Large masses of people were coerced by the mutineers into insurrection, if insurrection it could be called. Where again the mutineers were beaten and expelled, the country rapidly settled down to peace and order. Wherever our officers were able to hold their own, the people remained wholly or partially tranquil. Where British rule ceased utter disorder necessarily followed. And certainly the common belief in Hindostan was that the British dominion had been extinguished.[14]

However, as observed by many Europeans like Mrs Muter, wife of Colonel Muter and present at the Meerut uprisings, the passivity of many had limits. News of a British disaster at Delhi would have signalled to the masses that the hold of the English had finally slipped for good:

> The choice between the English who might again come into power, and the mutineers who were in power, was one of great difficulty to natives acting without fixed principles, and inclining to that side they expected to be most to their advantage. For months the scales had been evenly balanced; the prestige of empire was with us, but the belief throughout the land was that our sway had ended.[15]

Adding to the hesitation was the rough conduct of the rebel sepoys in many places. This was certainly the case in Delhi, where many of the mercantile and wealthier sections of the population of the city began to dread the anarchy of the rebel regime, the constant demands for money and the overbearing nature of the soldiers after their arrival at the city.

Ultimately, this very uncertainty helped the British as much of the country remained inert while the opportunity came and went as Delhi fell to the British Delhi Field Force. The mutiny was perhaps undone by sheer indifference among the masses.

*****

The story of the siege of Delhi can quite conveniently be split into three distinct periods.

The mutiny began in earnest at the Meerut cantonment on 10 May 1857. On the afternoon of that day, the three sepoy regiments stationed at Meerut – the 3rd Light Cavalry, the 11th NI and the 20th NI – full of resentment at their comrades having been imprisoned for refusing to use the new cartridges, broke into open revolt. The cantonment was burnt and the nearby prison broken into and their incarcerated colleagues freed. The mutineers would march to the imperial capital of Delhi, arriving the next day. From this time to 8 June, when the British Field Force reached Delhi, the mutineers were largely left to their own devices, with General Anson struggling to assemble a sufficiently strong force with enough carriage to advance to Delhi. The only significant actions during this time were at the Hindun River, where the smaller British force at Meerut that was attempting to join the main British force had two short clashes with the rebels from Delhi. At Delhi, meanwhile, the Meerut mutineers had been joined by the 38th, 54th and 74th NI regiments stationed at the city, making six regiments in total and turning the mutiny into something altogether more formidable. With the large Delhi magazine and the imperial capital of the Mughals in rebel hands, the mutiny assumed the aspect of a national uprising.

Despite the mutineers' disorganisation, there was a real danger that the revolt could sweep away British control of the entire north of the country in a matter of days. For the mutiny to succeed, it was paramount that other regiments elsewhere should rebel before they were disarmed by the alert British authorities. With the right leadership, the right decisions and a strong initiative, however, all was possible. Yet for various reasons this would never happen. It soon became apparent that the mutineers were better at destroying the old system than organising a new one. There was a failure to take full advantage of their strength during those vital few weeks. Time was wasted. A large army at Delhi sat virtually static, failing to grasp the initiative. Instead, they plundered the city. Delhi remained in chaos for many weeks after their arrival. The looting would continue after the arrival of the British Field Force.

The rebels had hoped to convince Bahadur Shah Zafar, the ageing Mughal Emperor, to join their cause and add legitimacy to the uprising. However, it quickly became clear that the monarch in his dotage was ineffective and could provide nothing in the way of money or organisation. A confused sort of leadership therefore remained among the rebels until the start of July. Meanwhile, the enormously advantageous telegraph system at Delhi allowed the British authorities to pacify the Punjab and other regions before news of the mutiny arrived there by ordinary means. Potentially large, dangerous mutinies were therefore smothered before they could break out and overwhelm the few European regiments stationed in the Punjab and elsewhere. More than this, the chaos in Delhi allowed the British commander-in-chief to take the initiative. A force was organised to try and retake Delhi before the rebellion spread out of control. It was obvious to everyone, most of all Governor-General Charles Canning and General Anson, that Delhi was the key. This was where the mutineers had decided to make their stand, and this was where mutineers from other cities were congregating. Possession of the city meant far more than its mere strategic value, for the rebellion would succeed only as long as the rebels held the city. The city had to be captured as a matter of urgency.

Given that the British never had sufficient numbers or artillery to break into the city in the early weeks, much of the rebel force could have been better deployed elsewhere rather than consolidating at Delhi. Initially, at least, the British authorities had been anxious at the accumulation of rebel sepoys at Delhi. However, as time went on it was realised that the rebels had no great designs beyond sitting at Delhi and awaiting the British advance. This worked to British advantage as the mutineers failed to take advantage of British weakness around the country and stir up further rebellion.

*****

The second period began with the arrival of the British Delhi Field Force in front of the city on 8 June and extended to 4 September. During this time, a sort of stalemate developed in which the mutineers would fail to dislodge the British force from its entrenched position on the Delhi ridge. As mentioned before, the British siege of the city was never a siege in real terms. There was never a ring of steel surrounding Delhi – the British lacked the numbers to accomplish an encirclement. Indeed, for the first half of the conflict the British largely considered themselves to be the besieged party. With no heavy guns and too few men to attack, the force merely clung to its position.

Over the next three months, the mutineers mounted a series of lacklustre and poorly coordinated attacks on the Ridge and were repelled. Without a strong guiding mind in the rebel camp, the sepoys generally showed little vigour. Scant imagination would be shown in organising counter-siege operations. Cutting off British supplies and ammunition from the magazines at Ferozepore and Phillaur, for example, seemed to be beyond the sepoy officers, and the British convoys were never seriously threatened.

Nonetheless, British casualties mounted in this slow war of attrition and it was generally felt that a more daring display from the sepoys might have forced the British to retreat, effectively signalling defeat. It is fair to say the rebels were singularly unaware of the weakness of the British position at times, and how close they really came to overthrowing British rule. Certainly the commanding officer at the Ridge at the time, Brigadier General Archdale Wilson, had seriously considered pulling his force back from Delhi.

The fate of the British East India Company and its rule over some 300 million people rested on two rather unlikely characters for much of the conflict. These were men who in normal circumstances would have been overshadowed by others.

On the British side, Brigadier General Wilson achieved the command of the British Field Force only after the death of Lieutenant General Anson, Major General Sir Henry Barnard and Major General Reid. Wilson perhaps never received the applause he should have under the circumstances, and was never much respected by his officers. Brigadier General John Nicholson, Chief Engineer Baird Smith, Capt. Hodson and others wrote rather disparaging remarks about their commanding officer, accusing him of indecision and questioning his ability to conduct a successful siege.

In the city, meanwhile, a humble subedar rose to become commander-in-chief of the rebel army. Bakht Khan, subedar in the Bareilly Brigade of mutineers, which would reach Delhi and reinforce the rebel army at the beginning of July, had the necessary commanding personality. But he would never quite manage to overcome the bitterness of other subedars and officers of the various regiments who were jealous of his promotion. The princes of the palace also showed him little cooperation, unwilling to accept the leadership of a commoner. Bakht Kahn had flaws of his own, which quickly became apparent on his arrival. The problem of dissonance between the various sepoy regiments would remain to the end despite his presence.

The third period of the siege could be considered to start on 4 September with the arrival of the British siege guns and end on 21 September with the capture of the city. Along with the siege guns had come significant reinforcements, shifting the scales decisively toward the British. Dejected mutineers had already begun to evacuate the city as the British heavy guns opened up on the city walls. British fire now became irresistible, and the city and its defences would be pounded without respite. Over the next ten days, the walls were repeatedly breached. British thoughts now turned to recapturing the city. In the early hours of 14 September, the assault on the city began with the detonation of the Kashmir Gate. British troops poured in through the destroyed gate and across the walls, beginning a week-long fight in the warren of narrow city streets that ended when the British flag was hoisted atop the palace and city walls.

The mutiny in Delhi was a pivotal struggle. British soldiers recognised that the capture of the city was essential for the survival of the empire in India. Mutineers, on the other hand, had strong religious motivations for rebelling against their paymasters and understood that they faced the noose if captured. Indeed, little or no mercy was shown to the rebels and few prisoners were taken. As one British officer at the siege would write, the enemy 'have not attempted to capitulate, because they know that nothing but death will satisfy English soldiers. Nought else shall they have at our hands.' Rebels in the city, wounded or not, were bayonetted where found. The city itself was looted in as systematic a fashion as possible under the circumstances, nearly three months being allowed for the uncovering of hidden valuables and plunder before order and sanity was ordered to be restored.

*****

It must be acknowledged that the mutiny had deep religious undertones. Of all the various religious communities in India, the motives and actions of the Muslim community perhaps received the most attention and suspicion among Europeans. Although Hindus easily outnumbered Muslims in India, the Muslim community had always been seen in a quite different light to the Hindus. They were seen as a much more restive population, always in ferment and turmoil. 'I cannot close my eyes to the belief that this race (Mussalmans) is fundamentally hostile to us and therefore our true policy is to conciliate the Hindus,' wrote Lord Ellenborough, Governor-General of India from 1842 to 1844, indicating an early interest in a policy of divide and rule.

There was a strong impression that Muslims were inveterate enemies of Europeans and Christians. The Muslim fought for his faith, to which temporal power could never compare. War against infidels was sanctioned and encouraged within the religion as Jihad, and anyone martyred in the process was guaranteed a physical and perfect paradise. The Muslim, it was felt, therefore had a genetic disposition towards war against unbelievers. This was amply shown in the north-western frontier with Afghanistan, where Muslim tribesmen in restive areas were almost constantly at loggerheads with the British. Muslims were thought to deeply resent the end of a thousand years of Mughal dominance at the hands of Christian infidels. How could this situation be allowed to remain? Was Muslim overlordship never to return? In the eyes of the British, therefore, the *summum bonum* of the Muslim in India was the re-establishment of Islamic dominance. This instinct for supremacy made them much more organised and gave them vitality. For the Muslim masses, then, the uprising against the East India Company instantly held a special resonance in contrast to the Hindu population, holding as it did the promise of a resurgence of Muslim power in Hindustan. For these reasons, Muslims were seen as the more combustible section of the population and the British authorities were correspondingly more wary of the community. In retrospect, perhaps the relationship between the Victorian Europeans, full of unbending Christian zeal, and Islam in India, an equally hegemonic belief, was always going to be uncomfortable and sometimes abrasive.

In stark contrast to their Muslim counterparts, Hindus were typically seen as less intractable and so were regarded with less suspicion. The Hindus, it was believed, were largely of a mild, non-violent nature, and held no inherent hatred for Christians. That was not to say that they had no aspirations or desire for freedom, or in fact grievances built up over the years against the British yoke. Indeed, the general belief was that Hindus had only picked up cudgels because they had genuine frustrations. They lacked the cutthroat fanaticism of the Muslim, which could turn a disagreement over the cartridge into a full-scale rebellion. The problem of the greased cartridge, among other issues, certainly was of deep concern to the Hindu community, but such a massive rebellion could never have taken place without the active ingredient of the Muslim.

Many Europeans were actually under the impression that the Hindus had been mere 'willing dupes' of the Muslims. 'There can be no doubt but that this was a Mahomedan rising and most skilfully had they prevailed on the Hindoos to join them though the latter appear now to repent their folly,'[16] declared Francis Spencer Wigram, joint magistrate at Meerut, where the mutiny originated. John Lawrence, Commissioner of the Punjab, suggested the issue of the greased cartridge initially concerned the Hindus more than the Muslims but that once the mutiny had begun it was the Muslims who turned it to their advantage and were the chief drivers of the rebellion: 'When once mutiny was in the hearts and minds of the Hindoos, it is probable that the feeling was fanned and inflamed by the Mahomedans. That which was in the first instance a mere desire to resist an infringement of their religion speedily extended into a great political movement.'[17] In a letter to the Government on 25 June, Lawrence wrote, 'The truculent fanaticism of the Mahomedan presents a disagreeable contrast to the soldierly spirit of the Ghurkha. It is remarkable fact that though this disaffection in the Native Army may be considered in its origin a Hindoo one, inasmuch as it commenced among the Native Infantry, still it has been taken up with especial fanaticism by the Mahomedans.'[18] Others like Sir James Outram, who played such a large part in putting down the rebellion at Lucknow, also thought it a Muslim conspiracy which had effectively hijacked the Hindu majority's grievances.

In the city of Delhi in particular, many Europeans believed the Muslim sepoys and inhabitants of Delhi had a far bigger hand in events than their Hindu peers. This belief ran through the British Field Force through to those decision makers in Punjab and farther afield to Calcutta. John Cave-Browne, chaplain to the British Field Force, was one of those who strongly believed so. The rebellion developed two faces as it gained pace, he speculated. One was the original Hindu movement, raised to recover lost privileges, to prevent the Christian missionaries and their schools from changing the religious and cultural milieu of Hindustan. This Hindu rebellion resulted from frustration and had no origins in any inherent hatred of the European. Nor did the Hindus want to destroy the British authority – providing concessions were offered. However, this rebellion had been hijacked by a Muslim revolt with greater pretensions. This was a political movement to recover the lost Muslim ascendancy, to proclaim Mughal rule in the country and, as Cave-Browne put it, to enact 'the annihilation of the Christian power'.[19] Cave-Browne pointed to a proclamation found in the tent of a Persian prince; it was found in Persian territory but was plainly targeted at the common man in India. The proclamation called for the expulsion of the Feringhees (Europeans) from India so that a Muslim king might be returned to power in Delhi.

Cave-Browne saw such Muslim antagonism as a continuation of the age-old conflict between the two religions:

> That the Mohammedan should conspire against the Christian, is not to be wondered at – his creed teaches it; the Koran demands it of him; and it would seem that during the last few years this obligation has pressed on his mind with more than wonted force; the mental thermometer of the Mohammedan has been rising to fever-heat of fanaticism. Not only in India, in Borneo too, in Arabia, in Syria – wherever the Mohammedan has come in contact with the Christian – this religious frenzy has burst forth.[20]

The Hindus, Cave-Browne argued, had their grievances – that much was clear – but were not the type to escalate such issues to violence and had now become honest dupes in the Muslim plan for domination. He therefore considered the uprising essentially Muslim in nature, with the Hindus who started it being swept along but lacking the venom and fanaticism required to propel it forward with energy. Quoting William Southey's poem *Roderick the Last of the Goths*, the chaplain would even compare the struggle in India to the reconquest of Spain in the fifteenth century, when Christian Europeans regained the territory from the Muslim Moors. Instead of the push to expel the Muslim from the Iberian peninsula, however, this struggle was to push Islam back from Hindustan.

The judge advocate general at the trial of the Mughal Emperor came to the same conclusions. In regard to a Muslim conspiracy, he pointed out that the prominent people involved were almost exclusively Muslim: 'A Mohammedan priest with pretended visions and assumed miraculous powers – a Mohammedan king, his dupe and accomplice – a Mohammedan clandestine embassy to the Mohammedan powers of Persia and Turkey – Mohammedan prophecies as to the downfall of our power – Mohammedan rule as the successor of our own – the most cold blooded murders by Mohammedan assassins – a religious war for Mohammedan ascendancy – a Mohammedan press unscrupulously abetting, and Mohammedan sepoys initiating the mutiny…' All these betrayed the strong Islamic undercurrent of the rebellion. He agreed with the consensus that the Hindus were generally peaceful, with the bulk of the firebrands being Muslim fanatics bent on destroying British ascendency. It would be Muslims who would benefit most from the implosion of British power, most of the nominal rulers in the country being Muslim. Certainly in the north of India, the King of Delhi and the former ruler of Oudh would perhaps benefit the most from having their power resurrected. Delhi and Lucknow were certainly seen as the two Muslim strongholds in the country.

This view was mirrored to some extent by others at Delhi. Jat Mall, an attendant at the palace working for the British, for example, on being asked whether there was the difference in attitude between the Hindu and Muslim citizens in relation to the mutiny, would reply, 'Yes, certainly, the Mahomedans, as a body, were all pleased at the overthrow of the British government, while the merchants and respectable tradesmen among the Hindus regretted it.' In the army, however, he observed the sense of alienation among Hindu and Muslim sepoys to be the same.

Some would comment on Hindus sepoys regretting that they had been 'duped' and blaming Muslims for their predicament during and after the conflict. Captain Gowan of the 18th NI, for instance, had managed to escape being killed by taking refuge with a friendly *zamindar* (landowner) near Bareilly. After the city fell, and having gathered the confidence to come out of hiding, Gowan talked to various dejected sepoys travelling down the road, encouraging them to return home rather than continue the contest. 'Homes! we have now no homes, we have rebelled against a Government that had always treated us well, – induced by promises from the Musselman, and now too late, we have found out our mistake,'[21] they replied to the captain.

Not everyone agreed with this analysis. Others would point out that the nominal head of the uprising had been the King of Delhi, Bahadur Shah, whom many wahhabis thought of as an apostate for his dabbling in and encouraging Hindu festivities and for his promotion of a syncretic society in Delhi. Not only that, but Hindus led the rebellion elsewhere. At Cawnpore, for example, the leader of the rebels, Nana Sahib, was a Brahmin Hindu. Syed Ahmad Khan argued against any interpretation of the uprising as a cause celebre for the Muslim community:

> The English Government does not interfere with the Muhammadans in the practice of their religion. For this sole reason it is impossible that the idea of religious crusade should have been entertained ... It must be remembered that the men who in those times raised so loud the cry of 'Jehad' were vagabonds and ill-conditioned men. They were wine drinkers and men who spent their time in debauchery and dissipation. They were men floating without profession or occupation on the surface of society. Can such fellows as these be called leaders of a religious war? It was very little that they thought about religion. Their only object was to plunder Government Treasuries and steal Government property.[22]

The only reason they had declared jihad, he pointed out, was to attract more plunderers and looters to the cause and to give the rebellion a stronger sense of legitimacy. This was a valid point in that the sepoy mutineers and their irregular compatriots had indulged in a considerable amount of looting of the city.

'Even the fanatic Moslem bigots who inhabit the hills around Peyshawur, far from joining any general conspiracy against us, have enlisted in our service, and have remained faithful. The city of Patna, supposed to be the hotbed of Mussulman intrigue, has been little moved, even though the sepoy brigade in the neighbouring cantonment of Dinapore succeeded in their tardy mutiny,'[23] wrote Martin Richard Gubbins, financial commissioner for Oudh, who detected no Muslim plot but did, like others, believe they happily exploited the mutiny for their own ends. 'This fact, however, is quite insufficient to prove that the *fons et origo mali* [source and origin of evil] was Mahomedan. On the contrary, it shows only what we are ready to admit, *viz.* that the Mahomedans, who dislike our rule in India the most, viewed with satisfaction the disaffection of the Hindoo soldiery, fanned the flame, joined in the movement, and endeavoured, with characteristic energy, to turn it to their own advantage.' By no means had all attention and energy been diverted to a religious war against the white infidels, he said, claiming like others that if the mutiny had been carried out with the vigour, fanaticism and martyrdom associated with religious wars then the result may well have been different.

An important additional point was the dim view of the mutiny among Muslims in Punjab and further west in areas like Peshawar. In these places, the Muslims enthusiastically opposed the rebelling Hindu sepoys to such a degree that British authorities deliberately moved various sepoy regiments into the trans-Indus area to stymy their hopes of rebellion, the sepoys being surrounded by unfriendly tribesmen inimical to their point of view. Muslims in Punjab and the frontiers weren't the only ones who failed to support the mutineers; the Nizam of Hyderabad proved loyal to the British, too. Even Dost Mohammad, the slippery Afghan ruler, failed to take advantage (although caution no doubt was part of the cause).

Whatever the case, it was apparent to all that the time for the mutiny had not been ripe. Deep divisions in Indian society led to a failure to unite for a higher cause, and on the other hand there was the desperation with which the English, small in number, marshalled themselves during the mutiny. These features were observed most succinctly by Capt. Hodson, head of intelligence in the British Field Force at Delhi:

> A nation which could conquer a country like the Punjab so recently with an Hindoostanee army and then turn the energies of the conquered Sikhs to subdue the very army by which they were tamed, which could fight out a position like Peshawur for years in the very teeth of the Affghan tribes and then when suddenly deprived of the regiments which effected this could unhesitatingly employ those very tribes to disarm and quell those regiments when in mutiny a nation which could do this is destined indeed to rule the world and the races of Asia must succumb. This is a proud feeling and nerves one's arm in many a time of difficulty and danger as much almost as the conviction that we must conquer or worse than death awaits us.[24]

# PART 1

# A Hundred Years of Twilight

# 1

# The Shadow of God

> ... Find out the role that God would have you play,
> The part assigned you, in the scheme of things[1]
> Aulus Persius Flaccus

> ... for he prided himself more on being a poet than on being a king ...
> Charles Freer Andrews

So drastic had been the fall in fortunes of the Mughal Empire during the first half of the eighteenth century that few at the time could have imagined its ruling Timurid dynasty lasting another hundred years. Prior to the death of Emperor Aurangzeb in 1707, Mughal authority had run from Kabul in Afghanistan to the delta of the Ganges in Bengal, and from Kashmir in the north to almost the extreme south of the subcontinent. However, Aurangzeb had practised policies of religious intolerance. This, along with a predilection for never-ending wars in the south of the country, had left the empire with both hidden and visible weaknesses. Wars of succession after Aurangzeb's death played their part, while foreign invaders and local powers took advantage of the rapidly declining central authority. By 1757, fifty years after Aurangzeb's death, the writ of the Emperor, the rather inconsequential Alamgir II (1754–59), ran little further than the walls of the city of Delhi.

The biggest blow came in 1739. The Persian adventurer Nader Shah, sensing opportunity, had invaded India and defeated a large Mughal army at the Battle of Karnal. Delhi itself was sacked and some 30,000 of its inhabitants massacred. The entire Mughal treasury, including the fabled Peacock Throne, was transported back to Persia in triumph. The Mughal Emperor at the time, Mohammed Shah (1719–1748), known by his sobriquet 'Rangila' or 'the Colourful', was forced to cede all territory west of the Indus River to the Persians. This disaster definitively brought to a close the golden period of the empire. Its frailties could no longer be disguised. Fortunately for Mohammed Shah, Nader Shah would soon pass away, eliminating the threat of another Persian invasion.

However, an arguably greater threat quickly surfaced in the form of Nader Shah's able lieutenant, the Afghan Ahmed Shah Abdali or Durrani. Capitalising on the continuing weakness of the empire, Abdali would invade Hindustan no fewer than seven times between 1748 and 1767, carrying away huge hauls of booty and further underlining the prostrate nature of the state. It's fair to say, then, that Emperor Alamgir II, occupying the throne in 1757 and weighed down by his own troubles, probably gave only passing attention to the news arriving from the far east of the country. On 23 June 1757, at the Battle of Plassey, the army of the Nawab of Bengal had been defeated by the force of a company of foreign traders named the East India Company, led by Robert Clive. The entire province would soon come under the Company's effective authority, laying the foundation for British rule in India.

A hundred years after the Battle of Plassey, and despite expectations to the contrary, a descendant of Aurangzeb still sat on the imperial throne. The city of Delhi seemed to have recovered its poise after the chaos of the previous century. In fact, the city had grown rich due to the stability of recent times. The walls of the city were well maintained. Some had even been renovated and strengthened, along with the Kashmir Gate to the north of the city. Outside, a tidy network of canals provided water to the neighbouring area and the city. Much else had changed. A new and alien style of architecture, in a European fashion, could be seen in the more upmarket eastern half of the walled city, which had developed a British presence. Many of these new structures caught the eye as one entered the city from the north and through the Kashmir Gate travelling towards the palace and the main commercial thoroughfares. A new Christian place of worship, St James' Church, now occupied a large and prominent plot on the road from the Kashmir Gate to the palace. Other European-style buildings and bungalows were dotted around close to the church and near the palace in the Daryaganj area in the south-east of the city.

This concentration of European-style buildings was strongest outside of the northern stretch of the city walls in a place called the Civil Lines, where European mansions, residences and administrative buildings stretched towards the Delhi ridge. These new developments pointed to the new rulers of the city. The British Resident, or Commissioner of Delhi, now had effective authority over the city while another European, housed in the apartments high above the main entrance of the palace of the Mughal Emperor, was now commandant of the palace itself. A large British cantonment lay just a couple of miles to the north of the walled city, guarding it. The Mughal Emperor had been retained as the nominal ruler of the city, but, like much of the rest of India over the previous century, Delhi had fallen into the hands of the East India Company.

*****

Prince Mirza Abu Zafar Siraj-ud-din Muhammad was born on 24 October 1775, during the reign of his paternal grandfather, Emperor Shah Alam II (1760–1806). He was the product of the union between Prince Mirza Akbar (later Emperor Akbar Shah II, 1806–1837) and Lal Bas, his Rajput Hindu wife. Mirza Abu Zafar seems to have had considerable vigour as a young man. He excelled in horsemanship, and displayed good skill with the sword and the firearm. As far as cerebral activities were concerned, his youth seems to have been well spent, with education in Persian, Urdu and Arabic. He showed a natural propensity towards the arts, however, including poetry, literature, calligraphy, music, miniatures and painting. He also excelled as a gardener. He was one of twenty-two sons and at least thirty-two daughters. He was neither the oldest son nor his father's favourite. In ordinary circumstances he would have taken the expected route, remaining in the shadows as one of the countless nobles whiling away their time in the imperial palace. Instead, Mirza Abu Zafar would be the last person to sit on the Mughal throne.

The era in which Mirza Abu Zafar was born and raised was a period of almost constant humiliation for his imperial line. It is difficult to put a definitive time and date on the transfer of supremacy in India to the British East India Company. Some would argue the Battle of Plassey in 1757 had been the moment, while others would say the Battle of Buxar in 1764 was a more definitive turning point. At Buxar, an army under Shah Alam II, together with the armies of the Nawab of Bengal and the Nawab of Oudh, had been bested by a British force under Major Hector Munro. By the subsequent Treaty of Allahabad, signed the following year, the Emperor was forced to cede the right to collect taxes in Bengal, Bihar and Odisha to the Company. Additionally, he would end up moving his court to Allahabad, placing him under the thumb of the Company for the following twelve years.

Continuing British expansion meant the authority of the Company finally reached Delhi on 11 September 1803, forty-two years after Buxar. This was the year in which an army under the command of Lord Lake defeated the Marathas of Scindia at the Battle of Delhi. The battle took place at Patparganj, just to the south-east of Delhi. The story goes that Shah Alam II, blind and helpless to influence matters, sat on one of the balconies of the palace in the direction of the battle, being told of its progress. On 14 September, Lord Lake would enter Delhi. Curiously, British arms would enter the city again exactly fifty-four years later, on 14 September 1857, following a protracted siege of the city. Lord Lake would have an audience with the Emperor, and the official Company records of the time describe the poverty and impotence of the monarch, caused by a collection of misfortunes and setbacks going back over nearly a hundred years.

> In the magnificent palace built by Shah Jahan the Commander-in-Chief was ushered into the royal presence, and found the unfortunate and venerable Emperor, oppressed by the accumulated calamities of old age and degraded authority, extreme poverty and loss of sight, seated under a small tattered canopy, the remnant of his royal state, with every external appearance of the misery of his condition.[2]

The records do not go into detail on which of the many princes were present in the Durbar (court) at the time. But there is no doubt that his grandson, the aforementioned Mirza Abu Zafar Siraj-ud-din Muhammad, then twenty-eight years old, must have watched the scene. Lake's visit must have impressed on all those in the Durbar, including the prince, just how drastically the power dynamics in North India had shifted during the last century. A company of traders who had pleaded with previous emperors for concessions now dictated the position of Shah Alam II as a simple pensioner of the East India Company. He was also deprived of what little authority he had retained till this time. The administration and authority over the city was, to all intents and purposes, transferred to a new Resident or Commissioner.

*****

In 1803, the Company considered it expedient to retain the Emperor as a puppet – for a time at least – rather than abruptly terminating the dynasty. There seemed to be profit in such a move. The holding of the 'Great Mogul' as a pensioner under its protection gave significance and prestige to the Company. As well as grandeur, his presence added legitimacy to their status as the new paramount power in India. Lord Wellesley, Governor-General at the time, certainly seemed to think retaining the Emperor in the Company's grasp would increase the standing of the British Government. That the Emperor was ageing and blind must have also elicited some sympathy among Lord Lake and his cortege at the Durbar. Sir John Kaye, the great chronicler of the mutiny, would write to this effect:

> It was solace to us in the 'great game' to know that we 'held the King' but it was a puzzle to us how to play the card. It was, indeed, a great political paradox, which Lord Wellesley's Government was called upon to institute and he did the best that could be done in the circumstances in which he was placed to reconcile not only the House of Timour but the people who still clung reverentially to the great Mahomedan dynasty to the state of things which had arisen out of those circumstances...[3]

With these arrangements it became clear to all that the imperial family were under the protection of the British Government of India, as made clear in a dispatch from the Governor-General to the Secret Committee on 13 July 1804:

> The deliverance of the Emperor Shah Alam from the control of the French power established in the North-West quarter of Hindustan, by which the Government of France has been deprived of a powerful instrument in the eventual prosecution of its hostile designs against the British Government in India, and the British Government has obtained a favourable opportunity of conciliating the confidence and securing the applause of surrounding states by providing a safe and tranquil asylum for the declining age of that venerable and unfortunate monarch, and a suitable maintenance for his numerous and distressed family.

It was under these circumstances that Mirza Abu Zafar's grandfather was kept as nominal ruler of Delhi. By late 1806, his father had succeeded to the throne as Emperor Akbar Shah II. Akbar Shah preferred another prince, Mirza Salim (also called Mirza Jahangir), as his successor. The mother of this prince, one of the many queens of the Emperor, had managed to persuade the Emperor to make her son, who was the third oldest of the princes, his heir apparent.

Mirza Salim was a tactless man who hated the new British ascendancy at Delhi. Rather than masking his true feelings till he gained the throne, Mirza Salim openly mocked Charles Seton, the British Resident in Delhi. One day, in 1812, in a reckless state of mind, he took a potshot at the Resident with his gun. He missed, but the man's hat was knocked off. Such audacity saw Mirza Salim exiled to Allahabad by the British authorities and wrecked his chances of gaining the throne. Although he was eventually allowed to return to Delhi, he was soon exiled to Allahabad once more for his attempts to poison his older brother. He died at the age of only thirty-one in 1821 from a debauched life defined by a strong preference for cherry brandy.

Akbar Shah now attempted to bestow the succession on another prince, Mirza Nali, but failed to obtain the consent of the British authorities. Mirza Abu Zafar's elevation to the throne, in reality to the role of *roi fainéant*, therefore owed much to providence. He eventually succeeded to the throne on 28 September 1837 at the advanced age of sixty-one, having received the Government of India's imprimatur. His full royal title would now be Mirza Abu Zafar Sirajuddin Mohammad Bahadur Shah Ghazi, or Bahadur Shah II. Bahadur Shah translates to 'Brave King' in English. Ghazi is the term for a Muslim warrior dedicated to fighting non-Muslims. These epithets would prove unsuited to the new Emperor, a gentle man and a lover of the arts. He himself preferred to be known simply by his *nom de plume*, Zafar, meaning victory, although time would tell whether this moniker fit any better.

A royal salute was fired at both Delhi and Agra on Zafar's accession. Agra was the capital of the North-West Province, the British administrative region which also included Delhi. Zafar happened to be a contemporary of Queen Victoria, who had ascended the throne just four months earlier. The comparison ended there, however. While the young Victoria was leading the British monarchy to its zenith, the ageing Zafar would be holding the last watch.

*****

What is known of Zafar's childhood is painfully limited. However, in his youth, during his grandfather's reign, he must have experienced the last faint residues of the prestige and glories of past emperors. Equally, he had seen enough during his during his life to fully understand the full litany of setbacks that had marred the reigns of his father and grandfather, leading to the complete loss of power. Lieut. Ommaney, who was in charge of Zafar as Emperor and who would escort him to his exile in Burma after the mutiny, describes a man that from his looks and personality must have caught the eye when he was in the vigour of youth:

> The ex-king was about eighty-five years old, and must have been a striking man in his prime; his face was of an aristocratic type, with marked features, especially in the nose. He must have been a powerful man too, as the muscles of his arms hung long and flabby in his old age. He had a pleasant expression, and a sense of humour. I should say he was too old to have initiated or taken any active part in the horrors of these days, and was the tool of the bolder and more truculent spirits, male and female, about him.[4]

Few images of Zafar survive. One potential photographer had arrived as early as 1850. In January of that year, Helen Douglas Mackenzie visited the monarch. Zafar had been smoking his hookah, one of his pastimes, when she entered his apartments. She described him as 'slender and feeble-looking, but with a simple kindly face, though he took no notice of me when I came in, which I suppose is etiquette'. He was lying on his bed with a woman rubbing his feet. Mrs Mackenzie had come armed with a camera, but it proved difficult to take pictures in the darkness of the room and the balcony was no better. The opportunity passed, although Mackenzie would make some drawings of Zafar's favourite wife, Zeenat Mahal, and her son. The coronation portrait of Zafar, made in 1837 by the Indian painter Ghulam Ali Khan, shows a confident man with an air of purpose, a subtle smile hinting at a general contentment.

Throughout his reign, from 1837 to 1857, Zafar made the best of his interest in the arts. He seemed most comfortable in his own restricted world, composing verses and presiding over *mushae'ra* (gatherings of poets). The missionary C. F. Andrews wrote of the role poetry played at this time:

> [It] was the one absorbing fascination for the high-born nobles, who formed a literary coterie round the Emperor and joined in his artistic pursuits. They vied with one another in their verses on every public occasion. Contests were held; the most highly praised poems were recited; prizes were awarded. The whole city was interested in these recitals to an extraordinary extent, and the fame of the prize-winners went abroad. Most of the nobles of the imperial court took part in these poetic contests. Each of them had his own literary title by which he was famous. The Emperor himself would often take part; for he prided himself more on being a poet than on being a king…[5]

The people of the city, for their part, seemed to cherish their poet-king, lauding him for his skill in this difficult art. The citizens were known to sing the Urdu and Persian couplets of Zafar's work in the streets of the city as they went about their work and leisure.

As well as poetry, Zafar had a liking for miniatures and excelled at calligraphy. Beauty appealed to him, and despite the parlous state of the treasury he found the funds to lay out the gardens at Shahdara, as well as the gardens below the palace walls. He also liked to play cards and chess. He was known to be a devout Muslim, although syncretic in nature and tolerant of the Hindu beliefs of the majority of the population. He allowed the court to partake in celebrations marking Hindu festivals such as Holi, Diwali, Dussehra, Raksha Bandhan and others with genuine spirit. He was seen as weak in character though, being influenced to an inordinate degree by his favourite wife, Zeenat Mahal. Syed Ahmad Khan, the famous Islamic philosopher of the nineteenth century, also hints at the Emperor having developed some level of imbecility in his later years: 'The Ex-King had a fixed idea that he could transform himself into a fly or gnat, and that he could in this guise convey himself to other countries, and learn what was going on there. Seriously, he firmly believed that he possessed the power of transformation. He was in the habit of asking his courtiers in Durbar if it were not so, and his courtiers were not the men to undeceive him.'[6]

Leaving aside these failings, the name of the King and his authority, though faded, still held a special resonance for the citizens of Delhi and beyond. Few of the population of Delhi thought that Zafar had any hope of reanimating the corpse of Mughal rule, true, but that didn't matter at this late stage. Zafar was well respected and loved despite his shortcomings, as C. F. Andrews testified: 'One of the survivors [of the British siege of the city], who had actually seen him in his Court, told me that he was dearly loved by Hindus and Musalmans alike for his "good manners." His very foibles and incompetence as a monarch were a part of his attraction for the multitude. He was very peaceful and unwarlike. His subjects would smile at his simplicity. They knew well how ineffective he was, but they loved him all the same.'[7] When the royal cortege used to travel through the city, the locals would respectfully dismount their horses and everyone would salute as he slowly went past on his elephant.

Zafar, for his part, seemed to enjoy this more personal relationship with the people, and the royal processions around the city were memorable. During Hindu and Muslim festivals, Zafar enjoyed watching the crowds milling in front of the palace from a tower in the fort; the crowds, spotting him, would make their obeisance. On these occasions a public recitation of his poetry would be addressed to the cheering masses.[8] The princes, meanwhile, would ride their richly dressed horses around the streets of the city to soak up some reflected glory. Perhaps the knowledge that Zafar was the last of his line invoked sympathy and affection, allowing his ineffectiveness to be forgiven; certainly, by the time of his reign the British Government of India had made it clear that the pretence of a Timurid dynasty and throne would not continue beyond Zafar's death.

*****

During the years following Lord Lake's visit in 1803, the East India Company's possessions had continued to expand and the Company had assumed the role of the paramount power in the country. The need to co-opt the prestige of the Mughal Emperor dwindled accordingly. There was perceived to be little merit in allowing the Mughal throne to continue, and therefore the Governors-General during this period made plain their intention to terminate the Mughal dynasty.

By this time, Zafar was a man in his seventies and in the twilight of his life. He would, inasmuch as the finances of his British pension allowed, continue to hold his diminished court and maintain the customs of his ancestors. The days of magnificent entrances by foreign ambassadors and governors were long gone. The Mughal Durbar had been shorn of its magnificence, although the rituals and etiquette carried on as before. Zafar himself was generally relaxed about his lack of legitimate power, having largely resigned himself to British plans for the dynasty. He had a strong faith in his court astrologer, who, sensing the winds of change, had predicted with certainty that Zafar would be the last of the house of Timur to sit on the Mughal throne. In his apathy, Zafar quite agreed with the astrologer. 'I am the last,' he would often declare to his courtiers in circumspect moments. According to Ahsan Ulla Khan, Zafar's physician, he was resigned to his heirs losing the palace as well: 'Indeed the King used often to remark that the Mirza (Fateh-ul-Mulk) had little reason to rejoice at his succession, for after him (the King), his successor would neither have any authority, nor would he be permitted to reside in the palace.' Faced with this inevitability, Zafar lost himself in the world of poetry and opium. He would write of his ambitious sons in one of his couplets:

My children have unjust dreams of Kingship
This order can't last for long
It will end with me
From Taimur to Zafar

It is said that the residents of Delhi showed much grief when they heard of Zafar's couplets on the impending end of the dynasty. Residents sung the couplet like a lament in the streets of the capital. In 1854 – three years before the mutiny – the prominent poet Ghalib epitomised anxiety about the demise of the Mughal Durbar when wrote to friend and fellow poet Junun, 'Inside the fort a few princes get together and recite their verses. Once in a while I attend these meetings. Contemporary society is about to vanish. Who know when the poets would meet next or meet again at all.'[9] Quite when the final curtain would fall was anybody's guess; Zafar seemed to be in relative good health up to the time of the mutiny. It seemed to most that a few years still remained for the Mughal throne, and for its fading imperial capital.

*****

British concerns about the continued existence of the Mughal dynasty had in fact begun during Lord Lake's time, fifty years earlier. Some felt that too much had been conceded to a dying dynasty, and that the disparity between the British power and the fallen house of Timur was too great to continue indulging in any pretence. Lord Lake had shown magnanimity in awarding a pension to the reigning Emperor, Shah Alam, which could be read as the British Government generously relieving the blind ruler of some of his worries. Allowing the Emperor to remain on his throne and to keep his title, however, was felt to have been a mistake. It meant that the servants of the British Government of India, Residents and even Governors-General were now having to display token and irritatingly visible subservience to the Mughal monarch.

The unequal nature of this relationship grew as the years went by. Europeans passing through Delhi would invariably seek an audience with the Emperor. Beyond idle curiosity in seeing the palace and meeting the man, many held little sympathy for the Timurid dynasty. With the Emperor lacking sovereign power and dependent on a modest British pension, the pomp and circumstance allowed to him was considered inappropriate. A British officer remarked upon the ridiculous degree of imbalance on display in everyday communication with the frequently penniless princes in the palace: 'One of these "kings" (a reference to one of the Mughal princes) who has no more than ten shillings a month to subsist himself and family upon will, in writing to the Representative of the British Government [Commissioner of Delhi], address him as *Fidwee Khass*, our particular slave; and be addressed in reply with, "Your Majesty's command (has) been received by your slave."'[10]

For the numerous princes of the palace, the continuing existence of the imperial throne and title during the decades after Lord Lake's visit allowed them to dream of a return to former glories; moreover, it meant they were open to plots and conspiracies. Exempting the residents of the palace from British jurisdiction also gave the princes a dignity and sense of importance that was not their due. Fears over the Emperor's residual authority were expressed early on by Lord Wellesley. The continuing pomp and circumstance, the maintenance of the Imperial title and the continuing residence in the palace, he suggested, would likely fill the mind of a future Emperor with ideas for retrieving the fortunes of the dynasty. 'Lord Wellesley saw clearly', Sir John Kaye wrote, 'that if the ancestral State of the Mogul were perpetuated – if he were left to reside in the Palace of Shah Jehan, with all the accompaniments of his former grandeur around him, in the midst of a Mahomedan population still loyal to the House of Timour – there might someday be an attempt to reconstruct the ruined monarchy in the person of one of Shah Allum's successors, which might cause us grievous annoyance.'[11]

David Ochterlony, the first Resident at Delhi (1803–06 and 1818–20), also voiced his opposition to what he saw as an over-generous settlement in 1803. Commenting on the arrangements agreed upon, he considered them 'as more injurious than beneficial' to British interests. Lord Wellesley, Governor-General from 1798 to 1805, with these misgivings in mind, had mooted the idea of moving – evicting, in truth – the Emperor from the palace as a precursor to the eventual abolition of the dynasty. His suggestion was that the Emperor give up his residence at Delhi and move to the district of Munger in Eastern India. If this was done, his memory would gradually fade away in the minds of the population of the city and Hindustan in general. Shah Alam, on hearing of these machinations, refused to agree to any such scheme that reduced his status in such a manner. He is said to have put his hand on his sword and declared that he was still alive, and that one could not put a living person into a grave. Wellesley quickly saw that the forcible eviction of a blind geriatric Emperor, especially against the man's will, would only cause embarrassment and bring no credit to the British Government of India. The matter was shelved for the time being.

*****

During the first half of the nineteenth century, the relationship between the Mughal Emperor and the various Governors-General and

Commissioners stationed in Delhi was friendly but frequently difficult behind the etiquette and professions of eternal friendship and amity. The first British Resident imposed on the Delhi Durbar was David Ochterlony in 1803. It is fair to say that Ochterlony showed some sympathy towards Shah Alam. Ochterlony himself had a liking for Mughal comforts and living, enthusiastically taking up the local culture by wearing a turban and adopting the local fashions. He kept thirteen wives (or concubines, as seen through British eyes) and had the habit of taking them all out on elephants during the Delhi evenings. A favourite tour was a trip round the Red Fort, each wife having her own elephant. His habit of a spectacular procession of elephants eclipsing anything the Mughal Emperor could conjure up underlined who was the real power in Delhi now. 'Where else could I live like a king?' he is said to have uttered when asked of his lifestyle and whether he ever wished to return to England. He lived a lavish lifestyle helped along by more than 400 employed servants.

Ochterlony was a diplomat too in the way he handled things in Delhi. Bishop Heber, the Anglican Bishop of Calcutta, visited him in Rajputana and remarked on his lifestyle: 'There was a considerable number of horses, elephants, palanquins and covered carriages. Ochterlony maintains an almost kingly state. He has been absent from his home country about 54 years; he has there neither friends nor relations, and he has been for many years habituated to Eastern habits and parade.' With his own royal lifestyle, Ochterlony perhaps had a sense of brotherhood with the Mughal Emperor. Future Residents, however, would adopt a more businesslike attitude.

Shah Alam lasted only three years after Lord Lake's visit. He died in December 1806 and was succeeded by Akbar Shah II. The British Resident also changed that year, with Archibald Seton (1806–11) replacing David Ochterlony on 25 June 1806. Seton also tended to be sympathetic to the plight of the new Emperor. Despite the poverty of the court, Seton tended to treat the monarch as what he was – a Mughal Emperor and the descendant of Timur. He showed no hesitation in displaying the necessary deference at the Durbar. Seton's view was that a certain show of obeisance, as well as giving way on small matters, did no harm. The Emperor was kept in good humour. Chipping away at the few privileges remaining to him would only annoy the Muslims of Delhi and bring little in return.

Akbar Shah was viewed in a different light to his predecessor, however. The British Government recognised that Shah Alam held real power during his life; he had commanded armies and ruled over territories, and was therefore a genuine ruler fallen on hard times. Akbar Shah, in contrast, had never tasted power and had assumed the throne as a pensioner of the British Government. It is little surprise that he was treated in a less deferential manner. His character and general demeanour, too, was said to have been less impressive. Some thought him a weak man. Sir David Ochterlony described him as 'imbecility personified under the guidance of a woman of low extraction, originally a servant of the household; weak, proud, and in the highest degree avaricious and rapacious'.[12]

Lord Minto, Governor-General from 1807 to 1813, commented on Akbar Shah's feeble attempts to try and revive the faded glories of the dynasty:

> Bent on his unattainable purpose but destitute of power to attempt it openly, and too feeble even to avow it, he stoops to every little artifice, engages in every petty intrigue, and is drawn into all the oblique and disingenuous courses which the ladies of his palace or councillors equally feminine can suggest and recommend to him. An opening is furnished for such practices by the liberal courtesies with which the exterior observances due to the real sovereignty of his ancestors are most properly extended to his nominal title, and under cover of the formal homage which a tenderness for his personal feelings alone prompts us to render him, he seeks to advance a silent and gradual claim to the substantial attributes of greatness.

Successive Governors-General therefore sought to avoid any show of inferiority towards the Mughal. An end to the charade of a Mughal throne was needed. In preparation for this, many tweaks were suggested regarding customs, formalities and court procedures in order to better represent the balance of power. Outward symbols of Mughal presence and prestige were gradually eradicated. Many of the royal prerogatives were done away with or seriously curtailed. At the same time, discussions over the matter of the dynasty continued. During the following decades, from 1803 to 1857, the treatment of the Emperor was downgraded and by degrees diminished in preparation for the termination of the dynasty.

It was the custom for visitors to present a *nazar* (tribute) to the Emperor as a display of his paramountcy. The British authorities used to present a *nazar* on the two Islamic Festival Days (Eids), during the Islamic New Year and on the Emperor's birthday. Earlier Governors-General and Commanders-in-Chief had presented the *nazar* when in audience with the Emperor. In 1813, however, during the reign of Lord Minto, this custom of high British officials offering tribute to the Emperor was ordered to be discontinued. Henceforth, only the Resident would offer a *nazar* on their behalf in the presence of the Emperor, cheapening the tribute. This change was met with consternation, and prompted the Emperor Akbar Shah to write to the Governor-General:

> I hope from your Lordship's high and pre-eminent character for justice and liberality that you will have the kindness to cause search to be made among the records of Government in Calcutta and on finding that such

> instructions were received from Europe, be so gracious as to pass the necessary orders in the Agent's name for the payment and presentation of the amount of *nazrs* for the past two years, and that the custom be regularly observed for the future. By doing this I will be gratified, and it will add to your fame.[13]

Lord Minto would remind Akbar Shah that his monarchy was only now accepted 'as a complementary recognition of a nominal sovereignty'. The *nazar* would in fact be done away with entirely by Lord Ellenborough in the 1840s. 'Since the time when, during the administration of Lord Ellenborough, the *nazar*, which used to be presented to the King or Delhi on the part of the Governor-General, was discontinued, the King was always very much grieved,' wrote Ahsan Ulla Khan, Zafar's physician. 'At first, he wrote on the matter to England, and he always afterwards used to complain against the order, and to express his dissatisfaction thereat.'

Meanwhile, policy in Delhi changed when Archibald Seton was succeeded as Resident by Sir Charles Metcalfe (1811–18). Metcalfe disagreed with Seton's softer policies. In fact, he had already voiced his concerns in 1807 when he was a subordinate:

> I do not conform to the policy of Seton's mode of managing the royal family. It is by submission of manner and conduct, carried on, in my opinion, far beyond the respect and attention which can be proscribed by forms, or dictated by a humane consideration for the fallen fortunes of a once illustrious family. It destroys entirely the dignity which ought to be attached to him who represents the British Government, and who, in reality, is to govern Delhi, and it raises, I have perceived, ideas of imperial power and sway, which ought to be put to sleep forever. As it is evident we do not mean to restore imperial power to the King, we ought not to pursue a conduct calculated to make him aspire to it. Let us treat him with the respect due to his rank and situation; let us make him comfortable in respect of circumstances, and give him all the means, as far as possible of being happy. But unless we mean to re-establish his power, let us not encourage him to dream of it. Let us meet his first attempts to display imperial authority with immediate check, and let him see the mark beyond which our respect and obedience to the shadow of a king will not proceed.

Metcalfe criticised Seton's tactic of conceding on numerous minor issues in the hope that the King would compromise on bigger issues as they appeared. He also disagreed with Seton's classification of many of the concessions as trivial, preferring an uncompromising attitude. 'Ideas of the exercise of sovereignty ought, I think, to be checked in the bud; it may be attended with difficulty to destroy them when they have been suffered to grow for some time; at least greater difficulty than there is in suppressing them altogether.'[14]

Some grievance, too, was shown against the Emperor himself. A feeling prevailed among Europeans that while the Mughal Durbar had lost its lustre and was now a poorer pageant than any other in the world, the Emperor himself remained perhaps the proudest. In other words, he was not recognising his dire situation. Akbar Shah's pretensions to greatness caused an issue in 1814–15. In that year Lord Hastings, successor to Lord Minto as Governor-General, travelled upcountry. A meeting between the two had been arranged, and Hastings had requested a chair on the same level as the Emperor during their meeting as a sign of the changed relationship. This was to be a meeting of equals. Akbar Shah, however, refused to see the meeting as anything other than a ruler meeting a subject and inferior. The request for a chair was refused. This no doubt irritated the Governor-General, who promptly cancelled the meeting. However, this particular royal prerogative managed to survive despite European disapproval. Nobody was provided with a chair during an audience with the Emperor, not even the Governor-General or the British Commissioner. Whatever their status, Akbar Shah continued to treat European servants of the Company as if they were his domestic servants. In 1828, for example, Lord Combermere, the British Commander-in-Chief, would visit the palace. A European in Combermere's party noted the aloofness of the Emperor:

> The old monarch, mindful of his dignity, scarcely deigned to notice, even by a look, the Commander-in-Chief as he approached to present his *nazir* ... He did not even condescend to raise his eyes towards the rest of the party, as we advanced one by one, salaamed and offered our three gold *mohurs*...

Nevertheless, times were changing and the British insisted on changes to protocol and etiquette. For instance, the Emperor used to call the British Resident his 'beloved son' ('*Farzand-i-Arjumand*') as a term of respect but also to show his seniority in the relationship. Charles Metcalfe had felt no need to change this. After Metcalfe, there were objections to this patronising form of address and the Emperor would be asked to refrain from addressing the Resident in such a manner. In 1827, Lord Amherst (Governor-General 1823–28) decided to dispense entirely with the pretence of the East India Company being a vassal of the Emperor. He declared that the British Government of India would not consider itself in any way subservient to the House of Timur and that it was the de facto sovereign power of the land. 'Your Kingship is but nominal; it is merely out of courtesy that you are addressed as King,' Lord Amherst would remind the monarch.

In 1835, it was announced the Emperor would henceforth be addressed merely as 'King of Delhi'. Alongside this was a move to brush away the remnants of anything implying the servants of the company were mere lieutenants of the Emperor. In the same year, the reference to the Mughal Emperor was taken off the coinage of the East India Company, with a new Company rupee bearing the image of the British monarch put into circulation. The text on all coinage was changed from Persian to English. The imperial mint in Delhi had already been closed on the orders of Lord Hastings back in 1816.

In 1838, Lord Auckland decided to travel to Delhi and meet the Emperor. Auckland, like Hastings in a previous time, wanted a meeting on 'a footing of perfect equality', and any etiquette inconsistent with the rank and dignity of the Governor-General, like the custom of the *nazar*, was to be dispensed with. However, Zafar, like his father before him, would not concede. The meeting never took place.

Until 1842, the Emperor still sat on his throne while receiving the British Resident and other British dignitaries. This was not the celebrated Peacock Throne, however, but a replica decorated with rubies and gilded peacocks. This throne was kept in the Diwan-i-Khas (Hall of Special Audience), a chamber in the Red Fort, and was used by Zafar when receiving the British Resident, among other state or formal occasions. However, in 1842, with the custom of the *nazar* already having been put aside, the throne itself was shut away in a room below the King's sitting room. It would not be used again till 1857 when the sepoys reinstated Zafar as Emperor of Hindustan. Lord Ellenborough also insisted that the Resident make clear to the Emperor that any successor to the throne must be approved by the British. The Earl of Dalhousie, Governor-General from 1848 to 1856, meanwhile, decreed that British officers should disregard the local custom of showing overt respect to the Emperor's cavalcade as it passed through Delhi.

By 1857, agreements made between the Durbar and the British meant that Zafar had no power beyond the palace. Only his immediate staff in the palace could show obeisance. He could only offer presents, titles and *khillats* (dresses of honour) to his immediate courtiers and hangers-on. He was not allowed to accept any token of sovereignty from any ruler or individual who accepted the supremacy of the East India Company. Moves were also made to prevent the Emperor and the royal princes, or in fact any of the *salatin* (relatives of the Emperor and previous Emperors residing in the palace), from travelling around the country without permission first being obtained from the British authorities. The Emperor and the heir apparent remained exempt from the law of the land – that is, British jurisdiction, as did the palace. However, once outside of the palace they could be arrested if accused of any crime.

Even inside the palace, Zafar's powers were now limited when it came to meting out serious punishment. During the reign of his father, Shah Akbar, for example, the Emperor could order an offender's hands, ears or nose cut off for any transgression – perhaps even on a whim. The unfortunate person could then be ejected from the palace. This prerogative was snatched away during Akbar's last few years by the British Resident, albeit in polite fashion. When the Resident suggested the draconian punishments be ceased, he is said to have replied, 'What! Am I not King in my own place?' 'Undoubtedly, your Highness is the Conqueror of the World and the Protector of Princes,' replied the Resident, 'but such a course is not pleasing to the Governor-General, and it would be a great evil to the world if the friendship of two such mighty and illustrious Sovereigns were to be interrupted!' Though aggrieved, the Emperor had no choice but to submit at that point, consoled somewhat by the retention of milder punishments.

# 2

# A State of Permanent Penury

> On this palace, once worthy of India, now the marble even cannot be seen from the filth. Would that I were King of India! I would make Moscow and Pekin shake. Before this no palace ever met my eye that excited a wish to become its master.[1]
>
> Sir Charles Napier, Commander-in-Chief of India 1848–49

Loss of authority over Delhi and life under the British thumb were not the only pains endured by Zafar and his father on ascending to the throne. Arguably of more immediate concern was the financial trouble created by the British pension arrangements agreed upon during Lord Lake's time. Soon after his reign commenced in 1806, Akbar Shah penned a letter to the Governor-General complaining that his stipend was insufficient to properly maintain his person, his court, his household and his palace, and requesting an increased allowance:

> It must be known to you that since our accession to the Throne the expenses and disbursements of the Royal Household have become more numerous while the receipts have continued the same as they were before. The arrangements for the establishments of the Princes, the Ladies of the Royal Family and ministers of Court are consequently suspended. Our sacred mind is confident therefore that in consideration of these circumstances you will now in a more satisfactory manner than ever fulfil the promises which were given to His late Majesty (the Emperor Shah Alam) with respect to a further augmentation of the sources of His Majesty's convenience and comfort. Considering our Royal favour towards you to be daily increasing; continue to transmit addresses to the Royal Presence.[2]

Akbar Shah would continue to lament his perceived financial embarrassments. Many years later, in 1830, he would even send an ambassador, Raja Mohan Roy, to England to plead his case. In the letter entrusted to Raja Mohan Roy, Akbar candidly expressed his predicament and the humiliations related to his desperate existence:

> I might remind your Majesty of the time when my ancestors ruled supreme over these countries where their wretched descendant and sole representative of their dynasty is compelled to drag on a dependent existence in a dilapidated palace exposed to the contempt or receiving the sympathy of the different classes of society both Europeans and Asiatics who resort to Dehli, with means utterly inadequate to support the dignity even of a nominal sovereignty or to afford a scanty subsistence to the numerous branches of his family who look to him as their only stay.[3]

Raja Mohan Roy's embassy bore some fruit: the East India Company Court of Directors offered a modest increase of 25,000 rupees a month. However, this was subject to conditions unpalatable to the proud Emperor. The pension arrangements Akbar Shah had agreed to in 1813 were for an annual sum of 12 lakh (1.2 million) rupees to be paid in monthly instalments with another clause indicating that in 1833 the pension would be increased to 15 lakh rupees. However, this clause had two conditions: the Emperor had to refrain from requesting further sums, and surrender the arrangement of pensions for the various members of the royal family and *salatin* to British authorities in the city. Akbar Shah had balked at this encroachment into his affairs, refusing the offer of the increased allowance; the pension had therefore stayed at 12 lakh rupees.

When Zafar took the throne in 1837, he asked for an increase and was offered the arrangement rejected by Akbar Shah. Like his father, he felt the conditions were overly punitive and refused the offer. The royal pension arrangements therefore remained unchanged for over forty years, with the British Government in Calcutta refusing to countenance an increase without further concessions from the Emperor. There was also some confusion as to the nature of the pension. In earlier times, what the British authorities considered a pension was welcomed by the Emperor as a *peshkash* or tribute, which signified a different kind of relationship between the two.

The British pension was not the only income the Emperor received. His coffers were bolstered by roughly 1.5 lakh rupees thanks to Crown lands on the banks of the Jumna and various properties in Delhi itself, with this money being administered in trust by the British authorities. In total, the Emperor expected to receive around 2.7 lakh (270,000) rupees a year. This was a fairly substantial income for anyone but a monarch. By Zafar's time, however, his own allowance from this sum amounted to only 79,300 rupees; the bulk of the money disappeared into pensions for the numerous members of the royal family, salaries for servants, courtiers and guards, and the general upkeep of the court and palace. Like his father before him, Zafar had attempted to enlist support in England for his case; he would employ an Englishman, the well-known abolitionist George Thompson, to help his cause – albeit with little success.

*****

Despite the straitjacket of the fixed pension, Zafar maintained the customs and rituals of the Durbar as best he could. Anyone wishing to have an audience with the Emperor had to go through a ritual that still preserved the prestige and mystique of more prosperous times. Zahir Dehlvi, an attendant at the Mughal Durbar and later a witness to the siege of the city, described the complex proceedings of an audience with the Emperor:

> When the emperor graced the court, there would be two rows of courtiers, standing according to their rank, on either side of the throne. They would have their gaze lowered. No one could move, smile, talk or even look at anyone else. The courtiers couldn't even scratch themselves. Two rows of attendants would stand on both sides of the Durbar, red sticks in their hands. If anyone transgressed even slightly, these sticks would be hooked on to their necks and the offender would be ejected from the durbar. There was no durbar in the country that could be compared to this.

Upon paying obeisance by performing three salaams, 'respectfully bending from the waist thrice with the hand on the forehead', a herald would be heard proclaiming, '*Mulaihza adab hai. Adab baja lao. Jahanpanah, Badshah Salamut, Alampanah*', meaning, 'Attention! Greetings, present your salutations to the Refuge of the World, long live the Emperor, the Refuge of the Universe!'[4]

After more ritual, the visitor would approach the throne and offer the *nazar*, which the Emperor would pick up and pass to the attending *darogha*, who was responsible for collecting tributes. The visitor would then respectfully retire – facing the Emperor all the while – before joining the rest of the nobles gathered for the Durbar. The expensive gifts of previous years had gone, however. Due to Zafar's financial predicament, the *khillats* given to the Emperor's visitors now tended to be made of tinsel and of little value.

The ordinary inhabitants of the city could have audience with the Emperor as well. The *jahorka darshan* was an age-old practice begun by Akbar Shah to provide an audience to his subjects and to listen to petitions. In the Red Fort this was carried out at the Musamman Burj, also known as the Saman Burj, on the east side of the fort where a balcony faced the river. The practice was called *Zer-e-jharokha*, meaning 'under the balcony'. When Zafar appeared, there would be a great cheer from the assembled crowd before proceedings began. Other formalities continued as well. Sixteen horses were used to pull the Emperor's carriage around the city on formal occasions, for example, while eight horses were used to pull Zeenat Mahal's carriage. Zahir Dehlvi was impressed by Zafar's ability to maintain the court while living within his means.

> If one were to glance at the income and expenditure of the court, one would be astonished, wondering how they could ever match each other. How was the revenue so blessed that there was never any shortage in meeting the royal expenses? These included expenses for royal workshops, personal bodyguards of the emperor, water department, dispensary, department of the royal wardrobe, department of the royal jewellery, artillery, camel shed, wagon house, workshop in charge of the umbrella and standards taken out in ceremonial procession of the Dignity of the Fish Emblem, office of the quartermaster, library, pigeon house, salary to the official in charge of collecting/tabulating the tributes paid to the emperor by guests, the official in charge of the carpets/furnishings, the official in charge of carriages, the official in charge of the porters who carried the carriage, office of the royal bodyguards, the official in charge of the eunuchs, the official in charge of executions and department of household expenses. It is impossible to write about them in detail, as it would become too long.[5]

The reality was that this pomp and circumstance cost a huge amount of money. Zafar tried his best to manage his outgoings and institute cuts, but sometimes his hands were tied. Royal weddings were one instance where parsimony was difficult. At the wedding of the prince Mirza Jawan Bakht on 2 April 1852, for example, much munificence was necessarily displayed. The whole city was lighted and decorated, and festivities went on for ten to twelve days, with numerous entertainments organised and dancers invited to entertain the crowds. Zahir Dehlvi described the opulence on display:

> All the royal employees and nobles of Shahjahanabad were presented with a tray or dish of various meats, called tora. People could either take the tora or Rs.50 cash instead. All the employees who were listed in the Court were given a tora by name. For instance, my father, my younger brother, my mother (who also received a fixed salary from the Court) and I were each given separate trays. I told the manager who was in charge of distributing the tora to send another one to the house, but only after eight days. The food was distributed very generously and lavishly. The day a tora came, we would send it to the houses of various friends and relatives. There were so many items in one tray that an entire gathering could eat to their heart's content. These trays would fill

> up the hallway of my house. Each tray had food weighing 5 ser: there were four or five different kinds of palao, many types of sweet rice coloured red, yellow and purple, 5 ser of sweets, salted baqarkhwani (a type of flat bread) and different types of naan. Every kind of food was present on these trays. In brief, I have never come across such a ceremony in any other kingdom, even though I saw this particular court in its decline.

The matter of how strong a military contingent the Emperor could retain was never considered by the British authorities in the agreement of 1803. After all, he was a pensioner of the British Government and could not support any meaningful force on his relatively small allowance. Nevertheless, for ceremonial purposes, the Emperor had managed to retain an armed contingent or bodyguard. This force totalled around 1,200 men, with three separate divisions of cavalry, infantry and artillery. There were also six serviceable cannon – there were others in reserve around the palace, but they were in need of repairs. This miniature 'army' was commanded by the eunuch Mahbub Ali Khan. The guard had little purpose beyond ceremonial occasions and was ill-trained and ill-fitted with what resembled European uniforms. These men could be seen ambling around wearing their poorly made uniforms, which were variously black, brown or dark blue, with red waistbands and turbans. There was a small special guard which wore red coats with dark blue turbans and waistbands.

Upkeep of the palace and the payment of numerous royal employees was no mean feat. Such outgoings combined with the inflexible pension arrangements meant that even the Emperor himself was frequently in debt, and in later years the Government would invariably send his allowance under a strong guard to prevent the money being hijacked by creditors outside of the palace. Many of the princes, too, reliant on portions of Zafar's pension, found themselves heavily in debt; the only thing in their favour was the sanctuary of the palace, which prevented their arrest. Plainly, Zafar's British pension was insufficient to meet the demands of such a large household considering the spending required of a ruler who wished to retain a modicum of aura and majesty.

The allowances of the *salatin* had shrivelled over time and were frequently paid late or not at all. Consequently, they lived in abject poverty in the palace. Some, in desperation, took out loans which they could not hope to pay off considering they were barred from employment. On hearing of this, Zafar forbid the *salatin* to take out loans as non-payment would necessitate an appearance before a judge at the court, causing acute embarrassment. However, financial difficulties led the Emperor himself to take out loans to satisfy the *salatin* as the complaints inside the palace walls proved too much for his ears. Somewhat to his embarrassment, Zafar was even forced to write to the British Resident in the city at one point asking him not to send his monthly allowance directly to the fort as plans were afoot by the *salatin*, no doubt helped by servants, to appropriate the treasure.

The *salatin*'s complaints of privation were quite genuine. Their living conditions shocked many visitors to the palace, with Cave-Browne referring to 'swarms of pensioned yet penniless hangers-on of that most profligate pauperised court'.[6] An earlier Emperor, Jahandar Shah (1712–13), had set a precedent by instructing royal family members to reside in the Red Fort and to spurn employment – labour being considered below the dignity of the royal family. Back then, the *salatin* compound must have been a gilded cage, with comfortable surroundings for its residents and sizeable allowances for all. However, as the fortunes of the dynasty declined and as the numbers of *salatin* increased with the years, conditions worsened in the compound. The situation was made worse by the generally large harems kept by Mughal Emperors, which were also accommodated in the enclosure. For example, Zafar's grandfather Shah Alam kept a harem more than 500 strong and ended up siring around seventy sons not to mention daughters. To many, the salatin quarters resembled a zoo with uncared for animals. Major Cunningham, a British officer visiting the fort, leaves one of the more colourful description of the *salatin* quarter.

> The salatin quarter consists of an immense high wall so that nothing can overlook it. Within this are numerous mud huts in which these wretched objects live. When the gates were opened there was a rush of miserable, half-naked, starving beings who surrounded us. Some men apparently eighty years old were almost in a state of nature, who from earliest infancy had been shut up; other young men, sons of kings whose mothers had either died or were not in favour ... other young children who had the space within these walls to look forward to as their world. The utmost allowed was a few blankets during the cold weather, distributed as if by the king, but in fact by a private charity of Seton.

There had been moves by the British Resident to open up a college inside the palace for the benefit of the princes so that they could achieve some level of education. However, the *salatin* felt there was little point in developing skills when they were forbidden to take employment. With little to do and much time on their hands, they idled away the days in the warren of small buildings inside the palace. To prevent escape, eunuchs guarded the walled enclosure and the doors of their residences were locked from the outside at night, the keys then being handed over to a head eunuch. In addition, the eunuchs did regular headcounts to ascertain if any had escaped. Despite these precautions, several princes are known to have disappeared over the years only to resurface in foreign courts asking for pensions or assistance; no doubt the eunuchs could be bribed if sufficient sums were handed over. After Delhi fell to the British in September 1857, the *salatin*, having spent their entire lives isolated from society, would be expelled from their enclosed compound and loosed on the city. Lacking the necessary skills to earn a living, most of them quickly sank into more visible poverty.

*****

The palace, which was known as the Qila-i-Mualla (meaning Fort of Exalted Dignity) but is more commonly known today as the Red Fort, was undoubtedly what gave purpose to Delhi as it was the seat of the Mughal Emperors. In Mirza Sangin Beg's narrative *Sair-ul-Manazil*, describing the city in the 1820s, the cost of building the palace complex and walls is put at sixty lakh rupees. The Diwan-i-Khas alone cost 14 lakh rupees to construct.[7] The walls and moat of the palace cost 21 lakh rupees. The height of the palace walls was set at 75 feet, rising to 110 feet above the ditch, with the distinctive red sandstone entirely dominating the east of the city.

The main entrance of the palace, the Lahore Gate, faced the Chandni Chowk (or Silver Street), the main commercial thoroughfare. Passing through the gate, a visitor would traverse a magnificent vaulted arcade or gallery, 375 feet long and generally reckoned to be one of the most impressive entrances of any extant palace. Also inside the arcade were various shops and businesses that serviced the *salatin* and workers of the palace. At the centre of the arcade was an octagonal space with staircases at the north and south leading to the apartments above the fortress entrance; these were the preserve of the commandant of the guard, who effectively had authority over the palace. Travelling through the arcade, a visitor would reach the Naqqar Khanna, a pavilion used to store the palanquins and musical instruments used on official business. In the heyday of the Mughal Empire, this had been where the nobility alighted from their elephants before being led into the presence of the Emperor. 'Above this building is a tall pedestal building and in this place kettledrums are played thrice daily, that is, in the morning, evening and midnight, and on Sunday drums are beaten throughout the day because this day is associated with the sun and similarly drums are beaten throughout Wednesday as it is the day of Hazrat Khalifa Rabbani Hazrat Muhammad Akbar Shah Badshah Ghazi's coronation,'[8] wrote Mirza Sangin Beg.

The palace was a city in itself with its own sizeable population. Inside the walls were the royal buildings, mosques and gardens complete with summer houses as well as living accommodation. In addition to this, the barracks inside the walls could house as many as three regiments. Here, in a peculiar forum-like atmosphere not found in any other palace in the world, could be seen beggars, sepoys, servants, locals and shopkeepers of the palace as well as royals. No count of the residents of the palace was ever made by the British after the capture of the city but an arguably conservative estimate suggested that the *salatin* compound held over

2,000 people. All in all, around 10,000 people would settle down to sleep inside the fort on any given night, with an estimated 12,000 people servicing the palace in one capacity or another during its heyday.

Among the droves within the walls was a small European contingent. By the 1820s, a British officer had assumed the position of commandant of the fort and palace; the first was one Capt. Macpherson, and the incumbent in 1857 was Capt. Douglas. The commandant had been allocated pride of place in the apartments above the Lahore Gate, of which there were three. One was in use by the ill-fated Capt. Douglas. The second was used by Revd Jennings, an Anglican missionary. The third, in May 1857, was used by the reverend's daughter, who was currently sharing the apartment with her friend, a Miss Clifford.

There also happened to be a large number of unofficial residents in the palace. Assorted ruffians, murderers and kidnappers had begun using the palace as a refuge because British jurisdiction stopped at the palace walls. The princes, always in dire financial straits, invariably accepted bribes from these criminals in exchange for sanctuary. Contemporary British accounts from visitors to the palace mention 'the whole vast complex being crammed with murderers, thieves, kidnappers and other criminals, who thumbed their noses at authority and lived safely in his [Zafar's] shadow'. The palace's role as a safe haven for criminals irritated the British authorities, but little could be done about the situation short of taking the palace and ejecting the royal family.

The palace complex itself was divided into three primary sections. On reaching the Naqqar Khanna, the magnificent state buildings could be found directly ahead, in the middle of the palace perimeter. Among them was the Diwan-i-am, where the Emperor would hold court, but without argument the most beautiful of the buildings was the Diwan-i-Khas, where the throne was kept. 'A seat of solid crystal like a block of massive ice was placed in a window, which from its delicate tracery seemed spun from marble – a fit spot for such a seat and not unworthy of him who styled himself "Ruler of the World,"'[9] was how one visitor recorded the magic of the scene. A red curtain used to hang on the entrance, separating the Emperor and throne from others.

Next came the northern section of the palace. This held the royal gardens, with the royal stables to the far north, while to the north-west of the fort were the various houses of the princes, including Mirza Mughal, as well as the Royal Cannon House. Water was raised into the palace at the Shah Burj in the north-east corner of the palace, where it cascaded down a small, picturesque cataract in marble canals amid buildings, gardens and fairy-tale fountains. Some of the buildings were designed to allow in a shower of mist from nearby fountains in the warmest months. The gardens bore the usual Islamic symmetrical pattern and contained a large structure of red stone which was surrounded by a moat fed by the canal. The denizens could take pleasure boats out on this moat.

The third major section of the palace took up the south of the complex, where stood the labyrinthine set of buildings inhabited by the Emperor, his sizeable harem, his family and the *salatin*, who occupied a rabbit warren of meaner buildings.

*****

With the onset of Mughal poverty in Shah Alam's time, a gentle ruin of the palace and its surroundings had begun. The massive sandstone walls of the fort, running nearly two-thirds of a mile from north to south and visible from the Chandni Chowk, required little maintenance and so retained the capacity to awe visitors. The inside of the palace, however, was a different story. Even a cursory glance would show how far the dynasty had fallen; the signs were apparent as soon as a visitor walked through the Lahore Gate. The gallery and courtyard were in a pitiful state when the American poet Bayard Taylor visited the palace in 1853:

> The vaulted gallery must have once been an imposing prelude to the splendours of the palace; but it is now dirty and dilapidated, and the quadrangle into which it ushers the visitor resembles a great barn yard, filled with tattered grooms, lean horses and mangy elephants. The buildings surrounding it were heavy masses of brick and sandstone, rapidly falling into ruin. But there was another gate before us, and I hastened through it, hoping to find something which would repay the promise of the magnificent exterior. There was, indeed, the Palace of Shah Jehan, but in what condition! Porticoes of marble, spoiled by dust and whitewash, exquisite mosaics with all the precious stones gouged out, gilded domes glittering over courts heaped with filth, and populated with a retinue of beggarly menials. This was all that was left of the Empire of Tamerlane and Akbar – a miserable life-in-death, which was far more melancholy than complete ruin.[10]

The formerly exquisite *pietra dura* work on many of the state buildings had been defaced, with the semiprecious stones gouged out to leave empty cavities. Many doors and windows were in a state of dilapidation. In order to preserve some of the splendour of the Diwan-i-Khas, artificial stone and glass had been inserted into cavities that once held gems; the effect was underwhelming, as they had none of the lustre of the genuine article. Gone also were the expensive silk carpets and curtains. Crumbling buildings met the eye in all directions, and a layer of dirt dulled once brilliant paintwork and hid the beauty of marble. Mud walls had been erected for the sake of economy, contrasting poorly with the existing marble. The palace mosque, the Moti Masjid, had fallen into a pitiful disrepair, with peepul trees (*ficus religiosa*) growing through its walls. As far as the palace gardens went, the trees and the walkways around the gardens were overrun by weeds, with the rose bushes unpruned, while the water tanks and fountains were covered by a thick scum. This was also the case in the gardens of the commandant of the fort, which surrounded the entrance hallway and were now filled with refuse and largely occupied by beggars who ambushed visitors with requests for alms. The water canals were neglected; dry and clogged with detritus, they perhaps presented an even sadder aspect than the prominent buildings. The only saving grace was the foliage of the gardens, which masked some of the neglect and decay.

Without the lifeblood of the water running through the canal system, one half of the beauty of the palace had disappeared. Even the most prominent buildings had been shorn of their original significance as the Durbars of old had come to a close. Various buildings, mean and unworthy compared to the splendour of those built during the heyday of the empire, had sprouted inside the palace complex, particularly to the north. Other buildings were decaying or used for purposes other than was originally intended. The artillery and magazine quarters, for instance, situated to the north of the entrance hallway, were no longer apparent; there was no army of artillery to be supplied anymore. The former location of the throne in the Diwan-i-Am, visitors found, was marred with bird-droppings; nests could be seen overhead in the roof of the structure. It was now full of lumber, broken palanquins and empty boxes while also being used by the King's private guard as a place to sleep. Only the high-pitched voices and laughter emanating from the nearby women's quarters compensated for the sadness of the surroundings.

Whether Zafar was ever fazed by the curious Europeans who came to visit him in his misfortune and poverty is difficult to say. He welcomed them warmly and kept up the pretensions of royalty as best he could in the circumstances. Europeans visiting the palace complex were invariably impressed by what they saw, for the palace still retained a faded grandeur. Zafar's state of poverty naturally generated some sympathy for the fallen dynasty. Bishop Reginald Heber, of Calcutta, visited Akbar Shah in early 1824. As he walked around the palace he was immediately enveloped by a swarm of beggars:

> All, however, was dirty, desolate, and forlorn, and I felt a melancholy interest in comparing the present state of this poor family with what it was two hundred years ago. There are, perhaps, few royal families which have practised, during their power, so many vices and so few virtues as the house of Timour. Yet their present circumstances are surely pitiable, and their reverses afford us an awful instance of the instability of all human greatness. But the gigantic genius of Tamerlane, and the distinguished talents of Achbar, throw a sort of splendour over the crimes and follies of his descendants; and I heartily hope that government will reverence the ruins of fallen greatness, and that at least no fresh degradation is reserved for the poor old man, with all the imaginable wealth and splendour, under the name of the Great Mogul![11]

3

# The Succession

> It has been determined that these appearances of subordination and dependence could not be kept up consistently with a due respect for the real and solid power of the British Government, and the same may be said of the title of King of Delhi, with the fiction of paramount sovereignty which attaches to it.[1]
>
> Lord Canning, Governor-General of India, 1856–1862

In addition to a host of concubines, Zafar had four wives: Begum Ashraf Mahal, Begum Akhtar Mahal, Begum Zeenat Mahal and Begum Taj Mahal. Of these four, Zeenat Mahal was much his favourite. During the 1850s, as Zafar aged, Zeenat Mahal would exercise the most influence over him while showing the most energy and ambition regarding the succession to the throne. She placed much less faith in the court astrologer than the Emperor and seems to have scorned British plans to bring the dynasty to a quiet end, harbouring aspirations for her only son, Jawan Bakht. However, Jawan Bakht was the fifteenth of Zafar's twenty-two sons and was therefore unlikely to succeed.

A natural schemer, Zeenat Mahal is said to have hated the British, whose authority over the city and over any succession to the throne rankled greatly, as did the imposition of a British commandant over the palace and numerous other indignities sustained over the years. For example, it was thought – but not proved – that Zeenat Mahal had grown furious with Sir Thomas Metcalfe, Commissioner of Delhi in 1853, during negotiations for Zafar's successor and had poisoned him. The widow of the Revd George Coopland would visit Zeenat Mahal during her incarceration after the siege of the city; her description of the queen, perhaps coloured by recent events, was a cold and uncomplimentary one:

> Seated on a charpoy we beheld a large bold-looking woman, with not the least sign of royalty or dignity about her. She seemed about forty; her complexion was tawny, and her face large and coarsely featured, with daring black eyes and wide mouth, and dark hair partially concealed under her white cotton chuddar. She wore a cotton dress of black print and but few ornaments; her small and well-shaped hands and feet were bare. Judging from her looks, she seemed capable of inciting the king on to deeds of blood, which she was accused of having done.[2]

Zeenat Mahal was she described as being 'old and ugly'. Certainly the queen looked older than her years; the only extant image of her from this time shows a rather tired old woman, although she was still only sixty-three years old. She seems to have the vanity expected of a queen. Helen Douglas Mackenzie also had occasion to visit Zeenat Mahal before the mutiny, and she offered to draw a sketch of her:

> She was so long in adorning herself, that it was dark soon after I began. They brought out boxes full of jewels; she put on about five pair of earrings, beside necklaces, a nose-ring with a string of pearls connecting it with the ear, rings for the fingers, besides ornaments for the head. Then she retired to change her dress, some of the women holding up the cotton *rezai* (wadded quilt) in which her majesty had been wrapped, as a screen. She came back dressed in red muslin spotted with gold, and sat down *huqa* in hand, with two female servants with peacock fans, or rather clubs, behind her. When I looked closer at her, I saw that she could not be old, but she is very fat, with large though unmeaning eyes, and a sweet mouth. Her hair, like that of all the other women, of whom there must have been about fifty present, was *a la Chinoise*.[3]

She added that the Empress laughed with her mouth open at some jest and that neither her or the other women in the room appeared to have done any work in their lives.

The British Commissioners of the city tended to be dismissive of Zafar's various sons. These princes were seen by the various British Residents as *bons vivant* minus the means. Although Zafar understood and seemed resigned to British plans on terminating the dynasty, this did not mean his sons felt the same. C. F. Andrews recalls an anecdote from a time when Zafar had fallen gravely ill. The news had caused a fierce quarrel among the princes as to who would ascend the throne after his death, which seemed imminent. So serious were the struggles that the British authorities posted a strong guard at the entrance of the palace in expectation of violence, albeit with orders not to enter the complex as per the agreement that it was outside British jurisdiction; the hope was that the guard's simple presence would prevent bloodshed. Zafar, on hearing of the troops, asked for their removal. He sent a message to the Commissioner: 'Sir, do you think that my dead body will fight against the English? May I not be allowed even to die in peace?' The Commissioner relented, and the troops were removed. The rivalry of the princes, however, had been made clear.

In all fairness, the princes, living in pensioned idleness, had little else to occupy them. With no real responsibility, they whiled away much of their time in idle pleasures. 'The favourite outdoor sport among the nobles, within the Fort, was cock-fighting. Immense sums of money would be won or lost in gambling upon the issue of a single cock fight. Such a decadent sport as this revealed a decadent age,'[4] C. F. Andrews wrote. 'But the greatest trouble always came from them [the princes]. They were turbulent and violent-tempered, incessantly quarrelling among themselves, and stirring up factions both in the palace and in the city. They impoverished themselves by spending money lavishly on their own parties and in endeavouring to crush their opponents. More than any other single cause, I was told, they brought about the final ruin of the House of Timur.'

Despite British plans to bring the dynasty to an end, the issue of heir apparent remained a topic of discussion and intrigue in the palace during the decade leading up to the fateful year of 1857. Prince Dara Bakht had originally been Zafar's eldest son and crown prince; he had been a popular man, and generally accepted as heir apparent by his brothers. His succession had earlier been given the assent of the British Government as well. However, Dara Bakht passed away on 13 January 1849. The general assumption, as the *Delhi Gazette* pontificated, was that his death signalled the end of the line for the dynasty:

> On Thursday morning departed this life Prince Dara Bukht, heir-apparent to the throne of Delhi, leaving Shahzada Fakir-u-din as heir, and with him we have some reason to believe that all the right of the Royal House to the succession dies out, such having been guaranteed to him individually and to no other member of the family. We sincerely trust that such is really the case, and that our Government will now be in a position to adopt steps for making efficient arrangements for the dispersion, with a suitable provision, of the family on the death of the King.

As the *Delhi Gazette* pointedly mentioned, the promise of the throne had extended only to Dara Bakht. Indeed, when the news of the death of the crown prince reached Calcutta, Governor-General Dalhousie mused on whether this was the moment to take the final step and do away with the Mughal throne. 'The British Government,' he wrote, 'has become indeed and in truth the paramount Sovereign in India. It is not expedient that there should be, even in name, a rival in the person of a Sovereign whose ancestors once held the paramountcy we now possess. His existence could never really endanger us, I admit; although the intrigues of which he might, and not unfrequently has been made the nucleus, might incommode and vex us.'[5]

Dalhousie consulted with the Supreme Council, which was then made up of Sir Frederick Currie, Sir John Littler and John Lowis. Their opinions varied considerably. Currie suggested waiting till Zafar himself passed away, at which time the curtain could be finally drawn on the dynasty; in the meantime, the matter of the succession should be avoided as the British Government agreeing to a successor implied somebody would eventually take the throne. Littler, on the other hand, adopted a more conciliatory line. The Muslim population of the country, he argued, held the Mughal in great esteem and warmth; to end the dynasty in any sort of forceful or abrupt fashion would rebound on the British Government and result in vocal Muslim dissent. Whatever the decision taken, there must be no coercion involved. Zafar or his successor should agree to the Government's proposals to end the dynasty, although persuasion in the form of concessions and increased pensions would make any agreement more palatable. The dynasty must not be extinguished with drama but with as little fanfare as possible. Finally, Lowis took the most strident view of the three. He argued that the Muslim population cared little for the moribund dynasty or its role as a focus for Muslim aspirations. If they did, then that was all the more reason to terminate the Mughal line in abrupt fashion:

> But, if these fears are not groundless, surely they afford a positive reason for taking the proposed step, because the result anticipated, as it appears to me, can arise only if the Muhammadans (no doubt the most restless and discontented of our subjects) have continued to look upon the representatives of the House of Taimur as their natural head, and to count upon the Palace of Dehli as a rallying-point in the event of any outbreak amongst them. If it be so, it is surely sound policy, on the first favourable opportunity, to remove the head, and to put the projected rallying-point into safe hands.[6]

Dalhousie would ultimately take Littler's advice. It was communicated to the Commissioner of Delhi that a new crown prince would be acceptable to the British Government. But whoever was approached for the role would be asked to concede on vital points. The royal family would need to leave the palace, and inducements would be held out in the form of an increased pension. If the prospective crown prince baulked at making these concessions, other princes would be approached with the offer. Since the palace was a competitive atmosphere, there was little doubt that one prince or another would be happy to accept the conditions offered, attractive or not. In any case, a refusal was considered unlikely. Faced with the risk of losing the title, whichever prince was approached would accept the offer with alacrity.

In the palace, meanwhile, after the death of Dara Bakht, Zafar had chosen Fakir-ud-Din (also called Mirza Fakhru) as crown prince. Mirza Fakhru was an amiable chap, thirty years old, with a liking for all things European and well intentioned towards the British. Malleable enough to agree to British demands, he was the favoured prince as far as the Governor-General was concerned. In a confidential meeting, Mirza Fakhru was told by the Resident, Sir Thomas Metcalfe, that he would have the full backing of the British Government but would only be allowed to succeed to the throne on the condition that he and the royal family vacated the palace and moved into more modest accommodation upon his accession. This was more than a matter of mere accommodation, however, for the royal family would lose their immunity to British law upon leaving the palace. Further, the British authorities would manage the royal estates and subtract management expenses from the King's funds. All court etiquette was to be done away with; henceforth the new King would meet Governors-General on terms of entire equality.

A house near the Qutb Minar close to the walled city was suggested as the new King's residence, and in preparation for moving the entire royal household from the palace – which, given Zafar's age, was expected shortly – the Commissioner of Delhi had been asked to draw up a list of royal family members. Only those immediately related to the crown prince would live in the new residence; everybody else would have to fend for themselves. Metcalfe would make a list of 2,104 members of the royal family, including illegitimate children. Of these, it was found that 815 were descendants of Zafar's grandfather Shah Alam.

Mirza Fakhru was canny enough to realise no succession could be possible without the backing of the British authorities. Pleased to have their support and anxious to prevent his brothers being offered the throne, he agreed to all the conditions. The agreement was then drawn up and the prince signed away his right to the palace. His agreement with the British had been kept secret, as he was well aware that his father would not have agreed to the concessions. As expected, when news of the agreement reached Zafar's ears he was said to have been very angry. But the deal was done. Dalhousie himself was quite jubilant, having managed to engineer the exit of the royal family from the palace, although he showed a little frustration at the East India Company Court of Directors for not allowing the complete abolition of the royal title just yet. Dalhousie's proposal for the emptied palace, meanwhile, was that it could serve as a new magazine.

> The young Prince – on condition of being hereafter recognised as successor – has agreed to all I wanted, including possession of the great fortified palace in the city of Delhi, which might be very mischievous in their hands, and will be splendidly convenient for an arsenal in ours. No doubt it is rather utilitarian to turn the famous hall

> [Diwan-i-Khas] – 'Oh, if there be an Elysium on earth, it is this!' – into a storeroom for portfires and perambulators. But this is the nineteenth century, you see, and Elysiums are a little out of date, while portfires are still in common use! Seriously, all the historical structures will be carefully preserved: the outer enclosure will be valuable for its security. I wanted to take his crown as well as his palace, and got leave; but the Court of D[irectors]. were in hysterics about it for some six months, and I waived my own wishes and opinions on the matter rather than distress them, poor old ladies.[7]

In 1856 there came a new twist when Mirza Fakhru unexpectedly died of cholera on 10 July, aged just forty. Once again, the issue of the succession prompted the usual excitement and jockeying for position inside the palace. Zeenat Mahal forcefully pushed forward her son, Jawan Bakht, convincing Zafar that he should be the new crown prince. The morning after Mirza Fakhru's death, Zafar sent letters to the Resident, Simon Fraser, asking for the approval of Jawan Bakht as the crown prince. Along with his request were papers bearing the seals of eight of the other senior princes agreeing to accept Jawan Bakht as the crown prince – and also agreeing that he would be the most suitable choice. It all seemed a settled issue to the Commissioner. However, all the agreements made with Mirza Fakhru would now have to be renegotiated with the new crown prince.

Dissent inside the palace soon surfaced. The following day, a letter from the palace was delivered to the Commissioner. It was from Mirza Korash (Mirza Korash or Kivash), the eldest of Zafar's remaining sons. The prince complained to the Resident that he and the other princes had been coerced into agreeing, with Zafar threatening to reduce their allowances if they disagreed and promising to increase their allowances along with other concessions if they assented. Mirza Korash said that, being the oldest, he should surely have been next in line to the throne. 'As in this view, my ruin and birthright are involved, I deem it proper to represent my case, hoping that in your report due regard. will be had to all the above circumstances. Besides being senior, I have accomplished a pilgrimage to Mekka [Mecca], and have learned by heart the Koran; and my further attainments can be tested in an interview,' the prince appealed to Metcalfe.

Leaving aside his pilgrimage to Mecca and knowledge of the Quran, if primogeniture was taken into account the prince had a genuine right to succeed his father. The Calcutta-based Lord Canning, who had succeeded Dalhousie as Governor-General by this time, had little knowledge of the circumstances in Delhi. However, he agreed that Mirza Korash should succeed Zafar. Like Dalhousie, however, Canning was averse to carrying on the royal line at all. 'It is as desirable as ever that the Palace of Delhi – which is, in fact, the citadel of a large fortified town, and urgently required for military purposes – should be in the hands of the Government of the country, and that the pernicious privilege of exemption from the law, which is conceded to the Crown connexions and dependants of the King now congregated there, should, in the interests of morality and good government, cease,' Canning declared. He was, if anything, even more firm than Dalhousie in the belief that the pretence of royalty should be swept away and that 'the nominal and now unmeaning title of sovereignty with all its inconvenient pretensions should be discontinued'. He therefore reiterated that Dalhousie's previous conditions must be met, along with some more. 'Mirza Muhammad Korash must not be led to expect that his recognition will take place on the same terms as Mirza Fakhru's, and that during the King's lifetime no communication is to be made, either to his Majesty, or to any other member of the family, touching the succession,' he advised the Resident.

Although Korash would be accepted as head of the family on Zafar's death, he would not be awarded the title of King; instead, he would have the title of *Shahzadah* (or prince).[8] Privileges would be extended to the sons and grandsons of the head of the family but no further. With the royal family moving out of the palace and into a more modest residence, and therefore no longer responsible for the upkeep of the palace, the allowance for the prince would be cut from the 100,000 rupees Zafar received to only 15,000 rupees a month. Other relations and sons, grandsons of former Emperors, would lose the pensions and privileges they enjoyed in the palace. They would become ordinary citizens.

While some felt the matter was settled, perhaps unsurprisingly some did not see it that way – chief among them Zeenat Mahal, who still harboured hopes for her own son. Zeenat Mahal had now seen two crown princes pass away, and felt that another could be done away with if the moment was right. She persuaded Zafar to take into his service one T. C. Fenwick, whose job it was to write to the Governor-General pleading for Jawan Bakht to be instated as heir apparent. However, the missive received scant attention, with the reply coming that the Government had already discussed the issue and that 'the pretensions of Mirza Jawan Bakht to be recognised as heir apparent had long since been rejected by the Governor-General'. Zafar would make one last attempt along these lines in late 1856; this time, the Government simply ignored it.

Jawan Bakht was an indiscreet and transparent young man of fourteen years. He had developed a hatred for the British, perhaps from his mother, and this had not been softened by the British preference for Mirza Korash. Meanwhile, his mother was said to be plotting other intrigues to stymy the conclusion of the succession dispute. One story has it that she was using the King's superstitious nature to advance her cause, advising him that she had, with the aid of astrologers, lost ten years of her life and transferred them to him so that he might live correspondingly longer. In return, she expected her son to be made regent after his death.

# 4

# 'The English peace'

> ... God's beings, the King's country and by the
> order of the Company Bahadur ...
>
> Delhi town criers' preamble before 1857

Compared to the other large cities of Hindustan, there was nothing special about Delhi in terms of wealth and size at this time. Despite its recovery during the first half of the nineteenth century, the heyday of the city in reality had passed with the decline of the Mughal Empire centuries before. Still, it had a certain glamour. The salient characteristic of the city – that it had been the capital of the Mughal Empire and that the Mughal Emperor was still resident there – meant that it still held an inordinate importance. Elizabeth Muter, a colonel's wife who visited the city shortly after its capture, summed it up well: 'Its name touches a chord in the Mussulman's heart, and its history gives it a political importance which neither its wealth nor population warrants.'[1]

Delhi, or Shahjahanabad as it was locally and properly called, is a relatively young city. It had been founded by the Mughal Emperor Shah Jahan around AD 1650. That is not to say the area in and around Delhi had been vacant and unpopulated; the River Jumna and the hilly ridge running close by made for a convenient and sheltered triangular strip of land in which to found a city, and therefore the area had been settled long before the new city was built. Extensive ruins of previous cities, running mile after mile to the south of Shahjahanabad, gave a good intimation of the age and importance of the settlement of this area to even the most unlettered person. These were the ruins of cities like Firozabad, Indrapat, Siri (Shahpur) and Tughluqabad, about 15 miles further south. There were several other settlements at Kilokhri, around a mile south of Humayun's Tomb (burial place of the second Mughal Emperor), and Mubarakabad still further south. Meanwhile, the old city of Delhi was about 2 miles distant and still had walls and several thousand inhabitants in the 1850s.

It was between 1638 and 1648 that the fort-cum-palace of Shahjahanabad was built, followed in quick succession by the city walls and the main mosque of the city, the Jama Masjid. The layout of the city and its defences had changed little in the intervening years. The great size of the city meant its walls were correspondingly long, running a length of around 6 miles in total and broken by strong bastions at regular intervals. At most places the walls were around 12 feet wide and 27 to 30 feet high. Damaged by a heavy earthquake in 1720, they had been repaired during the English period. An attack on the city by the Marathas under Jaswant Rao Holkar between 7 and 15 October 1804 led to British authorities in the city carrying out other work, including repairing the Kashmir Gate (also known as the Ali Burj) between 1804 and 1811. In that latter year the walls had been further strengthened, with more bastions built and Martello towers added at various points along with a glacis. The Kashmir Gate was rebuilt entirely under the aegis of a British military engineer, Robert Smith, in 1835. The defence of the city against Holkar had been marshalled by Colonel Burn, and this was recognised in the construction of the Burn Bastion. The renovated Water Bastion (also called Badar Bas Burj by locals) became more formally known as the Moira Bastion after the Earl of Moira, Governor-General from 1813 to 1823.

Colonel Baird Smith, the highest authority on siege operations in the British camp during the siege, and who would go on to plan the attack on the city, left one of the more detailed descriptions relating to the defences of the city:

> The eastern face of the city rests on the Jumna, and during the season of the year when our operations were carried on, the stream may be described as washing the base of the walls. All access to a besieger on the river front is, therefore, impracticable. The defences here consist of an irregular wall, with occasional bastions and towers, and about one half of the length of the river face is occupied by the palace of the King of Delhi and its outwork – the old Mogul fort of Selimghur. The river may be described as the cord of an arc formed by the remaining defences of the place. These consist of a succession of bastion fronts, the connecting curtain being very long, and the outworks limited to one crown work at the Ajmer Gate and Martello Tower, mounting a single gun at such points as require some additional flanking fire to that given by the bastions themselves. The bastions are small, mounting generally three guns in each face, two in each flank, and one in embrasure at the salient. They are provided with masonry parapets about 12 feet in thickness, and a relief of about 16 feet above the plane of site. The curtain consists of a simple masonry wall or rampart 16 feet in height, 11 feet thick at top, and 14 or 15 feet at bottom. This main wall carries

> a parapet loophole for musketry 8 feet in height and 3 feet in thickness. The whole of the land front is covered by a berm of a variable width, ranging from 16 to 30 feet, and having a scarp wall 8 feet high; exterior to this is a dry ditch of about 25 feet in height, and from 16 to 20 feet in depth. The counter-scarp is simply an earthen slope easy to descend. The glacis is a very short one, extending only 50 or 60 yards from the counter-scarp; using general terms, it covers from the besiegers' view from one-half to one-third of the height of the walls of the place.
>
> These details will, I trust, be sufficient to give a general conception of the nature of the defences of Delhi. They are, in a word, modernised forms of the ancient works that existed when the city fell before Lord Lake's army in 1803. They extend about seven miles in circumference and include an area of about three square miles.[2]

The Martello towers could each handle a single large gun on traversing platforms and were connected to the walls by drawbridges. These could then provide flanking fire as an enemy attacked the walls. Each bastion meanwhile was designed to accommodate between nine and twelve guns each. In total, if fully armed the walls would bristle with 120 to 140 guns. With the ditch 25 feet deep, the drop from the 16-foot walls was around 40 feet if not more in many places. Whether the ditch had ever been filled with water from the river is open to speculation as the city never came under attack during the heyday of the Mughals, only being threatened in the empire's decline when the rulers lacked the energy and resources to execute such action. The city walls were broken by as many as fourteen main gates and various smaller wicket gates, and were bolstered by two bastions resting on the river side: the Water Bastion covered the north of the city walls, while in the extreme south the Wellesley Bastion terminated the land walls at the river.

In anti-clockwise order, the Kashmir Gate and Mori (or Drain) Gate opened out to the north. From the Mori Bastion, the city walls then suddenly turned south with three gates – the Kabul, Lahore and Ajmer – opening to the west while the Turkman and Delhi gates opened to the south. The gates on the river side were the Daryaganj (Khairati) and Rajghat gates south of the palace, while to the north of the palace along the river were the Calcutta, Nigambodh, Kela and Badar Rao gates. The Calcutta Gate had been a new addition during British times, connecting the bridge of boats across the Jumna (there was no permanent bridge across the river at this time). The walls were weakest on the city's river side, which had the stream to protect it. The only gate protected by a crown-work was the Ajmer Gate. A certain level of extra protection was provided by the Salimgarh Fort, which adjoined the palace to the north and overlooked the river and the bridge of boats. The Mughals had mostly used it as a prison.

When the city was constructed, the natural ridge to the north was never incorporated into its walled defences. A flaw in the defence of the city was therefore ever present, although it was never utilised by any attacking force – until 1857, that is, and the advent of larger guns. The only arresting site, breaking the flow of the city walls, was an aqueduct that carried drinking water into the city from 75 miles away. The river was not generally used by the locals since its waters were coloured by natron, a natural mixture of sodium carbonate decahydrate and sodium bicarbonate, salt and sodium sulphate that was considered unhealthy.

*****

European references to Delhi were generally complimentary about its layout and construction. 'Modern Delhi was the largest and most picturesque native city I had then seen. The houses are of brick and stucco, painted in gay colours, and very few of them less than two stories in height. They have tiled roofs, which gives the place, when seen from a minaret, a strong resemblance to Smyrna, and other large Turkish towns. It covers an extent of about two square miles, but is very compactly built, and the population is reckoned at near 200,000 souls,'[3] enthused Bayard Taylor. The city itself was quite densely populated, with residences running close to the palace walls. Houses in this area largely belonged to the nobility and middles classes of the city. Around the year 1850, there were estimated to be roughly 24,000 houses within the city walls, mostly 'pucka' – that is, made of brick.

The city was a kaleidoscope of beliefs, cultures, ideas and languages, with all sorts of people – Hindus, Sikhs, Muslims, Afghans, Persians, Europeans and traders from Central Asia – mingling in the walled city. The 1854 census of the North West provinces of the Bengal Presidency showed the resident population of Delhi as almost equally divided between Muslim and Hindu at nearly 50 per cent each.[4] The figures were probably much the same in 1857. It was noticed that there was a sharp division of labour, with the commerce and business in the city largely managed by Hindus while Muslims held the bulk of the administrative jobs.

The Chandni Chowk was the main thoroughfare of the city, running due west from the palace to the Lahore Gate. This wide avenue originally had a stream running through the middle of it, providing a special beauty. However, the stream disappeared under the walkways as the city grew. Lt Vivian Majendie of the Bengal Artillery wrote that it was 'a splendid street, the broadest and finest I ever saw in an eastern town, with a stone aqueduct or canal, and a fine row of trees planted down its centre, and on either side shops glittering with the jewellery, scarfs, coloured silks, shawls and the other manufactures for which Delhi is celebrated'.[5] The bank building, an imposing and decidedly European work, was also located on the Chandni Chowk. Completed in 1808, it was originally a palace for Begum Samru, a rich widow who hosted many parties there before her death in 1836. At these parties, very lavish affairs by all accounts, the well-to-do mingled with Europeans of high station; even the Mughal Emperor was invited. By 1857, it was operating as a bank with Thomas Beresford as its manager.

*****

Besides the palace, the most prominent landmark in the city was the Jama Masjid. A large mosque of sandstone and white marble constructed over six years, it sat on a grand platform overlooking the neighbourhood and was reached by flights of steps on all sides. Due to its relatively central location, the Masjid would survive much of the devastation wrought by British guns during the siege of the city. Situated over a mile south of the northern walls, it only sustained damage from one shell and even this burst in the wide space of the courtyard, leaving the mosque itself unharmed.

There were other prominent buildings and structures quite incongruous with the seventeenth-century Mughal architectural style. A huge number of European residences, bungalows and civil buildings had sprung up during the last half-century. As well as residing in what were termed the 'Civil Lines' north of the city walls, European civilians and some Anglo-Indians – mixed race Christians – now lived on a fashionable strip running along the entire eastern half of the walled city, adjacent or close to the palace, from the Kashmir Gate down through the Daryaganj area all the way to the Delhi Gate. One of the first of these houses, situated in a large enclosure adjacent to the Kashmir Gate, was that of Mrs Foster, an Anglo-Indian. Next to the Foster house was the kutchery or court. The land that the kutchery occupied ran right up to the city walls facing the river, so anyone located on top of the kutchery had a fine view of the Kashmir Gate to the north, the river and the left bank, and the road from Meerut. The court also doubled as the British treasury in Delhi. Because of this, the grounds of the kutchery also had a strong sepoy guard. A mile further south of the Kashmir Gate neighbourhood could be found St James' Church. Construction began on St James' Church in 1830 and was completed six years later. It was said to have cost as much as two lakh rupees and was entirely funded by the Anglo-Indian James Skinner, who had been buried in the church after his death in 1841.

The southern stretch of the British-occupied area ran from the south of the palace to the Delhi Gate and the city walls; this was the area known as Daryaganj. The Daryaganj was effectively the English quarter, where many Europeans engaged in trade and commerce made their residences. Formerly the artillery lines, the area was now home to conductors and others working or attached in some way to the magazine on the other side of the palace, along with the various clerks and other administrative staff working in the government offices. The area was also popular with the various European retirees and pensioners. This thick eastern band also contained the Delhi press building and the palatial Skinner residence.

There was also the Delhi Mission, where Revd A. Hubbard and another missionary, Mr Sandys, were based along with one Louis Koch. The area was also home to the Government College. G. F. Taylor was the principal, with two other Europeans, Mr Roberts and Mr Stewart, being assistant teachers. The residences of various civil employees were also clustered here, along with the warehouses of European merchants and other administrative and public buildings.

By 1857, the British East India Company's stores and munitions were held in three principal magazines in North India. Two were in the Punjab, at Ferozepore and Phillaur, both around 300 miles north of Delhi. These held huge amounts of munitions and many heavy guns to guard the recently annexed region. However, the biggest arsenal was located in the city of Delhi itself. This new British magazine – one of the largest in all of India – happened to be situated just a stone's throw from the palace on the road leading to the Kashmir Gate. Construction of the Delhi Magazine was completed in 1830. By some quirk of the earlier agreement with the King, an unusual situation had developed regarding the magazine. British troops were banned from the city because it was, on paper at least, under the authority of the King himself. As a result, the magazine was manned by only a nominal host of European officers and men stationed inside, assisted by Indian staff and other employees. The magazine was big enough to supply a large army. In addition to years' worth of powder and shot, the magazine was also said to hold around 150,000 muskets, enough to supply several armies.

Concerns had been raised about the magazine being built inside the city, particularly by Charles Napier. On 15 December 1849, Napier, then Commander-in-Chief in India, had travelled through Delhi. Reflecting on his journey, he would write to Governor-General Dalhousie about the issue, suggesting the magazine be moved out of the city to a less vulnerable position. 'It is placed in a very populous part of the city and its explosion would be very horrible in its effects as regards the destruction of life,'[6] he explained, going on to emphasise the threat such an explosion posed to the palace itself and nearby government property. Indeed, it would raze not just the magazine but all the surrounding British administrative buildings and residences. Napier's next point was prophetic:

> It is without defence, beyond what the guard of fifty men offer and its gates are so weak that a mob could push them in. I therefore think a powder magazine should be built in a safe place. There is a strong castle three or four miles from the town which would answer well but I fear the repairs would be too expensive more so perhaps than what would be more efficacious *viz* to build a magazine in a suitable position near the city. I send a sketch of the Arsenal and some works which ought to be constructed for its security. They are not of my proposing but I consider them well adapted to their object and recommend their being ordered.[7]

Put simply, the bustling urban location of the magazine, almost impossible to defend and packed with gunpowder, was a disaster waiting to happen.

Within a year, Napier had resigned as Commander-in-Chief and departed India. After that, any impetus for the relocation or reinforcement of the magazine seemed to disappear. However, it is fair to say that Dalhousie also sensed some danger in both the palace-cum-fort and the magazine being outside total British control:

> Here, we have a strong fortress in the heart of one of the principal cities of our Empire, and in entire command of the chief magazine of the Upper Provinces—which lies so exposed, both to assault and to the dangers arising from the carelessness of the people dwelling around it—that it is a matter of surprise that no accident has yet occurred to it. Its dangerous position has been frequently remarked upon, and many schemes have been prepared for its improvement and defence; but the only eligible one is the transfer of the stores into the Palace, which would then be kept by us as a British post, capable of maintaining itself against any hostile manoeuvre, instead of being, as it now is, the source of positive danger, and perhaps not unfrequently the focus of intrigues against our power.[8]

In any case, no immediate steps were taken. Indeed, no attempt was ever made to move the magazine. However, a sepoy guard under a British officer was stationed at the Kashmir Gate only half a mile away; this was deemed important as the Kashmir Gate was the main entrance from the north and the British cantonment. The guard at the gate was changed every week. None of the other gates of the city held a British guard.

*****

During the early years of the eighteenth century, Delhi had been almost totally enclosed within its walls. Security was a matter of the city gates being opened and closed each morning and night. With the advent of the British period, however, fears of outlawry waned and the city began to spill beyond its walls. The area just north of the walled city was populated almost entirely by European civilian and administrative buildings in what was called the Civil Lines, or what the locals called the 'White town'. The road running from the Kashmir Gate north to the ridge and into the cantonments bisected this large, elongated triangle of flat land flanked on the right by the river and the left by the ridge. The Civil Lines could be said to start immediately after one departed the Kashmir Gate heading north along the road to Panipat. Much of the construction here had taken place in recent decades and was therefore relatively new.

Immediately outside the city walls on the right was the British Custom House, adjacent to the riverbank. This was a modern European building complete with out-offices and surrounded by gardens. A few hundred yards north of the Custom House compound appeared the Qudsia Bagh, also on the right of the road. Once an impressive walled pleasure garden, it had been named after Qudsia Begum, consort of the eighteenth-century Emperor Mohammed Shah Rangila, who had organised its construction around 1748. Set in Persian Charbagh style, the garden originally had water channels and a pleasure palace within its 50-acre spread. Featuring various archways and cloisters, and with its end open towards the river, the Qudsia Bagh made for an idyllic retreat from the walled city. As revenues decreased over time, funds to maintain the gardens vanished. By the time of the mutiny, the bagh was neglected and partly ruined. Nevertheless, one could still find peace among the citrus trees and rose bushes growing within its confines.

Many fine mansions and bungalows could be seen in the Civil Lines. Ludlow Castle, since 1831 the Residency at Delhi, could be found situated on the left of the road, around a third of a mile from the Kashmir Gate. The building had been built by Samuel Ludlow, the Residency Surgeon, shortly after 1813. Due to its tower and the crenellations on its walls, it quickly assumed the name Ludlow Castle. The present occupant was Delhi Resident Simon Fraser. The structure was built on a slight ridge that sloped down towards the Kashmir Gate. Along the base ran a drainage channel that departed from the ridge and emptied at the river near the Qudsia Bagh.

Metcalfe House was another prominent landmark on the right-hand side of the road. The large house was difficult to see from the road, being situated on a 1,000-acre plot (forcibly purchased from nearby Gujjar villagers) and surrounded by extensive gardens and orange groves. According to Emily Metcalfe, the grounds of the mansion, complete with gardens and artificial lakes, ran right up to the walls of the Qudsia Bagh. Large stables and a cow-house were also situated on the grounds on the south or city side. Metcalfe House was newer than most nearby buildings, with its construction having only commenced in 1830. The mansion was spectacular, with 24-foot ceilings. Around the house was a veranda, 20 to 30 feet wide and supported by stone pillars. The house was a veritable treasure trove, too, perhaps the most well endowed of any European residence in Hindustan. It boasted expensive furniture of marble, mahogany and rosewood, along with paintings and memorabilia and ornaments. It had a study and a library with over 25,000 books, accumulated over many years by Charles Metcalfe, who liked to have books shipped from England twice a year, preferably bound in Russian leather. The mansion was also home to the 'Napoleon gallery', which held perhaps the largest collection of Napoleonic memorabilia at the time. Charles Metcalfe's daughter, Emily, later wrote what she remembered of the treasures of the room:

> The room called the 'Napoleon Gallery', which was in the northeast corner of the house, was entirely devoted to the memory of Napoleon Buonaparte, of whom as I have said my Father was a devoted admirer.

> Its bookcases were filled with all the best and most interesting works relating to his life and career, and the walls were covered with fine engravings: portraits of the great hero, of his generals, and of all the events of his life. In one corner of the room on a marble pedestal stood Canova's marble bust of Napoleon, a beautiful work of art of which I now possess only the broken pieces, which I gathered out of the ruins of the house at Delhi two years after the Mutiny. The centre and side tables in the Napoleon Gallery were covered with beautiful bronzes and statuettes, all connected with the history of the Emperor. One especially fine bronze, three feet long, depicted the fight of the Bridge of Lodi, but this, like everything else, was either destroyed or carried off on the day the house was looted in the middle of May 1857. On the centre table, under a glass case, there was a beautiful marble stand with an exquisite silver statuette of Napoleon, and below the figure were hung the Napoleon gem, which I possess, the Cross of the Legion of Honour, and his diamond ring with the initial on it, which my Father purchased after the death of Mr Fraser, to whom they had all been sent by Napoleon's desire, in acknowledgement of the courteous and generous gift which he despatched to St Helena for the use of the Emperor, but which was lost at sea, and therefore never reached the exiled hero. The cross and ring were left to my eldest brother and were destroyed on the day the house was looted, as my brother was still resident at Delhi. But fortunately I had taken the Napoleon gem with me to England in 1854.[9]

The house would suffer grievously during the mutiny. The entire book collection and the family treasures were plundered and set on fire by the nearby Gujjar villagers in what must have been a sort of justice for their forcible eviction from the land. Outside, the British Delhi Field Force would do its share of damage, cutting down the extensive orange groves and surrounding gardens to give the guns and pickets a clear field of vision.

The only other structure of interest was a shrine to a Hindu swami or holy man which occupied the lower slope of the ridge to the right of the road. This was called the Swami's House, but British soldiers quickly corrupted the name to the 'Sammy house'. In addition, a second, smaller British magazine also existed close to the city. This was a powder magazine containing 1,000 barrels of powder around 2 miles upriver near the ridge.

Immediately beyond the Metcalfe House grounds, the road north ascended the back of the Delhi ridge towards the British cantonment. Here the entire area was cut up by 'ravines', or dried ancient water channels. Anyone climbing the gravel road on the ridge would find the whole vista of the city opening up behind them. One could see the river, the northern and eastern walls of the city and the palace and Jama Masjid. What caught the eye close to the northernmost extremity of the ridge, however, was the Flagstaff Tower. This was a small, circular Gothic structure built in red sandstone and barely 17 feet in diameter. Inside the structure, a spiral staircase led to the castellated top. As with other European constructions in and around Delhi, the tower was relatively new, built in 1828 to serve as a signal tower – hence its placement on the ridge, the highest point in the area.

The biggest structure on the ridge was a modern and spacious residence that had previously belonged to Raja Hindu Rao, a Maratha aristocrat with connections to the Gwalior rulers, for whom it was named. For political reasons, Rao had moved to Delhi many years before and built the house to suit his European tastes. Hindu Rao was completed in 1830. The raja died in 1855, and the mansion had sat empty since. Many points on the ridge gave good views of the walled city, but the best was from the top of the Hindu Rao. Mrs Muter, visiting the city after its capture, recalled the impressive view from the mansion:

> Through trees and bungalows wound smooth macadamized roads; beyond were the fortifications. Still farther away rose domes and minarets, and behind all were the dark red walls of the palace. From green trees peeped the roofs of houses, and these were broken by spires and pagodas; and I feel sure that, even during the worst period of peril and anxiety, many who looked from that height with the fierce determination utterly to destroy the city must have acknowledged in their hearts that its beauty was beyond that of any other they had seen.[10]

Lying snug to the north slope of the ridge was the British cantonment. Here were stationed the 38th, 54th and 7th Native Infantry regiments. To the south, and adjacent to the cantonments, was the Sabzi Mandi or vegetable market, situated in a large square serai (walled enclosure). In contrast to the mile upon mile of ancient broken settlements south of the walled city, to the north of Delhi and the ridge there stretched an arcadia of small villages and settlements, with the road from the ridge running directly northwards to Ambala and the Punjab.

*****

In 1857, the city was effectively governed by the British Resident in Delhi, Simon Fraser, who had taken up his post in November 1853. With Zafar's authority vanishing even in Delhi, the administration of the city largely fell to the British Resident, whose role was to function as a diplomat but also to oversee all of the affairs of the King and his family. Furthermore, he was responsible for governing Delhi, collecting revenues and administering justice. As happened in most other Indian courts where a Resident had been imposed, the Resident also gathered daily intelligence about goings on in the palace. This intelligence was then forwarded to the Government of India, as well as the East India Company's Court of Directors in England.

Among the best foreign witnesses to the last years of pre-mutiny Delhi were the Metcalfes, probably the most prominent European family in the area. Sir Thomas Metcalfe, 1st Baronet (1745–1813) had travelled to India in 1767, serving as a major in the Bengal Army before becoming a director of the East India Company until 1812. One son, the aforementioned Charles Theophilus Metcalfe, would become Resident from 1811 to 1818 and then again from 1825 to 1827. Another son, Thomas Theophilus Metcalfe, would serve as Resident from 1835 to 1853. This latter Thomas would gain a reputation for commissioning local artists to paint likenesses of the palaces, monuments and other striking scenes in and around Delhi, which he then collected into an album which he named *Reminiscences of Imperial Delhi* (or the Dehlie book) in 1844.

The family's connection with Delhi didn't end there. Theophilus John Metcalfe, eldest son of Thomas Theophilus, would be Chief Magistrate of Delhi on the outbreak of the mutiny; he managed to escape the carnage and reach Hansi. Emily Metcalfe was the eldest daughter of Thomas Theophilus and had spent her early childhood in Delhi before leaving for England. She came back to Delhi in 1848. Her time there provides an interesting glimpse into the lives of wealthy, influential Europeans in the city during the twilight years of the Mughal Empire. Fortunately for Emily, she left India in May 1857 – just before the mutiny erupted. However, she would return in 1859 and spend most of the next thirty years of her life there, finally leaving in 1878. She therefore experienced life in the city both before and after the mutiny. She wrote lovingly of the city as it appeared in 1848, when it still retained its early beauty:

> I used to enjoy driving through the streets of Delhi as everything was new and striking; the buildings of marble and red sandstone were so magnificent, the shops were so quaint, the colours of the cotton cloths hanging from the windows and across the streets were so gorgeous, the costumes so picturesque, and the crowds were so extraordinarily thick. Two syces rode at great speed in front of the carriage in order to clear the road, for the dashing little horses went at a good pace. On fete days the crowd in the Chandnee Chouk, or Silver Street, was so numerous and compact that the children could walk on the heads of the people, which was an astonishing sight to anyone fresh from England. But alas! after the Mutiny, these crowds were no more to be seen. For some years afterwards only a few scattered groups of people were to be seen on gala days in this celebrated street, and although more inhabitants have now returned to Delhi, it can never be again what it was in those palmy days which I am describing. Delhi was really a most beautiful city.[11]

The festivals were indeed celebrated in vibrant fashion in the city. The local elite, in particular, spared no expense when it came to finery, as one resident described:

> The daily intercourse and intermingling of the citizens in the streets were full of colour, variety and charm. Bright-coloured clothes were the fashion, and the nobles especially rivalled one another in their splendid costumes. The markets contained very few foreign goods; the country made goods were fine in quality and not expensive. They were also remarkable for their rich dyes. The horses, on which the nobles rode through the streets of the city, had gorgeous trappings, and there were frequent cavalcades with tinkling bells and costly equipage. You might have thought it rather tawdry, but we, who were boys at the time, can never forget its magnificence. We used to walk along by the side of the horses and join in these processions.[12]

Another European more visible around the palace and city than most was the fifty-year-old Cambridge graduate Revd Midgley John Jennings. A Church of England missionary, Jennings founded the Society for the Propagation of the Gospel to popularise Christianity in Delhi. Born in Stevenage in 1806, he reached India in 1832 and had been stationed at Cawnpore before moving to Delhi in 1851. Jennings was chaplain to the European community but also initiated several educational projects as part of his missionary impetus.

*****

Allied to the Europeans was the small community of Anglo-Indians and Christian converts in the city. The Anglo-Indians were mixed-race people or descendants of mixed marriages between European men and local women and were invariably brought up as Christians by their European fathers. These mixed-race Christians held a peculiar position, not fully accepted by either European or Indian society. As Christians, they had a spiritual association with European society and naturally gravitated in that direction. It was to their advantage to make the best of their Western blood and faith. However, due to their darker complexion they nevertheless occupied a separate perch in the social hierarchy. Most mixed-race Christians aped the Europeans in clothes, customs and culture as best they could, as well as having European names. Their incomplete understanding of European fashion caused some merriment among visiting Europeans. Emily Metcalfe, for instance, left some slightly contemptuous descriptions of her visits to the various Anglo-Indians in the city, like the prominent missionary David Thompson. On a morning visit she was somewhat bemused by the evening dress on display:

> ... when we arrived at the door Mr Thompson was waiting to receive us, dressed in evening dress clothes, black hat and white kid gloves. He and his family were all very dark, having a great deal of native blood in their veins, and this accounted for their utter ignorance of English customs as regards dress. As these visits were all paid in the forenoon, before luncheon, which in those days was the universal custom in India, you may therefore imagine my astonishment on being ushered into the drawing-room to find Mrs Thompson and five daughters waiting to receive me, seated in a row and wearing white gloves and white cotton dresses with low necks and short sleeves, while embroidered Delhi scarves of brilliant colours were thrown over the necks of some of the ladies ... The two sons were, like their father, in full evening dress with white kid gloves.[13]

Despite the tone of the above excerpt, Emily Metcalfe acknowledged how dear the family were to her father, who was a good friend of theirs. Other Anglo-Indians in the city included Mrs Foster, the widow of Colonel Foster, commander of the Shekhawati Battalion during the early years of the century. Mrs Foster lived with her sister, Mrs Fuller, possibly another widow. 'Both Mrs Foster and her sister Mrs Fuller were enormously stout people, and, being half-castes, were dark in complexion and spoke English with a very curious accent, 'wrote Emily Metcalfe. 'And as both were dressed in white cotton dresses made very like bed-gowns, they presented a curious spectacle to a newcomer. They were, however, excellent old ladies, and their sons and daughters were all connected with the British Army in India.'[14] Mrs Foster occupied the large house immediately adjacent to the Kashmir Gate and next to the kutchery.

The most prominent Anglo-Indians in Delhi were the Skinners. This large family was very wealthy, and its scions were not shy about flaunting it. Their home – more accurately described as a palace – stood on the opposite side of the road to the aforementioned St James' Church, built by Colonel James Skinner, and was next to a mosque that Skinner had built for Muslim friends. 'Colonel Skinner was a man of dark blood, and his wife was a native lady, and their children were all, of course, very dark in complexion, and spoke English with an extraordinary accent,' wrote Emily Metcalfe. 'Although they looked upon themselves as English people and held a prominent position in Delhi society they had very little education and were more native than English in their ways ... This Aleck Skinner [Colonel Skinner's son] had a large family of sons and daughters, who have, I suppose, succeeded to the large family property. He sent me their photographs sometime ago, and most of them were named after the royal family, but they were all black.'[15]

The Anglo-Indians' predilection for European clothing helped them stand out, marking them as Christians with Western allegiances. This would count heavily against them when the mutiny reached Delhi.

From 1803 to 1857, Delhi enjoyed a period of calm after a century of chaos. With British supremacy stretching to the Khyber Pass during this time, Delhi was not troubled by conflict. This quiet and peaceful time, a period of law and order, was termed the 'English Peace' by the locals. Whatever concerns they had regarding foreign rule, they welcomed the increased trade and prosperity as Delhi quickly recovered its former wealth. Fear of robbery, violence and murder was much reduced both in and around the city. Before the English peace, anyone of means expected danger when travelling out of the city. 'The city did not know what order was till the "English Peace" began,' an old resident told C. F. Andrews. 'My own father used to tell me how before that time looting and robbery used to go on in the open streets within the city walls, and how none could go outside the city boundaries without having an armed escort of sometimes thirty or even forty men. Even these would turn and rob the persons who hired them, and there was no remedy.'

# PART 2
# The Forewarnings

# 5

# Changing Times

In this city [of Delhi] the Imam al-Muslimin wields no authority. The real power rests with the Christian officers. There is no check on them. Promulgation of the command of kufr means that in the matter of administration and the control of people, in the levy of land-tax, tribute, tolls and customs, in the punishment of thieves and robbers, in the settlement of disputes, in the punishment of offences, the kafirs act according to their discretion ... From here to Calcutta the Christians are in complete control.

Shah Abdal 'Aziz', prominent
Muslim scholar, 1803

The calm and prosperity brought about by the 'English peace' wasn't without its cost. Christian missionaries had made relatively little impact in India during the eighteenth century. The East India Company, for its part, had made conspicuous efforts to keep a policy of strict neutrality on matters of religion and culture, as it was felt that missionaries sowed social discord. Their uncompromising call for the eradication of 'native superstitions' invariably caused tension, and any association with this would have hit the Company's commercial interests hard. Because of this, India managed to escape the worst of the Christian revivalism and fervour that emerged in Europe during the mid-eighteenth century. Indeed, as far as the people of India were concerned the Company had far-sightedly agreed in the last years of the nineteenth century to 'preserve to them the laws of the Shaster [Hindu holy books] and the Koran in matters to which they have been invariably applied, to protect them in the free exercise of their religion'.[1] The tide of missionaries was avoided for a time, and the religious status quo preserved.

During the decades after Lord Lake's visit to Delhi in 1803, the East India Company steadily became a more confident power in the country. This dominance gave it the confidence to tamper with the social and religious mores of the country. British attitudes to missionary activity abroad had also begun to soften during the early part of the eighteenth century, and the Company were subjected to pressure from various quarters over their stance on missionary activity. An example was the group of evangelical Christians known as the Clapham Sect who were, among other things, campaigning aggressively for the opening of India to missionary activity. The group included the abolitionist William Wilberforce. As early as in 1792, the British Baptist shoemaker William Carey had published the influential tract *An Enquiry of the obligations of Christians to use means for the conversion of heathens*. He would make his way to India the following year to begin distributing Bibles translated into various Indian languages.

Due to the pressure from such groups and individuals, the Charter Act of 1813 (or the East India Company Act 1813), which renewed the charter issued to the East India Company, allowed among other things for Christian missionaries to preach in Company territories. The Act went further still, assenting to the permanent presence of missionaries in the country and arranging for several bishops to hold office in India, with an Anglican hierarchy established in Calcutta. From this time, the informal relationship between missionaries and the British authorities was to become established in the minds of the Indian population. An evangelical in England triumphantly declared the coming end of heathen ignorance in India: 'The true cure of darkness is the introduction of light. The Hindus err because they were ignorant and their errors have never been fairly laid down before them. The communication of our light and knowledge to them would prove the best remedy for their disorders'. Missionary organisations from both England and America began marshalling their forces for the assault on the country.

There never was any suspicion in the villages and towns of India that the British authorities would try to coerce the country into Christianity. This was not the way the British Government worked, and it was felt that it would be grossly out of character for them to attempt even the smallest force in these matters. However, by the middle of the nineteenth century there was a widespread feeling that Europeans were masters of more subtle measures to achieve the same ends and that everything was now in place to bring about a supremacy of the Christian religion in the country; that by small degrees and actions – outwardly innocent – the conversion of the country was being planned. All rival powers to the East India Company had been eliminated in Hindustan, and the Company effectively ruled the entire sub-continent. The British Government would now look to annex the remaining princely states and begin the work of moulding Indian society in its own image. The introduction of Christianity to the masses was considered of prime importance. It was thought to be just a matter of time before Christians would begin receiving preferential treatment in the recruitment of Government staff.

Rumours abounded that the Government was providing missionaries with the funds to set up orphanages and distribute Bibles and religious tracts. How else could these missionaries afford their operations?

In 1863, a sepoy's account of life in the British Indian Army was published. Sita Ram Pandey's *From Sepoy to Subedar* was the first widely read account of experiences in the Bengal Army as seen through a sepoy's eyes. Sita Ram's village was near Rae Bareli between Allahabad and Lucknow. In his account, he noted the energetic evangelisation efforts of the Christian missionaries and the suspicions such actions aroused among the masses: 'I had also remarked the increase of Padre sahibs during recent years, who stood up in the streets of our cities and told the people that their cherished religion was all false, and who exhorted them to become Christians. They always maintained that they were not employed by the Sirkar [Government], but how could they have acted like this without the Government's sanction? Everyone believed that they were secretly employed by the Government; why else should they take such trouble?'[2]

With a population subject to British power and authority, the missionaries faced no danger and therefore saw no reason to hide their contempt for local beliefs. The war against the 'heathen' needed no tact or diplomacy. As early as 1807, the Serampore mission in the south of the country had printed an anti-Muslim pamphlet which had criticised the Prophet Mohammed as a 'tyrant'.[3] William Ward, one of the missionaries based at Serampore, had confidently predicted in 1803 that 'Hindoos and Mahomedans will as surely fall under the doctrine of the Cross as Greenlanders and Hottentots'.[4] Missionaries did not hesitate to use tactics considered dishonourable or underhand. In 1837, for example, a great drought hit the north of the country especially hard, increasing poverty, death and suffering among the villages and towns. The missionaries were quick to take advantage. Using the wealth of their organisations, they actively sought out orphans or the children of desperate parents. These children were taken away and brought up in the Christian religion in the well-funded missionary orphanages.

Other rabid manners of propagation of the Christian belief were also quite alien to the country. In Hindustan, open proselytization had almost never been observed before the arrival of the Christian missionaries. Hindu priests spoke in their temples while Muslim moulvis could address the congregations inside the mosques. Giving out religious tracts or books to nonbelievers in open squares, markets and other public places was never an Indian trait. Missionaries introduced this form of propagation and would go to extraordinary lengths with it, attending religious fairs and festivals to entice possible converts. Here the missionaries would openly attack or ridicule local beliefs while explaining the tenets of their own faith. While some converts may have been gained, most of the devotees attending these Hindu or Muslim religious gatherings were angered by the intemperate language of the missionaries, who were often protected by the local policemen to prevent any violence. A Baptist preacher named John Chamberlain, for example, had decided in the early years of the century to preach provocatively for a full twelve days at the Hindu holy centre of Hardwar at the time of the Kumbh Mela pilgrimage event.

One of the more aggressive proselytizers during this time was the German missionary Karl Gottlieb Pfander, whose stay in the country lasted from 1838 to 1859. He had been based at Agra, 120 miles from Delhi. While other missionaries targeted Hindus, Pfander specialised in the assault on Islam. He turned out to be one of its strongest critics, consistently launching scathing attacks on what he felt was 'a religion which knows nothing of a holy God, or where the glorious attribute of his holiness is only slightly mentioned'.[5] Muslims never call God their 'father' or themselves his children, he wrote, but simply his servants; in his eyes, they therefore believed in a much colder relationship than the warmer paternalism of the Christian God. Furthermore, Islam had borrowed wholesale from Christianity and Judaism with many of its stories and narrations of Muhammad's life, sometimes openly. In a swipe at Hindus, he sneered that the Muslim's only saving grace was that he had cleared his house of external idolatry; however, he had nonetheless 'fallen as much into the bondage of superstition as any of the heathen nations'.[6]

The five daily prayers required of the faithful were done in the most mechanical way by followers, Pfander said. Prayers being communal, with the masses being summoned by the call to prayer, meant there was no personal relationship with the Maker. It was pure ritual, with no passion or meaning compared to Christian worship, he argued. 'Prayer is therefore no delight to their hearts, but a heavy burden lodged upon them. And but for the good advice of Moses to Muhammad it would have been altogether intolerable; for according to a tradition which is related in the *Mishcat ul Masabih*, as well as in *Hayat ul Kulub* vol. ii leaf 176 God ordered them to pray 50 times a day but Muhammad on Moses advice bargained it down to five times.'[7] Here he was referring to the Islamic narrative of Mohammed having flown to paradise on a winged horse, on which journey he successfully managed to negotiate with the Almighty a reduction in the number of prayers Muslims were obliged to perform each day. Pfander also mocked the sensual nature of the Islamic paradise: 'They must force upon every thinking mind a conviction as clear as midday that a religion containing such stories tales and doctrines cannot possibly be a divine one however many good things it may otherwise contain. These traditions afford therefore only an additional proof.'[8]

Pfander would expound his beliefs in books such as *Mizan al-Haqq* (*The Balance of Truth*) and *Remarks on the Nature of Muhammedanism*. Among his other claims was a suggestion that Mohammed had been an epileptic, which he felt explained the Prophet's trances and revelations. Mohammed's capture of the Arabian peninsula meant 'spoils, dominion and prosperity', allowing his followers to 'shut their minds to his faults and failings'.[9] Military success and the subsequent financial windfalls encouraged followers to ignore the inherent weakness of Islam, he insisted. It was religion of the sword while Christianity was a religion of peace. Pfander provides a good example of the kind of confident and uncompromising missionary that was common in the country at the time. Perhaps not all missionaries were quite so aggressive, but they would have shared his confidence and contempt for local belief.

Allied to missionary efforts in the streets and public squares of towns and cities were the missionary schools that were popping up around the country. Along with the more conventional subjects, these schools taught the tenets of the Christian faith. Students underwent religious examinations, with children being asked questions like 'Who is your saviour' and 'Who is your God', with prizes being given out to children volunteering the most enthusiastic Christian answers. Again, many suspected there was Government assistance for these schools. Parents disliked the schools, but had little choice but to use them. Education was prized, after all, and while parents resented attempts to tamper with their children's minds, most nevertheless entered their children for the chance of Government employment or other opportunities only literacy could bring.

As they became established, Government-run village schools became synonymous with Christian missionaries even though they were not used for the propagation of Christianity. In the east of India, compulsion was used to force children to schools and this only served to increase suspicions. For a job in the public service, a certificate was required proving the child's education from school through college. Some viewed this as a measure to force children into schools – and when such schools were conflated with missionary schools, the conclusion was obvious. 'When the village Schools were established, the general belief was that they were instituted solely with the view of teaching the doctrines of Jesus. The *pergunnah* [subdivision] visitors, and deputy inspectors, who used to go from village to village, and town to town advising the people to enter their children at these schools got the nickname of Native Clergyman,' noted Syed Ahmad Khan. Girls were expected to attend the school unveiled, which infuriated the conservative Muslim population. In colleges, meanwhile, it was noticed that the study of Persian, Arabic and Sanskrit was reduced while Urdu and English became much more prominent. The study of Arabic, the language of the Quran, was particularly close to the hearts of many Muslims. Its neglect at school was thought to be a first step in the attempt to estrange Muslims from their scripture, and part of the preliminary groundwork for the introduction of the Christian religion to the Muslim masses.

Christian religious fervour wasn't restricted to missionaries. It was noticed in the Bengal Army that many European officers, full of zeal, would encourage their servants to listen to the preaching of missionaries or talk to their subordinate soldiers about matters of religion. General

Wheeler, commanding at Kanpur, was famous for his exhortations to his sepoys. 'I have told them plainly that they are all lost and ruined sinners both by nature and by practice,' he explained in April 1857. 'As to the question whether I have endeavoured to convert sepoys and others to Christianity, I would humbly reply that this has been my object.' While the inducements of employment or higher pay were never overtly suggested, no doubt many locals felt the adoption of Christianity would assist them in gaining the favour of their employers.

Meanwhile, the passing of the Caste Disabilities Removal Act in 1850 also caused profound suspicion. Before this Act was passed, anyone who changed their religion was stripped of equal rights when it came to legal inheritance. This naturally discouraged conversion, and many Christian missionaries in the country had commented on the reluctance of potential converts to take the final step of baptism due to this loss of inheritance rights. The Caste Disabilities Removal Act essentially removed this obstacle. Now, any person could convert with the knowledge that there could be no financial penalty by law. While this allowed more freedom of thought, it was widely felt to be a ploy by the Government to assist missionary activity. Since it was only the Christian missionaries who practised a virulent form of evangelism, they would be the main – if not sole – beneficiaries of the Act. Furthermore, the Act had been championed by prominent Christians. In any case, Lord Dalhousie, the Governor-General who had passed the Act, believed it would make little impact:

> We do preserve to Hindus their religion and their laws in the mass. We never pledged ourselves to maintain both *intact*; and after having, twenty years ago, interfered directly to prohibit *suttee* [*sati*, the sacrifice of a widow by burning on her husband's funeral pyre], I have not been disposed to yield to clamour (such as it was), or to abstain from interdicting what was an unjust penalty on Hindus who receive the Gospel, while the interdiction is no hardship on Hindus themselves. I wish that the Government should abstain from proselytising, because I believe they would impede at present, not promote, its advance; but abstaining from proselytising and permitting the continuance of grave infliction of injuries on those who become proselytes are two very different things.

*****

In 1855, an unusual letter written by a Mr E. Edmond Esq. appeared in Calcutta and achieved wide circulation. The letter was apparently sent to all senior government officials and carried more than the usual Christian zeal.

'The time appears to have come when earnest consideration should be given to the subject, whether or not all men should embrace the same system of Religion. Railways, Steam vessels and the Electric Telegraph, are rapidly uniting all the nations of the earth: the more they are brought together, the more certain does the conclusion become, that all have the same wants, the same anxieties, the same hopes, the same fears, and therefore, the same nature and the same origin. It is also very certain that death universally closes the scene,' wrote Mr Edmond. Was it rational, he asked, that God had given different nations different methods of obtaining happiness in this life and the hereafter? Only Christianity could offer the solution. The proof was apparent. Christianity was the only religion to have been spread by argument and not force. The nations who had embraced Christianity were the most thoughtful and civilised. His claims and arguments, although faulty, appealed to the Victorian's innate sense of superiority. Edmond talked of the evangelism of the apostles; surely others should emulate this work in India? 'We long to see churches thronged with the natives of this land, in which the glad tidings of the Gospel shall regularly be proclaimed by your own countrymen, and not by strangers only; in which women, as well as men, shall be urged to repent of their sins ... Would it not be an infinite improvement upon the foolish, degrading and wicked idolatry which now defiles the land?'

There was a general impression that the letter had Government approval and that it was to be circulated to Government staff before going into general circulation. Recognising that the Indian population already felt the missionaries were simply another arm of British authority, Frederick James Halliday, Lieutenant Governor of Bengal, was compelled to point out that the British Government in India was not an ally of any missionary organisations and had no interest in the promotion of Christianity. A declaration was issued: 'His Honor the Lieutenant Governor of Bengal, having heard that the people of the Country are unnecessarily apprehensive and uneasy on account of certain unreasonable and unfounded stories, fabricated and spread by people equally unreasonable and prejudiced, with regard to the religious rites and ceremonies of the Hindoos and Muhammadans, hereby notifies that Government has no intention of interfering in the matters of religion, rites and ceremonies of the country, nor can it ever have such an intention.' He was sorry that there was alarm among the population but assured them that the Government's intentions were honourable and that it would always protect local beliefs and customs.

> Some of the Calcutta Missionaries have, as is their wont, but without the sanction of the Government published religious discourses and circulated them amongst the natives who have wrongly understood them to have come indirectly from the Government. The Government has however had no hand in the affair. No attempt was ever made on behalf of Government to persuade the natives to embrace the faith professed by the Government. It is evident that the inhabitants of this country belong to different races and profess different creeds and religions, and are governed by different laws. They have now been long

> living under the protection of the Government, but the Government, instead of interfering in the religious rites and ceremonies of any class of its subjects, always regards them all as equal in its sight.

The declaration explained that, contrary to rumours, there would be no tampering with the religious practices of the population. Reports had spread in some newspapers that all Muharram (Muslim New Year) ceremonies, the *purdah* system of the Zenana (Muslim women being kept separate from males), the rite of circumcision and other customs practised under Muslim and Hindu laws were soon to be done away with by orders of Government. Halliday categorically denied the truth of these rumours.

The Lieutenant Governor also took the opportunity to address other issues like the change in prison routines, which had led to prisoners of all castes eating together during mealtimes and a single person cooking all the food. Both these changes were anathema to most Hindus as they broke caste. The beards and moustaches of new prisoners were also ordered to be cut when they were incarcerated, and this was taken as a great personal insult. 'To distinguish the Jail from the home, certain Jail Superintendents, ignorant of the customs and creeds of the country, divested prisoners of their necessary utensils used in eating and drinking, and of course without the knowledge and consent of the Government. But no sooner was this brought to notice of Government than orders were telegraphed to put a stop to their proceedings.'

On the issue of schools being used to propagate Christianity to children, Halliday denied any such motive and insisted that schools were established purely for the encouragement of knowledge and education. It was a matter of great regret that the motives of the Government should be treated as suspicious. English was being taught because the textbooks for most subjects were only available in English. 'H.H. Therefore notifies the above to H. Majesty's loyal subjects that they may rest well assured of the good intentions of the Government towards them, and take heart and work contentedly praying to God sincerely for the prosperity of their benign Government,' he concluded.

How much this calmed matters was moot. The following year saw the passage of the Hindu Widows Remarriage Act 1856, which allowed widows to remarry – much to the chagrin of Hindus. The abolition of *sati* had been accepted because it was aimed at saving lives, but this new Act was an attack on local taboos and therefore an interference in the social customs of the country.

*****

Although missionaries had fanned out across northern India during the early part of the nineteenth century, they had by and large remained distant from Delhi. An Arabic Bible had been sent to Emperor Shah Alam by missionaries in Calcutta shortly after the establishment of the British presence in the city in 1803, and some accounts mention debates between European padres and Muslim *alim* (scholars or leaned men), citing Charles Metcalfe as the intermediary, although the latter claim is hard to verify.[10] Shah Abd al-Aziz, one of Delhi's leading Muslim scholars, apparently debated with a missionary who asked him why Allah had not saved Mohammed's grandson Hussain from assassination if he was a prophet of God. Abd al-Aziz apparently retorted that God had declined to save the prophet's grandson just as he had declined to save his own son from crucifixion according to Christian belief.[11] In 1833, one of the leading alim of the city, Shah Muhammad Ishaq, was recorded to have had debates with the missionary Joseph Wolff.[12]

One of the first missions to open in Delhi during the British period was the Baptist Missionary Society, which was set up in 1818. The Anglo-Indian Christian John Thompson, from Serampore, was employed to win converts. He continued his work till 1850, but by all accounts had little joy in his preaching at the bazaars. He concentrated on trying to convert Hindus to his faith rather than Muslims, travelling regularly to the holy city of Hardwar on Hindu special occasions. While the Baptist Missionary Society's efforts made no impact, other Christian organisations left the city alone for fear of encroaching on Baptist turf. As a result, the city was effectively free of missionaries. As late as 1850, there was no sign of the schools, hospitals and orphanages typically used by missionaries to spread their message.

May 1852 signalled the arrival of Revd M. J. Jennings, an Evangelical Company chaplain. Jennings had earlier been stationed in Kanpur and also at Roorkee. Along with his daughter, Anne, he would take up accommodation in the palace, in an apartment on top of the Lahore Gate where palace commandant Capt. Douglas also resided. Jennings soon began to speak out against what he saw as the relative lack of missionary activity in Delhi:

> The only thing we have done is to establish a College, where everything is taught but religion, which is carefully excluded. There was a Baptist Missionary, some years ago: this has been the only attempt to Christianize Delhi. The Roman Catholics and the Free Kirk have both meditated taking possession of this neglected city; but it is hoped, if an efficient Mission be established, they will be dissuaded from commencing on a pre-occupied field.

Jennings seemed to be the stereotype of the aggressive missionary, which did not endear him to the population of the city. Jennings would also travel to the great Hindu festival of Kumbh Mela to seek converts. An correspondent of the *Delhi Gazette* observed Jennings' efforts at the festival and was unconvinced: 'The zeal of the missionaries is greater than their discretion in selecting this heathen pandemonium as the theatre of their exertions ... They have been preaching to the masses, but I should say without a shadow of success, having to compete with the four great anti-Christian powers – trade, crime, pleasure and idolatry – in all their most frantic forms.'[13]

After Jennings' comments, the Society for the Propagation of the Gospel (SPG) opened a centre in Delhi. The aim of this new mission was to bring Christianity to the upper classes of the city, be they Hindu or Muslim, rather than the downtrodden. Jennings was given 20,000 rupees along with the assistance of two other missionaries – Revd J. Stuart Jackson and Revd R. A. Hubbard – to take advantage of the opportunities that seemed to be present. Their efforts bore some fruit. Despite the SPG's target, the bulk of their converts were illiterate villagers. Such converts varied in their motivations; certainly the finer points of theology and of Christianity philosophy were beyond the understanding of the common unlettered villager. Some no doubt felt an attraction to the religion, while others converted for temporal gains and emoluments. Many of low caste had become Christians to escape the restraints of the caste system. Others converted in the hopes of being identified with the ruling European class and thereby gaining some reflected respect, and it was the view of many locals that this was the real incentive for most converts. By becoming spiritual servants of the Europeans, they had alienated themselves from the Hindu and Muslim masses.

*****

One of the more intriguing disputes concerning missionary activity surfaced quite unexpectedly at the famous Delhi College, where there was a change in the science curriculum. The culture of the Delhi College had been a strong mix of East and West, with the older section of the school functioning as a madrassa – a Muslim religious school – and teaching an oriental curriculum while the newer half of the college, opened in 1825, taught a Western curriculum. A drive to teach subjects in the local vernacular had emerged as early as the 1830s, under the principal of the college during this time, Frenchman Felix Boutros. In 1841, Boutros became the first secretary of the Delhi College Vernacular Translation Society (also known as the Society for the Promotion of Useful Knowledge), which spearheaded the translation into Urdu of various modern European science books. Delhi College therefore became the first college in India to teach using textbooks in the vernacular.

Delhi College was also different in another aspect, with Boutros promoting a more racially harmonious atmosphere. There were instances of European teachers being reprimanded for voicing or displaying some sort of race-based arrogance. One teacher, a Mr French, was even sacked for such behaviour towards his Indian colleagues at the college: 'All those

Indian teachers for whom he (Mr French) has such contempt are the students of this college. They are all highly respected people with knowledge of science and proficiency in English language. It's not surprising that they should feel offended at Mr French's behaviour. If they are not by all means "equal" to Mr French, they are certainly better than him in some ways,' wrote Boutros in defence of the dismissal. In consequence, Most of the European teachers employed by Boutros had a much more liberal and less aloof outlook than the typical European in Delhi.

One of the best-known individuals in the city connected with Delhi College was Professor Ramchandra. He had been a student at the college and in turn had become a professor of mathematics and science in the oriental section of the college in 1844, holding this post until the outbreak of the mutiny. By all accounts he had a brilliant mind, and the many scholarships and prizes he won in his early years are testament to that fact. Ramchandra was an active member of the Delhi Vernacular Translation Society as well. He felt it was essential that modern science be brought into the country and replace the Arab translations of old works that prevailed. Such was his interest that one of the three fortnightly papers he would publish, *Fawaid-ul-Nazarin*, in 1845 was committed purely to articles on science. Ramchandra came to prominence in Europe later for his book *A Treatise on Problems of Maxima and Minima Solved by Algebra*.[14]

Ramchandra would be the mentor and good friend of another well-known Delhi personality: the Muslim student Zaka Ullah. Moulvi Nazir Ahmad, who would become one of the leaders of the Muslim 'Aligarh school' and a well-known novelist, later called Zaka Ullah 'the greatest mathematician in India in his own generation'.[15] After leaving Delhi College, Zaka Ullah would join the Education Department of the Government of India. A prolific reader, he began learning English in order to gain access to the huge numbers of books available in the language. He would later become a prolific writer. In 1857, Zaka Ullah was a young man of twenty-five. Moulvi Imam Baksh, another major figure at the college, taught Arabic and Persian to Zaka Ullah and would later help the scholar Syed Ahmad Khan in writing his book *Archaeology of Delhi*. There were other notables as well. Shahamat Ali later became Prime Minister of Indore; Mukand Lal was one of the first fully Western-trained doctors in north-west India; Ziauddin and Muhammad Husain won fame for their literary works; Altaf Husain, whose *nom de plume* was Hali, would become one of the most renowned poets in Urdu literature.

The introduction and use of new science books translated from English to Urdu brought about a different curriculum. Beforehand, the more ancient and obsolete Ptolemaic wisdom had been taught primarily in Arabic in the schools of the city. Muslim belief of that time concerning the universe was, much like Christian belief of medieval times, decidedly geocentric. The Earth was believed to be the centre of the universe and the pinnacle of God's achievement along with mankind itself. The sun naturally rotated round the Earth, with the stars fixed in the heavenly firmament. This had been reinforced by translations into Arabic many hundreds of years before of ancient Greek manuscripts and books by Plato and other ancient philosophers. These books, or copies of them, had made their way to India and were still the basis of science education in the schools.

That the sun circled the Earth seemed natural and obvious to the naked eye. Human experience suggested the Earth was stationary while the heavenly bodies moved around it. This belief had never been subject to reasoned scrutiny before. The new textbooks taught a radically different idea. This was the Copernican or heliocentric model, in which the Earth circled the sun rather than the other way around. The new beliefs expounded by Copernicus and Galileo among others had delivered a considerable jolt to the prevailing religious dogma in seventeenth-century Europe, and harmonizing the parallel ideas was impossible; either the Earth was the centre of the universe or it wasn't. The new curriculum provoked a somewhat similar response in Delhi as it had in seventeenth-century Europe.

In fairness, the Copernican system wasn't entirely new to India, and some books on it had already been translated into Persian in Calcutta. However, these books were not used in schools and had not been noticed by Muslim clerics and so were largely ignored. In Lucknow, there seems to have been some discussion on the issue; a scholar of the city called Mazar Ali had been given an award by the Asiatic Society of Bengal for his research into the new system. It was in Delhi, however, with the arrival of the theory in schools, that the new cosmic model received wide publicity. The new teaching seemed to humble God's creation. Other ideas considered sacrosanct were declared invalid as well. Rather than God ordaining the sun and planets to move in orbits based on the supreme mathematical perfection of the circle, according to the new textbooks the Earth and the other planets moved in the humbler path of an ellipse. Moreover, the Earth was not only spinning but moving through the cosmos at incredible speed.

Students in Delhi, learning from these newly translated books on physics and astronomy, began openly laughing at the old teachings. Even those in the English department were seen to be mock the older beliefs, having been drawn into the new revolution. Both Hindu and Muslim beliefs were derided. Since Delhi College was taking the lead in this new teaching, its students felt themselves to be pioneers. Nazir Ahmad, one of the students at the time, would ponder on his time at the college. 'If I had not studied in Delhi College, I would have been a moulvi [Muslim priest], narrow and bigoted,' he admitted, suggesting these new ideas were even having an effect on students with religious leanings. Other beliefs once seen as unquestionable were at risk. For example, the teaching of medicine was still dependent on Greek wisdom gleaned from the translated works of ancient luminaries like Galen and Hippocrates while the new books on medicine had markedly different ideas. Such new theories were quickly given the moniker 'the New Learning' by students and locals in Delhi.

This 'New Learning', questioning as it did almost every aspect of the old wisdom, generated lots of publicity. In addition, since the new science books had been translated into Urdu, they could now be read, discussed and disputed by the common man. It was around this time that Professor Ramchandra, now a teacher at the college, began publishing the new ideas in his *Fawaid-ul-Nazarin* (*Useful to the Readers*) and *Muhib-i-Hind* (*Friend of India*) journals. These journals became notorious for their criticism of Muslim and Hindu dogma. Ramchandra's interest in religious belief would lead him to challenge prevailing doctrines; for instance, he railed against the Muslim Qazi of Delhi, Maulana Ulfat Husain, on the Islamic belief in the miracle of the splitting of the moon by the prophet Mohammed. These articles and their ideas particularly infected the young students studying at the college, and the journals proved popular.

This new teaching seemed nonsensical to the more religiously orthodox in the city. Parents and clergy were unsettled by the new ideas. The notion that the cosmic picture was far more complex than that painted in holy texts or even contemplated by the ancient Greeks struck at the heart of religious belief. Opposition to the new curriculum was widespread. 'The learned men, who lived in the city, did not like this innovation on their much-loved theories of the ancient Greek Philosophy, which had been cultivated among them for many centuries past,'[16] Professor Ramchandra recalled as news of these ideas began to circulate in the city. 'The result of this was, that many of our countrymen condemned us as infidels and irreligious. For this strange learning from the West, which had suddenly appeared, was already being openly called "Kafir," or infidel; it was openly said to produce atheists.'[17]

In Lucknow, some of the Muslim clergy took to vocally countering the new teachings. In Delhi, too, there was a reaction. Syed Ahmad Khan, serving as a *munsif* (petty judge) in the city and a well-known Muslim scholar of the time, would bring out a tract called *Qaul-i matin dar ibtal-i harakat-i zamin* (*Firm assertion with regard to declaring false the motion of the earth*) defending the Ptolemaic belief from the Islamic standpoint. To his credit he later came to accept the Copernican system, but at the time his leadership was vital in establishing the idea that the new teaching was dangerous to Islam and warranted suspicion. 'Indeed, there was even stronger objection on the part of the orthodox, as I have already intimated, owing to the singularly vivid fear that religion itself would be undermined. This was told me on every hand by those whose fathers had themselves taken part in the great change,'[18] wrote the missionary C. F. Andrews. According to what he was told, the fear seemed to be much greater in the Muslim community. 'The Muhammadan community in Delhi felt most keenly of all the impact of the New Learning. Though lavish Government scholarships were offered and a free education was given, the best families in the city, however poor, refused to send their children to the schools.'[19]

The Delhi College and the new learning soon became associated with missionary activities. In the 1850s, a new principal, a fervent Christian called J. H. Taylor, seemed to confirm local fears. The new learning and the new Christian tilt of the college was blamed, among other things, for the high-profile conversion of the Hindu Professor Ramchandra. 'It was then my conscientious belief that educated Englishmen were too much enlightened to believe in any bookish religion except that of reason and conscience, or deism,'[20] Ramchandra wrote on visiting a service at St James' Church, betraying the influence under which he had fallen. On 11 July 1852, Ramchandra was baptised at St James' Church. Baptised alongside him was Chiman Lal, a previously Hindu allopathic doctor and sub-assistant surgeon formerly in the employ of the King himself but now working for the Company. A host of Europeans attended the ceremony, among them Thomas Metcalfe, Commissioner of Delhi; A. A. Roberts, a magistrate; John Gubbins, a judge; and Captain Lewis and his wife, Ram Chandra's godparents. Ramchandra admitted that he had been contemplating conversion as early as 1850 but was put off by the rules regarding inheritance.

The baptism of these two converts drew much attention in Delhi, to such an extent that the British authorities thought St James' Church might be attacked during the service. A guard was therefore organised for the ceremony. Another person to convert later was Moulvi Imaduddin – later known as Padri (Padre) Imaduddin – who now became a vocal supporter of Christianity. Some believe that two other Delhi College graduates, the novelist Nazir Ahmad and the mathematician Zaka Ullah, came close to converting to Christianity as well. Since Zaka Ullah was close to Ramchandra, there was a suspicion that the professor had influenced his protégé and that perhaps he would convert very soon. Nazir Ahmad, his close friend since their college days, later refuted the notion: 'As far as one man can know the heart of another I believe Munshi Zaka Ullah to have been a strict Unitarian Musalman, trusting in one God with His full attributes as understood in Islam.'[21] Ramchandra's brother was also said to be contemplating conversion at the time.

This spate of conversions confirmed in many minds the toxic nature of Delhi College. The direct aftermath of these conversions was that the student count in the college went down heavily, with twenty-five students withdrawing immediately because of their parents' objections or their own. Ramchandra's journals also lost subscribers; he soon discontinued them in the face of hostility to the new learning.

Unaware of the rumblings of discontent, Revd Jennings revelled in the conversion of these high-profile converts. In May 1853, he also managed to convert a Muslim from a family of good standing. There were high hopes for more converts. The Bishop of Madras would write, 'The Delhi

Mission is one of the most hopeful and promising of our Indian Mission fields. The intelligent and well-informed converts ... the superior nature of the school, with its 120 boys, among the best I have visited in India, and the first-rate character for attainments and devotedness of the missionaries and schoolmasters are making an impression which is moving the whole of that City of Kings.'

It is difficult to know quite what the King thought of all this; certainly he kept his feelings to himself. Intelligence gathered from the palace noted that 'his Majesty made no reply'[22] when told of the conversions by missionaries. However, it seems that Zafar was more candid with his physician, Ahsan Ulla Khan, and seemed to think the British were actively trying to change the religious landscape of the country:

> It was the King's opinion that the Government really intended to change the religion of the people but I frequently explained to him that this was only a rumour set afloat by wicked people. For I added the British were wise people who would do nothing which was calculated to injure whole masses of people nor could I believe that they would seek to injure an army from whom they expected good service. This argument satisfied the King whenever I explained to him but he relapsed into his own way of thinking as often as he listened to the representations of his eunuchs.[23]

# 6

# Rumours of a Persian Invasion

> During the period of the war with Persia, some of the princes used to observe that if the Emperor of Russia were to aid the Persians, the English could be defeated, and the Persians would become masters of India; and the king himself coincided in this opinion.
>
> Ahsan Ulla Khan at the trial of Zafar

By the mid-nineteenth century there was a growing feeling in India that the day of reckoning was at hand for British military supremacy in the region. There had been the debacle of the First Anglo-Afghan War (1839–42), in which the entire occupying force stationed at Kabul had been annihilated in its retreat back to Hindustan. There had been the near disasters against the Sikh army at the battles of Ferozeshah and Chillianwala. More recently, the long-drawn-out affair of the Crimean War (1853–56) had shown that British strength was not all that it pretended to be.

One of the earlier predictions had been in circulation for some years before the mutiny broke out. It was said to have originated with the highly respected Shah Niamut Ulla Moulvy, who had pounced on a well-known anniversary that was coming into view: the hundredth anniversary of the Battle of Plassey. In this battle the East India Company had taken effective control of the province of Bengal, and by extension ushered in British supremacy in Hindustan. Moulvy speculated that British rule would definitively end one hundred years after the battle, which had been fought on 23 June 1757. 'After the Fire-worshippers and Christians shall have held sway over the whole of Hindostan for 100 years, and when injustice and oppression shall prevail in their Government, an Arab Prince will be born who will ride triumphantly to slay them,'[1] he had declared. By fire worshippers he presumably meant Hindus, although that was an ill-fitting description. The allusion to an Arab prince was also just as cryptic; perhaps he meant a Persian prince, for Persia was the only nearby Muslim power remotely vigorous enough to consider an invasion of India.

Not everyone waited patiently for the anniversary. There had been earlier attempts to dislodge the British. A half-baked plan for a jihad and the revival of Muslim ascendency had developed in the 1820s when Syed Ahmed Barelvi, a Muslim preacher committed to the puritanical Wahhabist form of Islam, travelled to the frontier region with Afghanistan hoping to establish an Islamic caliphate in the region. Leaving India in 1826 with a strong network of supporters and fighters, he led a force of around 500 jihadis in an attempt to combine with frontier tribesmen to form a Muslim army. He had declared war against the Sikh Empire of the Punjab in the late 1820s as a precursor to an attack on British-controlled Hindustan. However, Barelvi and his motley force of tribesmen and jihadis were massacred by the Sikh Army at the Battle of Balakot in 1831 and the jihad fizzled out. Support for Barelvi remained strong in Hindustan after his death, bestowing as it did a martyr status. One of his disciples, Moulvi Inayat Ali, now preached that the Muslim population would rise up in 1853 according to a seven-hundred-year-old prophecy he had uncovered called the Ode of Nimatullah.

> Then the Nazarenes [Christians] will take all Hindustan.
> They will reign for a hundred years.
> There will be a great oppression in their reign.
> For their destruction there will be a King in the West.
> The King will proclaim a war against the Nazarenes.
> And in the war a great many people will be killed.
> The King of the West will be victorious by the force
> of the sword in a holy war.
> And the followers of Jesus will be defeated ... [2]

Moulvi Inayat Ali would try and instigate a new jihad in line with the prophecy. He strongly criticised those who opposed religious war against unbelievers or preferred to stand on the sidelines:

> Those who would prevent others from hijra and jihad are in heart hypocrites. Let all know this: in a country where the predominant religion is other than Islam, the religious precepts of Muhammad cannot be enforced, [therefore) it is incumbent on Musalmans to unite and wage war with Kaffirs [infidels].[3]

Moulvi Inayat Ali had written to the Hindustani fanatics at Sittana in the north-western frontier in 1852–53 as they were being readied for war. However, their plan to unleash jihad in 1853 would fail before it even started. While British authorities in the area were ignorant of the impending jihad, Colonel Mackeson, in command at Peshawar, unwittingly pre-empted it when he led an attack on tribal positions in the area, disrupting Ali's plans in the process.

From around 1855, the Wahhabis began renewed efforts to convince people of the merits of jihad. In that year, their war song 'Risalat Al-Jihad' ('Message of Holy War') was printed and industriously circulated in Delhi, adding to the febrile mood of many Muslims and to the general feeling that British power was in decline. These assorted predictions perhaps preyed on the thoughts of the Bengal Army's sepoys, subtly preparing them for their own rebellion.

General speculations on jihad in the north-western frontier were soon overtaken by rumours of a large-scale invasion of India, either by the Russians or by the Persians as proxies of the Russians and bolstered with Russian aid and assistance. It was widely accepted that the Persians lacked the logistical and numerical capacity required to march through Afghanistan and launch a general invasion of India; even if they could, their army had little chance against the Company's forces on the borders of India. Since the Persians lacked the wherewithal for an invasion on their own, it was thought that any Persian advance would likely be supported by Russia. Perhaps it would even be a joint invasion.

The British Government was in accord with the Afghan ruler Dost Mohammad in its determination to block any encroachment by either the Persians or Russians into Afghanistan. The Afghan ruler had signed a treaty of perpetual peace and friendship with the British on 30 March 1855. For Afghanistan, this treaty provided a strong protector. The British in India, meanwhile, secured a friendly buffer state between themselves and two other powers. How long this treaty would actually hold was open to speculation. The recent Crimean and Anglo-Persian wars magnified speculation greatly. The early nineteenth century saw aggressive Russian expansion into the Asian republics, and the Russians were said to have territorial ambitions for Afghanistan and perhaps even India. For a while it seemed that Afghanistan would disappear into the maw of the Russian Empire. All this jockeying for position and influence over the same turf between the Russians and the British – later known as the 'Great Game' – lent itself to conspiracy theories and saw the formation of alliances both secret and overt.

The ambition of the Russian czars, with their huge reserves of manpower, was the salient factor. With Russian arms, guidance and logistics, a Persian army assisted or officered by Russians could very well cross Afghanistan and march into India despite the distance and the unfriendly terrain. If they managed this, the end result was anybody's guess. The British Government of India, over-dependent as it was on its huge sepoy army and the tacit acceptance of British supremacy by Indian princes, could collapse spectacularly if both withdrew their support and joined the Persians to overthrow British rule. In late 1856 and on into 1857, this was beginning to look like a plausible scenario.

In the palace at Delhi, several of the prominent princes began to expect a Russian-backed Persian invasion. Even Zafar himself was said to have been persuaded of the possibility. Indeed, according to one reliable source a Persian invasion was imminent. Hasan Askari was a Muslim priest resident near the Delhi Gate. After the mutiny, Zafar's physician would recall that Askari first came to the attention of the royal family around 1853. One of Zafar's daughters, Nawab Begum, had a house near the Delhi Gate very close to the mullah's home. She began visiting him and had quickly fallen under his sway, becoming a fervent disciple. Rumours around the city were that she may even have become his mistress.

Askari was a faith healer and mystic combined. His followers attributed to him various supernatural powers, including healing and the ability to interpret dreams. With the ageing King's health in decline, his daughter introduced him to Askari with the intention of revitalising his health. Askari took up the challenge, sending charms and potions to help Zafar's recovery as well as praying for his health. Zafar felt his condition improve, and so became a disciple. Nawab Begum herself died in 1856, but by then Zafar was well under the preacher's influence. Jat Mall, a British informer inside the palace, mentioned Askari whispering prayers and other incantations over the ailing King. One of his more curious acts was to breathe over the King to reinvigorate him – the air perhaps passing some life-giving qualities from one to the other. Through his supposed talents, Askari was said to have transferred twenty years of his own life to the monarch so that Zafar would live to a ripe old age – much as Zeenat Mahal had claimed.

Zafar, who saw Askari as a genuine visionary, would meet the mullah often. As time went on, Askari visited more and more. 'He used to come daily to the prisoner at various hours just as he was sent for, and frequently used to come uninvited – especially in the evening, when he would have secret audience with the King,' Jat Mall wrote. By the eve of the mutiny in 1857, this prototype Rasputin held an inordinate amount of influence over the King and the princes; it was said throughout the city that only the eunuch Mahbub Ali Khan wielded as much influence over the King.

Askari supposedly possessed the power of prophecy. One of his more well-known prophecies, particularly relevant to coming events, related to the affairs between Persia and the British Government of India in 1856. The city of Herat in western Afghanistan had fallen to the Persian army on 25 October that year, resulting in the British Government of India declaring war on Persia a week later on 1 November. When this news reached Delhi, Askari discussed it with the King. The mullah was of the view that the Persian army would march eastwards and enter Hindustan. Jat Mall described his prophecy:

> ... he had seen in a dream a hurricane approaching from the west, which was followed by a great flood of water devastating the country; that it passed over, and that he noticed that the King suffered no inconvenience

> from it, but was borne up over the flood, seated on his couch. The way in which Hassan Askari interpreted this dream was that the King of Persia with his army would annihilate the British power in the East, would restore the King to his ancestral throne, and reinstate him in his kingdom, and at the same time, the infidels, meaning the British, would be all slaughtered.

When the dust settled, Askari would categorically deny ever communicating any such prophecy to the King. He didn't deny his supposed supernatural abilities, however, claiming to have gained the King's faith after healing him with the famed curative breath. No doubt Askari was merely taking advantage of current events and existing speculation, but his pronouncement added to wishful thinking among the royal family as they chafed under British authority. The prospect of some sort of return of Mughal power, with the Persians and Russians doing the hard work of destroying the British, was too attractive to dismiss.

*****

The possibility of a Persian invasion and some sort of alliance had in fact reared its head several years earlier, and possibly through the actions of the King himself. Zafar's secretary, Mukand Lal, said at the King's trial that he had 'for some two years been disaffected against the Government and was disposed not to respect his obligations to the English'.[4] His bitter feelings against British authority were obvious to his family, so it is little surprise that some of his relatives were among those who tried to take advantage by fabricating an alliance with Persia and the ruler of Lucknow to destroy the British supremacy in Hindustan. Mirza Haider Shikoh and Mirza Murid were sons of Mirza Khan Baksh, who in turn was the son of Mirza Sulaiman Shikoh. Mirza Haider was therefore Zafar's nephew, and he had his uncle's ear.

These conspirators had agreed on a plan with Hasan Askari. The King was to be persuaded to approach the Shah of Persia for help. A grand alliance of the Persians along with the Nawab of Oudh was mooted, with a renewed Muslim ascendancy as its aim. The Nawab of Oudh had 70,000 troops at his disposal, and if a Russian-backed Persian army was added to his host it could extinguish British power with ease. First, the Persian army would move towards Hindustan. The British would no doubt react by pushing the bulk of their armed strength to the north-western frontier passes with Afghanistan. Once they had done this, the Nawab of Oudh could reveal his hand and declare war against the British, disrupting their supplies, preparations and logistics, and thereby hastening their collapse from the rear.

Was this scheme realistic? It is difficult to say. Nobody seemed to have consulted the effete Nawab of Oudh or even the far-off Russian court on these matters. As far as supporters were concerned, however, only one obstacle stood in the way: Zafar was a Sunni Muslim. The Nawab of Oudh was of the Shia sect, and so were the Persians. In order to cement a strong alliance and maintain a strong union between the three, Zafar would have to embrace the Shia faith. It was said that Mirza Haider was the prince who managed to persuade Zafar to convert for temporal gain. Court physician Ahsan Ulla Khan confirmed that Zafar had agreed to convert:

> He [Mirza Haider] was a hereditary Shia; both his grandfather Sulaiman Shikoh and his father Khan Baksh being of that persuasion. According to his faith it was a pious and creditable act to make proselytes, and he must have seen that he would derive much personal advantage, if he could succeed in converting the King of Delhi, inasmuch as he would in that case have three kings professing the same creed as his own, viz., the Kings of Delhi, Lukhnow and Persia…
>
> … There can be no doubt that the idea of communicating with the King of Persia was first suggested by Mirza Haider, who contemplated much advantage to himself; and it is probable that he desired that the conversion of the King should become known by means of a newspaper to the Shah of Persia, previous to the arrival of his brother, Mirza Najaf, in Persia so that the latter might be treated with consideration and honour.

In order to initiate negotiations of an alliance with the Persians, Mirza Najaf, a nephew of the King, had been sent to Persia in 1854. The Persian ruler apparently treated him well. 'I inquired from Mirza Ali Bakht, who was a great friend of Mirza Najaf, whether the latter had carried any letter from the King of Delhi to the Sultan of Persia. He replied in the affirmative, and described its contents to be to the effect that the King of Delhi had adopted the Shia creed, and the King of Persia should help him. Moreover, in that letter the King of Delhi described his miserable and helpless condition. Mirza Ali Bakht at the same time stated that no reply had been received from Persia,'[5] wrote Ahsan Ulla Khan.

Mirza Najaf's embassy seems to have been a failure, for he never sent any message of success. Several months went by with the Persian monarch remaining noncommittal. It was therefore decided to send a second embassy. This appeal for help to Tehran was to be led by Sidi Kambar, a highly trusted Abyssinian eunuch in charge of the Abyssinian armed guard at the palace. 'This letter, they [the conspirators] suggested, should represent that the English had made the King a prisoner, and had put a stop to all those marks of respect to which, as King, he was entitled, and had suspended the appointment of an heir-apparent. It was further to represent that his wishes in reference to the appointment of any particular son as heir-apparent were not attended to. Under these circumstances the letter was to request that such an understanding might be established that mutual interchanges of visits and letters might be the result,'[6] Mukand Lal explained. The letter, bearing the seal of the King, was given to Sidi Kambar by Hasan Askari himself. Sidi Kambar was also to find out why no answer had been given to Mirza Najaf's letter; in other words, whether or not the Persian monarch was genuinely interested in a compact. The embassy left Delhi in February 1855.

Under the agreement with the British authorities, the King was forbidden to make any communication with any court or power in or out of India unless he received prior permission. Like the last embassy, then, this one was sent in secrecy. Sidi Kambar was advanced 400 rupees to cover the expenses of the trip by Mahbub Ali Khan. The eunuch joined a *kafila* (caravan) heading to Mecca to disguise his true destination.

Zafar would later deny any involvement with Sidi Kambar's mission. 'As regards the Abyssinian, Kambar, he obtained leave from me to go on a pilgrimage to Mecca. I did not send him to Persia, nor did I send any letters by him to the Persian king. Someone has falsely circulated this story: Muhammad Durveshe's petition is no document of mine that it should be trusted: if any enemy of mine or of the Mian [His Honour or His Reverence] Hasan Askari has sent this petition, it ought not to be relied on.'[7]

Whatever the case, and despite the secrecy employed, news of Sidi Kambar's mission came to the attention of British authorities in Delhi. British informer Jat Mall had learned of Kambar's true purpose from Khwaja Baksh, a messenger of the King, and spoke with Ahsan Ulla Khan to find out more. He relayed his findings to Capt. Douglas, the commandant of the palace, who perhaps failed to treat the news with sufficient gravity but nonetheless asked Mall to gather more intelligence. Around three weeks later, Mall learned that Haider Hussein, the commandant of the palace artillery, and Hasan Askari had sent letters to Persia with the Abyssinian. Mall suggested to Captain Douglas that Sidi Kambar could be intercepted, but Douglas rejected the idea. It was unclear how far the eunuch had travelled and by which route, he said, and it would most likely be a waste of time to pursue him once he had such an advantage in distance.

After Sidi Kambar had departed with the letter, Mirza Haider and his brother had returned to Lucknow. Strangely, neither Mirza Haider nor the King or princes seem to have made any overtures to any of the other Indian rulers of the time. Perhaps they thought his was unnecessary – that a Persian or Russian force required no assistance in India to break British power. Or perhaps there was the fear other rulers may simply hand over the communication to the British authorities. A compact comprising only the Persians and Oudh was safer.

*****

The idea of a grand Shia Muslim alliance against the British was put to rest in the early months of 1856. On 7 February of that year, the state of Oudh was annexed by the East India Company. Matters in Persia then took a dramatic turn when, on 1 November, the British Government of India declared war against Persia after the latter captured the Afghan city of Herat in the west of the country on 25 October 1856. Herat was generally thought to be the key to any advance from the north (meaning Russia) or the west (meaning Persia) into India. This war, in which East Indian Company forces would attack territory in the Persian Gulf region, lasted five months and gave new impetus to rumours of a Persian or Russian invasion.

From November 1856 to April 1857, newspapers in Delhi were full of speculation on the war.[8] Magistrate Sir Theophilus Metcalfe would later note that there were many Indian newspaper correspondents in Kabul reporting on the Anglo-Persian War. It's quite possible that the idea of a Russian invasion was prevalent in the streets of Kabul, and that such rumours made their way to Indian ears through newspaper reports. The *Authentic News* in Delhi, for instance, reported that the Persian attack on Herat had only been a ruse, cover for a secret alliance with the Afghans prior to a war with the English. The Afghan ruler Dost Mohammad, who was on good terms with the British at the time, was going to change allegiance and join with his co-religionists (the Persians) and Russians in a war against the infidel British. On 26 January 1857, the *Authentic News* claimed to have gleaned from French sources that the Turkish Sultan and the King of France were as yet undecided on who to back in the war between the Persians and the British.[9] The British, meanwhile, were said to have sent embassies bearing gifts to dissuade the two countries from aiding the Persians, which was supposedly on the cards. The British adventure in Persia could in fact be used by the Russians as a pretext for a war to loosen the British hold on India.

> ... the Russians, however, they make no secret of the readiness with which they are assisting, and will continue to assist the Persians, whether it be with funds or with forces. It may be said that virtually the Russians are the cause of the war, and that using the Persians as a cloak, they intend to consummate their own designs, regarding the conquest of Hindustan. It is believed that the Russians will very soon take the field in great force.

On 16 March, the *Authentic News* published more detailed allegations that it claimed had come from the Persian court via papers in Bombay. There had been a meeting between the Afghan chiefs of Herat and the King of Persia about whether to push into India to fight the British. 'After due deliberation, they all advised him unanimously to declare war against the English, expressing their dependence that God would will his being victorious, for, said they, "Taking Herat you will be in a position as though you had reached the doorway into Hindustan."'[10] Urging him on, the chiefs told the King of Persia that this was the wish of the Russians and that he may as well make use of the Russian assistance, which would be considerable. The newspaper mentioned reports that the Russian Emperor was sending a well-equipped force of as many as 400,000 men to aid in the invasion of India. Rumours of the Russian army marching for this purpose apparently greatly pleased the Persian monarch and he 'spoke in terms of the highest praise for the Emperor Alexander of Russia, and issued instructions that funds for the expenses of the Russian Army should be defrayed from the treasury, and that the courier from the Russian army should not want for anything or suffer any inconveniences'. Such was the confidence in the Persian court that the various Herat chiefs were promised the governorships of various Indian provinces.

Ever since Nader Shah had sacked Delhi in 1739, the *Authentic News* continued, the Persian monarchs had longed to invade India once more. Previous rulers had neither the wherewithal nor the opportunity to emulate Nader Shah's feat, but now the time had now come. The Persian nobles and the various Afghan chiefs were supportive of the idea, while the Russians, in their eagerness to destroy British power in Hindustan, were lending a large army for this purpose. Also in Persia's favour were rumours that Dost Mohammad was fully supportive of a Persian invasion of India: 'On leaving for Cabul, the Amir [Dost Mohammad] wrote a letter to the King of Persia, that he was altogether a subject of the Persian sovereignty, and that he had no relations with the British government,'[11] the newspaper reported.

Further fuelling speculation were various tales of British difficulties and even catastrophic defeats in the ongoing conflict. Some rumours went as far as to say that the Persian army was already marching into India and had crossed the Indus and reached Attock. Another rumour was that they had instead traversed the Bolan Pass to the south of the Khyber Pass. It was understood that once the Persians entered India, the sepoy army, already discontented with the British yoke, would instantly rebel. 'I don't know whether any direct proposals came to the prisoner [Zafar], but the King's personal attendants, sitting about the entrance to his private apartments, used to converse among themselves, and say that very soon, almost immediately, the army would revolt and come to the palace, when the Government of the King would be re-established, and all the old servants would be greatly promoted and advanced in position and emoluments,' recounted Mukand Lal.

This was all to the satisfaction of the city's Muslim population according to Delhi-based journalist Chuni Lal, who described widespread delight at such a grand alliance of Muslims aided by Russians. Articles and news items on the war were of devoured by enthusiastic Muslims: 'It caused no excitement among the Hindus; but the Mahomedans took a marked interest in the news about Persia, and used to go about exulting and boasting that the Persians were coming, and would do this, that, and the other. As regards the general disaffection of the troops, the Mahomedans only seemed affected by it, and certainly appeared to be very much excited and interested.'[12] On being questioned later as to whether there was any talk of a Russian invasion as well, Chuni replied that there was, although talk of Persians was much more common than talk of Russians.

Around five to six weeks prior to the outbreak at Meerut, there was much discussion in the Delhi cantonments and beyond of a

100,000-strong Russian army sweeping through India from the north and toppling British rule. The princes in the palace had also heard the rumours of British defeats – and they were very interested.

*****

At this time, during the last days of March 1857, a significant discovery was made by the British force in Persia. It seemed to confirm the rumours of a Muslim grand alliance. After a battle at Mohammerah, victorious British forces discovered a letter, or rather a proclamation, in the tent of a prince who had commanded the Persians. It was highly incendiary. The letter accused the British of overarching ambition, of unnecessary aggression employed to add the entire east to its empire. The British Government might have been chastened in its recent disaster during the first Anglo-Afghan War, but apparently not enough. Further, it continued, the British Government was attempting to restrict relations between the Afghan rulers and Persia for its own ends, even though the two groups shared the Muslim faith (though the Afghans were Sunni and the Persians Shia). The British aim, the proclamation insisted, was 'to reduce the Government of Persia to the state of the Rajahs of Hindostan, and to destroy the religion of Islam in Persia, in like manner as the religion of the Mussulman in India'. For this reason, war was being conducted against Persia. The proclamation went on to claim that various forces were being sent in all directions, including Sindh and Cutch in India, and that the various Afghan rulers would be cooperating in this venture. Finally, it urged all Muslims to join the religious struggle against the infidel.

> ... it is necessary that the Affghan tribes and the inhabitants of that country who are co-religionists of the Persians and who possess the same Kuran [Quran] and kibla and laws of the Prophet, should also take part in the jahad [jihad], and extend the hand of brotherhood, and on receiving these glad tidings, act according to the words of the Prophet: 'Verily all true believers are brothers,' and 'also make manifest the decree of God.' 'Verily the Almighty will weigh the wicked in different scales from the pure and for the purpose of settling the quarrel, it is necessary that not only a small number of true believers should stand forth in the defence of the faith, but that the whole should answer our call ...'
>
> ... and they should join in the jahad [jihad] against the enemies of Islam, and be of the number of those to whom the Prophet sayeth, 'The grace of God dwelleth in those who fight in jahad.' And we are hopeful that after the publication of this proclamation, Dost Mahomed Khan, Ameer of Cabool, who always was desirous that the Persian armies should extend their conquests to Afghanistan, and who wished to be strengthened by their alliance, should also unite with us against this tribe of wanderers [the British] from the path of righteousness, and that he should become one of the leaders of the faithful in this jahad, and that he should become a Ghazi

> [Muslim bent on fighting non-Muslims] in Hindostan, for he cannot wish for the friendship of a tribe of whom the Prophet sayeth, 'Verily they do not love you, and neither do ye love them;' nor can he wish to sell his faith for a worldly price. And this proclamation is published for the information of all true believers; and please God the followers of Islam in India and Scinde will also unite with us and take vengeance upon that tribe (the British) for all the injuries which the holy faith has suffered from them, and will not withhold any sacrifices in the holy cause.

The letter was published by the *Bombay Telegraph and Courier* on 14 April 1857 amid a flood of news reporting the British victory in the Persian Gulf. The next month, British newspaper *The Sindhian*, quoting the *Bombay Times*, reported that the Persian city of Bushire had been recaptured from the British by a Persian army with the assistance of several Russian officers and around 3,000 Russians – but that it had now fallen to the British once more. However, a large Russian army was being assembled north of Afghanistan. If the Persians captured Kandahar, Dost Mohammad might switch sides.[13]

As late as May 1857, shortly before the mutiny at Meerut, these rumours of a Russo-Persian pact and invasion were still being discussed. In Delhi, for example, the Anglo-Indian John Everett, formerly a risaldar of the 14th Irregulars, was convalescing. On the morning of 9 May, one day before the Meerut mutiny, he received some inkling that not all was right. While conversing with an African employee of the King called Moujud, Everett was urged to join the King's service. '"You had better leave the Company's service, and with your troop come over to that of the King." He said this in the way of friendly advice. I asked him his reason. He said. "This hot weather you will see the Russians all over the place." I laughed at the fellow's ideas, and told him to go away just then, as I was busy, and I would see him some other time.'[14] The only thing delaying the invasion was the coming extreme heat of early summer before the monsoon rains; after this, an invasion could safely be conducted. In fact, he was told that six months earlier the King had even sent an envoy to the Russian court. Everett, though dismissive, had no qualms in reporting the information to the authorities.

* * * * *

In the cloistered air of the palace, news from Afghanistan and Persia was met with similar enthusiasm. Unlikely hopes were bandied about among the princes that somehow this was the beginning of the end of British influence and the resurrection of Islam in India. The Persians would raise the King to the rule of Hindustan, albeit as a vassal of Persia. Ahsan Ulla Khan later said that 'the King was always very anxious to obtain intelligence of the events which were occurring towards Persia during the time when war was going on at Bushire'. He had expectations of financial help, or perhaps of troops. He constantly asked about the course of the war. Informers continued to keep the British authorities abreast of the relevant conversations. Mohammed Dervish was one of these informers. He sent a warning in the form of a letter to John Colvin, Lieutenant Governor of the North-West Provinces, around six weeks prior to the outbreak of mutiny at Meerut. Writing on 25 March 1857 (and received at Agra on 27 March), Dervish, a newspaper correspondent who described himself as a 'mendicant of itinerant habits', claimed a conspiracy of the highest order related to the royal family themselves. He warned the Lieutenant Governor of the extraordinary influence of Hasan Askari on the mind of the King.

> In the palace, but more especially in the portion of it constituting the personal apartments of the king, the subject of conversation, night and day, is the early arrival of the Persians. Hasan Askari [the middleman] has, moreover, impressed the king with the belief that he has learned, through a divine revelation, that the dominion of the king of Persia will, to a certainty extend to Delhi, or rather over the whole of Hindustan, and that the splendour of the sovereignty of Delhi will again revive, as the sovereign of Persia will bestow the crown on the king. Throughout the palace, but particularly to the king, this belief has been the cause of great rejoicing, so much so that prayers are offered, and vows are made, while, at the same time, Hasan Askari has entered upon the daily performance, at an hour and a half before sunset, of a course of propitiatory ceremonies, to expedite the arrival of the Persians, and the expulsion of the Christians. It has been arranged that every Thursday, several trays of victuals, wheat-meal, oil, money in copper coin, and cloth should be sent by the king in aid of these ceremonies, and they are accordingly brought to Hasan Askari. Some of the higher functionaries of the government, drawn into a faith in this man by his frauds and deceptions, are in the habit of visiting his house, and consider his words and actions entitled to the greatest reliance. Where would be the use in my naming these traitors? May the Almighty God confound the enemies of the Government!

Dervish described Zafar's communication with the Persian monarch in previous years and claimed that further letters had been sent by Zafar to Constantinople via a caravan bound for Mecca. Perhaps the letters had as their purpose a treaty, or a request for assistance from the Ottoman Sultan. Dervish declared:

> [I have] learned for a certainty, that two men, with letters from the King of Delhi through the said Hasan Askari, proceeded about three or four months ago towards Constantinople in company with a caravan going to Mecca. Hasan Askari has now assured the King of Delhi that he has certain information that the Prince Royal of Persia has fully taken possession of and occupied Bushire, and that he has

> entirely expelled the Christians or rather has not left one alive there, and has taken many of them prisoners. and that very soon indeed the Persian army will advance by the way of Candahar and Cabul towards Delhi. He told the King also that his Majesty was altogether too careless about corresponding with the King of Persia. The king then gave Hasan Askari 20 gold Mohurs, and requested him speedily to despatch letters to Persia, and directed him to give the gold mohurs to the man who should take the letters, for the expenses of his journey. Hasan Askari accordingly took the money and returned to his house and has prepared four men to carry the letters, making them assume the coloured garments of religious mendicants, and it is reported that they will leave for Persia in a day or two. The petitioner has not been able to ascertain their names.[15]

Colvin's attitude upon reading the letter was dismissive, much as Captain Douglas had been upon being told of the royal embassies to the Persian court. He scoffed at the rumours, and he waved away concerns about the effects that these rumours, true or not, were having on the general population.

*****

In the weeks before the mutiny, proclamations mysteriously began to appear plastered on the walls of the Jama Masjid and several other prominent locations in Delhi. Some of the notices were brazen, calling for the followers of the prophet to wage war against the infidel, while others used more subtle language but nevertheless hinted at rebellion in support of an imminent Persian invasion. These notices were snatched down by the authorities as they appeared, but otherwise they were disregarded. Nevertheless, they will have been read by many and their message must have spread by word of mouth. One prominent example appeared on the walls of the Jama Masjid during March. It announced the imminent arrival of the King of Persia and his army, whose express purpose was to drive the infidel out of Hindustan, and exhorted all true Muslims to rise up and help in the overthrow of the nonbelievers. On 19 March, the *Authentic News* reported on the poster:

> The purport of it in a condensed form is, that people professing the true faith should, as a matter of duty, eschew assisting the Christians, and should, as being right and proper, exert themselves to the full extent of their ability to promote the welfare of the Mussulmans, that the time is at hand, when God willing, we, the King of Persia, will sit on the throne of India, and will make the king and people of that country contented and happy. In the same measure as the English have done everything to make them destitute of even the means of subsistence, we will exert ourselves to make them rich and affluent. We use no interference with any man's religion. Such is the substance of the proclamation.[16]

The *Authentic News* claimed that one Muhammad Sadiq Khan had contacted them and taken credit for the poster, as well as others around Delhi. He said he had reached Delhi from Persia on 4 March and quickly set about circulating the proclamation. According to him, by 6 March there were already up to 900 Persian soldiers in Hindustan, with around 500 in Delhi, including officers, ready to assist in fomenting unrest and helping to capture the city when the invasion finally took place. He also revealed that he was sending intelligence back to Persia, and that he would publish further proclamations as he received news of the Persian advance. It is unclear why this man would reveal so much in advance of a possible invasion, and thereby alert the British authorities. The Persian authorities disowned the proclamation, although they would later admit that a decision had been taken to foment unrest in India; the two countries were at war with each other, after all, and it was considered fair game to use such means to distract the enemy.

Within hours of the proclamation's appearance, the magistrate Sir Theophilus Metcalfe had it torn down and brought to him. Metcalfe described it as 'a small dirty piece of paper with a naked sword and shield depicted one on the right and the other on the left of it, and the purport of it was that the King of Persia was about to visit this country, and he called upon all the faithful followers of the prophet Muhammad to join with him in extirpating the English infidels, and offering landed estates and other large rewards to all who would do so; it was further stated that there were 500 men in Delhi at the time of putting up the placard, who were devoted to his interest'.[17]

The matter of 500 men already in the city planning unrest must have given the message added weight, suggesting as it did that an uprising was imminent. However, Metcalfe could discern no pretence of a Shia/Sunni accord or any attempt to meld the two elements of Islam together. His impression was that it was a false proclamation, and an obvious one at that. 'It was put up there at night,' he later recalled. 'I don't know the exact date, but it was about six weeks before the outbreak, and I suppose it may have remained up about three hours; in the morning a concourse of people was collected round it, and on hearing of this I had it taken down.'[18] His impression was that it attracted little interest or excitement, and as a result he didn't bother to discover its origins. 'It was considered altogether too contemptible. Any disaffected person in the city might have put such a paper and to have made a fuss about it would only have been investing it with undue importance,' he explained.

Metcalfe was probably wrong to suggest the proclamation was ignored by locals. Newspapers reported on similar posters found elsewhere in the city, and by carrying such news they rendered Metcalfe's censorship meaningless. There can be no doubt that news of a Persian invasion combined with the incendiary posters to prepare many for the possible downfall of British supremacy.

# 7

# 'The right arm, the hands and feet of the British government'

> The Government must be well aware that when a soldier has once or twice shown a disposition to mutiny he is useless as a soldier.
>
> Shaik Hedayut Ali, 8th NI

In the summer of 1857, European troops in India numbered around 40,000 in total. Of these 24,000 were queen's troops. European strength had been greater in the past. Several years earlier, the strength of the British regiments in India had reached a peak of twenty-six infantry and cavalry regiments. However, the outbreak of the Crimean War had meant a withdrawal of five regiments in 1854 while others had been transferred to the recently annexed area of Pegu after the Second Anglo-Burmese War (1852–53). Only one of these had been replaced, bringing the total to twenty-two regiments. During the recent Anglo-Persian War, three further European regiments (two infantry and one Light Dragoon regiment) had been sent from India, reducing the available regiments to nineteen.

The bulk of the European regiments were stationed in the north of the country, in the Punjab or nearby, specifically between the station of Ambala, 150 miles north of Delhi, and Peshawar on the far north-west border with Afghanistan. This was primarily due to the recent annexation of the Punjab and the assumption in British minds that any outbreak of violence would occur there or along the restless border with Afghanistan rather than in the heartland of India, which appeared to have been well pacified. The paucity of European troops meant that across the densely populated 600 miles from Meerut to Dinapore, for example, only two European regiments were present (the 3rd Bengal Fusiliers at Agra and 32nd Foot at Lucknow). Between Delhi and Calcutta in the far east, a distance of around 1,000 miles, just five European regiments remained: one infantry regiment at Calcutta, one at Dinapore, one at Lucknow, and one each of infantry and cavalry at Meerut. Another four European regiments were shared between the Madras and Bombay armies in the south of the country. None of the larger cities in the north and north-east – Delhi, Bareilly, Faizabad, Allahabad and Benares for instance – had a trace of a European garrison.

In contrast to the 40,000 European troops, the Company's sepoy regiments numbered just over 311,000. In other words, for every European soldier there were nearly eight sepoys. Everybody, whether English or Indian, knew that the military prestige and the seeming invincibility of British arms rested largely on the huge strength of the sepoy army. If the sepoys ever mutinied, all could be lost in an instant. The European regiments, few in number, scattered around the country and reliant on local supplies and logistics, would have little chance of retaining control of the huge country and its population. Of course, there had always been concerns about the disparity in numbers between sepoys and European troops. The sepoys themselves recognised it. The chances of a widespread mutiny were considered moot in European circles in 1857, however, and the question of whether the Company could retain control in such a scenario seemed entirely academic.

Nevertheless, it was apparent to all that discontentment was rife in the sepoy ranks; it was also clear that the situation had been worsening for quite a while. Some placed significant blame for the beginnings of the disaffection on a previous Governor-General, Lord Auckland, and his decision to invade Afghanistan in 1839. This move had been very unpopular with the Hindu soldiers, who believed they would lose caste once they crossed the Indus. Worse was to come when the British force under General Keane reached Afghanistan and cantoned in Kabul. The cold of the Afghan winter and the Muslim population irked the ordinary Hindu soldier for various reasons.

'Whatever they purchased in the Bazaar for their daily food, they were compelled to take from the hands of Mahomedans, because in the Cabool country all the Buneeahs with few exceptions are of the Mahomedan faith. The Hindoos being obliged as above stated to abstain from certain acts of their religion (bathing which to a Hindoo is almost as necessary as his daily food) and to receive their bread from the hands of Mahomedans, fancied they had lost their caste, and had been forced to become Mahomedans; they therefore became much dissatisfied and disgusted,'[1] wrote Shaik Hedayut Ali of the 8th NI, stationed at Ferozepore with his regiment. The units that had marched into Afghanistan had been stationed at Ferozepore, and when they were sent back he had learned much of their resentments and fears. To keep out the Afghan cold, the sepoy regiments had been issued with posterns – jackets made of sheepskin. These they had worn unhappily and with much regret, for traditionally only Hindus of low caste handled dead animals or their skin. Mutiny on these issues was never an option in Afghanistan, though; it would leave them stranded and leaderless among the puritan and uncompromising Muslim population of Kabul.

'They moreover thought that even if they did mutiny in that country, and killed all the English, they would be no better off, because the Affghans would compel them to become Mahomedans. Many Sepoys of the 27th and 54th NI who were wounded and taken prisoners, were converted to Mahomedanism. Don't let any English gentlemen think that the above is not true because they were not acquainted with it at the time: a native of Hindoostan seldom opens his mind to his Officer; he only says what he thinks would please his Officer. The Sepoys reserve their real opinion until they return to their lines and to their comrades,' wrote Shaik Hedayut Ali. 'It was said that the Sepoys of the 27th NI who were shut up in Ghuznee [Ghazni fortress] were all compelled to become Mahomedans.'

The sepoys were frank about their distaste for the campaign in Afghanistan. It had made them outcasts amongst their community, although paradoxically they also gained much sympathy for having been forced to march into that hated country. There were murmurs and mutterings in other regiments across the country that there might be more expeditions into Afghanistan and elsewhere. The Muslims of the sepoy regiments were angry too, but for different reasons. They had been made to fight against their co-religionists, which they said was forbidden in the Quran. 'The Mahomedans always boasted amongst themselves how they had evaded the English order by never taking aim when they fired,' wrote Shaik Hedayut Ali.[2]

Another troublesome issue had materialised ten years later in 1849. This was the matter of *batta*, the special allowance made to soldiers serving in the field. Sepoys stationed in the Punjab had grown accustomed to receiving double *batta* for the length of their stay in the territory. However, after the Punjab was annexed the relieving regiments were told that they would only receive their normal allowance; it was now British territory, so they were not on foreign service. This had been the direct cause of the mutiny of the 66th NI at Amritsar, which led to their disbandment in February 1850. Two other regiments, the 32nd and the 22nd, had also displayed signs of mutiny at this loss of earnings. It was later observed that British officers had hushed up or ignored discontent in their regiments during the mutiny of the 66th. The same habits would contribute to the events of 1857. Officers would withhold concerns from their own superiors for fear of losing respect either for themselves or for their regiments. As a result, nothing was done to address the sepoys' concerns. Not until the sepoys had definitively crossed the line was any action taken.

At least as far back as 1849, there was a considerable fraternity between the sepoy regiments of the Bengal Army. A lively correspondence existed between the regiments in Punjab and elsewhere regarding the reduction in *batta* and the disobeying of orders. Brigadier Hearsey, stationed at Wazirabad in the Punjab, had voiced his opinion to Sir Charles Napier, then Commander-in-Chief, that this communication should be opened and read by British censors. 'I told him that was quite impossible: that neither could Government abridge correspondence nor open private letters except on some occasion which would bear out such an act,'[3] Napier recalled.

Seven years later, in 1856, one of Lord Canning's first moves as Governor-General was the passing of the General Service Enlistment Act. By this Act, all sepoys of the Bengal Army could be called to serve abroad without extra pay. This had always been the case for the Madras and Bombay armies, but it was new to the Bengal Army, which was largely composed of high-caste Brahmins. As the sepoys understood it, this meant any and all units in the Bengal Army were liable to be called for overseas service. Overseas service naturally meant crossing the ocean, or *Kala Pani* as it was termed, and this would break caste. It also confirmed what had been feared after the war in Afghanistan – that sepoy regiments would have to face travel outside the country. The Act in fact only applied to new recruits, but the sepoys felt it was the thin end of the wedge – that soon the Act would be applied retrospectively to all units. Fear of losing caste was paramount among the Hindu sepoys. Class divisions were such that a cooking utensil could not be shared with others of a different caste. Travelling overseas on service in British troop ships therefore created a particularly difficult situation. In such cramped conditions, a high-caste sepoy would have difficulties making his own food on his own fire. To share implements or food meant immediate loss of caste and was therefore anathema.

Other matters played their own role. Shaik Hedayut Ali wrote that sepoys were greatly frustrated by the matter of promotion, as they could only rise to the rank of subedar. Moreover, promotion was based on seniority and not merit, so a sepoy could expect to wait an inordinate amount of time to achieve this rank. 'All the old men from length of service worth nothing as Commissioned or Noncommissioned Officers received promotion whilst younger men in every way fit languished in their lines saying, "What use is there in us exerting ourselves; we cannot get promotion until our turn comes and that time can't come until our heads are grey and our mouths toothless."' Pessimism was widespread among the young. The senior ranks, meanwhile, were full of old men declining in strength and generally incapable of keeping up.

The Company was very particular about recruitment. The soldiers were invariably high-caste men, largely recruited from Oudh and other princely states where the matter of caste was paramount. This homogeneity fostered a high level of fraternity, and union on some cause or another was all but guaranteed. The matter of losing caste, for instance, was important because the sepoys of the Bengal Army were drafted from Brahmin families. If the bulk of the sepoys had come from lowlier backgrounds, perhaps breaking caste would not have mattered so much. In contrast, the Bombay and Madras armies welcomed men of both high and low caste. When the financial commissioner for Oudh, Martin Richard Gubbins, asked a Bombay subedar why there had been little trouble in the Bombay army during the Mutiny of 1857, he explained the role of caste. '"On the Bombay side," said he, "I stood side by side with men of low caste, and who dared there say a word? Mahratta, Pasee, Brahmin, Chumar, Rajpoot, and many others, are there found in the same ranks. But here they are all one."'[4]

Another issue was the failure to keep a sufficient divide between Muslim and Hindu sepoys. Syed Ahmad Khan wrote *Causes of the Indian Revolt* in 1858, even as the conflict still rumbled on. He would go as far as to suggest that it had been a major mistake to enlist Hindu and Muslim soldiers into the same regiments. Kept apart, the gulf in religious belief would have maintained an invisible divide, preventing Hindu and Muslim from working in unison; however, over time, and despite their religious differences, the soldiers managed to develop a good sense of camaraderie as they lived and marched together. Put simply, a complacent Government of India had failed to maintain a policy of divide and rule in the regiments.

Perhaps the greatest danger was the growing pride and confidence among sepoys in the decades leading up to 1857. There had been a sea change in the way these men saw themselves. Looking at the paucity of European strength, the sepoys naturally thought they had done the lion's share of the work in the Company's recent conquests. Syed Ahmad Khan summed up the mood prevalent before the outbreak in frank terms:

> Owing to the paucity of the European element, the people of India only stood in awe of the sepoys who thus became puffed up with pride and thought that there were none like them in the world. They looked upon the European portion of the army as a myth and thought that the many victories which the English had gained were gained entirely by their own prowess. A common saying of theirs was that they had enabled the English to conquer Hindustan from Burmah to Cabul. This pride of the Sepoys was most marked after the Panjab was conquered. So far had it gone that they made objections to anything which they did not like, and I believe even remonstrated when ordered to march consequent on the yearly reliefs. It was precisely at this time, when the army was imbued with this feeling of pride and the knowledge or rather conjecture that Government would grant anything they stood out for, that the new cartridges were issued, cartridges which they really believed were made up with fat and the using of which would destroy their caste. They refused to bite them.[5]

Ahsan Ulla Khan went further, suggesting the sepoys had grown scornful of British authority: 'The mutineers spoke of the British with contempt. They called them Nasara [i.e. Nazarenes or Christians] and infidels but they did not use foul language against them.' When the mutineers from Meerut later arrived in Delhi, in their discussions with Ahsan Ulla Khan, Haider Hassan and others they gave their salient reasons for mutiny. Leaving aside the issue of the new ammunition, they listed short leave, the withdrawal of *batta*, the new directives on sending troops overseas and an emerging lack of respect from others. It was also apparent to the sepoys that the British did not have the means to combat them if they acted in unison, and that the Government of India would have to give way as it depended so much on the sepoys. Surely their overwhelming numbers would have to be taken into account.

The Earl of Dalhousie, Governor-General from 1848 to 1856, commented on the growing divide and was firm in his opinion that a strong hand must be kept on the Bengal Army. The sepoy must be taught his place as the European soldier's inferior so that the illusion of European invincibility did not shatter. Succeed in this, and the sepoy would never try his luck in a mutiny despite the disparity in numbers. Dalhousie felt that the Bengal Army was fat and pampered, and that mismanagement had led to the sepoy forgetting his place. He made his views clear in a letter of 17 November 1849:

> There never was mutiny in this army except from our own injustice or ill management. The sepoy is a child in simplicity and biddableness, if you make him understand his orders, if you treat him justly, *and don't* pet him overmuch. This C.-in-C. [Sir Charles Napier] is inclined to do so. He told 41st the other day that the sepoys were *better* than any troops in the world, except British troops, and *as good* as the British! Four days afterwards they refused to pile arms when coming off parade – in fact, took the first step to mutiny. That sepoys are as good as Britons (even if it were true) is not just the lesson to teach them while we are 25,000 and they 200,000 disciplined men. But it is *not* true, and whenever it becomes anything like the truth it will be time for us to be looking over our shoulders towards the Bay of Bengal and the outward bound.[6]

The general discontent prevailing around these and other issues was noticed by most European officers at the time, but it was largely dismissed. This is commonly explained away by reference to the increasing segregation of the Indians and the Europeans. In previous times they had mixed much more freely, with many European men taking Indian wives. These wives of officers, meanwhile, mixed with the sepoys of the regiments, providing a channel for gossip to reach the officers while also helping form an interracial bond. By the middle of the century, however, Europeans had generally become much more aloof;

now, European officers only married European women. A racial divide had materialised between rulers and ruled. The commonality between the two races was disappearing, and sepoys were no longer confiding in their officers as often as they once had. Many Europeans were now seen as aliens rather than brothers-in-arms. Because of this growing distance, most officers were quite oblivious to the strength of feeling in the sepoy cantonments at the time.

John Lawrence, Commissioner of the Punjab, summed up the changing mindset of the sepoy during the 1850s in his communication with the Government on 29 April 1858: 'They were, as they themselves said in their own phrase, the right arm, the hands and feet, of the British Government. Their strength consisted in their great numbers; in their unexampled power of combination from their being one vast brotherhood with common fatherland, language, religion, caste, and associations; and their possession of most of our magazines, many of our forts, and all our treasuries; while our weakness consisted in the paucity of European troops.'[7] He pointed to the increase in sepoy regiments over the last few years while the number of European regiments stationed in India in 1857 was as low as it had been for many years due to wars elsewhere. Furthermore, what European regiments remained in India were weak, many having not received fresh recruits for two years. 'These and all the other weak points of our system were patent to a Native Army having many intelligent men in its ranks, employed promiscuously from Calcutta to Peshawur and consequently well acquainted with our military arrangements. In short, it was a sense of overwhelming power acting upon men exasperated by a fancied wrong that led the Bengal Army to mutiny.'

Clearly, a combustible series of grievances was smouldering in the sepoy army at a time when its confidence and pride – as well as its contempt for the European soldier – was at its peak. And it was at this very moment that a new and much more potent issue suddenly appeared. The new Enfield rifle had arrived – with its new cartridge.

# 8

# 'A mine ready for explosion'

> ... should, which God forbid! any misguided men – dupes of fools and knaves, attempt to follow in the footsteps of the 19th and 34th, rest assured that Government, all powerful and irresistible, is not only prepared and capable, but will lose no time in inflicting such punishment as shall not easily pass away from the recollection of man.[1]
>
> Henry Lawrence, Lucknow

What finally triggered the Great Mutiny was a chance meeting between two men at Dum Dum, the large British arsenal adjacent to Calcutta, the British seat of power, in early February 1857. One was a *kalassie*, a low-caste worker, employed at the arsenal; the other was a sepoy of the 2nd NI (Grenadiers) from nearby Barrackpore. Barrackpore (literally meaning 'the town of barracks') was a large military station a few miles north of the British capital on the Hooghly River. No fewer than four sepoy regiments were stationed at Barrackpore – the 34th, 43rd and 70th Native Infantry regiments, along with the 2nd Grenadiers. The station was commanded by Brigadier Charles Grant. The division general was John Hearsey.

The *kalassie* had casually asked the sepoy if he could use his *lota*, a drinking vessel, to refresh himself with some water. The sepoy, a high-caste Brahmin, had refused to share the vessel with the man for that would have meant loss of caste. The spurned *kalassie* taunted the sepoy. He need not worry about losing his caste, the *kalassie* said, as that would happen soon enough. He explained that he was employed in manufacturing the new cartridges at Dum Dum, and they contained the fat of bullocks and pigs. The cartridges needed to be bitten as part of the new loading procedure, and therefore any sepoy using the ammunition would consequently have contact with the grease. For a Hindu, believing in the sanctity of the cow, this would mean immediate loss of caste.

The Brahmin sepoy, concerned by the news, returned to Barrackpore and immediately spread the word. Muslim soldiers were equally perturbed at the news, since pork was forbidden in Islam.

The disturbance soon reached the ears of Capt. Wright, the officer in charge of the Rifle Instruction Depot at Dum Dum, and he was the first to report the sepoys' feelings – albeit in a measured way. Writing to Major-General Hearsey, he mentioned 'a very unpleasant feeling existing among the native soldiers who are here for instruction regarding the grease used in preparing the cartridges, some evil-disposed persons having spread a report that it consists of a mixture of the fat of pigs and cows'. Many men, he had learned, were fearful of using the cartridges since the news had spread and they would be ostracised by friends, families and home town neighbours, who would refuse to deal or even sit with them. Capt. Wright had tried to reassure his men on the issue, explaining that the grease was made of mutton fat and wax. They remained suspicious. 'It may be so,' they replied, 'but our friends will not believe it. Let us obtain the ingredients from the bazar and make it ourselves, we shall then know what is used and be able to assure our fellow-soldiers and others that there is nothing in it prohibited by our caste.'[2] Meanwhile, Hearsey immediately sent Capt. Wright's report up the chain to the Government of India.

Another warning was raised by Major Bontein, who commanded the Depot of Musketry at Dum Dum. On learning of the soldiers' concerns from Capt. Wright, Bontein had decided to ascertain the level of dissent himself. During a parade, the soldiers were asked if they had any complaints. 'At least two-thirds of the detachment immediately stepped to the front including all the native commissioned officers. In a manner perfectly respectful they very distinctly stated their objections to the present method of preparing cartridges for the new rifled musket. The mixture employed for greasing cartridges was opposed to their religious feeling and as a remedy they begged to suggest the employment of wax and oil in such proportion as, in their opinion, would answer the purpose required.'[3]

Hearsey recommended that the officer commanding the Rifle Depot be authorised to obtain from the bazaar whatever ingredients might be necessary for the grease, which the sepoys could then make for themselves. The Government of India made no objection, so Hearsey allowed the organised collection of alternative ingredients from the bazaar – with the sepoys themselves permitted to mix the ingredients to calm any fears. The concession appears to have been a little too late, however. Rumours of the alleged composition of the cartridge grease had already spread. Sepoys writing letters to family, friends and fellow soldiers invariably mentioned their suspicions regarding the new cartridge fat. Their letters travelled across Bengal, up the north-west province, into Delhi and further north into Punjab and onwards to Peshawar and the borderlands with Afghanistan, as well as to the south of the country. Within a matter of weeks, rumours about the new cartridge had spread across the whole country.

On 9 February, Hearsey addressed the sepoys at Barrackpore and explained the situation with the cartridges. Although the troops showed no overt anger or defiance, it was obvious to their officers that discontent was simmering below the surface. Members of the 34th Regiment showed the most disaffection. In fact, they had voiced their mutinous feelings to men of the 19th NI and the 11th Irregular Cavalry, stationed roughly 100 miles north at Berhampore, who had also been angered by the news of the grease.

On 11 February, Hearsey wrote from Barrackpore that matters were rapidly escalating. 'We have at Barrackpore been dwelling upon a mine ready for explosion. I have been watching the feeling of the sepoys here for some time. Their minds have been misled by some designing scoundrels, who have managed to make them believe that their religious prejudices, their caste, is to be interfered with by Government; that they are to be forced to turn Christians. Any reasonable person would doubt, after the experience we have had, that such an absurd notion could possess them; but, nevertheless, it is a fact, and it will take time to dispossess their minds of this stupid idea.'

In mid-February, the men of the 19th NI at Berhampore became the first to refuse to handle their musket cartridges. Colonel Mitchell, their commanding officer, told them that the new cartridges had not yet been supplied to the station, but to no avail. In any case, Mitchell said, the Government had no interest in causing a loss of caste for the soldiers. When the men continued to demur over the next few days, an ultimatum was handed down. On 26 February, Mitchell declared that any man refusing orders would be court-martialled. This raised the ire of the men of the 19th NI. That night, they rose and armed themselves. Mitchell responded by ordering out the 11th Irregular Cavalry, which didn't seem as aggrieved, along with some guns. Tensions only worsened from there, although the men of the 19th NI were eventually persuaded to lay down their weapons.

On hearing of the growing discontent, the Government recalled a European regiment, HM84th Foot, from Rangoon. This regiment headed to Barrackpore, where the 19th NI had also been ordered to muster. The objective was to disarm the 19th NI before disbanding it, the regiment now being seen as beyond redemption. The disarmament was carried out while HM84th watched with a wing of HM53rd that had been sent from Fort William along with a troop of horse artillery and the Governor-General's bodyguard. Resisting this European host would have been futile, and the 19th NI duly accepted the disarmament and gave up their accoutrements.

Unbeknownst to the British, the 19th NI had been offered the assistance of the 34th NI at Barrackpore. As they were being marched down, a messenger from the 34th NI had advised them to kill their officers; the 34th NI was ready to mutiny at the same time and slaughter all its

European officers at Barrackpore. But the men of the 19th NI replied that they had no quarrel with their officers, only with the Government, and they refused to contemplate murdering their officers. As they marched to their disarmament, the sepoys of the 19th declared to passers-by that they had stood fast on their principles, choosing religion over money and refusing to lose their caste – whatever the penalty.

The issue for most sepoys at this early stage, then, was simply an unpopular Government policy. The matter could well have been settled if it had been handled with some sensitivity. However, the disbandment of the 19th NI was the first sign that the Government would not bend. In retrospect, it is plain to see that this is the moment when trust was lost. A significant estrangement between sepoys and their officers began to emerge. Sepoys elsewhere in the Bengal Army felt that the men of the 19th NI were loyal soldiers whose religious sensibilities deserved respect. The Government, they felt, had shown no willingness to compromise. Sepoy ringleaders duly began to communicate in secret all across India.

That isn't to say that the Government showed no understanding of the issue. After the disbandment of the 19th NI, in the hope of allaying the fears of the sepoys, an order had been issued to change the method by which the rifle was loaded. Instead of biting the cartridge, the sepoy could now simply break the cartridge open with his fingers. Various attempts were also made to explain the nature of the grease used – that it was merely composed of beeswax and clarified butter. However, no matter how the cartridge was loaded, it was going to be issued and the sepoys would have to use it.

Anxiety over the cartridges quickly merged with existing frustration regarding Christian missionary activity in the country. These cartridges, according to tales being circulated, were intended to break the caste of the sepoys and hence convert them surreptitiously to Christianity. Supposedly, this was a policy wholeheartedly endorsed by the new Governor-General, Lord Canning. The tug-of-war over the cartridge was starting to be seen as a trial of strength – was the sepoy army powerful enough to reverse the introduction of the new weapon? The sepoys wished for the grease – whatever its constituents – to be done away with entirely so that no mark of suspicion about caste could remain.

By this time, there were also concerns about the composition of the cartridge paper. Sepoys thought it seemed different, and the suspicion was that the paper itself had been impregnated with the suspect grease. Over the following weeks these rumours were further embellished. It was simply part of a larger conspiracy, some argued. Food was widely polluted by the British authorities. While the cartridges were meant to destroy the caste of the sepoys, flour was being contaminated to break the caste of the ordinary public. Gossip circulated that ground animal bones were being mixed into the flour, causing particular consternation in Meerut. Martin Richard Gubbins would describe the panic in Oudh during the early part of 1857:

> Government, it was said, had sent up cart-loads and boat-loads of bone-dust, which was to be mixed with the flour and sweetmeats sold in the bazaar, whereby the whole population would lose their caste. The public mind became greatly excited. On one day, at Sultanpoor, it was spread over the station that a boat had reached a certain ghaut on the river Goomtee, laden with bone-dust, and the sepoys were hardly restrained from outbreak. A few days later, at the station of Salone, two camels, laden with ammunition, arrived at the house of Captain Thompson, the commandant. It was rumored that the packages contained bone-dust, and a panic spread through the station. Not only the sepoys in their lines, but the domestic servants about the officers' bungalows, and the villagers and zemindars (landowners) attending court, hastily flung away, untasted, the food which they had cooked, and fasted for the day. At Lucknow, the rumors which were whispered about were perpetual, and the public mind was never allowed to rest. Now it was at one shop, the next day in another bazaar, that despatches of bone-dust had, it was asserted, been received.[4]

Other, more far-fetched rumours began to circulate in the coming weeks. In Oudh, Henry Lawrence struck up a conversation with Deybee Singh, a Hindu subedar of the Oudh Lola artillery battery, who ran through a litany of rumours. One of the most absurd was a plan by the British Government to import the widows of European soldiers killed in the recent Crimean War; these women were to be encouraged or even coerced to marry rich Hindu princes, aristocrats, landowners and merchants. The children of these marriages would then be brought up in the Christian faith. In this way, the vast bulk of India's land and wealth would be quietly transferred into Christian hands within a generation or two.

The authorities did little to counter these new rumours. It had been thought that the disbandment of the 19th NI would be sufficient to prevent further indiscipline elsewhere. Controversy surrounding the greased cartridges and the flour was largely ignored. In the Punjab, however, John Lawrence saw the disaffection of the sepoys. He correctly guessed that the sepoys felt they had no choice but to mutiny in the face of an unbending government. 'I would observe that the Native Army as a body fully believed that the introduction of the cartridge was a mere matter of time. They had heard that such would be the case; that sepoys had been punished even by death for refusing to accept and use these cartridges, and therefore concluded that the only chance of escape was to band together and refuse to take them.'[5] Although no force or coercion had been employed so far, it was only a matter of time.

So entrenched were theories about a European conspiracy to destroy the sepoys' caste and convert the country that it was quite impossible to argue otherwise. John Lawrence referred to a conversation he had with a sepoy of the 3rd Punjab Infantry on furlough when the eruption at Meerut occurred:

> After much enquiry and lengthened cross-examination, during which he only by degrees described what he had seen and knew, he affirmed that there was a general belief among all the *poorbeah* soldiers that it was the settled determination of the English to destroy their caste and their religion. So strong was this, he observed, that 'often when I talked with the relations and friends of sepoys and endeavoured to combat their views, I ended with almost believing that they were right. Then again when I talk to you and hear what you say, I see how foolish were such ideas.' He told us that the English officers little knew how strong the impression had become; that upwards of five years ago this impression had existed and nearly brought on an emeute; that it was supposed that all the serais, burdasht khanas and other conveniences which Government have constructed on the main roads for the comfort of travelers had been devised with the object of destroying their caste; and that before long food would be prepared in them which the people would be forced to buy and eat.[6]

*****

Meanwhile, at Barrackpore, news of the imminent disarmament of the 19th NI had alarmed the men of the 34th NI. They suspected their regiment would be next. Perhaps because of this, twenty-nine-year-old Private Mangal Pandey decided to make a stand.

On 29 March, two days prior to the disarmament of the 19th NI, Pandey arrived at the Barrackpore cantonment with a loaded musket and declared that he would refuse to take orders from his superiors. He said he would shoot the first British officer he saw, and asked his comrades to defend their religion. Sergeant-Major James Hewson soon arrived to investigate the matter. Pandey shot and injured Hewson, who managed to raise the alarm. Lieut. Baugh, the regiment's adjutant, mounted his horse to go and inform his commanding officer but on his way he passed Pandey in front of the regimental quarter-guard. Pandey, seeing the officer riding up, opened fire when Baugh was around a hundred yards away. He missed Baugh but struck the horse, which tumbled and brought down Baugh as well. Baugh responded with his pistol, although he missed his target. This allowed Pandey to saunter up, draw his talwar and send Baugh to the ground again with a cut on the head before delivering further blows to Baugh's head and hand while he was down. The injured Hewson tried to help the lieutenant. The jemadar present, Ishwari Prasad, watched the scene but refused to help the officers. It took another sepoy to pin Pandey to the ground and finally end the confrontation.

News of the violence had spread quickly, and most of the regiment had come out to watch the proceedings. Most showed little sympathy for their officers, instead being heard to shout, 'Kill the *feringhees* (Europeans)!' Mangal Pandey was not restrained, and continued to walk around with his musket. When a colonel arrived on the scene he ordered the regiment to seize Pandey, but nobody moved to obey him. In the end, it took Major-General John Hearsey's appearance to change the men's attitude. He declared he would shoot anyone not obeying his orders and stood there with revolver in hand: 'Listen to me; the first man that refuses to march when I give the word is a dead man. Quick march!' The sepoys followed this order, albeit begrudgingly.

Realising all was lost, Pandey attempted to kill himself but survived and was hospitalised. General Hearsey investigated the fracas and ordered Pandey's arrest. When he had recovered, he was brought to trial. Court-martialled on 6 April, Mangal Pandey was hanged two days later. On the 21st, Ishwari Prasad, the jemadar who had refused orders to overpower Pandey, was also hanged. Hearsey decided that seven companies of the 34th NI present at Barrackpore should be disbanded on 6 May. This, it was hoped, would be the end of the matter. The sepoy Sitaram recorded the nonchalance with which the danger of mutiny continued to be perceived by British officers at this tense time:

> It was the time of year for furlough – that is the month of April – and it was my turn to go on leave. Before I went, I told my Commanding Officer what I had heard, and I warned him that great madness had possessed the minds of all men. I could not say what shape the discontent would take, but I never thought the entire army would mutiny, only those men who might have suffered as a result of annexation of Oudh – and at present only a few of the really bad characters were disaffected. The Colonel sahib was of the opinion that the excitement, which even he could not fail to see, would pass off, as it had often done before, and he recommended me to go to my home.[7]

*****

From Bengal, the contagion of mutiny travelled upcountry. Lucknow and Ambala were particularly affected. Henry Lawrence had arrived in Lucknow at the close of March to take up his post as Chief Commissioner. He was the brother of John Lawrence, who was Chief Commissioner of Punjab. Henry's conciliating ways were thought to be ideal in soothing ruffled feathers due to the recent annexation of Oudh, where many locals felt they had lost out in status or in financial terms after the takeover of the state by the East India Company. HM32nd was stationed in Lucknow under

Colonel Inglis; it was the only European regiment in the whole province. Also based in the city were the 13th and 48th NI, the 7th Light Cavalry and one light field battery. Around 7 miles from Lucknow, at Moosa Bagh, was the 7th Oude Irregular Infantry. These men had fought for the King of Oudh, but annexation brought them into the Company's ranks.

The sepoys at Lucknow were well aware of the disbandment of the 19th NI and the feelings of their comrades at Meerut and Delhi and in the Punjab. The mood at Lucknow was uncertain, and this was not helped by news that Meerut's 3rd Light Cavalry had refused to use the new cartridge. The Lucknow sepoys waited anxiously to learn what punishment would be meted out to the men of the 3rd, but the expectation was that the judgment would be harsh. Attitudes quickly hardened, and some of the men at Lucknow also began refusing to bite the cartridges despite them being of the old variety.

It was known that some of the officers of the 48th NI were in league with relatives of the dispossessed King of Oudh, Wajid Ali Shah. Intelligence available to the European officers suggested that native officers were searching for a leader with sufficient gravitas to lead them and that they had already approached an Oudh aristocrat, said to be the brother of Wajid Ali Shah. Other sources had it that this brother warned the disgruntled officers of the punishment they would receive if they mutinied but offered to support them and pay them at least as much as the British. The sepoys apparently held nightly meetings, and it was obvious to their officers that some sort of intrigue was afoot; soldiers had begun showing much less deference towards their officers and Europeans.

On 28 April, some of the sepoys of the 48th NI were returning from target practice when they were confronted by disaffected soldiers of the 7th Oude Irregular Infantry, who taunted them for having surrendered to their officers' demands that they use the new cartridges. Lieut. Watson reported this to Brigadier Grey. A parade of the 7th Oudh Irregular Infantry was ordered at 4 p.m. that day. One Subedar, Ram Dyal Doobey, had volunteered to take the lead and bite the new cartridge. The men, watching him, shouted out that he could do what he liked but that they would not follow his example. 'You may bite it, we won't,' they shouted. Afraid of being ostracised by his men, the subedar took fright. 'I can't do so now, I am afraid,' he told Watson.[8]

According to Martin Richard Gubbins, the cartridges were blank. However, this didn't calm the sepoys at all. The parade was dismissed, and the men could be seen shouting in jubilation at their success. Watson immediately reported their actions to Brigadier Grey, who addressed the men himself on the parade ground that evening, warning them of the punishment awaiting them should they refuse to follow orders. Though they listened, the men seemed to show no great enthusiasm to comply. They replied that other regiments around the country had objected, so they must object as well.

On 3 May, a letter was given up by the officers of the 48th NI. Written by an officer of the 7th Oude Irregular Infantry, it asked the men of the 48th to take the lead in an uprising with the guarantee that the men of the 7th Oude would follow suit. Their resistance could either be active (mutiny) or passive (refusing orders). Whichever decision the men of the 48th NI thought wise would be accepted. The letter had been passed to a sepoy of the regiment, who had passed it to his officers. The letter was in turn handed over to Henry Lawrence. By this time the 7th were displaying open agitation; they even entered an officer's house and threatened to kill him. Captain Adolphus Orr, who commanded a regiment of military police, discovered a separate plot to alienate one of his men in order to seduce the man into mutiny.

The British officers of the 48th NI still had complete confidence in their regiment and protested that any action would only precipitate mutiny. Nevertheless, Henry Lawrence made his decision. He immediately ordered the 7th Oude Irregular Infantry to be disarmed prior to disbandment. Like others before him, he hoped this would discourage other regiments from refusing orders. After a short meeting with Brigadiers Gray and Handscomb, a force was organised. It was to be made up of HM32nd under Col Inglis, 7th Light Cavalry under Col Master, a wing of 48th under Lt Col Palmer, a wing of 71st under Capt. Strangways, a Light Field Battery and the 2nd Oudh Irregular Cavalry under Major Gall. This force immediately marched to the Moosa Bagh, where loaded guns were promptly wheeled to the front; the cavalry was positioned on the flanks with the infantry behind the guns. The men of the 7th Oude were told to surrender their weapons or else be fired upon by the guns. Gubbins takes up the tale:

> Gaps first appeared here and there in the line, and then the great mass of the regiment broke and fled. About 120 men stood still. A squadron of the 7th Light Cavalry galloped off to intercept the fugitives. Sir Henry rode up to the men that remained, and bade them lay down on the ground their muskets and accoutrements. The order was at once obeyed: the men laid down their pieces and took off their cross-belts, with subdued exclamations of '*Jye Company ki* [Victory to the company]', '*Jye Company Bahadoor ki* [Victory to the illustrious company]'. They were then told to go to their lines, where guards of the 4th O. I. Infantry and Gall's I. Cavalry, both of which had behaved well, were placed: and the affair was over. Before two in the morning, the troops had returned to their several lines.[9]

It turned out that around two-thirds of the regiment had fled – the primary cause being the portfire of a gun being lighted, giving the men the impression that were about to be fired upon. This was no organised retreat, however; the men simply threw their equipment to the ground to lighten themselves before fleeing. Almost all were caught by the cavalry and brought back to their lines to await punishment. Their colours, arms and treasure were removed to the city magazine. A court of enquiry was set up to ascertain the reason for the men's behaviour, but little was agreed upon. However, the ringleaders in the regiment were identified and put in irons.

Recognising that the problem with the new ammunition wasn't going away, Henry Lawrence organised a durbar for the various regiments on the lawn of the Residency House in the cantonments on 12 May. All native officers were invited, and each native regiment was to be represented by two non-commissioned officers and six sepoys. There he gave a strong and stern speech, railing against the rumours that the British Government was attempting to destroy the caste of the sepoys and convert them to Christianity by underhand means. He compared life under former rulers to what he argued was the enlightened and paternal rule of the Company, which brooked no interference in the matter of religion.

> Soldiers! Soldiers! some persons are abroad spreading reports that the Government desire to interfere with the religion of their soldiers; you all know this to be a transparent falsehood; you and your forefathers before you, well know and knew that for more than a hundred years the religion of your countrymen has never been interfered with.
>
> And those amongst you who have perused the records of the past, who have searched the annals of your country, and those who are familiar with the traditionary lore which has been carefully transmitted from generation to generation must well know that Alumgeer [Mughal Emperor Aurangzeb] in former times, and Hyder Ali [ruler of Mysore] in later days forcibly converted thousands and thousands of Hindoos, desecrated their fanes, demolished their temples, and carried ruthless devastation amongst their household gods. Come to our times: many here present well know that Runjeet Singh [Sikh ruler of the Punjab] never permitted his Mahomedan subjects to call the pious to prayer [5 times a day call from Mosques] – never allowed the Afghan to sound from the lofty minarets which adorn Lahore – and remain to this day a monument of their magnificent founders. The year before last a Hindoo could not have dared to build a temple in Lucknow. All this is changed. Now who is there who would dare to interfere with our Mahomedan or Hindoo subjects?[10]

The Company's rule had been and always would be meticulously fair and impartial, he declared. It would never interfere in the manner suggested. All were allowed to worship as they pleased. However, Lawrence did follow this assertion with reminders of the power of the British and threats of condign punishment if the sepoys continued to speculate on some form of mutiny:

> ... you know also that there is no government in the whole world to be compared with that of the British Government in power, in wealth, in resources, in money, in dominions; there is no sea on which its

> numerous navy does not float, no clime in which its soldiers do not abound ...
>
> ... If necessary, in a few brief months one hundred thousand European soldiers might be collected in any spot in India. A Government such as ours does not require to deal in deceit; what it does it enacts openly before God and man; and is at all times prepared to encounter, and capable of destroying foreign invasion or domestic factions ...
>
> ... The 19th has been disbanded – seven companies of the 34th have been disbanded. The guilt of many has been that they simply looked on at the vile wickedness of a few. Take warning![11]

After the address, *khillats*, ceremonial sabres and expensive shawls and cloaks were distributed to various officers and others who had shown loyalty. In addition, several sepoys received gifts of 300 rupees to sweeten their mouths after Lawrence's threats. Martin Richard Gubbins, who was present at the durbar, mingled with the sepoy officers and men after Lawrence's address:

> The bearing of these men was then decidedly favourable. Most of them eagerly declared their own attachment, and the part which they either had taken, or were willing to have taken, in the suppression of the recent mutiny. A number of sepoys were standing round the space appropriated to the durbar. We subsequently learnt that the remarks which they were overheard to make were of a different character; and that they attributed the whole proceeding to our fears.[12]

Although the sepoys had listened calmly to Lawrence's address, it had come too late. Even as he handed out rewards, the cantonment of Meerut, 250 miles to the north-west, lay in ashes. Further afield, fires swept through ransacked European residences in Delhi. Full-blooded mutiny, much more formidable than hesitant shows of defiance in Bengal and Oudh, had broken out at Meerut. On 13 May, Lawrence received a telegraph from the Lieutenant-Governor of Agra announcing that mutiny had broken out at Meerut and that the men had subsequently upped sticks to Delhi. The next day, a telegraph announced that the mutineers had seized Delhi.

*****

Ambala was the other station in the country where discontent was most apparent. This was an important station in more ways than one, having been chosen as one of the locations for a musketry school instructing sepoys in the use of the new Enfield rifle. One of the unforeseen effects of these musketry schools was that they allowed men of many regiments across the country to meet face to face. Dialogue and debate, potential plans and conspiracies could therefore take shape without the need for slow correspondence in a time when a letter written to Peshawar would take around a month to get there. This immediacy also allowed plans to be made at much shorter notice, of course. The musketry schools therefore radically changed the way the sepoys planned and organised their defiance. On arriving at the musketry schools, sepoys from all over could easily converse in private on the nature of the ammunition they were expected to use in future and what action they could take in response.

Those present included men and officers of the 36th NI, although the regiment itself was then serving as part of Commander-in-Chief General Anson's escort to the station as part of his tour of inspection throughout the north-west provinces. Two of the men in the escort belonging to the 36th Regiment, a havildar called Kassee Ram Tewaree and a naik called Jeololl Doobee, had recently been shunned by their comrades. They had become Christians, the other sepoys declared, by having followed orders and touching the new cartridges. The blow was all the harder for these two men as they were Brahmins. The two men registered their feelings with their officer Capt. E. M. Martineau. 'No reward that Government can offer us is any equivalent to being regarded as outcasts by our comrades,' they complained. Martineau, sensing this was not an isolated incident, wrote to Capt. S. Becher, the Assistant Adjutant-General.

'The affair is lamentable,' he wrote, 'as it discloses the actual feelings of the whole of the native army; and I hasten to put you in possession of the information I have subsequently received on the subject, as it is no longer possible to close our eyes to the present state of our Hindostanee regiments. The rumour has been industriously propagated (how it first originated no native knows) that the rifle-cartridges were purposely smeared with the mixture of cows' and pigs' fat with the express object of destroying caste. In fact the weapon itself is nothing more nor less than a Government missionary to convert the whole army to Christianity.'[13] Martineau warned that each regiment had formed *punchayets* or committees and that they were communicating from Peshawar to Calcutta. To present a common front they had agreed and determined on shunning and treating as outcaste any soldier who broke ranks and agreed to follow orders on using the cartridges.

The result was that General Anson, on reaching Ambala during his tour, personally addressed the sepoys to try and put their minds at rest regarding the cartridges. He declared 'on the honour of a soldier like themselves that it has never been, and never would be, the policy of the Government of this great country to coerce either those serving in the army, or the natives of India, in their religious feelings, or to interfere with the customs of their castes'.

The introduction of newer and better weapons had made the new cartridge entirely necessary, Anson explained, and the rumours of ulterior motives were quite absurd. He assured the sepoys that he would ask the officers to tend to their suspicions. He was sure 'that they will do everything in their power to prevent shame which must fall upon all who are faithless to the colours under which they have sworn allegiance to the Government, and they will prove themselves deserving of the high character which they have always hitherto maintained in this army'. After the address, Anson also asked Capt. Martineau to write a report on the feelings of the sepoys and whether they still harboured concerns. Martineau canvassed three officers who had been sent by the other officers to represent them and the regiment. On 23 March, he delivered his report.

> They respectfully beg to urge that they do not attribute any of the evil intentions to the Government of this country as described in his Excellency's address They know that the rumour is false but they equally know that for one man in Hindostan who disbelieves it, ten thousand believe it, and that it is universally credited not only in their regiment but in their villages and their homes. They are all ready to a man to fire when ordered, but they would wish to represent, for the paternal consideration of his Excellency, the social consequence of military obedience to themselves. They become outcasts for ever, unacknowledged, not only in their corps but also in their families and their homes. Their devotion to the service, and submission to the military authority, will inflict on them the direst and most terrible punishment they can undergo in this world. Their being selected as men of intelligence and fidelity thus becomes to them the most fatal curse. They will obey the orders of their military superiors, and socially perish through their instinct of obedience.[14]

Martineau also suggested a court of inquiry to investigate reports that the two men were still being ostracised and that certain sepoys wouldn't eat with them.

Over the next few weeks, incidents of arson were noted both in the station and nearby, indicating growing anger among the sepoys. On 26 March, an attempt was made to burn the property of Subedar Harbans Singh of the 36th NI. The subedar had shown willingness to use the new ammunition, much to the chagrin of the other sepoys. This was followed by another fire on 13 April. Two days later, another fire was seen in some outhouses in the compound of the 60th NI, the lines of the regiment being adjacent to the musketry depot. On the 16th, a large thatched building formerly used as a native hospital was set ablaze. A few hours later, in the early morning of the 17th, another fire destroyed a building full of beer casks and stores in the European Infantry Lines. The damage wrought that night was costed at around 40,000 rupees. Other fires raged in the cantonments over the coming days.

On the 17th, guards were arranged around the cantonments to watch the more important buildings. No other fires were seen, excepting some small ones set on lesser buildings. The Europeans' *chuppar* (shed) was burnt, and attempts were made to burn the houses of a jemadar and some havildars of the 5th NI. The jemadar had found powder and brimstone under his bed when the fire broke out, indicating the depth of feeling against those who contemplated following orders and using the new rifle. Up to this time, all the fires had been connected with the musketry depot in some way. However, more indiscriminate arson began to take place. On 21 April there were arson attacks on several huts containing property belonging to the 60th NI, who were on furlough leave.

It was thought the outbreak would subside as anger faded. Certainly this was the view of G. C. Barnes, the Commissioner of the Cis-Sutlej States, who wrote to Robert Montgomery, Judicial Commissioner of the Punjab, on 7 May: 'It is probable that these prejudices will subside as the minds of the sepoys become less excited and they perceive the groundlessness of their fears. At present the more rational among them are afraid of their fellow-soldiers and of the social penalties which the majority can always inflict.'[15] He was correct to some extent, for there fewer cases of arson as the days went by. However, this could also be attributed to British authorities growing more alert, and the increase in nightly patrols. Barnes also attributed the decrease in arson to the waxing moon, which removed the cloak of night. On 22 April, Robert Montgomery asked John Lawrence to sanction the reward of 1,000 rupees for any information on the arsonists. It was no use; no sepoy betrayed his colleagues. Brigadier R. D. Halifax, commanding the station, took the appropriate precautions. Mounted and foot patrols were organised all along the cantonment.

More serious news arrived at the end of April. A Sikh sepoy, Sham Singh of the 5th NI, reported to his officers that a general mutiny was being planned at Ambala. The plan was to capture the magazine, with the 4th Light Cavalry seizing the guns. Meanwhile, the horses of HM 9th Lancers, the only European force at Ambala, were to be let loose, destroying the effectiveness of the unit. When this was done, the European officers were to be massacred. A *pundit* (Hindu priest) was said by the *bazar kotwal* (head bailiff) to have predicted, using his astrological knowledge, that 'blood would be shed' within the week. Whether this would be at Ambala, Delhi or Meerut he did not say. The brigadier failed to take this warning seriously, even though more fires were set. In fact, sepoys were promised that they would not be disarmed. Meanwhile, any locals suspected of assisting in the arson or transporting messages was expelled from the cantonment.

On the very day that mutiny broke out at Meerut, it was noticed that the 60th and 5th NI were, in the Deputy Commissioner's words, 'in an excited state'. Rumour had it that all the regiments had decided to turn out with their weapons despite having no orders. General Barnard, who travelled to their lines, saw that many of the sepoys had loaded their muskets; some were even pointing them at European officers. Barnard gambled that he did not need to bring out the European artillery, and gradually order was restored. Around 4 miles away, a contingent of the 5th NI guarding the civil treasury had also been up in arms; however, all was calm by evening.

Capt. Martineau of the 10th NI later found the embittered sepoys quite frank and open in their opinions that mutiny was coming, such was their confidence. '[T]hey told me in plain language that there would be an outbreak; and there was every evidence of it in nightly fires at Ambala. The first fire commenced on the very day we fired the first Enfield cartridge, and continued nearly nightly, up to 10 May. We commenced using the Enfield cartridges on the 17th of April; the men themselves remarked, that although Government offered large rewards to anyone who would give information of the incendiaries, yet no one was found to do so; and that this was a certain sign of general dissatisfaction and some impending outbreak.'

The Deputy Commissioner of Ambala suggested changing the guard on the treasury, which was sure to be the first building pillaged in the event of a mutiny. However, John Lawrence agreed with the Brigadier and General Barnard that matters were tense and that any change might be seen as provocative action. '[U]nless the Regular Guard is considered untrustworthy, I suggest that they be not relieved. To do so is to distrust them, and perhaps bring on a collision which might be avoided. If the Regulars be relieved, European officers should be present. It will be a delicate matter, and will demand much careful and prudent management,' he telegraphed on 11 May.

# PART 3

# The Mutiny

# 9

# Mutiny at Meerut

There has been no acknowledgment of error, no expression of regret, no pleading for mercy.

Major-General William Hewitt, Meerut

Despite outward calm in Delhi and its nearby cantonment during the early months of 1857, something was not right. British officers in the cantonment had noticed a change in the atmosphere. News of the trouble at Meerut was well known in Delhi. Daily news of fires at Ambala, only 125 miles due north, also seemed to have stoked the confidence of the sepoys stationed at Delhi. According to Jat Mall, a considerable disquiet and a strong resolve had developed among the sepoys well before the eventual outbreak at Meerut. He mentions them talking about Ambala openly in front of locals (although not in front of their officers).[1] They vowed that they would not use the new ammunition when called upon.

After the mutiny, Captain Tytler of the 38th NI would declare that he had seen no change of attitude among his men in the Delhi cantonment. However, a servant of long standing had made a remark that struck him as odd. Tytler had told the man, who was departing on leave, to come back quickly: 'He on several occasions, with a sorrowful expression said, "Yes, Sir, provided your hearth is still in existence," that is, provided you and your family are in a condition to give me service. He made use of these expressions about a week or ten days before the [Meerut] outbreak. He left me about this time, and I have not seen or heard from him since.'[2] Similarly, Major Patterson of the 54th NI noticed nothing suspicious about his men but was informed by Lieutenant Vibart that the subedar major of the regiment, Sheikh Imam Baksh, had informed his officers that there had been men going about the lines encouraging rebellion. This had been around two months before the Meerut uprising. No action had been taken, and little concern given to apprehending these agitators.

At the Delhi magazine inside the city, Lt Forrest had noticed a difference in the bearing of the men under him. 'I noticed nothing in the dress of the men; but their behaviour for several days previous to the outbreak was insolent and overbearing, especially that of those who were Mahomedans. Mr Buckley and I had both remarked this, and spoken to each other about it. On the morning of 11 May when I went to the magazine, I remarked that the Sirdars and Durwans were well dressed, better than I had ever seen them before; also the magazine men did not appear in their usual working dress, but were much cleaner. This I remarked at the time to Lieutenant Willoughby, who coincided with me, and said the circumstance had struck him also.'[3]

In the houses of the Civil Lines and in the city itself there were further indications, though some would struggle to recognise them. Miss Florence Wagentreiber would write of an old nawab, a friend of her father, who warned that there would be trouble at Meerut. He had visited them on the night of 10 May and stated frankly that the 3rd Light Cavalry at Meerut would revolt, declaring that 'such stringent measures [court-martial and imprisonment with hard labour] were tyrannical and foolish at such a time, and the Government would rue their policy'.[4] Mr Wagentreiber retorted that the troops should have faced execution rather than imprisonment, which he considered unduly mild given such gross insubordination.

Sir Theophilus Metcalfe later recalled that the disaffection rife in the Delhi regiments over the new cartridges was no secret. Indeed, two weeks before the outbreak at Meerut the magistrate had received an anonymous petition asking that the Kashmir Gate be taken from British hands. Metcalfe smelled a rat: 'This gate being our chief stronghold in the city, and main connexion with the cantonments of Delhi, it would naturally be the first point seized in any attempt at insurrection in the city, and it was also the only gate at which there was any military guard, the importance of it, therefore, in a strategical point of view must have been obvious to all.'[5] Other sources indicate that authorities had dismissed widespread rumours of sepoys planning to capture the Kashmir Gate.

News of an imminent mutiny at Meerut had even reached as far as Hyderabad in the south of the country. Captain Skinner, Florence Wagentreiber's uncle, told her of strange rumours circulating there. His orderly had warned him to leave the country if he valued his life. When he asked why, the orderly referred to a 'massacre of the feringees'. Skinner had scoffed at this, but said that if such an act ever did occur it would be swiftly avenged.[6]

In the palace, too, open speculation abounded. Mostly people discussed how things might pan out once the Meerut sepoys took the vital step. The guards at the palace entrance could be heard suggesting that the Meerut sepoys would make their way to Delhi – that this had already been planned – and that they would receive a warm welcome from their comrades at the Delhi cantonment. A compact with the Delhi troops had already been arranged by the very officers who had been summoned to carry out the courts-martial in Meerut.

European visitors to the palace also commented on the behaviour of Jawan Bakht, the young and tactless prince. The young man exuded confidence, and was increasingly candid about his views on the British. Bazaar Sergeant Fleming related the experiences of his son, who had frequently taken the prince's horses out for exercise. In recent weeks, the prince's cordial manners had entirely vanished.

> In the latter end of the month of April 1857, he came from Mr Fraser's office, where he used to write, and told me that he had that day gone in the morning to the prime minister's house as usual, and had there seen the prisoner's son, Jawan Bakht, who resided in that quarter, and that this Jawan Bakht had then told him that he was not to come again; that he did not like to see the face of an English infidel, and that before many days he would have them all killed and under his feet. Jawan Bakht then spit at him. My son told Mr Fraser of it at the time, but Mr Fraser replied that he was a fool, and was not to listen to such nonsense. After this as far as I recollect, about the 2d of May, the prime minister sent for my son, to pay him up, and on this occasion again, the prisoner's son, Jawan Bakht, abused him still more, saying he would have his head off in a few days. This son of mine was killed in the place here during the rebellion.[7]

Sergeant Fleming's wife happened to be a regular visitor to Zeenat Mahal. She recorded a similar incident during a visit to the palace:

> I was sitting down with his sister-in-law, and Jawan Bakht was standing by with his wife. My own daughter, Mrs Scully, was also present. I was talking with Jawan Bakht's sister-in-law, when Mrs Scully said to me, 'Mother, do you hear what this young rascal is saying? He is telling me that in a short time he will have all the infidel English under his feet, and after that he will kill the Hindus.' Hearing this, I turned round to Jawan Bakht, and asked him, 'What is that you are saying?' He replied that he was only joking. I said 'If what you threaten were to be the case, your head would be taken off first.' He told me that the Persians were coming to Dehli, and that when they did so we, that is, myself and daughter, should go to him, and he would save us. After this he left us. I think this must have occurred about the middle of April, 1857.[8]

Jawan Bakht seemed to enjoy leaking his intentions in this way, although when challenged he invariably claimed to be joking. The older princes seem to have been more circumspect in their knowledge and in their dealings with Europeans; certainly they showed no outward hostility towards foreigners at this time. Not all were convinced, however. Major Abbott, commanding the 74th NI at Delhi, was one of those who voiced his doubts about the royal family's innocence. Writing on 13 May, immediately after fleeing the city, he argued that the King knew far more than he would later pretend.

> From all I could glean, there is not the slightest doubt that this insurrection has been originated and matured in the palace of the king of Delhi and that with his full knowledge and sanction, in the mad attempt to establish himself in the sovereignty of this country. It is well known that he has called on the neighbouring States to co-operate with him in thus trying to subvert the existing government.[9]

Ahsan Ulla Khan, on the other hand, remarked that this was never the case. According to him, the ageing king never courted such intrigue. 'I do not believe that any one was sent by the King to Meerut to procure information of the proceedings at Meerut, in regard to the refusal of the sepoys to receive the cartridges at the time when they were going on at that place. I did not hear that Zinat Mahal had sent any one to Meerut for the above purpose.'

*****

Meerut, the largest British cantonment in North India, was only around 40 miles north-east of Delhi. Major-General William Hewitt was the division commander. The city was also home to a school of artillery, the Dum Dum, which was commanded by Brigadier Archdale Wilson, who was also in command of the station. Unlike the plump and ageing Hewitt, Wilson was a thin, athletic man with a good reputation. Like Hewitt, however, he had seen little action. Certainly he hadn't experienced anything that would prepare him for the events that were about to unfold.

By the beginning of May 1857, the north side of the Meerut cantonment, the European half, housed the 6th Dragoon Guards (Carabineers) under Col H. Richmond Jones, the 1st Battalion of HM 60th Rifles (King's Royal Rifles) under Col John Jones, a troop of horse artillery under Major Tombs, and a company of foot artillery and light field battery commanded by Major Scott. To the north of the European barracks was a flat expanse of roughly 2 square miles which was used as the European parade ground. The southern part of the cantonment, meanwhile, was home to the sepoy regiments. This was larger than the European section, with sufficient space in the sepoy barracks for as many as seven regiments although presently it was occupied by only three. These were the 11th NI under Col J. Finnis, the 20th NI under Major Taylor, and the 3rd Bengal Light Cavalry under by Col G. C. Carmichael-Smyth. There was a contingent of Indian *golandaz* (artillery) stationed in the barracks as well.

The two halves of the cantonment were divided by the Mall Road, a fine, wide, tree-lined thoroughfare running east to west and forming a makeshift border between the European and sepoy sections. Dotted along adjacent and on both sides of the Mall road were the officers' bungalows with the rows upon rows of men's barracks situated immediately behind them to the north and south. Such was the size of the cantonment that the distance between the European lines and the sepoy lines was around a mile or so, and what was happening in one area wasn't immediately obvious in the other half.[10] In fact, between the opposite ends of the parallelogram-shaped cantonment – from the south-west to the north-east – the distance was said to have been as much as 7 miles.

The cantonment had no defensive capabilities to speak of. It had never been expected to double up as a defensive bastion; British strength in North India at the time of its construction was overpowering. Were any threat to materialise, the British force stationed at Meerut would surely advance and destroy it in open combat. A British garrison being bottled up in the cantonment by an enemy force was never considered a possibility, and therefore no defensive walls were constructed. Neither was a mutiny by its own sepoy regiments considered a remote possibility. The cantonment happened to hold the highest ratio of European to sepoy troops in India at the time of the mutiny, with 1,778 European soldiers and 2,234 sepoys. Naturally, one would assume that a sepoy mutiny wouldn't take place here; anywhere but where European forces were strongest. Paradoxically, this very strength was later blamed by many as the cause for the outbreak – only in a station like Meerut would the European officers have the confidence and the means to coerce or punish large numbers of sepoys for refusing to follow orders. In other stations, it was argued, officers without the support of European troops would have considered their actions more carefully for fear of precipitating a violent reaction among their men.

British officers at the station hadn't overlooked the simmering discontent about the new cartridges; the Meerut regiments were actually showing perhaps the most overt level of disaffection in the country. Mangal Pandey's stand at Barrackpore was big news in the station, as were the various disturbances elsewhere around the country. However, nothing serious had happened in Meerut during the early months of the year. In April, a *fakir* or holy man arrived and set up camp near the Suraj Khund lake. Around two months earlier, he had been seen at Ambala. Travelling on an elephant and leading a large retinue, the *fakir* attracted crowds of listeners from the sepoy and civilian populations. When the authorities found out that he was preaching against the use of the new cartridge, they demanded he move on. He simply upped sticks and moved elsewhere. Some accounts have him rather confidently moving into the cantonment itself. living within the lines of the 20th NI. Soon he would be seen accompanying the sepoys on a march to Delhi.

Colonel G. C. Smyth, in charge of the 3rd Light Cavalry at Meerut, was one of those who sensed the trouble more quickly than other officers. 'Nobody knew better than Colonel Smyth,' wrote the historian Sir John Kaye, 'that the Bengal Army was hovering on the brink of mutiny. He had, in the earlier part of the year, visited the great fair at Hardwar, where the disaffection of the 19th Regiment had been freely discussed. He had afterwards gone to Masuri [Mussourie], where he learnt from day to day what was passing at Ambalah, and he was so impressed by what he heard respecting the general state of the Sipahi [sepoy] regiments and their readiness for revolt, that he had written to the Commander-in-Chief to inform him of the dangerous state of the Army.'

On his return to Meerut, Smyth heard of the new order instructing officers that sepoys need not bite the cartridges during loading; they could simply tear the cartridge paper with their hands. Like many officers, he thought this concession might well satisfy the men. On 23 April, Smyth ordered a parade to be held the next day in which the sowars of the 3rd Light Cavalry would be instructed in the drill for using the new cartridges. He would show the troops the modified procedure – how to load the Enfield rifle without having to bite the cartridge. He called the havildar major and his orderly. 'I desired the havildar major and his orderly to come to me during the day, with a carbine and some blank ammunition,' wrote Smyth, 'that they might see how it was to be done; they came accordingly, and the havildar major's orderly fired off the carbine twice, but that night his house was burnt down, and also a horse hospital that was close to the Magazine.'[11] That night, it became clear that the 3rd Light Cavalry troops were not moved by the concession regarding the cartridge. The sowars met and agreed that on no account would they use the new cartridges. The Muslims swore on the holy Quran and the Hindus swore in the name of the Holy Ganges – their resolve would not soften. Even in the face of their officers' threats, they would resist.

Over that evening, Smyth was repeatedly warned that the parade would trigger an impasse. Officers from all six troops informed Smyth of the prevailing mood. Captain Craigie, commanding the 4th Troop, wrote that his men had 'requested the native Officer of the Troop, to solicit the Commanding Officer, through me, to defer the firing i.e. the skirmishing parade, until such time as the agitation, obtaining throughout the country in the matter of cartridges, should cease. As well as I can remember, the report was strictly to this effect. Feeling the importance of any request of the kind, I at once wrote to the Adjutant of the Regiment and urged in the strongest terms, my own solicitation with that of the Troop.'[12] At around 10 p.m.,

Capt. Craigie duly sent a strong written warning to the adjutant, asking him to inform the colonel that the men were attempting to ward off an impasse:

> Go at once to Smyth and tell him that the men of my troop have requested in a body that the skirmishing tomorrow morning may be countermanded, as there is a commotion throughout the native troops about cartridges, and that the regiment will become *badnam* (gain disrespect) if they fire any cartridges. I understand that in all six troops a report of the same kind is being made. This is a most serious matter, and we may have the whole regiment in mutiny in half an hour if this be not attended to. Pray don't lose a moment, but go to Smyth at once.

Smyth dismissed Craigie's worries; he believed the new instructions on tearing the cartridge would be enough. The parade was not cancelled, and Craigie instead received a severe reprimand for showing weakness by suggesting postponement. That night, the sepoys wrote to Smyth himself in a very respectful petition asking for the parade to be deferred until things had settled down elsewhere in the country. They complained that following the order to muster would see them scorned and ostracised by their families and by their fellow soldiers all over the country.

Smyth seemed to believe that everybody would calm down in the cold light of day. The revised drill would surely smooth things over. Moreover, their courage would fail on the parade ground; no trooper would be prepared to take that first fatal step. It has been suggested that Smyth wanted to soothe the feelings of the sepoys rather than present an ultimatum, that he had no motive in forcing the soldiers to choose between temporal order and spiritual edict. According to Sir John Kaye, however, Smyth may well have been the wrong man to defuse this most sensitive of situations. Kaye felt there were certain question marks over the man's character:

> He had graduated in the regiment, and had seen some service with it, but he had never earned the entire confidence of officers or men. He was not wanting in intelligence or in zeal, but he lacked temper and discretion, and the unquestionable honesty of his nature was of that querulous, irritable cast which makes a man often uncharitable and always unpopular. He had a quick eye for blots of every kind; and, being much addicted to newspaper writing, seldom failed to make them known to the public.

The decision to have the parade and therefore manufacture an impasse was also questioned by Hewitt, albeit after the eruption. Summoning Smyth, Hewitt is said to have cried, 'Oh! why did you have a parade? My division has kept quiet, and if you had only waited another month or so, all would have blown over.'[13]

*****

The next day, 24 April, the parade was held. On the parade ground, Smyth addressed his men: '[I] explained to them why I had ordered the parade, then made the havildar major show them how they were to load without biting the cartridge, which he did, and fired one off. I then ordered the cartridges to be distributed to the men, but with the exception of five non-commissioned officers they all refused to take them, saying they would get "a bad name" if they used them, but if all the men would use them they would do so. I then dismissed the parade, reported the circumstance in writing to the officer commanding the station, and in person to the General commanding the division.'[14]

Smyth had remonstrated with them, warning them of the repercussions of refusing the order. They had not been ordered to bite the cartridge, he said, so they had no grounds for objecting. The cartridges used were not the new ones, anyway; they were the old cartridges they had always used without complaint. 'You see the havildar-major has used one,' he had pointed out to them.[15] The men were unmoved. Of the ninety troopers of the 3rd Light Cavalry asked to use the cartridges, eighty-five had refused. These men – forty-nine Muslims and thirty-six Hindus – were too many to be arrested, so Smyth had simply dismissed them. Later they were collected and placed under a European guard comprising twenty-five men of the 6th Dragoon Guard and two companies of the 60th Rifles.

A court of enquiry was duly set up on the following day. Six sepoy officers were chosen to conduct proceedings – four from the infantry and two from the cavalry. Courts-martial would follow for the eighty-five men, all held between 6 and 8 May, with a tribunal made up of nine Hindu officers and six Muslim officers. Ten were from Meerut, but interestingly the remaining five had been summoned from Delhi, which meant that troops in Delhi would receive a blow-by-blow account of events at Meerut when the officers returned. The charge was as follows.

> For having at Mirath, on the 24th of April, 1857, severally and individually disobeyed the lawful command of their superior officer, Brevet-Colonel G.M.C. Smyth, commanding the 3rd Regiment of Light Cavalry, by not having taken the cartridges tendered to each of them individually for use that day on parade, when ordered by Colonel Smyth to take the said cartridges.[16]

The tribunal pondered the matter for three days, but the issue was clear cut. The prisoners for their part saw little point in cooperating with the investigation; they knew they would be found guilty. One havildar, Mattadin Singh, spoke for his comrades. He said that the colonel had treated the firing of the cartridges differently, and this had made them suspicious. Smyth was asked why he told the men that they would have to fire, rather than merely ordering them to do so. 'The parade was in orders the day before, and entered in the order-book as usual, and each man was ordered to receive three cartridges,' he explained. 'I wished to show them the new way of loading without putting the cartridges to the mouth, and attended the parade for that purpose. When I came on parade, the Adjutant informed me that the men had not taken their cartridges, and it was on that account I ordered the Havildar-Major to take a cartridge and load and fire before them; and it was then, also, that I said, that when the whole Army heard of this way of loading they would be much pleased, and exclaim, "Wah! wah!"'[17]

Whatever the manner of Smyth's instruction, it mattered not. The witnesses included men involved in the production of the cartridges and grease, and all declared nothing objectionable was used in their manufacture. It made no difference to the troops. A Muslim in the 3rd Cavalry voiced the fears of all: 'I have doubts about the cartridges. They may look exactly like the old ones, but how do I know that pig's fat has not been smeared over them?'

The tribunal would find the prisoners guilty by fifteen to one. The maximum sentence was ten years' hard labour, although recommendations were given for 'favourable consideration on account of the good character which the prisoners had hitherto borne, as testified to by their Commanding Officer, and on account of their having been misled by vague reports regarding the cartridges'. All were sentenced to ten years' hard labour. This was thought sufficiently punitive.

Despite his reservations over Smyth's approach, Hewitt endorsed the sentences with just one caveat. 'There has been no acknowledgment of error – no expression of regret – no pleading for mercy,' he pronounced. 'To the majority of the prisoners therefore, no portion of the sentence will be remitted. I observe, however, that some of them are very young, and I am willing to make allowance for their having been misled by their more experienced comrades, and under these circumstances I remit one-half of the sentence passed upon the following men, who have not been more than five years in the service.' There were eleven such men among the eighty-five; they were given shorter sentences of five years due to their comparative youth.

On 9 May, a Saturday, the entire garrison was called for a parade in the European sector of the cantonments. The objective was to make an example of the eighty-five prisoners and to give pause to any others considering a similar show of disobedience. The sepoy regiments were marched in without their ammunition and the sowars were dismounted. The European troops – HM60th, the Carabineers, Major Tombs' troop of horse artillery and a field battery – by contrast came fully armed, with the cavalry troops mounted and the artillery equipped with their guns.

The scene was dramatic by design. The European troops formed into a square with one open side. The 11th and 20th NI, plus the remainder of the 3rd Light Cavalry, were made to stand at the open end, in front of the armed Europeans. They were positioned so that if any showed support for their court-martialled comrades they could be shot by the European troops with ease should the order be given. The court-martialled men were then brought in, and made to stand in the centre of the square. The punishments to be meted out to the sowars were declared, and they were stripped of their uniforms and accoutrements. Horse artillery blacksmiths were brought forward to shackle the men. For more than an hour, the men were brought forward one by one under the hot May sun. All the while, the condemned men appealed to their disarmed comrades. Colonel Mackenzie of the 3rd Light Cavalry witnessed the scene:

> In sullen silence the two native infantry corps, the 11th and 20th, and my own regiment [3rd Cavalry], which was dismounted on that occasion, witnessed the degrading punishment. It would have been madness for them then to have attempted a rescue; for they would have been swept off the face of the earth by the guns of the artillery and the rifles of Her Majesty's 60th Foot, not to speak of the swords of the 6th Dragoon Guards, the Carabineers, all of whom were provided with service ammunition, and were so placed as to have the native regiments at their mercy. For more than an hour the troops stood motionless, their nerves at the highest tension, while the felon shackles were being methodically and of necessity slowly hammered on the ankles of the wretched criminals, each in turn loudly calling on his comrades for help, and abusing, in fierce language, now their Colonel, now the officers who composed the court-martial, now the Government.

Two hours passed before the prisoners were handed over to the civil authorities for incarceration in the jail east of town. The plan would have been to send them to one of the Government's central prisons, probably Bareilly or Agra. No European guard was placed over the jail; other sepoy troops guarded the prisoners instead.

Governor-General Lord Canning strongly supported the sentences. With the benefit of hindsight, however, he criticised the seeming pageantry of the proceedings in a private letter dated 5 June:

> The riveting of the men's fetters on parade occupying, as it did several hours in the presence of many who were already ill disposed and many who believed in the cartridge fable must have stung the brigade to the quick. The consigning the eighty-five prisoners after such a ceremony to the jail with no other than a native guard over them was, considering the nature of their offence and the known temper of a part of the army, a folly that is inconceivable.[18]

The deliberate and protracted humiliation of the prisoners had a predictable effect on their colleagues, Canning wrote. General anger and frustration became motivation for mutiny and the rescue of their imprisoned brothers. General Anson, the Commander-in-Chief of British forces in India, also fully agreed with Hewitt's ruling while expressing reservations about the gratuitous manacling of the prisoners in front of their comrades, which he saw as an unnecessary provocation.

Others later criticised the proceedings, albeit for different reasons. Many felt the public humiliation of the sepoys had fallen halfway between two better courses; it had neither been sufficiently punitive nor sufficiently conciliatory. The sepoy regiments had not been awed into submission by a show of British steel, and they had not been disarmed. The public humiliation of their colleagues had merely inflamed the situation. The sepoys, with arms in their hands and access to ammunition, were still the masters of their own destiny.

The proceedings ended without incident, and a general air of calm pervaded. Most of the European officers on the parade ground still seemed quite oblivious to the intense feelings of the sepoys. General Hewitt himself was one of them. After the parade was dissolved, he reported back to Army Headquarters that 'the majority of the prisoners seemed to feel acutely the degradation to which their folly and insubordination had brought them. The remainder of the native troops are behaving steady and soldier like.'

Other private letters from officers of the 11th and 20th regiments similarly suggested that all was fine and that the manacling and the threat of massacre had cured the sepoys of all ideas of independent action. Even the European sergeant majors who lived in the sepoy lines failed to notice any dissent or plotting that evening, with the sepoys apparently displaying orderly conduct. The prisoners, too, had marched away to the jail without further complaint according to H. M. Cannon, the superintendent of the Meerut jail. There was no sign of 'bad feeling', as he put it, when the prisoners were led through the gates. Perhaps they had come to terms with the sentence. During their conversations with palace courtiers at Delhi several weeks later, the sepoys recalled saluting the British officers as they marched into captivity.

*****

Things were different in the city itself. As news of the punishment percolated through the bazaars, news of disturbances and demonstrations began drifting into the cantonment. The Commissioner of Meerut, H. H. Greathed, wrote to his wife of that fateful night: 'We dined in the evening at Colonel Custance's. In the course of conversation, I related to him what I had heard – that placards had been seen in the city, calling upon all true Mussalmans to rise and slaughter the English. The threat was treated by us all with an indignant belief. Alas! One brave officer, Colonel Finnis, sitting with us at table, was, within twenty-four hours, one of the first victims to the infuriated soldiery.'

Men of the 11th and 20th NI who visited the less salubrious parts of Meerut and the Sadar Bazaar were taunted by the prostitutes that night. Their manliness was called into question; how could they have allowed their comrades to be humiliated and incarcerated? Others were taunted by their wives in the barracks according to Zahir Dehlvi, who had the chance to converse with the mutineers at Delhi:

> There were conspiracies being hatched in every house with group discussions and debates everywhere, especially amongst the womenfolk who have less power of reasoning and don't think of long-term consequences ... 'You are men and you claim to be soldiers,' they said, 'yet you are cowards, shameless and disreputable. We women are better than you. Aren't you ashamed that you stood and watched helplessly while your officers were handcuffed and you could do nothing? Here take these bangles and wear them and give your weapons to us. We will free the officers and bring them back.'[19]

Stung by the rebukes, the sepoys made plans. According to one rumour circulating among the men, the British authorities were short on manacles but had ordered 2,000 more pairs to clap on the remaining sepoys. Some locals referred to a competing rumour that the British were about to deprive the sepoys of their weapons, with possible disbandment on the cards. According to Dehlvi, the sepoys egged each other on and vowed support for one another: 'The entire army should refuse, and relinquish their duties, and if there is too much oppression, on a fixed day we should revolt all over Hindustan. Let us see if they can do anything then!' By nightfall, the men's minds were set: it would be outright mutiny.

The sepoys realised that Sunday would be a good time to rise up. Many of the European officers would be strolling around the Sadar Bazaar or indulging in some other leisurely pursuit, and most would attend the evening church service along with the rest of the Europeans – only sidearms there. The uprising, then, may as well begin at the same time as the church service. Quite how they would overpower and kill the Europeans – let alone what they would do afterwards – never seems to have been considered. However, in a rare early show of organisation, one thing was decided upon: a sepoy contingent would be sent to Delhi that very night to explain their plans and to ask for support.

The mutineers' bad luck, which would dog them throughout the next four months, started early. Unbeknown to them, the military authorities, mindful of the summer heat and the longer days, had organised for the church service to begin half an hour later than usual. As a result, the mutiny would not erupt at the best time. Many Europeans would assign this lucky coincidence to providence; the violence broke out before many

Europeans had been shut up in the church, giving them time to react and saving them from simple slaughter. 'In my firm belief, this change saved us from an awful catastrophe,' Colonel Mackenzie later wrote.

*****

10 May started off serenely enough. Some Europeans noticed a few of their servants were absent, but nobody saw the pattern across the households. Some other servants, of the sympathetic variety, tried to warn their employers but were ignored. Revd John Rotton, one of the chaplains at Meerut, and who would also act as chaplain to the Delhi Field Force in later weeks, was one of those given advance notice:

> The first intimation that I received of the outbreak was from a female servant, who came to my wife, and said to her with very anxious and troubled looks, 'O, madam don't go to church this afternoon.' The carriage was then at the door, ready to take us to church, and the service was appointed to commence in a quarter of an hour from the time this speech was made. Hearing this singular request addressed to my wife. I naturally enough inquired, 'Why should not madam go to church, this evening?' The servant replied, 'Because there will be a fight.' I asked, 'Who will fight?' The woman answered, 'The sepoys.'[20]

Dismissing the servant's warnings, Rotton continued to prepare for church.

The peace was broken at about half-past five in the evening. Some say a rocket was seen to be fired in the sepoy barracks as a signal for the mutiny to begin and that it happened at around 5 p.m. Europeans immediately came under attack in the bazaar and on their way to church. It was said that the men of the local *kotwali* (police station) quickly joined in, brandishing unsheathed swords along with the sepoys. Other sepoys were observed running back to their cantonments, where they broke into arsenals to obtain weapons and ammunition. Bungalows and other buildings in the cantonment were set on fire.

Some of the officers of the 3rd Light Cavalry still in the vicinity apparently attempted to calm the sepoys but to no avail. In the confusion, some men were wounded. Rotton was travelling towards the church when it became apparent that the servant's information was accurate: 'The sounds of musketry, and the pillars of smoke ascending into the air, and proceeding from the burning bungalows, or houses, in the native lines of cantonment, forced upon me the conviction that mischief had already commenced,' he recalled. Like the hundreds of other Europeans who managed to survive that evening, the Rottons had their own colourful story of how they managed to avoid death. Some fled or hid from the mob; some fought their way out. Others owed their lives to their Indian servants, who protected them in various ways.

Mrs Elisa, wife of Hervey Greathed, the Commissioner of Meerut, also received notice of a disturbance as she was beginning her journey to church. 'Shots and volumes of smoke told us of what was going on: our servants begged us not to show ourselves, and urged the necessity of closing our doors, as the mob were approaching,' she recalled. The Greathed family lived outside the cantonments and so were much more vulnerable. Loading his weapon, Hervey Greathed, with his wife and two other European women who had come seeking refuge, headed to the top of the house.

> The increasing tumult, thickening smoke, and fires all around, convinced us of the necessity of making our position as safe as we could; our guard were drawn up below. After dark, a party of insurgents rushed into the grounds, drove off the guard, and broke into the house, and set it on fire. On all sides we could hear them smashing and plundering and calling loudly for us; it seemed once or twice as though footsteps were on the staircase but no one came up. We owed much to the fidelity of our servants: had but *one* proved treacherous, our lives must have been sacrificed.

The house was set on fire but the Greatheds were rescued by their servant Golab Khan, who led the mob away from the area with the lie that he knew where the Greatheds were hiding.

Col Mackenzie found himself reading a book in his bungalow when the firing started. His bearer approached him with the news that a riot had begun and that the sepoys were now murdering Europeans:

> Not for an instant did I believe the latter part of his story, even though the rapid and frequent reports of fire-arms, which now broke the quiet of the Sabbath evening, made only too clear the truth of the first. The thought that flashed through my mind was that our men of the cavalry were attacking the native infantry in revenge for the sneers with which we all knew these others had freely, since the punishment parade, lashed their submissive apathy in witnessing, without an attempt at rescue, the degradation of their comrades.

Mackenzie quickly put on his uniform and rode towards his regiments' lines to find out what was happening. On the way he met the English quarter-sergeant of the 3rd Light Cavalry, who was fleeing in the opposite direction.

'Oh God! Sir, the troopers are coming to cut us up,' the man cried out, to which Mackenzie replied, 'Let us then stick together, two are better than one.' The quarter-sergeant appeared in too much of a panic for joint action, however. Looking back and seeing a cloud of dust kicked up by an approaching group of sepoys, he decided to continue his flight. He fled through the gates of Mackenzie's bungalow and began clambering over the wall separating it from the next house. At this point he was attacked by various people, including Mackenzie's own night watchman. One man, the *chowkidar*, thrust a spear at the sergeant, wounding him on his lip. The sergeant managed to fire off his pistol, killing the man, before clambering down the other side of the wall and making off successfully.

Mackenzie himself was attacked by an infantryman who had approached him. He managed to avoid the weight of the man's sabre blow, although he was wounded on the right shoulder. The assailant then ran off. Despite this, Mackenzie still had doubts as to the extent of the disturbance.

> As I turned from him and looked down the road to the lines, I saw that it was full of cavalry troopers galloping towards me. Even then it did not occur to me that they could have any hostile intent towards myself. I shouted to them to halt. This they did, and surrounded me; and, before I knew what was happening, I found myself warding off, as well as I could, a fierce onslaught from many blades. A few moments would have sealed my fate, when, providentially, the late Lieutenant Craigie emerged from his gate a little further down the road and came straight to my help. This diversion saved me. The troopers scattered past us and made off towards the European lines.

Both men hastened to the parade ground.

'Most of the men were already mounted, and were careering wildly about, shouting and brandishing their swords, firing carbines and pistols into the air, or forming themselves into excited groups. Others were hurriedly saddling their horses and joining their comrades in hot haste,'[21] Mackenzie wrote of the massing sepoys. He was joined by other officers, who addressed them variously with threats and friendly words in a bid to restore calm. 'To their credit be it said the men did not attack us, but warned us to be off, shouting that the Company's Raj was over forever! Some even seemed to hesitate about joining the noisiest mutineers; and Craigie, observing this, was led to hope that they might be won over to our side. He was an excellent linguist and had great influence among them, and he eventually managed to get some forty or fifty troopers to listen to him and keep apart in a group.'

News now came through that other sepoys had released the prisoners in the jail. Mackenzie, along with Craigie and another officer, Lieutenant Melville Clarke, led his group of soldiers to the jail in the hope of capturing the position and staunching the flow of convicts from the compound. 'The roads were full of excited natives who actually roared approbation as we rode through them, for they evidently did not distinguish in the dusk the British officers, and took the whole party for a band of mutineers,' Mackenzie wrote. [22] Along the way they would pass the burning hulks of European bungalows and other buildings, the air thick with smoke from the various fires. The telegraph wire hung limply from its pole – it had been cut.

The mutineers suffered perhaps their first casualty at this point, darkening the mood considerably. A sepoy trooper was seen thrusting his sword into an already dead European woman in a palanquin gharry, a sort of horse-driven carriage. Craigie, witnessing this, charged and killed the trooper. In turn, the slain sepoy's colleagues raised the shout of, 'Maro maro (kill, kill).' Despite this, Mackenzie and his group managed to extricate themselves. They arrived at the jail too late. Even as they rode up, they could see blacksmiths busy removing the prisoners' manacles while others escaped. The native infantry guards had obviously transferred their loyalty, as they promptly began firing at Mackenzie's group, forcing them to turn back.

As Mackenzie and his men made their way back to the cantonment, they could see utmost confusion and chaos all around. Most if not all the buildings were ablaze. Mackenzie split from Craigie at this point, heading off to his own bungalow with some of the troopers to protect his sister and Craigie's wife. Mackenzie's bungalow was burning, but Craigie's was not. In the latter he found both women, who had returned after aborting their journey to the church as all erupted around them. The house was approached several times by the mob, but, on seeing Mackenzie and others with guns, they declined to approach further. Lieutenant Craigie soon arrived, having made another unsuccessful visit to the parade ground to attempt a truce. A nearby Hindu shrine in the bungalow grounds was being utilised as a strong point. Mackenzie and Craigie would later make it to the British cantonments, although not without incident.

It was a contingent of the 3rd Light Cavalry that had forced its way into the jail to free the imprisoned comrades, creating the scene Mackenzie had witnessed. The Indian guards, perhaps sympathetic, had put up no resistance and blacksmiths had been summoned to break the shackles on their comrades. Not only were the sepoys freed, but all the other prisoners too. According to Hewitt's report of the outbreak, along with the military prisoners, around 1,200 other men were freed; the usual quota of riffraff, petty criminals as well as murderers and habitual jailbirds. According to some sources, many locals from nearby villages had made for the jail to help liberate incarcerated friends and family when they heard of the insurrection.

A lone European officer had been present at the jail. He tried to persuade the sepoy prisoners to stay put, offering to arrange for their pardon if they showed their loyalty and remained in the cells. Perhaps predictably, this offer fell on deaf ears; the Company, the sepoys replied, was not worthy of trust. A large flood of prisoners poured out of the prison.

Some of the mob had made for the treasury, but they were thwarted by a contingent of the 60th Rifles which arrived at the same time. Colonel Muter, having noticed the confusion, had made the decision to send a company of Riflemen towards the bazaar in order to protect the treasury and the records. The company reached the treasury just as the native guard showed its inclination to mutiny. Lieutenant Austin immediately ordered the guardsmen to 'ground arms'. Put on the spot, they obeyed. The European company promptly occupied the treasury and kutchery, saving the records.

Various officers had tried to restore order and received polite rebuffs from their own men, who apparently did not wish to harm them. Other officers, however, met with more violent refusal. The 20th NI had joined the mutiny with the 3rd Light Cavalry, and units of this regiment had moved towards the huts of the 11th NI to persuade them that now was the time. The soldiers of the 11th NI made attempts to save their officers from death. Their commandant, Col John Finnis, was a man generally well thought of by his fellow officers and men, and he had absolute confidence that he could successfully dissuade his men from mutiny. His reaction to the violence had been to ride out to meet his men. By all accounts, the men of the 11th NI were ready to listen to Finnis and it was apparent they still weren't set on joining the men of the 20th NI. Finnis would begin to address them.

Not long after Finnis had begun to parley with his men, a trooper of the 3rd Light Cavalry rode up and declared that the European troops were coming and that 'if they were soldiers and meant to do anything, now was the time to do it'. This intervention proved decisive. The men began to move towards their regimental magazine for their weapons. Finnis appealed to the men again, but he stood little chance. He had no opportunity to escape, either. A man of the 20th NI approached him and fired. He missed, but wounded Finnis' horse. A second shot wounded Finnis himself. Other sepoys now joined the fray, and Finnis died in a hail of gunfire. Once he had been killed, the whole of the 11th joined the mutiny. From this point, sepoys began to shoot other officers with vigour rather than merely warning them off. Capt. McDonald was killed, although other officers managed to flee. Lieutenant Humphrey had his horse shot from beneath him and was wounded but managed to flee to an outhouse of the nearby hospital. Capt. Taylor, Lieutenant Henderson and Lieutenant Pattle escaped as well, although this was only temporary respite – before long they would die at the hands of a mob.

Acts of mercy were also noted. Two sepoys of the 11th NI had taken pity on two European women with children and had personally escorted them to the European barracks before joining their comrades.

One of the officers missing, and who perhaps could have had more influence than others, was Colonel Smyth himself. Rather than joining his fellow officers in attempting to placate the rebellious sepoys, Smyth had made his way to safety in the European cantonments. In his defence, Smyth was field-officer at that time and was therefore perhaps in the right place. Nevertheless, many argued that he should have managed to find his regiment. Smyth later described visiting the Commissioner's house, then the General, whom he discovered had left in a carriage. He then sought out the Brigadier, before going to the artillery parade where he found the officer.

As the violence escalated, some of the sepoys travelled into the city to encourage the locals to rise up. Local thugs and assorted criminals joined the insurrection. When the dust had settled, Commissioner Williams would conclude that a certain level of conspiracy already existed between the sepoys and civilians of the city:

> Before a shot had been fired, the inhabitants of Sadr Bazaar went out armed with swords, spears, and clubs, any weapon they could lay hands on, collected in crowds in every lane and alley, and at every outlet of the Bazaars; and the residents of the wretched hamlets, which had been allowed to spring up all round it and between it and the city, were to be seen similarly armed, pouring out to share in what they evidently knew was going to happen.[23]

The local Gujjar villagers would travel into the city, also making their way to the Sadar Bazaar, looting and plundering the bungalows. Everywhere the shouts of 'Deen! Deen! (Religion)' and 'Allah-i-Allah! Mare Feringhee! (Kill the Europeans)' were heard as the mobs fanned out for looting.

Some Europeans were killed in their houses as the mob looked for victims. Others attempted to disguise themselves as locals. One woman had dressed herself as an *ayah* or servant but was recognised and set upon. Others, not grasping the gravity of the situation, were killed as they made their way to church. Two bedridden veterinary surgeons suffering from smallpox were killed as well. One managed to shoot at the mob, but there were too many of them and he was shot dead himself. His wife was burned alive; the mob feared to touch her, suspecting that she also had contracted smallpox, and instead threw a lighted material at her. One girl, the daughter of a non-commissioned officer, was found dead; a blow from a sword had cleaved her skull in two. The luckier Europeans in the city successfully fled to the cantonments when the chance arose.

*****

Brigadier Wilson, when informed of the mutiny, took prompt action. He immediately rode to the parade ground of the Rifles, and ordered the Carabineers and the artillery to join him there as well. Meanwhile, the men of the Rifles who had been heading to church were ordered to return and assemble with arms immediately. But a lengthy delay soon developed – there was a lack of ammunition. Wilson now made another mistake, rendering any immediate action impossible: he ordered the regiment to be mustered as for an ordinary parade. This meant the procedure was long-winded. All the while, fires were raging and soldiers could clearly hear and see the distant uproar, which demanded a more immediate response. Darkness was falling rapidly, adding to the confusion.

Once the force had been readied, a company of Rifles was sent to protect the treasury while another was assigned the protection of the barracks. Hewitt had appeared by this time, and he ordered the rest of the force to advance in the deepening gloom towards the sepoy barracks to force some semblance of order. Mrs Muter, the wife of Colonel Muter, recounts the swiftness with which the barracks were finally cleared:

> The sun had set and the moon had not yet lit up the scene. The illumination before him rising out of the thick blackness around was one of awful grandeur. For more than a mile three rows of thatched bungalows were on fire, and the spaces between seemed filled with a legion of fiends. As the skirmishers drew close, mounted Sowars with drawn sabres were seen riding furiously about in the light of the conflagration; but the troops approached in darkness, and it was not till the Enfield bullet in its deadly flight passed close by, that the mutineers knew their danger. Drawing rapidly to their left, the loud hum told the Brigadier they were congregating on his right. Some guns were unlimbered and the multitude was dispersed with three rounds of grape. This was the last ever seen of the Native army of Bengal in the lines of Meerut.[24]

With the bulk of the mutineers at the barracks having fled after this one action, the only sepoys left were a few stragglers and looters from the city and some Gujjar villagers who had arrived from the countryside to loot and pillage. Most disappeared into the jungle behind the cantonments as soon as the horse artillery guns fired a few shots. Wilson then organised a force to push the villagers away from the Sadar Bazaar; the battalion would advance along with a contingent of artillery and a small amount of cavalry. However, on reaching the bazaar it became immediately obvious that clearing the warren of shops would be no easy feat. The small force he had would have to break up into small parties to move through the narrow streets. This would be much more dangerous than the skirmish in the barracks. Wilson therefore exercised caution, bypassing the bazaar, and instead organised a parade of his force on the sepoy parade ground, hoping the display would awe the crowd. As night progressed, the remaining mutineers and looters melted away. The chaos of earlier hours was replaced by an unusual calm.

'In the streets not a human being was to be seen,' wrote Mrs Muter, 'though half-an-hour before they were filled with the predatory tribes for which, in former years, this neighbourhood was notorious. A few mangled victims were taken from the ditches and the force bivouacked on the Mall, throwing a chain of sentries around their lines.'[25] Most of the European troops stood on the parade ground, alert to the threat of attack but not intending to pursue anybody. One of the men, anxiously firing at what he supposed were sepoys, managed to hit an officer, Lieutenant Galloway, who had been hiding. In the nearby bazaar, which Wilson had opted to avoid, crowds of villagers still held supremacy. 'So continuous was the musketry in the bazaars that it seemed as if a great action were going on, wrote Mrs Muter, 'and amidst the cries of the frantic Goojurs and the blaze of the houses around, I venture to say that few slept that night within miles of the circle of Meerut.'

Wilson had placed no guard on the sepoy barracks during the night, thinking to keep his force together. This allowed the local Gujjar villagers to return when the opportunity arose, and they thoroughly ransacked the barracks with impunity. The villagers would also attack the other new prison inside the city. In all, 839 more prisoners were released and the buildings were set on fire, but not before everything of value had been looted, including doors and door frames, iron bars, cooking pots, bullocks and even the fetters of the prisoners.[26] Of more serious concern was the looting of 162 flintlock muskets and fifty cap rifles, plus a dozen boxes of ammunition.

*****

John Lawrence, in his correspondence with Charles Saunders, Commissioner of Delhi, mentions the testimony of a Munshi Mohan Lal who had conversations with some of the troopers of the 3rd Light Cavalry after their arrival at Delhi. According to Mohan Lal, the troopers told him that immediately after they had departed the area of the cantonment, they moved to the nearby village of Rithani. Brigadier General Neville Chamberlain later confirmed the truth of this in his own investigation. Here, many of the ringleaders from the three regiments congregated and a council of war was held as to what to do next. Taking advantage of the confusion in the European camp and launching an organised attack would have been a logical next step, but there seems to have been little appetite for this course of action. It was assumed that the European force could not be annihilated now that the element of surprise had vanished. Indeed, there was a real fear that a regrouped European force would attack at any moment. With an attack on the Europeans seemingly out of the question, the rebels had few other choices. They would march to Delhi and hope the other sepoy regiments there would join them.

Not only was Delhi free of European troops, but it also contained three sepoy regiments sympathetic to the mutineers' cause, a large fort and plenty of powder and shot in the large magazine in the city. Perhaps most importantly, Delhi offered the mutineers the one thing they desperately needed – a potential leader in the form of the King. The only other realistic option was to march towards Bareilly and Rohilkhand to the east and seek safety there with the native regiments who might rise up in sympathy. But Bareilly was over a hundred miles away as the crow flies, while Delhi was a third of that distance; not much more than a night's rapid march. Cries from the men helped make the decision. 'Quick, brother quick, Delhi, Delhi' was being uttered by some. Others shouted 'Dilli Chalo (Lets go to Delhi)'. The ringleaders took little time deciding. All the men of the three regiments were told to make their way to Delhi as fast as possible.

Unbeknown to the rebels, neither Hewitt nor Wilson had plans to impede their journey to Delhi. As darkness fell, Wilson had in fact suggested to Hewitt that the sepoys may well be circling around to attack the European cantonment from the north and that sending troops on the road to Delhi to pursue the mutineers might be an error. Hewitt agreed, and so after combing through the sepoy cantonments the European force consolidated its position in the European sector and assumed a long-term defensive posture. Not all agreed with Wilson. Capt. Rosser of the 6th Dragoon Guards had volunteered to attack or at least harry the rebels whatever their route. He had asked to lead a squadron along with several guns, but General Hewitt declined.

One of the few things the rebels had managed to organise between themselves was the destruction of the telegraph linking Meerut to Delhi. Hewitt was therefore forced to send a messenger by horse off to Delhi warning Brigadier Graves, commanding the Delhi brigade, that a large rabble of sepoys mixed with assorted other criminals from the jail was likely heading his way. Another mounted messenger was sent to Ambala cantonment.

During the day, thirty-one European corpses would be found, collected and buried, with the total eventually reaching roughly fifty. The figure could have been much higher if the sepoys had timed their attack right, or if they had embarked upon a deliberate campaign to kill all Europeans. In terms of damage, all the European bungalows south of the nullah were found torched. These included the residences of Commissioner Greathed, Major-General Hewitt and the commissariat officer. The government cable yard also went up in flames.

As dawn broke on 11 May, it became clear how thorough the mob had been in its work. Commissioner Williams describes the scene:

> The inveterate animosity with which the work of destruction was carried out may be judged of by the fact that houses built entirely of masonry, with nothing inflammable except the doors and the beams, which for a considerable height from the ground supported the roofs, formed of cement, resting on kiln-burnt bricks, were as effectually destroyed as the thatched bungalows. Property which the miscreants could not carry off was thrown out and smashed into fragments, evidently pounded with heavy clubs.[27]

Many were surprised to find that not all the sepoys had mutinied. The 20th NI guard stationed at the Pension Pay Office and Cantonment Magistrates had either stayed loyal or baulked at going through with rebellion. Only two officers and twenty men of the 11th NI remained, and of the 3rd Light Cavalry around fifty men had stayed put. Nonetheless, the seriousness of the situation was apparent to most. The bulk of three regiments had mutinied, and the authorities lacked the wherewithal to deal with the situation effectively. A line had been crossed. More sepoy regiments around the country were sure to follow suit. The scale of the emergency was fully understood.

'It was mid-day turned to black night – a picture of peace changed by magic to one of war,' Mrs Muter wrote. 'We felt intuitively that it was a great revolution – a cyclone that had merely its center at Meerut, destined to sweep with a violence that would startle the world, over the length and breadth of the land. Perhaps the framework of English rule would go down before the tempest, and, if so, what fate was reserved for us?'[28]

# 10

# Paralysis

> The state of panic at Meerut was shocking; all the ladies shut up in an enclosed barrack and their husbands sleeping in the men's barracks for safety and never going beyond the sentries. General Hewitt is in a state of helpless imbecility.[1]
>
> Capt. Hodson, 25 May 1857

On the morning of 11 May, it was by no means clear to General Hewitt and Brigadier Wilson that the mutineers were heading to Delhi. There were still suspicions that they might double back and attack the European cantonment from the north. There was also the threat of the looters and others in the city who might try and plunder the European houses and cantonment. Even more dangerous were the nearby Gujjar villagers, who might use the daylight to indulge in more plunder. News began to drift in that the entire area around Meerut was in a state of upheaval. Beset by such concerns, the Europeans at Meerut took on a strong defensive mentality just when the mutineers were at their weakest, retreating to Delhi.

With order established, Brigadier Wilson made preparations in earnest for the defence of the European cantonment. Measures would be implemented over the following days. Pickets were posted in outlying areas of the cantonment and beyond. Owing to its walls, the Dum Dum, situated behind the artillery section, became a sort of makeshift fortress housing families and civilians in its rooms and in tents within the walls. Due to the extreme heat inside the Dum Dum, thermantidotes – wheel-like devices fitted into windows and covered with wet tattties – were employed to reduce the temperature to a more pleasant level. Entrenchments were dug around the outside of the enclosure. The only other enclosed, easily defensible buildings in the cantonment belonged to the General Hospital complex behind the European infantry, and these were also utilised. The European cavalry barracks were abandoned, with only the infantry and artillery lines maintained, so as not to stretch the defensive perimeter. *Chevaux-de-frise*, spiked wooden obstacles, were positioned at vulnerable points. A vigilant eye was kept for an attack by villagers, with guards at numerous posts and some local workers organised into gangs to craft more defensive works.

Before 10 May, most Europeans dismissed the possibility of mutiny. However, by the 11th that had all changed. Paranoia reigned. Many suspected any and all Indians. Various rumours swirled around the European compound; for instance, they feared that the remaining Indian servants would poison them. Any local of the slightest martial bearing was seen as a threat. One man, a bearer for an officer in the camp, had the habit of curling up his moustache in a military fashion and wearing his *pagree* (turban) in a certain way. He nearly met the hangman because of this, but was recognised by another officer who explained his appearance. The man was advised by the officer to stop curling his moustache, to wear his *pagree* in a less ostentatious fashion and 'to drop his jaunty gait, and generally look as mean and dirty as possible'.[2] Confidence was interpreted as the loss of subservience. There was a general suspicion that the Indians inside the cantonment were either spies or perhaps assassins, ready to act if the opportunity arose. Some feared that the sepoys would return with reinforcements, presumably the Delhi brigade, and that there would be an attack on the cantonments on a coming Muslim holy day.

General Hewitt and other officers took to sleeping in a single building in the barracks. Each kept a loaded pistol under his pillow and his sword hanging next to him or resting on the chair beside his bed. The tension caused some misunderstandings. On one occasion, for instance, a *punkahwalla* was apprehended after a dozing officer, feigning sleep, observed the *punkahwalla* cease his fanning and approach to see if the man was sleeping. The officer grabbed him and announced, 'I've got him! I've got him!' Immediately the call went out to hang him, as well as the other two *punkahwallas* present. The poor man explained that he had simply got up as his shift was at an end and he could not call out to his replacement for fear of waking the officers. He had approached to see if they were asleep to ascertain if they would notice the fan had stopped.

No act of betrayal took place, and none of the rumours regarding the mutineers making another attack proved true either, but such anxieties succeeded in hobbling the British force. They were fully occupied guarding the cantonment day and night – sometimes with comic results, as this testimony from Frances Wigram, joint magistrate of Meerut, shows:

> [A]lmost every night, I take up my post at one of the pickets, as a volunteer. Last night we fully expected an attack; the alarm sounded, and as we fell in, the word came down the line of sentries, 'coming, coming,' when after being under arms a few minutes it turned out to be nothing more than a Carabineer being run away with, and a sergeant of the Sappers had shot and bayonetted a tree in the dark, the said tree having

> declined to 'answer' his challenge ... All the country round is in a state of insurrection; murders, dacoitees [robberies] and burnings are of everyday occurrence, and the country has been placed under martial law.

Col Mackenzie would relate the story of a fellow officer – he did not mention his name – whose appearance changed considerably during these days.

> That gallant officer rejoiced in a long and scanty moustache, which up to the moment of the Mutiny had retained the glossy black of youth. A few days afterwards, an officer who met me asked me if I had observed the terrible effect which late events had evidently wrought on the colonel. 'Poor fellow!' said he, 'his hair has turned perfectly white!' My irreverent laughter amazed and shocked him. He little knew that the blanching of the old gentleman's moustache was due to his not having had the time or the presence of mind to bring with him in his hurried flight from the mutineers his trusty bottle of hair-dye.

Occasionally, darkness and tension made for mistakes of a less humorous nature. As much as three weeks later, on 1 June, two carabineers mistook each other for mutineers in the dark and fought a duel. One man ended up wounded in the leg while the other had his horse wounded.[3] Meanwhile, the Gujjar villagers always seemed to be circling the cantonment waiting for an opportunity, and this kept the pickets occupied.

Worse still, various refugees were trickling in from Delhi. They told of massacres in the city.

At noon on 12 May, two days after the mutiny, with the telegraph wires fixed, a message was finally sent from Meerut to the Commander-in-Chief, then at Simla:

> Native troops in open mutiny. Cantonments south of Mall burnt. Several European officers killed. European troops under arms defending barracks. Electric telegraph wire cut.

*****

Four days after the mutiny, on the evening of 15 May, an unfortunate event occurred. A force of Indian sappers and miners had arrived from Roorkee, a station 65 miles due north of Meerut. This contingent had no intention to mutiny. However, with paranoia high among the Europeans, the new arrivals aroused great suspicion. That night, troopers of the 3rd Light Cavalry – or rather the small remnant of the regiment that had not mutinied – were being paraded by Col Mackenzie. Suddenly, shots were heard from the nearby sappers' camp, followed by sounds of uproar and shouting. Wigram had heard one explanation:

> [Y]esterday, whilst they were putting their ammunition into the magazine, a panic seized a large body of them, evidently from the assertion of a Taqueer (a race of men that should now be swept without mercy from the face of India, as they are, undoubtedly, the instigators of the rebellion) that they were to be made Christians the following day. They killed their commanding Officers and a Havildar who endeavored to restrain them, on the spot, and then fled across the parade grounds.[4]

A different story had reached Col Mackenzie's ears in the minutes after the shots: 'A rumour reached me – how I do not remember – that the Sappers had mutinied, had killed Alfred Light, the artillery officer who afterwards became so distinguished, and were about to fly into the jungle. Naturally I lost no time in dismounting and running in to the barrack to inform General Hewitt, whom I found in the dishabille of shirt and pyjamas.'[5] Mackenzie was joined by Brigadier Wilson, who ordered Mackenzie to gather his men and shadow the sappers, who were now leaving the camp, until a large force could be organised to annihilate them.

Only later was it discovered what had really happened. Major Fraser, the commanding officer, had been shot dead by an Afghan camp follower; neither the sappers nor the miners were involved. Given the atmosphere, however, the sappers quickly realised how it looked. Their only chance was in flight. Some were in uniform and some were not, but almost all fled for the nearby jungle with their muskets. They headed for the nearby Kali Nadi stream. A squadron of carabineers under Wilson and a couple of guns were sent against them. The sappers were soon overtaken. 'The poor fellows fought with the energy of despair. No quarter was given, and all were destroyed, except two who were made prisoners by myself, and who, I believe, were afterwards retained in the service, and proved perfectly loyal,'[6] Mackenzie recounted. This exchange saw the first European death during the mutiny in open warfare: a trooper called Frederick Kingsford. On the other side, fifty-six of the sappers and miners were killed while 280 survived, the vast bulk managing to make their way to Delhi and join the rebel camp in the following days. The few who had not fled agreed to be disarmed.

On the same evening, Col Mackenzie volunteered to set out with twenty-five of his men to try and rescue an assorted group of Europeans whom he heard had fled Delhi for Meerut. Holed up in a village en route, the escapees had sent a letter written in French indicating their desperate circumstances. Mackenzie would set out on the morning of the 17th with his group, accompanied by Lieutenant Hugh Gough (later Sir Hugh Gough VC). Mackenzie was unsure if his troopers would stay loyal. These men knew of the prevailing uncertainty in the Meerut cantonment, and he feared this may have had an effect on them. Luckily for Mackenzie, they proved loyal. His force reached a village called Hirchinpore, where many of those escaping Delhi had hidden, most of them with the help of a local landowner, an oriental Jew called Cohen.

> The fugitives of whom we were in search had in despair stowed themselves away in various hiding places, and when they appeared presented a pitiable spectacle from the effects of the hardships they had undergone. All that night we had to remain there while Cohen's people collected carts to convey the women and children. If one of our men or one of the villagers had bolted and carried to Delhi the news of what a haul could be made at Hirchinpore, two or three hours would have sealed our fate. But again Providence befriended us, and early next morning our little caravan started for Meerut, where we safely arrived that night.[7]

Some of the fugitives were officers of the various Delhi regiments who had chanced to flee across the Jumna. These included Colonel Knyvett, 38th NI; Lieutenant Salkeld, Bengal Engineers; Lieutenant Wilson, Bengal Artillery; Lieutenant Montague M. Proctor, 38th NI; Lieutenant H. Gambier, 38th NI; Lieutenant Vibart, 54th NI; and Lt G. Forrest, who had defended the Delhi magazine. There were eight civilians as well, most of them women.

*****

As confidence returned in the European camp at Meerut, retribution came to the fore. A few men from the city who could be identified were caught, and with martial law declared in the city they were promptly marched off to the nearest tree to be hanged. The vast bulk of the looters and plunderers were never identified. Curiously, some escaped prisoners, perhaps the less bold among them, gave themselves up after a few days; others left word with the jailors as to their whereabouts and their willingness to be returned to jail. One of them, a *zemindaar* (local landowner), even actively volunteered to help the authorities, presumably in the hopes of reducing his sentence. Perhaps it was felt that the British authorities would inevitably destroy the nascent mutiny and so it was better to give up voluntarily than wait to be captured further down the line.

A gallows was erected close to the burial plot of the victims of 10 May. The perception was that the Muslim butchers of the city had been the ringleaders of the local mob. Being popular shopkeepers, they were easily recognised. Col Mackenzie described them as 'a class of men who were among the most blood-thirsty actors on that night'[8] and seemed to have little sympathy for them. During the outbreak of mutiny, Mackenzie had ridden over the body of one butcher who had been killed during the fighting.

One of the first to feel the noose was a butcher who had killed a European woman. Lieutenant Moller of the 11th Regiment had come across evidence that a butcher murdered Mrs Chambers, the wife of the adjutant of the 11th, and went to the bazaar to search for the man. He brought him back at gunpoint. A drum-head court-martial was organised.

The butcher was found guilty and hanged from a mango tree on 14 May. Many other butchers who had led the mobs left with the rebels, and word was that they had taken part in the chaos at Delhi as well. When things settled down, some of the butchers actually returned to Meerut, perhaps feeling British authority was at an end, but they were apprehended and hanged. Various camp followers who had been seen joining in the looting were also strung up without delay. Proof of guilt was difficult to obtain for those apprehended in the riots, as Mrs Muter describes.

> It was difficult to obtain evidence, and they were sent round the garrison, drawn up in a row; while company after company and troop after troop was halted before them, and the men asked if they could recognized any of the number as having been engaged in the riots. Most of their faces wore a deadly hue—some could scarcely stand and all their lips muttered prayers, the name of Allah alone being distinguishable. The Natives condemned to death generally assumed a stoical indifference and moved with composure to the place of execution, sometimes picking their way over ground wet with heavy showers as if more concerned for their health than for their fate. It was then, and then only, in this terrible trial, they displayed any nobility of spirit.

Few could be definitively identified, and many got away with their actions. It was noticed later that the bazaar was full of looted goods, with locals betraying an air of satisfaction and 'showing belligerence'.[9]

Retribution was also sought from nearby villages. On 25 May, for example, a small force was sent out to destroy a village around 14 miles from Meerut. The events of 10 May and the lack of an immediate British response had encouraged local villagers to take part in the violence. Bereft of weapons, they had adopted rather desultory fighting methods during the outbreak. When the British came to seek revenge, they surrounded the villages before sunrise. All cattle belonging to the villagers were confiscated, and the inhabitants were driven away. Everything was then burned to the ground. Once the mutiny was over, land belonging to the villagers would be gifted to villagers who had supported to the British. Thousands of villagers were dispossessed in this way. Many of them died, but some did not. The *kotwal* of Meerut city, Bishan Singh, for example, was sympathetic to the rebels and warned the inhabitants of Gagol, Sisaree and Moorunugur of the impending retribution, allowing many to escape.

On 1 June, three weeks after the mutiny at Meerut, and with the rebels mostly pinned down in Delhi, it was decided that the roughly 120 loyal remnants of the 11th NI could be rearmed. This was recognised as risky move, but with British prestige damaged by an inability to effectively police the areas around Meerut it was considered a risk worth taking. 'We are living in a most isolated state at present for the road down country is so beset with Gujjurs that a mail rarely arrives from that side and the great part of the electric telegraph wire having been cut and carried away all communication by that means has been stopped I know not what is going on,'[10] a frustrated Francis Wigram complained.

News of the mutiny at Meerut had rippled out into the countryside, with the expected embellishments. A letter from a Muslim Inayatoollah of the Boolandsshuhr district to his brother, one Faisal Hassan, an extra assistant at Rawalpindi, provides an example of these exaggerated tales. It described the soldiers rising and killing all the principal Europeans in the cantonments. They had attacked the jail, calling up blacksmiths to free the captives from their chains. The treasury, he said, was sacked, and this chaos and looting continued for two days.[11] Not a single European bungalow survived, with the sepoys making their leisurely way to Delhi following the extensive looting. Other sepoys had also rebelled at Roorkee, he said. 'A moulvi from Meerutt and another from some other place have gone over to Dehlee with about 6,000 men to make religious war,' he wrote. While this is an exaggeration, tales of European caution and indecision at Meerut no doubt helped the mutineers' cause and swayed the minds of sepoys up and down the country who were still undecided on matters.

*****

Despite their organisation in the days following the Meerut mutiny, both Major General Hewitt and Brigadier Wilson would face serious criticism for failing to show the necessary command during the events of 10 May. Further criticism was levelled for their complete failure to pursue the mutineers. Had aggressive measures been taken that evening, the rebels would have been intercepted before they reached Delhi or destroyed as they tried to secure the city. The mutiny could have been crushed in its infancy. They had 2,000 European troops – more than enough to tackle the rebels. Even supposing an organised pursuit could not have been arranged for one reason or another, a small cavalry force could have been sent to Delhi to warn of the rebel army's approach. The gates to the city could have been closed and the bridge of boats connecting the city to the Meerut road broken, denying the rebels any chance to fraternise with their sepoy colleagues at the Delhi cantonment. No such measures were taken. Hewitt had kept the European force at Meerut entirely static during that vital time. Chronicler Sir John Kaye's verdict was damning:

> It is doubtful whether if the avenging Englishmen had that morning appeared under the walls of Delhi the Sepoy Regiments stationed there would have broken into rebellion and it is well nigh certain that in the presence of the British troops the Royal Family of Delhi would not have dared to proclaim themselves on the side of the mutineers.[12]

Nor did Brigadier Wilson step up and act with sufficient vigour. In fact, some later remarked that he tended to wilt in difficult situations, pointing to his similar display of pusillanimity during the siege of Delhi when he dithered over an attack on the city. Revd J. Rotton summed up what many felt at the time: 'In truth our military authorities were paralyzed. No one knew what was best to do, and nothing was accordingly done.' Hugh Gough, who was present at the Meerut disturbance, describes a more general confusion within the command. Of Hewitt he would write, 'He had more or less relegated his authority to Brigadier Archdale Wilson.'[13]

Hewitt was still failing to rise to the occasion two weeks after the events of 10 May. Capt. Hodson, for example, found a state of relative chaos when he reached Meerut more than a week later. 'The state of panic at Meerut was shocking; all the ladies shut up in an enclosed barrack and their husbands sleeping in the men's barracks for safety and never going beyond the sentries. General Hewitt is in a state of helpless imbecility,'[14] Hodson wrote on 25 May.

There were of course mitigating factors for this inertia. The European force was never as strong as it looked on paper. It had been difficult to organise the European troops, it was said. There had been the delay in supplying ammunition to HM60th Rifles. Many of the carabineers had not yet been supplied with horses. Only around half of the regiment could ride, made up as it was of somewhat raw recruits. Many of the horses supplied to the carabineers had not been broken in, either. Some of the European gunners were very young, and not as familiar with artillery drills as they should have been. Also, only two field batteries were fully equipped and ready to move. In any case, rather than swift action a roll call was decided upon to ascertain who was present and who had been killed. This proved slow to organise, and after it was done the gloom rendered any pursuit much more difficult. But then, if much of the force had left to pursue the mutineers, leaving only a token force behind at Meerut, the cantonments, already difficult to defend given their extensive perimeter, would surely have fallen to Gujjar villagers and looters.

The time of year was a factor, too. The sepoy rebels were used to the furnace heat of May. On reaching Delhi, they likely would have received succour and support in the form of water and supplies. The pursuing European force, on the other hand, would have to fend for itself. If the rebels had broken the bridge across the Jumna, then without boats the European force would have been forced to return empty-handed. Even if the river could be crossed, the tired and overheated Europeans would be facing six regiments should the three sepoy regiments at Delhi come out in support of their Meerut comrades – as indeed they did.

Despite this, the general feeling was that such excuses were entirely spurious considering the urgency of the situation and the British strength at Meerut. In fact, no reconnaissance missions were even made into the surrounding areas to prevent nearby uprisings. Nor was there any attempt to pacify and search the city of Meerut in the following days. This allowed looters to stow away their plunder, which is why so few individuals were caught and punished. The European force remained entirely inert, concerned solely with defending the European cantonments and civilians.

Whatever the mitigating factors, Hewitt's cautious approach left him open to charges of inaction. He would be removed from his position as a consequence. In his appeal against his removal from the divisional staff, Hewitt would argue that since the command of the station was in the hands of the brigadier, responsibility for immediate action lay with him. However, Hewitt was the senior officer, and many took a dim view of him shifting the blame for such a serious event. Brigadier Wilson would defend himself too, questioning Hewitt's assertion that it was his responsibility:

> I would beg to refer to the Regulations of the Bengal Army, Section XVII., which will show what little authority over the troops is given to the Brigadier commanding a station which is the Head-Quarters of a Division, and that I could not have exercised any distinct command, the Major-General being present on the occasion. As Brigadier, I only exercised the executive command of the troops under the orders of the Major-General. I may or may not have been wrong in offering the opinion I did to the Major-General. I acted to the best of my judgment at the time, and from the uncertainty regarding the direction taken by the fugitives, I still believe I was right. Had the Brigade blindly followed in the hope of finding the fugitives, and the remaining portion of the Cantonment been thereby sacrificed, with all our sick, women and children, and valuable stores, the outcry against those in command at Mirath [Meerut]would have been still greater than it has been.[15]

For his part, Brigadier Wilson's first concern was to protect lives and property at Meerut, to protect the city's treasury and magazine and to prevent the whole of the city and the European cantonment from falling. Hewitt, however, had bigger responsibilities. The Meerut Division included not only Meerut but also Delhi. Hewitt was not just responsible for Meerut, but also the old capital – and its magazine.

# 11

# Arrival at Delhi

> Unless you the King join us, we are all dead men, and we must in that case just do what we can for ourselves.
>
> Meerut sepoys to Zafar

Perhaps the earliest indications of the mutiny at Meerut could have been gleaned at Delhi by the afternoon of 10 May. At that time, Captain Tytler of the 38th NI was resting in his bungalow in the Delhi cantonments. At around 3 p.m., Tytler heard a bugle and the sound of carriage wheels clattering past his bungalow. Assuming that the carriage held those five Delhi officers who had been sent to carry out the court-martial in Meerut earlier that day, Tytler asked a servant to summon the subedar major of the 38th, who was one of the five and would be able to tell him all that had happened at Meerut over the previous few days. The servant came back with news that a carriage had indeed been making its way into the cantonment but that it wasn't carrying back the officers. Instead, it seemed to contain a large number of sepoys. None of them belonged to the regiments stationed at Delhi; they were from the Meerut Brigade. In fact, they were the men sent by the plotters to inform their Delhi comrades of the planned mutiny that night. The oblivious Tytler saw nothing suspicious in the arrival of these men, who were never asked what they were doing in Delhi.

Simon Fraser, Commissioner of Delhi, was another who failed to heed the omens – or even outright warnings. Late that Sunday, at around midnight, a letter from Hewitt was brought to Fraser's residence informing him of the mutiny. The letter urged appropriate measures to be taken, including the locking of the city gates, to prevent the sepoys from entering the city. Fraser never opened the letter; he had already decided to retire to bed. Some accounts claim that Fraser was awake but quite drunk when the letter arrived, and that he simply slipped it into his pocket, intending to read it the next morning. When the messenger realised that a reply was not forthcoming he pressed upon Fraser's servants the seriousness of the situation, insisting they wake Fraser, who had by now retired and nodded off. The servants refused; the Commissioner was known for his temper. When Fraser finally read the letter the next morning, matters were out of his hands.

There were other letters arriving from Meerut – but not for the British authorities. Some were delivered to the palace guard. The journalist Jat Mall later claimed that the palace guard was fully aware of the situation: 'The arrival of the soldiery from Meerut was expected in the palace. Letters came in from Meerut on Sunday, bringing intelligence that eighty-two soldiers had been imprisoned, and that a serious disturbance was to take place in consequence. Owing to this the guards at the gate of the palace made no secret of their intentions, but spoke openly of what they expected to occur, which was, that some of the troops after mutinying at Meerut, would come over to Delhi.'[1]

Whatever the case, Delhi was no different on the morning of 11 May. The daily hustle and bustle of the city and its bazaars was apparent, and business was in full swing in the Chandni Chowk. The usual congregation of Europeans and Anglo-Indians had visited St James' Church for the daily morning service. Inside the palace, too, daily routines were observed. Zafar had completed his morning prayers and was now seated on the *jharokha* (balcony) facing the river. He might have had plans to travel that morning, most likely to the gardens outside the palace, as his elephant had been prepared; a golden *howdah* with cushions and pillows was being readied. In the courtyard, several men of the bodyguard and various nobles could be seen awaiting the King's appearance. With them were around fifty or sixty porters dressed in smart red uniforms and turbans. Outside the fort, too, the main column of the King's party waited for him to appear before the cavalcade got under way. There were 200 special armed guards dressed in grey robes and turbans plus another thirty Abyssinians, also dressed in ceremonial uniforms and red turbans, along with a platoon of cavalrymen.

It was at this time, according to Ahsan Ulla Khan, that a sepoy who had no business in the palace confidently strode up to the palace gates and sauntered into the inner sanctum. This was not a rebel from Meerut, however, but a man from the 38th NI who should have been on duty at the Lahore Gate. He had come to make clear his loyalties.

> On the morning of the 16th of Ramzan [Ramadan], alias the 11th of May at about seven o' clock A.M., a Hindu sepoy of the 38th Regiment of Native Infantry came up to the door of the Hall of Special Audience in the palace, and said to some of the door keepers that happened to be on the spot, that the native army at Meerut had mutinied against the State, and were now on the point of entering Delhi; that he and the

> rest of them would no longer serve the Company, but would fight for their faith. My house is in the palace and close by the Hall of Special Audience; and I was immediately informed by one of the Mahomedan door-keepers of what the 38th sepoy had said.[2]

No more than a few minutes later, guards on the palace walls spied large clouds of dust in the distance, kicked up by what appeared to be a column of horsemen across the Jumna, fast approaching on the road from Meerut. Unbeknown to those on the walls, this was the vanguard of the 3rd Light Cavalry. Nobody was overly concerned at the sight; it was probably assumed that the British authorities had simply arranged to move troops to or from Delhi.

A few minutes later, the sowars reached the river and were observed securing the bridge of boats at the toll gate on the left bank. Here the first violence occurred. The toll keeper, a man called Mir Bahri, either challenged the party or refused them passage. He was killed, and the toll house was torched. A European crossing the bridge was murdered by the sowars as well. Some of the witnesses to these events were servants and employees of the palace. One of them was the chaprassi Kishen Singh. He had gone to the river with another chaprassi, Maharaj Singh, to bathe near the bridge. It seemed obvious to these men that trouble was brewing. 'The Darogha of the bridge told us to go off quickly for that there was a row impending. We returned to the Lahoree gate of the palace,'[3] Kishen Singh recalled.

Captain Douglas, the commandant of the palace, was the first person of any authority to speak with the mutineers in Delhi. One of the first of the rebel troopers to cross the river had made his way through the Calcutta Gate into the city, appearing at the main gate of the palace at the same time as Douglas. Makhan, Douglas' mace bearer, recalled the short exchange between the two: 'Captain Douglas asked the man what he wanted, when he replied that he had mutinied at Meerut, and arriving at Delhi had come to the guard for a drink of water and a pipe. Captain Douglas gave orders to seize him, when he immediately galloped off.'[4] Other witnesses tell a slightly different story, saying that the trooper declared to have come from Meerut where they had killed all the Europeans at the cantonment. Douglas had apparently ordered the subedar at the gate to arrest the sowar, who rode off before he could be stopped.

Those on the palace walls could now see smoke swirling up from the burning toll gate. A couple of horsemen sent to investigate had found the area near the bridge packed with fleeing boatmen and sentries as more and more mutineers began reaching the banks of the river. One of the horsemen asked a boatman if everything was alright. The man replied, 'Oh Sir, it is not good news! The army has come down and they have murdered Mir Bahri and set the toll gate on fire! They have looted the strongbox! We ran away to save our lives.' The cavalryman quickly returned to the palace to report his findings.

When Zafar was informed of the nature of the new arrivals, he ordered men down to the bridge to destroy or disable it and to lock the Calcutta Gate, the entry point into the walled city from the bridge. These orders were never carried out; having made their way to the Salimgarh Fort, the men sent to destroy the bridge saw that they were too late. The Calcutta Gate, too, was compromised. They returned to the palace with nothing accomplished.

Of those mutineers who had already crossed the river, a small contingent splintered off and rode along the palace walls adjacent to the river. They headed for the *jharokha* at the Saman Burj, where they hoped to have an audience with the King. Their approach was observed from the walls by the palace guards. When Zafar was informed of their wishes, he assented to an audience but asked Ahsan Ulla Khan to accompany him. The physician noted that the arrival of the sowars was a surprise to the King.

> I had hardly received this information when the King of Delhi sent for me. I attended on him immediately, and his Majesty said, 'Look, the cavalry are coming by the road of the Zer Jharokha.'[5] I looked and saw about 15 or 20 of the Company's regular cavalry then about 150 yards distant. They were dressed most of them in uniform, but a few had Hindustani clothes on. I immediately suggested to the King to have the gate fastened by which entrance to the palace from the Zer Jharokha is obtained, and this had scarcely been done when five or six of the sowars came up to the closed gate, which leads directly under the Saman Burj Palace, where the King has his own private residence in close contiguity with the apartments of the Queens and other secluded females of the establishment. The sowars commenced calling out, 'Dohai Badshah,' or 'Help O King! we pray for assistance in our fight for the faith.'[6]

Sheltering from the clamour outside, the sowars explained to the King their grievances about the new cartridge, and how they had no choice but to do what they had done to preserve their faith. They needed his help, they said. Mukand Lal, Zafar's private secretary, who was also present, recalled the troopers addressing the King in a more threatening tone:

> When the troopers arrived, they first came under the palace windows, and told the King that they had come to him after killing all the English at Meerut, and that they would slay immediately those that were here; and they further said that they would, for the future, consider the prisoner [Zafar] their King, and that now there was not an Englishman left in all India, – all had been slain. They further said the whole army would obey the King's orders. The King said that if they had a disposition to come that they should prepare themselves for all consequences, and if they were so prepared, they were at liberty to come and take the management of matters into their hands.

The sudden arrival of the mutineers that day must have bemused the old King. At a loss, he summoned Ghulam Abbas, whose title was Shamshir-Ud-Doulat, and asked the man to fetch Captain Douglas for advice. Douglas soon appeared at the Diwan-i-Khas; the ageing King followed, with the aid of a stick. A short meeting took place, in which Douglas was briefed on events at Meerut and the appearance of the mutineers at the *jharokha*. Along with Zafar had come several courtiers, including Ahsan Ulla Khan. Douglas had brought two chaprassies, Mohnum Singh and Moosahib Singh, as well as the jemadar Poorun Singh. Thanks to his earlier meeting with the sowar at the gate, Douglas already knew that the arrivals were mutineers. The important thing now was to decide on a plan of action.

Douglas's initial impulse was to address the mutineers himself. Rather than hailing them from the *jharokha* or palace walls, he explained, he would descend into the courtyard and exit the water gate, where he could challenge the troopers face to face. The King counselled against this: 'I won't let you go; they are murderers; they might kill you also,' he insisted. Ahsan Ulla Khan echoed Zafar. The physician urged Douglas to make his address from the balcony. Douglas relented; no doubt the boasts of the troopers outside that they had killed the Europeans in Meerut helped convince him.

From the balcony, Douglas could see thirty to forty sowars waiting for the King to appear. 'Some had their swords drawn, others had pistols and carbines in their hands, more were coming from the direction of the bridge, accompanied by men on foot, apparently grooms with bundles on their heads,' recalled Ahsan Ulla Khan. Douglas spoke up, asking the men what they were doing and why they had come. He warned that their close approach to the King's private apartments was disrespectful and that if they wished to air any grievances it would be better done elsewhere. He advised the mutineers to move towards the south of the fort rather than annoying the King further. If they assembled at the Kotila fortress at Ferozeshah, he would listen to their grievances. This seemed to placate the troopers. Watching them leave, Douglas reassured the King that things were under control. 'Don't be alarmed, the disturbance shall be put down at once; I will have the men apprehended,' he confided to the King.

Douglas understood the urgency of the situation. The gates of the city needed to be closed immediately to prevent more mutineers entering, particularly the Calcutta Gate. Confident that matters were in hand, Douglas quickly returned to the Lahore Gate. Bakhtawar Singh, stationed at the Lahore Gate, saw Douglas return in a state of excitement and head for his apartment atop the Lahore Gate, where the entire palace frontage as well as the river could be surveyed.[7] Only when Douglas looked out from this vantage point did the full scale of the crisis dawn on him. More contingents of the 3rd Light Cavalry were approaching the opposite bank of the river and proceeding across the bridge of boats toward the Calcutta Gate. Douglas hurried down to the arcade, where he was notified by Bakhtawar Singh that the Commissioner of Delhi had come by; a concerned Fraser had apparently showed up while Douglas was addressing the mutineers at the other end of the palace. Fraser had left a message asking Douglas to meet him at the Calcutta Gate so that the appropriate action could be taken. Lacking transport of his own, Douglas requisitioned a native officer's buggy and headed to meet Fraser with Bakhtawar Singh. Prior to leaving the palace entrance, Douglas gave the guards at the gate strict instructions not to allow anyone to enter the fort. This he hoped would prevent the rebels entering the palace itself, even if the city was already compromised.

Fraser had in fact become aware of the crisis even earlier than Douglas. On waking up in the morning, he had finally read the letter from Meerut. A little later, messengers announced that the mutineers had arrived. Fraser had taken immediate action, ordering one of his attendants to call upon the agent of the Nawab of Jhajjar to send some more troopers to help preserve order in the city. The nawab had personally contributed to Fraser's own guard. Then, in his buggy, and with an escort of Jhajjar sowars already present, Fraser hastened to the palace to secure Douglas's aid and ensure the mutineers did not get into the compound. Even before he arrived at the open spaces in front of the palace, however, it had been apparent that the various contingents of sepoys in the city had no intention of obeying orders. Zaka Ullah was one of those who saw the Commissioner driving around: 'I saw Mr Simon Fraser riding in a two-horse carriage. He stopped his carriage near the Magazine. There some Telego Soldiers were standing guard and were in uniform. He called the Subehdar of the Telego Company and asked him if he and his soldiers were loyal to him and the British. The Subehdar replied that they were loyal to their faith. They did not even return his salute properly.'

In his travels around the city, Fraser ventured as far as the Kashmir Gate; he found the guard there still willing to take his orders. He instructed them to secure the gate and then made for the palace. Once there, he had been told that Douglas was already aware of the situation and left his message asking Douglas to meet him at the Calcutta Gate. Fraser hoped the gate could be commanded by loyal troops and closed as a matter of urgency; the bridge and the Calcutta Gate were undoubtedly the keys to the city.

Douglas and Fraser weren't the only high-ranking Europeans to make their way to the Calcutta Gate area early that morning. Several others, on hearing of the disturbance, also arrived to see what could be done. Magistrate Mr Hutchinson's workplace happened to offer a particularly good view of the commotion caused by the sowars of the 3rd Light Cavalry as they entered the city that morning. The kutchery was situated inside the Water Bastion, around a mile from the Calcutta Gate, in the extreme north of the walled city. Looking downstream from the kutchery, the bridge could be seen less than a mile away. As he watched the rebels enter, Hutchinson noticed they appeared agitated and aggressive. With the toll house on fire, it was obvious something serious was happening.

Hutchinson took the initiative and rode to inform Brigadier Graves at the cantonment. He asked the brigadier to send troops as a precaution to ensure the peace of the city wasn't broken before making his way back into the city. Riding back through the Kashmir Gate, Hutchinson was warned by Lieutenant Proctor, the officer in charge of the main guard, that it might be best to stay out of the city for the time being. He dismissed the advice. 'I am the magistrate and I must go,' he replied. The officers at the cantonment were now aware of the mutineers' entry into the city, although they did not yet grasp the full weight of the situation; indeed, it is unlikely that anybody in Delhi understood the severity of the disturbance at Meerut and what it meant for them. Hutchinson next made his way to the Calcutta Gate to find out what was happening. He was soon joined by Mr Le Bas, the sessions judge at the old Custom House, as well as Mr Nixon, the Commissioner's confidential clerk.

Another prominent European to join the group at the Calcutta Gate was the magistrate Sir Theophilus Metcalfe. Metcalfe was at home when he heard about the mutineers and decided to travel into the city on his buggy to investigate. He went to the *kotwali* at the Chandni Chowk, where he ordered the chief police officer to send his men to the various city gates, which they were to close. Entry into the city was to be refused to all. Metcalfe would also visit the home of Lt Forrest, who had not yet made his way to the magazine. Metcalfe asked Forrest to accompany him to the magazine, where two guns could be collected. His plan was to place these on the bridge or thereabouts at the Calcutta Gate to discourage more rebels from entering the city.

When Metcalfe and Forrest arrived at the magazine, they found Fraser telling Lieutenant G. Willoughby to have the guns sent to the causeway of the bridge at the Calcutta Gate. But the guns never got there; it soon became clear there were no cattle inside the magazine to draw out the guns. Neither, it seemed, were there any artillerymen who could be sent with them. Metcalfe, Willoughby and Forrest then galloped to a nearby bastion on the banks of the river. Forrest would later describe the events to Colonel A. Abbott:

> On Sir Theophilus Metcalfe alighting from his buggy, Lieut. Willoughby & I accompanied him to the small bastion on the river face which commanded a full view of the bridge from which we could distinctly see the Mutineers marching in open column, headed by the Cavalry, and the Delhi side of the bridge was already in the possession of a body of Cavalry. On Sir Theo. Metcalf observing this, he proceeded with Lieut. Willoughby to see if the city gate was closed against the Mutineers. However this step was needless, as the mutineers were admitted directly to the Palace, through which they passed cheering.[8]

In fact, mutineers were now entering the city by another gate as well. The troopers that Douglas had directed south from the palace *jharokha* had followed his advice and moved to the Raj Ghat and the Khairati Gate, which gave access to the city from the south. These gates would normally have been closed at this time. The chronicler Khwaja Hasan Nizami narrated a fanciful story circulated around the city during the weeks following the arrival of the mutineers that a horseman descended from the heavens clad in green (the colour of Islam) and opened the closed gates for the rebels. Another variation of this supposed supernatural intervention was described by the *Delhi Urdu Akhbar* newspaper on 24 May, which reported claims that green-clad warriors had been seen riding into Delhi on female camels that day. Chuni Lal had a more plausible explanation for the ease with which the troopers entered through the gate, and includes details of what happened next:

> The Mahomedans of the Thanbi-Bazaar went to the Rajghat, and having made a solemn compact with the mutineers, opened the gates and allowed them to come in, when they immediately commenced firing the houses and killing the Europeans. Having killed the Europeans who resided in Daryaganj, and set fire to their houses, they murdered Chaman Lal, the native doctor, as he was standing in front of the dispensary. The Mahomedans of the city now told the troopers that Mr Fraser was at the Calcutta Gate. They immediately went thither…

It is unlikely that any order by Douglas or Fraser ordering the permanent closure of the gate could have reached the guard quickly enough to stop this. The troopers poured into the city from the south rather than congregating at the Kotila, and quickly manoeuvred round the palace walls to the main gate of the palace. Here they learned from the palace guard that Fraser and Douglas were at the Calcutta Gate. They immediately set off to confront them.

*****

At the Calcutta Gate, meanwhile, the small European clique realised little could be done. Fraser, Douglas and the others watched as various contingents of troopers entered the city, with more of the Meerut rebels crossing the bridge all the time. The police guard made no attempt to prevent the sepoys entering the Calcutta Gate either; they simply watched. The European group looked on helplessly. Even more conspicuous by its absence was any news of a European force coming from Meerut to deal with the mutineers. A large crowd of roughly 500 curious locals had gathered, most of them standing in a small area called the grape-garden, intending to watch the unfolding events although showing no overt sympathy for the rebels.

Much to his fortune, Metcalfe left the Calcutta Gate at this point; he must have only just avoided the arrival of the rebel troopers who had entered the city from the south. He had decided to return to speak to the local police at the Chandni Chowk *kotwali.* There he found the spell of European authority entirely broken. His earlier orders had been utterly disregarded, and when he gave a direct order the police chief spat on the ground while his men stood smiling. With the situation clear, Metcalfe would soon flee the city on horseback. He was half-heartedly pursued by some rebel troopers who spotted him, but with his sword drawn he managed to make his way through the Chandni Bazaar area and ride out of the Ajmer Gate, his haste saving his life.

The other Europeans at the Calcutta Gate were not so lucky. Plenty bore witness to what happened next, including the chaprassies Makhan, Bakhtawar and Kishen Singh, plus several of Douglas's servants who had accompanied him to the Calcutta Gate. The journalist Chuni Lal had also turned up. He had heard about the orders to close the city gates and had ventured out to sate his curiosity. At the Chandni Chowk, he could see police officers asking shopkeepers to close their businesses. He also saw Fraser trying to gain control of the situation at the Calcutta Gate.

> I went with the crowd in the direction of the Calcutta Gate. and there saw Mr Fraser and four or five other gentlemen. Mr Fraser's personal guard of Jhajjar troopers was with him. Mr Fraser went to the top of the gate accompanied by another gentleman and Sharif-ul-Hak, the chief police officer of the city, and at this moment the police officer of the second class at the Sabzi Mandi. After a while Mr Fraser came down and disposed the force present, by telling the Jhajjar troopers, to fall in and form, and at the same time made the Constabulary Guard form and draw their swords, himself taking a position between them.[9]

The only thing that gave Simon Fraser any confidence was his personal Jhajjar sowar escort, all twenty-two or twenty-three of whom appeared to be loyal at this time. Fraser had also been accompanied by the principal police officers of the city. Still thinking he had authority, and despite the rebels already coming through the gate, Fraser ordered it shut. This may have been the catalyst for what happened next.

Surprisingly, the first act of violence did not come from the troopers or locals at the Calcutta Gate but from the opposite direction. The rebels who had entered the city from the south were now close. Bakhtawar Singh recalled the mood quickly turning as they began to arrive. 'About this time there was a general cry that the troopers had come,' he recalled. Makhan Singh was watching the scene too. 'While he [Fraser] was there engaged, four or five cavalry troopers were seen approaching at full speed with drawn swords from the direction of the palace. One of them approached and fired his pistol at Mr Fraser, who immediately jumped out of his buggy, while Buktawar Singh, chaprassi, took a musket from the police guard at the gate, and handed it to his master. The musket was loaded, and Mr Fraser shot the trooper dead on the spot. This dispersed the man's comrades, who, however, before making off, wounded Mr Hutchinson in the arm.'

Accounts of rebel numbers vary. Chuni Lal said he saw seven troopers and two men mounted on camels riding up at fast pace; Jat Mall described ten to twelve sowars charging the Europeans. Whatever the case, the shots made dispersed the crowd in all directions and spread confusion.

In the charged atmosphere, with more violence on the cards, the Europeans decided to flee. Douglas jumped into the nearby ditch of the palace walls. However, he managed to severely hurt himself in the process. The wounded Hutchinson headed for the ditch as well, but clambered down with great care and managed to avoid further injury. Douglas and Hutchinson made their way along the bottom of the ditch to the palace gate along with Bakhtawar Singh and Kishen Singh. Fraser, meanwhile, showing more presence of mind, got on his buggy and, pushing his way through the assembly, drove to the Lahore Gate. The Commissioner's clerk, Mr Nixon, was not so fortunate; he was killed at the gate. All the while, Frasers's Jhajjar escort had stood idly by. However, when the troopers who had charged Fraser cried out, 'Deen! Deen!', invoking the Islamic faith to encourage the Muslim Jhajjars to join them, the Jhajjars fled rather than joining the sepoys. At the same time, according to Chuni Lal, the troopers reassured locals that they would not be harmed.

Fraser succeeded in reaching the Lahore Gate and was soon joined by the injured Douglas, who was helped by Hutchinson and Douglas's chaprassies. As they stood at the Lahore Gate deciding what to do, they were joined by the Anglican chaplain, Revd Jennings, who also lived in the apartments above the Lahore Gate. Jennings had almost certainly been watching the growing chaos from his apartment and had descended to help the injured captain. Douglas's condition was rapidly worsening, and he needed to rest. The party therefore passed into the palace's entrance arcade with what speed they could manage, Fraser ordering the guards to close the gates behind them – which was done in the most grudging fashion.

The party climbed the stairs to the apartments above the gate and laid Douglas down. The rooms happened to be occupied by two ladies – Miss Jennings, daughter of the reverend, and a Miss Clifford who happened to be a guest of the Jennings. Douglas had by now lost consciousness, and Miss Jennings began applying some oil to his head. Meanwhile, Fraser, conscious that the mutineers might enter the palace, sought help. 'Get from the King two guns with artillery, and place them at the gateway underneath us,' Fraser asked the chaprassies who had accompanied them upstairs, hoping a show of arms at the gate would deter the crowd from entering the palace complex. 'Send two palanquins with bearers immediately that the English ladies here may be taken to the Queen, and placed under her protection,' he added.

This wasn't the end of the matter. Fraser, it must be presumed, saw no need to stay in the apartments while the ladies were tending to Douglas. He duly went back downstairs to help maintain order in the palace entrance, for the guns he had requested would appear shortly. However, even from the apartments above the arcade it must have been obvious that trouble was brewing down below. A large crowd was gathering.

A large mob of locals outside the palace had in fact observed Fraser and the other Europeans fleeing back into the palace and had followed them to the main entrance. Here they found the gate shut as Fraser had ordered.

'Are you all followers of the faith or of these people?' the mob leaders asked the palace guard.

'Of the faith,' replied the guard.

'Then why had you locked the gate?'

Thus challenged, the wavering guards opened the gates. The mob flowed in through the arcade just as Fraser appeared at the base of the stairs.

It later emerged that the crowd had been led for the most part by three men. All three either lived in the palace or worked in the arcade at the entrance, so they were easily recognised. Mogul Beg was an orderly of Mahbub Ali Khan, one of the principal eunuchs of the King, and an occasional orderly for Jawan Bakht. The second ringleader was Wilayutee Mogul, also an orderly of the eunuch. The third man, an Abyssinian Muslim named Hajee Khan, was a regular sight at the arcade, where he earned his living as a gemstone polisher and seal engraver. Others played major roles; Bakhtawar Singh later said he saw another two men, Mohomed Buksh and Najee Khan, take the lead. Jat Mall would name Khalak Dad, a former resident of Kabul and armed retainer of Mahbub Ali Khan, as well as Sheikh Deen Muhammad, an armed orderly in the King's pay. In other words, the leaders of the mob were mostly armed orderlies from the palace. 'The physician Ahsan Ulla Khan had just left when we servants who were sitting there saw some five Mahomedans, King's servants, coming along the covered way calling out "Deen, Deen",' Bhakatawar Singh would recall.

The mood was tense. The mob had seen plumes of smoke spiralling into the sky from the Daryaganj section of the city as sepoys in the south of the city had begun burning European residences there. Meanwhile, mutineers who had entered the palace were already fanning out around the complex loudly shouting, 'Deen! Deen!' This was the situation when Fraser reached the base of the stairs. 'He got a gun and asked a sepoy on guard for a couple of cartouches but these were refused,'[10] recalled

Kishen Singh. With no ammunition to hand, Fraser asked for Kishen Singh's sword. He also asked Kishen Singh to order the guards to close the gate to the palace again. However, Fraser's authority had vanished. None of the guards moved to help or tame the mob.

There are varying accounts as to what happened next. Jat Mall described Fraser attempting to retreat back up the stairs.

> Mr Fraser had just come under the centre opening of the covered way, when by this time a great crowd of men and boys of all ages having collected, began clapping their hands as a kind of insolent bravado at what was occurring. Mr Fraser, seeing such marked feelings of hostility, began to return to Captain Douglas' quarters and as he reached the foot of the stairs, a Haji lapidary raised his sword to make a cut at him. Mr Fraser, who had a sheathed sword in his hand, turned sharply round, and thrust at him, with the sword in its sheath, saying to the havildar of the gate guards, 'What kind of behaviour is this?' Upon which the havildar made a show of driving off the crowd; but no sooner was Mr Fraser's back turned, than the havildar nodded with his head to the lapidary, to signify to him that now he should renew his attack. The lapidary, thus encouraged, rushed upon Mr Fraser, and inflicted a deep and mortal wound on the right side of his neck. Mr Fraser at once fell, when three other men of the names of Khalak Dad, a Cabuli Pathan, Moghal Beg or Moghal Jan and Shekh Din Muhammad who had been concealed in an out-house adjoining, rushed out and cut him with their swords over the head, face and chest till he was quite dead. Sheikh Din Muhammad was an armed orderly in the king's pay, and Khalak Dad and Moghal Beg were also armed retainers of Mahbub Ali Khan, the king's prime minister.

Maharaj Singh was watching the scene from a veranda above the arcade and told a similar story.

> [I] saw Mr Fraser standing at the bottom of the stairs with a wound in his left side. His sword was broken. I saw the Prisoner [Mogul Beg], and a Wilayutee Moghul, whose name I do not know, and Hajee, a seal engraver, with drawn swords, followed by a rabble armed with swords and sticks, rush upon Mr Fraser, and I saw the Prisoner Moghul Beg inflict a sword wound on him, so that he fell against the wall. I then entered the room and told Mr Jennings what I had seen. Mr Jennings went into the pantry and looked out of a window whence he could see Mr Fraser. He ran in, spoke to the others, who got alarmed and tried to hide themselves.[11]

It was at this time that Ahsan Ulla Khan and Ghulam Abbas, one of Douglas's servants, appeared at the arcade with palanquins and guns. Ghulam Abbas had been sent to the King to request help on Fraser's behalf and Zafar had complied, sending the guns and as many of the palace guard and the troops as he could muster in the fort. They and the palanquin bearers had reached the shops only in time to see Fraser being killed. His body was now sprawled at the bottom of the stairs, and they could only watch as the crowd surged over Fraser's corpse and up the stairs to finish off the other Europeans in the apartments above.

Reaching the second floor, the mob was temporarily frustrated. Makhan Singh, on seeing Fraser's murder, had quickly retreated further up the flight of stairs and locked the door at the first floor to prevent the crowd advancing to the apartments. However, some of the crowd simply flooded toward the other set of stairs at the southern end and made their way to the top floor of the arcade without further issue. Having used the alternative flight of stairs, some of them now descended the northern stairs to let the rest of the crowd in. They then made for the apartments directly above the Lahore Gate. Hutchinson and the rest of the party, thinking they would be safe in the apartments, had neglected to lock the doors to their rooms. There was nothing to stop them coming in.

With Fraser dead, the remaining Europeans in the apartments were the wounded Hutchinson, the unconscious Douglas, Revd Jennings, his daughter and Miss Clifford, plus another man who was never identified. Maharaj Singh, who was tending to Douglas with various other chaprassies, saw the crowd making their way towards the apartments and entering the dining room. The ringleaders showed their anger at Douglas's servants for standing by him:

> Moosahib Khan was standing between the door and Captain Douglas, and he got two slight sword wounds from one of the ringleaders, and I also received a back handed blow from the tilt of the Prisoner's sword, and the scar of the wound then inflicted is still visible on my forehead. We chuprassees and jemadar [Pooran Singh] went to the verandah of the room, and I saw the Prisoner [Mogul Beg] wound Captain Douglas with his sword, and other of the rabble also cut at him. I did not see any of the others killed for they had concealed themselves.[12]

Maharaj Singh and the other servants, fearing for their lives, slipped away. As they escaped, Maharaj Singh heard the sounds of the ringleaders cutting down the other Europeans; concealment in the small apartments was impossible.

Only one man seems to have stayed to watch. This was a thirty-two-year-old gold-twist maker named Boolun. He was working as a chaprassi for the King as events unfolded, and was one of those who had been tasked with delivering the palanquins that Fraser had requested. Boolun had followed the mob upstairs to watch proceedings:

> On reaching the stair-case I saw Mr Simon Fraser's corpse lying at the foot of the stairs, and going up I found Captain Douglas leaning

> against the wall. From the opposite side of the room, I saw Nubboo, two sowars of Mr Fraser, and another man rush up and despatch Captain Douglas with their swords. In an outer room, not that in which I saw Captain Douglas, I saw the Prisoner (Moghul Beg) and Khalikdad Khan and Hajee Khan standing over two murdered ladies with their drawn swords. They asked me who there now was to send to the King. I then left.[13]

According to Makhan Singh, however, Douglas had not yet succumbed to his wounds:

> On this I ran down the staircase. As I got to the bottom, I was laid hold of by one Mamdoh, a bearer in the service of the King, who said, 'Tell me where Captain Douglas is, you have concealed him.' He forced me upstairs with him. I said, 'You have yourselves killed all the gentlemen already'; but on reaching the room where Captain Douglas was, I saw that he was not quite dead. Mamdoh perceiving this also, hit him with a bludgeon on the forehead and killed him immediately. I saw the other bodies including those of the two ladies. Mr Hutchinson was lying in one room, and the bodies of Captain Douglas, Mr Jennings and the two young ladies in another, on the floor, with the exception of that of Captain Douglas which was on a bed.[14]

The only survivor of the attack on the apartments seems to have been the unknown European. However, he did not last much longer. 'The stranger who had arrived that morning from Calcutta contrived to get out on the ramparts of the palace wall,' recalled Jat Mall, 'and had gone unobserved as far as Mirza Kochak's house near the Delhi Gate of the palace, when he was fired at by somebody, and wounded in the shoulder. On this he retraced his steps, and was eventually cut down at the foot of the southern staircase leading to Captain Douglas' apartments.'[15]

Between the crowds arriving at the Lahore Gate and the last European being despatched on the wall, just fifteen minutes had passed. The plundering of the apartments soon commenced. According to Kishen Singh, this plunder seemed to be reasonably well organised: 'I saw the Prisoner [Mogul Beg] directing the people who were bringing down Captain Douglas property where to put it. Allahee Buksh, elephant driver, told the Prisoner [Mogul Beg] that some of the things he had got were his.'[16]

There seemed to be considerable excitement at the killings and the loot obtained, with the ringleaders proceeding down to the arcade shouting, 'Deen! Deen! We have done it!' and boasting to the crowd downstairs of having killed the Europeans. Mogul Beg was later observed brandishing the bloody sword and walking around the palace grounds narrating the story of the killings to various palace servants. Amir Alli, a twenty-three-year-old shawl embroiderer who worked in the palace as a guard at the King's sleeping apartments, witnessed the jubilant scenes: 'Arriving there I met Nubboo, alias Deen Mohomed, the Prisoner, Hajee Khan, and Wulatee with naked swords bloody. They were boasting, one that he had killed the ladies, one that he had killed the clergyman, and so on. They drank water and went towards the King's quarters.'[17] Mogul Beg had taken as a prize the pistol worn by Captain Douglas, and busied himself showing it off around the palace.

The ringleaders of the mob, as it turned out, would have varying luck escaping British retribution after the mutiny. Mogul Beg would be arrested in 1860, 150 miles away in Jaipur. He had fled the city and managed to take service in the employ of a Capt. Gholam Ali in the armed force of the Raja of Jaipur. He was found guilty on 1 February 1862, with the recommendation he be hanged in the open space between the palace and the Chandni Chowk – in front of the Lahore Gate. The Abyssinian Hajee was arrested some years after the event and brought to trial. Meanwhile, the apartments were never cleaned; traces of blood could still be found in the rooms when the siege was over.

With the deaths of the Fraser and Douglas, and the flight of Sir Theophilus Metcalfe, all recognisable sources of civil authority in the city had vanished. The only European of any authority who could bring order and calm was Brigadier Graves, commanding officer at the Delhi cantonment 2 miles north of the walled city.

12

# 'We are not seeking loot but life'

There are three things of such a sort,
that they produce merciless destruction
when they get the upper hand.
One is a flood of water,
another is a raging fire
and the third is the lesser people,
the common multitude;
for they will not be stopped
by either reason or discipline.
John Gower, *Mirour de l'Omme*, 1378

Although the bulk of the British officers in Delhi were stationed at the cantonments outside the city, on the morning of 11 May there was a small British military presence inside the city: a contingent of British officers held the magazine close to the palace, and the Kashmir Gate was in British hands. These positions, in the north-east of the walled city, were separated from each other by half a mile. The rest of the walled city slipped wholly into the hands of the mutineers and the various mobs roaming the streets. European civilians found themselves entirely at the mercy of the mobs. News of the murders in the palace had rippled through the city. Mutineers confidently rode around the city picking off Europeans and burning their homes. All British authority had vanished. With the sepoys on their side, locals felt free to do as they pleased. The common man's frustration at fifty years of European mastery found an avenue for release. Many of the city plebeians quickly lost their inhibitions and took full advantage. The mobs delighted in the unprecedented satisfaction of seeing Europeans driven off, humbled in some manner or even dragged out and butchered in the streets. Predictably, Indian Christians were also seen as fair game.

The common people were joined by a rougher contingent. Not all the Meerut sepoys had crossed the river by the bridge of boats; many crossed a little further downstream, the river being at a low level at this time of the year. Some then made their way to the prison just outside the city walls and released hundreds of resident criminals. Many from this assorted group of miscreants, being opportunistic by nature, headed into the city. Another group of the same mind were the local gangsters. These men had apparently begun to ally themselves with the more unruly elements of the sepoy regiments. The criminal elements along with the locals and armed sepoys made up a powerful mixture; even had the local authorities been up to the task, they would have struggled to stop the marauding mobs. Everywhere the sound of 'Deen, Deen' was heard, while elsewhere in the city the sepoys, sundry people and mobs could be heard loudly declaring, 'Mulluk Badsha, hukkum Sepai! (The country is the King's, by the will of the sepoys)'[1] as they went about their business.

Prominent European buildings and institutions in the city were obvious targets. The telegraph office on Lothian Road, close to St James' Church, was not spared. The office was manned by telegraph master Mr Todd and his assistants William Brendish and I. W. Pilkington. Todd had left the office very early on the 11th as he had discovered that the line to Meerut was down and wanted to investigate. His assistants continued manning the post, confident the authorities in the city could handle the situation. Neither assistant had much to do till around 2 p.m. However, things began to develop rapidly thereafter. The first message was sent at 3 p.m.:

> We must leave office. All the bungalows are burnt down by the sepoys from Meerut. They came in this morning. We are off: don't roll today. Mr C. Todd is dead, I think. He went out this morning, and has not yet returned. We heard that nine Europeans are killed. Good-bye.[2]

They were right – Todd had been killed. However, their message failed to convey the critical nature of the situation. A second message, sent later, showed much more urgency; this time the sender was Brigadier Graves.

> Cantonments in a state of siege. Mutineers from Mirath [Meerut] – 3rd Light Cavalry – numbers not known – said to be a hundred and fifty men cut off communication with Mirath. Taken possession of the Bridge of Boats. 54th Native Infantry sent against them, but would not act. Several officers killed and wounded. City in a state of considerable excitement. Troops sent down, but nothing certain yet. Further information will be forwarded.

Out at the cantonment, Brigadier Graves had sent word into the city urging all Europeans to make for the ridge and the safety of the Flagstaff Tower. After sending their telegram, Brendish and Pilkington followed this advice and fled. A well-known but false story has it that Brendish was cut down while signalling the final message; in fact, he survived and retired on a special pension that equated to full pay in acknowledgement of his services during the rebellion. The messages sent by Brendish and Pilkington, regardless of their degree of urgency, were sufficient to raise the alarm at Lahore, Rawalpindi and Peshawar, along with a few other cantonments in the north of India.

Other British establishments were attacked. The treasury was an attractive target. The dak bungalow (post office) was ransacked, too, as were neighbouring residences, and two Europeans were killed in the vicinity. The bank on the Chandni Chowk was attacked around noon. Mr Beresford, the manager, managed to escape with his wife and daughters to one of the outbuildings and up to the roof of an adjacent building. They had managed to arm themselves in the short time they had; Mr Beresford took hold of a sword while his wife handled a spear. Since Beresford guarded the top of the stairs, none of the rabble decided to hazard that approach; instead they climbed the building's rear walls. Beresford and his wife managed to kill or wound several of the attackers, but finally they were overpowered. The Beresfords died, and the bank was overrun.

Zahir Dehlvi was witness to the attack on the bank, which ended with the building going up in flames. 'The rebels looted as much as they could carry away. Each shoemaker took approximately three bags of cash. The residents of the Kaghazi Mohalla, who had been economically backward, were now flush with money. There is a famous saying: "Maal-muft, dil-e-Brahma (freely got, lavishly spent)." How much can anyone loot? There were 14 lakh in the bank, but who would leave money behind? Within an hour, the thieves had looted everything. They even took away the strongboxes. This pandemonium lasted for two hours.'

At around the same time as the bank was attacked, the troops that had entered by the Calcutta Gate came upon Delhi College. Principal G. F. Taylor and assistant teachers Mr Stewart and Mr Roberts were cut down, and sepoys looted and destroyed the college library. English books were torn up and burned; witnesses later spoke of torn pages littering the college gardens. Books in Arabic, Persian or Urdu were kept and sold for money.

The *Delhi Gazette* press buildings went the same way as the bank. Compositors at the press had been busy producing 'extras' focussed on the breaking news about the mutiny at Meerut when, around midday, the building was overwhelmed by rioters. Some of the staff managed to escape; some didn't.

St James' Church came in for special attention. The looters took the time to ring the bells, mocking the Europeans, before detaching them from their fixtures and allowing them to plummet to the church floor. Anything of value, including the church plate, disappeared. The building was then vandalised, with large sections of the internal wall pulled down.

Most of those targeted realised that showing a clean pair of heels was the wisest option. Some managed to gain the ridge as Graves had instructed, heading north to Meerut and elsewhere from there. However, would-be escapees weren't always so lucky. Many were assaulted and humiliated by having their clothes torn off. Outside of the city, villagers who baulked at murder would heap insults on the refugees as they trudged past: 'Where are your servants, your iced water, your fans and *punkahwallas*?' Others, however, treated the dispossessed with kindness; many refugees were sheltered by villagers to await a relieving British force. Even in the city, some sympathetic locals hid victims – although several were sniffed out.

Plenty of the locals were sympathetic to the sepoys, of course. 'They [the sepoys] were shouting "Deen, Deen". When these shouts were heard by the residents, crowds of Muslims gathered around them and started bringing sweet drinks for the soldiers to drink,' wrote Zaka Ullah, who witnessed some harrowing scenes as the sepoys worked their way through the city casually dispatching Europeans. Others were shepherded towards the palace, as Zaka Ullah also described:

> I witnessed, a Memsahib, a British lady surrounded by the rebel Indian soldiers. She had a baby in her arms and was trying to cover it with a towel. She also had a toddler with her. On the way the soldiers were showing them their swords and making gestures to indicate that they wanted to cut off their heads. The young boy kept clinging to his mother in fear and this continued until they reached the Red Fort.

Europeans were dragged out of their homes and killed in the streets. One woman who managed to lay hands on her husband's pistol was seen shooting two sepoys before being bayonetted in the back. Once all residents in a particular house had been killed, the residences were invariably plundered and gutted.

Mr Wagentreiber, sub-editor of the *Delhi Gazette*, and one of those trapped in the city with his family, described their modus operandi:

> Private houses were entered by troopers (their horses being held at the gates of the gardens), who said that they did not come for loot but life, and when they were disappointed in their greed for European life they let in the *budmashes* [hoodlums] of the city, who, in the space of half an hour, cleared out the best-regulated houses from punkah to floor cloth. They then either set fire to the house, or, if it were not of an inflammable nature, they pulled out the doors and window-frames, &c., in some cases the beams from the roofs.[3]

Meanwhile, near the Kashmir Gate, many of the *chamar* (low-caste) women combed through the houses for fugitive Europeans. In the process, they took whatever they wanted. At some places, would-be victims made a stand. One example was at a bungalow owned by a Mr Aldwell. The Aldwell house was situated on the riverbank side of the Daryaganj district, with the upper stories overlooking the walls. The family knew sooner than most what was to come; between eight and nine in the morning, a *syce* (horse groom) had urged them to flee, warning that the sepoys from Meerut were murdering Europeans on their way into the city. The Aldwells, like many in the area, assumed order would quickly be restored; far better, they thought, to stay put and safeguard their house and property from looting. Their neighbour, a Mr Nowlan, was of the same opinion. Between them it was decided that the Aldwell residence, being the stronger and more defensible of the two houses, was the place to make a stand.

Other nearby European families were invited to the Aldwell house with instructions to bring their weapons. A motley bunch of fugitives trickled in, including Baptist missionary Revd Mackay, Conductor Nolan, Subconductor Settle, Sergeant Connors and various women and children. Mr Aldwell and Mr Nowlan also hit upon the idea of asking the guards at the nearby hospital for help. 'This guard was composed of native infantry sepoys,' recalled Mrs Aldwell, 'and Mr Nowlan and Mr Aldwell asked them whether they would assist in defending us, adding that the Europeans would, in return, render them all assistance that might be in their power. "Go and mind your business, and we will mind ours," was the reply given by these sepoys. At this time, shortly after eight o' clock, the Meerut sepoys had not even crossed the bridge, and could not therefore have communicated with this guard.' Realising they would get no help, the two men returned and commenced barricading the property, pushing all the furniture against the doors and windows. Large stones and boulders were placed behind the gate of the house outside to further reinforce the grounds of the residence. All six men present then went to the second floor with their guns in order to deter any sepoys or looters from venturing near.

Various other people arrived looking for sanctuary at the Aldwell house over the next few hours; eventually the house held about thirty fugitives. From the roof, they could see some of the troopers of the 3rd Light Cavalry making their way into the city. The sowars eventually rode directly past the house, and some of the troopers fired shots at the Europeans, but they showed no interest in breaking into the place. Sensing the shift in the city's balance of power, the majority of the servants of the house turned against their masters and departed the house, taking care to break the water urns in the residence as they did so.

At around ten in the morning, as houses near them were put to the torch, those holed up in the Aldwell house realised that an attack was soon to take place. One of the ringleaders of the mob, who had presumably killed others already, made his intentions clear to Mrs Aldwell:

> About this time, one of the city people, a Mahomedan, and a dyer by trade, rushed into our grounds with a drawn sword in his hand, reeking with blood, repeating the *kalima* [Muslim declaration of faith, i.e. 'There is no God but Allah, and Muhammad is the messenger of Allah'] and calling out to know where the Europeans were. Mr Nowlan asked him who and what he was, and on his not replying shot him dead. This man was the only one who had entered the grounds, but then 50 or 60 of his followers, city people, collected at our gate.[4]

The dyer's allies, perhaps unarmed, made no attempt at revenge. All around the house, though, rioting and turmoil prevailed. Soon after, around eleven in the morning, one Mrs Foulon reached the safety of the house; she had been wounded in the head by a mob, but was brought through the crowds and into the house by a sympathetic local.

There was respite around midday, with the rabble outside seemingly distracted by the burning and looting of the nearby hospital. However, it soon became apparent that the mob was organising itself and that guns were being brought up to blast through the gates of the Aldwell property. At last, around midnight, armed sepoys appeared. Mrs Aldwell suggested to her husband at this point that she should escape with their three children in the two doolies left in the house. The plan was to discard their European clothes and dress in the servants' clothes; disguised in this fashion, they would be transported to sanctuary by the few servants that remained. They would head to the residence of Mirza Abdulla, a prince and grandson of the King, where she felt sure they would receive protection. The plan was a success to begin with; they reached the house, and Mirza Abdulla offered them sanctuary. However, he soon turned against them and asked them to leave his property. Mrs Aldwell and the children then asked to be transported to the palace to join other Europeans who had been captured in the city:

> On reaching the Lahore Gate of the palace, we were made prisoners by some of the King's police stationed there as a guard. These men took us to Mirza Moghal, who ordered us to be confined with the rest of the European prisoners then in confinement. We were accordingly taken there on Wednesday night, 13 May. As far as I can guess, I should say, men, women, and children included, there were from 46 to 50 persons imprisoned.

The rest of the party was still holed up at the Aldwell residence. Night passed without event. In the morning, however, the residence received more attention as the sepoys brought up more infantrymen and attacked the gates. By 4 a.m. on the morning of the 13th, with ammunition, food and water running out and Conductor Settle killed in the last attack on the gates, the remaining members of the party decided that breakout was the only option. The plan was to make it to the nearby riverbank, where a strip of jungle afforded some protection, and then flee northwards along the bank. In the end, the only two to make it out alive were Mr Aldwell and his son; the rest were killed in the attempt to escape. Their bodies were dumped in the ditch flanking the city wall.

Another four Europeans were discovered hiding in the residence of a wealthy merchant named Muhammad Ibrahim. They were killed and the house was given over to plunder in retribution. One European woman, attempting to flee the city disguised in native clothes, was apprehended near the Ellenborough tank close to the palace and killed by the sepoys. Jat Mall, Chuni Lal and others in the city report hearing of a large massacre. Several European clerks had managed to take shelter in a large property belonging to Rajah Kalyan Singh, of Kishangarh, and brought their wives with them.[5] The sepoys, hearing of this holdout, approached the house but were driven off by the armed defenders. They returned with two guns, at which point the clerks withdrew to an underground chamber. There were twenty-nine men, women and children crammed inside. 'On their ammunition failing they were brought out from an underground apartment and killed by some of the Mahomedan inhabitants in concert with some of the mutinous troopers,' Chuni Lal wrote. Others killed in the city included Dr Dopping of the 54th NI, assistant magistrate Mr Galloway, Revd Hubbard and the missionary Mr Sandys.

One unnamed man had a more than fortunate escape. He had been cut down by sepoys and left for dead on a bridge. After a while, he regained consciousness. With much effort, he dragged himself to the water's edge where he heard a familiar voice – it was a servant of his who had witnessed the attack. This servant helped him to flee the city despite the danger to himself. He was not alone in receiving the help of kindly locals. Sessions Judge Smith, on hearing of the tumult and firing in the city, dismissed the court and mounted his horse to ride for the city. He was met by an old tailor who knew him. 'Sahib, why are you going towards your death?' the tailor asked. He took hold of the horse's reins and turned it around, and convinced Judge Smith to stay away.

*****

Mr Le Bas, the judge, was one of the first civilians to reach the Flagstaff Tower. He had been at Metcalfe House when he decided to visit the Kashmir Gate to investigate the chaos. The crowds had been too thick, however, so Le Bas headed to the kutchery in the Water Bastion and then returned along the riverbank to Metcalfe House before making his way up to the Flagstaff Tower.

The Wagentreibers were early arrivals at the Flagstaff Tower. While still at their residence they got word that troopers of the 3rd Light Cavalry were causing trouble, although they heard conflicting reports about rebel numbers, ranging anywhere from fifteen to over two hundred. Alert to the possibility of danger, Mrs Wagentreiber sent some servants to warn her husband at his workplace, the offices of the *Delhi Gazette* near St James' Church. Perhaps wary that her husband might not heed a simple warning, Mrs Wagentreiber had instructed the bearer to tell him, 'The Mem Sahib is very ill, and desires his immediate return.' Mr Wagentreiber at this time had only got as far as the Kashmir Gate. Finding it closed, he had remonstrated with the guards. Fortunately for him, the delay allowed the bearer to catch up with him at the gate and give him the message. On his return, Mr Wagentreiber offered help to a Dr Balfour resident nearby. The Wagentreiber residence had a tiled roof, unlike the doctor's residence, meaning it was less likely to burn quickly. The doctor declined the help, however, saying that any show of panic would only increase the danger.

As the morning progressed, news emerged from the city that Europeans were being massacred. There were rumours that the Commissioner himself had been butchered by a mob. Shots could be heard, and plumes of smoke could be seen rising from the city. The Wagentreibers now decided that flight was the wisest option. The family made for the cantonments, with the husband bringing along his weapons and ammunition. They used the road to the ridge instead of the direct route to the cantonment, thus avoiding many bands of armed sepoys – but not all. Those they did pass were not violent but had shorn themselves of all deference to Europeans. On being challenged by the Wagentreibers and asked where their officers were, they casually replied, 'Go, and find them.' Others jeered and mocked the family. Meanwhile, beggars in the area were unleashing their frustrations, throwing stones at the carriage and asking the family to salaam them.

The Wagentreibers' plan had been to head to the brigadier's house once they reached the cantonments, but when they got there the brigadier was nowhere to be seen and the servants either could not or would not say where he was. They then decided to return to their house, and before entering met a neighbour, Mr Murphy, who urged them to come to his residence. Here the family joined a party of other anxious Europeans, which with their arrival numbered around twenty. Many of them were armed.

As the clock passed noon, Mr Murphy's servants began slipping away or disregarding orders. An hour or two later, a large crowd of locals and sepoys emerged from the city's Mori Gate and headed towards the Civil Lines. Barricading the house and making a defence against the hordes was impossible. The entire group – bar one who thought getting to Meerut was a better bet – made a rapid exit, fleeing to the Flagstaff Tower before the mob reached the house. The bulk of the group made it, although one of the men, a civil servant named Mr McWhirter who was already suffering from a fever, expired on the way in the tremendous heat. At the tower they discovered a fair number of other Europeans had already made it. These included Dr Balfour, the civil surgeon. With him was his sister-in-law, Miss Smith. Merchant Mr Marshall was present, as was Lieutenant Thomason of the settlement survey.

One Mrs Leeson, an Anglo-Indian Christian, also found good fortune if her recollection is to be believed. She had managed to join up with around thirty other men, women and children in a large house near St James' Church adjacent to the city walls. The house had a *tykhana*, an underground apartment used for respite from the hot weather. The *tykhana* had a passage and door adjoining the city wall itself. The party stayed hidden in the *tykhana* for the whole of 10 and 11 May. A longer stay proved impossible owing to the children in the party, who risked the group's discovery when they began wailing in hunger, so the decision was made to attempt an escape. On the morning of the 12th, the party used the passage to exit the city near the Water Bastion, moving north between the city walls and the river towards the ridge. However, at a nearby gate they were caught by two sepoys. By this time the rebel sepoys had orders to round up all Europeans and bring them to the palace, so the group were ordered to follow the two sepoys back to the city.

Some of Mrs Leeson's story grew a little contrived at this point, at least to the Wagentreibers, to whom she later narrated it. As the party was being escorted back into the city through some scrubland, the sepoys seemed to change their mind about the prisoners. They shot a woman in a precursor to a general massacre. Her two daughters attempted to hide in the bushes, crying, 'Oh, they have shot mamma!' but the sepoys shot them as well. Then the sepoys turned their guns on the rest of the party, disposing of them one by one. Apparently nobody in the sizable party attempted to flee or overpower the two sepoys when they opened fire on the first woman; all simply awaited their deaths with quiet resignation, according to Mrs Leeson. In time she too was shot; the sepoys fired at the baby she held, which was killed, but she herself was only wounded. Her other two children, she said, must have been killed as well.

Mrs Leeson says she was rescued by a young man, an Afghan who was training to be a *moulvi*. 'It is right to kill the men but not right to kill the women and children,' the man had said on finding her alive. He gave her a drink of water and some bread, and in the evening had her transported to his master's house in a bedstead where she was promised sanctuary. In this way, Mrs Leeson managed to survive almost the whole siege, albeit spending a large time recuperating from fever and having her wounds bandaged in rough fashion. According to the Wagentreiber retelling, despite kind treatment Mrs Leeson was despondent about her ultimate chances:

> She felt she was an alien and in their power, that at any moment in spite of their tolerance of her, that the hatred to her race was too deeply grafted to be completely veiled, and she could see they were only waiting the course of events. Should the English be victorious they might restore her to her own people. If they failed it would mean death, or worse, and so in the midst of sorrow and suffering and uncertainty, with little to hope for, and less to live for, the days sped on apace. They almost persuaded her to accept their faith, and repeat the *kulma* (creed) urging that should there be no rescue she would have to remain with them and become a Mussalman, but for all her weakness and misery she said she would rather die in her own faith.[6]

When a British force eventually arrived outside the city, Mrs Leeson asked the moulvi to have her transported to the British camp where he would be well rewarded for his charity. The moulvi seemed to agree, and so contact was established. Capt. Hodson at the British camp received a letter on 8 August, three months after Mrs Leeson had taken to hiding. 'She is still concealed in the Affghan's house,' he wrote. 'I heard that there was a woman there and managed to effect a communication with her through one of the Guides and to send her money &c and so I think the poor creature may be preserved till we enter Delhi if we fail in getting her free before. I fear she is the only European or rather the only Christian (for she herself is hardly European) left alive from the massacre. Her husband was the son of Major Leeson and a clerk in a Government office in Delhi.'[7]

Sometime after this, Mrs Leeson was dressed in Afghan clothing – presumably a burka, which would have disguised her completely – and driven out of the city on the moulvi's oxcart. Women in burkas were rarely checked by the sepoys, and the story given was that the moulvi was transporting his Afghan lady to another place. The moulvi went through the Sabzi Mandi and managed to reach the ridge area, where some grass cutters working for the British were alerted and passed the news to Major Chalmers. However, Mrs Leeson's ordeal wasn't quite over. Chalmers took her to Brigadier General Nicholson, who refused to believe the words of a dark-skinned half-caste woman. 'He would not believe that a Christian woman could live so many months in Delhi,' wrote Florence Wagentreiber, 'and told her, much to her indignation, that she was a spy! but he nevertheless put her in the charge of the only European lady in camp (Mrs Tytler). There she remained for a few days and was then sent off to Meerut, where she was ultimately joined by her husband who was at Agra during the outbreak.'[8]

Some Europeans protected by locals were being discovered by mutineers even twelve weeks after the outbreak. On 19 August, the Anglo-Indian wife of a European sergeant appeared at the Sabzi Mandi having escaped the city. Her children had been killed – one before her eyes – and she had been wounded. Her name was Mrs Collins. Protected by a local, she too was guided to the safety of the ridge and the care of Mrs Tytler.

The party of Anglo-Indian missionary Revd David Thompson, comprising his wife, four daughters and two sons, had no such luck; all were murdered. The only survivor of the family was a fifth daughter who happened to be in Meerut at the time of the mutiny. She had managed to send a telegram to Delhi warning her father just before the line was cut, but it was not delivered until early Monday – too late.

John Everett, an Anglo-Indian and a risaldar of the 14th Regiment of Irregular Cavalry, managed a lucky escape. He had been convalescing in his house in the city on sick leave when he saw the sepoys arrive in the city and set about their grisly business. Realising he was in danger, Everett laid low until nightfall. Under cover of darkness, he crept into the palatial Skinner residence, where he spent an anxious night in hiding. Early the next day, he sought shelter at Mirza Azim Beg's house, knowing the man was a pensioner of the 1st Irregular Cavalry. Mirza Azim Beg agreed to have him in the house, but after two days the neighbours voiced their suspicion that Christians were sheltering next door. Keeping Everett company was George Skinner, another half-caste Christian who had come seeking sanctuary.

Mirza Azim Beg probably realised it wouldn't be long before his property was searched, and he decided to travel to the palace and ask the King's protection for the men. It is likely he asked Ahsan Ulla Khan, who happened to be his relative. Ahsan Ulla Khan, however, rebuked Beg for sheltering the men and endangering his own life. Perhaps frightened by this, Beg asked the two men to leave. Everett then attempted to take shelter in an old mosque but was recognised by some sepoys. Taken prisoner, Everett – along with George Skinner, who had been arrested at Beg's house – was driven towards to the *kotwali:*

> Both of us were being taken to the *kotwali*; but before we had reached it, about 11 troopers from the 3rd Light Cavalry came galloping up and asked the sepoys, 'Who are you taking prisoners? Are they Christians?' They replied 'Yes' when some of the troopers drew their pistols, and said 'Why take them to the *kotwali* at all; why not kill them here?' The others replied, 'The *kotwali* is not far off, let them go there, and you can then do as you like.'[9]

The cavalrymen had themselves been bringing two European children to the *kotwali*; presumably their parents had been killed. Once they arrived, one sepoy grabbed George Skinner, put him against a wall and shot him.

> I stood before the *kotwali* thinking they would come and take me; but the troopers, after killing Mr Skinner, galloped off to the fort. I was then ordered by the havildar at the Kotwali, to go and sit among

the prisoners; and there I remained for 25 days with 40 others, men, women, and children, all Christians; after which we were released in consequence of a moulavy, by the name of Muhammad Isma'il, giving evidence that we were all Mahomedans, and that if there were any Christians they would become Mahomedans, and that it was not lawful to kill such as turn to Mahomedanism of their own accord. We were not, however, allowed to leave the city. I then went to live with an African of the name of Moujud.'[10]

Moujud was a former employee of Colonel Skinner who had worked for the King since 1842. He had actually warned Everett about an uprising a few days earlier, urging him to find employ with the King, but the Englishman had dismissed the notion.

The famous Christian professor Ramchandra was another of the lucky ones. He managed to escape to the nearby village of Matola before travelling to Roorkee. His enemies searched in particular for him according to another survivor, Rai Piyare Lal Sahib. At around 10 a.m., Sahib had seen Zaka Ullah, one of his former students, racing towards Delhi College ostensibly to save Ramchandra in spite of the danger afoot. It soon became apparent that Ramchandra had heeded an earlier warning by a well-wisher and was hidden somewhere in the city. One of his own students was able to help him out of the city when things calmed down.

Others mistaken for Christian converts were also attacked. Seth Badri Chand, deputy inspector of Delhi schools, was attacked having made the mistake of wearing European clothes on that fateful day. The Kashmiri Pandit Mohan Lal was attacked on the 12th; he had in fact converted to Islam and was now called Aga Hasan Jan, but he too had taken to wearing European clothes. The sepoys were about to dispose of him, thinking he was a convert, when his acquaintance Nizam Uddin Chisti Nizami fortuitously passed by and informed the sepoys that the man was a Muslim.

By the evening of 11 May, perhaps seven or eight from the targeted groups had been seized and brought to the palace. This number would climb beyond fifty in the following days. The sepoys in the palace urged Zafar to let them execute the prisoners, but the King refused, insisting they be handed over to him. The sepoys agreed to this although with the condition that the guards guarding the prisoners would be from their own ranks. They may have feared that the King would help the prisoners escape.

*****

Amid the chaos, looting became commonplace. Not only European residences but local businesses and properties came under attack. Fearful traders had closed their shops when the mutineers arrived, but it had little effect. The large markets of the city, and the shops in the areas of

Khari Bavli, Chandni Chowk, Dariba and Chawri were ransacked in broad daylight. Three of the more prominent businessmen in the city – Vali Mohammed, Hussain Baksh and Qutubuddin – all had their shops looted with impunity in broad daylight.

Wealthy merchants now had their houses plundered. Journalist Chuni Lal records the sepoys attempting to loot the house of Saligram, the palace treasurer. Initially they were thwarted by the formidable gates and walls protecting the property, but they showed patience. Not until midnight did they succeed in creating a hole large enough to get in and carry away their ill-gotten gains.

The criminal element was quick to take advantage. One of the most feared men in the city was a gangster called Ghami Khan. This man had ingratiated himself with the sepoys and their officers, and he used these new connections to have people tortured or even killed to obtain valuable items. Various shops were looted at his urging. Dehlvi, travelling to the palace, saw various bands looting the city with the gangster:

> [I] rode off in the direction of the Qila [fort]. My horse had just moved a few steps ahead when I saw the rogue, Gami Nahrwala, the local bodybuilder, dressed in a kurta and his trademark loincloth, and with a cap on his head, holding a stick and leading a group of fifty profligates in similar loincloths and with cudgels in their hands, going in the same direction. On reaching Ashraf Beg's apartment, he hit his stick on the lantern hanging there, and when it shattered he said, 'I have killed one more infidel.' Saying this, the group started breaking the lock of a draper's shop. I just urged my horse forward and left...
>
> ... I went via the Kotwali to the Khooni Darwaza and saw that there was a huge crowd of scoundrels looting the shops of bankers and moneylenders. Amir Khan was hesitant to go with me. When I reached the walls of the Qila, I saw some fifty sawars near the moat, and pages of English books flying in the air. There was a strong wind blowing and the pages were drifting towards the Qila door. A little way away from the Qila Darwaza, there was a completely nude, drunken man, holding an old English shoe. Pages of the books were flying towards him, and he was hitting at them with the shoe and abusing them in anger.[11]

Ghami Khan was not content with mere plunder; he will resurface later in the story of the siege.

Some residents were able to ward off the roving bands of looters. One eyewitness later related how to sepoys attempted to enter Nagar-Seth Street. The residents had managed to close the gates to the street, and had armed themselves with brickbats and other missiles. They pelted the sepoys, driving them off.

As night fell, a great uneasiness settled over the walled city. Pillaging continued. Numerous bright fires turned night into an unnatural day.

## 13

# The Magazine

A puff or white smoke, followed by a magnificent coronal of red dust, rose above the walls, and told us that the magazine had exploded![1]

Eyewitness at the Delhi ridge

Less than a third of a mile from the northern walls of the palace and a stone's throw from the Calcutta Gate lay the huge British magazine in Delhi. This was a prominent landmark, lying as it did on the wide Lothian Road linking the palace and the Kashmir Gate. The magazine held such a wealth of weaponry, ammunition and supplies that its early capture should have been considered a *sine qua non* by the mutineers. However, many of the rebels, arriving in batches and tired from their night march from Meerut, instead headed for the palace. Others had simply begun killing Europeans or searching for plunder in the city. For several hours, no mutineers paid the British magazine any attention. This was a cardinal mistake as it turned out, for the magazine had few real defenders and could have been captured with ease.

Lieutenant George D. Willoughby of the Bengal Artillery, commissary of the ordnance, was the man in charge of the magazine. With him were lieutenants William Raynor and George Forrest, conductors John Buckley (assistant commissary of ordnance), William Shaw and John Scully, subconductor William Crow and sergeants Benjamin Edwards and Peter Stewart – nine Europeans in all. Much of what happened at the magazine would be revealed by Forrest, one of just three of the men to survive the events of 11 May.

From the edge of Lothian Road, the magazine stretched all the way back to the banks of the river. The eastern walls of the magazine, overlooking the river, gave an exceptional view of both the bridge of boats, the Calcutta Gate and open areas adjacent to the palace. Early on the fateful day, the European officers present had observed the rebel troopers crossing the bridge of boats. The burning toll bridge and the sound of musket fire had made it obvious that something was wrong, but neither Lieutenant Willoughby or any of his men were aware that Simon Fraser and the other Europeans in the palace had been slaughtered. Forrest personally saw mutineers march into the city.

> I first saw them, viz., some cavalry in front (nearly a regiment) followed by the 11th and 20th regiments of Native Infantry crossing the bridge on the road from Meerut. They were coming up in military formation. I would say in subdivisions of companies with fixed bayonets and sloped arms, at about nine o' clock. I did not see any of them previous to this; but I was informed that a small portion of the cavalry had arrived on the Delhi side of the bridge much earlier viz., about seven o' clock.

Forrest and Willoughby had not been at the magazine for that earlier entry; they were at home when Sir Theophilus Metcalfe alerted them to events at Meerut, which had prompted them to journey with him to the Calcutta Gate. There they had seen that closing the Calcutta Gate to the mutineers was impossible, so Willoughby and Forrest had quickly made their way to the magazine to take precautions to prevent the sepoys from gaining entry to the compound. Both men knew full well the implications if the magazine fell to the mutineers.

Willoughby was quite confident he could hold on to the magazine until the expected help arrived. Within the magazine complex was a complement of several hundred guardsmen and workers. With the gates closed and guns manned, these numbers would be more than sufficient for a time. No doubt Brigadier Graves would send assistance from the cantonment shortly to quell the disturbances in the city and deal with the mutineers. Like many others in the city, Willoughby must have assumed that a European force would soon arrive from Meerut in pursuit of the rebels. All would be well in a few hours. Nevertheless, he ordered further barricading as a precaution in case the rebels attempted an attack. Guns were moved out to strategic positions. Forrest takes up the story:

> Inside the gate leading to the park, we placed two 6-pounders double charged with grape, one under Acting Sub-Conductor Crow and Sergeant Stewart, with the lighted matches in their hands, and with orders that, if any attempt was made to force the gate, both guns were to be fired at once, and they were to fall back on that part of the magazine in which Lieutenant Willoughby and I were posted. The principal gate of the magazine was similarly defended by two guns, with the *chevaux de frieze* laid down on the inside. For the further defence of this gate and the magazine in its vicinity, there were two 6-pounders so placed as both to command the gate and a small bastion in its vicinity. Within

> sixty yards of the gate, and in front of the office, and commanding two cross roads, were three 6-pounders and one 24-pounder howitzer which could be so managed as to act upon any part of the magazine in that neighbourhood. After all these guns and howitzers had been placed in the several positions above named, they were loaded with double charges of grape.[2]

All in all, ten guns were placed in position to discourage anyone from trying to force an entry, although there were only nine Europeans to man them. This wasn't considered an issue, as it was assumed that the staff in the magazine would help defend the place. Willoughby also ordered Buckley, Scully and Stewart to lay several trains of powder to destroy the magazine if the worst should happen. Once lit, these would blow up the sections of the magazine containing ammunition and small arms. The train to the powder site was laid right to the foot of a large lime tree in the yard, where Conductor Scully was stationed to light the train as soon as he saw Conductor Buckley raise his hat or at any time when resistance seemed doomed.

Defending the magazine turned out to be a far more difficult business than Willoughby had envisaged, mainly because the vitally important guards and other assistants stationed inside the magazine turned out to be manifestly sympathetic to their sepoy comrades outside. Willoughby needed their numbers, and couldn't turn them out even if he wanted to. He gambled on them staying loyal, and they were issued with arms. Forrest describes how things went wrong from this point: 'The next step taken was to place arms in the hands of the Native establishment, which they most reluctantly received, and appeared to be in a state not only of excitement but also of insubordination, as they refused to obey orders issued by the Europeans, particularly the Mussalman portion of the establishment.'[3]

The magazine's doorkeeper, a Muslim called Karim Baksh, was rumoured to be entirely sympathetic to the rebel cause and waiting only for an opportune moment to throw open the gate. In fact, he seemed to be signalling to the men outside – sufficient reason for Willoughby to order him to move away from the gate and threaten to shoot him if he tried anything.[4] Later, Forrest would describe Baksh as 'an intelligent man and also a good scholar capable of writing Persian well'. After the mutiny, Forrest would learn from a hospital sergeant called Goddard that Baksh had been actively spreading rumours regarding the new cartridge well before the mutiny: 'The serjeant then said to me that a native had been to him that morning and informed him that someone in the magazine at Delhi had been sending circulars to all the native regiments to the effect that the cartridges prepared in the magazine had been smeared with a composition of fat and that they were not to believe their European officers if they said anything in contradiction of it.'[5] Karim Baksh would later hang for his crimes.

The other main weakness of the position was the inherently flawed design of the magazine itself, as it was overlooked by various houses. Men stationed in these houses could fire into the compound at will. In addition, the southern wall of the magazine abutted a European cemetery containing several large monuments and obelisks that overlooked the walls and could easily be climbed.

Despite these issues, Willoughby and his men had nothing to do for a while. The crowds gathering in front of the palace were thinking only of Fraser and the other Europeans within. However, around 9 a.m., roughly two hours after the mutineers began arriving in the city, the magazine fell under their gaze. The first part of the complex to be attacked and ransacked held the magazine workshops; these were separate buildings located on the opposite side of the road to the magazine proper. The workshops had no guard, and there was nothing Willoughby could do. Soon after this, the inevitable happened and the mutineers turned their attention to the magazine itself.

The first contact between the mutineers and the magazine's guard was initiated by a contingent of men from the palace who asked Willoughby to surrender the magazine in the name of the King of Delhi. They wore a blue uniform with a forage cap bearing the badge of a gun in brass. These were the artillery soldiers of the palace guard, who had also decided to thrown in their lot with the rebels. A subedar of the 38th Native Infantry led the group and did the talking. Forrest takes up the story:

> Between the hours of nine and ten a subadar of the 38th Native Infantry who was commanding the magazine guard outside, informed me through an aperture, that the King of Delhi had sent a guard to take possession of the magazine, and to bring all the Europeans there up to his palace, and that if they did not consent to this, none of them were to be allowed to leave the magazine. I did not see the guard at this time, but I saw the man who had brought this message. He was a well-dressed Mussulman. We told the subadar of the guard that he was to pay no attention to any orders he might receive from any one, unless it was Lieutenant Willoughby or myself; but we held no communication with, nor did we deign any answer to the man who had brought the above message.[6]

Soon after this, another contingent of the King's guard arrived at the magazine under the command of a native officer. The officer went on to allocate twelve men to each of the gates of the magazine, thus eliminating the possibility of Willoughby and his men bolting out in an attempt to escape. 'These men took up their posts in regular military style, posted their arms, received their orders and behaved altogether like regular soldiers. They were all in the full uniform of the King,' wrote Forrest. 'This was some time between ten and eleven in the morning, about an hour after which the door keeper on the outside of the gate called out that he wished to speak either to Lieutenant Willoughby or myself.'

Willoughby and Forrest approached the gate together, and the man informed them that the government stores outside the magazine were being carried away. This was true; they could see through the apertures of the gate that labourers were busy transporting the supplies away under the direction of the King's soldiers. The defenders were asked once more to surrender. The guardsman said he and his men were fighting for the cause of his Imperial majesty, the Emperor. Neither Forrest nor Willoughby gave any response. There followed a lull; the mutineers likely hadn't thought of a plan in the event that the Europeans refused them entry. One casualty was sustained when another European, Park Sergeant Hoyle, was shot by the King's men while attempting to reach the magazine at around 11 a.m.

Desultory hostilities began about an hour after midday, and soon the mutineers were keeping up a steady musket fire on the magazine. Little or no fire was returned from the magazine; the Europeans were sticking by the heavy guns, and the guards in the magazine, reluctant to fire on their colleagues outside, simply fired into the air if they fired at all. Forrest tried to ascertain who was leading the mutineers outside: 'Lieutenant Willoughby and myself frequently went to the gate which was close by and asked who was leading or commanding the attack and the same answer was given us on every occasion viz a son and a grandson of the king's were present organising the attack on us … Another message about one o' clock came in the King's name to say that if we did not surrender he would mine and blow up a part of the wall which was known to be weak and so effect an entrance.'[7]

Eventually, at around 2 p.m., scaling ladders were brought up to the magazine and appeared on the walls. These were apparently sent under order of the King, and Forrest says that this was the final straw for the Indian troops and staff: 'On the ladders being erected against the wall, the whole of our native Establishment deserted us by climbing up the slope sheds on the inside of the Magazine & descending the ladders on the outside, after which the enemy appeared in great numbers on the top of the walls & on whom we kept up an incessant fire of grape, every round of which told well as long as a single round remained.'[8] He also noted that all the men who ascended the scaling ladders and entered the magazine were sepoys of the 11th and 20th regiments NI – not men of the King's guard.

With the attack now in full flow, firing continued till around half-past three. A small group of mutineers managed to clamber into a small turret after scaling the wall. Four guns manned by Forrest and Buckley fired grape at this group – two guns at a time to ensure two others were always ready. Willoughby and Raynor, meanwhile, strode around ensuring the other guns were ready for firing as and when required. Another two guns were placed at the other gate under Crow and Edwards, and another was faced toward the river under Shaw. Orders were to hold fire until the mutineers breached the gates.

The situation became untenable after each gun had fired four rounds. Buckley had been shot in the arm at this point, and Forrest had two musket balls in his hand. Their ammunition was exhausted. Defence was impossible; rebels had breached the compound in two places. The local guard had entirely vanished by this time, save for a solitary Bengali writer. Realising the game was up, Willoughby gave a signal to Buckley, who in turn signalled Conductor Scully by raising his hat. Scully fired the train immediately.

Estimates vary as to the time of the explosion. Some said the magazine was blown around 3 p.m. while others put it as late as 5 p.m. Whatever the case, the explosion was spectacular. The sound was heard loud and clear within the thick walls of the palace, rocking even the inner buildings. At the time, Zafar had been in prayer with his various courtiers. Zahir Dehlvi recorded what happened:

> A prayer for peace was on everyone's lips when suddenly there was a tremendous noise. Even if 1000 cannons had been fired, their noise would not have been so loud. The Khan-samaani building is from Shah Jahan's period and its walls are 4 feet wide. It is made of lime and mortar. The ceiling of the hall is very solidly constructed of red sandstone and salmon-coloured stone. After this noise, dirt and mud started falling from the walls and everyone was covered in dust. The earth shook as if there had been an earthquake…
>
> … When we turned our eyes to the west, we saw a column of smoke rising from the ground to the sky and corpses of men flying around in the air like crows and kites. Three minutes later, it seemed as though pieces of the mountains were raining on earth.[9]

The first impressions in the palace at that time was that the mutineers had attacked the magazine and blown it up themselves although it later became known that the British officers had done the deed.

A great plume of dust dominated the landscape. The explosion was so violent that around 50 yards of the city wall bounding the magazine on the riverside disappeared, with bricks and rocks being thrown as high as half a mile into the sky. Hundreds of sepoys who had entered the compound were killed, along with several European women and children who had fled there for safety. Hundreds more, principally bystanders, were killed and wounded by falling debris. The explosion was heard as far away as the cantonments at Meerut, 40 miles distant. 'What a bad man the general is to kill our people in this way,' remarked a sepoy to his comrades as they sheltered outside the compound.

The savage explosion killed most of the European officers in the magazine. Scully, who had fired the train, died instantly and Crow,

Edwards and Stewart were not seen again, presumably dying in the explosion. The other Europeans took advantage of the maelstrom of dust, confusion and chaos to escape, which in other circumstances would have been impossible. They quickly fled through the sally port on the riverside. Shaw managed to escape to the Kashmir Gate but was shot by a sepoy of the 64th NI. Willoughby and Forrest managed to get past the Kashmir Gate; Willoughby was killed days later by villagers on his way to Meerut, but Forrest made it. Of the conductors, Buckley and Raynor eventually managed to reach Meerut as well. All three would receive the Victoria Cross for their exploits.

To Forrest, it must have seemed like the magazine had been utterly destroyed. 'After crossing the river on the night of the 11th, I observed the whole of the magazine to be on fire, so that I am in hopes that little of the property fell into the hands of the enemy,' he would write to Colonel Abbott on 27 May.[10] He was wrong. Most of the stores and ordnance remained quite untouched. Perhaps the trains of gunpowder had been incorrectly or hurriedly laid to certain portions of the magazine. Unfortunately, over the next few bloody months the rebels never lacked ordnance from the magazine. Despite the appreciable number of mutineer casualties, the explosion might not have done the Europeans any good. The only thing that can be said with certainty is that the explosion dissolved what scant loyalty remained among the sepoys at the cantonment, at the Kashmir Gate and elsewhere.

14

# The Flight

A sepoy of the light company then put his arm on my shoulder and told me I had better go or I should be shot down.

Major Patterson 54th NI

The British cantonment at Delhi was situated on the western slope of the Delhi ridge, 2 miles to the north of the city. Due to this distance, the arrival of the mutineers at the city was not immediately apparent to the British officers. At sunrise on that day, though, during the morning parade of the brigade, the sepoys of the 38th, 54th and 74th NI made their feelings clear. They had already been informed of the Meerut mutiny the day before; the sepoys at Meerut had sent messengers. There were plenty of soldiers at the cantonment who held sympathy for the cause, so what happened at the morning parade must have hardened opinions still further.

When the general orders were read out that morning, one announcement stood out: the court-martial and hanging of Ishwari Parsad, the jemadar at Barrackpore in Bengal. Parsad had refused to follow orders and subdue Mangal Pandey, the sepoy who had fired on his officers. The news was met with a significant murmur of disapproval among the men of all three regiments. 'Though it lasted but a few seconds, it struck me forcibly as something extraordinary, never having witnessed anything like it before,' noted Captain Tytler of the 38th NI. Rumblings of discontent would continue after the parade, although there was no overt show of anger. Most of the British officers, meanwhile, still largely oblivious to the great frustration among the sepoys, went about their duties as normal, stopping for a leisurely breakfast.

Shortly after parade, news arrived that large numbers of sowars had ridden into Delhi and even entered the palace. Capt. Tytler was told by a servant who himself had heard the news from Lieutenant Holland. Meanwhile, Brigadier Graves had been made aware of events by Mr Hutchinson, the magistrate, before he rode back to the city and met his grisly end in the palace. Graves at this time had no knowledge of the bloodbath in the palace, and so was unaware that he was now responsible for retrieving the situation in the city as the most senior figure alive. Still unaware of the severity of the situation, Graves made no immediate move to restore order. Instead of sending a force into the city, he asked Capt. Tytler to take two companies of the 38th NI (his own company and Capt. Gardner's) – around 200 men – towards the smaller, secondary magazine outside the city by the river. The objective was to keep an eye on the river from there and prevent rebels crossing for access to the smaller magazine. A nearby house commanded an excellent vantage point, but before Tytler could make use of it he had to summon and equip his men:

> Captain Gardner and I went immediately to the lines; we found the men of our companies rather excited, and it was with some slight difficulty that we succeeded in completing each of our companies to 100 strong. A slight delay now took place in serving out the ammunition and after sending repeatedly to the magazine to ascertain the cause, I went myself, and the khalassies said, 'What can we do? the sepoys about here who have come for ammunition are quarrelling and squabbling with us about the cartridges and caps, and we cannot give either without counting them.' I hurried the work and returned to the company. When the cartridges and caps were being served out, many of the men seized more bundles than they were entitled to; therefore, to prevent further delay at the time, I had these men marked, that I might punish them afterwards. Captain Gardner also remarked to me that the men of his company showed the same anxiety to secure more ammunition than they were entitled to.[1]

After eventually organising the two companies, Tytler led his men towards the house near the magazine. The men now showed their true feelings, with shouting and acts of indiscipline which the officers were powerless to punish. At the house, Tytler organised various lookouts and sentries while the bulk of the men were told to pile arms.

After sending Tytler to protect the secondary magazine and watch the river, the brigadier planned for men with artillery to take command of the bridge of boats across the Jumna. Since the bridge was being used by the mutineers, this made eminent sense. However, any units sent from the cantonment for this purpose would have to enter the city through the Kashmir Gate before proceeding through the walled city to the Calcutta Gate, which connected to the bridge. The Kashmir Gate ordinarily had a small guard of around fifty men, the duty being rotated among the three regiments stationed at Delhi; on 11 May it was the turn of two companies of the 38th NI under Lieutenant Proctor. Graves was confident the gate would be safe to use. Col Ripley, along with Major Patterson, was therefore ordered to take the whole of the 54th NI into the city by this route. They would be bolstered by two guns from Capt. de Teissier's Native battery under Lieutenant Wilson. The 54th NI was thought to be the most loyal and reliable of the regiments, and Graves reckoned this show of force would be sufficient to bring order to the city. However, the guns were delayed and the regiment could not move as one. Instead, two companies of the 54th NI were ordered to stay behind and accompany the guns when they were ready. Col Ripley commenced the march towards the Kashmir Gate with the remaining eight companies.

The 54th NI made it to the Kashmir Gate, where a sepoy sent from the main magazine by Willoughby arrived with the message that assistance was required to keep it from falling into rebel hands. Col Ripley therefore chose to press on down the road, passing the guard of the 38th NI at the gate. The regiment managed to make some headway towards the magazine, reaching as far as St James' Church – about halfway there – when they came face to face with the troopers of the 3rd Light Cavalry and a throng of locals. Seeing the mutineers, Col Ripley asked his men to load their muskets. Reluctant to fire on their comrades, the men baulked at this precursory act; their sympathies were clearly with the rebels. Their hesitation broke the authority of the officer. The crowd in front, encouraged, moved forward. This was the cue for some of the rebel sowars to attack. They began firing at the European officers. Except for Ripley, all of them – Capt. Smith, Capt. Burrows, Lt Edwards, Lt Waterfield and the quartermaster-sergeant – were shot dead. Ripley himself, though wounded in seventeen places, managed to survive. Almost the entire 54th NI now merged with the rebels and melted into the city. Playing dead, or perhaps too weak to show signs of life, Ripley stayed still until the crowds dissipated. When the coast was clear, he struggled back to the Kashmir Gate.

Lt Proctor, the officer at the Kashmir Gate, heard the gunfire quite clearly. On learning of what had happened, he had the presence of mind to realise the mutiny might well spread to the cantonment and his own regiment, the 38th, as well as the 74th. The best thing to do, he decided, would be to close the gate and refuse to allow anyone near the cantonment. This would delay any news. He also asked the guard at the gate – his men of the 38th – to advance up the road and fire on the rebels, but like Ripley's men they demurred. Many showed open contempt at the order, even going so far as to allow deserters from the 54th to saunter up to the Kashmir Gate and inflict further wounds on the sheltering Ripley.

Things were looking bleak for Proctor, who must have worried for his own safety, and just minutes later some troopers of the 3rd Light Cavalry could be seen moving towards the Kashmir Gate. Fortunately for him, at this very moment the two guns that had been delayed finally arrived under Lt Wilson, along with the two companies of the 54th under Major

Patterson. This temporarily shifted the balance of power, and the rebel troops retreated. Patterson:

> On our arriving within about 100 yards of the Cashmere Gate, I was met by Captain Wallace, 74th Native Infantry, field officer of the week, who requested me to hasten in as fast as I could, as the cavalry mutineers had arrived, and had shot down all the officers of the 54th Native Infantry. I immediately ordered the two companies to load, and while this was being done, Colonel Ripley came out of the Cashmere Gate, wounded in several places, and supported by the fife-major.

Patterson, like Ripley earlier, would attempt to seize the initiative by advancing past the Kashmir Gate with his two companies. However, the rebels had retreated and he encountered no resistance; not even the men from the other eight companies of the 54th could be seen. Nevertheless, he had to be extremely careful. Guarding the gate to his rear, the men of the 38th were now known to be of dubious loyalty. Captain Wallace had told Patterson how they had done nothing to help Ripley. They might show their true colours at any time.

Advancing up the road, Patterson could see the scattered corpses of the officers of the 54th. It was clearly too risky for him to push further into the city; with the bulk of the 54th having joined the rebel cause, there was a clear danger that his remaining two companies might desert as well. He therefore withdrew towards the Kashmir Gate, where the two guns had been set up. Consulting with Lt Vibart, who had accompanied him, he decided to retrieve the dead officers' bodies. However, the men of the 54th advised against this, saying that the rebels would kill them and that it was much safer for a party of sepoys to go. Patterson agreed. A party of sepoys from the 74th NI would later arrive and accomplish the task.

*****

Despite Proctor's desire to close the Kashmir Gate to prevent news reaching the sepoys of the 38th and 74th at the cantonment, word had already arrived. The barracks were full of excited talk, with the sepoys no doubt mulling over what they should do. Lt Gambier was on the scene:

> The 38th and 74th had not long been under arms when news reached us that the 54th refused to fire; that Colonel Ripley and other of their officers had been shot or cut down. We then moved down the Artillery parade ground where were De Tessier's guns and some companies of the 74th. Thence we moved to the Flag Staff Tower, where the midday gun fires, and formed line along the high ground.[2]

This was a precaution taken by Brigadier Graves to protect European civilians fleeing from the city and looking for refuge by heading towards the ridge, as it was by now clear that the situation was much more serious than first thought. Graves had decided to send two guns to the Flagstaff Tower. A contingent of the 38th NI several hundred strong was sent to accompany the guns along with the remnants of the 74th NI. Christian band-boys of the regiments went too, supplied with muskets and ammunition.

The defection of large elements of the 54th must have worried Graves. When he found out, he sent another force to the Kashmir Gate to bolster the guard of the 38th and the two companies of the 54th that were still nominally loyal. This time, he sent 150 men of the 74th NI along with another two guns (under Lt Aislabie of Capt. Teissier's battery) all under the command of Major Abbott.

Graves had earlier decided that the Flagstaff Tower would be the most appropriate gathering point for civilians fleeing the city. At the tower, a collection of European refugees from the city had already begun to congregate. Lt Gambier wrote of the pervading confusion and anxiety there:

> We remained at the Tower all day; the ladies and residents some in their carriages some walking gradually flocked there. Thomason with brain fever threatening him and Glubb just recovering from it paced about in the sun. Dr Stewart had marvelously escaped from the City and told us of the fate of Colonel Ripley who was not dead but removed to the Artillery Quarter Guard ... It was so inexplicable to us why troops from Meerut did not arrive. Looking towards the City we saw fires blazing and heard the firing of heavy guns which left us in uncertainty as to what was taking place.[3]

Abbott's force reached the Kashmir Gate around noon. However, they could do little more than entrench their position to hold it. Abbott realised early on that the men of the 38th NI at the gate were most untrustworthy. These men, albeit still reluctant to commit to mutiny, had generally adopted a very insolent outlook towards their officers. The 74th NI, meanwhile, were still relatively loyal and even drove off an advance by the mutineers of the 54th. It was these men who now moved in to retrieve the bodies of the 54th NI officers slain by the troopers of the 3rd Light Cavalry. Nearby mutineers were heard to cry out, 'The Company wished to take away our caste, on this account have we killed them.'

Abbott could hear distant sounds of musket fire, but could not ascertain the source. What he was hearing was Willoughby's defence of the Delhi Magazine. He dithered over whether to investigate; in truth, his 150 men were hardly sufficient for any major confrontation and he must have known it. Abbott instead held the gate with his guns. While this kept the gate in British hands for a while, giving citizens a safe route to the cantonment, British authority in the wider city vanished.

This was the way matters stood at the Kashmir Gate in the afternoon. The magazine, as we have seen, preoccupied the rebels at this time. Some way into the afternoon, however, the detonation of the magazine shook the city. This destroyed almost all residual loyalty among the sepoys at the Kashmir Gate, regardless of regiment. At the secondary magazine near the river, too, the explosion of the city magazine had an impact. The two companies of the 38th NI guarding the smaller magazine on the river had already been on the point of mutiny; Tytler writes that they had been discussing matters and ignoring his orders:

> When I went into one of the rooms, I remarked, for the first time, a native, from his appearance a soldier, haranguing the men of the companies, and saying that every power or government existed their allotted time, and that it was nothing extraordinary that that of the English had come to an end, according to what had been predicted in their native books. Before I could make a prisoner of him, the magazine in the city exploded, and then the men of the two companies, with a tremendous shout, took up their arms and ran off to the city, exclaiming, 'Prithivi Raj Ki Jai! [Victory to the Sovereign of the World!]'

Tytler and his fellow officers went unmolested; the sepoys said they had no wish to kill them. Seeing discretion as the better part of valour, Tytler and his fellow officers did not attempt to stop the sepoys. Instead, they made their way to the Flagstaff Tower.

At the ridge, Brigadier Graves was struggling to work out a plan. The Flagstaff Tower was great strategic site, overlooking the city and boasting good defences. Both the cantonments and the city could be observed from it. If the mutineers from the city tried to attack it, they could certainly be held off for a few hours. However, sepoys of the 74th NI had been moved to the ridge and it was clear that they would not want to fight their comrades. To show any suspicion towards the sepoys would perhaps have precipitated a more immediate break, so Graves decided to keep them at the tower, which he considered better than sending them back to the cantonment or the city, where they would most likely join the mutineers. It all hinged on how many men of the 38th and 74th at the tower stayed loyal. Their loyalty was required only for a short time, Graves reckoned, as the European troops at Meerut would already be marching down to relieve Delhi. In fact, he was puzzled as to why the European force at Meerut had not already arrived. From the summit of the Flagstaff Tower, a watch was kept over the opposite bank of the river and the road from Meerut in preparation for it.

After the explosion at the magazine, matters accelerated at the Kashmir Gate. Graves ordered Major Abbott to retreat with the apparently loyal 74th NI. However, instead of the cantonment they were to withdraw to the Flagstaff Tower; the cantonment was now in rebel hands. A huddle of European civilians had gathered at the Kashmir Gate with Abbott's men, having previously decided against travelling up to the Flagstaff Tower unprotected. One of them was the deputy collector, Mr De Gruyther, who insisted that the European officers should stay at the gate; the guard of the 38th NI, he said, could not be trusted. De Gruyther apparently sought a private audience with Brigadier Graves to clarify the situation, but he never got it. After leaving Abbott's presence, he was never seen again.

Abbott ordered his detachment of the 74th to prepare for retreat, with the guns at the rear. However, only around 120 men of the 74th NI obeyed. Abbott must have been dear to the sepoys, for they warned him of the danger: 'A jemadar said, "Never mind sections. Pray go on Sir." My orderly havildar then came up to me and said, "Pray Sir, for God's sake, leave this place, pray be quick."'

The bloodshed could not be postponed indefinitely. As those sepoys of the 74th who remained loyal marched out of the Kashmir Gate, the guardsmen of the 38th NI quickly closed the gate before the guns could be brought through. Abbott himself had barely got a hundred paces when he heard firing. The men of the 38th, now in open mutiny, had begun shooting the various European officers and civilians still trapped inside the gate.

Abbott's initial reaction on hearing the shouting and gunfire was to try and force his way back in to help his fellow officers. 'I then ordered the men with me, about a hundred to return to their assistance,' he recalled. 'The men said, "Sir it is useless. They are all killed by this time and we shall not save anyone. We have saved you and are happy. We will not allow you to go back and be murdered."' In any case, forcing the doors would have been impossible. Resigned, Abbott turned and marched away with his men.

The major was only escorted part of the way to the ridge before his own sepoys left him. 'We have protected you so far; it will be impossible for us to do so much longer. Pray fly for your life,' they urged him. The colonel and adjutant of the 38th, who had been fortunate enough to get out with Abbott, were similarly advised. The sepoys said they would no longer take orders from the Europeans, and would now join their colleagues, but wanted to let the officers escape.

When Abbott marched away, he left a group of officers and a large contingent of civilians at the mercy of the 38th. Capt. Gordon of the 74th was the first to be shot, dropping from his saddle without a sound. Lt Reveley, also of the 74th, came next; he had a loaded pistol, which he fired at a group of rebels before he died. Capt. Smith of the 54th was also shot dead. However, the other Europeans were luckier. Perhaps there was still some residual loyalty, or perhaps the sepoys were reluctant to kill civilians. Others later said that most of the sepoys at the Kashmir Gate were more concerned with the nearby treasury, for most headed in that direction rather than staying to massacre the remaining Europeans. Whatever the case, this sudden reticence among many of the sepoys allowed several of the Europeans to escape what had seemed an impossible situation.

After the first shots, Major Patterson and Ensign Elton forged a path up the ramped walkway of the bastion to the guardroom and were followed by the group of civilians. Closing the door behind them, they took account of the damage; a Lt Osborn was wounded, as was a Mrs Forest. Inside the guardroom, a gun embrasure offered the opportunity to jump clear of the walls; however, this was easier said than done. The height of the wall and the depth of the ditch beneath meant a drop of roughly 30 feet. Then, even if the jump was accomplished successfully and without injury, there was the counterscarp to negotiate. The officers had a better chance of negotiating the drop and escaping, but they were burdened by the less mobile women.

A round-shot flying over their heads from a gun inside the gates removed any reluctance. To lessen the height for the jump, the officers took off their belts and fastened them in the fashion of a short rope which they all used to lower themselves some way down the wall. The party then climbed the scarp, though not without difficulty, and clambered on to the crest of the glacis before running from the city walls. Some decided to head for the Flagstaff Tower; others decided to take their chances at Metcalfe House. The gathering dark helped, as did the fact that the sepoys showed no interest in pursuing the fugitives.

*****

Over the course of the day, Europeans and Anglo-Indians had trickled into the Flagstaff Tower. The space around the tower teemed with all manner of horses, carriages, carts and other makeshift transports while the air was filled with anxious conversation, children's cries and the entreating voices of mothers trying to console their progeny. Among the European families buzzing about the tower was Miss Wagentreiber.

> Here we found a large gathering from civil lines and the houses nearby – mostly ladies and children and their attendants (ayahs and bearers, carrying infants), all huddled together in the interior of the tower (a space some eighteen feet in diameter). Many of the poor ladies were in a terrible plight owing to extreme terror and the excessive heat. Some had little ones who were crying and clinging to them which they were vainly trying to soothe and comfort. All wore that expression so near akin to despair. Here were wives made widows in one short hour, sisters weeping at the report of a brother's death, and there were those whose husbands were still on duty, in the midst of peril, of whose fates they were as yet ignorant. It was a sight not to be forgotten. It was a

> black-hole in miniature, with all but the last horrible features of that dreadful prison, and I was glad even to stand in the sun to catch a breath of fresh air.[4]

While the tower filled with refugees, the British officers talked to the sepoys in an attempt to ascertain their loyalties. The brigadier had earnest discussions about whether anything could be done to remedy the situation in the city. One rather desperate plan he conceived during the afternoon was to seize the initiative with a surprise attack on the mutineers. A rumour had reached the ridge that the men of the 3rd Light Cavalry, tiring of the killing and looting in the city, were now resting from the day's heat along the banks of the river. If this was true, they could quite literally be caught napping if a sufficiently strong force was mustered. Capt. Tytler of the 38th agreed that a surprise attack might work and got the approval of the roughly 200 men still under his command. However, when he ordered them to fall in, the sepoys demurred. They were ready to fight their enemies, they said, but they could not fire on their own comrades.

With the bulk of his men now lost to mutiny, and those nominally loyal in fact unreliable, Graves had just two choices: continue waiting for a European force from Meerut that might never come, or flee before the mutineers in the city organised themselves and turned their attentions to the ridge. The brigadier opted to stay at the tower; he felt confident that succour would shortly be coming from Meerut.

It was imperative to find out what was happening at Meerut. One man, a nephew of the Delhi merchant Mr Marshall, volunteered to ride to Meerut to get help. The brigadier agreed. With a horse and a brief letter for General Hewitt, the man was sent on his way with the hope that he could cross the river upstream of the bridge of boats. Alas, he never made it that far. As he descended the ridge and approached the secondary magazine, he was spotted by mutineers of the 38th NI who were guarding it. He was shot as he forded the river.

Another volunteer came forward with a different plan. This was Dr Batson, the surgeon of the 74th NI. He too would head for Meerut and General Hewitt, but he would be sent disguised as a local; he stained his face and hands to darken his complexion in an attempt to fit in. Batson dressed as a fakir and set off with the letter. The disguise failed to protect him; the colour of his European eyes betrayed him, and he was set upon by sepoys and other villagers. He was allowed to live, but his clothes were torn from him. He would eventually reach Meerut naked – and far too late.

Meanwhile, the issue of the sepoys at the tower was addressed. Protecting the approaches to the tower were two guns of the Light Field Battery and a company of the 38th Light Infantry. Graves suspected these men since their comrades in the regiment had already joined the rebels. If they followed suit, the whole European assembly at the tower was in danger of being massacred. Some of them were seen having intense conversations with the gunners, presumably debates about joining their comrades. In light of this, several of the European civilians who had brought firearms were told to stand near the guns in readiness to protect them.

'The Brigadier tried to reason with the men,' wrote Miss Wagentreiber. 'He reminded them of their good services in the years that were past, and told them it would be well to their interest to remain staunch and loyal to their oath and the salt they had eaten for so many years. They immediately showed their distaste for the "salt" by expectorating about in a disgusting and disrespectful manner; one who seemed to have influence called out, "Don't listen to the Boorao (old imbecile)!" and were altogether so insolent and offensive in their replies that it was evident nothing was to be gained by reason and argument.'[5]

Graves knew time was short. A crowd could be seen emerging from the Mori Gate, seemingly advancing towards the Flagstaff Tower. Reaching the base of the ridge, the group stopped, reluctant to move within range of the European guns. Their cries of 'Mare Feringhee (Kill the Europeans)' nevertheless continued, unsettling the sepoy contingent on the ridge. It was clear the advancing mutineers would find the courage to climb the ridge before long.

The stalemate was interrupted by the spectacular explosion of the magazine in the city. As elsewhere, it had a visible effect on the sepoys. Many rushed to their piled guns, and although they refrained from violence, little vestige of loyalty remained. Many of their comrades were sure to have been killed in the explosion, and they knew it. Some of the more vocal sepoys standing nearby had begun shouting, 'Deen! Deen!'

Shortly after this, the Europeans observed two carts being driven out of the city and up the ridge. As the carts drew near, it became obvious that they were filled with the corpses of Europeans killed in the city. The drivers mocked those gathered at the tower, crowing that they would suffer the same fate before nightfall. The sepoys at the tower simply smiled and laughed. Around this time, Major Abbott's party returned from the Kashmir Gate. Abbott had passed by the cantonment and had seen that the sepoys there would no longer obey orders. Indeed, they could mass for an attack on the Flagstaff Tower at any moment.

These events pretty much decided matters for Graves. The risk of a massacre was increasing by the minute, and an immediate decision was required. With just nineteen European officers present, scant personal loyalties and traces of discipline were all that kept the sepoys on the ridge from hostile action.

'At last one of the officers suggested that we should get away while we could,' Mr Le Bas recalled. 'At first the brigadier would not hear of such a thing. He said that he could not abandon his post – that we should soon have aid from Meerut; but the question was agitated, and the idea of a retreat gradually became familiar to men's minds.' Many others agreed, pushing for immediate flight while it was possible. If the mutineers organised themselves and concentrated their attentions on the ridge, the road to Karnal and the north might easily be blocked. If that happened, there would be no escape. Every minute was vital. A short meeting was held in which the brigadier, after discussions with Captains Nicoll, De Teissier, Tytler, Wallace and civilians like Mr Le Bas, agreed that waiting for the Meerut force was a waste of time.

Their decision was reinforced by the arrival of Ensign Elton of the 74th NI, who together with Patterson had led the escape from the Kashmir Gate. He told Graves how a number of officers had not made it out. If there had been any doubts, they were now dispelled. The sun was setting now, and some of the European civilians, seeing the brigadier's indecision, had already taken the initiative and left for Ambala or Meerut in their carriages and buggies, or on foot if they had no transportation. By the time darkness fell, most of the Europeans had fled. Only the British officers and the sepoys remained at the Flagstaff Tower.

Around sunset, the remaining sepoys of the 38th approached their colonel and adjutant. They politely advised the officers to leave, saying they would no longer accept orders. Brigadier Graves and his officers were told to go, for 'this was no longer a place for them'. Graves himself was apparently held in high regard by his men and by the men of his previous regiment, and this helped to save his life as well as those of the other European officers still present. Graves recalled some men of the 16th NI visiting him back in April. They had been passing through Delhi on their way to Oudh from the Punjab and had stopped to pay respects to their old commanding officer. Many of the men had then urged Graves to leave for England, or failing that to leave for the cool climate of the hills – the pretext being the coming heat. The advice had struck Graves as very strange at the time, although he failed to heed it. The men of the 16th nevertheless asked their colleagues in the 38th not to harm their old commanding officer, and the request was honoured.

Graves had not given up on his men. As the sepoys milled around waiting for him to depart, he decided to sound the assembly, hoping they would rally. It was too late; just one man of the 74th NI stepped forward. He was the only sepoy to leave with the European officers as they departed the ridge on horseback.

Reluctant to leave his guns at the tower, Capt. De Teissier ordered the drivers to take them up the road to Ambala. There was a half-hearted attempt by the men of the 38th NI to prevent this, but the drivers managed to get through. However, about four miles up the road the drivers refused to go any further. Ensign Glubb of the 38th NI urged them on, but the drivers refused to countenance any more orders. De Teissier therefore had to abandon the guns; he himself escaped in his own carriage with his family and some friends who had no transport of their own. Glubb, meanwhile, hitched a lift in another carriage bearing European fugitives from the tower.

Brigadier Graves was one of the last to leave the ridge. He had hoped to destroy the secondary magazine, depriving the mutineers of powder, but he simply didn't have the numbers. All he could do was drench the ammunition that had been brought to the Flagstaff Tower, rendering it useless. In one of the most curious cases of loyalty during the mutiny, the sepoys allowed him to do so. With this small task complete, Graves mounted his horse and galloped off.

For those fleeing the ridge, whether civilian or soldier, safety was either 130 miles north in Ambala or 40 miles north-west at Meerut. Nobody could say which journey was safer; it was a gamble. Speed, camouflage and stealth proved essential. Many hid in abandoned buildings or patches of jungle outside the city. Most traded their European clothing for local garb. The officers and soldiers either abandoned their bright uniforms or tore away their epaulettes, which glinted in the moonlight.

The reception these refugees received along the way varied considerably. Some friendly locals helped the unfortunates. Capt. T. W. Holland, for example, was cared for in one village by a sweeper called Paltu, who even brought him milk from nearby villages to maintain his health. Holland was also sheltered by a Brahmin called Jamna Das for almost a week. 'He gave me the best part of his house to live in, and the best food he could,' Capt. Holland reminisced. Such luck was not universal. Some were killed; others were stripped naked and sent on their way. Occasionally, locals would feign friendliness but betray the Europeans at the right opportunity.

Several of the fleeing Europeans managed to meet up in a village near Panipat. The group comprised Brigadier Graves, the Wagentreibers, Mr Le Bas, Capt. Nicholl, Lts Grant, Taylor, Mew, Martineau and Drummond, and a sergeant-major of the 74th NI. This group headed to Panipat itself, and then moved on to Karnal. Finally, word reached them that British troops would soon be moving down from Ambala. They were safe.

# 15

# Empire *ex nihilo*

... A courageous chief only is wanted.
Abbé Raynal, 1780

In normal circumstances, the only armed men inside the palace would have been the Emperor's bodyguard and the palace guard, a unit of around 1,200 men used largely for ceremonial purposes. But 11 May had been different. During the early morning of that day, the sowars of the 3rd Light Cavalry had entered the palace. They were soon joined by the bulk of the two Meerut infantry regiments, the 11th NI and 20th NI, who trickled into the city over the later morning and afternoon. Tired from their rapid overnight march, these sepoys needed rest. In the chaos and confusion, many of them bedded down in the open spaces and gardens of the palace.

By late evening, it became clear that the European officers had fled the cantonment and the ridge. Sepoys from all three regiments stationed at Delhi, having cast off their loyalty to the British Government of India, made their way to the palace as well. They could be seen milling around near the Diwan-i-Khas and other state buildings, as well as near the King's private apartment. Emulating their Meerut comrades, and showing equal contempt for the palace authorities, many of them also bivouacked in the palace courtyards and gardens, and in the Diwan-i-Khas and Diwan-i-Aam. Other soldiers approached the windows of the female apartments with little regard for etiquette, while some begged food from the palace staff.

The men of the 3rd Light Cavalry had casually brought their horses into the palace courtyards, turning the palace entrance into a makeshift stable. Mingling with this growing crowd were hundreds of curious servants and orderlies who worked in the palace. The sepoys conversed with palace workers and staff amid the sound of pistols, carbines and muskets being fired into the air in triumph. Jubilant cries rang around the palace grounds. Chants of 'Deen! Deen!' went up all night. All around the palace and inner sanctum, confusion reigned. The senior palace staff could only look on in bewilderment.

Before long, parties of soldiers began asking to see the Emperor. 'There was no regular court that day,' wrote the King's physician, Ahsan Ulla Khan, 'but the King came out some three or four times to the Hall of Special Audience, where the mutineers were lying about all over the place; and the mutinous troopers came flocking into the palace the whole day and even after the night set in.'[1] A bemused Zafar complained to the soldiers of the trouble they were causing. He asked them why they had come and what they wanted. Everywhere was a cacophony of voices, the noise growing to uncomfortable levels. Zafar soon retired, no doubt mulling over the extraordinary events of the day.

Over the next few days, various conversations took place between the King and the mutineers. All followed a similar pattern. Zafar would later say that he was approached immediately after the killing of Capt. Douglas and the others in the palace gate apartments, and that the soldiers who spoke to him then did not display the politeness that had been evident when they first arrived in the city:

> ... the mutinous soldiery rushed into the hall of special audience, crowding into the court-yard, the hall of special audience itself, and the hall of devotion, surrounding me completely, and placing sentries on all sides. I asked them what their object was, and begged of them to go away. In reply, they told me to remain a quiet spectator, saying that they had staked their lives, and would now do all that might be in their power. Fearing that I should be killed, I kept quiet and went to my own private apartments.[2]

Perhaps seeing an indecisive king in his dotage frustrated them. Zafar showed no immediate enthusiasm for their cause, yet the sepoys absolutely needed his support to grant them legitimacy. Only with him as their leader could the mutiny have a chance of success. With the King's support, a mere mutiny – albeit a large one – would become a national movement to oust a foreign occupier. Zafar, in turn, could not understand what they hoped to achieve. He tried to explain the impotence of his position. 'Badshah Salamat, please keep your hand on our heads and give us justice,' the rebels implored. '*Hum deen par bigad kar aaye hain* [our faith has been corrupted].'[3] Zafar's reply was less than encouraging:

> Who calls me Badshah [Emperor]? I am but a mendicant who is somehow living a sufi's life in the fort with my progeny. The empire went away with the emperors. My ancestors were emperors, those who had Hindustan under their control. But the monarchy left my house a hundred years ago ... I am a recluse, Why have you come to trouble me

> now? I have no treasure that I can use to pay your salary. I have no army that can help you. I have no estate from which I can collect revenue and employ you. I can do nothing. Don't entertain any hopes of help from me. It's between you and the British. Yes there is one thing in my power. It may be possible for me to broker peace between both parties.[4]

Ahsan Ulla Khan, among other courtiers, had also attempted to explain the situation to the sepoys. 'The Emperor has neither troops, magazine or treasury,' he explained, 'and he is not in a position to pay you. You are used to regular British salary.' The sepoys were adamant. 'We will bring you the treasury of the entire country, just lend us the legitimacy of the Emperor's name.' As for the soldiers requiring food and provisions, Ahsan Ulla Khan explained in no uncertain terms that feeding six regiments from the King's slender resources was impossible. 'From where can we give you provisions? Yes, we have some gram, which comes once a month for the horses of the royal stables. That is available. Apart from that we don't have a grain. The Emperor's horses will die of hunger, but you fill your stomachs! How long will the gram last? It won't last you even a day.' On this point the physician caved somewhat, however. To placate the hungry sepoys, he arranged for them to receive three ser of gram each.

As the initial excitement faded and the soldiers made themselves comfortable in the palace, emotions were mixed. Sometimes the rebels showed confidence in their venture, promising to establish the King's authority over the whole of Hindustan again.[5] They declared themselves confident of annihilating the British power as the other regiments of the Bengal Army would undoubtedly mutiny. The British would soon be fleeing to their ships and sailing back to England. At other times they were more introspective, betraying a more realistic attitude about the logistics of being paid, fed and armed. Sometimes they showed frustration and anger towards the King, who seemed unimpressed by their cause. Ghulam Abbas recalled one of the more cordial meetings between the King and the men of the 3rd Light Cavalry in the Diwan-i-Khas. The sepoy officers, after hushing their men, explained their cause and the issues now arising from the mutiny. They reiterated that his assistance was paramount. 'I did not call for you; you have acted very wickedly,' Zafar complained. 'Unless you the King join us,' they insisted in reply, 'we are all dead men, and we must in that case just do what we can for ourselves.' Defeat or capture would invariably mean a British noose.

Amid the clamour, the rebels nonetheless managed to show decorum and respect to the elderly king at times. In a show of obeisance, many of the mutineers approached Zafar as he sat on his chair, bowing before him in expectation of him placing his hand on their head and thereby showing acceptance of their support. This show of humility seems to have struck a chord with Zafar, and he duly placed his hand on their heads, giving their cause his nominal blessing if nothing else. However, whether polite or intemperate, their message to him remained the same: you must be our leader. A refusal could not be countenanced.

During the meetings, it became quite apparent that Zafar's authority would only be nominal. Even in the palace itself, his orders and commands were given little weight by the soldiers. In one instance, Zahir Dehlvi witnessed a cloth merchant bringing his materials to the palace. The cloth was to be used for the funeral shrouds of Europeans massacred in the city, in accordance with Zafar's wish that they receive a proper burial. The soldiers opposed this scheme. When they saw the palace servants readying the shrouds, they challenged the decision. 'What are these things?' they asked roughly. 'We are trying to make amends for your actions. You started the fire; we are dousing it,' replied Ahsan Ulla Khan. 'Arrey!' spat the ringleader. 'You are all dishonest Christians. Arrey! You are all infidels. You have eaten the leftovers of the British.'[6] The mutineers then took the cloth for themselves, and the British bodies remained in the streets.

The matter of provisions was perhaps foremost in the minds of the Meerut soldiers, who had brought little or nothing with them. The palace employees struggled to explain to each new arrival that they had little to offer. One group of 300 cavalrymen, for instance, began milling around insisting on provisions. Dehlvi recalled a courtier fuming, 'What arrangements can we make? You have already killed those who used to make arrangements for the city. You have created an uproar in the city and the city is being looted, shops are shut. So what arrangements can we make for your food now? Make your own arrangements from wherever you can. Because of you, even we don't have any means of getting food for ourselves.'[7] In response, the cavalry officer said the King should order the bazaars to be reopened so that food could be procured. The courtier was aghast. 'You have already looted the shops! What is left in them that you want them reopened? And why should shopkeepers open their shops? You have created an atmosphere of strife in the city. The shops can only be opened if there is peace.' The officers assured the man that they would establish order, posting guards at regular intervals throughout the city if the shops were reopened. The courtier was unconvinced. 'First, promise that you will not kill anyone, of whatever faith, neither will you loot and plunder the markets. We will send out the royal proclamation, and you set up guard posts at all points.'[8]

*****

The day after their arrival, on 12 May, the soldiers were quick to go through the formalities of reinstating the dithering Zafar to the position of his ancestors. Early in the morning, the Imperial throne was brought out and placed in the Diwan-i-Khas. The silver throne had been stowed away below the Emperor's sitting room since 1843, when

Lord Ellenborough had discontinued the custom of British high officials presenting *nazar* to the Emperor and the custom of royal durbars had vanished. Zafar now took his seat on the throne, signalling the beginning of his new reign as 'Emperor of Hindustan'.[9] A salute of guns was fired to mark the occasion.

At around 3 p.m. that day, Zafar was proclaimed Emperor by a beat of drums in the city. The declaration rang out that 'God was the Ruler of the World and Bahadur Shah was sovereign of the country and had the supreme authority'.[10] All references to British authority were ordered to be erased. Prior to 11 May, for example, the city criers would preface their announcements with, 'God's beings, the King's country and by the order of the Company Bahadur.' From now on, news was introduced with the simpler and shorter, 'God's beings, the King's country.'

At midnight, the firing of a royal salute proclaimed the new order. For the first time in more than fifty years, the King's government had authority over the city. In the palace, celebrations were ordered by the officers. Mahbub Ali Khan, the eunuch, was instructed to organise a feast for the new army. Confectioneries were duly handed out, and officers received monetary gifts. All around the palace, courtiers, civilians and sepoys were celebrating. So great were the crowds gathered to witness Zafar on the imperial throne that Ahsan Ulla Khan had no chance to approach him all day.

It is difficult to say quite what Zafar was thinking during his enthronement. A pensioner for his entire life, he must have known he was a poor choice. He had no experience of government or military leadership, not to mention revolution. However, he had little choice in the matter; the soldiers would brook no refusal. It is fair to say that Zafar, for his part, had little confidence in the soldiers either. Despite giving them his blessing, he was uneasy. Ahsan Ulla Khan stepped in on the King's behalf:

> On the evening of the same day on which the troops arrived, I represented to the King that nothing good could be expected from them, inasmuch as they had mutinied against their masters. And I addressed a letter to the Lieutenant-governor of Agra, on the part of the King, informing him of the arrival of the troops, after they had murdered their European officers, and representing the King's inability to take any measures against them, and begging for help in the shape of European troops.[11]

When Ghulam Abbas arrived at the palace on the morning of the 12th, he met Ahsan Ulla Khan in the Diwan-i-Khas. Abbas questioned him on the King's feelings and what he planned to do. Ahsan Ulla Khan replied that a letter had been sent by camel to the Lieutenant-Governor of Agra asking for instructions. Agra never did reply; the messenger was told only that a response would follow shortly. In another revealing conversation, this time with courtier Hasan Ali Khan on 13 May, Zafar voiced his indecision. 'The army has collected in the palace, what is to be done?' he sighed.[12] Hassan Ali Khan replied that the troops could not be trusted, having already turned against their masters; what was to stop them doing the same at Delhi if things didn't go their way?

While Zafar struggled, some of the royal princes, unburdened with supreme responsibility, were elated. The mutiny was an opportunity to resurrect the glories of their ancestors. The prophecy that European rule would end had not just been wishful thinking. There was to be no more subservience to British authority. An army of six regiments, trained and armed by the British, sat before them. Outside the palace, a vast magazine, while damaged, held plenty of munitions with which to supply and equip this new army. Moreover, regiments elsewhere were sure to join them. Many of the princes, untroubled by their lack of military experience, were anxious to gain commanding positions in this new army.

The officers of the regiments from Delhi and Meerut had already begun to look to Prince Mirza Mughal as their superior. He was around forty years old and Zafar's most senior legitimate son. Like the other princes, he had neither experience nor education in warfare. But he was the natural choice; he had the required air of authority. Many of the soldiers showed their support for him to be installed as commander-in-chief. Various other princes – Mirza Kochak Sultan, Mirza Khizr Sultan, Mirza Mendu and Mirza Bakhtawar Shah – asked to be made colonels of the various infantry regiments, and Abulbakr, one of Zafar's grandsons, coveted a role in the 3rd Light Cavalry.

Zafar was more circumspect about his sons becoming generals and colonels, as he later explained: 'After these occurrences [of 11 May], the rebellious troops brought Mirza Moghal, Mirza Khair Sultan, and Abulbakr, and said they wished to have them as their officers. In the first instance, I rejected their request; but when the soldiery persisted, and Mirza Moghal in anger went off to his mother's house, from dread of the soldiers.' Wiser figures concurred; Ahsan Ulla Khan, for instance, voiced his doubts: 'I represented to the King that they were not of sufficient age and experience for such appointments, nor would they understand any of the duties, and they [the princes] were much displeased in consequence.'[13] Such concerns were swept aside; Abulbakr became a colonel in the 3rd Light Cavalry, and the three princes were given two guns each and ordered to take charge of their regiments at the Kashmir, Lahore and Delhi Gates so that they might help bring about order in the city.

One week after the arrival of the rebels, on 18 May, during a durbar at the Diwan-i-Khas, journalist Chuni Lal saw the appointments formalised:

> The bands of the five regiments attended and continued playing English music. The King bestowed arms and dresses of honour, varying in grandeur, by reference to their appointments, on Mirza Moghal as

> Commander-in-Chief of the whole of the forces, on Mirza Kochak Sultan, Mirza Khair Sultan, Mirza Mendu, and on others of his sons as Colonels of infantry, and on his grandson Abulbakr as Colonel of the regiment of Cavalry.[14]

Another ill-considered decision was made the following day when the sixteen-year-old Prince Jawan Bakht was named prime minister of the state, being given the title 'Prime minister to the King of the conquered territories'. Jawan Bakht was presented with an expensive *khillat* along with a silver inkstand by Zafar; in return, the prince offered ten gold mohurs in tribute.

Zafar made other errors in selecting his inner circle. Mahbub Ali Kahn, the eunuch vizier, was perhaps the only one to inspire confidence. Hasan Askari, the prophesying priest, was there. Several of Zafar's own household were included, among them his wives Zeenat Mahal and Ashraf-un-Nissa and daughters Nani Begum and Agha Begum. The wiser, more capable Ahsan Ulla Khan was never invited to the meetings. Mukand Lal, Zafar's loyal secretary, was frozen out too. This inner circle exemplified what plagued the mutineers on a wider scale: the lack of strong and inspiring leadership.

Despite these missteps, appointing leaders for the new army and government was a simple task. Outside the palace, the city was convulsing with chaos. Projecting a stable government, raising revenue, controlling soldiers and organising defences – these would be the true challenges.

The true shape of the mutiny must have puzzled Zafar. Was this a genuine rebellion that could encompass the whole of the Bengal sepoy army? If it was, the East India Company's authority could crumble within weeks. The writ of the sepoys could run from the borders of Afghanistan to the British capital at Calcutta. Equally, the mutiny might just fizzle out. Was a strong British response already preventing uprisings from taking place elsewhere? The Company might have already restricted the mutiny to Delhi; certainly they had more experience here than Zafar. The King must have been conflicted. However, he had reluctantly accepted the role of leader; there was no going back. His new administration had to reanimate Mughal authority in the city – or vanish forever in the attempt.

# 16

# Reign of Terror

> Thus, without my knowledge or orders, they plundered, not only many individuals, but several entire streets, plundering, robbing, killing and imprisoning all they chose; and forcibly extorting whatever sums of money they thought fit from the merchants and other respectable residents of the city, and appropriating such exactions to their own private purposes.[1]
>
> Zafar

During the month-long interval before a British force appeared before Delhi, Zafar attempted to carry out the administration of the city and surrounding areas. Papers and documents captured in the palace and elsewhere after the recapture of the city showed the efforts made and the almost insurmountable difficulties faced in calming the disorder in the city. Chaos and plundering continued unabated in the days following the arrival of the mutineers, with neither police nor sepoys upholding the law. Lawless elements took advantage, with many street lamps being destroyed and all twelve *kotwalis* in the city being attacked. The sepoys continued to loot commercial premises and private residences alongside their attacks on the civil and judicial court buildings and the empty cantonments outside the city. Those European bungalows still standing were set ablaze. Some locals, seeing the behaviour of the mutineers, dressed up as sepoys to give themselves licence to plunder; on 16 May, for instance, two weavers were caught looting while disguised as infantrymen.

Ten days after the rebels reached Delhi, the febrile atmosphere remained. On 18 May, a journalist wrote to Randhir Singh, Raja of Kapurthala, detailing the dire situation in the city and the King's failure to restrain the troops. The letter was passed by the Raja to the Deputy Commissioner of Jalandhar.

> The whole place is in disturbance. The King has sent his son to inspire confidence, but the ill-disposed are plundering everywhere. The King has encamped outside the city with six regiments. He is old. The officials are those of a worn-out government. The *jageerdars* in deference to the English have not girded their loins. There is no arrangement for any provision, much less for anything else.[2]

The sepoys, he went on, were not averse to taking citizens' lives on a whim. The King had asked for many of the principal men of the city to come forward to help make arrangements for its government, but many pleaded sickness in an attempt to avoid both the responsibility and the risk of being labelled as rebels if the British authorities recaptured the city. 'The state of the people is not to be described,' he lamented. 'They are alive, but they despair of their lives. There is no cure for such a curse. The sepoys are without a leader.'

Even on 24 May, two weeks after the mutineers' arrival, the jemadar in charge of the remains of the Delhi Magazine, Rajab Ali, was forced to petition the King with a warning about the ever-present chaos:

> The disorders and disturbances prevailing in the City, being beyond all limits, we present ourselves at the Royal threshold, and pray that orders, under Your Majesty's Seal, may be issued to all the Police Officers, that they maintain efficient arrangements, in the several jurisdictions, for the protection of the houses of the Magazine servants; moreover, your Slaves, residing in the Khalassy lines which are situated in the Nigambodh Police Station, as well as the rest of the inhabitants, wearied of their lives, by the excessive oppression they are suffering, pray that the present Police Officer may be transferred to some Station outside the City, so that your petitioner may obtain rest and quiet. Petition of the Slave, Rajab Ali, Jemadar of the Delhi Magazine.[3]

In some cases, rebel soldiers themselves were boldly robbed. For example, on 24 May a petition was lodged by Sekh Bansu, a corporal of the 44th NI, with sixty men of his regiment. Before the mutiny, Sekh Bansu had been transporting ninety Arab horses from Agra to Meerut, presumably for the garrison there. The mutiny had broken out when he was at Bulandshahr, and he immediately joined the rebel cause and elected to bring the horses to Delhi. In Bulandshahr, looters had already broken into the treasury, although Bansu managed to save a portion of the money to present to the King for the imperial treasury. In his petition, Bansu complains of the conduct of civilian and rebel plunderers on his arrival in Delhi:

> On our arrival at the bridge of boats, there remained in our possession 83 horses and the treasure, minus 45,000 rupees, which were laden on two waggons and were plundered from us on the road. When we

> crossed the bridge, we were met by numbers of the townspeople who beat the grooms, and forcibly took away several of the horses. Had your slaves not been under the impression that these men had been sent by your Majesty for our protection, your slaves would have used resistance. The treasure and the twenty-two horses which remained with us have been made over to the Government. The missing horses are however still with the cavalrymen and others who took them from us, and can be recognized by the grooms. We therefore pray that orders may be issued to [prince] Mirza Moghal, to recover them, as they are pointed out by the grooms, from the men, in whose possession they are, and to restore them to the State.[4]

Even the policemen of the city weren't averse to a spot of plunder. Chuni Lal describes a police officer stationed near the Lahore Gate brazenly threatening to arrest citizens unless they handed over 1,000 rupees. The shopkeepers complained of this demand, and Ahsan Ulla Khan was forced to use his limited influence to issue orders for the arrest of the police officer.[5]

The extensive looting paradoxically worked to the benefit of some traders. Weighed down with valuable items, many sepoys had been approaching them to exchange their rupees, jewellery and other goods for gold coins, which were far more portable. Some embittered merchants craftily paid out counterfeit gold mohurs, knowing the sepoys couldn't tell the difference.

*****

Murders, lynchings and other forms of mob justice were ubiquitous over the following weeks, often ordered or even carried out by suspicious sepoys. It was quite obvious after the mutineers' arrival that many hankered for the stability of British rule, and this inevitably led to accusations of spying for the British. On 17 May, for instance, one of the palace sweepers working for Mirza Mughal was severely beaten by soldiers who doubted his loyalties. He was eventually released on the word of the prince. Chuni Lal records another man being captured that day while carrying a suspicious letter from Meerut. The man was apparently tied to an artillery piece, but whether it was used to kill him is not explained. Others treated roughly included anybody dependent on Europeans in some manner for their livelihood. Former employees were understandably displeased with the new order, having lost their jobs. Others marked out by their loyalty to Europeans were also suspect. The wealthy mercantile class, too, had much to lose from the recent breakdown in law and order.

Latent jealousies and feuds came to the fore, and private vendettas raged. On 15 May, a goldsmith was arrested for killing a rival in the confusion of the early days. Those harbouring a grudge could successfully bear false witness against their neighbours. This was a good time to accuse others of European sympathies. Simply inform the rebels that so-and-so had given shelter or some form of assistance to Europeans fleeing the city and the sepoys would ransack the home of the accused. One notable example of this was Quazi Panu, an employee of the state of Alwar who was resident in Delhi. His own nephews accused him of giving refuge to Europeans, and his house was promptly plundered of considerable wealth. When they had taken everything they could, the sepoys murdered Quazi and his son.

Parties of mutineers worked their way through the city, arresting locals suspected of harbouring fugitives. On 12 May, Nawab Mir Hamid Ali Khan was arrested, the rumour being that he was helping conceal some Europeans. He told the troops to search his property if they liked; it had already been looted anyway. Owing to his high station in life, he was hauled before Zafar instead of facing the usual summary execution. The Emperor apparently sent Mirza Abulbakr to search the house, declaring that he would be released if no Europeans were found. None were found, and the nawab walked free. The troops were asked to return his property, and did so.

Other prominent residents were also suspected of harbouring Europeans. Ram Charan Das, deputy collector of the city, had his house searched. A priest called Shah Nizam-Ud-Din was accused of sheltering two European women in his haveli; he challenged them to search his house, saying they could plunder at will if they found anything incriminating. Another man called Aga Muhammad Khan had his house plundered on the same day for the same reason. More fingers were pointed in the following days. When Narayan Das Naharwala was accused, the intelligence turned out to be accurate; the fugitives were killed and the house was looted as punishment.

No one was exempt from suspicion, with the sepoys extending their investigations to the servants and courtiers of the palace and even the royal family itself. Various palace servants were accused of being informers. In particular, Ahsan Ulla Khan and Mahbub Ali Khan were singled out. On 15 May, an assembly of officers confronted Zafar about these two men, claiming they were secretly in league with the British. Mahbub Ali Khan assuaged their fears by swearing an oath on the Quran that his motives were transparent, but Ahsan Ulla Khan's house was ransacked by the soldiers and he was detained to await execution. Zeenat Mahal was also challenged at various times; one day the soldiers went to her house seeking plunder, but they were thwarted by its sturdy doors. Even her father was arrested. On 17 May, Zafar toured the Salimgarh Fort, which was occupied by some of the regiments, and took the opportunity to talk to the soldiers. According to Chuni Lal, he endeavoured to assure the soldiers that he was 'associated with them in a common cause, desiring them to place every confidence in the physician

Ahsan Ulla Khan, Mahbub Ali Khan, and the Queen Zinat Mahal, and telling them he would slay with his own hands any Europeans they might seize and bring to him'.[6] Thanks to this intervention, suspicions were allayed for a time and the physician was released.

The palace guard, attendants and employees were also accused. Zahir Dehlvi was one of a group stopped inside the palace and addressed by a band of soldiers: 'You are all without faith. Arrey, you are all Christians! You write letters to the British!' The attendants had heard enough. 'Kill us once and for all. That will be better than daily harassment,' they shot back. Some sepoy officers nearby defused the situation and led the sepoys away.

Suspicions extended still further to the students of the Delhi College, who were perceived to harbour little enthusiasm for the revolution. One of their professors, the convert Ramchandra, had disappeared[7] and was presumed to have been killed by the sepoys (although it was later discovered he was still alive). The death of the principal, Mr F. Taylor, was common knowledge. The students were in a quandary; they had little interest in a chaotic revolt that might be ruthlessly crushed by the British, and to side with the rebels seemed a betrayal of the new learning that was their passion, but many had no wish to go against their own countrymen. It seemed wrong to resist the sepoys. Be that as it may, not a single student joined the rebels over the coming weeks. Their equivocation did not go unnoticed.

Meanwhile, the hunt for European fugitives hiding in the city dragged on. On 12 May, two Europeans attempting to escape the city passed in front of the main *kotwal* of the city in local guise but were recognised and killed by the sepoys. On the 14th, a European woman was captured and brought to the palace. News arrived two days later that some Europeans were hiding in a house belonging to the treasurer Mathura Das, but nobody was found after a search. On 20 May, two Europeans who had decided to hide in the Mubarak Bagh gardens to the north of the cantonments were discovered by some troopers and killed. Khwaja Hasan Nizami wrote of another discovery around this time: 'In the same way there was a tailor, it was found that he had hidden three British in his house; the rebel soldiers killed the British and looted the house. In this manner two or three people suffered every day.'

Looting and lawlessness wasn't restricted to the sepoys and criminal elements in the city. Disorder had spread to the countryside and towns around Delhi. Learning of the anarchy in the city, villagers decided to take advantage. On 13 May, Mewati villagers from Jaisinghpura plundered the house of the local railway officer and managed to get away with around 4,000 rupees plus possessions. The Gujjars and Ranghurs, local peasant villagers who needed no prompting to indulge in looting, were by far the greatest nuisance. By 14 May they had looted their way into the Civil Lines, aiming for the wealthy European residences and official buildings. The house of Simon Fraser was found to be entirely devoid of furniture.

Records too had been destroyed – all papers of the Commissioner and of the Agency to the Lieutenant Governor had been burnt.

By the 18th, the Gujjar villagers had begun reverting to self-rule. Anyone passing through their lands, whether under the authority of the Emperor or the Company, was relieved of money and valuables. 'Goojur ho ya Oojur (either Gujjar or Oojur)' was the motto adopted by these fierce villagers, meaning territory was either Gujjar land or it was devastated. Travelers coming into Delhi brought news of thousands of Gujjar villagers scouring the area. Two sowars returning after delivering a message to Alwar described their encounter with these villagers. The villagers declared they had no respect for the authority of the King, and consequently robbed the sowars of their money, possessions and horses. When the sowars produced a letter from the King, the villagers simply tore it up and handed back the pieces. After much begging, the sowars were given back their horses – but nothing else. Another messenger, on his way to Farrukhnagar to deliver a message to Nawab Ahmad Ali Khan, was simply stopped on the road by villagers and refused permission to proceed.

Although universally disliked for their lawlessness, one thing that gained the Gujjars favour among the mutineers during their destructive spree was that they invariably hacked down telegraph wires where they could, hampering British communications.

*****

With the sepoys continuing to loot despite the best efforts of Zafar and the officers, shops remained shut. As a result, ordinary people could not obtain supplies. Bringing stability to the city was the most important thing of all, and it was proving impossible. In desperation, Zafar asked the sepoy officers to place their men at strategic points across the city. They assented, and a plan was finally carried through. One regiment was stationed directly outside the palace, while most were spread across the Delhi, Ajmer, Lahore and Kashmir Gates. Smaller contingents guarded the other gates and key locations like the Farash Khana and the Darya Bazar.[8] Suitably parcelled out, the regiments could now make camps and organise themselves. At the same time, Mirza Mughal, seated on an elephant and accompanied by a company of infantry, visited the main *kotwalis* in the city to inspire confidence. Proclamations rang out warning that anyone found plundering would have their nose and ears cut off.

On 12 May, by beat of drum, shopkeepers were ordered to open their shops under threat of fines or imprisonment. Zafar, deciding his presence was necessary, ventured out with Jawan Bakht amid considerable pomp and circumstance, escorted by two regiments of infantry and guns plus musicians. Chuni Lal recorded what he saw:

> He got on his elephant and roamed the markets. The royal canopy was on display, the royal fish symbols, camel mounted cannon, black soldiers, and a number of Telanga soldiers shouting 'long live the Badshah', 'long live our religion' preceded the King's procession. The Royal Criers were shouting the Badshah's orders to open the shops. The procession was followed by Turk Soldiers who were shouting Allah o Akbar. The result of these actions was that the shops were reopened.[9]

Zafar declared that the behaviour of the sepoys thus far was an aberration; the citizens would be protected now, for the soldiers wished to gain the support of the people not their hatred. A twenty-one-gun salute had been fired when Zafar set out from the palace, and another was fired on his return to mark the new state of things.

The royal proclamations gave some shopkeepers the courage to reopen, allowing supplies to be distributed – with the strict instruction that soldiers were to pay for their goods. To further promote a semblance of order, on the 13th a new *kotwal*, Meer Nawab, was appointed to lead the police. On that day he recruited 200 men, who were duly placed at appropriate locations to prevent looting. There were even some arrests; two dubious characters called Kuli Khan and Safaraz Khan had gone on a looting spree with other men in the Teliwara and Sabzi Mandi areas, and they were apprehended. Lesser miscreants were also being dealt with. In his diary, Chuni Lal records the arrest of two water carriers who had brazenly stolen butter from a shop. The 13th also saw Zafar appoint Mirza Manir-Ud-Din, the former *kotwal* of Paharganj, as governor of the city, tasked with organising the city's food supply.

The next day, Meer Nawab made his presence known around the Sabzi Mandi, Pahari Durrung and other areas. To reinforce his authority, he was bolstered by troops of the 38th NI regiment who had agreed to cooperate to prevent the further wrecking of the Delhi cantonments. However, residents did not always find the patrols reassuring. It was noticed that the sepoys sauntered around with drawn swords, frightening the ordinary citizens. There was a palpable atmosphere of violence. Many merchants were still dreading opening their shops. Chuni Lal writes that Zafar attempted to remedy the situation by ordering that nobody should go about the city with a drawn sword.[10] To discourage locals assisting Europeans fugitives, meanwhile, a proclamation was posted around the city warning that anyone caught harbouring Europeans would be punished severely.

While law and order was being shored up, arrangements were made to put out the various fires still raging in the city. The magazine, in particular, had been burning all through the 12th after the explosion the previous day, and the conflagration was threatening to spread. Lots of the gunpowder had not yet caught fire, so there was a danger of further explosions rocking the city. Rebel soldiers found that many of the firearms in the magazine had already been appropriated by locals, but the artillery, shot and other *matériel de guerre* had been left behind. This was quickly claimed in the name of the King, as were the contents of other small British caches dotted throughout the city.

*****

Another vital plank for any new administration in the city was the preservation of good relations between Muslims and Hindus – no easy feat at a time of such great religious fervour. Despite his recently avowed faith, Zafar had to address the Muslim practice that most incensed the Hindu population: the slaughter of cows. One of the most significant orders given out in the city after his coronation was the ban on consuming beef. Muslim butchers were given strict instructions to cease killing kine, and Khwaja Hasan Nizami writes that these orders were strongly enforced:

> The first law he promulgated was to forbid the slaughter of cows, and the punishment for anybody slaughtering a cow would be to be blown to bits at the mouth of a cannon. After that the rule came that even at the time of the Eid Festival for Muslims nobody would slaughter cows. For four months, the cow butchers stayed hidden in their houses, any of them venturing outside their houses were caught and killed by the mutinying soldiers, who would say to them that the way you slaughter our holy cows we will slaughter you.

Not satisfied with Zafar's sympathy on this matter, the Hindu community would eventually push for the law to extend beyond the mere slaughter of cows. It had been noticed that bulls were being laden down with the human waste of the city, which was transported out of the city walls to be used as fertiliser in the surrounding areas. Petitions were sent to the King to proscribe such use of bulls by Muslims, as it was considered degrading. Orders duly went out that donkeys should be used for this task instead of bulls. Mrs Aldwell, the Anglo-Indian Christian who survived the events at Delhi that summer, claimed there was general cohesion on this issue, with the killing of cows largely stopped: 'I believe that not a single oxen was killed in Delhi during the whole time of the rebellion. On the festival of the Bakr-Eed when the Mahomedans usually slaughter an ox a disturbance was expected but the Mahomedans refrained from doing so.'[11]

However, some of the more uncompromising figures among the Muslim population were quick to show their anger at the new directives. Moulvi Mohammed Said, a doctor in the city, was such a man. He was supported and accompanied by various other Muslim doctors and mullahs, who brought many fervent followers to the cause. On 19 May, they organised a march to the Jama Masjid where they raised the green flag (the standard of Islam) on the mosque, declaring jihad against nonbelievers.

Their intention was to stress that the war was now a religious one, and that it was incumbent on all Muslims to rise – 'the doctors having represented the great merit of slaying the English, who, they said, were infidels' in the words of Chuni Lal.[12] As far as these protesters were concerned, Zafar was going too far with his attempts to inspire fraternity. 'The Muslims got annoyed with this and Moulvi Mohammed Said placed a flag in the Jama Masjid to assemble the Muslims for actions saying this was not a Muslim Government and that the Hindus were dictating terms to the Badshah [Emperor],' wrote Khwaja Hasan Nizami.[13] This call to arms proved successful, with several thousand Muslims agreeing to join the struggle. This caused concern in the palace, for the jihad could be turned against the Hindu community at any time.

Zafar pointedly refused to see the rebellion as an Islamic struggle. He summoned Moulvi Mohammed Said to the palace, and in discussion it became clear that the doctor's interest was in a general religious jihad, not a politically motivated struggle for independence from Britain. Chuni Lal writes of the disagreement:

> The King remarked that he (the doctor) had erected the Mahomedan standard in the Jama Masjid against the English: but that as they had been all killed, there had been no necessity for doing so. The doctor replied that it had been sent up against the Hindus. On this the King remarked that he regarded Hindus and Mahomedans alike, and he was not disposed to acquiesce in a religious war against the Hindus; further remarking that, as for the Christians, all there had been of them, had been already killed. After this, the officers of the army attended and complained that the Mahomedans had raised the Mahomedan flag against them; but the King assured them that the object of its being erected was the slaughter of the English.[14]

Zafar explained to the moulvi that it was important for Muslims and Hindus to stay united against the British, that anything else would be complete folly. Another Muslim priest, Moulvi Sadr-ud-Din Khan, was then sent to the Jama Masjid to reason with the crowd, and he successfully prevailed upon them to take down the green standard. On 21 May, to reassure the Hindu population, another proclamation was issued. By beat of drum, it was decreed that there must be no quarrels between the two communities and that together they must strive to oust the British interlopers from the country.

By his prompt actions, Zafar had prevented violence and suspicion from dragging the rebellion into the mire. Nevertheless, the ephemeral relationship between the two groups had been starkly exposed. Without strong central authority, all could be lost.

# 17

# Puppet Emperor

Do you know what the outcome of the events unfolding before us will be?
Zafar

Huzoor, your glory has been revived after 150 years. The empire which had been taken away has been returned.
Hameed Khan

Freed from the constraints of British authority by the mutineers, it soon became apparent to Zafar that life and liberty was little better under a different thumb. It must also have been plain that governing the city was going to be harder than expected. Law and order was just one of many immediate problems facing the King. There was no money to pay the troops, and there were no supplies for their daily needs. Their anarchic attitude, their indiscipline, their continued looting of the city and their refusal to show deference presaged a difficult relationship. Nevertheless, Zafar tried to make the best of the situation. He endeavoured to direct the rebellion so that it might bear fruit.

The matter of raising revenue for the payment of troops had to be resolved quickly or else Zafar's nominal influence over the troops would vanish. The sepoy officers had already begun requesting daily allowances for their men beforehand, and Zafar had extended another 400 rupees per regiment for their supplies on 13 May. The next day, he asked his treasurer, Saligram, how much money remained in the depleted treasury. This the treasurer did not know – finding out thus became yet another matter to address. However, it was inevitable that whatever money did remain would be minuscule next to what was required. Zafar also invited the city's principal grain dealers to the palace and asked them to open the granaries again, and to sell under regulated prices.

The only quick way to raise money was to appropriate British treasuries in the nearby towns, which were already at risk of being looted by the marauding Gujjars. Two such treasuries were at Rohtak (around 60 miles north-west of Delhi) and Gurgaon (around 25 miles south-west). It was imperative that troops were sent to guard these places. On 15 May, news arrived in Delhi that the magistrate of Rohtak had fled and that the treasury in the town was in imminent danger. The treasury at Gurgaon, meanwhile, had reportedly been plundered already. Anxious to secure the large sums at Rohtak, Zafar ordered a regiment to march on the town and bring back the treasure. Two days later, on 17 May, word reached the King that the several lakh rupees at the Gurgaon treasury had been discovered untouched. The treasure was being brought to Delhi by some sepoys, but the column was under attack by nearly 300 Gujjar and Mewati villagers. In response, two companies of infantry and a troop of cavalry were immediately sent to help protect the treasure and bring it into the city. On 19 May, there was good news: 17,000 rupees had been collected by a party of troopers at Garhi Harsaru in Gurgaon. The money had been abandoned by the local collector, who had fled as soon as disturbances broke out in the area.

In all, eight British treasuries fell to the rebels in the Delhi area. Some further afield would also be captured or looted by nearby regiments as the mutiny spread. The Haryana Light Infantry Battalion, for instance, had in its possession the areas of Sirsa and Hissar. Gouri Shankar Sukal, one of the officers of the unit, wrote to Delhi informing the authorities of his intention to bring them captured treasure.[1] However, Sirsa was over 150 miles north-west of Delhi, and the officer had little confidence he could make it to Delhi safely given the uncertain conditions on the roads. All along the route, Gujjar villagers were waiting to swoop on the column. The officer urgently asked for reinforcements.

Raiding nearby British treasuries would only alleviate the financial shortfalls temporarily. Revenue would have to be raised, and taxes formerly collected for the British treasuries needed to be collected for the royal treasury instead. With this in mind, Mahbub Ali Khan was asked to prepare a list of the wealthy residents of the city. On the eunuch's list were the more prominent merchants of the city, including men like Ramji Das Gurwalla, Saligram and others. These men were told that, with the daily expenses involved in maintaining the various regiments in the city reaching 2,500 rupees a day, it was necessary that they should provide five lakh rupees for the treasury. This would be sufficient to pay the troops in the short term. The merchants expressed much dismay, protesting that they had already been looted of much of their goods and wealth by the troops. How were they to come up with such sums?

*****

In terms of reinforcements, there was some early good news. On 17 May, additional men arrived in the form of five companies of sappers and miners from Meerut. These were the men who had come from Roorkee to help the Europeans at Meerut before suspicion and confusion had led to skirmishes in which a number of them were slain by the Europeans. On the 18th, the officers of this contingent were granted an audience with the King to give their version of events at Meerut. Upon reaching the city cantonment, they had found the Europeans of the city, both soldiers and civilians, busy entrenching themselves in the Dum-Dum. Here is where the story diverges from the earlier, European narrative. The Roorkee men said that they were approached by the European officers, who asked for their loyalty. The men claimed to have refused, despite an offer of higher pay. In the face of their steadfast refusals, they said, the Europeans began firing on them at about three o'clock in the morning. The Europeans then pursued them out of the city, killing around 200 of them; the rest had made their way to Delhi. Zafar welcomed their allegiance, and arranged for them to be quartered in the Salimgarh Fort.

A few days earlier, orders had been given to recruit more troops. In all, 400 infantry and a regiment of cavalry were required, with the salary for infantry set at 5 rupees per month and 20 rupees for the troopers. Enthusiasm seems to have been lacking, however, given all the uncertainty. By 15 May, only 200 new recruits had been gathered.

It quickly became apparent that this new army had little inclination to take any initiative or even venture beyond the city walls. Much like the European force at Meerut, the rebel army was almost entirely static after reaching Delhi. This was not for want of trying; one week after the mutineers' arrival, with colonels chosen to lead the various regiments, plans were laid. On 18 May, Prince Mirza Abulbakr led out a regiment of cavalry in an attempt to tame the nearby Gujjar villagers, who had been continuing to indulge in plentiful looting.[2] He made it to the villages of Chandrawal and Wazirabad, but the villagers melted away before he arrived and nothing was achieved. On the same day, orders were also given to bring order to the districts neighbouring Delhi.

'Intelligence was received that the Goojurs of Chand Rawal were every night plundering the shops in Sabzi Mandi, Teliwara, Rajpur, Mandersa &c.,' writes Chuni Lal, 'and Mirza Moghal was ordered to suppress these evil practices of the said Goojurs. Mirza Abulbakr accordingly went to the village in question with his regiment of cavalry, and had it plundered and burnt.'[3] But the Gujjars were a fratricidal people. Villages would frequently turn on one another, usually due to territorial disputes; there was no central authority to which the authorities could appeal. It seems that the sepoy officers, unable to subdue the Gujjars, may have decided to offer them the hand of friendship. 'I am of the opinion that no agreement was made between the Goojurs and the mutinous troops beforehand. But afterwards certain mutinous officers caused the King to grant a dram and standard to two Goojurs of the neighbourhood of Delhi who were enjoined to plunder the provisions of the British camp,' wrote Ahsan Ulla Khan. After a while, some of the leading Gujjar chiefs were given command of certain villages and territory in exchange for accepting the nominal authority of the Emperor.

During the first few days after their arrival at Delhi, the general feeling among the sepoys was that a strong British force was sure to march from Meerut within days. On 14 May, news – incorrect as it turned out – was received from four men who had just come from Meerut. They said that a European force was marching on Delhi and that it would arrive in a matter of hours. 'The soldiers were not pleased at this intelligence, and placed the four men in question in arrest,'[4] Chuni Lal recorded. However, in consequence, two men were sent towards Meerut to ascertain the truth of their claim. Three days went by with no sight of the enemy on the opposite bank of the river. The two scouts finally returned on 17 May with the news that, far from marching on Delhi, the British were barricading themselves in at the Meerut cantonment. There were said to be about 1,000 soldiers there, but they were encumbered by many civilians. Various fortifications had been constructed for an expected attack by the rebels. The mutineers couldn't believe their luck. However, the scouts had been very lucky to return safely; they barely escaped the attentions of the Gujjar villagers now waylaying any unfortunates on the route between the cities.

Buoyed by the news that the British force at Meerut was too weak to advance on Delhi, the sepoys began to talk about attacking Meerut. Intelligence arriving from Meerut on 19 May seemed encouraging; two troopers brought news that violence had broken out in the city. Some native troops had apparently arrived from Bareilly and Moradabad with artillery and treasure. However, they had heard about the hostile reception received by the sappers and miners from Roorkee before them. In this tense atmosphere, the British apparently fired on the troops, who answered in kind. 'Through the direction of God a shot from the latter fired the mine the Europeans had laid, and the whole area enclosed by their entrenchments was blown up,' reported Chuni Lal. 'On receiving this intelligence the whole of the troops and the King were highly delighted, and fired five guns at Salimgarh in token of their joy.'[5] Not everybody trusted this intelligence, however; when Chuni Lal approached officers of the 20th NI at the Salimgarh Fort, they dismissed the story. Nevertheless, these rumours gave an added fillip to the rebels. An interesting petition later came to light; written by fifty men previously employed in the constabulary force at Meerut's jail, it beseeched the authorities to let the men join a force under Mirza Mughal that was due to attack Meerut.[6]

On 20 May, forces were mustered to march on Meerut. Quite how much motivation and energy remained after two days of talking was unclear, however. The plan was to send four regiments of infantry as well as cavalry units under the command of Mirza Mughal. 'The said Mirza suggested that Mirza Amin-ud-Din Khan, Mirza Zia-ud-Din Khan, Hasan Ali Khan, and other great chiefs holding extensive territories, might be sent with him and promised to exterminate the English. On hearing this suggestion, the chiefs preferred to remain silent,' wrote Chuni Lal.[7] Zafar, perhaps changing his mind, then chose another prince to lead the force: Mirza Abulbakr. In the end, nothing happened. Idle words aside, the soldiers had no great desire to leave the comforts of Delhi. The idea of seizing the initiative never progressed beyond mere speculation.

Such dithering defined the coming days. Even maintaining the peace in the area around Delhi proved beyond the new authorities; Gujjar villagers reigned supreme. Crucially, there was never a plan to march north to persuade the cis-Sutlej rulers to join them or to attack the British presence at Ambala or elsewhere. The British forces might not have attacked yet, but it was surely a matter of time. This window of opportunity could have been used to great effect. Instead, it was squandered.

*****

Despite the aborted attack on Meerut, morale was high among the soldiers and officers. Around a week after their arrival, Haider Hassan, Commandant of the King's Artillery, overheard sepoys who were clearly hopeful: 'If we continue united together, we shall not be defeated by the Government troops but shall become masters of the country.'[8] Haider Hassan had good relations with the rebel officers, and in conversations with them heard their plans to take various princes and make them viceroys of various parts of Hindustan as British rule crumbled across the country. Despite these ambitions, however, nobody suggested a way to bring these goals to fruition. Perhaps it was hoped that the whole of the Bengal Army would mutiny, causing the British to simply give up.

Despite the reservations of the common folk, the soldiers received support from various quarters. Scholars from both the Muslim and Hindu faiths encouraged the sepoys, suggesting to them that they were invincible. The newspapers of the city joined in as well, as exemplified by this piece from the *Delhi Urdu Akhbar* of 24 May:

> God is all powerful. O' countrymen the intelligence of the English, trade, good administration and the expansion of their government and wealth, treasury and income and expenses have probably disheartened you as to how such a big government can be destroyed in such a short time. But the Muslims and Hindus all should enlighten their hearts with their faith (Iman) and knowledge obtaining inspiration from their religions ...
>
> Thus when you see that how big Rajas after sometime are destroyed by other caste people then how do you not understand that God has

> arranged through his absolute powers evidently that that nation which has established its power for the last one hundred years and treating the people of God with contempt and calls your kith and kins blackman (Kala Aadmi). God has shown his game...
>
> It is imperative for you to eradicate fear from your hearts and not to flee abandoning the city with fear and despondency. It is to degenerate power of God. O dear brothers if you are anxious in this war and do any work with satisfaction or are afraid and tremble with fear of them, you are bound to be called sinners. This is the sign of weakness of your faith. You possess two hands, your opponents have also the same. Every one of you is a brave person who is like a lion.[9]

Among the common populace, the divide was stark. According to Mrs Aldwell, who survived the siege in the city, there was a marked difference between the attitudes of the Hindus and the Muslims. Aldwell noted much more enthusiasm and fervour in the Muslim community: 'The Mahomedans always seemed glad that the mutiny had taken place and during the Muharram festival, I heard the Mahomedan women praying and teaching their children to pray for the success of their faith and these prayers were generally accompanied by execrations against the English.'[10]

*****

Whatever the case regarding the organisation and morale of the rebel army, Zafar was never in doubt as to the true feelings of the sepoys towards him. Even on the day of their arrival, he had been treated with scant deference. His coronation seemed to have changed little. The contempt of the soldiers and officers as they strode about the palace left much to be desired. From the time they had first entered the palace, the sepoys had refused to follow the required etiquette, striding about imperiously within the palace complex, and the sowars had refused to dismount at the appropriate gates, riding wherever they pleased. Zafar later made his feelings clear:

> These are places which not even Nadir Shah nor Ahmad Shah nor any of the British Governor-Generals of India ever entered on horseback ... As regards the behaviour of that rebellious army, it may be stated that they never saluted me even, nor showed me any other mark of respect. They used to walk into the Hall of Special Audience and the Hall of Devotion with their shoes on. What confidence could I place in troops who had murdered their own masters? In the same way that they murdered them, they made me a prisoner, and tyrannised over me, keeping me on in order to make use of my name as a sanction for their acts.[11]

Some semblance of decorum had in fact returned to the palace on 17 May, when the sepoys and subedars agreed in principle to move out of the

Diwan-i-Khas and other buildings. This allowed new carpets to be laid, replacing those ruined by the soldiers and allowing the inner sanctums to return to their previous state. However, the arrogant bearing of the soldiers continued to trouble Zafar. How could matters progress when the soldiers showed no deference to his authority? The soldiers, in turn, seemed not to think his assent was required for orders and declarations. He was just there to rubber stamp their decisions, and this was clear to him.

> As regards the orders under my seal, and under my signature, the real state of the case is, that from the day the soldiery came and killed the European officers, and made me a prisoner, I remained in their power as such. All papers they thought fit, they caused to be prepared, and bringing them to me, compelled me to affix my seal. Sometimes they brought the rough drafts of orders, and had fair copies of them made by my secretary. At other times they brought the original letters intended for despatch, and left copies of them in the office. Hence several rough drafts in a diversity of hands have been filed in the proceedings. Frequently they had the seal impressed on the outside of empty unaddressed envelopes. There is no knowing what papers they sent in these or to whom they sent them...
>
> ...whoever wished, had orders written as he chose, without my authority, not even acquainting me with their purport, while I and my secretary being in jeopardy of our lives, could not dare to say anything in the matter.[12]

Zafar explained how officers began bringing orders written by themselves or the army committees and asking him to rewrite them in his hand to provide legitimacy. Sometimes vague threats were issued that those who did not consent to the sepoys' wishes 'would be made to repent their conduct'.[13] At other times, they would threaten to unseat him and make Mirza Mughal the King instead, saying he would be more pliable.

Their inconsiderate language and their threats, real or imagined, preyed on Zafar's mind. As early as ten days after their arrival in Delhi, Zafar wrote a revealing letter to Mirza Mughal voicing his frustration at the disrespect he experienced. On the matter of money and supplies, Zafar personally informed the soldiers that he had no treasure but that he would try his best to assist them. Arrangements had been made to take out loans to pay the soldiers their daily allowances. The soldiers, he said, had understood his financial embarrassments and had agreed to obey him if he assisted them. He had asked the officers to arrange to manage the magazine and treasury so that supplies could be managed in the most efficient way possible. Instead, their indiscipline untamed, the men had set up camp in the inner sanctums of the palace as well as the Mahtab Gardens and refused to leave. Realizing the delicate nature of relations, Zafar asked his servants not to interfere.

> Repeated injunctions have been issued prohibiting plunder and aggression in the city, but all to no purpose; for although ten days have now elapsed, the same evils are prevailing to the present time. Moreover, without reference to night or day, they enter and plunder the houses of the inhabitants on the false plea that they have concealed Europeans. They force locks and shop-doors and openly carry away the property from the shops, and they forcibly loose the horses of the cavalry and take them off. They commit these excesses in the face of the fact that all cities taken without military operations have ever been exempted from sack and slaughter. Even Jangiz Khan [Genghis Khan] and Nadir Shah, kings execrated as tyrants, gave peace and protection to such cities as surrendered without resistance. Moreover, the men of the army go about threatening and intimidating the royal servants and the inhabitants of the city.

Violence and oppression prevailed in the city. How was revenue to be raised to pay the soldiers if the city and its neighbourhood could not be policed? Moreover, their looting and plundering reflected badly on Zafar, for the people would think he was in league with the rebels. Zafar had done all they said; as aforementioned, he had appointed the princes as commanders of the regiments. Yet the sepoys refused to bend to discipline. Nonetheless, Zafar's biggest grievance was the lack of respect given to his person:

> Setting aside all these points, it may be remarked that whenever the most distinguished officers of the highest ranks in the service of the British Government visited the palace, they dismounted at the door of the Hall of Public Audience, and came from thence on foot. These soldiery, however, used, till recently, to come galloping up to the Hall of Special Audience on their horses, and as a last resort, both the gates were closed a wicket only being left open; but they still ride up to the Hall of Public Audience, and the Jalwa-khana, unsuitably dressed, and without their turbans, in utter disregard to the forms of respect due to royalty. The officers of the army too make a practice of coming into court carelessly dressed, wearing caps instead of turbans and carrying their swords. Never during the British rule did any members of their profession behave in this way.

All in all, the King was very pessimistic as to whether a new government could be maintained.

> Accordingly, nothing but the total desolation of the city and country can be expected as the inevitable end of this state of matters...
>
> ...Under these circumstances, how is it to be believed that these people can have the welfare of the state at heart, or that they cherish

> any desire to yield subjection and obedience to the royal authority? It is further to be considered, that there is no money in the royal treasury, and the city merchants having been plundered and ruined have no longer the ability to provide a loan. How then are the daily allowances to be paid for any length of time? and when they shall, of necessity, have been discontinued, and the supplies from the country shall also have ceased. What will be the state of things then?

Zafar contemplated abdicating the throne and removing himself from the scene entirely: 'Wearied and helpless, we have now resolved on making a vow to pass the remainder of our days in services acceptable to God, and relinquishing the title of sovereign fraught with cares and troubles, and in our present griefs and sorrows, assuming the garb of a religious mendicant, to proceed first and stay at the shrine of the saint Khwaja Sahib, and, after making necessary arrangements for the journey, to go eventually to Mecca.'

The only way to save the situation, he told Mirza Mughal, was to organise a meeting with the officers of the various regiments and ask them in no uncertain terms to agree to a written declaration that they would obey the royal command, put a stop to the looting and make their men police the area and collect revenue. All murmurs and grumblings must stop, and orders must be obeyed. If their endeavour was to succeed, every effort had to be made to bring the state to an even keel. If the officers did not accept this ultimatum and affix their seals to the document, Zafar would abdicate and take up the life of a beggar, sweeping the floors of mosques.

# 18

# Divine Cull of the Unbelievers

> On the day fixed for the slaughter arriving great crowds of people were flocking to the palace ... [1]
>
> Chuni Lal

The number of European and Christian prisoners held in the palace had grown steadily since 11 May. Some had made their way to the palace voluntarily during the chaos of the 11th or in the following days, thinking they would receive sanctuary from the violence in the streets. Others had been brought in, Zafar having requested that any Europeans or Christians taken captive in the city come into his custody rather than face summary execution. A steady trickle of European fugitives into the palace had persisted. All the same, any captured European's survival was subject to the whims of the sepoys they faced; many were shot on sight. Death didn't necessarily mean the end of degradation, either. On the 14th, the police officer in charge of the Nigambodh area ordered the bodies of Commissioner Simon Fraser and Captain Douglas to be fetched from the palace and buried, but the other European corpses littering the city were collected and thrown into the river.

By the 16th, the total number of prisoners in the palace amounted to just over fifty – mostly women and children. At first the sepoys had guarded the prisoners themselves, but they were soon handed over to the palace guards and housed in a makeshift prison in an underground chamber, sometimes called a kitchen, close to the Mehtab Bagh. During Zafar's trial in the wake of the mutiny, the presiding judge would examine the 'kitchen' himself. 'The building is 40 feet long, 12 broad, and about 10 high,' he wrote. 'It is old, dirty, and dilapidated, and without the vestige of plaster; but it is worse than this, for it is dark, has no made flooring, no windows, and is entirely without the means of ventilation or of light. There is but one aperture to it, a miserable, small wooden door.'[2] Here the prisoners languished while their future was decided upon by the sepoys, their officers and the princes.

One issue raised during the later trials was whether or not Zafar could have saved the lives of some of the prisoners by offering them shelter in the women's apartments in the palace. The sepoys would have been reluctant to enter the seraglio, which was a sequestered area. Even if the sepoys had thrown aside their reluctance and entered, there were known to be numerous secret recesses and passages where the prisoners could have been hidden for a time. Perhaps, mused physician Ahsan Ulla Khan, a more resolute stance by Zafar could have saved the prisoners. Instead, he was party to a massacre.

> If the King had kept the women and children in his own female apartments, and on their being demanded, had explained to the latter that he would only agree to their (the Christians) being murdered, after his (the King's) own women and children had been first put to death, it was very probable that the sepoys would not have dared to enter the royal seraglio to forcibly seize and kill the Christians. The King could safely have said and done so. He frequently spoke to the sepoys as resolutely. Had the King's sanction not been given it was not possible that a false entry could have been made in the official documents to the effect that his sanction *had* been given.

Despite the physician's testament, it is difficult to gauge how much Zafar could have done. Many later claimed that any major effort on his part to save the prisoners – or even a strong show of sympathy – would have compromised his own position. Perhaps he feared that such an act might precipitate a break with the sepoys without even helping the captives. For his part, Ahsan Ulla Khan advised Zafar as to what he thought was the best way to keep the prisoners alive: approach the Islamic authorities in the city and obtain a fatwa from them stipulating that the prisoners were not to be killed. Since the prisoners were mainly women and children, he explained, and Islam forbade the slaughtering of women and children prisoners, the fatwa would surely be granted. Such a ruling could then be shown to the rebels, removing some responsibility from Zafar himself. Lacking the sanction of the King and assent of the Muslim authorities, the sepoys would probably abandon the idea of executing the captive Christians.

There were other advantages to preserving their lives as well, as the physician explained to the King in a conversation on 14 May, invoking the ill-fated British campaign in Afghanistan less than twenty years before:

> I explained to him that such was the line of conduct adopted by Sirdar Mahomed Akbar Khan, of Caubul [Kabul], to those who became his prisoners during the Afghan war [First Anglo-Afghan War]. I pointed out to the King how, in consequence of such conduct, Akbar Khan succeeded in procuring the liberation of his father, the Ameer Dost Mahomed Khan, from confinement in the hands of the British, and how the Ameer

> was ultimately restored to his country and kingdom. The effect of my suggestions was, that the King, at that time, withheld his sanction to the murder of the Christians, and for two days their lives were preserved.

Another person with influence at Zafar's court was Nabi Baksh Khan, agent of Akbar Shah, the former emperor. He petitioned the King on the subject, offering similar advice. He recommended obtaining a fatwa from the Muslim authorities in the city as well as a *bywasta* (a ruling by a Hindu pundit) on the subject. If both these religious authorities agreed to the slaughter, then the soldiers should be allowed to proceed; if they did not, as was more likely, Zafar must show courage and declare to the soldiers that they would have to go through him to get to the captives. This would be sufficient to discourage the soldiers from committing a massacre.[3]

Other parties in the palace also tried to dampen the soldiers' hankering for blood. Zahir Dehlvi and some colleagues approached Gulab Khan, risaldar of the 3rd Cavalry (from Meerut) and a subedar, Qadir Baksh of the Safar Meena Paltan. These men, senior figures aged roughly sixty, no doubt commanded respect among the sepoys. Dehlvi thought that if these seniors could be convinced, there was a good chance of the prisoners being saved. Like Ahsan Ulla Khan and Nabi Baksh Khan, Dehlvi also stressed the religious aspect. Some of the prisoners had indicated they would embrace Islam and were even heard uttering the *kalima* in a gamble to save their lives; how could it be right to kill them? One of Dehlvi's group firmly addressed the sepoys:

> Listen, O Muslims! You say that the foundation of this dispute is your faith, and that you have come here after your religion was endangered. Therefore it is obligatory and compulsory for you to listen to the elders of your religion and follow the rules of Islam and Islamic law. If you behave of your own accord and allow bigotry to creep in, then you will no longer be worthy of being called a Muslim. In the age of the Prophet (peace be upon him) or in the age of his Caliphs, when wars were fought against the Jewish and Christian sects on the basis of religion, they were presented with three conditions which, when accepted, were enforced. The first condition was: If you follow Islam and read the *kalima* and accept the oneness of Allah and the prophethood of Mohammad, then you are brothers. You are what we are. And there's no difference between us. We have nothing to do with your property, possessions, wife and family. The second condition was: If you don't accept Islam but agree to pay *jeziya* [the Muslim tax on non-believers], then you are under our protection and we will never break our promise to you. The third condition was: If you refuse to agree to either of the two stated, then the Sword hangs between us. If these people had decided to fight and it reached the stage of do or die, they would be punished, but no one has ever lifted a finger against women and children. Women

> and children were exempted from the punishment and those who came into the community as *zimmi* [or *dhimmi* – non-Muslims accepting the temporal supremacy of Islam and Muslims] were not harmed by anyone. It is astonishing that these people are reciting the *kalima* and accepting Islam, yet you want to murder them. What faith is this and which religion are you advocating? No religion condones the murder of women and children.[4]

Tempers seemed to be soothed by these well-delivered rebukes, and the sepoys asked Dehlvi and his colleagues what could be done with the prisoners. 'You should hand them over into the custody of the Badshah-e-Islam [i.e. Zafar] and he will convert them and get them suitably married as per their choice,' one of them replied.

However, this plea for mercy only had a temporary effect. The common soldiers had been calling for their execution from the beginning, as Zafar would explain. 'Near evening [11 May], these traitors brought, as prisoners, some European men and women whom they had found in the magazine, and resolved on killing them. I had recourse to persuasion and succeeded in getting their lives spared for the time.'[5]

Impatience grew among the sepoys over the following days, and they questioned why the prisoners were being kept alive for no purpose. Some of the Muslim officers asked for five European women prisoners recently captured to be handed over to them. Zafar, in turn, asked for advice from Mahbub Ali Khan as to where the matter stood according to Islamic law. A moulvi was summoned. 'The Moulavy presented the opinion required, ruling that the slaughter of women was not legal according to the Mahomedan code,' wrote Chuni Lal.[6] The women had escaped death for the time being. Zafar's influence, paired with the moulvi's ruling, was enough. The soldiers certainly still desired the King's sanction to give their actions legitimacy.

Before long, patience was wearing thin again. The soldiers clamoured for blood once more. According to Ahsan Ulla Khan, there was a strong circle of influential people in the palace who were actively in favour of disposing of the prisoners. It appears the princes, especially Abulbakr and Mirza Khizr Sultan, were among those who shouted loudest for executions. Several of the sepoy officers joined in, most prominently Gulab Shah of the 3rd Light Cavalry; he was supported by officers of the 11th NI and 74th NI. However, perhaps the most belligerent of the group was Basant Ali Khan, the eunuch chamberlain. Jat Mall described him as 'a man notorious for his savage disposition' who 'went among the soldiers and instigated them to insist on the murder of the Europeans'. Basant Ali Khan was also known to have whipped up anger at the King's reluctance to shed captive blood. Zafar had his work cut out for him.

Meanwhile, in the makeshift prison downstairs, the captives waited for a final judgment. Mrs Aldwell, one of the few prisoners to survive, records little of those six days save for occasional threats from the sepoys:

> We were all confined in one room, very dark, with only one door, and no window or other opening. It was not fit for the residence of any human being, much less for the number of us that were there. We were very much crowded together, and in consequence of the sepoys, and everyone who took a fancy to do so, coming and frightening the children, we were obliged frequently to close the one door that we had, which then left us without light or air. The sepoys used to come with their muskets loaded and bayonets fixed, and ask us whether we would consent to become Mahomedans, and also slaves, if the King granted us our lives; but the King's special armed retainers, from which the guard over us was always furnished, incited the sepoys to be content with nothing short of our lives, saying we should be cut up in small pieces, and given as food to the kites and crows. On Thursday [14 May] some of the sepoys came and told the ladies that they intended to kill us all by mining and blowing up the palace. We were very indifferently fed; but on two occasions the King sent us better food. Nothing further of consequence occurred till Friday afternoon, when one of the King's special servants asked one of the ladies (I think it was Mrs Staines) if the English were ever restored to power, how they would treat them; and she replied, 'Just as you have treated our husbands and children.'[7]

Aldwell and her daughters had taken precautions after their capture. No doubt helped by her half-Indian blood, she had managed to convince the guards that she and her children were from Kashmir and were Muslim. 'Since the outbreak on Monday, I had learnt and had taught my children the Mahomedan confession of faith, and we were all able to repeat it. It was from believing us Mussulmans that our lives were spared.' For this reason, she was also treated better than the Europeans and had been given food separately from the other captives, eating with Muslim servants in the palace. Another woman prisoner was also spared. A Muslim resident of the city, she had been arrested for giving food to some fleeing Europeans.

*****

On the morning of the 16th, things came to a head. When Zafar went to hold court in the Diwan-i-Khas, he was confronted by a sizable contingent of soldiers and officers. One of the officers held a letter with the seals of both Ahsan Ulla Khan and Mahbub Ali Khan. The letter had been intercepted with its messenger as he tried to leave via the Delhi Gate. The soldiers announced that the letter was proof that the two courtiers were in league with the British. Apparently, it promised help to defeat the rebels from within once a British force arrived to recapture the city. Both vehemently denied all accusations and declared the letter a forgery.[8] This the soldiers refused to believe, and heated conversations followed. Several of the soldiers drew their swords on Ahsan Ulla Khan as they railed against his Christian sympathies and what they perceived to be his self-serving duplicity.[9] Tempers were already running high among the sepoys as they had engaged in numerous fruitless searches based on rumours of Europeans being sheltered by sympathetic locals.

Mukand Lal recounts how Mirza Mughal and Basant Ali Khan decided to confront the King with their suspicions. Accompanied by a party of sepoys, they went to Zafar. 'The King was at this time in his own apartments; Mirza Mughal and Basant Ali Khan went inside while the soldiery remained without; they returned in about 20 minutes, when Basant Ali Khan publicly and in a loud voice, proclaimed that the King had given his permission for the slaughter of the prisoners, and that they could take them away.'[10] The prisoners were now fair game.

Zafar would later protest that he was powerless to stop the enraged sepoys by this stage:

> On the last occasion, though I again did all in my power to reason with the rebellious soldiery, they would not heed me, and carried out their purpose of slaying these poor people. I gave no orders for this slaughter. Mirza Mughal, Mirza Khair Sultan, Mirza Abul-Bakr and Basant one of my own personal attendants, who had leagued with the soldiery, may have made use of my name; but I have no knowledge that they did, nor do I know that my own armed retainers, acting independently of my orders, joined in the slaughter. If they did so, they may have been urged on to it by Mirza Mughal. Even after the massacre, no one gave me any information regarding it.

Mirza Majhli, one of the princes, to his credit was seen trying to prevent the massacre.[11] However, the hostility was so great that the prince himself had to flee for his life. Others also thought to prevent the atrocity. Zahir Dehlvi had informed Ahsan Ulla Khan of eunuch Basant Ali Khan's plans to carry out the massacre, and the physician tried to formulate a plan to save the prisoners with Zafar's help. However, sepoys were on hand to make sure nothing got in their way.

*****

At around eight in the morning, the prisoners were herded out of the makeshift jail by a force led by eunuchs Basant Ali Khan and Sidi Nasir. Only Aldwell and her daughters were left behind, along with the other Muslim woman. Aldwell relates what happened next.

> On the morning of the 16th of May some of the King's special servants, attended by a small number of infantry sepoys, came and called out to our party that the Christians were to come out of the building, and that the five Mahomedans were to remain. The women and children began

> crying, saying they knew they were going to be murdered; but the Mahomedans swore on the Kuran, and the Hindus on the Jumna, that such was not the case; that they wanted to give them a better residence, and that the one they were in would be converted into a magazine. On this they went out, were counted, but I do not know the number; a rope was thrown round to encircle the whole group, the same as prisoners are usually kept together when on the move; and in this manner they were taken out of my sight, and as I heard, brought under the pipal tree by the small reservoir in the courtyard.[12]

As the prisoners walked to the reservoir they had to run the gauntlet of sepoys and guards uttering invectives. Word must have spread rapidly, for a large concourse of people had quickly gathered to see the execution. Jat Mall had heard about it, and decided to make his way to the palace. 'I got into the palace among the crowd. This was about eight o'clock in the morning. On my reaching the first courtyard of the Palace, I saw the Europeans seated in a row, with their hands tied behind their backs along the edge of the square reservoir, and also along the small canal leading to it; there were men, women and children.'

The wait continued till around 10 a.m., with people gathering all the while. Some seemed to be of the type to revel in executions. 'There were about 200 Mussulmans standing at the reservoir uttering the coarsest abuse against the prisoners,' wrote Chuni Lal, who was also present.[13] The princes were of course in attendance, enjoying the view from a terrace of Mirza Mughal's house overlooking the courtyard. Mukand Lal, in the crowd below, observed the princes savouring the moment, laughing and encouraging the sepoys.[14]

Earlier, the prisoners had been pushed to convert to Islam. Facing oblivion, some broke down. Zahir Dehlvi watched some of the women concede on the matter of faith.

> We got up to see them and found they were covered in dust and blood. They were in a state of fear and panic. When they saw us standing near the tasbihkhana, they started pleading for water. We called two water carriers from the water house who brought two water skins and helped them wash their faces and hands and drink water by cupping their palms to hold it. Some infants couldn't drink from the cupped palms and I felt very sorry for them. I got two paper cups from the water rooms and gave them to their mothers to help the children drink. When they had washed themselves and drunk water, they said, 'Brother Muslims, La 'ilaha 'illa-llah, Muhammadur Rasulu-llah! We all are converting to Islam. Don't take our lives!'

It was no use; the soldiers were in the mood to kill. The offer to convert simply came too late. The prisoners were told to stand in a line in front of the Naqqar Khana (where musical instruments were stored) by some of the King's servants. The original intention was to shoot the prisoners, and some shots were fired with a carbine. Farcically, somebody missed and killed one of the King's armed retainers. In consequence it was decided that, in light of the danger posed by the large crowd, dispatching the prisoners with the sword was the better option. The dubious honour was granted to the King's own armed retainers. Eyewitnesses told Mrs Aldwell how it went down:

> [The captives were] murdered with swords by the King's private servants. None of the sepoys took part in killing them. The privilege, for it was so considered, of murdering them was particularly reserved for the King's own servants, as it was believed by them that the killing an infidel would ensure them a place in paradise. I was told of this at the time by the wife of a sweeper, and afterwards, when residing in Delhi during the whole time of the rebellion, frequently heard this circumstance confirmed.[15]

According to a bystander called Gulab, between two and eight people did the killing: 'I did not observe any signal orders given but on a sudden the men just mentioned drew their swords and all simultaneously attacked the prisoners and continued cutting at them till they had killed them all.'[16]

Once the executions were complete, the crowd was ushered out of the palace. Two carts were brought in and loaded up with bodies. The palace sweepers would take the carts towards the Salimgarh Fort, where the corpses were thrown into the river. Chuni Lal talked to the sweepers, who said they had taken fifty-two bodies in total – all but five or six were women and children. At this point, the journalist was warned about his curiosity: 'You collect news for the English,' one of the King's servants sneered. 'If you continue to do so, you shall be served in the same way as these have been.'

Despite some of the sepoys doubting her professions of faith, Mrs Aldwell and her children, having been spared execution, were released. They were taken to the house of their tailor, a friend, although they were later arrested again by authorities looking for Christians. This time they were held in Capt. Douglas's apartment on top of the Lahore Gate. While here, the only surviving Europeans Mrs Aldwell heard about were a European woman and her daughter. The two had been sequestered in a house meant for the *salatin*.

'This court was also occupied by some of the mutinous sepoys, who, attracted by the little girl's prattle, showed her some kindness,' wrote Florence Wagentreiber. 'When orders came for the prisoners to be brought before the King, they concealed her and her child under a *charpai* and covered them with a sheet.'[17] The sepoys and other inhabitants of the house protected the mother and child for the duration of the siege. Although they warned the mother that they couldn't do so indefinitely, nobody ever found out.

1. View of the crowded streets of the walled city with the main city mosque, the Jama Masjid, in the distance. The mosque along with the palace formed the two focal points of the walled city. (Felice Beato, 1858, J. Paul Getty Museum)

2. Chandni Chowk, the picturesque main thoroughfare and commercial heart of the walled city. The Delhi bank as well as the main police station could also be found on the road. (Samuel Bourne, 1866, J. Paul Getty Museum)

3. Part of the long frontage of the palace/fort, showing the barbican protecting the main entrance, the Lahore Gate, in the foreground. The apartments used by Capt. Douglas, the palace commandant, and Revd Jennings were situated at the top of the gate (below where the Indian national flag can be seen).

4. Bridge of boats across the River Jumna used by the mutinous sepoys from Meerut to enter the city. After crossing the river some parties entered the Salimgarh Fort situated immediately to the right of the bridge, through which they entered the palace, while others travelled adjacent to the river to attempt an audience with the Emperor. (Felice Beato, 1858, J. Paul Getty Museum)

5. Saman Burj of the palace in front of which the mutineers from Meerut gathered to talk to the Emperor and Capt. Douglas. Douglas was dissuaded from confronting the mutineers directly by using the water gate (immediately below the balcony).

6. The palace ditch (shown in front of the barbican) was substantially deep in places. A fearful Capt. Douglas jumped into the ditch after a clash with the mutineers near the Calcutta Gate, hurting himself badly in the process, but was helped back into the fort. Commissioner Simon Fraser meanwhile had managed to make his way in his buggy to the palace gate. They and other Europeans then fled to the apartments at the top of the Lahore Gate.

*Above:* 7. Lahore Gate of the palace, where the large crowd of sepoys and their sympathisers in the city congregated before entering to kill the European party which had a short while earlier fled through the gate.

*Left:* 8. Much-faded interior of the 350-foot-long arcade inside the Lahore Gate. The impressive decorated vaulted ceiling has now been whitewashed over. The arcade at the time of the mutiny contained various shops of artisans and gem polishers.

*Below left:* 9. Octagonal opening in the middle of the arcaded entrance from which two staircases, one on each side of the arcade, led to the apartments above the Lahore Gate. The north staircase – opening to the left of the shop on the right – was where Commissioner Fraser was killed by the mob leaders as he tried to address the crowd.

10. Narrow staircase on the north side leading up to the apartments at the top of the Lahore Gate, along which the crowd, led by several ringleaders, ascended. They found a locked door barring their path, so then ascended along the other south staircase to kill the Europeans in the apartments above.

11. The apartments at the top of the Lahore Gate where Capt. Douglas and other Europeans were murdered. The ceiling of the vaulted arcade is to the left.

12. Revd Midgley John Jennings, Chaplain of Delhi, spearheaded Christian mission work in the city. He was murdered in the Lahore Gate apartments along with several other Europeans including an unconscious Capt. Douglas. The apartments were then ransacked by the ringleaders of the mob.

13. The large British magazine adjacent to the British cemetery on the Lothian Road heading from the palace to the Kashmir Gate. The low walls of the compound meant the magazine could be entered by the mutineers with little difficulty. Part of the magazine was successfully blown up by the defenders. The remaining ammunition and supplies largely powered the rebels' defence of the city during the siege. To the right is the British graveyard in the city. (Robert Tytler, 1858)

14. One of two of the extant gates of the magazine, facing west on to the main road (Lothian Road) leading from the Kashmir Gate to the palace.

15. Memorial plaque on top of one of the magazine gates dedicated to the European contingent of the Bengal Artillery who defended the compound on 11 May.

16. Second of the extant magazine gates, a few metres south of the first.

*Above:* 17. Picture taken from where the former magazine wall would have run. With the magazine gone, and the Lothian expanded into a dual carriageway at this point, the gates are now on an island between the two roads. The road on the left now runs through what would have been the inside of the magazine. The telegraph memorial can be seen at the end of the island.

*Left:* 18. British telegraph memorial a few feet away from the magazine gates, dedicated to the staff who manned the Delhi telegraph office on 11 May 1857.

*Below left:* 19. British graveyard immediately adjacent to the magazine. A modern wall now runs where the old magazine wall would have run in the far background. Mutineers used the graveyard to clamber over the walls of the magazine using ladders. The cemetery was founded soon after the British recaptured the city, with graves as old as 1808 found by the author.

20. Inside the Kashmir Gate. One of numerous large and small city gates, this happened to be the only one guarded by British sepoys. The gate was important in that it connected the British magazine in the city to the Civil Lines as well as the British cantonment 2 miles from the walled city.

21. Picture of Lothian Road taken from near the Kashmir Gate. The Lothian Road led from the Kashmir Gate to the British magazine half a mile up the road and beyond to the palace. British officers on 11 May 1857 made several attempts to lead sepoys towards the magazine from the gate to quell the chaos in the city but failed, only managing to advance a few hundred feet. Later that day the troops at the Kashmir Gate also mutinied and joined the Meerut rebels in the city.

22. The Flagstaff Tower on the Delhi ridge, where Europeans fleeing the city congregated for protection under the officers at the cantonment. Note the open, barren nature of the ridge at that time. (Felice Beato, 1858, J. Paul Getty Museum)

23. The Flagstaff Tower in 2019.

*Above left:* 24. For the many Europeans who had fled to the ridge, the inside of the small Flagstaff Tower afforded little in the way of space or protection from heat.

*Above right:* 25. View from the top of the Flagstaff Tower towards what would have been the British cantonments in the distance. One can see the Najafgarh Jheel canal less than a mile away, and the road north to Ambala, along which most of the fugitives decided to flee for safety.

*Below:* 26. The Delhi Bank in Chandni Chowk, which was ransacked the same day that the mutineers arrived from Meerut. Along with his wife and five daughters, George Beresford, manager of the Delhi Bank, fell victim to the mutineers. (Felice Beato, 1858, J. Paul Getty Museum)

*Above:* 27. One of the former gates of the large square Badli serai in the distance with the inside of the serai now a park. The serai, which no longer has its walls, was occupied by the mutineers during the battle.

*Left:* 28. A British memorial at Badli to the men of HM75th hangs precariously to life. Very little of the large flat mound remains, the earth having been largely utilised by locals. The mound formed the centre of the mutineers' position, with several large guns stationed here during the battle.

*Below:* 29. Close-up of the memorial to the soldiers of HM75th who died in the battle.

*Right:* 30. Grave of Lt Alfred Harrison, HM75th, adjacent to the British memorial at Badli.

*Below:* 31. River Hindun, photographed from close to the modern bridges, which now stand on the site of the old bridge. The curve of the river can be seen, along which the British cavalry went and outflanked the mutineers to their left. During the battle the river was little more than a film of water, allowing for an easier crossing by British cavalry than would have normally been possible.

32. The large Najafgarh Jheel canal, situated to the west of the British cantonment and ridge, effectively protected the British camp from attack on its weakest side, as well as providing plenty of fresh, clean water during the siege. The housing on the left is situated on what would have been the edge of the former cantonment.

33. The Sammy House (a corruption of 'Swami's House') on the southern lower slope of the ridge was the former residence of a swami or holy man. The house was used as the advance picket during the siege of the city, being the British position closest to the city walls just half a mile distant. (Felice Beato, 1858, J. Paul Getty Museum)

34. The Hindu Rao mansion on the ridge. The structure received considerable attention from rebel guns as it was key to the British defensive position. (Felice Beato, 1858, J. Paul Getty Museum)

35. A British battery was constructed at the ruined observatory on the ridge. Being too far from the city, its guns did little damage before they were brought forward. The heavily damaged Hindu Rao mansion can be seen in the distance. (Felice Beato, 1858, J. Paul Getty Museum)

36. Position of the Crow's Nest battery on the western side of the ridge. The Crow's Nest battery, like the other batteries, had limited range and did little damage before the siege batteries arrived, although it could target the Sabzi Mandi area of the city, from where the rebels launched the bulk of their attacks on the British camp. (Felice Beato, 1858, J. Paul Getty Museum)

37. Metcalfe House, situated in the Civil Lines adjacent to the river. The mansion was sacked by mobs after the arrival of the mutineers from Delhi. Along with its grounds it later formed the advance picket line for the British force to the east of the ridge. (Felice Beato, 1858, J. Paul Getty Museum)

38. The well-built Metcalfe House stables housed a strong British picket to prevent a rebel advance on the ridge from the east. (Felice Beato, 1858, J. Paul Getty Museum)

39. The line held by the British pickets, stretching from the slope of the ridge through the Metcalfe House grounds to the river beyond. This was taken close to the ridge facing Metcalfe House (extreme left) and the stables (right). In the distance can be seen the river and opposite bank. (Felice Beato, 1858, J. Paul Getty Museum)

40. The Sabzi Mandi or vegetable market section of the city adjoining the ridge and where much of the skirmishing took place during the siege. Walled houses and gardens in much of the area made the fighting difficult. (Felice Beato, 1858, J. Paul Getty Museum)

41. Shattered remains of the Qudsia Bagh mosque located close to the river, photographed from the rear. The mosque sat in the midst of a large walled *bagh* or garden. Later in the siege, a British battery was installed adjacent and immediately to the north of the mosque to utilise its cover, which meant the structure received heavy attention from opposing rebel guns. Notice the hole in the rightmost dome of the mosque, caused by a rebel shell, and the ruined section of the mosque to the right and rear. (Felice Beato, 1858, J. Paul Getty Museum)

42. Qudsia Bagh mosque in 2019, photographed from the front.

*Right:* 43. The damage inflicted on the mosque by rebel shelling is still evident on its right.

*Below right:* 44. A photograph taken from the former position of the British battery at Qudsia Bagh, with the mosque in the background. The gardens still exist, although the walled perimeter is gone.

*Below:* 45. Remnants of the Custom House, which was situated adjacent to the city walls and near to the Kashmir Gate. The Qudsia Bagh mosque immediately to its north can be seen on the extreme right. The Inter-State Bus terminal now stands on the site of the Custom House. (Felice Beato, 1858, J. Paul Getty Museum)

46. The damaged Kashmir Bastion with the Kashmir Gate to the far right of the picture. (Felice Beato, 1858, J. Paul Getty Museum)

47. Damage to the Mori Bastion. Along with the Kashmir Bastion, the Mori Bastion received the most attention from the British guns. (Felice Beato, 1858, J. Paul Getty Museum)

48. The breaches made by British batteries to the Water Bastion, forming the extreme northern point of the city defences and adjoining walls. (Felice Beato, 1858, J. Paul Getty Museum)

49. The Kashmir Gate after the capture of the city by the British. (Felice Beato, 1858, J. Paul Getty Museum)

*Above:* 50. Kashmir Gate in 2019, with the repaired Kashmir Bastion to the left. The right leaf of the gate was blown up by British engineers during the assault on the city on 14 September 1857.

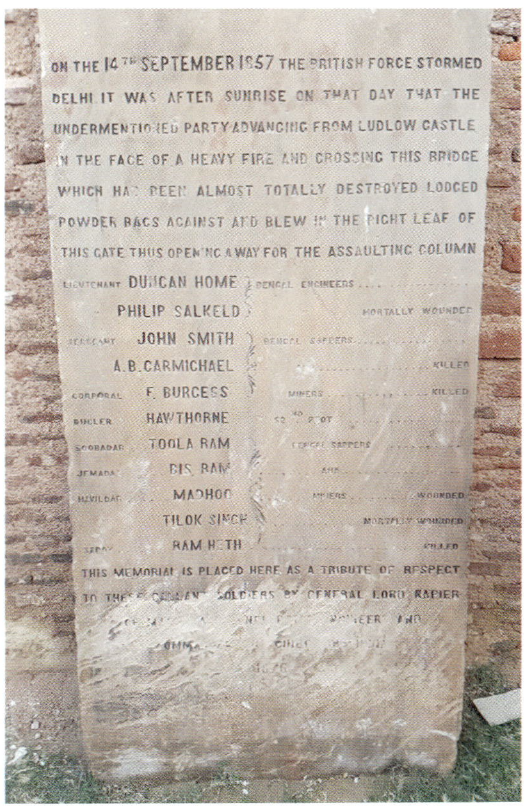


*Right:* 51. British memorial to the Bengal Engineers, miners and sappers who blew the Kashmir Gate during the assault on the city.

52. Nicholson Road, 200 feet from the Kashmir Gate, runs adjacent to the city walls and leads to the Mori Gate half a mile to the west. Brigadier General Nicholson was shot and wounded here as he led the British troops against the Burn Bastion. After entering the city, British columns advanced along the road, quickly capturing the Mori and Kabul Gates before being repelled at the Burn Bastion.

53. The Delhi Gate in the south of the city. After stiff resistance on the first day of the assault, rebels gradually began deserting the city through the Delhi, Turkman and Ajmer Gates to the south as the British advanced.

54. Ajmer Gate, a mile to the west of the Delhi Gate, is one of only five gates to survive along with the Kashmir, Delhi, Turkman and Nigambodh Gates.

55. Humayun's Tomb, 3½ miles south of the city, was where the Emperor, several princes and a large number of dejected rebels congregated after evacuating the city. Zafar was apprehended here by Hodson and brought back to the city after he gave himself up having been promised his life by General Wilson.

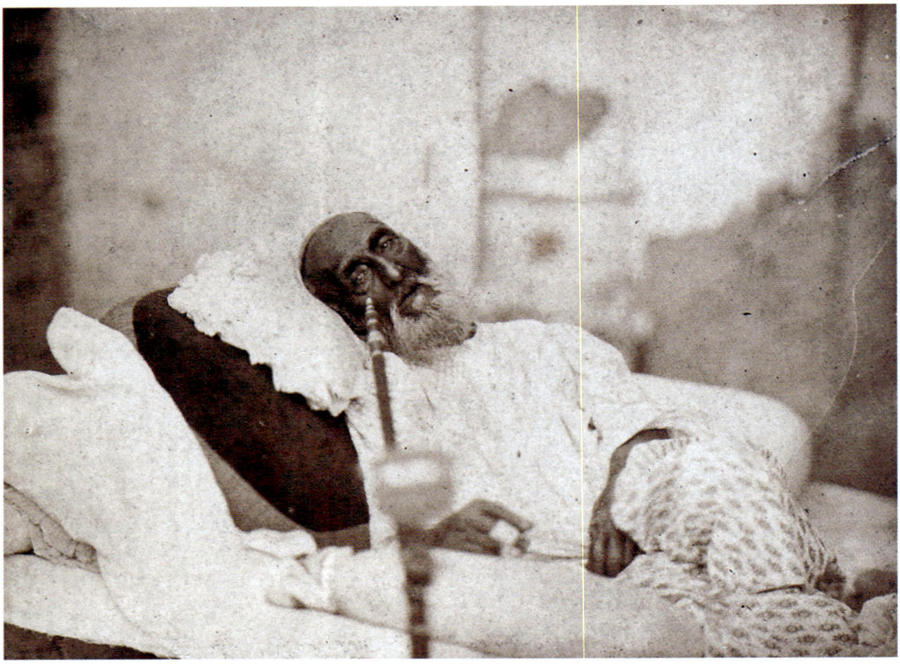

56. Bahadur Shah Zafar in captivity in 1858, photographed after his trial and before his exile to Burma. (Robert Tytler, 1858)

57. The house in which Zafar was kept in the palace complex after his capture. (Felice Beato, 1858, J. Paul Getty Museum)

*Above:* 58. The Diwan-i-Khas, the inner sanctum of the palace, was utilised as an office by General Wilson. (Felice Beato, 1858, J. Paul Getty Museum)

*Below:* 59. A wide band of the city in front of the palace was razed to the ground after its capture to allow the British garrison a clear line of fire in case of another uprising. Photograph taken from the Jama Masjid. (Samuel Bourne, 1864, J. Paul Getty Museum)

60. St James' Church was used as a canteen by rebels during the siege and a hospital by British after they entered the city. The church holds a considerable number of memorials related to the mutiny and to other personalities of that age.

61. British memorial to Christians who died in Delhi on 11 May at St James' Church.

62. Close-up of the memorial to Christians who died in Delhi on 11 May.

63. Memorial to William Fraser, Commissioner of Delhi prior to the Mutiny, in St James' Church. He was killed in 1835 having served three tenures as commissioner during the 1820s and 1830s.

*Above:* 64. The Nicholson Cemetery, the large British cemetery situated less than half a mile north-west of the Kashmir Gate.

*Left:* 65. Nicholson's tomb, close to the entrance of the cemetery bearing his name.

*Below left:* 66. Ramchandra's tomb at the Nicholson Cemetery. The Christian convert professor at Delhi College managed to escape the upheavals of 11 May, returning to the city after its recapture.

*Above right:* 67. The memorial to the soldiers of HM8th, Nicholson Cemetery.

*Below right:* 68. The defences to the south of the city were untouched during the siege and still survive up to the Delhi Gate in perfect condition.

*Bottom right:* 69. The British Martello tower near the Delhi Gate, built after the capture of the city in 1803, when the defences of the city were refurbished.

*Below:* 70. The now jungled rough slopes of the Delhi ridge remain as difficult to negotiate as in 1857. The road on the spine of the ridge, along with other roads and paths down the ridge, however, allow for exploration.

71. The British Mutiny memorial on the Delhi ridge. The Gothic sandstone memorial was erected on the southern section of the ridge in 1863 in memory of the officers and soldiers of the Delhi Field Force. The 115-foot memorial also marks the position of Taylor's battery during the siege of the city.

PART 4

# The Empire of Four Months and Four Days

19

# The Response

Every exertion must be made to regain Delhi.
Every hour is of importance.
Lord Canning to John Lawrence,
16 May 1857[1]

General Anson, the fifty-eight-year-old British Commander-in-Chief in India, happened to be at the summer playground of Simla, just north of the plains of India, when the mutiny broke out at Meerut. Communication with Simla was rather slow at the time, the retreat having yet to be connected to the telegraphic network. Telegraphs for Simla were received on the plains and taken on horseback into the hills by one of two roads: one passed via Sabathu and was around 41 miles in length from the plains, while the other passed via Dagshai and was around 50 miles long. The first, although a little shorter, was more difficult to travel, being more or less a bridle path. The other, longer road was wide enough to be used by bullock carts.

The news of the uprising at Meerut therefore took longer to reach Simla than elsewhere on the telegraphic map, only reaching Anson's ears on the afternoon of 12 May. In fact, two messages arrived at roughly the same time – one at 3 p.m. and another an hour later. The first came from Ambala and was composed by Capt. Barnard, *aide-de-camp* to Sir Henry Barnard (and also his son), commander of the Sirhind Division. He reported that six regiments had now mutinied in total – three at Delhi and three at Meerut. The second message came from Meerut, where the repair of the telegraph system had finally allowed General Hewitt to detail the events of 10 May.

Anson had only become Commander-in-Chief in November 1855. Sir John Kaye described him as better than most in the sense he was not an old man by the time he became C-in-C: 'He could hear and see; he could ride and walk. He was of a light spare figure, well framed for active exercise; and his aspect was that of a man who could "stand the climate".' He had left Calcutta in September 1856 and had been touring the north of the country, travelling through Lucknow in November 1856 before reaching Ambala in March 1857. Despite Kaye's assertion, Anson had never been happy with the Indian climate and remained in poor health, travelling to Simla to recuperate. Still recovering in early May, he therefore found himself propelled into the biggest challenge of his career when he was perhaps least fit to cope with it. Anson has never been given much credit for how he dealt with the situation; while he knew action needed to be taken to protect the British civilians at Delhi and Meerut, many claim that he failed to see the greater pattern. Nevertheless, he took immediate measures. He had already addressed the men of the 36th NI at Ambala to reassure them about the cartridges, so he wasn't entirely unaware of the issue.

Anson only had three European regiments at his disposal nearby, each at a separate British station up in the hills. Luckily for him, all three were much closer to the plains than he was. At Kasauli, closest to the plains, HM75th Foot stood ready. Around 5 miles east of Kasauli was Dagshai, home to the 1st Fusiliers. Sabathu, roughly 5 miles north of Kasauli, hosted the 2nd Fusiliers. In addition, at Jatogh, less than 5 miles from Simla, a Nusseri Gurkha regiment stood at readiness. Together, these troops could form the strong nucleus for any force marching on Delhi. The Sirmoor battalion based at Dehra Dun would be ordered down as well, Anson decided, but it would be sent to Meerut to strengthen forces there.

At this time, the Punjab, close to Simla, was under heavy British occupation; in all, it had about 15,000 European troops and 65,000 sepoys stationed inside its borders. Which of these sepoy regiments could be trusted was difficult to say. What was clear was that, due to the depth of feeling among the sepoy army, many more regiments were expected to mutiny. From a strategic point of view, therefore, it was considered quite dangerous to remove European troops from the Punjab and the trans-Indus region in case the sepoy regiments there rose up once they heard about events at Meerut and Delhi. Put simply, the European regiments had to stay to watch over the sepoy regiments. Furthermore, there was the constant fear of a general Muslim uprising all along the turbulent trans-Indus region adjacent to Afghanistan. A sizeable force was required to keep these forces in check. Anson also wasn't sure which way the Sikh population of the state would go, having only been defeated eight years prior.

Realistically, the bulk of any force to retake Delhi could only be constructed from the European regiments stationed in the Simla hills, the European contingent at Meerut and the Gurkha regiments (who were considered loyal beyond doubt). Along the way, this force would be supplemented at Ambala and elsewhere by any sepoy regiments or irregular troops considered free of mutinous intent. Anson therefore ordered the 75th Foot to move into the plains immediately, with the

1st and 2nd Bengal Fusiliers to follow as soon as practicable. The force to retake Delhi was to assemble at Ambala, around 40 miles south of Kasauli and on the direct route to Delhi from the Punjab. What heavy guns there were at Phillaur in the Punjab were to be sent to Ambala as well, with the Nusseri Gurkha regiment at Jatogh tasked with escorting them down to Delhi along with the 9th Irregular Cavalry. Aside from the guns, some artillery at Nurpur and Kangra was also sent for.

The plan was for this force from Ambala – led personally by Anson – to march south and join the European force at Meerut prior to the last march on Delhi. This, Anson thought, would show the British determination to retake Delhi and discourage mutiny elsewhere, although the coming hot season would complicate matters. Phillaur Fort and its guns would be organised by Lt Griffith, Commissary of Ordnance. It was his job to arrange a siege train and the host of supplies that would be sent with it. This was an urgent task, for it was the time of the year when the River Sutlej rose. Phillaur was on the right or north bank of the river; it was feared the bridge of boats might be swept away, preventing the siege train from being brought south.

Meanwhile, measures were taken to prevent a repeat of Meerut or Delhi occurring elsewhere. Of chief concern were the various magazines and treasuries around the north of the country and the Punjab – arms and money were the only two things that could fuel a mutiny. The East India Company had two great arsenals in the Punjab, Phillaur and Ferozepore, which held all the heavy guns. Both were in the hands of sepoy regiments. If the men stationed at these locations mutinied in sympathy with their fellow sepoys and took control, assembling an army at Ambala to advance on Delhi would be utterly pointless because not only the guns but all ammunition and supplies had to be drawn from these two magazines. At Ferozepore, therefore, the magazine was to be placed under a European guard of HM61st. The fort at Phillaur was to be manned by two companies of HM8th, while the important fortress of Govindgarh, guarding Amritsar, would be guarded by HM81st.

In order to prevent further mutiny and to calm the situation around the country, Anson would immediately issue a general order halting all drill and target practice. This he hoped would defuse the situation in some cantonments and prevent an impasse such as had arisen at Meerut. Furthermore, a few days later, on 19 May, another general order would be issued to clarify that nobody would be compelled to use the new cartridge – although it was stated once more that the grease contained no objectionable matter. Anson said that he understood the predicament of the sepoys; that even though many of the soldiers believed the government had no desire to offend them in any way, they nonetheless felt that using the cartridges would alienate them from their friends, families and fellow villagers, who refused to believe the cartridges were inoffensive. The adoption of the new cartridge would be halted:

> His Excellency, therefore, has determined that the new rifle-cartridge, and every new cartridge, shall be discontinued; and that, in future, balled ammunition shall be made up by each regiment for its own use, by a proper establishment entertained for this purpose. The Commander-in-Chief solemnly assures the army that no interference with their castes or religion was ever contemplated, and as solemnly he pledges his word and honour that none shall ever be exercised.[2]

Despite Anson's attempts, a general panic spread throughout the European colonies across north India in the face of this seemingly enormous insurrection and its manifestation at Delhi. Within a matter of days, a local mutiny had evolved into a rebellion led by the King of Delhi and aimed at overthrowing British power in India. More sepoy regiments were likely to mutiny all across north India and the Punjab. Indeed, the military was not immune to this panic, as exemplified in this record from Revd John Cave-Browne, a chaplain stationed at Nowshera in Peshawar:

> A report did float about the Panjab, the truth of which we have never heard denied, that one member of the Staff suggested that all European troops should concentrate on Philur [Phillaur], and, taking boat down the Satlaj, make for England as fast as possible; another, however – one who, alas! fell among the earliest victims of the rebellion – suggested that the Philur Fort, with its large magazine, might be made available for a very different purpose. Hence the idea of a siege-train.

Increasingly cognisant of the emergency, Anson would leave Simla on the 14th, travelling towards Ambala to lead the force to retake Delhi. Shortly before he left, he wrote to Lord Canning of his impressions at the time:

> … This is a most disastrous business, and it is not possible to see what will be the result. They say the King of Delhi is at the bottom of it. I doubt it; but I have no doubt that he has taken advantage of the opportunity, and is assisting the insurgents …
>
> … If the mutineers, having possession of the city, make their stand behind the walls, we shall want a good force and artillery. This must be collected at Karnal, as it would not be wise, I think, to divide the force we shall have and send part from Mirath [Meerut] on the opposite side of the river. But I hope to hear something which will enable me to decide what is best to be done when I get to Ambalah.[3]

With the European regiments having departed the hills, the European civilians in Simla explained their fear of the mutiny spreading to the town. The local chaplain, Mr Mayne, asked the departing Anson if some European troops could stay behind for the protection of the women; there were already some unsavoury characters in the bazaars plotting to take advantage of the situation, he warned. When Anson said he had none to give, the chaplain asked, 'What, then, are the ladies to do?' The general replied, 'The best they can.'[4] One month on the civilians at Simla were still restless, complaining of the lack of protection in a memorandum to John Lawrence, Commissioner of the Punjab, by a Col C. D. Blate on 7 June:

> We the undersigned residents and others now living at Simla earnestly beg to bring to your notice the present state of this station, in which are not less than 300 women and nearly double that number of children, almost all of whom are without protection against any sudden outbreak of the bazaar Mussulmans and bad characters or the incursion of any band of wandering marauders. There is a vast amount of private property to excite cupidity besides the treasure in the bank, and it is to be feared that many will be actuated by the spirit of revenge when they hear of the retribution inflicted on their countrymen in Delhi; while any reverse there would also be stimulant to all their evil passions. In the large and there are only 46 Policemen of the ordinary stamp, and we therefore earnestly request that you will be pleased to entrust a Military officer with the defence of this station, invested with full powers to proclaim Martial law, and in conjunction with the Civil officer to enrol as a Militia the few Europeans remaining in Simla, call in the contingents, seek aid of European Troops, if they can be spared from the neighbouring depots, and take such other measures as may appear necessary.[5]

Nothing could be done with the few troops available. From Lawrence there came the reply: 'All our available soldiers are required to fight the mutineers and hold the country.'[6] They were advised that the fifty policemen and one hundred Rajputs in the neighbourhood were quite sufficient, but if they felt it necessary they were welcome to organise a body of special constables equipped with firearms.

Anson reached Ambala on 15 May and was met with vital good news: the Maharaja of Patiala had signalled his loyalty and his willingness to assist the British cause as much as he could. The same was true of the rulers of Nabha and Jhind, as well. This meant that communication and supplies from Ferozepore and Phillaur would not be in danger, with the three rulers' forces patrolling and helping escort supplies over the 200 miles from the Punjab to Delhi. However, Anson still had other issues to contend with, not least the absence of heavy guns. In correspondence with John Lawrence, he commented on the difficulties in mustering a sufficiently powerful force as well as problems of a logistical nature:

> The second European regiment only arrived this morning, and all of them having been brought in such a hurry and so quickly, they have nothing with them. We hear that many regiments have joined the mutineers in Delhi, the gates of which are closed, and guns mounted on

> them. The walls would be nothing against guns of heavy calibre, but we have none nearer then Phillour, and only two troops with 6-pounders. At Meerut there is a light field battery of 9-pounders. My intelligence from Meerut is very scanty.

The mutiny had taken the British authorities completely by surprise, and Anson was finding it difficult to organise a force with sufficient resources. The main issue was that of carriage – hardly any was obtainable – while tents and other general supplies had to be procured. Anson already knew taking Delhi would be difficult. The sepoys were trained along European lines and if led well could put up a stout defence. Having mutinied and killed European officers and civilians, they had only the noose to look forward to and therefore could be expected to fight to the death. Anson wanted to wait until more troops and guns were available for an overwhelming attack on the city. An inadequate force with insufficient heavy guns to batter the walls and with few if any supplies or ammunition could lead to disaster. Any setback, any repulse or show of impotence, could have enormous repercussions elsewhere. In these circumstances, one can understand why the general expressed to Lawrence his doubts about the ability of his small force to retake Delhi successfully and quickly.

> It becomes now a matter for your consideration whether it would be prudent to send the small European force we have here in an enterprise upon Delhi. I think not. It is wholly in my opinion insufficient for the purpose. The walls could of course be battered down with heavy guns when we got them up. The entrance might be opened and little resistance offered, but so few men in a large city with such narrow streets and an immense armed population who know every turn and corner of them would, it appears to me, be in a very dangerous position. And if six or seven hundred were disabled what would remain? Could we hold it with the whole country armed against us? Could we either stay in or out of it? My own view of the state of things now is by carefully collecting our resources, having got rid of the bad materials which we cannot trust and having supplied their places with others of a better sort, it would not be very long before we could proceed, without a chance of failure, in whatever direction we might please.

John Lawrence, not being a military man, had entirely differently considerations in mind. 'Delhi would open its gates on the approach of our troops,' he confidently predicted, such was the prestige of the EIC army. The alternatives could not be contemplated. British troops 'cooped up in their cantonments tamely awaiting the progress of events' could only lead to disaster. Lawrence gave the example of Clive of India, who with a small number of troops had defeated the large and unwieldy army of the Nawab of Bengal at the Battle of Plassey. This was a similar situation, he said, and it required the same kind of proactive response. A small, disciplined force could move quickly to overawe the leaderless mutineers.

Whatever his private apprehensions about having insufficient men and resources to capture Delhi, Anson nevertheless saw the truth in Lawrence's argument and continued his approach to the city. As his troops began reaching Ambala, he sent an advance force of five companies of the 2nd Fusiliers, a squadron of the 9th Lancers and two horse artillery guns towards Karnal, 50 miles further south, to ensure the route was clear of mutineers. Assuming the path was clear, the plan was to join up with the European force at Meerut under General Hewitt before advancing to attack Delhi. Hewitt would be ordered to bring all the men he could spare, bearing in mind the Meerut cantonments still had to be defended. Once the Meerut forces were merged, Anson expected to have around 3,000 European troops, 1,000 Indian troops and twenty-two field guns. The Gurkhas at Juttogh would escort the siege train from Phillaur, supplementing the main force later.

Very early in the planning, the British forces almost suffered a major setback. Perhaps undecided on whether or not to join the rebels, or maybe due to grievances of their own, one of the companies of the Gurkha regiment had shown its discontent by robbing the treasury at Kussowlie before advancing towards Simla, and even looting Anson's baggage as it was brought down to Ambala. Meanwhile, the rest of the regiment was in what could best be described as an indecisive mood. This only increased the panic among the Europeans of the hill stations, who began fleeing to the plains by whatever method they could. Luckily for Anson, the Gurkhas were won over by diplomatic means. The men who had been plundering the treasure and the commander-in-chief's baggage were handed over; in return, the British officers, in desperate straits themselves and reliant on the Gurkhas' support, turned a blind eye on what in ordinary circumstances would have merited harsh punishment.

Anson received further good news on 16 May: all was well in Ferozepore, and the fort at Phillaur had been secured. There would be no issue with ammunition and supplies. In addition, the whole of the Punjab was generally quiet. The sepoy troops at Lahore had been disarmed. With the rulers of Patiala, Jhind and Nabha assisting, the rear of Anson's army was as safe as possible in the circumstances.

On the same day, Capt. Hodson of the 1st European Fusiliers was appointed assistant quartermaster-general by Anson. Hodson had previously been in command of the Guides in the Punjab. He was also asked to raise a force of a hundred sowars and fifty infantry to be used for intelligence-gathering purposes and to double up as a personal escort. Among this force was a one-eyed moulvi called Rajab Ali who would prove particularly useful to Hodson and the British in days to come. Hodson had been well trusted by Henry Lawrence during his stint in the Punjab; he was supposed to have good contacts, and on arrival at Delhi was expected to unearth whatever valuable intelligence could be gleaned in the city.

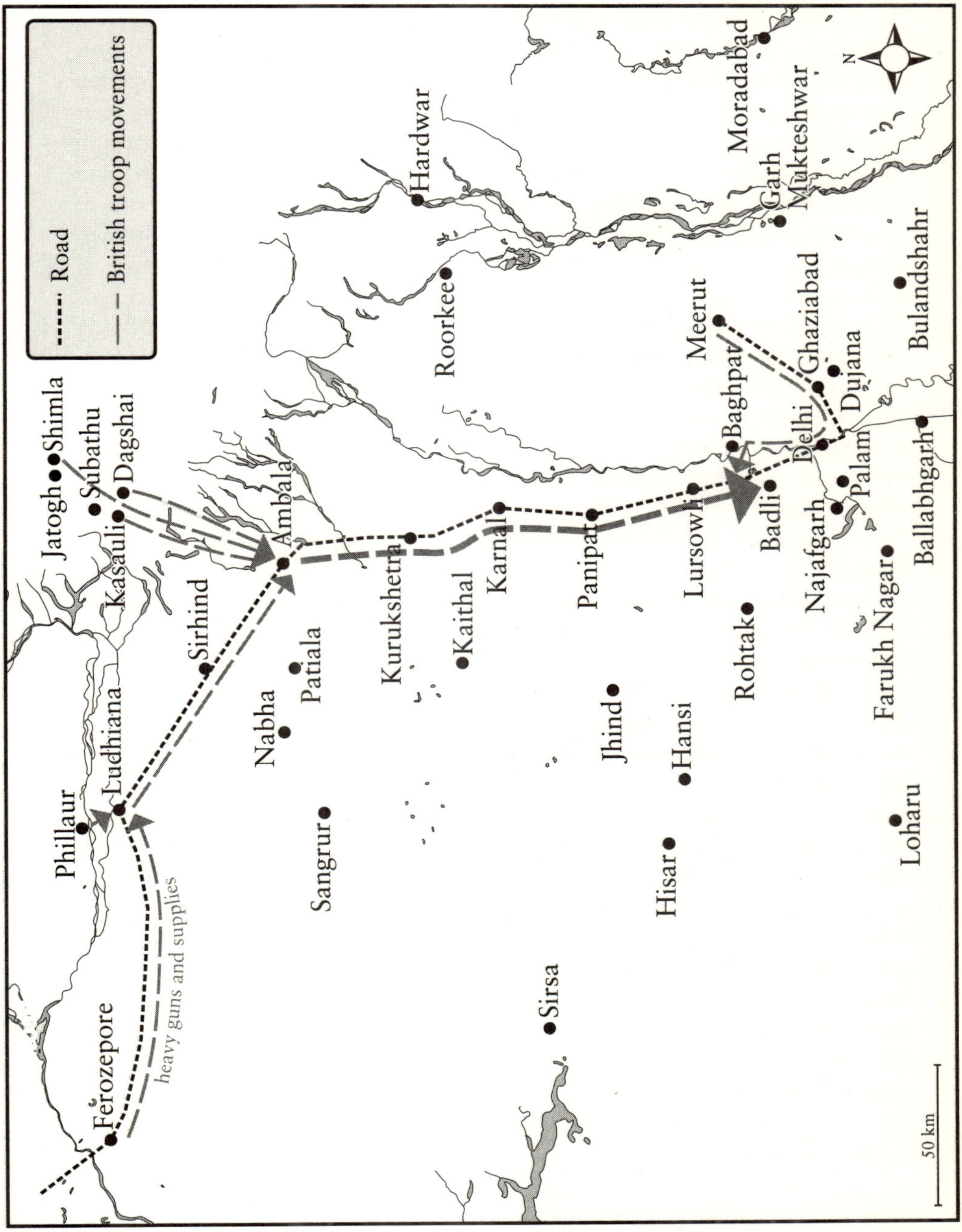


The British advance on Delhi.

The sepoys stationed at Ambala were known to be mutinous but had not shown their hand as yet, so Anson was torn over whether he should disarm them before proceeding to Delhi. John Lawrence was most vociferous in wanting them disarmed. It was dangerous, he pointed out, to leave armed sepoy regiments behind to their rear as the force marched south. To take them as part of the force was equally dangerous, as it was expected that they would simply go over to the rebels on reaching the city. Hodson also felt uncomfortable with Anson's mildness, and agreed with Lawrence that the sepoys should be disarmed: 'Here alarm is the prevalent feeling, and conciliation, of men with arms in their hands and in a state of absolute rebellion, the order of the day. This system, if pursued, is far more dangerous than anything the Sepoys can do to us.'[7] The problem was that the commanding officers at Ambala had already promised their men that they would not be disarmed.

Anson, reluctant to be seen as an oath breaker, went with his gut and allowed the Ambala sepoys to remain under arms. However, as a precaution he left four companies of the Fusiliers under Major-General Sir Henry Barnard to hold Ambala and keep an eye on the sepoys. He also ordered a rough defensive compound to be constructed at the city, with the church having entrenchments dug around it for use by Barnard's detachment. The Europeans in Ambala were formed into a militia to aid in its defence, and the magazine, treasury and commissariat stores were moved into the reinforced church. Any men too sick to fight were sent to the hill stations for safety, and the civilians were sent with them.

With the issue settled, Anson finally began the advance towards Karnal on 17 May. The Raja of Jhind's men arrived there on the 18th and the Maharaja of Patiala now held Thaneysur with another 1,000 men, meaning much of the route towards Delhi was secure. Advance units of Anson's force reached Karnal on 19 May. It was only another 60 miles from Karnal to Baghpat, where the Meerut force was expected to cross the river before joining the main force at Alipur.

During this time, Anson heard little about events elsewhere; the telegraph lines linking Delhi, Meerut and Agra to the Punjab had largely been destroyed. What little information was trickling through augured well for the column, although messages like Governor-General Canning's order to 'Make short work of Delhi' were met with some derision. However, according to one officer Canning's actions inspired more confidence than his words:

> We heard, with satisfaction, that he had taken measures to stop the China expedition; and trusted soon to have troops sent from home overland to our aid. It was hoped in camp, however, that a blow struck at Delhi might save the rest of the army from overt rebellion. Indeed many could scarcely believe that the sepoys there would not run away on our approach, or come out with clasped hands to solicit pardon.[8]

Despite the good omens, logistical problems persisted. On 18 May, Barnard, back at Ambala, complained of a lack of ammunition:

> And now that they [the European regiments] are collected, without tents, without ammunition, the men have not twenty rounds apiece. Two troops of Horse Artillery, twelve guns, but no reserve ammunition, and their waggons at Lodiana – seven days' off! Commissariat without sufficient transport at hand. This is the boasted Indian Army, and this is the force with which the civilians would have us go to Dehli.[9]

On 23 May, Anson sent a message to General Hewitt: 'I propose to advance with the column from Kurnaul towards Delhi on 1 June, and be opposite to Bhagput on the 5th. At this last place I should wish to be joined by the force from Meerut.'[10] In order to accomplish this, Capt. Hodson was tasked with leading a force of 400 sowars of the Raja of Jhind to Meerut to establish communication with Hewitt.

At the same time, Capt. MacAndrew continued with his advance force south for reconnaissance purposes. 'I hope to push on some more troops tomorrow, but we have no doolies for sick and bearers. They cannot be got,'[11] wrote Anson. MacAndrew's force was to act as the vanguard, always keeping around 20 miles in advance of the main force. As they passed Baghpat, a contingent of this force stayed behind to protect the bridge, which secured communication and supplies from the left bank of the Jumna but more importantly would allow the Meerut force to cross and join the main army.

Anson informed Lawrence that his spies were receiving wildly different accounts regarding the state of the rebels in Delhi. Some said they were entirely bereft of organisation, while others stated quite the contrary. Also, there was some confusion as to who was joining the rebels. There was news that the 9th Regiment from Aligarh had reached Delhi, and some of the sappers and miners from Roorkee were also said to have joined by this time. The exact strength of the rebels could not be discerned. The main issue for Anson, however, was still the want of carriage. By this time, 500 carts had been procured along with 2,000 camels and 2,000 coolies as well as 30,000 maunds of grain, which would be stored at Ambala and sent down over the following weeks to supply the force. This was not enough. Anson complained to Lawrence of the lack of camels and elephants on 25 May, and also bemoaned Hewitt's lack of activity: 'The Meerut force has been useless in that division; the civil authorities apparently the same.' Despite Anson's complaints, however, Lawrence was bullishly confident that Delhi would easily be captured:

> I served for nearly thirteen years in Dehlee, and know the people well. My belief is that with good management on the part of the Civil officers, it would open its gate on the approach of our troops. It seems

> incredible to conceive that the mutineers can hold and defend it. Still I admit that on military principles, in the present state of affairs, it may not be expedient to advance on Dehlee – certainly not until the Meerut Force is prepared to act, which it can only be when set free.[12]

Anson would never see the junction of the two British forces. Having made it to Karnal on the 24th, Anson died of cholera three days later. His death meant Major-General Sir Henry Barnard, who had been left behind at Ambala to manage affairs and protect the British supply lines, was now the senior officer and must take command of the force heading to Delhi.

Barnard was an experienced soldier. He had commanded a brigade in the Crimea under Lord Raglan. After Raglan's death, he became General Simpson's chief of staff. He had no experience of India, however, having only arrived in April 1857 to take up command of the Sirhind Division. Not everyone was impressed with Barnard, but Hodson summed up the prevailing mood: 'Sir H Barnard is a fine gentlemanly old man, but hardly up to his work. However, we must all put our shoulders to the wheel, and help him over the crisis. I trust he will act with vigour, for we have delayed far too long already.'[13] But Barnard, like Lawrence, was highly optimistic. He decided against waiting for the siege train from Phillaur; instead the force would hasten to the city without heavy guns, marching by night to avoid the punishing daylight temperatures of the hot season.

Meanwhile, as the force neared Delhi, summary justice commenced in nearby villages.

A few weeks before, European fugitives from Delhi had fled north towards Ambala. Now, the British force marched south down the same road. Many villagers had harmed or mocked the dishevelled fugitives on their way to safety; those Europeans who made it to Ambala had told Barnard and his officers which villages and villagers had been friendly and which had not. On 3 June, five villagers accused of heaping insults on two European women escaping Delhi were captured. They had been betrayed by other villagers; perhaps personal enemies, perhaps genuine witnesses. The five were summarily hanged, becoming the first casualties of British retribution against rebels and their sympathizers. Some in the British camp regretted this move, considering it a precursor to future savagery. One officer wrote of his concerns:

> Officers now went to courts-martial declaring they would hang the prisoners, whether guilty or innocent, and the provost-marshal had his cart waiting for them at the tent door. Some brought the names of offending villages, and applied to get them destroyed, and plundered on the strength of vague report. The fierceness of the men increased every day, often venting itself upon the camp servants, many of whom ran away. These prisoners, during the few hours between their trial and

> execution, were unceasingly tormented by the soldiers. They pulled their hair, pricked them with their bayonets, and forced them to eat cow's flesh, while officers stood by approving. The fury of one of the peasants, a tall powerful young Jat, broke out in boasting and curses as he was led to execution. The village was burnt and plundered; they spared not even the house of the old *zamindarin*, who had in vain tried to save the ladies from insult. Prudent and humane men began to fear that our just vengeance on Delhi would be stained with a general massacre of the inhabitants, and a course of judicial slaughter, which would surpass the horrors of the Reign of Terror. But the slightest whisper of anything short of indiscriminate vengeance was instantly silenced by twenty voices. How dangerous it is to entrust to mankind the power of taking even the justest retribution![14]

The British force passed the village of Rai on 4 June. By 5 June they had reached Alipur, around 10 miles north of Delhi. Hodson, meanwhile, with a contingent of sowars from the Maharaja of Jhind, pushed on towards the cantonments. This advance group made it all the way up to the Delhi ridge unharmed. Back at Alipur, the main force waited for the Meerut force to cross the Jumna. By this time, more stories of the bloodshed in Delhi had spread. Further news was coming in from Hansi and Hissar, where more European civilians had reportedly been murdered by sepoys. The European troops grew increasingly frustrated as they waited for the Meerut force, demanding an immediate move on Delhi despite their relative weakness. William W. Ireland, a surgeon in the Bengal Horse Artillery, described the mood:

> Many an oath was sworn that they would grant no mercy to a black face. The phlegmatic nature of the British soldier disappeared under the burning desire of havoc and revenge. None doubted of a complete and easy victory. Most of the men believed that one battle would decide the fate of the mutinous regiments. They would fight in the morning; they would drink their grog in Delhi at night.

Nobody foresaw a prolonged siege outside Delhi. Some thought the rebels would simply flee as soon as the British force appeared. Expecting an easy rout, many of the sick troops, eager not to miss out, implored those in charge to release them from their beds. 'Every man whose strength was not hopelessly gone was let out, and few returned for days after,' added Ireland.

# 20

# The Battles of Hindun River

When the sepoys, who returned defeated on that occasion, came back to the city, the men began talking despondingly, saying they would have no chance against the English.

Mrs Aldwell

Surprisingly, the first real engagement between British forces and the mutineers didn't involve Barnard's force from Ambala but the almost entirely static Meerut force. On 23 May, Anson had ordered the Meerut force to combine with the Ambala force marching south to Delhi. On receiving the instruction, Brigadier Archdale Wilson had organised the units at his disposal. His force was assembled and readied by the evening of the 26th. On the 27th, seventeen days after the mutiny had erupted, the European troops at Meerut began marching out. Wilson had managed to muster around 1,200 men in total. Because the Meerut cantonment had to be defended, not all the men at his disposal could be taken. Wilson had elected to take with him two squadrons of HM6th Dragoon Guards (carabineers) under Lt-Col W. N. Custance, the 4th Irregulars (cavalry), a wing of the HM60th Rifles (1st Battalion) under Col John Jones (around 500 men), and two companies of native sappers with artillery including two 18-pounder guns commanded by Lt-Col Murray Mackenzie. The guns were all manned by Europeans. In addition, Mr Hervey H. Greathed, Commissioner of Meerut, would accompany the force in the role of role of political agent. Colonel Muter, meanwhile, was left in command of the wing of his regiment at Meerut to oversee the defence of the cantonment.

Progress out of Meerut was slow to begin with. Like Anson, Wilson had decided to march at night and rest by day due to the extreme heat. The first camp, on 28 May, was made just 7 miles from Meerut. News of Anson's death arrived at this time. The following day, 29 May, the force made camp at Muradnagar. Early on 30 May, the village of Ghazi-ud-din Nagar was reached and preparations for camp commenced. The village lay south of the road to Delhi and was roughly a mile from the left bank of the River Hindun, a tributary of the Jumna River that gradually wound closer and closer to it before joining around 25 miles south of Delhi. At Ghazi-ud-din Nagar, the Hindun was still more than 10 miles east of Delhi. The Meerut–Delhi road crossed the valley of the Hindun by an iron suspension bridge flanked by causeways on both sides. A toll house had been built at the end of a 600-yard road beyond the bridge on the right bank. Usually the stream had a good flow, but in the strong heat of May the river frequently dried to little more than a film of water over a mass of mud; some sources mention patches of quicksand. The Hindun could be crossed, then, but moving carriages on the riverbed would be very difficult. It was therefore essential for any army on the left bank to have control of the bridge.

The surrounds were tranquil and picturesque, with the few small villages on each side of the river showing no disquiet, so the British troops settled down to sleep for the day. Wilson had largely dismissed any chance of the rebels challenging his force before his junction with the Ambala force; two weeks of relative inactivity by the mutineers at Delhi showed they had little desire to march out of the city. The common perception in the Meerut continent was that the rebels would only be inclined make a stand behind the city walls. Mr Greathed was certainly one of those who predicted a peaceful journey: 'We seem to have Delhi by the nose. I expect that a reconnaissance will be made to-morrow up to the banks of the Jumna. I believe the only idea the mutineers now have is to defend the Fort [of Delhi]; I suppose it is the only plan on which they could agree.' It was immediately after Greathed's letter was despatched to Meerut that a scout returned with the surprising news that a strong rebel party was advancing towards them from Delhi. Two British videttes tasked with watching the right bank of the Hindun then raced in with news that the rebels were approaching accompanied by heavy guns. Furthermore, the rebel force had brought plentiful carts packed with sandbags and entrenching tools.

Days before, outriders for the mutineers had reported back to Delhi that the British force at Meerut was on the move. This was a good opportunity to destroy Wilson's small force before it reinforced Barnard, which would in turn make that larger contingent more manageable. According to Dehlvi, the rebel force left the city by the bridge of boats around 10 a.m. on the 30th. The rebels were estimated to number around 5,000, including men from the 11th and 38th NI, and Syed Ahmad Khan writes that morale was high. Just as the British felt confident that the mutineers would flee upon seeing the force come to challenge them, the sepoys were sure that their compatriots in the British force would desert when they saw their comrades on the opposing side.

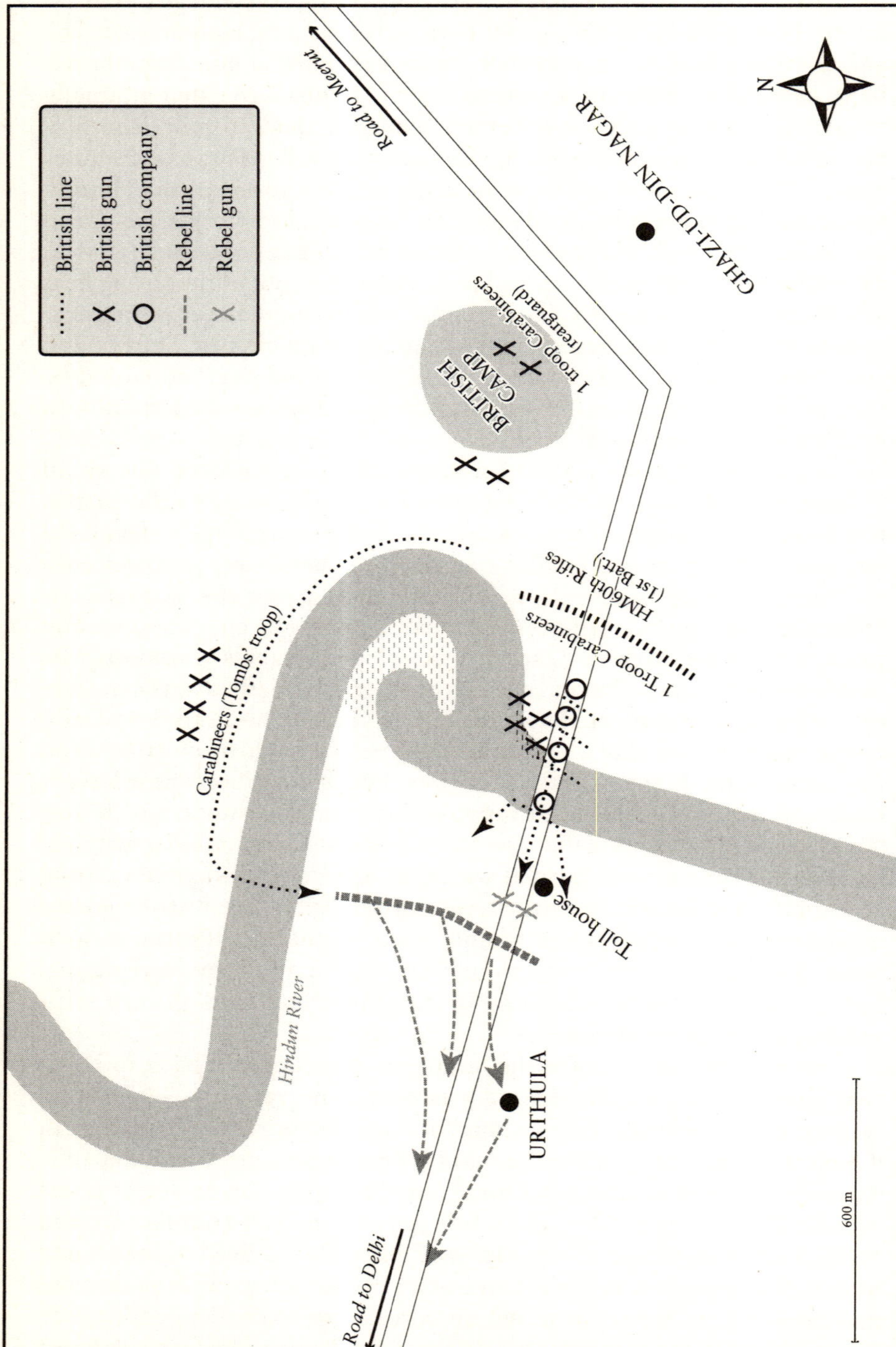


The Battle of Hindun River.

From Delhi, the journey to the Hindun was short; the rebel force came within sight of the right bank of the river around 4 p.m. Had they arrived a day or two before, they could have dug in quite effectively and prevented an easy British crossing. In the event, Wilson's force had beaten the rebels to the bridge and spent the day resting, gathering their strength. Even so, the rebels had greater numbers and a better position; Wilson, confident the rebels were far away, had made the mistake of camping on the left rather than the right bank of the river. With good organisation and stout determination, the rebels could still prevent a British crossing. As soon as they arrived, the rebels dug in on the slight ridge on the right bank and readied themselves for a fight.

The British bugler sounded the alarm as the rebel heavy guns fired the first shots, prompting an immediate reply from the British 18-pounders. One of the first rebel shots, from an 18-pounder, managed to maim two palkee-bearers who happened to be waiting outside the carabineers' hospital tent. Wilson immediately made plans to cross the river and attack. The Rifles, he decided, would cross the suspension bridge and launch a full-frontal attack. At the same time, the carabineers, accompanied by four guns from Major Tombs' troop, would ford the stream a few hundred metres upstream and turn the enemy's left. Initially, one company of the 60th Rifles was pushed forward to gain the bridge, which happened to face the right of the rebel line, while a second company moved behind in support. The response from the rebels was to open up on both columns with their guns. As the carabineers and Rifles moved off, Major Scott's battery (four guns) was moved under the bridge. Meanwhile, another two companies of the 60th were moved up in support on the bridge, along with the sappers and a troop of carabineers who took cover along the walls of the causeway. With so many committed to the assault, only a troop of carabineers and two guns were left to protect the camp.

The two heavy guns brought from Meerut were also employed, firing from inside the British camp toward the far side of the bridge at the toll house. Wilson:

> The first few rounds from the insurgents' guns were admirably aimed, plunging through our camp; but they were ably replied to by our two 18-pounders, in position under Lieutenant Light, and Major Tombs' troop, most admirably led by Lieutenant-Colonel M. Mackenzie, who, raking them in the flank with his 6-pounders, first made their fire unsteady, and in a short time silenced the heavy guns.[1]

Meanwhile, Tombs and the carabineers managed to cross the river and wheeled to the left to turn the flank of the rebels. At the same time, the two companies of the Rifles who had moved towards the bridge charged the rebel guns from around 80 yards away, causing most of the sepoys to flee. Two of the rebel heavy guns on the causeway adjacent to the toll house were the first to be captured. 'The charge was made in a most gallant manner, the enemy were now seen deserting their guns,' wrote Revd Rotton, accompanying the force. 'This result was partly attributable to an admirable flank movement of our artillery, under the able direction of that excellent officer (now alas! No more), Lieut-Colonel Murray-Mackenzie, and partly to the very effective fire of the Enfield Rifle.'

Showing little cohesion, the rebel force made no attempt to stand and fight. One of them managed to fire a tumbril loaded with ammunition before retreating back up the road to Delhi, however; Capt. Andrews and four of his men died in the explosion. It was later found that the rebel responsible was Havildar 'Deveesing' of the 11th NI, who had been pardoned prior to the mutiny for his refusal to use the new cartridge and granted leave. The Rifles caught up with Deveesing and bayonetted him. Others were overtaken and killed or wounded near the village. The rest of the rebel guns were abandoned, and the carabineers pursued the rebels for some distance. 'I cannot cease talking of the splendid behaviour of Tombs' troops; the gun-carriages are pitted with grape and shot marks, and Tombs continues the same gentle modest fellow. He has lost killed and wounded, thirteen men out of fifty, but the action of the troop never ceased for a moment. Colonel Mackenzie, too, has proved himself a splendid officer,'[2] wrote Greathed.

The only determined stand made by the rebels was at a village to their rear where a small number holed up; they were soon forced out. Around fifty rebels who had occupied an adjacent nullah were also killed, and the village was subsequently burnt by the British force. After this, the intense afternoon heat caused the British to give up their pursuit.

In the final accounting, the British force suffered thirty rank-and-file killed or wounded, with Capt. Andrews killed and Lt de Bourbel of the carabineers wounded. The dead were buried in the evening under mounds between a babool tree and a milestone marker next to the road from Meerut to Delhi. Five rebel guns had been captured: two 24-pounders, an 18-pounder, a 10-inch howitzer and an 8-inch howitzer, plus entrenching tools.

The sound of gunfire from the battle had been heard as far away as Delhi. Dehlvi reckoned the clamour lasted around two hours before it petered out. He also saw the rebels returning to the city claiming victory.

> At around 5 p.m., as I left the Qila [fort], I saw the Indian forces returning to the chatta of the Lahori Darwaza, their wooden carts bearing artillery leading the way. A young man was sitting propped up against a wooden box holding the cannonballs on the cart, but he was unconscious. I thought he was wounded and asked the front rider, 'Where has he been hurt?' The rider said, 'He isn't injured. He was hit by a *thanda gola* [spent cannonball] and fainted from the impact.' I saw that the cavalry and infantry were all joyously trooping along, blowing

> trumpets. I asked one of the sawars, 'Why did you return so quickly?' The sowar said, 'We were victorious and the *goras* [Europeans] ran away from the field, hence, we returned.' I questioned him further. 'What kind of battle did you fight?' He said, 'We were on this side of the embankment and they were on the other. There was artillery fire from both sides, and we prevailed. We fired shot after shot but the *gora* could not tolerate the heat of the day. We could see from afar that they were standing up to their knees in water, and when our cavalry attacked them they ran away in panic. They took their artillery guns with them.'[3]

Other mutineers returned more perturbed. Many had been robbed by Gujjar villagers as they straggled back to the city, stripped of the plunder they carried everywhere. Some were robbed of their firearms; some even lost their clothes. On their return to Delhi, they met with a cold reception. Zafar, guessing the truth, reproached the men for their cowardice and the loss of the heavy guns, urging them to return to the Hindun River the next day to put things right.

*****

With Zafar's words ringing in their ears, the rebels attacked again at midday the next day, a Sunday. Like last time, they positioned their guns on the ridge and commenced firing at the British, who had returned to their camp on the other side of the bridge. Wilson pushed a troop of carabineers across the bridge with two guns under the command of Capt. Rosser, who dug in at the toll house. Meanwhile, the Rifles moved on to the bridge.

While this went on, the two 18-pounders under Lt Light had been pushed to the edge of the river to provide support. With them were two guns of Major Scott's battery and a troop of carabineers. Capt. Rosser at this point communicated to Col Jones of the Rifles that he was under fire from the village on their left, Urthula, so Jones pushed two companies of the Rifles towards the carabineers to join them. They were also joined by two guns from Major Scott's battery. A cannonade between the two sides continued for roughly two hours. Once the Rifles reached the rebel line, they wheeled to the left to attack Urthula, which quickly fell. However, after two hours of bombardment the Rifles decided to pull back. The village was practically ruined, with many houses burning, and the heat of the day was intense.

The British troops decided to bypass Urthula and attempt to attack the rebel guns. However, shortly after, orders arrived from Wilson to hold the village. Col Jones complied, pulling the companies back into Urthula. The rebels were gradually retiring at this point, the large amount of grape being fired signalling their intention to move off. The British troops advanced to the top of the ridge, where a stop was ordered.

No guns were captured, the British troops being too tired for any pursuit. Some men, desperate in their thirst, picked up vessels left by the rebels thinking there was water in them and died from drinking poison or some corrosive substance.

The rebels had suffered twenty-three killed in the battle, and more bodies were seen strewn along the road to Delhi. Wilson, meanwhile, lost nine, with three of these dying from sunstroke. Lt H. G. Perkins of the Royal Horse Artillery was one, and the assistant-surgeon of the carabineers was severely wounded; he died later. An ensign of the 60th Rifles, a young man called Napier, was wounded; his leg had to be amputated. The heartbroken lad kept murmuring after the operation, 'I shall never lead the Rifles again – never lead the Rifles again.' He died a few weeks later. Counting both battles at the Hindun River, the British force had lost four officers and fifty men.

In Delhi, meanwhile, the mood was downbeat. Mrs Aldwell, the survivor of the palace massacre, was still being held in the apartment of Capt. Douglas. She was finally released shortly after the second battle. Aldwell noted early dissension among the sepoys as to their poor performance at the battle:

> When the sepoys, who returned defeated on that occasion, came back to the city, the men began talking despondingly, saying they would have no chance against the English. The Hindu sepoys especially upbraided the Mahomedans, saying 'This is your first engagement with the English; is this the way you intend to fight for your faith?' They also already spoke in terms of much regret of the turn that affairs had taken, reproached the Mahomedans for having deceived them on pretences of their religion, and seemed to doubt greatly whether the English Government had really had any intention of interfering with their caste. Great numbers of the Hindu sepoy at this time declared that if they could be sure their lives would be spared, they would gladly go back to the service of the Government; but the Mahomedans, on the contrary, used to assert that the King's service was much better than that of the English, that the Nawabs and Rajahs would supply the King with large forces, and they must eventually conquer.[4]

Following the two battles, Wilson allowed his men to recuperate for four days before continuing the march to join Barnard's force. They were strengthened the next day, 1 June, by the arrival of the 2nd Gurkhas, the Sirmoor battalion under Major Charles Reid, which had marched from Dehra Dun. This contingent, 500 strong, was a welcome addition considering the casualties sustained in the battles. Roughly a hundred more men of the Rifles also arrived, having been released from their duty to defend Meerut. On the 2nd, the village of Urthula, across the bridge and to the left of the road, was destroyed. Elephants were brought in to bring down the mud walls of the village houses. Greathed observed the affair with some regret:

> The poor inhabitants are certainly to be pitied, but the destruction is a necessity: they were unluckily 'Jats' who are for the most part our friends. There were twenty-three of the enemy, all Sepoys, lying together in the ditch at the back of the village; they had been killed in a mass by a party of Rifles. There were several dead bodies outside, of the enemy who fell on the 31st; and Light, who went down the road with the patrol for three and a half miles, found dead bodies at that distance, and abandoned ammunition waggons blown up or burnt. We could see Delhi plainly from the bridge occupied by our outlying picket.

On 4 June, Wilson received word from Barnard instructing him to cross at Baghpat and join the main force at Alipur, north of Delhi, and duly marched his men north. Before leaving, they damaged the bridge over the Hindun to make it impassable. The advance was delayed somewhat by the camp followers sacking Urthula, but by the evening of 5 June Wilson had reached Khekurah on the banks of the Jumna, and the next night they crossed the bridge of boats at Baghpat. The next morning, they marched down the right bank of the river to reach Alipur and join the main force. Stormy weather had closed in, and the lashing rain and high winds disrupted their progress, but the Meerut force was cheered loudly as it marched into camp with the guns captured at the Hindun River.

21

# The Battle of Badli-ki-Serai

… the advance of our troops towards Delhi and the victory at Badlee Serai near that city on the 8th June proved to the country that there was vitality in our cause and power on our side.

John Lawrence

The rebels soon had a third chance to stop the British advance on Delhi a week after the battles at Hindun River, although with Wilson having reinforced Barnard it was a more difficult proposition this time around.

On 7 June, Barnard, now based around 12 miles from Delhi at Alipur, had been informed that the rebels had dug in around halfway between his position and Delhi at a place called Badli-ki-Serai. Battle must be joined the next day. Armed with this insight, Barnard had some of the more suspect sepoy troops sent back towards Ambala on dubious pretences to pre-empt any treachery during the battle. The dismissed troops were essentially a squadron of the 4th Cavalry along with a wing of the 9th Irregular Cavalry. They were told to head back up north and keep a watch on some supposedly hostile villages. With this done, the rest of the evening and night was spent preparing for the coming battle.

Barnard's infantry now consisted of six companies of HM60th Rifles, HM75th Foot, the 1st Fusiliers, six companies of 2nd Fusiliers, the Sirmoor battalion and 150 Indian sappers and miners. As for mounted troops, he had HM9th Lancers and two squadrons of carabineers. All in all, Barnard's army now totalled 2,400 infantry, 600 cavalry and twenty-two field guns (sixteen horse artillery guns and six horse battery guns). Behind them, a siege train was being organised at Ferozepore that comprised eight 18-pounder guns, four 8-inch howitzers, four 8-inch mortars and a 5½- inch mortar with a company of European artillery and recruits.

On the morning of 8 June, around 2 a.m., the force moved out to meet the rebels. The baggage was left at Alipur, and the advance towards Delhi was commenced in battle array.

The advance column was composed of the following: the 3rd Troop of the 3rd Brigade of Horse Artillery under Major Frank Turner with four guns of the 2nd Troop of the 1st Brigade under Major Tombs, all under the command of Lt Col Murray Mackenzie; three squadrons HM9th Lancers under Lt Col Yule; and around fifty Jhind cavalry commanded by Lt Hodson. This advance column was placed under the command of Brigadier James Hope Grant.

The main force was organised into two infantry brigades – one under Brigadier Showers and one under Brigadier Graves, the last man to leave the Flagstaff Tower. The second column, commanded by Showers, was composed like so: nine companies of HM75th Foot and the 1st European Bengal Fusiliers; a party of sappers (mostly European) with entrenching tools under the command of Lt Chesney of the Bengal Engineers; one squadron of 6th Dragoon Guards (carabineers); four heavy guns; and four guns of Major Scott's battery. The third column, commanded by Graves, was composed as follows: the 1st Battalion of 60th Royal Rifles; the 2nd European Bengal Fusiliers; the Sirmoor Battalion; a party of sappers under Lt Salkeld of the Engineers; the 2nd Troop of the 3rd Brigade under Capt. Money; and a squadron of HM9th Lancers.

The rearguard, left behind to protect the baggage at Alipur, was commanded by Major Cobbe and comprised one company of 2nd European Bengal Fusiliers, one squadron of 6th Dragoon Guards, the Jhind contingent and two guns from Major Scott's battery.

Barnard's plan was for the second column to form the right flank while the third column formed the left flank, with the heavy guns positioned in the middle and the lighter artillery divided between the left and right flanks. Most of the European regiments were not at full strength; the forces under Showers and Graves amounted to 1,900 infantry and 170 cavalry with fourteen guns. The two brigades were to launch a full-frontal attack supported by a flanking cavalry force of roughly 350 cavalry and ten guns.

The rebels, meanwhile, had decided on a defensive position so far as the surroundings would allow. The Badli-ki-Serai included various houses and gardens, which were utilised to form a good line. The camp had been set up at the serai itself, on the west side of the road to Delhi. A deep canal or *jheel* protected the rebel right, while another canal (the Najafgarh *jheel*) protected their left flank, which abutted the village of Sahipur. Furthermore, the ground on the rebel right was soft and marshy, making it difficult to advance upon. Various water and drainage channels would also prolong any direct advance.

The rebel line ran in front of the serai. Around 150 yards in front of it, facing the advancing British line, were two ruined summer houses

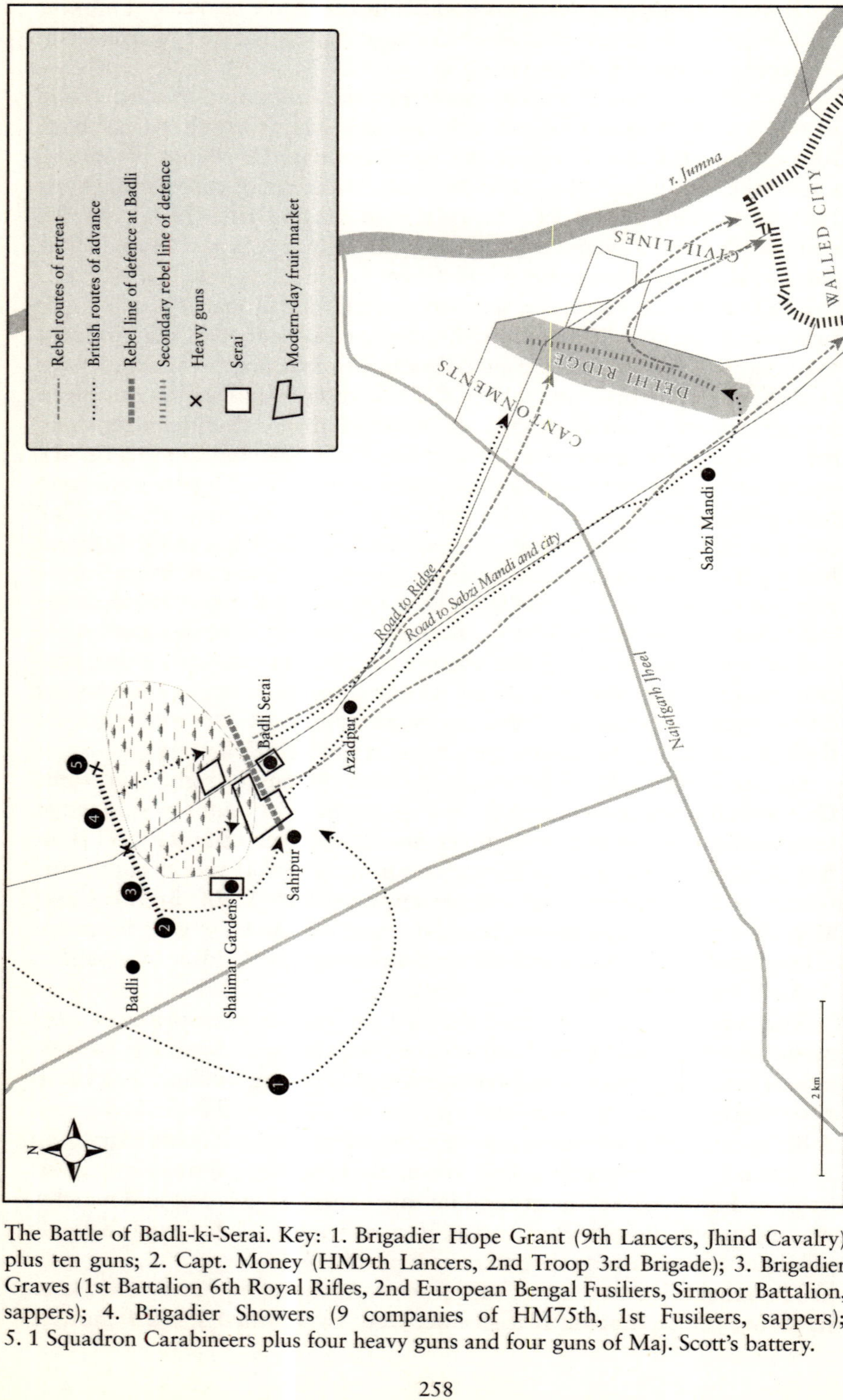


The Battle of Badli-ki-Serai. Key: 1. Brigadier Hope Grant (9th Lancers, Jhind Cavalry) plus ten guns; 2. Capt. Money (HM9th Lancers, 2nd Troop 3rd Brigade); 3. Brigadier Graves (1st Battalion 6th Royal Rifles, 2nd European Bengal Fusiliers, Sirmoor Battalion, sappers); 4. Brigadier Showers (9 companies of HM75th, 1st Fusileers, sappers); 5. 1 Squadron Carabineers plus four heavy guns and four guns of Maj. Scott's battery.

which had been garrisoned and were protected by a battery each, plus some other light field pieces. The rebel artillery, meanwhile, was spread all along the line. Having arrived a few hours earlier than the British force, the rebels had placed large, white earthenware jars at various distances from their line to aid their gunners in finding the right range. Near the two summer houses there was a mound on which four (some say three) heavy guns, along with an 8-inch howitzer, had been placed in a sandbagged battery. On the rebel left, the houses and garden walls of Sahipur afforded good cover for the infantry.

All in all, there were said to be seven regiments (or elements thereof) present, perhaps joined by parts of two other regiments. Apparently this included Delhi's 38th and 54th NI, Meerut's 11th and 20th, Meerut's 3rd Light Cavalry and Delhi's 4th Bengal Irregular Cavalry. It is hard to say whether these were really all soldiers or if their numbers were bolstered by volunteers and general riffraff from the city hoping for plunder. The rebels supposedly boasted in their line a number of Gujjar villagers as well. One could put their number at 6,000 infantry – assuming the regiments had turned out in full force.

In addition to greater numbers, the rebels had the upper hand in heavy guns. They had brought thirteen, including an 8-inch howitzer, two 24-pounders and two 18-pounders. The guns were worked by the 3rd Company of the 7th Native Battalion Artillery, supplemented by a motley bunch of artillerymen from the palace guard more used to firing guns on ceremonial occasions and retired gunners resident in the city, plus a few gun lascars who had previously worked at the British magazine.

Since the rebel position was difficult to attack from the flanks, Barnard sent Grant's cavalry force in a semi-circular motion to the west of the rebel line so that it might turn up at the rebel rear around the same time as the two British infantry brigades attacked from the front. To effect this, the cavalry column would set off around half an hour before the rest of the force, taking a road that veered right across a canal. Barnard would move ahead to engage the enemy at the same time, with Showers leading his column on the left and Graves leading his on the right.

The British force began its 5-mile advance at 1 a.m. and arrived at Badli-ki-Serai just before daybreak, when the rebel fires could still be seen burning. As the British line approached, the rebels opened fire; British guns responded in kind. By all accounts, the fire of the rebel batteries was very accurate and had a telling effect.

Early on, there was confusion in the British line. While Showers' column was under fire, Graves' troops were stuck behind a confusing mass of baggage, pack animals and other supplies, so there was delay before they could help their comrades. At first the rebels had the better of things thanks to their heavier artillery; the lighter British guns were powerless against the 18- and 24-pounders. In another mishap, at one point somebody called out, 'Prepare for cavalry!' The men of the 75th duly formed a square, but no enemy cavalry charge appeared. The square made for a tempting target, however, and round shot came bounding in almost immediately, causing death and injury. The mistake was soon spotted, and Brigadier Showers led the men against the rebel line.

The 75th made it to the rebel line first, reaching the rebel guns and mounting a bastion. In the process they lost nineteen killed and forty-three wounded, including officers. The 1st Bengal European Fusiliers moved in support, although the brunt of the fire was still trained on the men of the 75th. Lt Norman recounted the combat:

> The fire of the enemy's heavy battery, aided by several light guns, began to tell seriously. The bullock-drivers of our heavy guns ran away with the cattle, and one of the wagons blew up; our men fell fast, and the staff offering a tempting mark, two officers (Colonel Chester and Captain Russell) were killed, and several horses of the staff lost in the course of one or two minutes. Time was precious, there was no sign of any flank attack by our cavalry on the insurgents, and it was evident that our guns could not silence their artillery sheltered behind a parapet, so Sir Henry Barnard ordered the 75th Regiment to charge and take the heavy battery. This corps, led by Brigadier Showers and Colonel Herbert, carried out this duty in the most spirited manner. They were supported by the 1st Bengal European Fusiliers, who in their advance suffered somewhat from a musketry fire opened from an enclosure on their right.[1]

According to some of the soldiers, Showers' advance was so rapid that the rebels could not depress their guns fast enough and so fired their shot and grape over the heads of the onrushing British column.

The men under Graves also reached the rebel line soon after, although they had to contend with knee-high water as they advanced. There was a short period of intense fighting, especially in the serai. The rebels made a half-hearted defence, some fighting furiously while others wilted. At this time, and a little later than planned, Grant's cavalry and horse artillery appeared at the rebel rear having been delayed somewhat by the water channels crisscrossing the area. The cavalry charge triggered a confused retreat by the rebels. HM9th Lancers charged and took the rebel guns, which were swiftly turned on the fleeing rebels.

Francis Wigram later heard that the British forces had employed subterfuge, making use of intercepted communications between the rebels and the suspicious sepoys of the 4th NI, who had been sent away before the battle:

> Just before this action, a spy was intercepted carrying a letter from the men of the 4th NI Cavalry (Lancers) to the insurgents, telling them they were to be placed on the left and not to fire on that quarter, as they would as soon as the action commenced go over to them; the letter

> was allowed to pass into the city, and the 4th N.I. Lancers ordered to Meerut, while the 9th Queen's Lancers took their place on the left dressed in blue. The insurgents consequently were rather taken by surprise to find their friends on the left suddenly amongst them cutting them up without mercy.[2]

Barnard extended the British advance all the way to the village of Azadpur, where the road to Delhi forked. The left path led through the Delhi cantonment and the ridge, while the other led directly into the city through the Sabzi Mandi.

*****

The ridge and cantonment area would in fact have made a far better defensive position for the rebels than Badli-ki-Serai, for in front of the cantonment ran the large, deep Najafgarh canal. Only the cantonment bridges spanned this canal, which was much too deep to wade through. If they had dug in behind the canal and destroyed the bridges, the British would have had great difficulty in capturing the ridge; a full frontal assault against a rebel line along the banks of the canal would have been impossible. However, without a guiding mind, the rebels retreated from Badli-ki-Serai all the way back into the city, leaving a relatively small number to defend the ridge. The bridges, meanwhile, had not been put out of action. The rebels had damaged them, yes, but not destroyed them; they remained sturdy enough even for artillery to cross. The rebels hadn't even placed a guard at the bridges. Barnard was alive to the opportunity; he knew his force must immediately cross the canal and capture the ridge.

The British force wasn't large enough for a full-frontal attack along the breadth of the ridge. Instead, Barnard split the force into two main brigades. Graves led one (supplemented by Money's troop of horse artillery) in an advance along the road to the cantonments, while Wilson (with the rest of the artillery and cavalry) led the other along the road to the Sabzi Mandi. The Sirmoor Battalion, left out of the two larger forces, advanced over the ground between the two roads. Since both roads passed the ridge – one to its north, the other to its south – the two brigades could attack the rebel position on each flank while the Sirmoor Battalion preoccupied the defenders with a frontal assault. The Royal Rifles were now moved ahead in skirmishing order.

Up on the ridge, the rebels could be seen hastily forming a defensive line. They had anchored their right flank at the Flagstaff Tower, where three guns had been placed. These guns opened up as soon as the British left column, led by Graves, moved into range. In the face of this barrage, the column crossed the canal by the bridge opposite the Flagstaff Tower. Once across, the brigade fanned out in line and began advancing through the cantonment; the rebel guns were barely slowing them down.

Once through the cantonment, the line found itself within a few hundred yards of the rebel guns at the Flagstaff Tower. The British guns under Money now opened up, silencing the rebel guns. This was followed by an advance by the 2nd Bengal European Fusiliers and the 60th Rifles on the left before the guns were taken from the flank. The whole column then moved along the crest of the ridge, driving the rebels back towards the Hindu Rao buildings.

As they approached the Hindu Rao, the retreating rebels found themselves facing Wilson's column, which had captured an 18-pounder en route. Graves' men were not in the clear, however, for they now found themselves within range of the rebel guns in the city. Several were killed by the rebel shot, and one British gun had its limber destroyed, but the bulk of the rebels had fled back into the city. The time now was coming up on 9 a.m. Brigadier Graves had been the last European to leave the Flagstaff Tower; now he was one of the first to recapture it.

Graves and his men also found evidence of the events of 11 May at the ridge. In particular, he saw the cart loaded with European corpses that had been driven up to the tower shortly before he had fled for Ambala. The extreme heat and the attentions of local carrion eaters had rendered them almost unrecognisable.

*****

The British force during that day suffered fifty-one killed (four officers) and 131 rank-and-file wounded. The bulk of the casualties had been taken by HM9th lancers (fifteen killed and ten wounded) and HM75th (twenty-three killed and forty-three wounded). Among the casualties was Adjutant-General Colonel Charles Chester, who was killed by the first shot the rebels fired. Captain Claud W. Russell (54th NI), Chester's orderly officer, also died, as did Captain J. W. Delamain (56th NI). Another orderly officer, Lt A. Harrison (HM75th), was a casualty as well.

Rebel losses are difficult to discern, but Lt Henry Norman (later Field Marshal Sir Henry Norman), estimated they suffered more than 300 casualties:

> Of the troops opposed to us it was said that a thousand of those who came out never returned to Delhi. This may be an exaggeration, but their losses were undoubtedly heavy, probably three or four hundred killed and wounded, besides a good many who were said to have gone off to their homes after or during the action.[3]

According to spies, most of those rebels unaccounted for had simply lost heart and set off home with the loot they carried. Thirteen rebel guns had been captured at Badli-ki-Serai and twelve at the ridge, plus one at Sabzi Mandi, meaning twenty-six guns had been captured that day. Among them were two 24-pounders, two 18-pounders an 8-inch howitzer; the rest were 9-pounders. All the ammunition supplies the rebels had brought out to Badli-ki-Serai also fell into British hands.

*****

Standing atop the Flagstaff Tower on the ridge that morning, looming roughly 80 feet over the city before them, Barnard and his officers would have had a magnificent view of the city and the land before it. On a clear day they would have been able to take it all in: the city walls, the palace, the Jama Masjid, the bridge of boats – not to mention the burnt-out, looted wrecks of the European residences between them and the city walls, including the grand Metcalfe House. The British position was ideal, and Barnard knew it. On its southern limit, the ridge was almost adjacent to the walled city; the Mori Bastion, situated at the north-western end of the city, was little more than half a mile away.

The rear of the British position was protected by the canal running along the northern perimeter of the cantonments. In the hot season this canal tended to dry up completely, but intense rains earlier in the year had completely filled the various basins and lakes upstream, so the canal was still full of fresh water; indeed, it would stay that way for the duration of the siege. To the east of the ridge lay the curve of the Jumna, which at this point was too deep to be forded easily. It was also wide enough to prevent any artillery guns stationed on its left bank enfilading the position on the ridge opposite.

If the rebels wanted to attack the British position without tackling a steep climb or deep water, they had to come from the south, through the Sabzi Mandi. Where the ridge met the plain to the south it was thick with bazaars, houses and walled gardens, offering crucial cover to any approaching force. The southern end of the ridge was also relatively close to the city walls – just 1,200 yards to the south and within the range of rebel guns.

The defensive strength of the ridge would save the British force several times over during the coming months. The nearby canal, and the fact that it was overflowing with water, ensured a steady flow of drinking water, a continued focus on hygiene, and respite from the intense heat of the summer. If it wasn't for the providential high water, the British would have been reliant on the handful of wells in the cantonments, which frequently brought up brackish water, or the river itself, which was 2 miles distant and promised a gruelling uphill climb with heavy pails of water.

Barnard ordered camp made on the parade ground below the ridge. Meanwhile, British pickets were organised. For now, the British position on the ridge would run approximately one mile, from the Flagstaff Tower in the north to Hindu Rao House further south, with pickets at these points and also at an old mosque situated between the two. The picket at Hindu Rao House was the largest. Major Reid's Sirmoor Battalion and two companies of the 60th Rifles were ordered to hold the position, which was the key to the British right flank and provided good protection. A further picket was organised for a large mound (later nicknamed the 'General's mound') as it was ideally situated for the commanding officer to martial the defence of the British camp, pivoting in whatever direction required attention. While this went on, the British guns were pushed forward and batteries were organised at the mosque, the Hindu Rao and the nearby observatory, as well as at the Flagstaff Tower. The wide span of the batteries meant all the approaches to the ridge from the city were covered. Meanwhile, cavalry patrolled the extreme north of the ridge to protect the British left while another cavalry picket constantly guarded the canal to the rear. The position was effectively locked down.

A strong defence was well and good, but offence was another matter entirely. The city could not be bombarded in any meaningful way from the ridge; the nearest battery was still over 1,500 yards from the city walls, and the guns were too light to reduce the city walls anyway. Defence would have to do.

At around 2 p.m., the rebels opened up with the city's heavy guns. Two 24-pounders were moved out of the city walls to fire on the ridge. At the same time, a large contingent of rebels moved up as if to contest the ridge and the whole of the British force was called out to form up for defence. It was a half-hearted attack, however; indeed, it proved to be the first of many weak and disorganised attacks on the British camp over the following months. The fighting petered out as the evening drew on.

*****

The victory at Badli-ki-Serai and the almost bloodless capture of the Delhi ridge was crucial. It allowed the British force to approach the city and take a strong defensive position, and it proved that the rebels, although greater in number, so far lacked the spirit and organisation necessary to put up a good fight. John Lawrence was triumphant; his confidence had been vindicated. Anson and his officers had not wanted to march on Delhi so soon, but now the loyalty of the Cis-Sutlej states of Patiala, Nabha and Jhind had been cemented when they might have been wavering. 'The advance of our troops towards Delhi and the victory at Badlee Serai near that city on 8 June proved to the country that there was vitality in our cause and power on our side,' Lawrence enthused.

In the city, the early setbacks had caused much dismay in the rebel ranks. John Everett, the aforementioned ex-risaldar of the 14th Regiment who had hidden in the city, recalled conversations with an African named Moujud who harboured him for a time. Moujud, a royal attendant, was constantly at Zafar's side. He told Everett of the uncertainty among the princes and the loss of morale after the defeats:

[Moujud] used to return home at night and give me the news of the day and on one occasion he told me that the King had assembled all his sons and his men of note at a public durbar, and remarked to them that since the battle at Ghazi-ud-din-nagar [Hindun] he had observed that they had been gradually sneaking away from their attendance on him, and that he imagined this must be through a fright. The King added, that this was the time when they should all unite, and heartily combine to drive the British off the ridge. 'If you do not do so,' said he, 'mark my words; if the British ever enter Delhi again, they will not leave one soul alive of the descendants of Taimur Shah.'[4]

22

# The Possibilities of a *Coup de Main*

At Dehlee 8 regiments (natives) have mutinied. But don't you be misled by the words of any, because at last the rule of the British Government will be restored over Dehlee.

Lal Singh, Gurkha sepoy, Nusseri battalion

Barnard was pleased with the successful capture of the Delhi ridge on 8 June. However, he found himself in a quandary now that his force faced the city. Both Lord Canning and John Lawrence were insisting that he take the city with all possible haste; all eyes were on Delhi, so the city's swift capture was imperative in order to dampen the mutinous instincts of the sepoy army around the country. Every day the city remained in rebel hands tarnished British prestige in the country and increased the chance of wavering sepoy regiments joining their comrades in mutiny.

With an early assault essential, the idea of a *coup de main* was mooted. John Lawrence knew the city well. He had spent four years there as a magistrate and tax collector, and had previously served as a civil and sessions judge in the city. As early as 6 June, before the British Field Force had even reached Delhi, Lawrence had suggested a surprise night attack on the city utilising an underground passage that passed beneath the city walls and came out in a European residence within:

> Opposite the Church inside Delhy, on the wall, is a house which Mr Egerton occupied. In it are rooms underground, and a wide passage which leads outside. A man well acquainted with the locality could sneak along the banks of the nulla at night and ascertain if the passage is guarded. If not guarded, a picked body of men going down secretly about 2 in the morning, when guards are negligent, might get into the

> town, when turning sharp to the right, and going through the Kucherry compound they could win that bastion and even the Cashmeer Gate. This latter is cut off from the town by a wall. A body of troops concealed behind the old Customs House outside the Cashmeer Gate might then advance, and get in by the Cashmeer Gate.[1]

In case the plan failed, the men were to bring bags of gunpowder with which to blow open the gate as a last resort. Lawrence suggested that a local man, suitably bribed with 500 rupees and the promise of double if the plan succeeded, should be employed to check if the plan was feasible and lead the party into the city if so. 'Great secrecy is essential if the scheme be tried. If we have to make regular approaches the troops will be worn out,' Lawrence warned.

However, neither Lawrence nor Canning had a military background. For Barnard, surveying the city from the ridge, the difficulties of an immediate attack on the city were obvious. His guns could not possibly compete with the rebel guns, which were more numerous and of heavier calibre. He lacked sufficient troops to maintain the position and protect the baggage, let alone consider an attack. Nor, in fact, did he have sufficient sappers to make regular approaches towards the city defences. Taking everything into consideration, Barnard decided that the best thing was to simply sit tight and await reinforcements. The rebels, leaderless and incoherent, were unlikely to mount an effective attack on the British position, and Barnard was confident that the ridge could be held so long as they didn't launch a full-blooded attack. Chief Engineer Major Laughton, Brigadier Wilson and other officers were of the same opinion, concurring with Barnard that no active operations should be carried out until reinforcements arrived.

By 12 June, however, Barnard had been swayed by the urgency of the situation. A rather audacious plan was dreamt up utilising all 1,800 infantrymen he had at his disposal. Capt. Hodson, along with engineers Greathed (no relation to H. H. Greathed), Maunsell and Chesney, had been called upon to organise the plan. The idea was plain and uncomplicated. Two gates, Kashmir and Lahore, would be blown open with powder bags at dawn. Hodson:

> We drew up our scheme and gave it to the General, who highly approved, and will, I trust, carry it out; but how times must be changed, when four subalterns are called upon to suggest a means for carrying out so vitally-important an enterprise as this, one on which the safety of the empire depends! ... Simple but 'perfectly-feasible' plan of four subalterns: blow open gates with powder, and go in with bayonet.[2]

After the Kashmir and Lahore gates were detonated, the force – divided into three columns – was to advance into the city. One column would pass through the Kashmir Gate and another through the Lahore Gate while the third attempted to scale the walls with ladders at a suitable point. Beyond that, it was simply hoped that rebel resistance would collapse once the gates had fallen, allowing the British force to establish a strong toehold in the north from which to push on and capture the rest of the walled city.

Understandably, the plan caused some concern among the officers, who felt the plan was doomed to failure. There was little prospect of such a small contingent of men being able to successfully capture the gates, they argued. Even if they could, a force of fewer than 2,000 men could hardly be sufficient to capture a city of Delhi's size. Casualties in the city would surely reduce the force further still. A repulse and retreat after those casualties would be much worse than an attack never taking place, as it would be certain to boost the morale of the rebels. Furthermore, if the rebels showed any initiative, they could counterattack the weakly guarded British camp and utterly destroy it.

Despite these reservations, Barnard, under pressure from John Lawrence, approved the plan. Orders were given for an assault at dawn on 13 June – the very next day. The scheme was kept entirely secret; so much so that even the chief engineer was not informed of the plans. Any sign of preparation could alert spies in the camp. However, as dawn approached, all was not well. Advance pickets under Brigadier Graves, roughly 300 men in total, were still on duty at the Flagstaff Tower. Graves had been given no written order regarding the assault; he had only received a verbal notice, and, doubting its authenticity, had disregarded it. By the time his men arrived to join the assault, the cover of darkness had been lost, and with it the element of surprise. The assault was postponed.

In retrospect, most later agreed the idea had been foolish. 'There are few who do not now feel that the accident which hindered this attempt was one of those happy interpositions on our behalf of which we had such numbers to be thankful for,' wrote Lt Norman. 'Defeat or even a partial success would have been ruin, and complete success would not have achieved for us the results subsequently obtained, or, as far as can be seen, would it have prevented a single massacre, most of which indeed had already taken place.' An exception was Hodson, the architect of the plan, who remained bemused:

> I am much annoyed and disappointed at our plan not having been carried out, because I am confident it would have been successful. The rebels were cowed, and perfectly ignorant of any intention of so bold a stroke on our part as an assault; the surprise would have done everything. I am very vexed, though the General is most kind and considerate in trying to soothe my disappointment – too kind, indeed, or he would not so readily have pardoned those whose fault it is that we are still outside Delhi.[3]

With the plan cancelled, Barnard reverted to watchful waiting. A reward was promised for destruction of the bridge over the Jumna, which would halt rebel supplies and reinforcements from the east; there was talk of a gunboat or fire raft being sent down to destroy it, but nothing came to fruition.

On 14 June, General Thomas Reed arrived on the ridge to assume command of the force from Barnard. However, Reed's health was not good and there was a delay in the transfer of power. The idea of a *coup de main* was raised with Reed to gauge his feeling; with the pressure to capture the city so great, the notion was constantly being considered and rejected. In a meeting on 15 June, for example, Barnard again decided to await further reinforcements. John Lawrence by now seemed to have sensed the magnitude of the task: 'I am quite of opinion that Delhy should not be attacked until the reinforcements now on their way arrive. A repulse would be a calamity, and even partial success unsatisfactory. The repeated punishments which the mutineers receive in the meantime will tell both on them and the country,' he advised Barnard.

Reinforcements were drifting in all the while. British strength had been supplemented on 9 June by the arrival of Capt. Daly's Guide Corps from Mardan, Peshawar. This force boasted three troops of cavalry and six companies of infantry. Its men had covered the distance of 580 miles in just twenty-two days, equivalent to a marathon every day. The corps was effectively the advance guard of the reinforcements that were now moving from the Punjab to help Barnard capture the city on John Lawrence's orders. The new arrivals were received enthusiastically at the ridge; Hodson, who had once been in charge of them, wrote that they had a positive effect on other Indian troops in the camp who may or may not have been privately wavering in their loyalty. The unconditional loyalty of the Guides likely strengthened bonds in the camp, and they would go on to distinguish themselves in the fighting to come.

Further reinforcements arrived between 24 June and 3 July. This next contingent was headed by Brig. Gen. Chamberlain, who would take up the post of adjutant-general. It comprised a wing of HM8th Regiment; a wing of HM61st Regiment; a squadron of the 5th Punjab Cavalry; the 1st Punjab Infantry (Coke's Rifles), led by Major Coke; contingents of newly recruited Sikh sappers and artillery; a contingent of European reserve artillery from Lahore; two guns of the 1st (European) Troop, 1st Brigade, Horse Artillery; and two guns of 5th (Native) Troop, 1st Brigade, Horse Artillery. On the 29th, Capt. Taylor arrived to strengthen the Engineer Brigade, with Chief Engineer Major Laughton retiring through illness. Laughton would be replaced on 3 July by Lt Col Baird Smith, who would take up the post of chief engineer with Capt. Taylor as his second-in-command. With these arrivals, the British force camped on the ridge slowly grew to around 6,600 men. However, while heartened by the boost to numbers, Barnard was concerned at the severe shortage

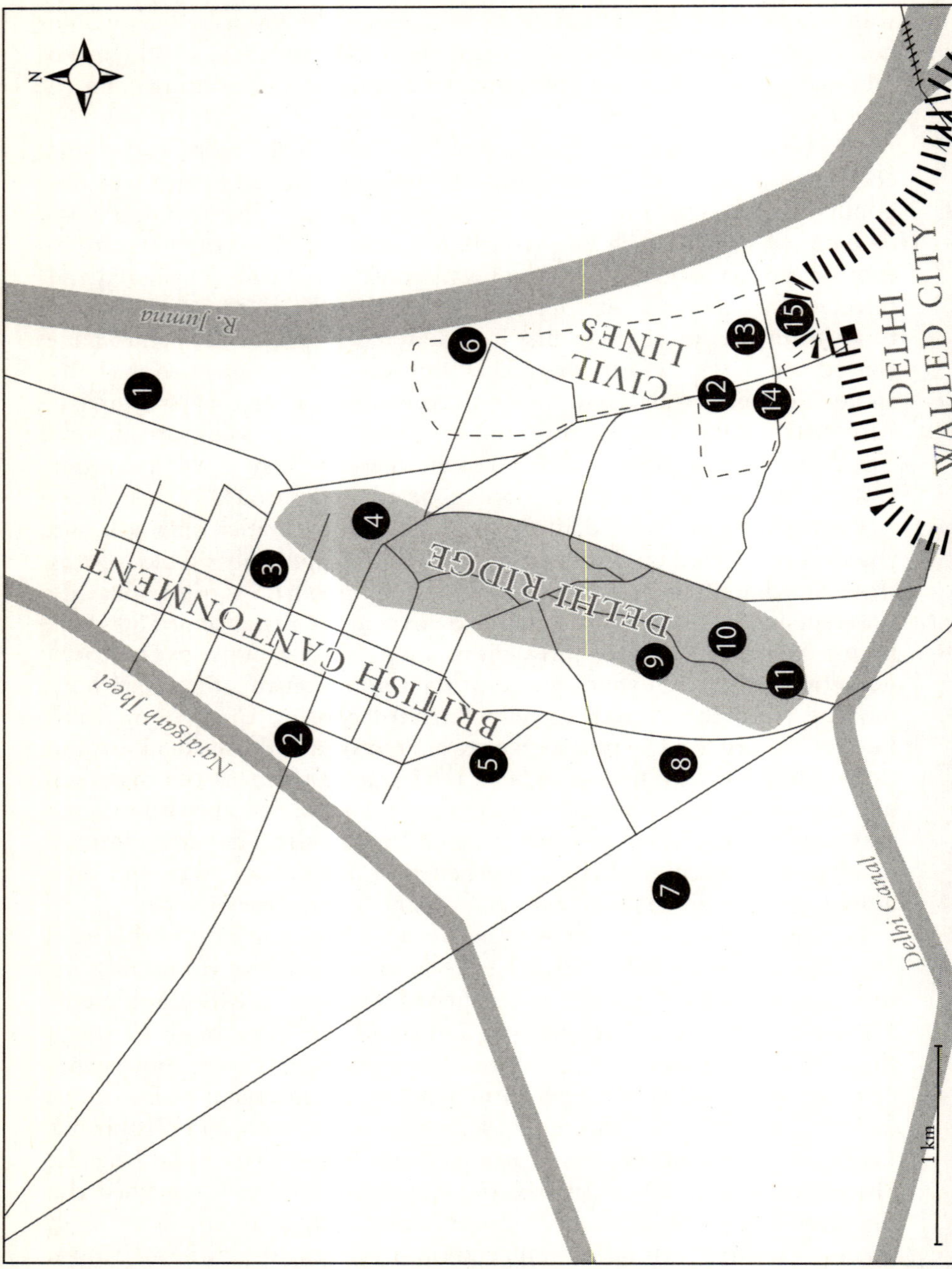


The Ridge and the Civil Lines. 1. Secondary magazine; 2. British cemetery; 3. Sadar Bazaar; 4. Flagstaff Tower; 5. The General's Mound; 6. Metcalfe House; 7. Roshanara Gardens; 8. Sabzi Mandi; 9. Hindu Rao; 10. Mutiny memorial; 11. Sammy House; 12. Ludlow Castle; 13. Qudsia Bagh; 14. Nicholson Cemetery; 15. Kashmir Gate.

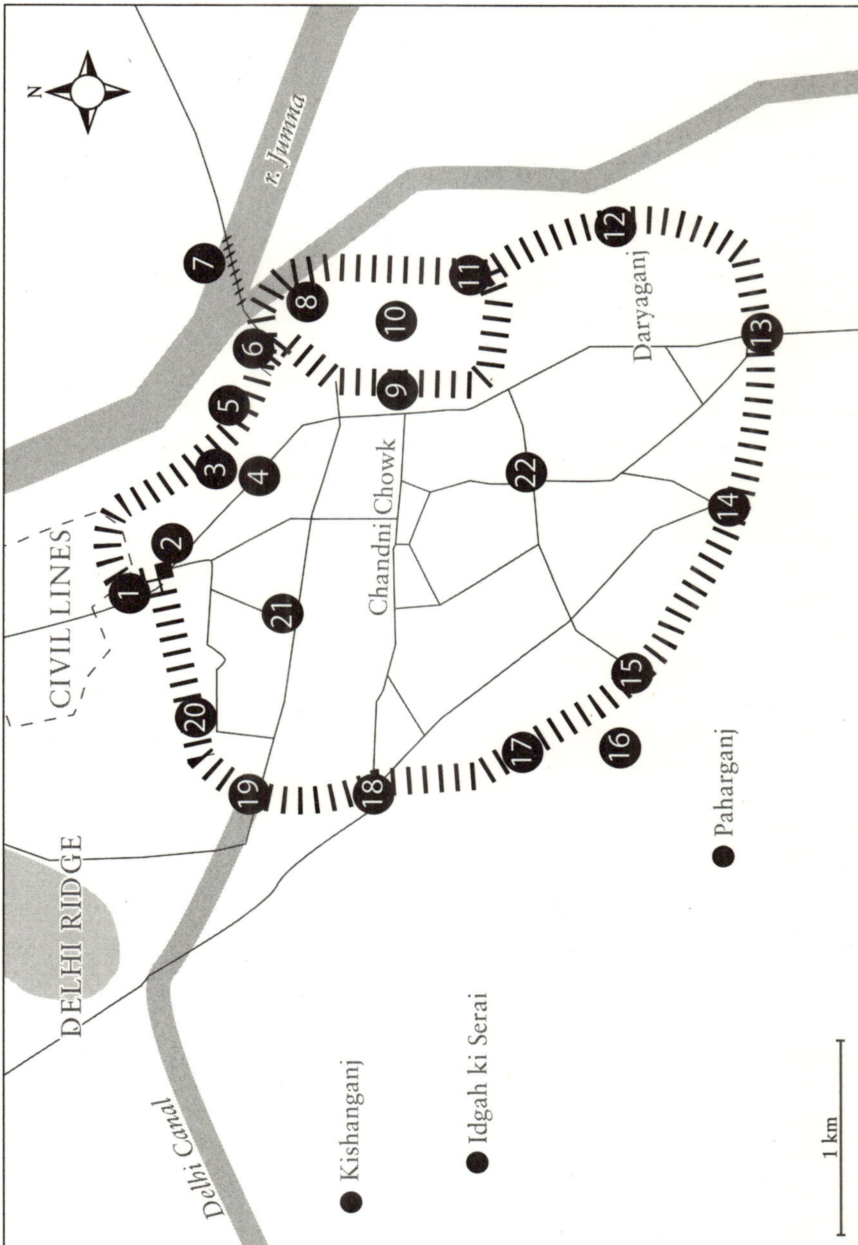


The walled city. 1. Kashmir Gate; 2. Skinner's House; 3. British Magazine; 4. Telegraph office; 5. Kellah Gate; 6. Nigambodh Gate; 7. Bridge of Boats; 8. Salimgarh Fort; 9. Lahore Gate (inner); 10. Palace; 11. Delhi Gate (inner); 12. Daryaganj Gate; 13. Delhi Gate (outer); 14. Turkman Gate; 15. Ajmer Gate; 16. Delhi College; 17. Farash Khana Gate; 18. Lahore Gate (outer); 19. Kabul Gate; 20. Mori Gate; 21. Begum Bagh; 22. Jama Masjid.

of artillerymen. John Lawrence would oblige him by recruiting as many Sikh artillerymen of the old Khalsa Sikh Army as he possibly could.

Sometimes officers arrived at the Delhi camp without men. On the morning of 11 June, for example, several British officers of the 60th NI had reported in after a close encounter with their own men. The 60th NI had originally been part of the Delhi Field Force but had been detached when the force reached Karnal as their loyalty was considered suspect. Separated from their comrades and denied any post, the men of the 60th had protested their loyalty and as a result their commander, Colonel T. Seaton, had taken the risk of trusting them. On the morning of 9 June, the troops were finally allowed their post, from which they learned more of what was happening around the country. They learned that the 5th NI, comrades from a posting in Ambala, had been disarmed. Angry at this news and fearful of disarmament, the men of the 60th made their decision and began plotting how to kill their officers. Unfortunately for them, one of Seaton's servants overheard the conspiracy and warned the officers – but not before saddling the officers' horses, which they used to escape. Because of this rushed flight they had arrived at the Delhi ridge with nothing but the clothes on their backs. Officers such as these were labelled 'refugees' by their fellow Europeans in the camp.

There was also the issue of whether the small contingent of sepoys in the British camp could be trusted. On 2 July, a plot by a group of sepoys in the camp was uncovered. One of the Sikh soldiers in a regiment recently arrived from the Punjab was approached by several men who tried to encourage him and his comrades to join the rebel army, saying they had been in touch with rebels inside the city and had hatched a plan. They asked the Sikh soldiers to desert and offered large bribes for doing so. Revd Rotton heard of the plan:

> The will of Heaven was to take away the Raj from the English and to give it over to the descendant of the Great Mogul; and that it could be no benefit to them to continue any longer in the British service, as by so doing they would only incur the displeasure of 'Shah Bahadoor Shah' which would rest upon the Sikhs, and follow them from place to place, till destruction completely overtook and overwhelmed them. If, however, on the other hand they made choice of the winning side, the King would gladly enrol those of the Sikhs who were officers among his Colonels and Generals, and would give large pay to one and all.

The Sikh soldier promptly told his commanding officer of the discussion, and the three sepoy officers were arrested, put on trial and hanged that very night. Their company, now under suspicion, was turned out of the British camp and no doubt joined the rebels.

John Lawrence, meanwhile, candidly warned both Barnard and the Government of India that he could spare no more European troops from the Punjab to help recapture Delhi. By 25 June, the whole of the Punjab excluding Peshawar was held by British prestige alone. A measly 1,200 European infantrymen were now stationed in the large province (100 at Phillaur magazine, 100 at Jalandhar, 150 at Govindgarh Fort near Amritsar, 500 at Lahore and 350 at Ferozepore), not counting a wing of the Bombay Fusiliers at Multan considered essential to protect the long supply line from Bombay to Lahore via the city. Meanwhile, across the Indus in Peshawar, there were three European regiments amounting to 2,400 men and twenty-four guns, while at Attock, which protected the Indus crossing, there were another 240 men. These numbers also excluded the moveable column under John Nicholson, comprising 800 men of HM52nd. All in all, north of Ambala and up to the Khyber pass, a distance of nearly 450 miles as the crow flies, the total number of European troops amounted to not much more than 4,500 men.

John Lawrence knew it was essential to send more men to Delhi, however. For a time he even considered withdrawing all British troops from Peshawar, effectively abandoning it to achieve a better hold on the rest of the Punjab and the south:

> If we retire from Peshawar and Kohat, we could probably hold all the country cis Indus, and at any rate have all our European Troops in hand ready to act together. We should be among a peaceable and not, as in Peshawar, among a hostile population … Brigadier General Cotton, Colonel Edwardes and Nicholson are all against this plan, and consider that Peshawar must be held to the last, even though we have to give up all the intervening country between it and Lahore. They consider that we could not retire from Peshawar with safety, and that such a movement will be the signal for a general insurrection.[4]

Lawrence's own personal view was that British troops could retreat from Peshawar in safety since the population was unarmed: 'It is doubtless a choice of two evils, neither of which I would adopt until the last moment, but it is a choice which we may have to make, and, if we make wrong one, may prove fatal,' he explained to the Government of India on 25 June.

Beyond morale and sheer numbers, the reinforcements Lawrence were vital for another reason. Cholera had begun killing in the British camp as early as 9 June – the day after the arrival at the Delhi ridge – and there had already been some deaths on the march down. Among the early victims were some of the few medical men available. Worse still, monsoons were expected, and would only strengthen cholera's grip on the camp. The rain began on 3 July, and continued almost solidly for another five days. The British camp effectively became a series of lakes. Drainage became the foremost concern. Several died from cholera on just the first day of rain. Meanwhile, the wounded and sick were packed off to Ambala and Meerut.

While disease raged and the abandonment of Peshawar was considered, strong orders went out instructing the men at the ridge to disregard any overtures from the rebels. By this time, it was common knowledge that the King had been browbeaten into leading the rebellion and that he had considered helping the British on the day the rebels arrived. There was a possibility the King would try further overtures through emissaries. On 20 June, a telegraph was passed to the Lieutenant Governor of the North-west Provinces insisting that no promises be made when considering any overtures the King might make to the British force on the ridge. Only Zafar's unconditional surrender would be accepted. If this occurred, he and the family must be kept under confinement pending a decision by the Governor-General.

Gathering intelligence about rebel plans was essential, and Capt. Hodson soon began developing network of spies. 'For this appointment,' wrote his brother in a letter to *The Times*, 'which was then a most responsible one, as intelligence of the enemy's movements and intentions was of the utmost importance, his long acquaintance with Sikhs and Affghans, and his having been similarly employed in the Punjab war, had peculiarly fitted him. Of course, there were always plenty of traitors in the enemy's camp ready to sell their own fathers for gain, or to avoid punishment, and he was invested with full power to promise reward or punishment in proportion to the deserts of those who assisted him.'[5] By the end of June, Hodson had recruited a network of industrious spies and informers in the city. The British camp heard about everything: the chaos in the city, the conditions and preparations of the sepoys, their fading morale, their dwindling supplies.

Spying was dangerous work; any man caught was invariably executed – and as we have seen, simply being accused, perhaps by a business rival, was enough to land somebody in hot water. On 10 June, for example, orders were given for the arrest of two men, Gulab and Jowalla Singh, who lived in the Pahari Dharang section of the city.[6] According to intelligence received in the city, they were in the British camp at this time – presumably spotted by rebel spies themselves working in the British camp. Orders were put out to arrest them and any associates working with them. On 28 June, a British informer named Ameer Chund reported that a man caught with papers destined for the British camp had been shot by sentries.[7] Some of those who assisted the British had friends in high places. Man Singh and Turab Ali, for instance, managed to get themselves released thanks to their friendship with the princes. Raja Ajit Singh, the uncle of the Maharaja of Patiala, was arrested twice but also released. Others were not so lucky. Baldev Singh, a resident of the Korya Pul area, was accused of being a spy and shot; his body was displayed outside one of the police stations. Others went in more spectacular fashion: Professor Pyare Lal was blown from a gun. Execution was not saved for informers alone; some bakers near the Mori and Kashmir gates, suspected of supplying bread to the British lines for profit, were shot.

The British camp was no place to be caught spying either. As the siege dragged on, so many suspected spies were apprehended that instead of being brought to camp for trial they were judged by the officer commanding the picket that had caught them. Executions carried out on these terms were a daily occurrence throughout the siege. Spying was difficult to stop; the plain fact was that the camps were too close, trade was too intertwined, and camp followers were too indistinguishable.

With reinforcements arriving every day, Barnard was soon proposing a *coup de main* again – this time for 30 June. The plan was as ambitious as the last. The force was to be divided into four columns: one was to enter through the Kabul Gate after it was blown up; a second column would enter through the Kashmir Gate; a third column would use scaling ladders to attack the Kashmir Bastion; and a smaller fourth column would advance past the Water Bastion and attempt to force an entrance by one of the gates facing the river. The plan relied almost totally on surprise, and it was never put into practice because only 3,000 infantry could be drummed up – not enough. On the evening of 2 July, Barnard once again suggested a surprise attack after a meeting of regimental field officers. The intention was to attack immediately, or early the next morning, but once again the plan fell through.

Putting aside the proposed surprise attack, Barnard's strategy during June and July was to keep his force almost permanently on the defensive. It was clear that he would have to wait for the heavy guns from Ferozepore and Phillaur if he wanted to compete with the rebel guns and tear a breach in the city walls, and he really needed more boots on the ground as well. Despite the nomenclature, for now the British force remained more besieged than besieger.

# 23

# Fighting in the Sabzi Mandi

I receive accurate reports of conversations among sepoys from my spies. One of them was rebuking the mass for hiding in the town like women, while the English remained on the *maidan* [field] and yet sustained no defeat.

H. H. Greathed, political agent, 7 July 1857

Following the loss at Badli-ki-Serai, the rebels spent the month of June mulling over how they might drive Barnard's army off the ridge before British heavy guns and reinforcements arrived. With the British camp protected by the Jumna to the north and the deep canal to the west, the position could really only be attacked up the ridge or through the Sabzi Mandi directly south of the British camp. With the ridge a forbidding prospect, attacks through the Sabzi Mandi became de rigueur for the rest of the month, along with the occasional attack on the British supply lines utilising the road south from Ambala. According to Revd Rotton, there were twenty-six rebel attacks before the picture changed in August, although minor skirmishes were an almost daily occurrence. Most attacks were not pursued with sufficient vigour; if they had been, the British force could have been starved of ammunition and supplies. The rebels instead kept their distance, preferring to take potshots from afar rather than risk close-quarters combat. Similarly, most of the rebel attacks failed to take advantage of their superior numbers; many of the mutineers opted to let new arrivals do the fighting, feeling that they had already done their share. Others were simply more interested in their loot.

Many sepoys had converted their loot into small gold coins or bars – although, as we have seen, plenty had been defrauded in the process by embittered traders. Most kept their gold in cummerbunds of muslin or linen wrapped around their waist or tied to their legs under their clothes, and these bulging cummerbunds marked a mutineer out as a member of the first wave of rebellion. When a sepoy fell, it was a race to get to the body and recover the loot. All soldiers in the British force, whether European, Gurkha or Sikh, invariably sprinted to fallen rebels to claim their loot. Cummerbunds were quickly torn off – sometimes causing an argument as to who was first to touch them. Sometimes considerable wealth was relieved from the sepoy, who had no care for it now – one grenadier of the HM61st found the princely sum of twenty gold mohurs, equivalent to £32.

On 15 June, political agent H. H. Greathed noted the discord sown among the mutineers by the matter of loot:

> I do not think the position and strength of the enemy will be improved by the delay that attends our operations. They only acquire numbers, and there is a jealousy between the old and new mutineers; the former are gorged with plunder and think they have done enough, and wish to leave the hard work to the new arrivals, but have no inclination to give them a share of the spoils. The Rifles say it is scarcely worthwhile to kill the new Pandees, they have nothing about them.

This is not to say that full-blooded fighting never happened. When the rebels first attacked the ridge on 9 June and were driven back through the Sabzi Mandi towards the city walls with the help of the Guides, who had just arrived, they destroyed a large veranda encircling the Hindu Rao with their 24-pounders. Some of the British heavy guns had been moved up towards the Hindu Rao in order to counter them, but the distance was too great. All that could be done was to compete with the rebel guns on the nearby Mori Bastion. The rebels attacked the Hindu Rao position again the next day, and there was fighting in the gardens of the Sabzi Mandi and on the other side of the ridge near the river as well.

During these early days, the rebels would try their utmost to persuade the Gurkhas and other non-Europeans to desert the British force. On 10 June, for example, when in close proximity, the rebels shouted to the Gurkhas. 'Come on, Gorkhas, we are not firing; we want to speak to you, we want you to join us.' 'We are coming,' a Gurkha replied, and they approached as if to parley; once they were within twenty paces of the sepoys, the Gurkhas fired a volley which killed nearly thirty. The skirmishing continued until around eight o'clock in the evening.

On the morning of 11 June, fighting began around 4.45 a.m. with both British flanks under attack. Barnard ordered the whole force out:

> On my ascertaining that both flanks were being attacked, the usual supports were not only sent up to the position on the heights, but the whole of the troops under my command were speedily under arms and marched up to reinforce the pickets and to drive back the enemy. This was first accomplished on the left, the enemy falling back under the fire

> of the troops, and after being beaten back from the right, they came on again for a second attack, under cover of the thickly wooded gardens near the Subjee Mundee [Sabzi Mandi]. The 1st Bengal European Fusiliers were sent against them, under the command of Major Jacob, and succeeded most gallantly in not only driving the enemy back, but pursued them, skirmishing all through the thickly wooded gardens of the Subjee Mundee. It was about half past 7 am when the troops began to be recalled, and the assembly first sounded for the skirmishers.

Worse was to come the next day. In the grounds of Metcalfe House, half a mile east of the Flagstaff Tower, several deep nullahs ran between the Flagstaff Tower and the river. Units of the 75th NI, supported by horse artillery, concealed themselves in the nullahs and began to creep forward shortly after daylight, cresting the ridge north of the Flagstaff Tower and fighting hard with the British pickets. Several men, including Capt. Knox, were killed. The element of surprise and numerical superiority saw the rebels push to the other side of the ridge and close on the British camp before British reinforcements managed to repel them. With the defenders still catching their breath, they learned that a separate rebel contingent had pushed through the Sabzi Mandi and was attacking the Hindu Rao picket. Major Jacob with the 1st Bengal European Regiment then reinforced the picket and drove the rebels back toward the market. 'A sharp fight for four hours, ending as usual. They have never yet been so punished as today,' recorded Hodson. In reality, this had been a dangerous day for the British force. The rebels had almost overrun them.

While thoroughly looted, the Metcalfe mansion and its outbuildings stood largely intact, so British pickets occupied the Metcalfe mansion from this day on to prevent a repeat of the attack on Flagstaff Tower. Three separate pickets were arranged to cover its vast grounds. One contingent – around 150 men – was positioned on a mound west of the main building. Some of the men of this contingent occupied a house commanding the road that led to the Kashmir Gate. The second contingent occupied a cowshed midway between the river and the mound. Further east, the third contingent occupied the mansion stables adjacent to the river bank. These picket points, in a rough west-to-east line, were hard to see from the city walls due to the profusion of tree cover in the gardens. These positions were gradually strengthened by the engineers over the weeks, making any rebel attacks much more difficult. Meanwhile, a guard of 100 men and two guns was placed on the Flagstaff Tower and stayed in close contact with the pickets in the Metcalfe grounds.

Early on 15 June, roughly 5,000 rebel infantry and cavalry along with two 9-pounders advanced within 100 paces of the ridge. The green flag of Islam was planted, and the British position was charged. The rebels were driven back but managed to retreat in good order and with their two intact. The action lasted till around 2 p.m. An attack on the new Metcalfe picket was also made at this time; the river had less water than usual on the 15th, and a gap had appeared between the riverside picket and the river itself. The rebels decided to attack across the sandy banks of the shrunken river. The pickets on duty, from the 75th Foot, nonetheless managed to repulse the rebels.

Two days later, a rebel shot from a 24-pounder blasted through the portico of the Hindu Rao, instantly killing seven men and an officer and wounding four others, two of whom later died. Investigations concluded that the shot had been fired from the Eidgah in the Kishanganj, an open-air enclosure where the rebels were building a new battery that, if completed, would allow the rebels to enfilade the ridge. This could not be allowed to happen; accordingly, at 4 p.m. that day, a force of two companies of Rifles, two companies of Gurkhas and Tombs' troop of guns was assembled to destroy the position. The force was organised into two columns under Majors Reid and Tombs. Tombs would lead the right column and attack the enemy left with four guns, thirty Guides cavalry, twenty sappers and miners and two companies of the 60th Rifles. At the same time, Reid, commanding four companies of the 60th Rifles and the Sirmoor Battalion, would attack the rebel right at Kishanganj. There was sharp fighting at the Eidgah, with Major Tombs having two horses shot under him. The doors of the Eidgah were eventually blown open, and the rebels within – around fifty in all – were killed while the battery was captured. A 9-pounder gun was brought back by Major Tombs while Major Reid destroyed the battery and burned the surrounding houses. A mosque which had been occupied by the rebels was also blown up. The British force lost three men killed and fourteen wounded.

The next day, 18 June, a man named Latafat Alee was sent into the city to spy for the British and brought back news of lethargy and discord among the rebels. He visited Syed Hamid Allee Khan, who was also working for the British:

> The Syud said that every body, high and low, fervently prayed to be rid of those rascally sepoys. ... The sepoys abused the sowars (500) for not charging [in the battle at Kishanganj]. The sowars made no answer, but got behind the seraee walls. They had 3 standards, 1 for the Regular Cavalry, 1 for the Lucknow Irregulars, and 1 for the riff-raff of Delhee. On the near approach of the British Force the sepoys bolted, taking 1 gun away with them. The other was captured. They then began to abuse one another, and talked about returning to retake the captured gun, but not one could be got up to move. Some went into the city, but 800 went out to Pahar Ganj. The 60th Regiment went out to the Old Fort.[1]

At the camp, 18 June – the anniversary of the Battle of Waterloo – passed by relatively quietly, although Revd Rotton heard mutterings that the date should have been marked by some sort of attack on the rebel positions:

> I well remember someone said in the Rifle mess, 'The 18th of June is a day of success and triumph with the British. The enemy ought either to have engaged us, or we them, on this day above every day in the year. Our success could not have been otherwise than sure.' 'Ah!' replied a Crimean hero, 'it was a day of disaster and defeat during the Russian war; though even the Emperor of all the Russias professed to wish both us and our allies well, even at the expense of his own good fortune.'[2]

The rebels in fact obliged that day with a half-hearted attack that was repelled by the Gurkhas and the 60th Rifles.

A fierce contest was fought on the 19th. Shortly before sunset that day, rebel forces moved to within a mile and half of the British camp. Brigadier Grant, in charge of the safety of the camp, was sent with 500 cavalry and twelve guns to force them back. Reinforcements from the 60th Rifles soon arrived as the fighting heated up. Grant describes the combat:

> The enemy had taken up a position about half a mile in rear of the Ochterlony gardens, and thence opened a very severe fire of round shot, grape and canister. I advanced our guns right up to them, and our artillery replied to their fire with the greatest spirit. As long as it was light, we succeeded in driving the rebels back, but in the dusk of the evening the enemy, who were in great numbers, very nearly succeeded in turning our flank, and for some time two guns were in great jeopardy. On the left flank two squadrons of the 9th Lancers under Colonel Yule, one troop of the Carabineers under Lieutenant Ellis and the Guide Corps under Captain Daly proceeded in support of Major Tombs's and Major Turner's guns. The former proceeded with the Guide Corps, the latter with the 9th Lancers in support to the left of the Ochterlony gardens and both opened fire. A squadron of the 9th Lancers under Captain Anson then charged down the road and the third squadron under Lieut. Jones with Colonel Yule followed in support.[3]

Bitter fighting continued as darkness fell, with the guns falling quiet around 8:30 p.m. The only major British loss was a wagon of Major Scott's battery that was detonated by rebel fire. The rebels for their part left a 9-pounder gun, which was brought into the camp early the next day. British losses amounted to twenty men killed (including three officers) and seventy-seven wounded (including seven officers), plus seventy horses killed or wounded. The officers killed were Brevet Lt Col Yule of the 9th Lancers, Lt Humphrys of the 20th Regiment NI and Lt Alexander of the 3rd Regiment NI. Grant had his horse shot beneath him in a charge at the rebels but was fortuitously rescued by several of his own men and some sowars of the 4th Regiment Irregular Cavalry. The rebels were believed to have suffered severely, for quite a few bodies were scattered about.

The next morning, just before 10 a.m., a detachment of the 75th Foot along with the whole of 1st and 2nd Europeans advanced toward the rebel position along with guns and cavalry. On seeing this force, the rebels withdrew. Two guns were captured along with three ammunition wagons. In fact, one of the wagons carried eight wounded rebels for transport back to the city. No quarter was given; the abandoned rebels were killed.

When the fighting over 19 and 20 June was done, the rebels were estimated to have lost around 300 dead against British losses of around eighty killed and wounded. 'Since then the insurgents are said to be greatly dispirited, and had kept quiet. Provisions are said to be carried into the town from the left bank of the Jumna, and to be tolerably plentiful,' Lawrence wrote to the authorities.

There were several days of quiet before 23 June – what would be the hundredth anniversary of the Battle of Plassey. The feeling in the British camp was that a determined attack would surely take place to mark the date. Spies were reporting that various Muslim clerics in the city prophesied a climactic battle on that day, with the British vanquished and Mughal rule re-established on a sure footing. Rotton had heard the details:

> It was said that both Hindoo and Mussulman would combine for the purpose of securing to the country a native instead of a foreign rule. Their prophets and religious teachers had promised them certainty of success. 'It is written,' said they, 'and therefore must be literally fulfilled – not a word shall fall to the ground.' The only conditions which they imposed on their credulous adherents, in order to ensure success, were the absolute necessity of immediate and strenuous effort on this selfsame day. 'Now or never' was the word which proceeded out of the lips that kept knowledge. The believer in the false prophet, and the infatuated devotee of paganism, listened to these words, and looked around and about them, and in that look found satisfaction, when they saw the defences of Delhi, and all her numerous appliances of war, and could call them absolutely their own.

Morale in the city had been buoyed a day or two before the 23rd by the arrival of the 6th Light Cavalry along with the 3rd, 36th and 61st NI, which had risen up at Phillaur and Jalandhar in the Punjab and significantly increased the rebel strength. Perhaps the relative calm of the 22nd could also be attributed to the extreme heat – it was the hottest day of the year so far. Whatever the case, both sides prepared for a trial of strength. Barnard himself expected the anniversary to bring the hardest fighting yet. Fearing the worst, he sent a message to Major Olpherts, marching south with treasure and reinforcements, to move with all speed through the night.

Major Olpherts had with him six guns of horse artillery, a weak wing of the 2nd Punjab Cavalry, a company of the 75th Foot and four companies of the 2nd Fusiliers previously at Ambala. When Barnard's request was received, this force, comprising 850 men and six guns, was around 22 miles from Delhi at Rai. The decision was made to leave the treasure at Alipur under guard until the route to the British camp was secured and to move on at speed. If the rebels attacked the rear of the British position on the 23rd via the Sabzi Mandi, with a bit of luck, Olpherts' force would appear at just the right time to attack the rebels' own rear.

Around 5 a.m. on the 23rd, the expected hostilities began when an estimated 6,000 rebels attacked the Hindu Rao. Against them were sent the Rifles, Guides and Gurkhas. Some field pieces were set up against the attackers as well, prompting replies from the guns in the city. The fighting seesawed back and forth, with the rebels driven back into the Sabzi Mandi six times. To make matters worse, it was even hotter than the previous day. At around 4 p.m., with the rebels showing no signs of retiring, the Rifles, Guides and Gurkhas were ordered to advance and capture the Sabzi Mandi. Rebels dug in on the rooftops were killed as the houses were cleared one by one. Fortunately for the British, Olpherts' reinforcements arrived from their long march just as hoped; they were immediately thrown into the contest without the chance for rest. Eventually, the 2nd European Fusiliers and the 4th Sikh Infantry managed to push the rebels back behind the city walls around 6 p.m. The rebels left perhaps a quarter of their men – over a thousand – dead or wounded on the battlefield.

Those in the British camp rejoiced at the day's success; the rebels had thrown everything at them and failed. Against the massive rebel losses, the British force suffered thirty-nine killed (including one officer) and 121 men wounded (including three officers). Balanced against this was the fact that the Sabzi Mandi had fallen into British control. A strong picket could now be maintained at the market, which had heretofore been the main route of attack for the rebels. Barnard ordered permanent pickets in two of the market's larger buildings: a serai on the right of the main road and a Hindu temple on the left. Each would hold around a hundred men. Over time, breastworks were dug from this position to the ridge, further securing the entire right flank and rear of the British position.

Rebel morale was sapped for a time by the defeat on 23 June, with subsequent attacks on the British position lacking vigour. For the next four days, they barely made an effort. According to intelligence received by Henry Lawrence, by 27 June the men of the Nusseerabad Brigade were sick of the inactivity of the other regiments:

> This morning the Nusseerabad Force represented to Mirza Mughal that the regiments inside the city should all be sent outside, or they would come inside. Of the old mutinous regiments few are now left. But the

> officers still draw money for them. The Nusseerabad Brigade also asked for their pay. Out of every regiment two of the companies were selected for the attack on the British Camp.[4]

Perhaps prompted by the complaint, the rebels managed to gather themselves for a stronger attack on the British flanks that day; heavy fighting broke out at the Metcalfe and Sabzi Mandi pickets, and the British suffered thirteen men and one officer killed and forty-eight wounded.

There was other good news for the rebels on the 27th, as news came in that a rebel regiment with 400 sowars and two guns had been sent to Baghpat to disrupt British supplies and communications from Meerut. From what spies ascertained for the British, the force was accompanied by between 300 and 400 Gujjar villagers. 'There was apparently great joy in the city that the Baghpat bridge had been destroyed,' reported the spy Jawahur Singh. 'The guns at Baghpat were plundered, although the Mahajuns offered 30,000 rupees ransom. The Baghpat mutineers had sent in for reinforcements, and then they would cross the river and take the [British] camp in the rear.'[5] The following day, the rebel force managed to close the road to Meerut via Baghpat, cutting off communication. Hearing of this, Hodson was sent to recapture the bridge.

By 30 June, intelligence had it that the rebels were going to attempt to erect another battery in the Kishanganj. In order to counter this, Brigadier Showers advanced with a troop of Carabineers, a troop of 9th Lancers, a wing of HM75th Regiment and the 1st Fusiliers plus six horse artillery guns under Major Olpherts. When the force arrived at the site of the supposed battery, they found no activity. However, in a nearby house they found saltpetre, sandbags and entrenching tools; everything was either confiscated or destroyed.

On 3 July, a large rebel force poured out of the city. Their destination was Alipur, about 11 miles north of Delhi, and their objective was to disrupt British supplies arriving from the Punjab. 'It is generally reported in the rebel army that the British have no money left, and the ammunition is nearly expended, and sickness is on the increase,' wrote G. C. Barnes, Commissioner of the Cis-Sutlej States, to John Lawrence. 'It was reported that a lot of Europeans had fallen sick, and had been sent to Umballah. And eleven lakhs of treasure were coming from Ferozpor. On this account the Rohilkhand mutineers joined with the Nusseerabad mutineers to waylay the treasure and to murder the sick and wounded, and with this intent the rebels went out to Aleepoor.'[6] The secondary objective was to punish the villagers of Alipur, who had been cooperating with the British. Pickets observed thousands of rebels emerging from the Kabul and Ajmer gates. Fearing an attack, they raised the alarm and a force was readied to the rear of the canal, but nothing of note happened; the rebels ignored them and headed north.

Alipur's sole protection, under Lt Young, was a squadron of 5th Punjab Cavalry made up of just fifty or sixty Sikhs. Young elected to retreat with his force to the village of Rai, allowing the rebels to loot the village before setting it on fire. In response, at 2 a.m. the next morning, Major Coke was sent with 1,500 men including infantry, cavalry and artillery to intercept the rebels. This force comprised a squadron of Carabineers, a squadron of 9th Lancers, the Guide Cavalry, a wing of HM61st Regiment and 1st Punjab Rifles (Coke's Rifles) along with twelve guns. The force marched north for roughly 3 miles before cutting west in an attempt to take the rebels as they retreated with their booty. Unfortunately for Coke, the road – if it could be called that – was flooded. Swampy fields stretched between his force and the rebels. The advance was nonetheless continued for around 2 miles until Coke's force reached a canal with trees lining each side. Pickets sighted the enemy, and Coke moved his force across the canal with the guns ordered to the front.

Before the British force was a fairly open plain about a mile long. At the northern end there was a village, and this was where the rebels were taking up position. Coke placed his cavalry on either side of the guns, with the infantry forming behind the guns. Guns from both sides soon opened up, with the rebel force turning to face the threat. However, the rebels quickly packed up and moved to the British left to carry on their retreat to the city. Coke attempted to follow, but his troops and guns were bogged down in the mud. Stragglers caught in the village were killed, and some treasure and plunder taken from Alipur was recovered, along with two ammunition wagons but no guns. Coke sent the guns and cavalry back to the ridge and told his infantrymen to rest. Soon after, they were attacked by some rebels who had circled back; however, the rebel attack was cut short when six horse artillery guns arrived to assist the resting infantrymen. Across the two encounters, it was estimated that roughly a hundred rebels were killed. On the British side, three men and seven horses had been killed while twenty-three men and seven horses were wounded.

*****

Over the course of June, the British force had averaged between thirty and forty casualties daily, with spikes between 100 and 150 on the bloodiest days. Barnard knew this was not sustainable. A slow war of attrition would destroy his force; reinforcements could not arrive fast enough or in sufficient number to rectify the losses. Furthermore, there was ammunition to worry about. The British force had kept up the tit-for-tat with the rebel guns, but after three weeks shot for the big guns was running low. On 4 July, Chief Engineer Baird Smith inventoried the ordnance supplies in the artillery park. Only 150 round shot and 240 shells remained for the 24-pounders. The 18-pounders were better off, with 628 shot remaining. For the 8-pounders there were only 192 shells:

> For shells we were better off, but still very badly; and the commandant of Artillery told me he had no hopes of receiving any large supplies soon. It was therefore clear that all thoughts of a siege in even its most irregular form must be abandoned, as our artillery means were inadequate to even one day's open trenches. Of Engineer means we had practically none at all, and so I put all formal operations quite on one side for the time being.

In terms of ordnance powder for the seventeen guns, there was 11,600 lbs – apparently only sufficient for one day's firing. Musketry powder had decreased to 12,900 lbs.

> The Engineer Park was quite as insufficiently supplied for even the briefest formal operation. It is questionable whether batteries could have been maintained even if their first construction had been practicable, as riveting materials were in extremely small numbers. Hence there was no hesitation whatever in abandoning all idea of operations of this class.[7]

Worried about the levels of ammunition, Baird Smith arranged a meeting with Barnard on the morning of 5 July to discuss the matter. An order duly went out for camp followers and locals to gather up spent 24-pounder shot fired by the rebels, which could be fired back. The prize for bringing in shot was 1–2 annas per piece. The reward provided a lively contest for the camp followers, who chased the large missiles as soon as they were seen to have fallen. Since most of the rebel shot fell on the incline of the ridge, it would frequently roll down the slope; catching up and hauling it back to the camp was no easy task after a merry chase down the incline, especially with the shot still being red-hot from the guns.

'Our Artillery officers themselves say that they are outmatched by these rascals in accuracy and rapidity of fire; and as they have unlimited supply of guns and ammunition from our own greatest arsenal, they are quite beyond us in many respects,'[8] Hodson wrote of the frustration of the British gunners. However, the British guns were clearly having a telling effect in the city; by the end of June, in light of British shelling, rebel officers had decided to move large supplies from the Delhi magazine into underground chambers. Some was being moved into the Salimgarh Fort as well. The Delhi magazine, close to the Kashmir Gate, was vulnerable.

## 24

# The Imperative of Law and Order

> If the Princes Royal, delegated to protect the subjects of the State and the poor, begin themselves to plunder and oppress, where then can there be any safety for the subject?[1]
>
> Delhi merchants' petition to Zafar

Having checked several attempts to push his force off the Delhi ridge, Barnard must have been buoyed by news that the rebels were in disarray. It must also have become clear to him that the issues faced in his camp were the opposite of those hampering the rebels in the city. Barnard had throughout June been dogged by a shortage of ammunition, which had to be dragged the 300 miles from Ferozepore and Phillaur. Neither were there sufficient heavy guns or troops for any large initiative. In some ways, though, Barnard had more fortune. Treasure was being escorted into the British camp at regular intervals, so payroll was never an issue. Morale didn't pose a problem, either; despite scant troops and dwindling ammunition, the discipline of the British force remained. Spirits were high, and there was a quiet confidence among those in the camp that they would be victorious.

In Delhi, by contrast, the rebels seemed to have an inexhaustible supply of ammunition, guns and *materiel de guerre* thanks to the Delhi magazine. Indeed, they had more guns than gunners. The rebel camp also boasted an embarrassment of troops, which was in fact a bad thing as they simply could not pay everybody. Spies and informers were quick to alert Barnard to the dire situation in the city. As June gave way to July, rebel morale swung wildly. Each setback led to bickering over which regiments were pulling their weight and which were not. Petty jealousies surfaced. It became clear that the rebel army was little more than a congeries of regiments led by subedars rather than a cohesive force headed by an experienced core.

The foremost problem for the rebels was indiscipline. Instilling restraint in the troops and maintaining law and order were vital if the rebels were to foster a sense of confidence in the population. Despite a month-long grace period spanning the mutineers' arrival at Delhi on 11 May and the British arrival on 8 June, Zafar and the sepoy officers never managed to engender the necessary obedience within their ranks. Looting and plundering continued without respite, and getting the various regiments to cooperate in an attack on the British camp was always hard work.

Letters and documents captured after the fall of the city list numerous complaints and petitions given to the King regarding the behaviour of the sepoys during this time. Their contempt for the Delhi populace was evidently widespread. The local merchants complained of sowars casually tying their horses in front of shops without regard for the merchants' loss of trade. Others more brazenly commandeered shops, considering the properties more comfortable than outside quarters. A petition by merchants Jogal Kishwar and Sheoprashad complains of continuing exactions by the princes and soldiers; the two had already paid 1,200 rupees into the royal treasury in exchange for a document signed and sealed by the King protecting them from further demands for money. Despite this, sepoys were hassling them for money every day, darkly threatening violence if they didn't pay up. These sepoys were being sent by the princes themselves, the merchants complained, begging Zafar to reason with his sons: 'If the Princes Royal, delegated to protect the subjects of the State and the poor, begin themselves to plunder and oppress, where then can there be any safety for the subject?'[2] They concluded their petition with a request for protection from *kotwals* rather than the untrustworthy sepoys.

Other petitions were addressed to Mirza Mughal. For instance, locals living in and around the Old Fort in the south were also being harassed for money. On 18 June, Zafar wrote to Mirza Mughal that soldiers were failing to heed his orders to leave the locals alone: 'It is surprising that, up to the present time, no arrangement should have been made, and that you should not have given effect to the prohibition, by sending out some Cavalry. It is the business of the Army to protect, and not to desolate and plunder. The officers of the Army will, therefore, immediately restrain their men from the commission of these improprieties.'[3] He asked for the soldiers camping in the Old Fort to vacate the structure and make camp elsewhere – after all, he wrote, the British had no ambition to attack the south of the city.

Around a week later, on 27 June, Zafar expressed to both Mirza Mughal and Khizr Sultan his anxiety at the unruly behaviour of the soldiers. Apparently four or five local men disguised as soldiers had openly extorted what they could from their neighbours before making off into the countryside with a substantial amount of loot; they were not challenged by sepoys on guard, who presumably considered them comrades.

> It is a matter of some surprise, that from the lawless doings of but four or five men, so much plunder and devastation in the City, and so much ruination of the people generally, should result; and that, on their capture alone, the establishment of order should be expected to depend; for not a day has elapsed, since the arrival of the Army, and its taking up quarters in the City, that petitions from the towns-people have not been submitted, representing the excesses committed by numerous Infantry Sepoys, about whom there could be no suspicion of disguise, and that orders have not been issued, day after day, to you, our Sons, to take measures with the aid of a Military force, to suppress these disorders.[4]

The unruliness of the sepoys was evident even in the palace grounds. Ever since they had made camp within the palace walls, Zafar had been suggesting that they go elsewhere. There was the Salimgarh Fort adjacent to the walls, as well as the spacious, tree-covered riverside area nearby. On 26 June, a frustrated Zafar again attempted to move them out. Perhaps he thought the rebels would listen to his son Mirza Mughal, who along with Mirza Khizr Sultan and a few other princes seemed to have at least a shred of influence over them.

> ... orders have, day after day, been issued to the Officers of the Cavalry to vacate the Garden, and they have, till now done nothing, but make excuses and promises. Definite orders are therefore now issued, to the intent that you, our Son, will summon the Officers, and will tell them that if they consider themselves the servants of the State, they will not go to the Batteries to-morrow, but will leave the Garden.[5]

Not that the sepoys seemed to take any more notice of the princes than the King. The ageing monarch continued to face open contempt. The soldiers were often heard declaring that they could topple Zafar and raise one of the princes to the throne if they so chose. The new king, they joked, would be crowned with a pair of shoes on his head.

It wasn't only in the city but also in surrounding villages that inhabitants continued to feel the exactions of the sepoys. On 19 June a petition was delivered to Zafar by the residents of Jysinghpur and Shahganj, otherwise known as Paharganj, which lay outside the Ajmer Gate. They complained that the troops, upon exiting the Ajmer Gate, would as a matter of routine pass through the neighbourhood helping themselves to the wares in the shops:

> Frequently the Troops of the State, emerging from the Ajmer Gate, visit Paharganj, and oppressing the shop-keepers, forcibly take away their wares, without the payment of prices, and also, entering the dwelling houses of the destitute and indigent, forcibly carry away all such articles, as beds, woods, vessels, etc., that they can lay hands on,

> and wound with fire-arms and Swords, those who may supplicate their forbearance ... [we ask] that they desist from oppressing us, and the other poor residents of Paharganj.[6]

On 29 June, the people of Firozabad Khadir complained that they could not pay their taxes owing to the harsh weather and the fact that the sepoys had taken their farming implements, including ploughs, meaning they could not cultivate their land. The sepoys had even looted the woodwork on the wells. If this wasn't bad enough, the sepoys' failure to police the area had allowed the Gujjar villagers of Mallanji, Hasangarh, Alipur and Aliganj to carry on their own plunder and robbery.[7]

*****

Despite the British force in front of the city and the disorder within, new mutineers continued to trek to Delhi and join the rebel ranks during June and July. On 13 June, two days after the officers of the 60th NI traipsed into the British camp, its sepoys arrived at the city to bolster the rebel numbers. Three days later, fifty regular sowars arrived in the city with some Ranghur villagers from Jhajjar; later that day 100 men of the 8th Irregular Cavalry and a company of infantry joined them. These men had brought word from the Nusseerabad regiments, whom they said would arrive with a light field battery on the 19th. Around this time, the moulvi Rajab Ali, gathering intelligence for Hodson, noted the arrival of roughly 100 rebel troops from Jaipur. On the 22nd there were rumours in the British camp that force from Nusseerabad had arrived comprising two infantry regiments and six guns. Reports had it that a rebel force from Mhow was just four marches away. Three days later, rebel sepoys from Jalandhar were encamped outside the city. 'They have quarrelled with the 6th Cavalry, who are following behind,'[8] reported Rajab Ali. Inside the city, the mutineers learned that the brigade at Bareilly and the troops at Gwalior had mutinied and would be with them by 1 July. Altogether, these troops would add nine regiments of infantry, three corps of cavalry and five field batteries to the rebel army. There were even rumours that the Bareilly brigade would try to capture Meerut on its way to Delhi. The Neemuch contingent was making its way to the city as well, and a small force of roughly 100 men had thrown off the authority of the Nawab of Jhajjar on 1 July.

Not all recruits to the rebel cause were regular troops; with them came plenty of criminals and wanderers. The brigade from Meerut had been supplemented by a general assortment of ruffians sprung from the prison there, enticed by the promise of plunder. Prisoners freed from the jail at Delhi had swelled numbers as well. An assortment of jihadis and ghazis were arriving all the while to face the infidel in battle, although their dedication to the mutiny was suspect.

Perhaps unsurprisingly, it proved difficult to maintain good relations between the original mutineers, the new additions, the various jihadis and the citizenry. 'One of the native officers of the Guides (you know how ingenious they are at disguise) got into the city as a spy, and remained there four days,'[9] wrote Hodson in a private letter on 24 June. 'He reports great dissension and quarrelling among themselves. Robbery and fighting, and everything that is bad, between the newly arrived rebels and the city people. This account my own native newsletters confirm. The 9th Native Infantry had already decamped, and thousands would follow if they dared.' Hodson was referring to the 9th NI regiment, whose frustration at the chaos in the city had seen them abandon the cause.

Many of the rebels cared little for their duties, even neglecting to man the city gates. G. C. Barnes was optimistic in his report to Robert Montgomery in mid-June. He passed on intelligence detailing the mutineers' sloppy practices, especially when it came to security:

> There is very slack guard kept up at the Kela Ghaut Gate. Two advances made by the British Troops had the best effect. Indeed, in one it was reported in the city that the British Troops had entered the city. The Lahoree Gate was left for a considerable time wide open, all the Sepoy Guard having run away. If only half a dozen British Troops were to appear inside the city, the whole rebel force would decamp. The old body of the mutineers has had all the fighting taken out of them, and they quarrel on the slightest grounds, Sumand Khan, the leader, is not to be found. At Agra and Meerut it is reported that great consternation prevails. If they could only see Delhee and the state of the rebel force, they would soon revive.[10]

Two days later, Barnes reported that rebels were deserting: 'The mutineers are very dispirited. 100 sepoys of sorts had bolted, 25 were retaken and plundered. Many desert ... The gate between the Ajmer and Lahore Gate is unprotected. Two guns are stationed there, but no ammunition. There is a great want of Artillerymen, and there is no arrangement in the Ordnance Department.'[11] He passed on intelligence estimating rebel strength at around 13,000 infantry and 1,300 cavalry: 'About 3,000 are without arms. The 11th Regiment, 54th Regiment and the 74th are very rich and show no disposition to fight.'

Some of the city newspapers, meanwhile, tried to help lift rebel morale. The *Delhi Urdu Akhbar* in its issue of 21 June declared that God had removed the fear of the English from the hearts of their servants and thrown the entire army and treasury at the feet of the King. 'Then do you not believe in the power of Almighty God? You should not be fearful of the continuous gunfire of the white people. No one dies before his appointed time. If the white people capture one or two of your guns you should not worry. You should see that how they fire thousand times but by the grace of God except for few persons none is harmed.'[12]

*****

Regardless of their ill conduct and the lackadaisical way in which they engaged the British, the sepoys expected to be paid. Zafar duly sent orders out to tax collectors in nearby districts where British authority had crumbled, ordering them to bring the revenue they had collected for British treasuries to Delhi instead. They were also told to ensure that order was preserved as a matter of urgency, to ease revenue collection. This required funds in itself, leading many to ask in turn for help, money and troops to keep order. At Najafgarh, for instance, due to a lack of funds, some of the policemen and staff at the *kotwali* had already deserted their positions. The police chief there had written begging for funds so that the police force could be maintained and armed. The petition had been sent, the police chief added, through cartmen who had themselves experienced ill treatment.

There were still untapped treasuries to be appropriated, and Zafar would frequently receive tipoffs about them. One sepoy at Meerut, for instance, had written urgently about sizeable British treasuries at Babugarh, Aligarh, Chataur and elsewhere:

> Cherisher of the Poor, at Babughar there are 20,000 rupees under the safe custody of 24 military men and at Chataur there are 20 lacs of rupees in the charge of Mardan Khan guarded by 600 Jats while the treasury at Aligarh is forthcoming guarded by three companies of regular infantry. Moreover there are 1,500 horses at Babughar together with the money for their necessary current expenses. If your Majesty will take immediate steps for despatching troops and for establishing arrangements in the above places it is to be expected that the whole of the above said property will be secured and will come into your Majesty's possession but if a delay of one or two days is allowed to occur there is undoubted room for apprehension that it will be all lost. There is not a man of the English army in the whole of the space between the two rivers from Saharunpoor to Agra who will offer to oppose one regiment of infantry sent by your Majesty.[13]

The sepoy wrote that all that the villagers needed was a display of armed strength to show that the authority of the King encompassed them; if that was done, the reassured villagers would aid the King, enlist in his force and pay taxes.

Zafar knew measures to extract money from such treasuries was essential; indeed, he was already beset by demands for payment. As early as 1 June, Mirza Mughal had warned his father that the men at the Shahdari battery had been waiting two days for their daily allowances and would soon be clamouring for payment. A sum of 15,000 rupees was required to cover the back pay and to provide a placatory advance payment.

# 25

# The Arrival of Bakht Khan

In early July, important events occurred in both camps to change the course of the mutiny. Arguably the most important change in the British camp came on 3 July, when the new chief engineer arrived from Roorkee. The previous chief engineer, Major Laughton, had broken down and been recalled. Capt. Taylor filled in for a time, and the plan was for Lt Greathed, who had been Barnard's *aide de camp*, to take the position up on a permanent basis. However, another name was put forward: Lieutenant Richard Baird Smith. This man happened to be very knowledgeable about the city, for he had been employed in its canal department since 1840; as recently as September the previous year he had been in the city for ten days working on the canals. During his stay he had taken the opportunity to wander in and out of the walls, examining the defences and terrain. 'My camp was pitched upon the ground we carried our operations over, and on the whole I had, before I joined the force at all, a tolerably minute knowledge of the important features of the ground both inside and outside the place,' he wrote. Baird Smith got the job.

Early on the morning of 5 July, Barnard had a three-hour meeting with his new chief engineer. Barnard himself was very anxious about the British position and the casualties depleting his force. Baird Smith, however, was ebullient:

> I had been familiar with Delhi for nearly sixteen years, and knew the ground well. It offered singular facilities for an attack [on the walls] by reason of the perfect cover that existed close up to the walls, and under which our columns might be formed without serious risk from the enemy's fire. The fortifications posed no formidable obstacles to escalade. The counterscarp was an earthen slope, down which men could pass with but little difficulty. The ditch was dry; a berm wall of 8 feet and bastion faces of 16 feet high were not frightful heights to

> surmount. The main gate was known not to be retrenched, and to be easily destructible. The habits of the Mutineers were notoriously lax, and their capacity to stand face to face with our men of the smallest. We could muster about 3,500 men for the assault, all in the best possible spirit, and keen for the work. On the whole it seemed to me that a fair chance of success existed for an assault just at dawn, when natives are always asleep, and I accordingly recommended that we should make one at once, and prepared all the details.[1]

Another meeting was scheduled for noon the same day. Baird Smith later wrote that Barnard seemed relaxed and in good health; he showed his usual anxious and world-weary expression, sure, and his eyes seemed a little dim, but that was all. He even perked up on hearing Baird Smith's encouraging assessment. Only an hour or two after the meeting, however, Baird Smith was told that Barnard would not be available for the next meeting as he wasn't feeling well. Later that same day, cholera claimed its most prominent victim in the British camp: Barnard died at around 3 p.m. 'Tell them I die happy,' he told his son, Capt. Barnard.

Before his death, the departed general had written Baird Smith a message asking that the chief engineer defend his honour. This was never required; it was widely understood that Barnard had too few men and guns at his disposal to attempt any significant action during his tenure. Indeed, many blamed his death on the pressure of the job; the survival of the British in India hinged entirely on his behaviour. All eyes were on him, and the knowledge had taken a heavy toll. Others blamed excessive sunlight, for Barnard was out almost all hours of the day marshalling his troops. '[Barnard] was terribly harassed for the last month, and has sunk under the weight of his anxieties and troubles. I am very sorry we have lost the good old man,' Baird Smith wrote to his wife on 5 July. The next day, the old general was buried in a simple ceremony. In the meantime, General Reed took over as the new commanding officer of the Delhi Field Force.

Along with the promotion of Baird Smith and the death of Barnard, Governor-General Canning made waves on 9 July with his firm ruling concerning mutineers:

> The Right Hon'ble the Governor-General in Council is pleased to direct, and hereby notifies, that it shall not be competent to any authority whatever, save only to the said Governor-General of India in Council, to exercise the power of pardoning any mutineer, or any rebel who has opposed the troops of the British Government by force, or who, in the course of recent events, has committed any heinous outrage; or any public officer, or State stipendiary, or Native Chief, who has joined or in any way whatever assisted mutineers or rebels, or any person belonging to the family of any such public officer, State stipendiary or Native Chief.[2]

Further to this, on 10 July, Canning authorised the payment of rewards for captured rebels. Fifty rupees would be awarded for an armed sepoy, and thirty for an unarmed sepoy. A similar reward system was also declared for information that led to any rebel being arrested – the reward being paid on conviction. Further rewards would be given for the retrieval of any arms, supplies, property or horses looted from government properties.[3] Meanwhile, it was ruled that any former sepoy who encouraged others to rebel, or even neglected to inform the authorities of mutinous activity, would be punished and deprived of his pension. It was hoped that such announcements would coax wavering civilians and sepoys off the fence.

*****

In the rebel camp, the most significant event came on 1 July when the Bareilly brigade arrived. Most importantly, among their number was the man who would lead the rebel force at Delhi for most of the remainder of the siege: Bakht Khan.

The 3,000-strong Bareilly brigade – composed of the 8th Irregular Cavalry and the 18th, 28th, 29th (from Moradabad) and 68th NI, along with No. 15 horse battery and two 6-pounder guns – had mutinied on 31 May. After indulging in looting for a while, these men had opted to march on Delhi. With them came ammunition and considerable money taken from the local British treasuries. In addition to regulars, this force had been joined by roughly 400 Muslim jihadis and ghazis loyal to Moulvi Sarfaraz Ali. If used wisely, the large force could easily have swung the balance decisively in favour of the rebels. For now, its arrival provided an enormous fillip for the mutineers in the city.

The man chosen to lead the Bareilly brigade to Delhi was Bakht Khan. Many rumours swirled about his background. He was a Pashtun, supposedly related to the Rohilla chief Najib-ul-Daula, and Munshi Jeewan Lal wrote that he claimed to be related to Zafar when he met the monarch on 2 July. A subedar in the 8th Foot Artillery at Rohilkhand with forty years' service under his belt, Bakht Khan had seen plenty of action. He was at Jalalabad during the First Anglo-Afghan War, after which he had been promoted to subedar. Initially stationed at Neemuch, he had later been transferred to Bareilly, and he was there when the mutiny erupted at Meerut.

It is said that Khan, who had a reputation as a good soldier and an able leader, had little intention to mutiny before Moulvi Sarfaraz Ali, who was his mentor, encouraged him to do so. His erstwhile commanding officer, Captain Waddy, described him, although any British assessment of the man must be taken with a pinch of salt: 'He is 60 years of age and is said to have served the Company for 40 years;

his height 5 feet 10 inches; 44 inches round the chest; a very bad rider owing to large stomach and thick thighs but clever and a good drill.'[4] Colonel Bourchier, who knew him well, wrote that 'Bukht Khan, like the Nana, was always very fond of English society. At one time, when studying Persian, he used to come twice a day to my house to read and talk with me. He was a most intelligent character, but a more dreadful hypocrite never stepped on earth.'[5]

Bakht Khan carried some gravitas but was nevertheless a subedar. He was not the kind of man who stood far above others in terms of his leadership and presence, nor did he command total authority. Inevitably, then, his rise would be dogged by the jealousy and rivalry typically directed at unspectacular people thrust into leading roles. His fellow officers and subedars would chafe under his orders, often delivered in an abrasive manner. However, Khan undoubtedly had military expertise, and this put him beyond the princes. He was far better qualified to plan attacks on the British camp than the princes, whose attempts thus far had been amateurish.

Bakht Khan originally had no plan to march his men to Delhi. Instead he had joined Khan Bahadur Khan, a local rebel leader and grandson of Hafiz Rahmat Khan, the Rohilla chief of Bareilly. It was Khan Bahadur Kahn who advised the subedar on 11 June that a move to defend Delhi against the approaching British Delhi Field Force would be wise. The brigade then set off westward. By 19 July he had reached Tigree, just 2 miles from the Ganges. The river was crossed by the 25th, and advance units sighted Delhi on 30 July.

Word of the Bareilly force had reached Delhi during late June, with rumours that they were bringing over a thousand carts of supplies and loot, and between six and eleven lakh rupees. These tales weren't entirely wrong. The arriving column was impressive, complemented by a huge retinue of carriage as well as forty to fifty elephants, carts and tumbrils full of ammunition and their own tents and baggage. Furthermore, they had brought 550 colts along as well as innumerable camels.[6] Such a huge addition to the rebel army was cause for celebration, and the father-in-law of the King progressed out of the city with a large retinue of his own to greet the column, which began crossing the bridge of boats across the Jumna in the early hours of 1 July.

Inside the city, the Bareilly men were warmly received. Witnesses in the distant British camp could hear jubilant shouting and the strains of the rebel band playing 'Cheer Boys Cheer', a British military song. The brigade settled in a space stretching from the Turkman Gate to the Ajmer Gate, where the Phillaur and Nusseerabad regiments had camped as directed by Mirza Mughal. The confidence of these recent arrivals seems to have been infectious: 'The Rohilkund mutineers asked the King to kindly give them the most difficult battery to take, and they would soon capture it,'[7] Barnes wrote to Lawrence in an intelligence report. Meer Mohumud Alee of the 9th Irregular Cavalry, a spy in the city, described the high spirits: 'The mutineers outside and in amount to 20,000 men. They are all ready to die!'

*****

Up on the ridge, the British could see the Bareilly force accumulating on the opposite bank of the river before crossing into the city. There was nothing they could do; their guns were too far away to target the bridge. As bad as it already looked, the British could not know that in the new arrivals the mutineers had found their leader. The only consolation was that the British camp was also receiving reinforcements, with a wing of the HM61st (450 men) arriving around the same time. Amusingly, these men in their turn were welcomed by a band playing 'Cheer Boys Cheer'.

There was considerable unease at the manner in which the Bareilly brigade had been able to make its leisurely way to Delhi. Criticism was mostly directed at General Hewitt, the commanding officer at Meerut. During their march west to Delhi, the rebels, weighed down with plunder and baggage, had crossed the Ganges at the town of Goormuktesur, a mere 30 miles from Meerut. There was no bridge here, nor were there any boats; the British authorities had already ordered the burning of all boats in the vicinity to hamper any rebels making their way to Delhi from the east. The rebels therefore lost several days building rafts. Despite eventually finding three boats, the rebels took five long days to cross. Doing so while under fire from the opposite bank would have been impossible, making this an ideal place for the Meerut force to intercept the rebel brigade with little risk.

The European strength at Meerut at this time happened to be 386 Rifles (45 in hospital), 440 Dragoons (40 in hospital) and 372 Artillery (30 in hospital), so a usable force of just over 1,000 men. Also available were the loyal remnants of the native infantry regiments: the 4th Light Cavalry (200 men), 3rd Light Cavalry (70 men) and 11th Native Infantry (60 men) plus Craigie's new levies (30 men), for a total of 360 men. Altogether, then, Hewitt had more than 1,400 men. This was considered by most to have been quite sufficient to both protect Meerut and prevent the rebel crossing of the Ganges. Yet the force stayed static. One officer at Meerut voiced his frustration in a letter on 12 July:

> The Artillery officers here told me they could have taken out 10 field guns and 6 heavy guns, and then there would have been a number of heavy guns left for the protection of this station. No troops left Meerutt for Delhi at the time the Bareilly rebels crossed, nor have any left since; and my opinion is, I have no hesitation whatever in saying, that had a move been made with 500 men and 6 guns from this, not a man would or could ever have crossed the river, and that had we attacked them at Baboughur could not fail to have given them a tremendous pounding.

John Lawrence in particular was incensed that the rebels had not been challenged, especially since they had passed so close to Meerut. He dismissed any notion that Hewitt lacked sufficient resources, insisting that he could have spared at least half of the men at his disposal to contest the heavily laden rebel crossing of the Ganges.

> … Our people at Merutt [Meerut] were in an entrenched post, defended by heavy guns. Under such circumstances it must be obvious that a few men might have held the place with perfect safety against large numbers. Indeed, it was so strong that the Rohilkund mutineers would not even approach it …
>
> Such a body under an enterprizing and efficient officer would have prevented the mutineers from ever crossing the Ganges, and even under the supposition that they had crossed previous to his arrival, which was almost impossible, would have harrassed and impeded their march throughout the whole line of their route. So that it is only reasonable to suppose that not half the number would have reached their destination. Encumbered with plunder, rapid movement was impracticable …
>
> When officers like General Hewitt are permitted to retain the command of our soldiers, it is not surprising that disaster and misfortune should occur: indeed it is only wonderful that more mischief does not happen. The British Troops are able and ready to face any dangers, but they should at least be efficiently commanded.[8]

Allowing the rebel troops to march on Delhi unmolested was complete folly. Lawrence felt strongly that the arrival of the Bareilly troops, as well as the Jalandhar troops, had increased the morale of the rebels immeasurably and perhaps even prevented the city from falling into British hands already:

> The almost triumphant advance of these large bodies of troops showed to the insurgents that the British Government were nearly powerless over wide and important tracts of country. The moral influence of such a circumstance must been very great. And that such was the effect of our mistakes must be evident when it is considered that the most resolute and powerful attack on a troops invariably followed the accession of each reinforcement to the enemy. As a spy heard them remark after one of their defeats – 'We are continually gaining aid, whilst the English get none: we may be often beaten, but in the end we are sure to win.'[9]

Moreover, the triumphant march had sent a strong message to chiefs all along the route to Delhi: British authority was finished.[10]

*****

In the city, Bakht Khan met the King for the first time on 2 July. At this audience, some of his failings became immediately apparent. To honour the subedar, Zafar presented him with one of his own swords and a buckle. Khan, however, failed to present a *nazar* to the King, neglecting royal protocol and showing a certain indifference towards the monarch. It also turned out that he had a blunt and irreverent way of conversing, as displayed starkly in his words to the King: 'Your good-for-nothing princes enjoy full powers over your military. Give all the power to me as no one else but I know the norms of the English army; who knows them better than me?' Zafar acknowledged that Khan spoke the truth, albeit in rougher fashion than was necessary; Mirza Mughal had done little to justify his position as commander. Despite whatever private reservations he harboured, Zafar appointed Khan as commander-in-chief of the rebel army, dubbing him Governor-General, with all previous arrangements and appointments superseded. Mirza Mughal was downgraded to the role of adjutant general and now answered to Bakht Khan.

Khan might have showed little deference to the royal princes, but his advice on their conduct was sound. He told Zafar that everybody knew the princes were siphoning off taxes gathered from the city businesses. This had to be stopped. With the royal treasuries dwindling, such brazen corruption made it harder to pay the troops. One of Zafar's sons, Mirza Khizr Sultan, was particularly overt; Zafar and Khan duly cajoled him into returning his ill-gotten gains. Khan warned the princes against interfering in military affairs. Administrative affairs, too, were best left to those with the expertise. He was frank about the princes with fellow officers as well, declaring that 'everyone knew that they were good-for-nothing fellows'. Predictably, the princes came to deeply dislike the new commander.

Whatever the princes might think, Zafar had such hope in Bakht Khan that he was given carte blanche to punish sepoys or civilians caught plundering or abusing their authority. Khan's all-encompassing role could be divided into five key missions. The most obvious, and paramount, was to pulverise the British or at least push them to retreat from their eyrie on the ridge. The second was to sort out the disorder among the troops and instil discipline, in the course of which he was to move them into camps outside the city walls where they could do less damage. His third role was to organise suitable salary arrangements for the troops. The fourth role, linked to the third, was to improve and oversee revenue collection; the treasure that the Bareilly brigade had brought them was substantial, but would only last a few weeks. His fifth task was to increase policing around the city and punish the local ruffians and gangsters who continued to loot at leisure.

These missions, each considerable in themselves, would have presented quite a task for any experienced administrator in wartime, let alone a subedar in a new city. However, Bakht Khan apparently went about his new role with some gusto. On the matter of law and order, he delegated responsibility to the *kotwal* of Delhi, warning the man that his life would be forfeit if his efforts failed to impress. As a check on the depredations of the princes and their henchmen, Bakht Khan allowed merchants and shopkeepers to arm themselves and ruled that any sepoy caught plundering or extorting money would have his hands cut off. To offset the reduced opportunities for plunder, Khan then promised the soldiers regular salaries and *jagirs* (land grants) for their services, and successfully convinced the King to agree that any sepoy wounded in the conflict would receive a pension and a *jagir*. There were various administrative changes in revenue collection as a consequence, with taxes on salt and sugar lifted to ease the burden and ensure that regular supplies reached the army.

Aside from his five main tasks, Khan suggested the rebel force be organised into three divisions: the first would comprise the Delhi and Meerut troops, the second the Bareilly and Neemuch brigades along with some other units, while the third would be made up of all the jihadis, ghazis, irregulars, new recruits and various other troops.

There was also a firm effort made to prevent spies in the city passing information to the British camp. Several spies – or alleged spies at least – were caught and summarily executed. A spy named Hurchand informed the British camp at this time that thirty-two new standards had been distributed by the King, allowing the troops to discard their old British standards. This may also have come from the mind of Bakht Khan. The rebels, wrote Captain Charles Griffith, had now shorn themselves of all visible British accoutrements and uniform: 'The enemy … appeared entirely in white, having soon discarded the dress of their former masters; and it was a pretty sight to see them turning out of the gates on the occasion of a sortie, their arms glittering, pennons flying, and their whole appearance presenting a gay contrast to the dull, dingy dress of their foes.'

In his continuing campaign against the princes, Bakht Khan managed to persuade the King to relieve them of all commands in the army. This was a popular decision among the city people, soothing general anxiety as crime inevitably began to fall. How the soldiers felt about this drastic step is more difficult to say, however. Despite their lack of success, Mirza Mughal and Mirza Abulbakr were popular with the soldiers. 'The troops as a body were offended at the title of Governor General having been granted to Bakht Khan,' wrote Ahsan Ulla Khan. 'They actually addressed a petition to the King in which they signified their unwillingness to be commanded by Bakht Khan. They represented that Bakht Khan was only an artillery officer unfit for the office of governor.' However, Zafar knew that Bakht Khan's experience was more valuable than the prestige of the princes, and so he fully supported his general. On 6 July, he confirmed Bakht Khan's elevation with the royal seal.[11]

In the meantime, new plans were made for an assault on the British position. Gone were the days of tame, haphazard attacks. After almost daily attempts on the ridge throughout June, the British position now went unchallenged for eight days while the rebels gathered their strength. With these radical changes, Bakht Khan breathed new life into the rebel cause.

*****

Excluding the jihadis accompanying the Bareilly force, there were plenty of other ghazis, wahhabis and other malcontents travelling to Delhi and volunteering their services for the higher cause. Wahhabism was an austere and puritanical form of Islam compared to the mainstream belief, and its adherents were flocking in from all over the country. Captured records later indicated that most came from the prominent Muslim centres of Bareilly, Bhopal, Hansi, Hissar, Jaipur, Nusseerabad and Tonk. Their inspiration came from firebrand priests like Moulvi Abdul Ghaffar, Moulvi Sarfaraz Ali, Imam Khan Risaldar and Ghaus Mohammad Khan. The group from Tonk had travelled 250 miles; they wished to fight for the cause of Islam, they said, but the Nawab of Tonk had offered little support.

A substantial number of the jihadis were supporters of the late cleric Syed Ahmed Barelvi. A wahhabist, Barelvi dreamt of destroying infidel control of the country and reviving Muslim rule. A magnetic, energetic personality, he drummed up a sizable following in his travels around the country in the 1820s and decided to initiate a jihad from the north-west region bordering Afghanistan, where the hardy and equally puritan Pathans would be natural allies. Together they launched a jihad against the Sikh Empire of the Punjab. Barelvi had little luck, meeting his end at the hands of the Sikhs during the Battle of Balakot in 1831 as his force was annihilated. Unfazed by his demise, his supporters in Hindustan continued to grow the movement. Many of his disciples, eyeing the growing mutiny, now saw their second chance to realise his dream of Muslim ascendency.

'In Delhi,' wrote Zaka Ullah, 'when the highest authorities of the rebel forces, Bakht Khan, Ghaus Mohammad Khan and Imam Khan Risaldar assembled and with them arrived Moulvi Abdul Ghaffar and Moulvi Sarfraz Ali, then there was a great assembly of the Wahabis in Delhi. Moulvi Sarfaraz Ali became the Commander-in-Chief of the Wahabis and Bakht Khan became their supporter ... These jihadis issued a proclamation addressed to the Muslims to take up arms for Jihad.'[12] Bakht Khan was apparently a wahhabist himself, as were some of his officers. In this vein, Moulvi Sarfaraz Ali would be made Amir-ul-Mujahidin, leader of the Jihadis and Wahhabis and all those who wished to join the ranks of the ghazis fighting the infidel British.

Sources vary as to the number of jihadis in the city by early July. Some say as many as 3,000 or 4,000 jihadis were there by the time the Bareilly brigade arrived. By mid-July, 600 more jihadis had arrived from

Tonk. Estimates of jihadi numbers now ballooned to around 6,000. Based on information his spies had gleaned, Barnes wrote that one of the ghazi leaders, Sooraj-ood-Deen of Tonk, found that he had around 7,000 ghazis and jihadis by late July. Considered alongside the 12,000 to 15,000 regulars in the rebel ranks, this was not to be sniffed at.

The effectiveness of these religious fanatics is difficult to gauge. Most were bereft of military discipline. 'Most of the jihadis were hunger stricken. They were also not having proper dresses on their bodies but they possessed a sword and a dagger in their vest and a muzzle loading gun on their shoulders,'[13] Zaka Ullah observed. Not being regular soldiers, they received no salary from the King so could not buy food. In desperation, they protested to the King that they required funds; Zafar told them that the treasury was empty but nonetheless asked the citizens to give them assistance. Some stepped forward to help; a well-known artist in the city, Mohammad Sharif, offered up his entire house as well as his wife's jewellery. Another, Nawab Mohiuddin Khan, donated 2,000 rupees.[14]

These jihadis could also prove to be an embarrassment. Their calls for jihad were hardly in the general interest, and could only alienate the Hindu soldiers who might baulk at the rebellion being hijacked for Muslim interests. These wahhabis and jihadis would pressure the mullahs of the city to declare that the country would, when the British were expelled, revert to a 'land of faith'. The city mullahs – thirty-seven in number – were also pressured into putting their seals on a fatwa declaring jihad against the Christians. There was some confusion later as to whether this was a forgery or a genuine agreement to declare a religious war. The mullahs would later argue that their hand had been forced. Syed Ahmad Khan could not verify the document's veracity: 'I am told that when the mutineers arrived at Dehli from Meerut, some persons expressed a wish for a Futwah [fatwa] as to the expediency of a religious war. Every opinion given was against such a step. I have only seen a copy of the Futwah I allude to. The original has been lost and it is impossible to say how far the copy may be authentic.'

A second fatwah relating to waging jihad was released as soon as the Bareilly mutineers arrived in the city, but this was suspected to be a forgery as well: 'The man who had it printed, and who was a turbulent fellow, a noted scoundrel, attached certain names to it in order to deceive the public, and gained for it thus a degree of credit. He stamped it, by the way, with the seal of a man who had died before the commencement of the mutinies. It may be added that some of the Bareilly mutineers and their rebel brethren caused several seals to be forged. This fact has become a matter of notoriety.'[15]

Certainly Zafar was entirely against making the rebellion a Muslim struggle. The cry of jihad, though, was heard more frequently after Bakht Khan's arrival as he was known to be friendly to the cause. Zaka Ullah would also describe leading Muslims preaching the same in the city's mosques and urging locals to join the armed cause while issuing the dire threat that a British victory would see their families slain by the infidels.

Not all the Jihadis were men, as Zahir Dehlvi recorded:

> There was one old woman who would wear a headband and tie a dupatta around her waist and be right in front during the fighting, instigating the soldiers: 'Come on, Sons, let's go for Jihad!' We didn't know who she was. She would gather people from the market every day and take them to fight. Though she led them, she always returned safe and sound while hundreds were slain because of her. When the army [British force] entered the city, no one could find her. She simply disappeared.[16]

Meanwhile, in the British camp, another woman who showed much commitment to the rebel cause was noted. 'She is a "Jehadin", a religious fanatic, and sports a green turban, and was probably thought to be inspired,' commented Greathed. The woman, referred to in the camp as 'Joan of Arc' or the 'Maid of Delhi', was not so lucky, being apprehended on 18 July. Hodson:

> I have sent one of our few prisoners up to Forsyth at Umbala [Ambala] whom we ironically call the 'Maid of Delhi' though her age and character are questionable and her ugliness undoubted. She actually came out on horseback and fought against us like a fiend. The General at first released her but knowing how mischievous she would be among those superstitious Mahommedans, I persuaded him to let her be recaptured and made over for safe custody.[17]

Not all the recruits were anything like as committed as the 'Maid of Delhi'. All sorts of ruffians, criminals and other opportunists came along for assaults but hung back from the fighting, instead rifling through the clothes of the fallen. These included the gangster Ghami Khan, who was mentioned by Dehlvi:

> The state of Delhi was such that when the sawars went to attack the enemies, the mischief-makers would also go with them and collect money, weapons and horses from the injured and dead. No Hindu or Muslim from the city ever accompanied the *fauj baghiya* [rebels] – not at the beginning of the fighting, nor at the end. From the very first day, it was these ignoble people who looted the city, along with the purbias. They looted houses, the bank and even the *bakshikhana*, and now they had purchased horses and entered the service of the rebels. Most of them were from Kaghazi mohalla and from the area around Kashmiri Darwaza. They consisted of butchers, paper sellers, shoemakers, local musclemen such as Gami, cudgellers and sundry ruffians – there was

> no genteel person among them. In fact, the decent people had stopped coming out of their homes as they were busy trying to overcome their own troubles.[18]

In terms of morale, spirits were high after the arrival of the Bareilly troops. Further reinforcements arrived on 16 July in the form of the Jhansi Regiment, whose officers were warmly invited into the palace where they presented their swords and pistols to Zafar as a token of their allegiance. Zafar in turn gave the regiment 2,000 rupees to buy supplies and ordered them to camp at the Ajmer Gate. [19] The following day, 17 July, two regiments of infantry from Ambala arrived as well. Confidence grew further on hearing that the Neemuch brigade would arrive shortly. These men were led by 'General' Sudharee Singh and Sheikh Ghous Mohummud. Bakht Khan, with his officers, had written to the brigade on 8 July urging them to reach Delhi with all possible haste to help in a strong assault on the ridge:

> Mohummud Bukht Khan, the Governor Buhadoor, all the troops present in the capital of Delhi, and all the officers of the troops detailed, send you greeting and congratulations ... Brethren! your King and all of us are night and day labouring for the annihilation of a small body of Christians, those infidels having from fear of their lives entrenched themselves on the top of a hill which is neither practicable for Cavalry nor assailable by the Artillery. God willing, in a short time the plain of Delhi will be cleared of the existence of these impure Nazarenes. But now, brethren! you should march expeditiously without halting and reach the presence of your (both secular and spiritual) King and unite with us in the extirpation of the infidels. Render your King happy by your presence inasmuch as this is the most important enterprise, after the successful termination of which we propose to invade Meerut, Puttiala, Hansee, Lucknow and Agra, &c.; as a few Europeans still remain at those places. Therefore you must come over without a moment's delay. We are anxiously awaiting you.[20]

The sheer number of rebels arriving in the city during July was becoming problematic. The 9 July petition of a risaldar called Muhammad Murtaza reveals the tensions that could easily surface with the absence of discipline and authority. He complained to the King that his regiment of cavalry had made its camp in one of the King's sheltered gardens but that another regiment from Gwalior had now come and taken over the place. 'I therefore pray that orders may be issued to the men of the regular cavalry directing them not to disturb us in our occupancy but to search out some other quarters for themselves or at least to occupy one half themselves and to leave the other half to us,'[21] the risaldar wrote. Zafar would in turn ask Mirza Mughal to arrange matters between the two regiments so that the garden was shared in friendly fashion. It was decided that the

Bareilly and Nusseerabad rebels would camp outside the city walls from the Ajmer Gate to the Delhi Gate, while the 60th NI camped at the Old Fort and the 20th NI at the Lahore Gate. The rest of the regiments were scattered at various gates and inside the Salimgarh Fort, while the cavalry would bivouac at Begum Sumroo's garden inside the city.

The jihadis had desires of their own. A certain Syad Muhammad Khan would complain to the King of the lack of accommodation for the men he was leading: 'Your slave the petitioner has been in attendance since yesterday, but has not a place so much as to sit or stand in. I therefore pray that some quarters may be assigned to me and my companions, in all 84 jahadis, where we may rest ourselves. It was necessary and we have submitted it.'[22] The reply from the King was noncommittal, although he did bestow some funds upon them: 'You know what the state of the revenue just now is. May the jahadis be amply commended for all the meritorious deeds they are performing.'

*****

As the days of July ticked by, the major unresolved issue remained: there was no stable and authoritative command of the rebel army. Petty issues and jealousies had quickly begun to chip away at Bakht Khan. The princes and officers were irritated by the commander's rough manner and usurpation of complete power, and the other subedars found it difficult to accept a fellow subedar becoming their commander. The Neemuch commanders, Ghaus Kahn and Sidhari Singh, both seemed to have issues taking orders from Bakht Khan. Their support for his various plans tended to be lukewarm at best, and they constantly disagreed with his decisions. Zafar would sometimes attempt to clear the air with these men, but there was never more than superficial warmth between the former subedars. As early as 5 July, the court or military council of rebel officers would remonstrate with Bakht Khan on his general attitude towards them and his abrasive manner in dealing with Mirza Mughal. One letter captured the fractious nature of the relationship:

> The kingdom of Delhi which has sprung up by the grace of God is in its infancy and resembles a child. We believed that God had sent you to foster this child, and relying on God we hoped that you would manage the affairs of this infant kingdom in a satisfactory manner …
>
> Here in the first fierce struggle [up to the time Bakht Khan arrived in Delhi] everything was managed by the Commander-in-Chief, Mirza Moghul, and he still directs the affairs. And first he is a Prince of high dignity and in this respect superior not only to ourselves, but to all. Secondly, he is Commander-In-Chief.
>
> Thirdly, he is your predecessor in the office, so that in every respect he is your superior …

> Nevertheless up to this day you have never submitted the 'Present State' of your Brigade, nor ever asked permission to issue any order. All this is foreign to 'Rajneet' [Laws of Government]. If you will not obey your superiors how will your inferiors obey you?[23]

Khan was accused of being big-headed owing to all the troops and treasure he had brought. Perhaps someone else would bring even more troops and replace him as commander-in-chief? This would not happen if he did everything according to proper laws and protocols of administration, of course. 'We Sirdars who compose the Court have only this duty to perform, viz., to see that the affairs of the kingdom are properly managed and the administration is strong and not undermined by any one's acts; that everything be conducted according to "Rajneet"; that the sepoys and minor officers obey the great Sirdars; and that everything is in its proper order. We have written as we thought.'[24]

Mirza Mughal was apparently open in his refusal to follow Bakht Khan's commands, and tried to poison Zafar against him. Some of the differences between the two men surfaced in dramatic fashion. Mirza Mughal, of course, had opted for almost daily attacks on the British camp by one regiment or another. One day, as the army marched out, the recently arrived Bakht Khan overruled the prince and stopped the attack. Mirza Mughal complained to his father:

> ... your Majesty is cognizant that before Muhammad Bakht Khan came, active operations of war were carried on daily, and without intermission and Your Majesty knows likewise that since the arrival of the Bareilly General, several engagements have taken place. It so occurred to-day that your slave, purposing to make an attack, had formed the army and taken it outside the city, when the above named general interposed, and for a long time kept the whole force standing inactive, wanting to know by whose orders it had gone out; and saying that it was not to proceed without his permission, caused it to return. A proceeding like this, even an open enemy would not attempt, namely, that the army should be proceeding to an attack, and one should interfere and cause it to return. Your slave therefore supplicates, that if the entire control and management of the army have, from the royal presence, been bestowed on the said general, your slave may be directed, by written order, to refrain from interfering in all military matters, and he will no longer interfere, but will acquaint the officers of the army that, for the future, they are to remain with the said general, and are to yield obedience to him. Having his orders reversed cannot but cause vexation and chagrin to any officer, high or low. If, on the other hand, the control of the army is supposed to be vested in your slave, the said general should not interfere. He has entire authority over his own regiments. Such demands as are made for the services of his regiments from this, he should invariably comply with.

# 26

# The Heat and Flies of July

> O brothers, countrymen, specially for the army men it is essential that Hindus and Muslims unite and become one, should understand one another as their arms. For the destruction of this group of people make complete endeavour and don't take rest until they are completely routed.
>
> *Delhi Urdu Akhbar*, 19 July

In the British camp, the main worry during early July was the superiority of the rebel guns. The soldiers liked to nickname the rebel guns that were causing the most trouble. One was nicknamed 'Whistling Dick', for example, while another was called 'Tambourine Sal' for its continuous firing. Humour aside, the plain fact was that the British at this stage had no answer to the heavier rebel guns. 32- and 24-pounders had been placed on the city walls along with 13-inch mortars. To counter this disparity in hardware, on 17 July General Reed requested extra siege guns from Ferozepore in addition to the ones being readied at Phillaur. The convoy from Ferozepore was to consist of six 24-pounders, eight 18-pounders, four 8-inch howitzers and four 10-inch mortars. As well as these, there would be two 10-inch howitzers from Phillaur. An additional three heavy guns (18- and 24-pounders) had already been readied and were being sent. Once these arrived, the British camp would have sixty-three guns.

The good news for Reed was that the dwindling supply of shot for the guns was now being topped up by deliveries from the north. A small force was sent to Alipur on 13 July to escort a convoy of hackeries full of ammunition. Meanwhile, despite the disparity in artillery, the rebels weren't having it all their way. The British battery at Hindu Rao had been increased and was now battering the Mori Bastion, which was being reduced to rubble.

In order to further discourage the rebels, a false rumour was spread at this time that General Wheeler was marching on Delhi with four

European regiments; the general was in fact dead, massacred at Kanpur with his men. 'Alas! for the credit to be attached to the voice of rumour,' lamented Revd Rotton. 'At the very moment when with wistful eyes and longing hearts, the Delhi Field Force – in ignorance of the tragedy that had been enacted at Cawnpore – was reckoning with confidence on the General's skill and succour, and looking forward to his advent as the harbinger of salvation, the poor General, with his small garrison, were inhabitants of another and I hope a better world.'

Meanwhile, to prevent the rebels from attacking the rear of the British position or the supply lines beyond, Reed – as advised by Baird Smith – had ordered that all bridges across the canals moving north and parallel with the Grand Trunk Road be destroyed. Only one, the bridge at Painbari, would be retained; this was in British hands and allowed troops and cavalry to cross for offensive purposes while denying the rebels an easy crossing from the west. There were two sets of bridges to be destroyed. One comprised several bridges spanning the Najafgarh Jheel, while another set spanned the western Jumna Canal. On 7 July, Lt Greathed and Lt Fulford were sent out to blow up the Shalimar, Badli and Shumapoor bridges. A force of 400 cavalry and 1,000 infantry (sappers and pioneers) along with eighteen guns accompanied them. The next day, Lt Geneste and Lt Champain were sent to blow up the Busaye bridge on the Najafgarh Jheel, which was by now the only bridge left standing within striking distance. Baird Smith was effusive in his praise: 'We reached the ground just as daybreak, when the sappers began work at once. When the explosion took place it was beautiful, and the necessary demolition of the most perfect kind. The enemy not only never looked near us but bolted into the city as soon as we made our appearance.'[1]

The next day, the more distant bridges spanning the canal between the ridge and Alipur were taken down by Lt Stewart and Lt Carnegie. Some of the bridges happened to be constructed out of wood although being covered with masonry. Wood was in very high demand in the British camp, being required for the artillery park, so small charges were used to blow away just the masonry, with the rest of the bridge being deconstructed and the wooden planks and beams being ferried back to the camp. With this done, all that remained was to destroy the Pulchadar Aqueduct, which carried water into the city. This was accomplished on 9 July. It was not expected to make a big difference to the rebels, however, for the city was amply supplied by the Jumna River and numerous wells.

Nine days of relative peace was broken on 9 July, the day of Bakht Khan's first serious attack on the British position. Early in the morning, a cannonade opened up from the city and was followed by rebel attacks on British pickets. On the British right was the mound on which an infantry picket and three 18-pounders had been placed to confront any attack from the Sabzi Mandi. Adjacent to the mound, a few hundred feet to the right on level ground, were stationed two horse artillery guns along with a troop of carabineers. It was the turn of Major Tombs' troop to take the position on this day, with the guns under the command of Lt James Hills. The carabineers were commanded by Lt Stillman. Further to the right of the horse artillery gun picket was a fakir's house where a contingent of the 9th Irregulars were stationed, with two men pushed forward around 200 yards down the road to provide further early warning of an attack. Being stationed on the Grand Trunk Road, they could see roughly 700 to 800 yards down it towards the city. On either side of the road, however, private residences and walled gardens restricted visibility and hid any movement on either side of the road. Although a suitable outpost in other respects, the fakir's house also had the disadvantage of being out of sight from the ridge.

The morning had seen almost continuous rain, and some guards had grown complacent. At around half-past nine in the morning, some sowars clad in white advanced towards the 9th Irregulars; no alarm was raised, for the 9th Irregulars themselves wore white and assumed they were looking at friends. The rebel horsemen, realising they had not been recognised, charged with roughly 100 men. Some of the British officers suspected treachery; according to Revd Rotton, some of the rebel cavalry were guided in by a treacherous picket of the 9th Irregulars. Greathed, too, claimed that pickets had shown the rebel sowars the road into the camp. The British soldiers would not fire at the sowars in white for fear of hitting their comrades in the 9th.

Whatever the case, the rebels' large numbers gave them away, causing suspicious British artillery to unlimber the guns. The rebels were aiming for the guns of Tombs' battery. Lieutenant James Hills, manning the guns, charged the rebels and killed two men in the hopes that he would buy time for others to unlimber the guns and fire, but there was no time before the horsemen reached them. Hills had a lucky escape; a rebel horseman was just about to cut him down Major Tombs shot the attacker. Hills scrambled to face another man, who cut him badly on the head. Tombs shot this man as well, saving Hills' life. Both Hills and Tombs were later awarded the Victoria Cross for their acts of bravery. Passing Tombs and Hills, the rebel sowars took further advantage of the confusion to urge a native troop of horse artillery to join them. The men refused, and the rebel sowars then galloped away. The situation was rescued by the guns of Olpherts' European battery, which opened fire on the rebels. Men of the 75th then arrived, which was enough to ensure the retreating rebel cavalry didn't turn about.

Thirty-five rebels were killed in the action, which Greathed summarised:

> It was a momentary affair and by the time we got to the mound the cavalry had disappeared and the only signs of the raid were Tombs' two dead men and other corpses and the bodies of a few poor camp followers. The mistake of leaving an inlet into camp to be guarded by

> Hindostanees will not again be committed. Brigadier Wilson had in vain protested against it but knows better than anyone else and now we see the results.

Confusion about the rebel uniform did not go away. Hodson and the Guides, ordered to pursue the retreating rebels, actually rode in parallel with them under the mistaken impression that they were friends; they only realised their mistake when the sowars crossed a bridge and entered the city.

This skirmish was just a prelude to a larger attack. At around 10 a.m., rebels poured from the city while a terrific cannonade was kept up by the city guns to keep the British busy. The rebel force moved towards Kishanganj in order to launch an attack on the right rear of the British position while a force under Brig. Gen. Chamberlain moved toward Kishanganj in order to intercept them. The force comprised Maj. Scott's horse battery, contingents from the 8th and 61st Foot along with the 4th Sikh Infantry and two companies of the 60th Rifles under Col J. Jones. The infantry brigade was commanded by Brigadier W. Jones. In all, the force boasted 700 men and six guns. A short while after crossing the canal, the terrain opened into a plain and the two forces caught sight of each other. Skirmishers were sent out and the guns began firing. The rebels made an orderly retreat, occasionally unlimbering their guns and firing before turning to retreat again as the British advanced. The field was characterised by profusions of a prickly-pear type of cactus which made it difficult to move in line. Then the rain started up again, drenching the combatants. Meanwhile, the British guns on the ridge fired over their men into the rebel line, thinning it out. The British column gradually swept through the Sabzi Mandi, pushing the rebels back. There was strong resistance at several serais, which offered makeshift defences. The fighting continued until sundown, despite the rainfall continuing for the rest of the day.

British losses for the day were heavy. One officer and forty men were killed, eight officers and 163 men were wounded, and eleven men were missing. These casualties meant HM60th Rifles, along with the Guides and Gurkhas, had all lost around a quarter of their strength by now. Estimates on the rebel casualties meanwhile were as speculative as ever, with some saying as many as 500 killed and 1,000 wounded.

Following this heavy encounter, Reed ordered various parapets, abattis of trees and trenches constructed in the area of the mound to protect against similar attacks. Garden walls, clumps of trees and other obstacles were cleared by the Engineers giving British pickets at the Hindu Rao a better view towards the city. The large mound nicknamed the 'general's mound' was chosen as the site of a new battery of three heavy guns, and work began on cutting an approach for troops.

Later in the day, suspicions in the British camp fell not just on the 9th Irregulars but also the 4th Irregulars concerning the earlier skirmish where rebels had reached the mound. The common perception was that the rebels had managed to penetrate the British camp because men of the 4th had assisted them. It was decided to send both regiments back to the Punjab, although the headquarters of the 4th Irregulars (around a hundred men) would stay behind. These men never deserted, but they were relieved of their weapons and horses and used only as orderlies in the camp. Now hardly any sepoys remained in the cavalry, which consisted of six squadrons of Dragoons, five squadrons of Punjab and Guide cavalry and Capt. Hodson's corps of Sikh horse, which was now being raised. The only sepoy contingents remaining were stationed a little way north at Alipur to protect the village.

Some good news for Reed at this time was the arrival of reinforcements comprising 300 Punjab sappers under Lt Gulliver and 600 unarmed pioneers under Lt. H. A. Brownlow. Brownlow's men would work tremendously hard in dangerous conditions to construct batteries and other siege operations. Brownlow had also brought in plentiful supplies from the engineer park at Roorkee. The 1st Punjab Cavalry, composed of Punjabis and Sikhs, also arrived.

Discounting the endless tit-for-tat exchanges of the heavy guns, the British camp enjoyed a few days' respite after 9 July thanks to a heavy rain that fell throughout the 10th and 11th. On the morning of the 14th, however, rebels appeared at the Kabul and Lahore Gates making for the Sabzi Mandi. They kept up a heavy fire, with British guns replying. In order to repel the rebels, a column of around 1,500 men was mustered. The column soon found itself in heavy fighting and began taking casualties, with other men wounded by the rebel guns, which, although more than 1,100 yards away, managed to land some accurate hits. Gradually, the rebels were driven back into the Kishanganj district. Part of the British force managed to reach within a few hundred metres of the city walls but was driven back by the guns on the walls; generally the British abandoned pursuit around 600 yards from the walls in order to avoid grape and shot from the rebel guns.

The next day, the British faced another powerful assault. Capt. Griffiths noticed the difference Bakht Khan had made: 'Unusual bravery was shown by the rebels on this day: they stood fairly in the open, and also attacked the pickets with great pertinacity, assaulting one called the "Sammy House" for hours, and leaving eighty dead bodies in its front, all killed by the infantry of the Guides, who most gallantly held the picket against overwhelming numbers.' Rebels attacked the right flank in the morning, focusing on the batteries on the Hindu Rao. Firing from the ridge failed to drive them off, so Brig. Gen. Chamberlain ordered Brig. Showers to lead off a column consisting of Maj. Coke's corps of Punjab Rifles, the 1st Fusiliers under Major Jacob, six horse artillery guns under Maj. Turner and Capt. Money, some contingents of the Guide Cavalry,

Hodson's Horse and the Kohat Risalah. Rotton recorded what must have been considered a wasted opportunity:

> The battle was long and furious; the enemy were driven in and followed up by our men almost to the Lahore gate. We committed, however, a sad oversight on this occasion. It appears that the enemy, retreating before our gallant soldiers, left six guns on the field; which guns were at one time so situated that we were between them and the mutineers, who had originally brought them out. This fact seems to have been forgotten, and the rebels, to our mortification. How it was we committed such an error I cannot possibly say; but we did, and the enemy must have laughed at us heartily for our negligence.

*****

These last few assaults had caused a rapid increase in British casualties. Among the wounded were Brig. Gen. Chamberlain, Lt Roberts, Lt Walker, Lt Geneste and Lt Carnegie (Bombay Engineers), Lt Faithfull and Lt Rivers (75th Foot), Lt Penton Thompson (3rd Troop, 3rd Brigade Horse Artillery), Lt Tulloch (20th NI) and Lt Pollock (1st Punjab Infantry). The fighting since 9 July, when Bakht Khan had taken charge, had seen British losses of 500 men killed and wounded.

Mounting deaths meant a considerable number of items went up for auction. Such sales had had been going on ever since the force had reached Delhi, but early July saw a particularly large auction for the possessions of the departed commanders Anson and Barnard.

The other enemy was the monsoon weather. The rain and extreme heat made for a very muggy atmosphere, with temperatures as high as 44°C in the shade. Swarms of flies were everywhere. Capt. Griffiths, for one, was miserable:

> The heat was insupportable, the thermometer under the shade of my tent marking 112 °F.; and to add to our misery there came upon us a plague of flies, the like of which I verily believe had not been on the earth since Moses in that manner brought down the Wrath of God on the Egyptians. They literally darkened the air, descending in myriads and covering everything in our midst. Foul and loathsome they were, and we knew that they owed their existence to, and fattened on, the putrid corpses of dead men and animals which lay rotting and unburied in every direction. The air was tainted with corruption, and the heat was intense. Can it, then, be wondered that pestilence increased daily in the camp, claiming its victims from every regiment, native as well as European?

To avoid the heat, the British soldiers took to swimming or fishing in the canal at the British rear; the first to catch a fish won a bottle of beer.

Meanwhile, cholera continued to take its toll, primarily within HM8th and HM61st. The sick of both regiments were under one roof, their hospitals sharing the same building on the extreme left flank of the line. The men of HM8th had a long central room while HM61st the side verandas. As early as 7 July, fourteen hospitals had been erected around the camp. They were manned by only two priests – the Anglican Revd Rotton and an unnamed Catholic priest – who found themselves in high demand.

# 27

# Wilson's Doubts

> I never served under a man, and I have now served under or with a considerable number, for whom I had less respect, or on whose judgment and capacity I had less reliance.
>
> Baird Smith, 1 November 1857[1]

Reed's tenure as the commanding officer at the ridge would prove to be short. He had in fact arrived on the ridge to relieve Barnard on 14 June, roughly three weeks before actually taking charge, but he was unwell. Upon Barnard's death on 5 July, Reed had no choice but to assume command despite continued ill health. Baird Smith, the chief engineer, remarked that Reed was barely able to ride his horse. 'Oh for a man to command us!' he wrote to his wife on 7 July.[2] The idea of executing a *coup de main* was discussed with Reed as well, with talks dragging on for several days. Due to the commander's condition, Baird Smith's advice on an early attack didn't receive the required urgency; the senior officers voted it down. In the following days, casualties sustained during Bakht Khan's series of assaults rendered moot all arguments about a *coup de main*; there weren't enough healthy men in the British camp to launch an attack anymore.

As the days went by, Reed's health rapidly declined. Increasingly confined to his tent, he was advised by the camp doctors to retire to the hills on medical leave right away and duly moved off on the 14th. He had been commander for less than two weeks. With his departure, the responsibility of leading the Delhi Field Force fell on Brigadier Archdale Wilson, who had led the Meerut contingent to Delhi and who would now be assigned the rank of brigadier general. 'These orders gave great satisfaction,' wrote Revd Rotton, 'and none rejoiced more in the appointment than his own little army, who had gained for him and themselves imperishable honour on the banks of the River Hindun.'

On becoming commanding officer, Wilson told John Lawrence that he was confident of capturing the city but that he lacked sufficient numbers to do so. 'I have consulted with Colonel Baird smith, the Chief Engineer with the force, and we have both come to the conclusion that any attempt now to assault the city of Delhi must end in our defeat and disaster.' He had at this time only 3,700 men (2,200 European and 1,500 Indian) against a far greater force. The rebels lacked order, true, and their largely incoherent attacks on the ridge could be repelled in the short term, but behind defences and walls they had too much of an advantage; and while the mutineers waited, the heat and unsanitary conditions would deplete the British force. 'In fact, this force is, and has been ever since we arrived here, "besieged" rather than "besiegers",' he opined. 'To enable me, however, to hold this position I must be *strongly* reinforced, and that *speedily.*' Since the various British contingents were busy elsewhere around the country, he begged for more reinforcements from the Punjab. 'I candidly tell you that unless speedily reinforced this force will soon be so reduced by casualties and sickness that nothing will be left but a retreat to Kurnaul. The disasters attending such an unfortunate proceeding I cannot calculate.'[3]

It soon became apparent that Wilson was filled with great anxiety. Indeed, so worried was he that a withdrawal from the ridge back across the Jumna was considered.[4] On the very day that he took over command, Wilson had privately asked for an audience with Baird Smith at which he wished to extol the advantages of moving the camp to the left bank of the river. He planned to argue that it was a safer position in which to await reinforcements and allowed easier communication with Meerut. Baird Smith was aghast:

> The step was never deliberately proposed to me for my opinion, but a friend gave me a private intimation that it would be proposed, and that I had best be prepared for it. I hated the very idea of such a movement, regarding it as wholly uncalled for, weak and mischievous. I did not wait therefore for any formal reference on the subject, but on the day General Wilson assumed command, I took the opportunity of his sending for me to consult with me on the whole question of our position, to urge in the most earnest terms I could employ, the absolute necessity of our holding the grip we then had on Delhi like 'grim Death', not receding a foot from the ground we held, and I cheerfully undertook the responsibility of making the position tenable against any assaults.[5]

The chief engineer suggested that the rebels had never managed to destroy British communication, nor had they prevented supplies from the Punjab or even showed the necessary spirit to attack the camp in earnest. With that in mind, he could not think of a single reason to retreat. In fact, a retreat would be disastrous. 'All India would at once believe that we retreated because we were beaten; and in circumstances like ours a belief of this kind was equivalent to the severest defeat we could sustain,' he wrote.[6] Moving the camp would also unsettle allies, in particular the rulers of the Cis-Sutlej states, who may reassess their position. If this happened, and the rulers of Patiala, Nabha and Jhind withdrew their support, all communication with Punjab would be lost and the chance for reinforcements and heavy guns would vanish with it. Beyond this, the boost to enemy morale would have been enormous.

Wilson reluctantly bowed to Baird Smith's point of view, reassuring his chief engineer that he would not consider a retreat. Given Baird Smith's assurances that he could marshal the defence of the ridge and prevent it falling, both men agreed that the best strategy was for the British force to remain strictly on the defensive to await the arrival of siege guns and reinforcements, at which point operations of a more offensive nature could be considered. The bullish, optimistic Baird Smith had of course wanted to assault the city when he first arrived, but the losses sustained in recent battles had cooled his fervour. Baird Smith wrote that Wilson expressed a willingness to attack if he had 2,000 more men. 'I told him I was ready for this whenever he was. And so it was agreed that I was to strengthen the position as much as my means would permit, and he was to be very cautious in the use of the troops during the enemy's attacks.'[7]

Baird Smith generally got on with Wilson, as recorded in his private letters, although his esteem for the man was never very high due to what he considered Wilson's excess caution. Over time this difference would see their relationship cool, although Wilson seemed to trust Baird Smith and was happy to consult him on most issues.

There seemed to be a consensus on Wilson's risk-averse nature. Another who held him in scant regard was Brigadier General Nicholson, a later arrival, who apparently disliked Wilson personally and considered him to be an indecisive ditherer. Hodson, too, doubted Wilson's ability to deal with the situation, although he accepted Wilson's arguments against an attack: 'I fear our movements wait upon theirs. We have no one in power with a head to devise or a heart to dare any enterprise which might result in the capture of Delhi and alas one cannot but admit that it would require both a wise head and a very great heart to run the risk with so reduced a force as we have here now.'[8]

John Lawrence, himself desperate for troops to hold the Punjab, gave thought to Wilson's plea for reinforcements. He had to decide whether to gamble all and send what he could to Wilson or protect himself and retain the Punjab regardless of what happened at Delhi. He only had seven European regiments in total; five had already been stationed in the province, while the Bombay Fusiliers had recently made their way up, as had a combined force of 250 men of HM8th and a wing of HM61st. Three regiments were currently stationed in Peshawar, one held Lahore, another Multan and Ferozepore while another held Rawalpindi,

Amritsar and Jalandhar. One regiment was therefore free to join a moveable column. Also, there were around 800 to 1,000 artillerymen available. Excluding the sick, European regiments accounted for no more than 4,700 fit men. However, new Punjabi regiments were already being drilled and trained. The problem for Lawrence was that there were still 6,000 armed sepoys in the Punjab who might turn against their masters, while another 12,000 had been disarmed but required careful watching. A large host of troops was therefore required not only to keep Punjab stable but to watch the sepoys.

Despite this, Lawrence had always been foremost among those urging for a push towards Delhi and he now felt he should do his utmost to prevent the force being pushed back. He therefore decided to offer up as many troops as he could to help the Delhi Field Force; after all, if they retreated all was lost. Over the following weeks he pushed troops south, chief among them the large column led by Brigadier General John Nicholson which left Amritsar on 23 July.

As with General Reed, Wilson's health also began to suffer. By the end of July, little more than two weeks into assuming command, the general impression in the camp was that he would break under the pressure and be replaced. Nevertheless, Wilson began his reorganisation of the camp in energetic fashion. New measures were taken to improve the speed with which outlying pickets could be reinforced. A contingent of fifty European troops would become mosque picket when an alarm went up, while another fifty from the 4th Sikh Infantry would move to the breastwork between the mosque and the observatory and fifty more would stand ready to reinforce them. The 2nd Brigade would help defend the Sabzi Mandi or Hindu Rao whenever these positions were under pressure, while the men of the 3rd Brigade were to assemble on the cemetery road and help defend the rear of the camp if it was attacked. Major Coke's column was to assemble near the bridge adjacent to the mosque and attack any rebel units that managed to penetrate into the camp. The Guide Cavalry and reserve guns, meanwhile, were to assemble on the road to the Flagstaff Tower. The sappers were held in reserve to plug gaps wherever they appeared. The cavalry under Brigadier Grant would continuously patrol the camp. These precautions came in addition to all the pickets already in place. Capt. Griffiths was satisfied:

> The fruits of General Wilson's accession to the command of the army, and the stringent orders issued by him for the maintenance of order and discipline both in camp and on picket became more and more apparent every day. All duties were now regulated and carried out with the utmost precision; each regiment knew its allotted place in case of a sortie, and the officers on picket had to furnish reports during their term of duty, thereby making them more attentive to the discipline and care of their men.

In terms of tactics, too, there were changes. The order was given not to pursue rebels close to the city walls, which made life easy for the rebel gunners and sharpshooters. More organised methods were introduced for the various duties that the troops had to carry out in the camp, and more recreation was offered. For public safety, countless animal carcasses that littered the camp were ordered cleaned up, with adjutants asked to organise work parties without extra pay. In the matter of uniform, too, Wilson ordered more discipline: 'Many corps had become quite regardless of appearance, entirely discarding all pretensions to uniformity, and adopting the most nondescript dress,' wrote Griffiths. 'One in particular, a most gallant regiment of Europeans which had served almost from the beginning of the siege, was known by the sobriquet of the "Dirty Shirts," from their habit of fighting in their shirts with sleeves turned up, without jacket or coat, and their nether extremities clad in soiled blue dungaree trousers.'

Wilson also investigated rumours that the men were selling percussion caps to traders in the regimental bazaars. This was done innocently enough, but the caps were supposedly sold on – presumably after a good mark-up – to the rebels, who were apparently short of caps. Searches were carried out at the bazaars, but nobody was apprehended; either the rumours were groundless, or the traders were discreet enough to hide their stashes.

*****

By the middle of August, pressure on Wilson to capture Delhi would be greater than it ever had been on Barnard or Reed. By this point, the British force had been sitting on the ridge for more than two and a half months and was no closer to capturing the city. Lawrence strongly feared an uprising in the Punjab, which would be galvanised by the British failure to take Delhi. Governor-General Canning also showed frustration at the slow progress. Wilson would write to Baird Smith on 20 August to complain:

> A letter has been received from the Governor-General urging our immediately taking Delhi, and he seems angry that it has not been done long ago. I wish to explain to him the true state of affairs, that Delhi is seven miles in circumference, filled with an immense fanatical Mussulman population, garrisoned by fully 40,000 soldiers, armed and disciplined by ourselves, with 114 heavy pieces of artillery mounted on the walls, with the largest magazine of shot, shell and ammunition in the upper provinces at their disposal, besides some 60 pieces of field artillery, all of our own manufacture, and manned by artillerymen drilled and taught by ourselves.[9]

Canning, he lamented, had no understanding of the scale of the task; the Delhi Field Force was insufficient to undertake any sort of assault on the city. He considered the safety of the force and of the Empire to be best served by waiting till further reinforcements arrived. Wilson asked Baird Smith for his opinion before formulating an answer. Perhaps swayed by Canning's urgency, however, the chief engineer suggested an immediate assault of the city. He understood the dangers of attacking the city with a small force, he said, but continued inaction was arguably worse in the effect it had on the general population, who would come to see the British as impotent. Although rebel resources dwarfed their own, there was little union apparent in their actions and they lacked expertise. Both men had valid points; Wilson overstated the task while Baird Smith took it too lightly.

Pressure on Wilson increased when news reached camp on 21 August that the 10th Light Cavalry, stationed at Ferozepore in the Punjab, had mutinied. Lawrence's fears had been realised. The 10th had been considered a loyal unit, having stayed true even when their colleagues in the 45th and 57th had mutinied. Delay in taking Delhi was blamed entirely. Eventually, in a meeting on 23 August, Wilson agreed to Baird Smith's proposals:

> It is evident to me that the results of the proposed operations will be thrown on the hazard of a die; but under the circumstances in which I am placed I am willing to try this hazard, the more so as I cannot suggest any other plan to meet our difficulties. I cannot, however, help being of opinion that the chances of success under such a heavy fire as the working parties will be exposed to, are anything but favourable. I yield, however, to the judgment of the Chief Engineer.[10]

Baird Smith was perhaps was the most candid in offering his low opinion of Wilson. As time went on, their relationship frayed. In a letter to his father written after the siege, he voiced his frustrations on working with Wilson.

> You will perhaps be somewhat surprised that I should have said nothing of General Wilson who commanded the force. The simple truth is that I have such contempt for his military capacity, and found him throughout the siege operations so uniformly obstructive by his dread of responsibility, and his moral timidity that I say as little about him as I can.
>
> I believe his mind to have been off its usual balance all the time we were at work, and he was literally more difficult to deal with than the enemy. It was only by constantly reminding him that if he interfered with my plans I would throw the whole responsibility for the consequences on him that I could get on at all.[11]

*****

Matters were worsened by the fact that little information was being received from around the country. Letters tended to get through from the Punjab, but little news from the south reached camp. A message had been sent to Kanpur on 15 July; General Wilson had been told on 25 June that General Wheeler, unable to hold out for much longer at Kanpur, would be surrendering to the rebels. A reply finally came from Kanpur on 3 August. The Europeans had been massacred, and General Wheeler was dead.

On 5 August, a misleading letter from Colonel Fraser-Tytler to Capt. Earle illustrated the dangers of miscommunication: 'Havelock has thrashed the Nana ... will relieve Lucknow in four days ... we shall soon be with you.' In fact, it would be another four months before Lucknow was relieved. No troops from Lucknow would come to the aid of the Delhi Field Force.

# 28

# War of Attrition

From hence to Allahabad the fort of Agra and the Residency of Lucknow are the only spots where the British flag still flies. We are more to be considered now as an isolated band fighting for our very name and existence in the midst of an enemy's country than as an avenging army about to punish a rebel force.

Capt. Hodson, 20 July

Casualties in the British camp were not letting up. Wilson was particularly anxious about his European troops, thirty to forty of whom were invalided out each day during mid-July, due to a mix of combat, fatigue, disease and heat. Exacerbating the latter was the fact that the ridge was increasingly bare of foliage, with the once fertile lower reaches denuded by artillery fire and the need for firewood. With supplies plentiful, however, the hospitals were in far better shape than they had been during the recent Russian campaign. 'Our position here is very different from that in the Crimea and at Scutari,' wrote Hodson. 'There the men died from want of care and of the ordinary necessaries of life. Here there is no absolute want of anything except a genial climate and well built hospitals neither of which you could supply. The men are attended to immediately they are sick or wounded and within an hour sometimes half that time of his being wounded a soldier is in his bed with everything actually necessary and the greatest medical attention.'[1] Care for the wounded was further augmented on 30 July with the arrival of Revd F. W. Ellis, erstwhile chaplain at Ambala. His presence took some of the burden from Revd Rotton, who wrote of the struggles in the camp at this time:

> Most men were complaining, and acknowledged to a constantly distressing feeling of sickness, especially before and after breakfast. I was a martyr to it myself, and attributed much of this nausea not

> only to the quality of the food which we ate, and which was at times very coarse and inferior, during the rains, but to the presence also of an overwhelming number of flies, who soiled everything which they came in contact with. As I have before observed, the misery arising from these creatures only, was something almost intolerable; they sought you out in your tent, at your meals, when occupied in the discharge of duty; and the only time you could secure rest from this annoyance was during the hours of sleep at night, when they themselves felt the necessity of repose. Whatever might be the dish you selected to feed upon as soon as it was uncovered, a legion of flies would settle upon it; and even so simple a thing as a cup of tea would be filled in a few minutes, unless you were very watchful, the surface of the liquid presenting a most revolting dark appearance from flies floating thereon, some dead and others dying.

A general mood of optimism nevertheless prevailed into August. The feeling was that Delhi must fall – that it was only a matter of time. As rebel attacks tailed off, there was found to be more time for other pursuits. Popular games in the camp included football and quoits. Fishing in the canal remained popular, and cricket matches and pony races were organised. Food was plentiful, although luxuries were expensive. News such as that from Kanpur dented morale for a time, but rather than causing despondency it was mostly channelled into a determination to assault the city and end the siege, as in Hodson's case:

> We have fresh accounts from below that every European woman and child have been ruthlessly murdered at Cawnpore. The details are too revolting to put on paper and make one's blood boil. Mothers with infants in their arms murdered with fiendish cruelty and worse than all two young girls just arrived from England are said to have been only saved to meet a worse fate in some Mussulman's zenana. There will be a day of reckoning for these things and a fierce one or I have been a soldier in vain.[2]

Wilson was feeling the strain. He had been resting, having been ill for a few days. 'He is older however by ten years than he was,' wrote Hodson. 'The responsibility and anxiety of what is certainly a very difficult position have been too much for him and he has got into the way of being nervous and alarmed and over anxious even about trifles which shakes one's dependence on his judgment ... These men are personally as brave as lions but they have not big hearts or heads enough for circumstances of serious responsibility.'[3]

On the evening of 29 July, the camp was informed of a private court-martial that had taken place a day or two before. A sergeant had been tried for killing a classie called 'Oree' who had been attached to the

2nd European Bengal Fusiliers. There had been incidents recently where camp followers had been abused by European soldiers, and some deaths had been reported on 9 July. This had caused unease among the camp followers, and some were known to have already slipped away. Anxious to retain the loyalty of the camp followers, Wilson was determined to stamp out such behaviour. The court, however, acquitted the sergeant of the murder.

Suspicions dogged the remaining sepoys in the British camp, and this was not helped when it was discovered on 16 August that ordnance charges had been sabotaged. Some guns had been badly off target in recent days, and they would flash several times when firing. The blame was put on the gun lascars, who were accused of filling the vents of the guns with powdered glass, which prevented rapid firing and offered a visual signal to the rebels when the guns were fired. Two lascars were caught and, after a summary trial, hanged the next morning. A sharp lookout was kept against such happenings thereafter, with the powder magazine carefully guarded and entrenchments dug round to prevent anyone slipping in.

*****

Skirmishing continued into August. The rebel officers were seemingly unaware that the casualties they wrought on the British were not being remedied by reinforcements, for they failed to press home the advantage. Brevet Major Anson, 9th Lancers, was nonplussed: 'They steal up in great numbers to within eighty or ninety yards of the picket, and, firing off their muskets, run away as hard as they can, one of our batteries helping them to do so with a good grace. Our men being safe behind breastworks, their noisy volleys are perfectly innocuous.'

A major rebel attack took place on 18 July in the form of a two-pronged assault on the Sabzi Mandi and the Hindu Rao. The alarm in the British camp went off at 9 a.m., and in accordance with Wilson's new system the picket at Hindu Rao was quickly reinforced with 100 men of HM1st Battalion of 60th Rifles. To push back the rebels, Lt Col J. Jones of the 60th Rifles was put in charge of contingents of HM8th, HM61st, the 75th Foot and the 2nd European Bengal Fusiliers along with two companies of Sikh Rifles, Coke's regiment and Hodson's irregular cavalry plus four guns. The force pushed into the Sabzi Mandi around 1 p.m. and cleared the rebels, though they encountered some stiff resistance at the serais. British casualties were twelve men killed and sixty-six wounded, while one officer – Lt Crozier of HM75th Foot – was killed and three others were wounded. Two men were missing. In addition, Lt Walter of the 45th NI died of sunstroke right after the skirmish. The rebels were said to have lost around 400.

This was the last serious rebel attack via the Sabzi Mandi. By now, the British engineers had destroyed almost all the walls, gardens, old buildings and serais along the no-man's land in front of the camp, freeing up the field of fire for the British pickets and guns manning the various outposts. The breastworks protecting the pickets now extended from the Hindu Rao right towards the canal and beyond, limiting the rebels to potshots from afar. By this time, the rebels had made thirty-six sorties against the British position since 8 June – a testament to their mediocre leadership, divisions within their ranks and a lack of resolve despite their superior numbers.

On 20 July, one Capt. Greensill was shot by his own men in an unfortunate incident. He had gone to reconnoitre an enemy position, telling his party to stay at a certain spot. It was pitch-dark, however, and when he returned his signal was not recognised; the escort party fired at the shadowy figure approaching, only to realise his identity later. The wounded captain did not recover, dying overnight.

In mid-July, Hodson reckoned the rebels to number roughly 36,000 fighting men while the British strength was less than a fifth of that. However, it wouldn't be obvious to anyone observing an exchange of fire:

> Our position however is much strengthened and we now beat them with half the trouble we had at first, their appetite for fighting being considerably lessened by having been so repeatedly driven back but alas we only drive them back while we do not advance an inch …
>
> The people within it [the city] are immensely disheartened and dissensions are rife among them. A split between the Hindoos and fanatic Mahommedans is almost inevitable and above all money is getting scarce. Meantime this waiting race is very wearying to heart and body.[4]

Another large rebel attack came on 23 July, this time on the British left flank. Exiting from the Kashmir Gate with six guns, the rebels advanced at around 7 a.m. Their guns were placed in the Ludlow Castle grounds, with fire directed at the left of the ridge. The rebels moved the guns frequently, making it impossible for the British gunners to target them effectively. The rebels also attacked the picket at Metcalfe's House close to the British left flank, managing to get close to the ridge itself. Brigadier Showers was dispatched to repel them, as Griffiths recorded:

> To punish their temerity, a force of all arms was sent out from camp under Brigadier Showers, with the intention of attacking their right flank. We moved up a deep gorge, and coming on them by surprise, force them to remove their guns, which quickly limbered up and made for the city. There was a great deal of skirmishing in the gardens and ruined houses before the infantry followed the example of their comrades; but the fight was not nearly so severe as during the sorties on the right, nor did the enemy suffer any very great loss. On our side, we had in all fifty offers and men killed and wounded.

The rebel hold on the Ludlow Castle was temporarily broken as they were pushed out of the building. When Showers' men moved close to the city walls, however, they inevitably came under fire. Brevet Captain W. G. Law, nominally of the Bengal 10th NI but attached to the 1st Punjab Infantry, was killed while Brevet Lt Col R. Drought of the 60th NI was wounded.

A week later, on 31 July, the rebels launched a major assault. A large force came streaming out from the Kashmir and Ajmer Gates. The force that had exited the Kashmir Gate moved towards Ludlow Castle with several light field pieces and fired some desultory shots at the old mosque and centre batteries; the pickets replied in kind. The guns in the city then began firing, the 24-pounder battery at the Mori Bastion causing the most discomfort as the other guns fell short. Revd Rotton reports what the Kashmir Gate contingent did next:

> A rule seems to have prevailed in Delhi that troops who went out to fight should not return within the walls of the city sooner than four o'clock in the afternoon. So the rebels were said to have contented themselves upon this occasion with sitting down behind rocks, and smoking their hookahs, taking now and then a sly and occasional shot at us at a distance of 1,000 yards. This was their practice on the left; but their brethren on the right adopted another policy, often coming within 100 yards of our batteries.[5]

The rebels coming out of the Ajmer Gate, meanwhile, moved along the road to Rohtak. This force consisted of both cavalry and infantry along with twelve guns. Their aim, it was suspected, was to intercept a convoy carrying seven lakh rupees' worth of treasure and ammunition to the British camp. In response, Wilson sent around 200 men of HM75th under Capt. Brookes plus Coke's Rifles and eight guns under Major Tombs. Coke went north to Alipur but lost track of the rebel force and returned. The convoy was nonetheless saved by a hard rain, which bogged down the rebels and caused them to head back to the city.

The important Muslim festival of Eid-ul-Adha or Feast of Sacrifice fell on 1 August this year, and at first there was no fighting; indeed, it was thought that the Muslim soldiers in the rebel army would indulge in feasting instead. The rebels always attacked in the morning if they attacked at all; only once before had they attacked at night. As the sun set, however, a large contingent emerged and attacked the British pickets on the right flank and the ridge. Spies later informed the British that the attack was headed by the Neemuch contingent and sections of the Gwalior and Kotah rebels; the custom was to send new arrivals out to prove themselves, and it was their turn. In response, reinforcements were sent to man the breastworks at Hindu Rao. A huge amount of yelling and shouting filled the air as the rebels pushed for the position. Griffiths:

> Darkness came on – a lovely night, calm and clear without a cloud in the sky. The batteries on both sides kept up a terrific cannonade; and our men, effectually concealed behind the earth-works, poured incessant volleys of musketry into the enemy. The roar and din exceeded anything I had ever heard before, and formed one continuous roll, while all around the air was illumined by a thousand bright flashes of fire, exposing to our view the movements of the rebels. They had also thrown up breastworks at no great distance to our front, from behind which they sallied at intervals, returning, however, quickly under cover when our fire became too hot for them. And in this manner, without a moment's intermission, the combat continued all night long, with no advantage to the assailants, and with few casualties on our side.

The fighting continued into the next day, with fire at the British position maintained till around 2 p.m. when the rebel guns fell silent after seventeen hours. Finally, everybody could get some sleep. The fighting had cost the British fifty men killed and wounded. The rebels had lost 200 men just in front of the British position, and possibly others elsewhere. This was certainly the longest battle that had been fought between the two sides so far, and possibly the fiercest.

With some time to think now that the battle had died down, Wilson spent a while watching the constant flow of traffic on the bridge of boats across the Jumna. He decided that now was the time to blow it up. On 5 August, several rafts were loaded with barrels of gunpowder and readied around a mile upstream from the bridge. A slow fuse was lit so that the gunpowder should blow just when the rafts reached the bridge. However, two of the rafts caught on a sandbank and blew up prematurely. The third had a more promising journey but was spotted by rebels, and some gutsy individuals floated toward the raft on *massaks* (inflated sheep-skins) as it drifted down and managed to put out the fuse just before it blew. The raft was then towed to the river bank, with the gunpowder no doubt being utilised by the grateful rebel gunners.

Baird Smith was unperturbed by the failure:

> We are making efforts to-day to destroy the enemy's bridge, as yet without success. One of the infernal machines, popularly called 'devils,' stuck on a sandbank, and exploded, apropos to nothing in particular, with a diabolical row. There are five more to go off, so it is to be hoped one will reach its destination. These all act by explosion. We send off a huge raft this evening which is to act by pressure and obstructing the water-way. I wanted these operations to be connected with some others against the enemy himself, but the General doesn't like anything at all risky, and so when we've demolished the bridge we've got only to stand and admire our success, but get nothing from it.[6]

Apparently the scheme was to be tried again later in the day. Twelve marksmen from the Rifles were duly moved to the river bank to pick off any rebels who tried to intercept the second convoy of rafts, but the rafts weren't readied in time. In the end, the bridge was left alone. Hodson was authorised to offer 6,000 rupees to anyone inside the city who could engineer its destruction, but this scheme petered out.

A week later, the British force launched one of its first concerted attacks on an enemy position. Up to this point, Wilson had not attempted any large assault on the rebel positions in order to preserve his dwindling troop numbers before reinforcements justified an assault on the city walls. However, on 12 August it was decided to push the rebels from Ludlow Castle in order to alleviate pressure on the Metcalfe House picket. For several days, the rebels had been advancing on the picket. Moreover, their guns were within shooting range of the Flagstaff Tower. Wilson decided that enough was enough; these positions had to be recaptured and the rebels driven back into the city walls.

Early that day, Wilson met with his officers. Brigadier Showers was to lead the attack with a force comprising portions of the 75th Foot, the 1st and 2nd European Bengal Fusiliers, Coke's Rifles and also the Guides. With the attack would go four horse artillery guns of the 1st Troop 1st Brigade. Showers was to advance down the Flagstaff road while it was still dark and attack the rebel picket at Ludlow Castle. The attack was to be carried out with stealth while the guard was at its weakest and before the rebels could be reinforced. According to Zahir Dehlvi, the night guard manning the position was made up of some of the most undisciplined rebels:

> Now let me tell you a few things about the night guard. It was these very men who had looted the *bakshikhana* and the bank. They were often in a state of stupor thanks to drinking *bhang* and eating *kalakand* and *laddu peda* during the day. When they reached the *kothi*, they were alert at first, but when the night came and a cool breeze started blowing they were unable to stay awake. They kept the guns at an angle and, spreading their *dhotis*, fell into deep sleep.

Showers' surprise attack was a complete success. One man was even bayonetted while in the act of lifting up the portfire. Most of the rebel force retreated, leaving their guns. Four guns – two 9-pounders, one 6-pounder and a 24-pounder howitzer – were captured along with fourteen horses. Once the element of surprise was gone, however, the fight became intense. The British suffered 117 killed and wounded including officers, with Showers wounded along with Major Coke, Capt. Greville and Lt Owen, Lt Sherriff and Lt Lindsay. The rebels were said to have lost 300 men, with many wounded. Those left behind were shown no mercy by the British, who bayonetted them where they lay.

Around this time, the British camp was buoyed by the arrival of Brigadier John Nicholson with his sizeable force. Nicholson himself had ridden into camp on 8 August in advance of his column, which arrived within the week. The reinforcements he brought totalled 3,000 men (some say 4,200). Greathed was ecstatic:

> It was a fine sight this morning to see Nicholson's column march in. There were great greetings among both officers and men, and they received a hearty welcome...
>
> They are pitched close to us. They were followed by a splendid regiment of Seikhs, the biggest men I have seen for a long time; they also had a band. The column was played in by the 8th. Altogether it was a cheery sight and would have struck gloom among the Pandees, if they could have seen it. The battery is commanded by Bouchier so the best part of the force is connected with Meerut.[7]

The column consisted of HM52nd regiment (600 men), the left wing of HM61st from Ferozepore (around 400 men), a body of Multan horse (200), plus 1,200 Sikh and Punjabi soldiers. Also included was Bourchier's battery of European artillery. In all, roughly 1,100 of the troops were European. Also accompanying the force were two 24-pounders and three 18-pounders pulled by elephants. The column stretched for 13 miles. The British force now had more than 8,000 fighting men on the ridge and another 2,000 invalid, making 10,000 troops overall, although many of the sick had been moved to Ambala. As if this wasn't enough good news, word came in that the siege train vital to any attack on the city had finally left Ludhiana on 17 August. Meanwhile, the siege train from Ferozepore, escorted by a wing of the Belooch Battalion and a Punjab regiment, was just 75 miles away.

A new battery was completed on 22 August, 300 yards in the front of the Sammy House. The Sammy House, at the southern tip of the ridge, had till now been the most advanced post, closest to the city walls. The new battery had a trench leading to the Sammy House, and its purpose was to provide a staging post for the siege guns to hit the Mori gate once they came in. Existing batteries on the ridge overlooked the new one, protecting it. The rebels had heard the working parties toiling away over the last few days, but despite firing grape they were unable to prevent its construction.

By this time, the rebel batteries in the Kishanganj had been silenced. With the arrival of Nicholson's column, it was now suggested that the British position be widened to encompass the Kishanganj area and attempt to take hold of the Eidgah ridge – the natural extension of the ridge southwards, which faced the western and south-western walls of the city. However, Wilson felt that such a move would stretch the British line too far. The current position could support the greater troop numbers and was well protected. With the siege train expected imminently and an expectation that the guns would be stationed to the north of the city, a strong force would be required at the line of operations. The entire force would stay on the ridge, and the western walls and gates would go undisturbed.

# 29

# '... no money whatever remains in the Treasury'

> The Bareilly mutineers are out of heart and demand their pay. They are promised payment when they take the Hill batteries. It is not unlikely that they will refuse to attack without their pay.
>
> G. C. Barnes, Commissioner and Superintendent, Cis-Sutlej States[1]

By the middle of July, Zafar was struggling to pay his troops. Almost two months after the sepoys had appeared at Delhi, almost all the money was gone. Even the considerable hoard brought by the Bareilly brigade seems to have been exhausted. Zafar had begun warning Mirza Mughal on 8 July that 'a very small balance of cash remains in our Treasury ... there is no immediate prospect of revenue from any quarter ... the little money which remains must of necessity be very soon expended'.[2] He asked the prince to collect together the officers of the army so that the issue of raising new funds could be addressed. They were to come up with schemes as a matter of great urgency:

> It is a necessary measure of prudence and precaution, to make arrangements in this matter before the Treasury is quite exhausted. Moreover, as no private Treasury was ever kept by us, and as the contributions to the State loan have not been realised, all our servants, old and new, are now in pecuniary difficulties. The money amounting to a lac and twenty thousand rupees, which was levied last month as a loan at interest from the merchants of the City for our private expenses was not all received accordingly. Under these circumstances, how are the expenses of others to be provided for? You will explain all these points, particularly and clearly, to each officer, and have their answer put into writing, and will not fail to submit it tomorrow of our consideration.[3]

Mirza Mughal duly assembled the court of officers and several schemes on raising revenue were mooted. Typically, the first idea was that further loans should be extracted from the merchants in the city, to be paid off when the British force was annihilated and order restored, at which point revenue collection could fill the royal coffers.

The second idea was to secure revenue collection by sending a sizeable force of around 2,000 men (1,500 infantry and 500 cavalry with two guns) around the nearby villages and towns to reassure people that the new government was here to stay and its revenue collection effort was legitimate. To effect this, police stations would be established along with revenue offices. The *dak* (postal service) was to be re-established. The sepoy force would then begin to collect the revenue, although Mirza Mughal understandably opined that 'it should be thoroughly impressed on all its members, that such of them as shall commit any act of plunder, tyranny or oppression will be severely punished'. A senior noble of the court should go with the sepoys to inspire confidence. This nobleman, too, would be warned about taking bribes or oppressing the people.

In line with the first idea, Zafar asked local traders and businessmen for a loan of 20 lakh rupees. Perhaps understandably, they immediately raised their hands in protest. How could they provide such money when it was proving so difficult to carry out their business? With anarchy both inside and outside the city, they were trading little if they were trading at all. Some urged the authorities to search their homes; go and see if you can find any money.

As word spread that the treasury was empty, the troops grew restless. On 13 July, Mirza Mughal informed his father that many troops were reneging on their agreement to accept monthly payment. A risaldar of the 1st Lucknow Irregular Cavalry named Karim Baksh, for example, presented a petition to the prince on 12 July asking that his regiment receive daily payment; other regiments were already paid this way, he noted. He also requested arrears of payment amounting to nineteen days for his regiment. Troops who had recently arrived from Hansi and Hissar joined the clamour; in their petition they reminded the King that they had brought in money from British treasuries and had dutifully paid the money into the royal treasury.[4] They risked their lives daily in fighting, they declared, and wanted their salaries to be paid. Zafar agreed to pay them one month's salary for the time being. 'The real state of the matter is, that these people have learned that there is very little money in the Treasury, and it is on this account they now apply for daily allowances,'[5] complained Mirza Mughal. Zafar in response stressed that those who were paid monthly would have to remain on that schedule.

By 15 July, arrangements were finally hammered out for a loan from the reluctant city merchants, a rate of interest of 1 per cent being offered.[6] Whether the merchants were browbeaten, cajoled or threatened into agreeing is unclear, but it was known that those who refused to cooperate had been arrested and incarcerated in the palace – presumably until they agreed to pay up. However, in such troubled times even these arrests didn't go smoothly; relatives of those arrested sometimes bribed the sepoy guards, who let them go.[7]

Fortunately for Zafar, the very same day a *harkara* (courier) named Megh Raj reported that a large amount of treasure was being brought into the city by the 14th Irregulars and others from Jhansi. When the treasure arrived, it was immediately parcelled out among the troops. Each sowar would receive 610 rupees, and each sepoy 400 rupees. Camp followers received 100 rupees and fakirs were given twenty-five rupees. The contingent also brought two elephants from the Rani of Jhansi as a present for the King. This influx of money relieved Zafar's worries for a little while, but as ever it would only hold off the inevitable. Two weeks later, things were once again looking dismal. On 28 July, Zafar wrote an order to Mirza Mughal:

> Son, – The illustrious and valiant Mirza Zohur-ud-din, otherwise Mirza Mughal, Commander-in-Chief Bahadur! Learn that no money whatever remains in the Treasury for paying the daily and monthly allowances of the Troops, nor yet for defraying the daily urgent expenses of the Magazine, the Artillery, and the manufacture of powder. Without powder the active operations against the infidels must be interrupted.

The merchant creditors were to pay up any of the money they had yet to provide, and they should be enticed with the promise that their cooperation would see them considered for important positions. However, threats would do just as well:

> But if, notwithstanding such assurances, and the hopes of advantages thus held out, any of the people mentioned do not exert themselves to arrange for the money, but advance unfounded excuses, you, our Son, are empowered to chastise them as may be proper, so that severity may bring them to the path of propriety, and obedience to our Royal orders may be the result, and the expenses of the Magazine, the Artillery, and the manufacture of powder, may not be interrupted, and all necessary operations may be prosecuted daily.[8]

Such was the need that the money was arranged to be paid into the treasury within three days. Many of the merchants still baulked at the excessive demands, but on 6 August Mirza Mughal announced that they had finally agreed to advance loans. While they acquiesced, the merchants nevertheless suggested that all inhabitants of the city be urged to contribute according to their means. In this fashion, a much larger sum could be collected, and more equitably: 'The Hindus will be assured that your majesty regards Hindus and Mussalmans with equal favour, and the army will see, that the whole of the inhabitants, whether Hindus or Mussalmans, are sharers in the arrangements for raising funds to meet its expenses.'[9]

As for the second idea, about sending men out in a show of force to collect revenue from Delhi's surrounds, around 4 August Bakht Khan attempted to send some of his soldiers out for this purpose. However, his fellow officers were apparently jealous when they heard of the plan. 'Dissensions have arisen in consequence,' wrote a spy to the British. 'There is no end to the daily quarrels and jealousies. No pay has been issued now for 20 days. The soldiers complain loudly, and many intend to leave.'[10]

To supplement the revenue from loans and taxation of the surrounding villages, Mirza Mughal suggested creating a city mint so that precious metals might be converted into coin.[11] A man had already offered to carry out the work of the mint on contract. Zafar agreed to the plan, although it is unclear today whether anything came of it.

By 8 August, some 40,000 rupees had been collected from Punjabi merchants. It was not enough. Three days later, a desperate Zafar issued a proclamation urging the people of the city to chip in. He also asked for volunteers to help fight the British:

> To all Hindus and Mahomedans who wish the advancement of Religion. Be it known to you That Falak ud Din Shah being one of those who have pledged themselves to fight for the Mahomedan faith in the religious war against the infidels and being director of finance and the army is sent to collect ghazis as well as money for the expenses of the armies bestowed by God which have come from all directions and have assembled at the royal threshold for the destruction of the Christians and which have already sent thousands of the British soldiery and others of the English to hell. It is incumbent on you to consider well your own advantage and to forward to the royal presence such amounts of treasure as he may determine at the same time sending your accredited agent also. You will moreover give the above named Falak ud din Shah such aid in military forces for arrangements on the way and for the slaughter of Christians as he may demand. Those who will join in the cause of the faith and of religion will receive distinctions and those who will confederate with the Christians will be utterly despoiled of life and property.[12]

Paradoxically, the lack of pay was keeping large numbers of soldiers in the city as the rebel cause flagged during August; they couldn't go anywhere else. Some soldiers began looting again. In early September this included the brazen robbing of the shop of a tinker called Pirbaksh Beg in the palace itself. The tinker supplied culinary vessels and other materials to the royal household. The soldiers, in their pique, destroyed the tinker's forge and occupied his house.[13]

By late August, the lack of money gave rise to curious rumours that a considerable number of guns had been buried in the grounds of the

Salimgarh Fort during a previous age. These claims were being made by old servants and veteran palace workers who also said that substantial amounts of treasure had been buried around the fortress by earlier emperors for safekeeping; they even pointed to the spots where the gold could be found.[14] The result was a bizarre scene in which the fort's grounds were pockmarked with makeshift excavations. Nothing was found.

The cash-flow issues were exacerbated by the fact that the princes were still siphoning off money. Embezzlement wasn't limited to the princes either; the Raja of Bullubgarh, for instance, had sent 10,000 rupees in recent days but the money had been appropriated by the queen, Zeenat Mahal. The council, deciding they had to bring such chicanery to an end, directed the people of the city to pay money only to the secure 'Kote'. The blatant corruption of the princes combined disastrously with the desperation of the soldiers to bring matters to a head on 1 September, when spies reported a large tumult in the palace as soldiers demanded money from Zafar.

Toorab Ali described three princes – Mirza Mughal, Abulbakr and Khizr Sultan – being present along with the various officers of each of the regiments. Other men of various regiments, a group of around 500 soldiers, could be seen milling around the Diwan-i-Khas wanting their say. These men would surround the princes, voicing their own suspicions about them and about Ahsan Ulla Khan. They shouted for the latter's death and called for the princes to be imprisoned; once this was done, they said, they would divide the city into sectors, with each sector given over to a certain regiment. The regiments would then extort money directly from their sector if pay wasn't forthcoming. Toorab Ali describes what happened next:

> The king declared he had no pay to give them. The troops rejoined that in that case they would plunder both the palace and the city and massacre all the court. Upon this the King rose and threw down the hassock on which he usually sits in Durbar, and gave orders that all the property of the court, the horses, elephants, caparisons and even the ornaments of his Begums [wives] should be immediately made over to them, and then turning his face towards Mecca he burst into tears, exclaiming that he was well punished for his sins. Had he been included in the massacre of the English, he might have been spared this humiliation. Hearing these passionate cries, the whole court and the Begums were moved to tears and even the soldiers were ashamed of their violence, excusing themselves on account of the extreme distress and hunger to which they were reduced.[15]

As tempers cooled, an agreement was hammered out. The King would raise 40,000 rupees – the amount it was estimated he could scrape together – and Mirza Mughal would hand it over as a first instalment.

The agreement on how to pay the troops was settled as follows: a risaldar would receive 12 rupees, a naib risaldar 8, a jemadar 6, a duffadar 5, a trooper 3, a sepoy 2 and a camp follower 1.[16] This reduced salaries to a third of what they had been. Even at these measly rates, it was difficult to work out where the money would come from. Zafar had evidently decided to use whatever he had left. Gowree Shunkur reported silver being stripped from ornaments, furniture and items of state including the King's *howdahs* as well as the various staffs of office.[17] All silver utensils in the palace were collected to melt down. Even this was insufficient, and so a call went out to raise additional money from the city's already burdened population. 'One lac of rupees is to be raised from the city people, Mooftee Suddur-ood-deen being security on behalf of the Mussulmans and Lalla Mokund Lall on behalf of the Hindoos,' reported British spy Futteh Mahomed. 'These two have agreed to pay this sum in 15 days, but hope that the city will fall to the English before that date.'

In their desperation, the sepoys contemplated various forms of harassment and torture. Toorab Ali records two of the moonshees of the palace – Aga Jan and Waris Alli – having been intimidated into promising to pay 1,000 rupees each on 31 August. However, with the money not forthcoming the soldiers threatened torture. They heated the ramrods of their muskets, declaring they would burn holes in the moonshees' bodies till the money appeared.[18] Aga Jan bravely replied that they could kill him, but his relations stepped in to pay for him. Other citizens, tiring of the continuous demands, had other methods to avoid payment. Mooftee Sudder-soddeen was one of these, for instance, decided to spend his money on forming a guard instead of submitting to threats. Barnes reported on this: 'He was sent for to the palace in order to get money out of him, but he would not go. He summoned a lot of fanatics to his house, and engaged to give them 24 Rs. a day for rations. He not only refused to pay, but threatened the Palace folks with raising a war and of dying in arms against them. It is more commendable, he said, to attack and fight such people than to wage a religious war against the English.'[19] By September, other bankers and traders in the city were plucking up their courage and refusing to extend or honor loans.

*****

If there was one piece of good news in the city during July and August, it was the relative peace between the Muslims and Hindus. Indeed, this unity had been put to the test. Eid-ul-Adha had occurred on 1 August, marking the day when Muslims commemorated Abraham and his willingness to sacrifice his son. Plenty of animals were slaughtered in the city during the festival; sheep and goats were the norm, but there was fresh concern that some Muslims would flout the law on killing cows. In order to prevent this, as early as 9 July Zafar had announced that killing kine would be punishable by death – specifically, transgressors would be blown from a gun. With tensions rising as Eid approached, another proclamation was made on the 28th:

> The people of God, the country of the King and order of the chief of the army,
>
> Whoever during this festival of Baqre Eid or prior or after it sacrifices cow, oxen, calf or she calf, buffalo or she buffalo secretly in his house, he would be regarded as enemy of the Emperor and he would be put to death and who ever falsely makes allegations after inquiry by the court and if the allegation is proved to be correct the offenders would be punished otherwise who makes allegation would be given death punishment.

To lessen opportunities, Zafar forbade animal traders to bring in cows, oxen or buffalo for the six days prior to Eid. Mubarak Shah, *kotwal* of Delhi, was given orders to count all cows owned by Muslims before and after the feast day. Furthermore, he was to gather all cows and remove them from their Muslim owners for the duration of the festival. Such measures greatly bolstered respect for Zafar in the Hindu community and helped maintain harmony. However, given the number of cows in the city the order proved difficult to enforce. Some in the Muslim population instead suggested a signed guarantee by Muslim owners that they would not slaughter cows during the festival.

Despite the precautions, some in the Muslim population were apparently determined to flout the law. On 29 July, Rajab Ali reported Hindu soldiers killing five Muslim butchers for ignoring the order and continuing to kill kine. G. C. Barnes suggested to Lawrence that this was part of a wider rift between the Hindus and Muslims in the city:

> Dissensions have sprung up and increase daily between the Hindoos and Mahomedans. The King, with the view of preventing an open rupture, has also lately interdicted the sale of beef and even goat's flesh. The Mahomedan fanatics are greatly disgusted, and vow they will offer a sacrificial cow in the open street on the day of the Eed, and if the Hindoo sepoys try to prevent it, then they will wage a religious warfare with them, and die as martyrs for the faith, or conquer. It is equal glory to die in battle with the opponents of cow-killing as with the detested Feringhees [Europeans]. First, they say, we will settle this dispute, and then we will turn our arms against the Feringhees. It is very likely indeed that there will be bloodshed and fighting among themselves on the day of the Eed.

In the event, the festival passed largely without incident. Zafar's approach appears to have been successful. The rebels fired a royal salute to commemorate the festival, and Zafar himself sacrificed a camel to mark the occasion.

# 30

# A Shortage of Gunpowder

> The sepoys obey no orders. Assaults are planned, but the sepoys refuse to execute them. Those who do go out loiter here and there, sneak back at night ... The numbers of the rebels may be from 20,000 to 25,000 men, but there are few fighting men among them.[1]
>
> Letter to H. H. Greathed, 20 August 1857

As August wore on, rebel efforts to cannonade the British position were increasingly hampered by dwindling supplies of gunpowder. Zafar had been warned as early as 20 June that the gunpowder in the Delhi magazine was all but gone. Local manufacture had filled the gap, but the gunners were expending so much on a daily basis that the powder makers in the city could not keep up with demand. Zafar therefore asked Mirza Mughal to arrange for groups to search the city for gunpowder barrels, presumably looking for those looted from the magazine on 11 May. He also asked the prince to urgently pursue the purchase of more materials for increased production.[2] Some regiments still had the stocks of gunpowder they had brought with them, but they proved reluctant to share. According to Mirza Khizr Sultan, the 74th NI at the Lahore Gate were sitting on a healthy 232 barrels; meanwhile, the guns at the Kashmir Gate, which were using up the most powder, only had seventy barrels left.

By 27 June, sufficient saltpetre for the manufacture of gunpowder had been obtained and large vessels were sited in the godowns of the city for its refinement. One of the main areas for production was just behind the Jama Masjid. 'Immense preparations are being made for the manufacture of gunpowder under the superintendence of Mirza Mogul,' Barnes reported to Lawrence on 5 July.[3] Spies estimated the production rate to be somewhere from 6 to 15 maunds (roughly 200–600 kilograms) every day, depending on supply levels and the weather. Over six rainy days at the end of July, the rebels produced just 20 maunds.

With the authorities failing to organise the equitable distribution of gunpowder, Rajab Ali reported that the shortage triggered a rush to stockpile: 'The 74th and 54th have a private stock of 500 maunds of powder, which they will not give up. They say they know their lives are forfeited, as they raised the rebellion. They keep this powder for emergencies. There are about 400 maunds cutcha of saltpetre, but no sulphur, in Delhee.'

On the afternoon of 7 August, a large explosion rocked the city after a makeshift magazine in the city caught fire. The entire building was destroyed, with many casualties. Zahir Dehlvi reckoned as many as 700 men were killed in the explosion.[4] From his house he could see a huge column of smoke and dust climbing into the sky. At the scene, a huge crowd converged to dig out dead relatives. Nearby houses caught fire. Desperate people clawed at the rubble all night. On top of the fatalities, a further 100 people were estimated to have been wounded. The death toll could well have been worse had the building contained more than a humble 20 maunds of powder; so acute was the shortage of gunpowder in the city that it was taken away as quickly as it was produced, meaning the magazines were usually almost empty. The explosion was quickly noticed on the ridge, and the British troops reacted with jubilation, as Greathed describes:

> As we were returning along the ridge towards the Flagstaff my attention was directed towards the city and I saw a magnificent column of white smoke arise. It shot straight into the air and then assumed the shape of a mighty mushroom and slowly floated on. It ignited by accident and carried with it into the air some 500 artificers employed in the manufactory and the stock of sulphur and saltpetre. There was of course great cheering from the batteries though we could not claim the credit of the explosion.

There would be recriminations. In their anger, the sepoys would turn on Zafar's physician, Ahsan Ulla Khan. Claiming to have unearthed a letter written by him to the British camp, they set fire to his house. Barnes reported that Ahsan Ulla Khan was forced to stay in the fort for his own protection, with only the King's influence protecting him:

> The soldiery demanded his surrender and even menaced the King's life, and those of his family, if their wishes were not complied with. At last the King gave up the Hakeem into their hands, but said that if his life was injured he would not survive his servant. For this purpose the King always carries about his person a small diamond. [It was the belief in those days that swallowing a diamond would mean death.] Zeenut Muhul is also an object of strong suspicion.

As the days went by, others were suspected of complicity. The man in charge of the elephant stud was also suspected of having a hand in the destruction of the magazine, seemingly because he happened to live nearby.

The destroyed magazine had been in the south of the city, safely away from the range of British guns. However, spies now began reporting the manufacture of powder at a property in the north of the city. If the British guns could be brought closer to the walls, they said, the new manufactory would be in range.[5]

By 12 August, Rajab Ali was reporting serious issues with the quality of the powder that was being produced. 'A gun cartridge was taken out of the ammunition waggon seized along with the four guns on the 12th and opened in camp,' he reported. 'It was filled with new powder, very coarse and of inferior quality. This fact confirms the reports that they have no good powder left, but are obliged to make their daily supply. Shortly brimstone [sulphur] will run short, and then they will not be able to make even this powder, bad as it is.' Another spy reported this issue on the same day: 'Some good gunpowder for small arms has been obtained from the merchants in the city. But the powder for the guns is very poor. Ahmad Mirza Khan has supplied 500 maunds of good saltpeter.'[6] The latter spy also reported that the rebels were forced to cast their own musket barrels, cartridges and cannon balls, with predictable results.[7]

The acquisition of sulphur continued to prove problematic as the weeks wore on. Extensive searches continued within the city. Toorab Ali reported on 14 August that sulphur was being seized from shops, with 35 maunds being taken from one shop alone. On 16 August, no powder was manufactured due to the dearth of sulphur. Finally, the Delhi regiments were successfully cajoled into sharing 150 maunds they had appropriated from the British magazine in May.

By 20 August, reports were emerging that charcoal, equally essential in the manufacture of gunpowder, was being made from bamboo instead of hardwood. A week later, spies related that 50 maunds of gunpowder were being produced daily; the guns were using at least this much each day. By the beginning of September, the issue of the shortage of sulphur was once again acute. It was thought that supplies could be obtained from Rewaree, and moves were made to arrange this. 'The day before yesterday 27 barrels of gun-powder newly manufactured were carried off to the palace, and about 60 maunds in an incomplete state are lying in the manufactory,' wrote Barnes on 1 September. 'No more sulphur is to be had at any price. On account of the badness of the powder recently made, some fire-work makers of Coel were sent for to Delhee, but they have not come.'[8] The next day, the production of gunpowder was halted completely. All supplies of sulphur in the city had been depleted.

Another significant problem arose at this time. By 27 August, the supply of ammunition guncaps was running out in the city. Although grapeshot and round shot could be cast more easily, manufacturing gun caps wasn't easy. Toorab Ali wrote that just two blacksmiths, Alla Buksh and Hussain Buksh, were tasked with their manufacture. It is unlikely that the two men alone could have kept up with demand.

*****

If the problems regarding ammunition weren't enough, there was continuing friction between the various regiments and their officers. On 16 July, it was reported that the Delhi and Meerut regiments were deeply unhappy to discover that, having given up all their treasure to the palace, the Bareilly brigade was keeping its hoard for itself. If the King would not demand they hand over the money, they would force the brigade to share it with the original mutineers.[9] The Bareilly soldiers, meanwhile, had their own issues with the Delhi and Meerut regiments. 'The Bareilly mutineers accused the 54th of shirking duty, and said that the 54th sit at ease and count their money,' Barnes told Lawrence on 22 July. 'After much wrangling, it was at last settled that four regiments should go out daily, and every regiment should take its share of the fighting.'[10] Other regiments also complained of a lack of support. The 14th Regiment Irregulars, for instance, dismounted and fought on 20 July without any other regiments helping, and lost ten sowars killed and sixty wounded. 'Their Resaldars, Muhammad Hyat Khan and Fya Tulb Khan, were much annoyed, and openly declared they would not fight again,' Barnes reported.

Perhaps in light of these complaints, by August the rebel force had been reorganised into four divisions – Delhee, Bareilly, Nusseerabad and Ferozepore – with the main rebel brigades being the core of each division. The divisions were roughly equal in size, with six infantry regiments and roughly 1,000 sowars accompanied by a certain amount of artillery. The plan was for the divisions to take turns attacking the British position. In this way there would be constant pressure on the enemy. Quite why nobody considered a concerted attack by *all* divisions is unclear. Predictably, strong coordination and *esprit de corps* remained elusive. Complaints about one regiment or another failing to support an attack were commonplace. In one petition, Ghulam Mu'id-ud-din Khan, one of the foremost risaldars, expressed his disgust at the general passivity evident in many of the regiments.

> To the King! Shelter of the World!
>
> Respectfully Sheweth, – That your slave has come to this city from Tonk, accompanied by nearly 500 men who are organised as a body, and by nearly 1,500 besides, who have come devoting their lives, to fight in the religious war against the infidels. That he and his followers joined in the attack yesterday, that eighteen infidels were dispatched to hell by your slave's own hand, and that five of his followers were killed and five wounded.

> Your Majesty! The rest of the army gave us no help whilst we were engaged in combat with the infidels. Had they even stood by, only to make a show of support, it was to have been expected that with the help of Providence, a complete victory would yesterday have been obtained. But there is no remedy against the will of God. I trust that some arms, together with some trifling funds, may be bestowed on my followers, so that they may have the strength to fight against and slay the infidels, and in doing this, may realise their desire.

One moulvi bravely criticised the rebels and suggested a different path. They had mutinied for their own aggrandisement, he said, and not for religion. They had no hope for victory considering their fitful performance; surely it would be better to try and obtain terms from the British? If amnesty was not forthcoming, so be it.[11]

Meanwhile, the various subedars of the regiments remained at loggerheads. Generals Gauss Khan and Sidhari Singh of the Neemuch brigades in particular were blinded by jealousy. Both were supporters of Mirza Mughal, and they were still smarting from Bakht Khan's appointment. So bad did the situation become that they were said to have held back their troops during the daily skirmishing, forcing Bakht Khan and his column to fight on alone. Not content with this, they accused the commander of being a British spy, claiming his failure to capture the British position on the ridge was due to his secret association with the British.

If one thing united the officers, it was the knowledge that mutiny rendered their lives forfeit. The only option was to keep going. On 14 August, therefore, with bad news and dissension dogging the ranks, it was decided that another compact between the officers was required. In a tense meeting between the King and the officers, a general agreement was reached. Toorab Ali reported on it:

> This morning a general assembly of all the Native officers of the force took place. Each throw a pinch of salt into a lotah of water (thereby swearing that as the salt dissolved in the water so might they dissolve and melt away if they proved faithless to their oath). It was settled that as the English would never spare them, so no one should be afraid to meet death. No one should return from battle alive. Either he should give up his life in the field or conquer… [12]

Zafar, in his apathy, asked why the rebels were having no success. 'It is evident that you cannot compete with the small British Force in camp,' he lamented, 'so it is better for you to crave their mercy, and not to destroy both the city and me.'[13] Declaring he would surrender himself to the British, he ordered his elephant readied but was talked down from the ledge.

On 20 August, Zafar held a durbar at which the men of the Meerut brigade were granted an opportunity to voice their concerns. Their issue, they said, was that Bakht Khan and other subedars had been given the roles of generals and colonels. These men never personally went out to do battle, they complained, and still held on to the treasure they had brought with them. The Meerut brigade, meanwhile, had been going out nearly every day to do battle and had handed over all its treasure. Despite their sacrifices, they were not even being paid. Such was the anger that the soldiers threatened violence in the city. 'Our intention is to plunder the palace and the town and to start for some place where we can maintain ourselves. You can defend your city with your Generals and Colonels,' a spy named Data Ram quoted. Zafar tried to reason with them, but the soldiers would not listen, shouting abuse and generally showing much insolence in their bearing towards the King.

After these talks, the conduct of war was once again reordered near the end of August. A new system was agreed upon in which a ten-man court of administration would oversee all orders. Six councillors came from the army (two from the artillery, two from infantry and two from cavalry), and four were selected by the King.[14] Two councillors were chosen to become president and vice-president. The Military Court of Administration, as it became known, was neither western nor oriental in its makeup and held two kinds of meetings. One was the ordinary daily meeting, which typically lasted five hours a day. The other was a kind of emergency meeting which could be called anytime day or night depending on the circumstances.

Generally, the council proved no better than the previous setup; the friction between the Bareilly and Neemuch generals had not subsided. They were united on one matter, however: payment. On 22 August, an order was issued to the army: 'When complete victory shall have been obtained, and the revenues of the conquered countries shall again, as heretofore, be paid into the treasury, the pay of the troops will be regulated according to the following scale' the proclamation began.[15] A trooper of regular cavalry would receive 20 rupees a month, and a private in the regular infantry 10 rupees; other irregular troopers would receive 14 rupees, and irregular infantry would receive 8 rupees. 'The monthly allowances of all others will be fixed by reference to their qualifications and exertions, and as the protection of the people is very much desired, all those who will oppress or ill-use them will receive due punishment. You are urged to trust in God's blessing, and cherish full hopes of victory, and of the realization of the revenue, and, thus animated, to exert every energy for the welfare of the State, and with full confidence of success, to fight with courage and intrepidity.'[16]

*****

There were days of optimism inside the rebel camp. News of cholera wreaking havoc in the British camp raised spirits considerably. Arriving reinforcements provided frequent chances for celebration too, as did news of uprisings elsewhere in the country. On 13 July, for instance, news reached Delhi of the supposed fall of Agra, and Zafar ordered a twenty-one-gun salute to mark the occasion. Much rejoicing could be seen in the palace, and the musicians of the regiments played jovial tunes on their English flutes, clarinets and drums.[17] 'The king constantly upbraids the rebels with their defeats,' Barnes wrote, '[but] they quiet him by saying "our forces are on the increase day by day, whereas the English Army gets no reinforcements. We must win in the end."'[18]

However, the lack of pay, petty rivalries among the officers and dwindling gunpowder supplies gradually sapped the morale of the army as time went on. Spirits dropped amid recriminations as to who was to blame for the failure of the day's attack. At other times, perhaps when there was little sign of payment, other frustrations came to the fore. According to intelligence Greathed had received in August, the sepoys were getting most disconsolate at their lack of ability to capture the ridge:

> The effects of the Pandees failing to make any impression on our position after having received their last reinforcements are already visible. To cover the disgrace of their failure they for the first time exaggerate their losses and estimate them at 3000 men and they openly tell the king they have no chance of taking our batteries and numbers are asking for leave to return to their homes to protect their families as their safety is endangered by the presence of our forces in Oude. We may therefore soon expect their power of resistance to be diminished while ours will be largely increased by the 18th of this month.

As August progressed, the malaise within the rebel camp grew. Desertions became commonplace. On 14 August, Toorab Ali reported that around 1,500 sepoys and troopers had deserted in recent days. The Nawab of Kumooud, who was supporting the rebels, had decided to leave the city given the disorganised manner of the rebel army. 'In the 62nd Regiment scarcely 100 men are left for duty. Some have been killed and some deserted on 11 August,' Ali wrote. Other spies gave different figures. On 16 August, according to information supplied by another spy, Mohumud Shuffee of the 8th Irregulars, as many as 3,000 sepoys had fled the city in the last four days. On 17 August, an informer called Sedoo reported to the British that 200 sepoys had deserted the day before disguised as *fakirs*. Ten sepoys lately enrolled who had also decided to leave were caught however. On 18 August, an even more damming report emerged: 'The mutineers quarrel more and more every day, and many desert. At least 1,000 men have lately deserted ... the sepoys inside the city are all ready to desert, but wait for their pay.'[19]

Around 20 August, British informant Data Ram entered the city. According to him, roughly 1,000 rebels – both infantry and cavalry – had deserted the city over the preceding three days. So bad was organisation in the army that the officers did not know how many men remained in each rebel regiment.[20]

Attacks on the British position were petering out. Food and money were scarce. While the rebel sepoys were getting some sort of pay, albeit intermittent, the jihadis were having less luck and had begun to drift off. In order to increase morale, the officers told the troops that as many as twenty-two battalions of infantry and ten regiments of cavalry on their way up from Bombay, and would reach Delhi in little over a week. There was also talk of mutinies among the sepoy regiments in the Punjab. However, the lack of money in the treasury could not be explained away. They men would not fight without their pay. Either the officers organised their pay, or they would go home – or resort to plunder.

On 14 August, the British force attempted a count of all the regiments and men that had reached the city based on observations and reports from spies. G. C. Barnes estimated around 4,000 cavalry and 12,000 infantrymen in the city, supplemented by 1,000 cavalry and 3,000 infantry from undisciplined levies.[21]

## 31

# The Battle of Najafgarh

Their general Bhukt Khan is accused of being in league with us.
H. H. Greathed, 27 August 1857

On 25 August, the rebels launched what proved to be their last major attempt to take the initiative. They knew that the British siege train making its way from the north would provide the rapidly expanding force on the ridge with the means to destroy the city walls, which would spell certain defeat for the mutineers. The siege train had to be stopped.

On the 24th, a large contingent of rebel troops was readied to march due west to fool the British camp into thinking significant elements of the rebel force were either deserting or leaving the city for some other destination. This force was then to veer clockwise and backtrack northwards on to the road to Ambala to intercept the British convoy as it travelled south. A force of 6,000 men – some sources say as many as 9,000 – was readied with thirteen guns. The bulk of the force came from the Neemuch and Nusseerabad brigades, and there were also men from the Kotah contingents. The Bareilly brigade would act as the vanguard, with Bakht Khan leading his own brigade.

Under the watchful eyes of the British, the large force marched out of the Lahore and Ajmer Gates on the western walls. The bulk of the force travelled 15 miles west and crossed the canal near the village of Najafgarh before making camp there. Bakht Khan, however, kept his Bareilly force on the eastern side of the canal. According to Zahir Dehlvi, the other officers asked Bakht Khan why his men were not crossing with the rest of the army. Khan's reply made sense: the British could simply blow the bridge if his men crossed, cutting them off from the city.

Shortly after the bulk of the rebel army had crossed the canal, an unusually heavy downpour inundated the already waterlogged area. The northward advance had to be delayed. Such was the ferocity of the rain that some of the men in Sidhari Singh's camp, sited in a hollow near the Najafgarh Lake, were submerged to their waists. It was decided that the camp would remain at Najafgarh till rain abated.

In the British camp, a force under Brigadier Nicholson was organised and sent to pursue the rebel force early on the 25th. Nicholson had around 2,500 men and eighteen guns. His force consisted of 1,600 infantry and four squadrons of cavalry (450 men) from HM61st, the 1st European Fusiliers, the 2nd Punjab Infantry (Sikhs), Coke's Rifles and a party of sappers and miners under Lt Geneste of the Engineer Corps. Accompanying the force was a squadron of 9th Lancers under Capt. Sarel as well as the Guide Cavalry and the Multan Horse. A familiar figure from the beginning of the mutiny came along with the party: Sir Theophilus Metcalfe, the magistrate, who knew Delhi and its surrounds better than most and so acted as a guide.

Leaving around 4 a.m., Nicholson marched north, before turning off the Grand Trunk Road to follow the road going west. The objective was to reach a small village called Nanglooi 6 miles distant. The severe rains that were hampering the rebels hit the British force too: 'The day was very wet, and the roads were well-nigh impassable; the country for miles round was nothing more than a marsh,' wrote Revd Rotton. A brief rest of two hours was called before the march resumed at noon. The men found themselves ankle deep in mud on the road, and when they had to traverse swampy ground they sank to their waists; it proved necessary to carry ammunition pouches on their heads to prevent spoiling. Camels struggled in the muddy swamps, spilling their burdens and further slowing progress. The guns kept getting stuck and had to be hauled out by hand. The short journey to Nanglooi took more than three hours.

When the first men reached the village, they learned that the rebel army was just 12 miles away at Najafgarh. It was another six hours before the guns were dragged into Nanglooi, but Nicholson opted to move his men ahead. By 4 p.m., he had sighted the rebel force. His men crossed the canal via a nearby ford, the passage inexplicably left unguarded by the nearby rebels. Less than two hours later, the opposing lines came within sight of one other.

On hearing of Nicholson's approach, the rebel officers had organised their line adjacent to the canal; the right was anchored at the bridge across the canal and the left at a large serai on the outskirts of Najafgarh. In all, the line stretched for roughly a mile and a half. Four guns had been placed in the serai, while nine guns were spread along the line. According to some British accounts, the rebels had constructed entrenchments with parapets and embrasures. This seems unlikely given the swampy conditions and the fact that the rebels hadn't expected Nicholson's force; it is more likely that some makeshift defences were thrown up as scouts returned with news of Nicholson's imminent approach.

Night was coming on fast, but Nicholson was reluctant to delay battle until the next day. He moved his force forward, leaving 120 Punjab

Horse and a contingent of the 2nd Punjab Infantry to protect the baggage. 'One hundred men from each corps formed the reserve,' wrote Major Norman. 'The 61st Foot, 1st Bengal Fusiliers, and 2nd Punjaub Infantry were formed up with the Artillery on either flank, supported by the 9th Lancers and Cavalry of the Guide corps.' HM61st and the 1st Bengal Fusiliers were led by Nicholson himself; to their right, those of the 2nd Punjab Infantry not left with the baggage advanced. Rather than advancing directly opposite the rebel line, Nicholson cantered his line on the village of Najafgarh. If he could capture the serai on the rebel left, it would be relatively easy to veer inside and roll up the rest of the rebels.

Before advancing, Nicholson rode along the line offering encouraging words and advising the men to hold their fire until they were close to the rebel line, and then to charge with fixed bayonets. 'Remember, men, the experience which others have gained,' he said. 'Take for your example the 93rd, and other regiments in the Crimea, who spurned to waste ammunition while at a distance from the enemy. Reserve your fire for a close range, and victory will be yours.'[1] He then gave the order: 'Line advance!' The men moved off with a cheer. As soon as they were within 200 yards of the rebel line, he ordered the charge.

The battle was short and swift, with the rebels failing to show much resistance. When roughly 100 yards separated the lines, the British fired a volley and charged at the serai. Lt Gabbett was the first man to reach the building, making it through an embrasure before falling to a rebel bayonet. The serai was soon taken without much difficulty, and four guns with it. The rebels fled. After this, the line advanced along the rebel position, capturing the other nine guns. 'Now the sepoys tried the efficacy of flight: they made for the bridge, and there vainly endeavoured to maintain a stand,' Revd Rotton recalled. 'It was worse than useless. The precision of our artillery fire was the admiration of our own force, and the terror and destruction of the enemy.'[2] Harrassed till nightfall by the horse artillery and 9th Lancers, no attempt was made to make a stand. Although the contest had been short, heavy rain was falling, hampering the movements of both sets of soldiers.

The only position at which the rebels put up strong resistance was behind the lines in the village of Najafgarh itself. This was stormed by the 1st Punjab Rifles after a stiff fight, with Nicholson eventually having to send the 61st Foot as reinforcements. The rebels held on for a while longer before evacuating by moonlight and withdrawing to the city. Curiously, Bakht Khan and the Bareilly brigade stayed on the opposite side of the bridge throughout the battle and now simply watched their fellow soldiers streaming away. Rajab Ali would go further, saying Bakht Khan had struck camp as soon as he saw the defeated soldiers and returned with all haste to Delhi with his brigade, leaving the rest of the men to make their way as best they could.

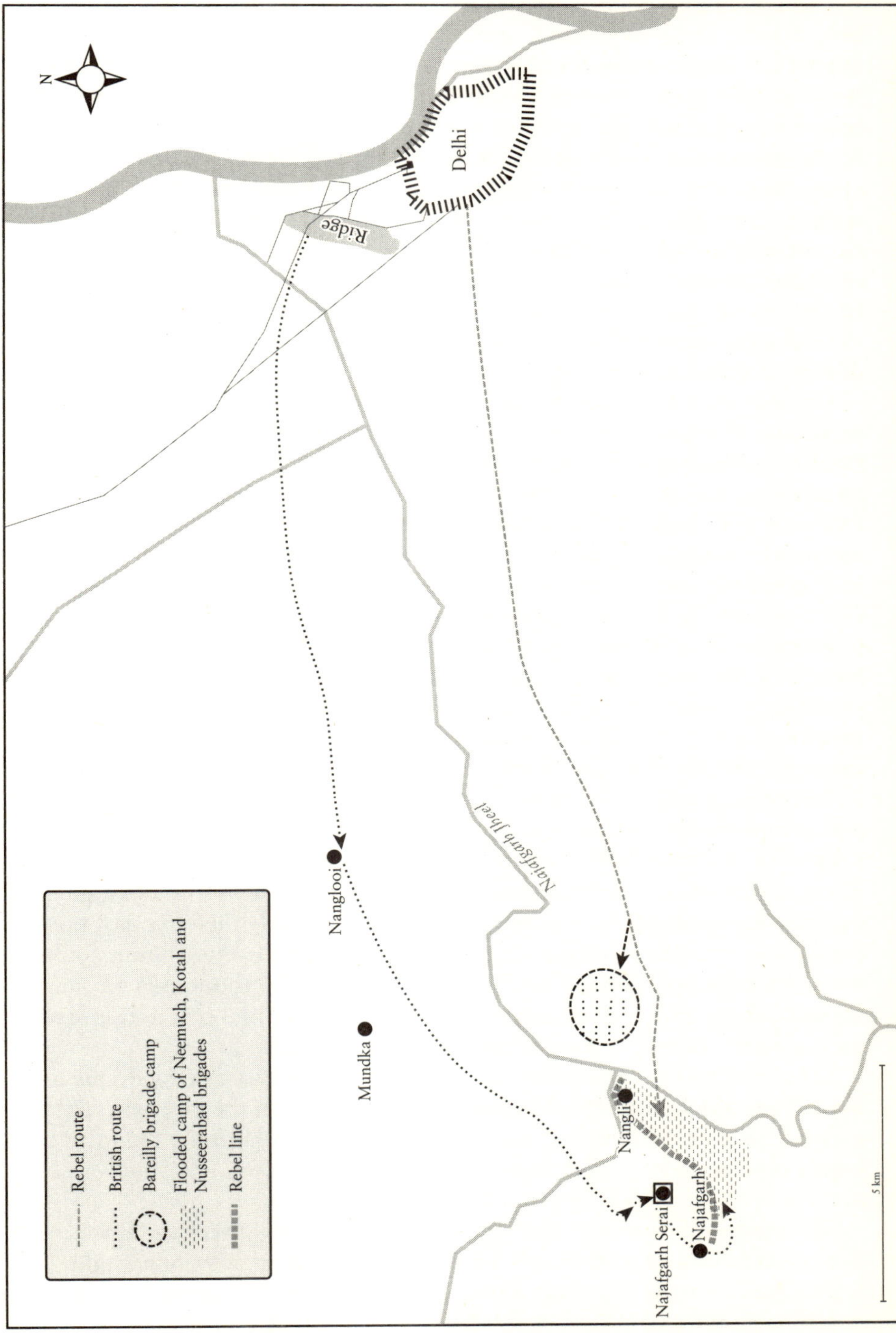


The Battle of Najafgarh.

Casualties amounted to twenty-five killed and seventy wounded on the British side. Lt Lumsden of Coke's Rifles was killed, and Lt Gabbett of HM61st Foot succumbed to his bayonet wound. Gabbett's charge on the serai led Nicholson to write a letter to the man's mother saying he would have recommended Gabbett for a Victoria Cross had he survived. One of the stranger tales told of the battle was that of Elkington, an eighteen-year-old of the 61st Foot who had joined the regiment a few months earlier. After his death in the battle, it was found that he had divided his personal effects and valuables into separate parcels, specifying where each parcel should go in the event of his death. Normally gregarious, Elkington had not said a word to his colleagues during the march from the ridge prior to the battle. It was thought that he must have somehow understood that his end was near.

On the rebel side, the Neemuch brigade had faced the brunt of the fighting and subsequently took most of the casualties. It was said in the British camp that as many as 800 rebels had been killed or wounded; Megh Raj, a *harkara*, reported less embellished numbers of around 300 to 400 killed. Rajab Ali reported one Mahalum Singh, a witness to the battle, saying that around a hundred rebels had been killed either in the process of crossing the bridge or by drowning as they tried to swim across the canal. Meanwhile, the baggage, supplies, treasure and ammunition, not to mention all thirteen guns, were left to fall into British hands. Nicholson arranged for it to be taken back to camp. The bodies of the rebels were searched and gold mohurs, money and valuables were extracted. The remaining tents were then looted by the local villagers and camp followers while the village of Najafgarh was entirely gutted.

Nicholson opted to make camp at the routed village, with his exhausted troops having eaten nothing since their departure from the ridge. The constant heavy rain made the night difficult; few men got any sleep. Meanwhile, British sappers attempted to destroy the Najafgarh bridge; they succeeded sometime after midnight. Early the next day, they blew up all the tumbrils and ammunition wagons that the column could not take back with them. 'We heard the explosions about two am and thought there had been a night attack the sound of the real action had scarcely been heard,' recorded Greathed at the ridge.

Unwilling to spend another day and night at the waterlogged village, Nicholson ordered the force to march straight back in the morning. They arrived back in the British camp at 5 p.m., to cheers and the regimental bands playing them in. Greathed:

> The main body was preceded by the baggage and followers and it was amusing to see the different descriptions of plunder that were brought in. One fellow mounted on a pony had a live peacock under his arm with an immense tail. A good deal of money was picked up and a rare assortment of cooking pots and lotas. There were thirteen guns

> taken two are of native make 3 pounders but as heavy in metal as our 6 pounder guns. The force came in in high spirits and have just reason to be elated with their success.

Other plunder included the buggy used by Bakht Khan. The sheer quantity of goods meant the loot went for around half its actual value when auctioned in the British camp later.

There had actually been fighting closer to the ridge on the day of the battle at Najafgarh. Many of the rebels remaining in the city had kept the British pickets busy with gunfire, and at 10 a.m. an attack had been made on the British camp. Since Nicholson had taken a large contingent of troops towards Najafgarh, it was supposed that the British camp would be more weakly defended than before. The north of the ridge and the Metcalfe picket was attacked. Alongside this, the rebel battery at Ludlow Castle and the guns on the left bank of the river also opened up. The attack was never pushed forward with much vigour, however, and little was achieved. Gowree Shunkur, a spy, reported that this attack had been led by prince Mirza Mughal, who advanced with all the men he had. Several other princes had accompanied the force; even the armed guard of the King had come along. Fifty were wounded, among them the prince Ghulam Mustapha. There were insufficient doolies to carry back the wounded, so the rebels improvised stretchers from crossed muskets.

There was much gloom in the city following the debacle at Najafgarh. Many rebels had grown disillusioned at their inability to win. Toorab Ali reported only 500 men of the Neemuch brigade returning from the battle, although others claimed it was even fewer. Gowree Shunkur witnessed the rebel force re-entering the city, the Neemuch infantry marching 'in most woeful plight', although more may have trickled in over the following hours and days. 'The sepoys who were surrounded at Nanglee are tumbling into Dehlee in very bad plight, and about 200 of them have come in. The Neemuch brigade weeps for the loss of their guns. They say that there were no guns like theirs. Directly the portfire was applied, the enemy was swept out of sight. In sunshine or rain, they always worked well. There were also 1,000 splendid shells; there are none left like them.'[3] The rumour going around the British camp was that the rebels were too fearful of admitting the loss of so many guns and had instead claimed they were simply being slowed down by the rains. The broken Neemuch brigade appears to have made no effort to retrieve its baggage. On 28 August, Hodson travelled to Najafgarh and managed to collect three ammunition carts and other supplies that Nicholson had been unable to take with him.

By 1 September, news from the city was that the Neemuch brigade had all but melted away. Many men had simply deserted after the battle, heading for their homes. No wounded were seen returning to Delhi; they had been left in the flight. The brigade had lost as many as 800 men from its ranks. Many were said to have stayed in the nearby villages rather than return to Delhi. By a week after the battle, thirty sowars from the 3rd Light Cavalry were sent to scour the nearby villages for these men. Two sowars returned to say that nobody had been found.

Men of other brigades mocked the remaining Neemuch men. On 2 September, for instance, the men of the brigade were due to take over watch of the batteries from the Delhi brigade. However, when they reached the batteries the men of the Delhi brigade taunted them as 'runaways' and refused to hand over the guns to such 'cowards'. Arguments raged for several hours, and there were altercations between the two contingents before the matter was settled by the men of the Bareilly brigade, who agreed to take over the watch themselves.

Zafar was apparently much dismayed by the disaster. He blamed Bakht Khan for the defeat, saying he had not supported the Neemuch brigade in timely fashion. The general in turn retorted that he was his own master. 'He is not to show his face and is well abused,' Gowree Shunkur reported.

In the British camp there was jubilation. 'From the accounts of the spies from the city this defeat has caused great sensation, and desertions are becoming more frequent. No more than 600 of the Neemuch and Kotah Force appear to have returned. They lost all their guns, ammunition, equipage and, many of the men who escaped, their arms,'[4] John Lawrence's secretary wrote to the Government of India.

32

# Overtures from the King

It is not at all improbable that the Bareilly Troops will fall out and kill Mirza Moghul. Every brigade is clamourous for pay; indeed they are actually in want of food. There is not a stiver in the treasury. The Cavalry constantly desert to their homes.

Barnes to Lawrence, 1 September 1857[1]

With their continuous losses, by September the rebel army had been reduced to only fifteen field guns; the rest had been either lost or captured by the British. Six of the remaining guns had been brought by the Bareilly brigade, while five were those of the Nusseerabad contingent. Another four had already been in the palace prior to the mutiny. The Neemuch brigade had lost their guns at Najafgarh. Recriminations raged over responsibility for the disaster, and rifts widened between the officers and men. Even the simplest decisions were becoming difficult to make according to Charles Saunders, Commissioner of Delhi: 'Each Cavalry Regiment is now split up into small "thokes" or federacies, comprising those who are residents of a particular tract of country. For instance, the Hansee fellows form one "thoke", the Kalanoor men another "thoke", and so on through the whole body. Not one agrees with the other … and are all on the eve of deserting. They wait however for the promised issue of pay.'[2] Around this time, in early September, various ambassadors from other had come in from Lucknow and Bareilly. They expressed disappointment at the state of the army and the failure to push the British force of the ridge.[3]

It was plain that something had to be done, and a new 'Kote' or military council was formed in the wake of Najafgarh. This was comprised of three different contingents. In the first group were the various subedars and risaldars of the various regiments and brigades. Second were a group of Muslim priests including the moulvi Fuzl Huq. Bakht Khan had also chosen moulvi Sarfaraz Ali of Bareilly and moulvi Imdad Ali of Pulwul to advise the council, both of whom were apparently close with the King and attended his durbars. The third contingent comprised five sepoys chosen from the various regiments present in the city to represent and voice the opinions of the common soldiers. Many of the soldiers had threatened to stop attacking the British position unless they received adequate support and reinforcements from other regiments, while others complained that there was no overall effective command. Some asked Zafar himself to lead them. Jeewan Lal records a tired Zafar remarking in response, 'You alone have the power to act. Whatever you think you are able to accomplish, do that.'

This collection of common soldiers, Muslim priests and subedars would decide on policy matters and how to conduct the war from now on. Certainly there was a feeling that they were fighting for a common cause and must cooperate with each other. 'Yesterday evening the officers of the Neemuch, Bareilly and Nusseerabad brigades met at General Bukht Khan's quarters,' Futteh Mahomed reported. 'Their swords were placed in the middle and each and all swore solemnly to stand together for life or death.'[4] They also agreed, in a rare show of cooperation, to give some of their artillery to the Neemuch brigade, which had lost its own at Najafgarh. Among other decisions taken was the repair of the Shah Bastion, which was steadily being reduced to rubble by fire from a British battery. The Neemuch general, meanwhile, agreed to lead his force in an attempt to capture or destroy the offending battery in the near future. The subedars got their wish: Mirza Mughal was again appointed nominal commander-in-chief on 2 September.

Zafar held a meeting with Bakht Khan on 5 September enquiring as to his plans to defend the city from an expected British assault. If he was not confident of managing to repel the British, the King asked, would it not be better to open the gates of the city now? The general said no; he was confident that the British could be repelled.

Meanwhile, others in the city tried to drum up morale despite the bad tidings. Toorab Ali in his report of the 28th singled out Moulvi Fuzl Huq from Alwar, who harangued the soldiers while issuing dire warnings of what would happen to them should the city ever come under British control again: 'Ever since Moulvee Fuzl Huq arrived in this city, he has been unceasingly employed in stirring up the army and the city people against the British. He declares he has seen in the Agra Gazette a decree of the Imperial Parliament directing the wholesale slaughter of every living soul in Delhee and the entire destruction of the city. Only one minaret of the Juma Musjid is to be left standing as a memorial to future ages that on this spot the city of Delhee once stood.'[5] Many of the city's frightened population, now impervious to his exhortations, were taking the chance to leave the city before the expected British attack. Cartloads of people were seen streaming from the city every day by the Delhi Gate to the south.

*****

As had been the case for Wilson, Barnard and Reed, the strain of the siege was affecting Zafar. The King seemed to vacillate between shows of energy and utter apathy. There were reports that he contemplated opening the gates of the city or the palace on the river side and allowing the British to enter. He recognised this might mean his death at the hands of the sepoys, but at least it might save his family. He was apparently stopped by Ahsan Ulla Khan.

Tired of managing the rebel army's demands, a frustrated Zafar sometimes threatened to abdicate his throne or worse. On 9 August, he wrote to the officers of the 38th Regiment saying he had pleased the army as best he could and treated them as his own children despite their shows of *lese majeste*. 'The petulance of one's own child has to be borne with, and so I have borne with yours, indulging you in all your wishes. But it is to be deplored that you have, notwithstanding, shown no concern for my life, and have had no consideration for my old age,' he rumbled. He complained not only of the soldiers' contempt for him but also for Ahsan Ulla Khan, who was constantly accused of being in league with the British. Ever since the physician's house had been burned down, he had been kept from Zafar's side. If they had proof that he was a spy, Zafar wrote, they must provide it. Simply causing a nuisance on suspicion alone was to be deplored. Zafar asked for all looted property to be brought back and the plunderers suitably punished. Tired of being treated as he was, he wrote of withdrawing from public life:

> If you are not disposed to comply with these requests let me be conveyed, in safety to the Khwaja Sahib [a Muslim shrine near the Kutb Minar]. I shall there sit and employ myself in the Occupation of Mujawir [sweeper of a mosque] and, if this even is acceded not to, I shall relinquish every concern, and go away. Let those who think they can detain me attempt to do so. Not having been killed by the hands of English, I shall be killed by yours. Further the oppression that is at present on the people, is not inflicted on them, it is inflicted on me. It is incumbent on you all to take measures to prevent it. Or let me have my answer [i.e. Tell me in plain words that you do not wish to obey me] and I shall swallow a diamond and go to sleep [ie. kill myself].[6]

At other times, Zafar harboured dreams of leaving the cares of the world and leaving on pilgrimage to Mecca. On 12 August, the soldiers relented and Ahsan Ulla Khan was released on the condition that he refrained from any influence on the government of the city – he was to act only as Zafar's physician. The princes Mirza Mughal, Abdoolla and Khizr Sultan would accompany him home.

Zafar himself had always been open to negotiations with the British camp, and as the siege wore on and the fortunes of the rebel army declined further these thoughts must have grown stronger. He had always been a hesitant figurehead. As early as 4 July, a messenger had appeared in the British camp with a letter from the King. In it, Zafar wrote of his eagerness to make an agreement. All he asked was that his position as king remain and that his pension continue as before. In return, he would cooperate with the British to end the conflict in their favour. General Reed consulted Lawrence as to his view on this overture: 'If the King can give us possession of Delhy, I would recommend that his position and pension be guaranteed provided it can be shown that he did not order any of the murders which were perpetrated on our countrymen,' Lawrence replied. 'But I would not give him the Palace and he should quit Delhy. This seems to me essentially necessary. I have no idea what orders Government have given, but there are my views.'

On 8 July, after mulling over the matter further, Lawrence wrote a more optimistic letter than was warranted: 'If the King will let our troops into the Palace, which he may be able to do, unknown to the insurgents, the city would be untenable for the latter. We might simultaneously assault every quarter from within and from without. Indeed I doubt if the insurgents would stand. It will be necessary, however, to guard against treachery.'[7] Although seemingly promising, nothing came of this dialogue.

In mid-August, Greathed received a telegram from the Government of India on the matters of overtures by the King. Greathed was given strict instructions to refuse the conditions: 'The Governor-General wishes it to be understood that any concession to the King of which the King's restoration to his former position should be the basis is one to which the Government (as at present advised) cannot for a moment give its consent.'[8] Furthermore, Greathed was to submit any negotiations to the Government prior to committing it to anything.

A further overture would come on 21 August, this time from the queen. 'An emissary came out from Zeenut Muhul, the favourite wife of the King, a great political personage, offering to exercise her influence with the King, to bring about some arrangement,' wrote Greathed. 'I sent word, we wished her personally all happiness, and had no quarrel with women and children, but could hold no communications with any one belonging to the palace.'

During mid-August, many members of the royal family seemed to have realized that the cause of the rebels was failing. Many of the princes were short of money and worried for the future. Spies reported that some were ready to flee to the British camp if an opportunity arose. Others sent letters pledging friendship and asking what they could do to assist a British victory. This was confirmed by Greathed on 19 August: 'I am beginning to get letters from the princes declaring they have been all along fondly attached to us and that they only want to know what they can do for us. They must find out for themselves for I shall not answer and tell them.'

A week after the battle of Najafgarh, a downcast Zafar again offered to surrender to Wilson. This time, the rebel officers themselves seemed to be contemplating surrender. On 31 August, a very gloomy, downcast day, a messenger arrived in the British camp from the city carrying a message from the King in concert with the council of sepoy officers. The letter contained Zafar's conditions, which were that his pension be continued and that the sepoys be taken back into British employment. In reply he was told that unconditional surrender was the only thing that would be countenanced and that no negotiations would be carried out.

However, Wilson did consider another plan. This was to offer an amnesty, which would have the effect of dividing the rebels and therefore weakening resistance in the city prior to any British assault. Considering the hopeless divisions already blighting the rebel camp, amnesty would be made solely to the irregular cavalry in the city. 'Great gain may be attained by detaching Irregular Cavalry from the mutineers; important overtures have been made,' Wilson told Lawrence on 2 September. The Commissioner himself was hesitant on this issue due to its implications: 'I do not think that under the Government notification you could pardon mutineers. But you could recommend for pardon, which would almost certainly be attended to, provided the parties were not murderers,' he replied.

After further reflection, Lawrence wrote back on 4 September to give his assent. Government policy on the matter of amnesty was sufficiently cloudy to allow the leeway that the difficult circumstances demanded. 'As you are aware, I have no authority whatever at Delhi or in Delhi matters. But I consider every officer ought to aid the State to the best of his ability, and to assume responsibility where that course is advisable. If therefore you deem it expedient to receive the overtures of corps, or portions of corps, which have not murdered Europeans, and find it necessary to give distinct pledges for pardon, I am quite prepared to share the responsibility.'[9] There were other benefits to the amnesty. The rebel cavalry had done little so far in terms of hostilities; if they could be lured into switching sides, they could still perform good service around the country. 'The combination has been so extensive, the mutiny so general, that it is impossible for us to carry on a war of vengeance against all,' Lawrence wrote. 'We cannot destroy all the mutineers who have fought against us. The sooner we open the door for escape to the least guilty, the better for all parties.'

At around the same time, Greathed finally received his directions from Governor-General Canning not to consider any offer of surrender. The message had been sent from Calcutta on 20 August, but the poor state of the telegraph system had seen the message bounce from Kanpur to Agra before finally reaching the Delhi ridge. Canning again warned the political agent not to receive any advances from the King or princes. The city was to be captured with no promises.[10]

# 33

# The Demons of Destruction

> By the latest trustworthy accounts which come down to the 1st September, copy of which is annexed, it will be seen that the mutineers are without leaders, are split up into small factions, have no united plan of operations, and are deficient in munitions of war and in money. Humanly speaking it may be fully anticipated that they will not be able to withstand our assault, and that the first regiment which enters the town will be the signal for a general rout.
>
> John Lawrence to Government of India,
> 7 September 1857[1]

After the disaster at Najafgarh, there had been few attempts to attack the British position. In fact, the rebels gave away a key position. Ludlow Castle had always been in rebel possession, and although they had been driven out of it several times they had always reoccupied it later. This had happened on 23 July and on 12 August. Generally Wilson made no attempt to hold on to the position Ludlow Castle permanently, as it was too far forward to work as an outpost. The British line at this time ran in an oblique pattern anchored on the left at Metcalfe House through a series of outposts up to the Flagstaff Tower. All these positions were well chosen and formed a strong line. However, the rebel presence at Ludlow Castle made the British positions on the ridge vulnerable to shelling.

From the 26th to the end of the month, the rebels had kept up concerted shelling on the Hindu Rao and had also tried to disrupt the sappers at work in the trenches below the ridge. A strong attack had been expected on 29 August: 'On the last day of the Mohurrum [the first month of the Islamic calendar] astrologers predict some severe fighting. The Moosulmans expect martyrdom if they fall on that day,'[2] a British report warned. In the event, the day passed without great incident; low morale in the rebel camp dampened any ardour for fighting. On the

30th, elements of the 60th Rifles and Gurkhas successfully attacked the advanced breastworks at Ludlow Castle.

The first day of September was very hot, with temperatures around 37°C. Such days tended to be quiet, but on this particular morning a rebel shell made the difference. The rebel battery on the left bank of the river had thus far done little damage to the British pickets at the Metcalfe House, and just after sunrise members of the stable house picket were milling around waiting for their grog. The group was estimated to be around 100 strong, and included rank-and-file, officers, Sikh soldiers and various attendants. Without warning, a shrapnel shell fired from the battery, roughly 2,000 yards distant, burst among the crowd. Charles John Griffiths was present at the picket outpost when it landed:

> The bullets scattered around, and the scene which followed it is almost impossible for me to depict. Many threw themselves flat on the ground, falling one on top of the other, while groans and cries were heard. One soldier fell mortally wounded by my side, and on looking around to count up our losses, we found that two of my regiment had been killed outright, besides six others severely wounded. Two Sikhs and a *bhisti*, or water-carrier, also met their death, and two doolie-bearers were wounded – thirteen men in all. One very stout old officer was in the act of having his morning bath when the shell exploded, the *bhisti* standing at his side and pouring over him, when squatted on a tent-mallet, his massuck of water. He rolled over and over on the ground, presenting such a ludicrous appearance in his wet, nude state, and covered with earth, that, notwithstanding the awful surroundings of the scene. I and others could not forbear laughing. The shot had been quite a chance one, but it proved how deadly was the effect of a shrapnel shell exploding, as this had done, only a few feet in front of a large body of men.

*****

During the first few days of September, with the siege train's arrival imminent, Baird Smith encouraged Wilson to devise an attack on the city. Since the number of reinforcements yet to arrive was unlikely to add substantially to the total, the force could be already considered complete. Baird Smith was emphatic that the assault must be delivered soon. In this, he was strongly supported by Nicholson, Capt. Daly, Capt. Hodson, Capt. Taylor and Lt Norman. Nicholson in particular showed his frustration at the continuing delay. According to Lt Roberts, who happened to be in Nicholson's tent before he left to attend a meeting, Nicholson had confidentially declared, 'Delhi must be taken, and it is absolutely essential that this should be done at once; and if Wilson hesitates longer, I intend to propose at today's meeting that he should be superseded.' Roberts replied that with Chamberlain *hors de combat* this would see Nicholson in command of the Delhi Field Force; his meaning was that Nicholson's move would be taken as self-aggrandisement. Nicholson replied that he had already thought this through and that he would propose Colonel George Campbell of HM52nd to be the next commander.

Hodson expressed his own frustration at Wilson:

> He is a good artillery officer with an undue estimate of his own arm of the service. He seems to realize the old saying that officers of a special arm such as artillery and engineers do not make generals. Wilson for instance looks upon guns as engines capable mathematically of performing perfect results and acts as cautiously as if in practice such results were ever attained by Asiatic gunners forgetting all our glorious Indian annals all the experience of a British army and hesitating before an Indian foe. I never hear these old gentlemen talk without thinking of Sir Charles Napier's remarks on the Duke's comments on Colonel Monson's retreat and the heroic way in which he had read and profited by the lesson.[3]

Wilson was adamant that any attack wait until the siege engines had reduced the defences. However, with Baird Smith ill, he did ask the man's second-in-command, Capt. Taylor, to draw up plans for the breaching batteries since the arrival of the siege train was expected.

In terms of reinforcements, around 26 August, some 100 men colourfully dressed and draped with chainmail reached the British camp along with some cavalrymen. These men were Afghans sent by Dost Mohammad to show his support for the British troops besieging the city. It was only a nominal force, and the common perception in the British camp was that the men were simply spies sent to monitor the British struggle at Delhi. They certainly took little part in the action.

The more substantial force that Wilson awaited came from the Maharaja of Kashmir, Gulab Singh; the force was close, having reached Ambala. The British had gifted Gulab Singh the state of Kashmir in 1846 as a reward; although a former vassal of the Sikh state of Lahore, he had aided the British by keeping his troops back and engineering the downfall of the Sikh army during the First Anglo-Sikh War. He owed a large debt to the British government for his elevation to the throne, and the British in their need had asked him for troops. However, inclement weather and Gulab Singh's own death – he was succeeded by his son – slowed the troops. The force of 2,600 men was divided into four regiments of infantry and 150 cavalry, and they had six horse artillery guns and twenty-four swivel guns. The contingent was made up largely of Dogras, i.e. Rajputs from the hills, although a sprinkling of Afghans acted as orderlies. Their chief weapon was the *hurmur*, a flintlock with a considerable range, although they had no bayonets.

The quality of the troops from Kashmir was a worry. It had been said that they had little enthusiasm to fight for the British cause and that they would refuse to go south of Amritsar. Captain Lawrence had therefore decided that he would look them over at Ambala and lead them to Delhi if he considered them good enough. If they were found wanting, they would be deployed in support roles elsewhere.

On 26 August, the contingent crossed the Sutlej River after a halt at Jalandhar on their way to Ambala. John Lawrence spent three whole days walking and talking with the men to evaluate their temperament; he felt this was vital, for it would be an utter disaster if such a large contingent mutinied at Delhi. The nominal commander of the column was Dewan Hari Chund, brother of the staunchly pro-British Prime Minister Dewan Jowala Sahai. To cement the men to the British cause, Lawrence offered the soldiers as much as he could without being unseemly: a present of 5,000 rupees was given to the troops, with pensions offered to the wife or son of any officer or soldier killed in action. There would also be gratuities for wounds depending on their severity. The officers themselves were given *khillats*. Lawrence also reminded the men that the new maharaja's father had been put on the throne by the British government and said that now was the time for him to prove his gratitude. As examples he pointed to the Cis-Sutlej states that were aiding the British as well as the Gurkhas.[4]

Capt. Richard Lawrence, brother of John Lawrence, was promoted to lieutenant-colonel and placed in charge of the contingent. Brother John advised him to keep an eye on the temperament of the troops while at Delhi as he still held suspicions:

> As you have already been demi-officially informed, you will communicate to that officer [Wilson] without reservation your opinion of the character and merits of these troops. While their presence at Delhy, if thoroughly reliable, would form, an important addition to our means, on the other hand, if the soldiers are not to be trusted they only become a source of danger and inconvenience. A grave responsibility will therefore attach to your opinion, which must necessarily have much weight with General Wilson.[5]

It was also important for Capt. Lawrence to remember that the troops needed to be led into battle by their own officers rather than Europeans; the latter would be perceived as a slight. The British officers were only there to assist. They were not to drill or discipline the men in any way either, only offer advice in battle. These men had to see that they were allies, not subordinates.

The impending arrival of the Kashmir contingent was welcome news to Wilson, who was troubled by casualties from skirmishing and disease. The temperature was stable at roughly 37°C in early September, and cholera was not loosening its grim on the camp, with the 52nd and

61st regiments continuing to suffer disproportionately. By 3 September, 2,500 men in the British camp were hospitalised. Of these, around 1,100 were Europeans – more than a fifth of all the Europeans in camp.

*****

During the latter part of August, a huge British convoy could be seen wending its way south towards Delhi from the Punjab. This was the British siege train dispatched from the arsenal at Ferozepore in mid-August. A vast collection of supplies was packed into 800 wagons, 2,000 hackeries and innumerable carts, forming a line 8 miles long. The most important part of the convoy was the collection of heavy guns: six 24-pounders, eight 18-pounders, four 10-inch mortars and six 8-inch mortars. Each of the heavy guns was pulled along by two elephants. The convoy would reach Lursowlie, around 30 miles from Delhi, on 1 September, having been delayed considerably due to the recent rains; a large part of the road to Delhi was underwater. By the next day, the siege train reached the village of Rai – 20 miles to go. Wilson ordered No. 17 Battery along with two squadrons of the 9th Lancers out to escort the siege train to the camp. Early on 4 September, the vanguard of the siege train was finally in sight of the ridge. Wilson sent out additional cavalry to escort it into the camp.

The entire convoy had been readied by Captain Lewis, Commissary of Ordnance at Ferozepore. Escorting the train and acting as further reinforcements for the Delhi Field Force were HM8th Regiment, 400 men of the Belooch Battalion drawn up recently from Sindh into the Punjab, the same number of men from the new Punjab Corps of Infantry, and a Bombay irregular corps. All came under the command of Col Farquhar. The Raja of Jhind also sent a cavalry force to assist in escorting the train. The guns would almost double Wilson's arsenal. He now had fifty-six guns, howitzers and mortars ready to rain down death on the city, battering and breaching its walls in preparation for a full-scale attack.[6]

Further reinforcements arrived from Meerut on 6 September: 200 Royal Rifles and 100 artillery recruits. Meanwhile, the 4th Punjab Infantry arrived on the 7th. The same day, many of the wounded and sick were moved off to Ambala. More reinforcements arrived on the 8th; this was the Kashmir contingent commanded by Lt Col Richard Lawrence. They were met personally by Wilson and escorted into the camp. In addition to the siege train, these reinforcements represented almost all the men and material Wilson would receive. Put simply, there was nothing left to give.

With these reinforcements, the strength of the British force stood at 9,988 men (3,766 being European and 6,222 being Indian). Around two-thirds, 6,089 men, were infantry (2,672 European and 3,417 Indian). There were 1,827 cavalrymen (514 European and 1,313 Indian). Another 1,350 men made up the artillery contingent (580 European and

770 Indian). The remaining 722 men were Indian engineers, sappers, miners and so on. The force included newly raised Sikh levies, lascars, artillery drivers and other units. 'On their fidelity we could only depend so long as their interests were ours, and the prospect of plunder was before them,' wrote Col Bourchier, 'added to which, no support was nearer than Lahore, distant 300 miles. From this it will be seen that General Wilson's position was one to try the strongest nerves.' This was just the British force, however. There were also allied troops present totalling around 3,000 men. The Maharaja of Kashmir's force totalled 2,200 men with six guns, forming the bulk of this force, while the Maharaja of Jhind had sent around 400 cavalry with the siege train. All in all, then, the grand total of the British force including allies on the ridge stood at nearly 12,600 men.

*****

With the arrival of the siege train, plans to take the offensive with the big guns were in full swing. The day after the arrival of the siege train was a busy one in the engineers' park. An estimated 10,000 gabions and as many if not more fascines along with an estimated 100,000 sandbags had already been manufactured and lay in small hills everywhere, waiting to be moved towards the city. Alongside these were all sorts of entrenching tools along with sandbags, scaling ladders and platforms for the construction of batteries and field magazines under Lt Brownlow. 'The ordnance park is also a busy scene, and has a formidable appearance,' wrote Greathed. 'Hogge is the life of it, and every one works hard and cheerfully under him. The guns will have to be taken down by bullocks, as elephants cannot be trusted under fire; they have a great sense of self preservation. Every exertion and precaution has been made and taken to ensure success; and any one who sees the extent of the preparations that are requisite, would not be disposed to think that much time has been lost.'[7] Oxen gradually brought the heaviest batteries forward, with the assistance of many of the 9th Lancers.

In terms of where on the walls to focus fire, and therefore where to locate the siege batteries, there was little choice. The force occupying the ridge was never sufficiently numerous to encircle the entire city along its west and southern walls; to attempt this would have spread the units too thin. The ridge and the north could not be abandoned as this position protected the road to the Punjab, the source of British supplies. The only practical option was to position the batteries on the ridge and to the north of the city.

But attacking the north of the city had other advantages. The batteries stationed in front of the walls would have their flanks protected by the river on the left and the British position at the Hindu Rao on the right. Secondly, there were many buildings and residences in the Civil Lines scattered around this area between the walls and the ridge which provided much-needed cover for the troops protecting the batteries.

The west of the city, in comparison, was much more exposed. From the north, the siege guns could be pushed forward with relative impunity. When the city was to be stormed, the British columns could approach very close to the city walls before emerging from cover.

Wilson saw that an attack from the north would also work best once the city had been entered. The west and south of the city formed a warren of small streets and tightly packed housing. The north of the city from the Kashmir Gate to the palace, meanwhile, was wide open and would allow the troops to make their way along the wider thoroughfares without the necessity of storming numerous shops and residences that might allow ambushes. This latter point was Wilson's main concern. The rebels lacked the organisation to make their numbers count in open battle, true, but in the crowded urban environment of the city, where every door, window and rooftop provided a good sniper position and every house could be barricaded, advancing European troops could quickly become bogged down.[8]

The rebels don't seem to have reacted to the siege train. In fact, they had made the cardinal mistake of withdrawing pickets and posts from Ludlow Castle and its vicinity. 'To our surprise we had been allowed to take possession of the Ludlow Castle, within six hundred yards of the city walls, without opposition; the enemy doubtless thinking that the assault was intended from the right, where our batteries had from the first been erected on the ridge; and the attack on the Mooree Bastion confirmed this belief,'[9] wrote Col Bourchier. The area around Ludlow Castle and Qudsia Bagh was gratefully seized on the morning of the 8th. Ludlow Castle was only around 500 yards from the city walls, so it made an ideal site for constructing batteries to target the nearby defences. If they were stealthy, British patrols could now approach very close to the city walls without being detected.

The stage was now set for a bombardment of the city defences in earnest. Preparations were made for making parallels and approaches and for the erection of batteries. Trenches were dug, with much of the army being employed in this activity. Work would go on day and night. Since Baird Smith was ill at this time, Capt. Taylor deputised for him. Taylor was well thought of as an engineer and appeared to be well liked and trusted by those under him. The evening of 7 September was arranged to be the time for the tracing of the batteries. The logistics involved in the construction of the batteries and defences was considerable. Eight hundred camels were used to transport the fascines to the batteries while 300 more camels would be employed to shuttle up and down the ridge transporting ammunition for the big guns. When they began firing shells, these guns would do so at a frantic pace; a constant supply of ammunition from the ridge was therefore vital.

The most advanced position was the Sammy House at the southern tip of the ridge. Here a trench had been dug just beyond, facing the city walls. On 6 September a light field battery was placed in the trench, comprising four 9-pounders and two 24-pounder howitzers (some accounts say six 9-pounders and two 24-pounders). This was to target rebel guns at the Mori Bastion, only 950 yards away, and any other safe houses for the rebels between the Mori Bastion and Kishanganj. It also had the dual purpose of protecting the right flank and discouraging rebel sorties from the Lahore and Kabul Gates aimed at the batteries. Behind this battery, higher up on the ridge, was another of four heavy guns, and behind that, at what was called the crow's nest, were two light field pieces. These three batteries were under the command of Capt. F. F. Remington. 'The men, ragged and exhausted, often worked at night in preparing the batteries, for during the day the temperature exceeded 90 degrees under cloudless skies,'[10] wrote Brev. Maj. Anson of the 9th Lancers.

Four main batteries were to be organised. No. 1 Battery was to be below the ridge around 700 yards from the Mori Bastion, which formed the north-west section of the walls. It had been positioned to the south of the ravine, with the ravine wrapping round it and thereby protecting its flanks from any surprise attack. The ravine could also be used to ferry wounded back to the ridge in safety. The battery was completed by the morning of the 7th. This was the first battery to be readied, the hope being that the rebels would think the attack would come from here rather than the north of the city. Ten heavy guns and mortars were to be placed at No. 1. Of these six, the first division – the right portion, of five 18-pounders and one 8-inch mortar – were to direct their fire at their counterparts on the Shah Bastion, where the rebel guns and their defences were to be destroyed. Their secondary purpose was to protect the assaulting columns when the city walls were finally attacked. The second division of the battery – the left portion, consisting of four 24-pounders – was to fire at the rebel guns of the Kashmir Gate battery while protecting the parties at work constructing the No. 2 battery 300 meters to the east. This left portion was to be commanded by Major Turner, and the right side by Major Brind.

The rebels were slow to realise the battery was being constructed, and not a single man was lost in its construction. As the crews toiled, shells whizzed over them toward the Hindu Rao instead. Much work was done on the night of the 7th, and by the next morning one gun was mounted and began firing. The rebels now caught on and began directing grape and shot at the position, but it was in vain. Soon there were two guns firing from either division in the battery. By the end of the day, all ten guns were in position and firing.

Three days after its construction, the left portion of Battery No. 1 was in danger of being destroyed. By now, Major Turner had been wounded and Major Kaye had taken command. The guns were being fired without rest, which caused a fire. Noticing the conflagration, the rebels directed their fire towards the battery with renewed enthusiasm. In order to save the battery, Lt Lockhart with two companies of the 2nd Gurkhas bravely moved into the open and brought sandbags to extinguish the flames. This naturally

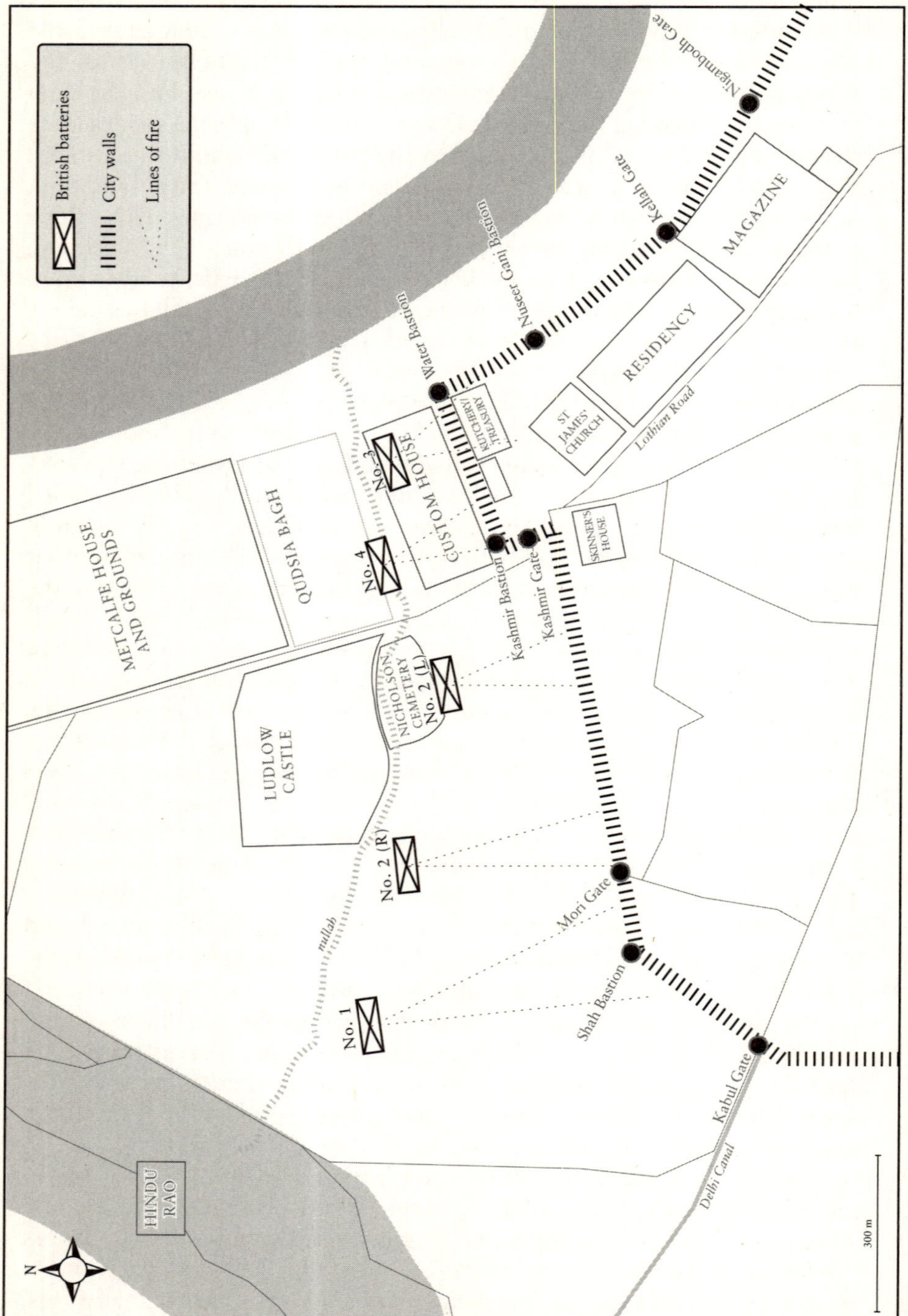


The British batteries.

exposed them to the fire of the defenders on the walls, and two of the Gurkhas were killed along with Lockhart, who was shot through the jaw. The fire was put out and the battery continued to do its work. Such was the destructive fire of the British guns that the opposition was quickly silenced.

'I went up again to the Flagstaff at six yesterday evening,' wrote Greathed. 'Major Brind had got his ten guns at work, and was firing salvos at the Moree and Cashmeeree. The effect on the Moree, which is the nearest, is very telling; every shot strikes home, and sends up a column of dust, and the shells burst inside it.' Little more than a day and a half later, on the morning of the 9th, anyone peering over the British trenches in front of the Mori Bastion would see a pile of ruins.

A heavy howitzer was moved into position by the battery, pointing towards the Kishanganj area as the rebels tried to target the battery from that quarter. Two light guns and rockets were used by the rebels to enfilade the battery position, although the rebel marksmanship was poor. 'It was a very pretty sight,' Greathed recorded, 'and if we had only known, as now, that they failed to do any harm, it would have been highly enjoyable, but some seemed to go so near, and a rocket inside a battery would be an ugly customer. One rocket flew right across from Kissengunj into Metcalfe's grounds at one bound; another pulled up on the road, 300 yards from the Flagstaff; several ended their careers in the ravine. It was very exciting.'[11]

No. 2 Battery was to be placed to the left front, before of Ludlow Castle and just 500 yards from the Kashmir Bastion. Work was commenced on the 8th and the battery was armed two days later with nineteen pieces of heavy artillery – two 18-pounders, nine 24-pounders and seven 8-inch howitzers. Like No. 1, No. 2 was divided into left and right divisions both independently commanded. The left was by far the most powerful battery, with all the 24-pounders, and was situated directly in front of the castle. The right division, situated around 200 yards to the right of its counterpart, was to target the rebel guns on the Kashmir Bastion itself and destroy the parapets on the bastions and wall for the 200 yards to its left. There was also a small tower close to the bastion that was to be reduced.

'The first salvo from this battery from nine 24-pounders showed what might soon be expected,' wrote Col Bourchier. 'The Cashmere Bastion attempted to reply, but was soon silenced, and became almost as great a wreck as its twin brother the Mooree; neither were portions of the curtain walls in a much better plight.' The artillerymen and others stationed in the battery cheered as the guns opened up for the first time. The rebels in this sector were ready, however, and as soon as the artillerymen removed the screen hiding the battery a round shot went through the embrasure. 'On regaining my feet,' Roberts wrote, 'I found that the young artilleryman, who was serving the vent while I was laying the gun, had had his right arm taken off.' That same evening, a shower of grape wounded Col Campbell. Capt. Johnson duly took command of the battery.

No. 3 battery, to the left of No. 2 battery, was traced by Lt Medley on the evening of the 9th. It was closer to the river, being situated in an out-office of the Custom House and pointing at the Water Bastion just 80 yards away. Being so close to the defences, the men building and manning it suffered greatly under musket fire from the defenders; during the first night, as the battery was being placed, thirty-nine Gurkhas lost their lives as the defenders desperately tried to prevent the process. Melancholy scenes were enacted as each Gurkha fell; his comrades were seen to 'stop for a moment, weep a little over a fallen friend, place his body in a row along with the rest and then set to work again', according to a European witness. The battery, composed of six 24-pounders and commanded by Major E. W. S. Scott, was finished on the night of the 11th. Also with this battery, under the command of Capt. Blunt, were twelve 5½-inch mortars. The object of the mortars was to bombard the interior of the Kashmir and Water Bastions along with the ground close to the church while Scott's 18-pounders hammered the Water Bastion itself. Like Battery No. 2, No. 3 would begin firing on the morning of the 11th.

No. 4 Battery, consisting of ten heavy mortars (four 10-inch and six 8-inch mortars) was situated in front of the Kashmir Gate, positioned in the Qudsia Bagh under the command of Major Tombs. The garden was a picturesque place prior to hostilities. Situated only 250 yards from the city walls, the garden of the mosque had been populated with fragrant orange and lemon trees. A visitor could walk through the garden towards the terrace on the river's edge. However, necessity required the cutting of the trees for the battery. The compound itself was ideal, being walled on three sides (it was open to the river) and therefore work on the battery could be finished without the rebels being alerted. The sound of workmen and their tools nevertheless gave it away after a while, and the fire was trained on the garden. Targeting the mortars was difficult due to the high walls, however, and most of the shots simply sailed overhead. The battery was traced and readied on the morning of the 10th. Tasked with reducing the walls from the river to the Kashmir Bastions, it opened up at 10 a.m. the next morning.

Once the batteries opened up, they would pummel the walls until shortly before the assault on the city. Night and day, the guns pounded away. A mishap near one of the batteries illustrated the dangers of the task beyond the fire from the walls. One of the workmen had been unloading live shells from a hackery, and, deciding to save time, he tilted his cart to allow the shells to fall to the ground. The impact of the shells triggered a giant explosion. Five workmen were killed instantly, while another two were injured along with three European artillerymen.

*****

All in all, around fifty guns were now trained on the city walls and gates. They poured shot and shell into the city day and night.

Confidence soared in the British camp as the first of the big guns began firing. As early as 6 September, Hodson had written of his optimism:

> Tonight I believe the engineers are really to begin work constructing batteries so that in two or three days Delhi ought to be taken. If General Wilson delays now he will have nothing left to take; all the Sepoys will be off to their homes or into Rohilcund or into Gwalior ...
>
> The Sepoys in Delhi are in hourly expectation of our attack and the cavalry keep their horses saddled night and day ready to bolt at a moment's notice so say the news letters I suspect that the moment we make an attack in earnest the rebel force will disappear.[12]

Hodson's good cheer was not misplaced. The cannonade was most spectacular at night, creating an unnatural day. Brilliant flashes from the guns broke in the gloom, with shells exploding over the city and lighting up the rooftops and minarets. In between the thunder of the guns could be heard the crackle of musketry and small arms along with the hissing of rockets. Revd Rotton was effusive:

> The din and the roar of cannon had been hitherto deafening ... roll after roll of ordnance thunder, in a succession almost momentary, fell with electric effect upon the ear. Nothing can be grander, nothing more fearfully imposing, than the circumstances attendant on a bombardment. And yet, terrible and grand as unquestionably they are, among them none is more so than the sight of living shell traversing the air, with more than the brilliancy of many falling meteors simultaneously, and in brightness rivalling at times the tremendous glare occasioned by continuous flashes of lightning during a stormy night. This sight will detain you, in spite of weariness and want of sleep, and hold you for the hour together, gazing in wonderment and admiration, not unmixed with awe.

*****

The rebels weren't entirely idle during this time. The few days prior to 4 September had been fairly quiet in the city, but when they observed the construction of the batteries they put up some resistance. British soldiers were harassed in their work from the trenches before the city walls. A Martello tower provided a platform for firing rockets towards the British lines. The defenders made occasional attempts to knock out the batteries. One of these attempts came on the night of the 8th, when the rebels attacked No. 1 Battery. They were repelled but skirmishing continued well into the night, with Capt. Remington's battery firing grape to help them on their way.

Two more attempts were made to disrupt the British batteries. The first was against No. 2 Battery as it came into play. The rebels had control of a parallel trench around 300 yards from the battery, and they kept up a tremendous fire from there all night. Another attack was made on No. 3 Battery, with the rebels launching an assault covered by gunners on the ramparts of the Water Bastion. Among the casualties in the battery was Capt. Fagan, who was shot in the head as he broke cover to check for damage. An enfilading battery was quickly constructed across the river to harass the No. 3 Battery. At the same time, guns in the Salimgarh Fort kept up their fire. Frequent attacks were also made on the British positions in and around Ludlow Castle. This area was much more difficult to attack; the British had the river on their left and were therefore completely protected. Although they were met with a concerted response from the rebels, the pickets at Ludlow and Qudsia Bagh were never greatly troubled in these exchanges.

Still, the resistance of the rebels made life difficult. All in all, the British suffered around 350 casualties during the bombardment. At No. 2 Battery, for instance, the rebels managed to fire a 3-pounder gun from a hole in the city walls. Despite all efforts, this gun continued to fire. One day, an officer at No. 2 put his head over the parapet for little more than a few seconds before a shot from the 3-pounder completely took of his head.

Indecision hampered the rebels, however. Several times cavalry and infantry was seen to come forth from the city gates only to disappear back into the city after a while, showing no direction or motivation to attack. Revd Rotton:

> Some time during the day a body of their horse crossed the canal, and drove in a picket of our Irregular Cavalry; with what definite object, except annoyance, it would be difficult to determine. This was a movement in the rear; but the Guides, supported by some mounted Punjaubees, were hurried on to the rescue. An engagement took place in which the enemy were worsted and fled; our men pursued and overtook many of them; twenty-five of the mutineers were killed, including a native officer. We lost in killed and wounded twelve men and fifteen horses; not including Lieut. Watson, who was wounded.

The rebels used a trench parallel to the British ones for harassing the work crews of the batteries. However, around twenty rebels had the misfortune of being killed or wounded by just one shot when a mortar dropped into the trench. There was some desultory fighting in the Sabzi Mandi area, too. Around 200 rebel troopers had decided to carry off some British camels and bullocks grazing to the north, as related by Baird Smith:

> They formed up in column when they first saw a detachment of our cavalry but broke when the distance was lessened to 500 yards and made for the canal. They were however met by another party of eighty of the Guide Cavalry under Sanford 3rd Cavalry and two of

> the enemy's native officers and twenty five sowars were killed. They probably thought the attention of every one was directed to the front and that they could help themselves to baggage animals with impunity.

By 12 September, hardly any of the city guns were firing back. Only the boom of the British guns could be heard, although the crackle of return fire from rebel muskets did not fade.

According to Futteh Mahomed, No. 4 Battery at the Qudsia Bagh was creating the greatest disturbance in the city. Other informers, including *harkaras* Kulloo and Mohun, mention that by the 12th the British guns had managed to turn a length of roughly 200 yards around the Kashmir Gate into ruin. The walls could be breached.[13]

*****

Other plans were made while the city walls were being reduced. With an assault imminent, orders were given out for each division and brigade to elect prize agents in anticipation of the sack of the city. The same day, a notice was sent out in which Wilson laid down instructions on the matter of plunder and the necessity for perfect discipline:

> The force assembled before Delhi has had much hardship to undergo since its arrival in this camp, all of which has been most cheerfully borne by officers and men. The time is now drawing near when the Major-General commanding the force trusts that its labours will be over, and it will be rewarded by the capture of the city for all its past exertions, and for a cheerful endurance of still greater fatigue and exposure. The troops will be required to aid and assist the Engineers in the erection of the batteries and trenches, and in daily exposure to the sun, as covering parties.
>
> The artillery will have even harder work than they yet have had, and which they have so well and cheerfully performed hither to: this, however, will be for a short period only, and when ordered to the assault, the Major-General feels assured British pluck and determination will carry everything before them, and that the bloodthirsty and murderous mutineers against whom they are fighting will be driven headlong out of their stronghold, or be exterminated. But to enable them to do this, he warns the troops of the absolute necessity of their keeping together, and not straggling from their columns. By this can success only be secured.
>
> Major-General Wilson need hardly remind the troops of the cruel murders committed on their officers and comrades, as well as their wives and children, to move them in the deadly struggle. No quarter should be given to the mutineers; at the same time, for the sake of humanity and the honour of the country they belong to, he calls upon them to spare all women and children that may come in their way.

> It is so imperative, not only for their safety, but for the success of the assault, that men should not straggle from their column that the Major-General feels it his duty to direct all commanding officers to impress this strictly upon their men, and he is confident that after this warning the men's good sense and discipline will induce them to obey their officers and keep steady to their duty. It is to be explained to every regiment that indiscriminate plunder will not be allowed; that prize agents have been appointed, by whom all captured property will be collected and sold, to be divided, according to the rules and regulations on this head, fairly among all men engaged; and that any man found guilty of having concealed captured property will be made to restore it, and will forfeit all claims to the general prize; he will also be likely to be made over to the Provost-Marshal to be summarily dealt with.
>
> The Major-General calls upon the officers of the force to lend their zealous and efficient co-operation in the erection of the works of the siege now about to be commenced. He looks especially to the regimental officers of all grades to impress upon their men that to work in the trenches during a siege is as necessary and honourable as to fight in the ranks during a battle.
>
> He will hold all officers responsible for their utmost being done to carry out the directions of the Engineers, and he confidently trusts that all will exhibit a healthy and hearty spirit of emulation and zeal, from which he has no doubt that the happiest results will follow in the brilliant termination of all their labours.

Wilson considered prize agents essential. His force was small compared to the city, and if his men began looting before the fight was over there could be disastrous results. The troops had to be prevented from any search for plunder – until it could be managed in an organised fashion, anyway. Three separate classes of prize agent were made ready: general and field officers; queen's service, for all ranks below that of major; and Company army. Capt. Fagan would end up being chosen to represent all field officers and the general. Capt. Campbell of the 60th Rifles was chosen to represent the queen's officers below the rank of major, while Capt. Wriford of the 1st European Bengal Fusiliers would represent Company men. All three nominees were very popular with the rank and file, and were considered to be the best men for such a delicate job.

# 34

# The Plan of Attack

> All goes well, except that I am satisfied Wilson had gone off his head. It is of course the responsibility, and he is at present the only obstacle to the vigour.
>
> Baird Smith[1]

While the rebel camp was riven by dissension, the British camp also had its problems. There was intense pressure on Wilson and his officers to capture the city. During the run-up to the assault, tempers were high and relationships grew strained. Wilson's officers did not have confidence in him, and he in turn was perhaps more open with his reluctance than was wise. Nicholson's contempt for Wilson was growing, and he was frank in his view that Wilson was not up to the job of capturing the city. Nicholson had begun to question Wilson's energy soon after he had arrived at Delhi: 'Wilson says that he will assume the offensive on the arrival off the heavy guns, but he says it in an indecisive kind of way which makes me doubt if he will do so ... He is not at all equal to the crisis, and I believe he feels it himself,'[2] he wrote to John Lawrence.

Nicholson had expected an attack shortly after the siege guns had arrived. However, Wilson let the guns pound the defences for nearly ten days. Nicholson also got the impression that Wilson didn't want to be overshadowed by anybody else: 'It appears to me that he is becoming jealous of me, lest I should earn more than my share of kudos. He will not even show me the plan of assault now, though I feel pretty sure his nervousness will make him do so before the time comes.'[3] Perhaps it was Nicholson's own manner that was grating on Wilson; Major Charles Reid thought Nicholson had a 'haughty manner and peculiar sneer'.

Baird Smith's relationship with the general was worsening as well. Wilson clearly had a habit of writing perhaps more than he should; to Baird Smith alone there are over sixty letters extant, and thirty-two of them were written between 4 and 14 September. Baird Smith wrote of his exasperation on the 6th:

> I was very angry again yesterday with the General, he is the most obstructive being ever created for the worry of an unfortunate Chief Engineer's mind. I had been urging him to do some of what he called 'Baird Smith's impossibilities,' and he wrote me one of his impertinent letters. I was half disposed to run rusty, but then the thought of the great interests at stake, and my knowledge of the fact that in reality he leans almost exclusively on me; came to compose me; so I didn't run rusty, but kept my temper, and satisfied myself by proving to him that he was egregiously and absurdly wrong. He came up last night, and we had a long talk about things in general, and he agreed as usual, to all that I proposed. It will be a strange story, the story of the capture of Delhi, I mean its secret history, but it will never be told, and all memory of the General's absolute obstructiveness will be buried under the glare of success. However, if we only do succeed, it will matter but little.[4]

The next day, Wilson was candid in a letter to the chief engineer about the pressure he was under to take the city with what he thought were insufficient resources:

> My dear Smith, we shall never get on in this manner, because I told you, you were asking more than the means at my disposal would allow me to sanction. You say all your calculations are valueless, and even waste labour; and seem inclined to throw all the work as well as responsibility on me. I have already more than I can manage, and my head gets into such a state that I fell nearly mad sometimes. For God's sake don't drive me quite so.[5]

On 9 September, Wilson complained of Baird Smith not wanting to open up the siege batteries till No. 3 Battery was ready. He entirely disagreed with this, feeling that by not opening all the batteries they were undoing all the work done by Battery No. 1 over the last few days – not to mention wasting valuable ammunition. 'A great and useless delay has, in my opinion, also taken place,' he wrote, 'which will greatly encourage the enemy and discourage our own troops, more particularly the working parties, who were led to believe they would only be called upon for such exertion for a very short period, but will now by the miscalculation and want of arrangement on the part of the Engineer Dept. be continued for four days and nights, perhaps longer.'[6]

However, Wilson bowed to the wishes of the chief engineer in an indication of the friction between them, commenting, 'I shall not, however, oppose myself to the wishes of the Chief Engineer, but as I cannot coincide with him, it will be better that in future he makes all his requisitions regarding the arming of the batteries, direct to Major Gaitskill, commanding the Artillery, and for working parties to the Asst. Adjt-Genl. of the Forces.' Baird Smith in turn acknowledged that anxiety was playing heavily on Wilson's mind:

> He is quite off his balance, and now he has 'cut' me, and we don't communicate officially at all except through his staff! It is a great relief, and the result is pretty much as poor Walker anticipated, and I find myself somewhat in the position of commanding the army in a quiet way. I command the General anyhow, and as things stand he is conscious of it, and doesn't like it, and takes a congenial revenge by abusing myself and brigade whenever he can.[7]

Part of Wilsons's problem could be attributed to his health. Perhaps there was an element of truth in what was said by the men – Wilson was known to suffer from insomnia and what he termed 'dreadful cramps' in his legs and feet. He also complained of the excessive heat. 'I get so exhausted and my head gets so confused that I at times almost despair,'[8] he wrote. Sleep, it had to be admitted, was generally fitful for everyone, whether in the city or on the ridge.

*****

Regardless of these issues, preparations continued in full swing. On the morning of 12 September, with the batteries working, a council of war was arranged by Wilson. All regimental commanding officers were invited, and the assault on the city was discussed and agreed – although no date was settled upon. On Sunday 13 September, in the Anglican service, the first lesson quoted a violent tract from Nahum 3:

> Woe to the bloody city! it is all full of lies and robbery, the prey departeth not;
>
> The noise of a whip, and the noise of the rattling of the wheels, and of the prancing horses, and of the jumping chariots.

During this day, the breaches in the city wall were examined. Two officers, Lang and Taylor, went along with four men of the 60th Rifles during the day. The rebels on the walls must have been snoozing as the two officers managed to reach the glacis and have a look at the ditch and the two breaches without being shot at. Lang reported back that the breaches could be negotiated in an assault. Two engineers also went to the batteries that evening to survey the breaches. They were accompanied by Nicholson, who stayed at a battery. He was apparently well pleased with their work as he surveyed the broken walls: 'I must shake hands with you fellows; you have done your best to make my work easy tomorrow,' he declared.

Further confirmation was necessary before a decision could be made as to when to begin the assault. To confirm earlier findings, later that night Medley, Lang, Home and Greathed were sent up close to the city walls to examine the breaches at the Kashmir and Water Bastions. Wilson wanted to make sure they were sufficient for ingress so that no misfortunes occurred on the day. Greathed and Home ventured close to the Water Bastion, while Medley and Lang inspected the Kashmir Bastion. Lang also jumped into the ditch to measure its width there – 16 feet. Venturing so close to the walls was fraught with danger. As they completed their task they heard the cries of the defenders, alerting them to their discovery. They managed to make it back unhurt despite a volley from the sepoys. It was now official: the breaches were of a reasonable size and could be used for ingress. However, the musketry parapets at the Water Bastion were still intact and could cause some problems. With the breaches fully appraised, Wilson made his decision: they would launch their assault the very next morning.

That night, Wilson gave precise orders as to the position of each regiment, the organisation of the columns and their objectives, although he was still coy about the exact time of the attack. 'Gentlemen, I do not myself know the day nor the hour of the assault; and if I did, I freely confess I would not tell you, for fear, in some happy moment, or at some social board, the secret might casually and unwittingly escape,' he explained before dismissing them.

Wilson had roughly 8,000 fit men at his disposal. This force was to be assembled into five storming columns, with Nicholson in overall command of four of the five columns. The four columns under Nicholson would attack the city while the fifth was to be kept in reserve. Two of the attacking columns would enter the city by the breach in the Kashmir Bastion; the other two would enter via the Kashmir Gate, which was to be blasted open.

Column 1 was to be led by Nicholson and consisted of around 1,000 bayonets: 300 men of HM75th, 250 men of the 1st European Bengal Fusiliers and 450 men of the 2nd Punjab Infantry. Attached to the column were Lts Lang, Medley and Bingham of the Engineers and around sixty other men who were to turn any captured guns on the enemy if the assault was successful. Half the column was to attack the breach near Kashmir Bastion while the other half was to escalade the walls to the left of the breach.

Column 2, around 850 men, was to be led by Brigadier William Jones (HM61st) and consisted of 250 men of HM8th, 250 men of the 2nd European Bengal Fusiliers and 350 men of the 4th (Rothney's) Sikhs. Lts Greathed, Hovenden and Pemberton of the Engineers were attached to the column with around twenty others, again to turn any captured guns on the enemy. Column 2 was to attack the breach near the Water Bastion.

Column 3, around 950 strong, was to be led by Colonel George Campbell (HM52nd). This comprised 200 men of HM52nd Light Infantry, 250 men the Kumaon Battalion (Gurkhas) and 500 men of the 1st Punjab Infantry (Coke's Rifles). Lts Home, Salkeld and Tandy of the Engineers were attached and twenty others of a Bengal artillery detachment. Column 3 was to attempt to enter through the Kashmir Gate – assuming it had been blown up successfully by Salkeld, Home and Tandy.

Column 4, around 860 men, was to be led by Major Charles Reid (Sirmoor Battalion) and was comprised of the various pickets, European and Indian, from the Hindu Rao position (380 men) including the Gurkhas, 50 men of HM60th Rifles, 80 of HM61st, 160 of the 1st European Bengal Fusiliers, 65 of the Kumaon Battalion, 25 from Coke's Rifles as well as some of the Kashmir contingent. Lts Maunsell and Tenant of the Engineers were attached. Column 4's role was to attack the Kishanganj area from the ridge and, once cleared, to enter through the Lahore Gate. Once inside they were to join up with the other three columns.

Column 5, headed by Brigadier John Longfield (HM8th Regiment), was to be the reserve column. This comprised 250 men of HM61st, 450 men of the 4th (Wilde's) Punjab Infantry and 300 men of the 1st Belooch Battalion (one wing only). Meanwhile, HM60th Rifles would act as the skirmishers and 300 Jhind troops were attached as well as Lts Ward and Thackeray of the Engineers. The column was to follow Column 3 into city.

Meanwhile, the Cavalry Brigade would be under the command of Brigadier Grant. This comprised HM9th Lancers, the 1st Punjaub Cavalry, the 2nd Punjaub Cavalry, the 5th Punjaub Cavalry, the Guides and Hodson's Horse – in total 610 men. The role of the cavalry would be to position themselves to the right of Column 1 (facing the Mori Gate and adjacent to Kishanganj) and to thereby protect the flank of the attack while also protecting the camp from any counterattack by the rebels. This was a token force, however, and it was recognised that if the rebels were sufficiently organised and mindful of British strength they could easily brush this force aside and capture the camp. It was a risk that had to be taken. The force was supplemented by all the sick and wounded in the camp.

There was also the Cavalry Reserve, commanded by Lieutenant-Colonel William Custance and comprising members of HM6th Dragoon Guards, Hodson's Horse, the Guides, the 3rd Bengal Light Cavalry and some units of the 1st, 2nd and 5th Punjaub Cavalry as well as the Multan Horse. Meanwhile, the defence of the camp and the batteries was left to Colonel John Dennis, HM52nd Light Infantry.

In front of the columns would be a 200-strong covering force of HM60th Rifles under Colonel John Jones which would screen the advance of Columns 1, 2 and 3 before joining the reserve column. The directions of each column once the city was entered had been decided, and each commander was given a plan of operations on oil paper to take with him.

The assault was finally confirmed at 11 p.m., with the columns to assemble at their allocated places at 3:30 a.m. There was little sleep in the British camp that night. Other instructions came through: no prisoners were to be taken as there were no men to guard them. Women and children were not to be harmed. Given the situation, any man or officer who fell during the advance or in the city was to be left where he was – all men must be spared for the attack. The wounded could be picked up after the assault if it was a success; if the assault failed, they would be left to the mercy of the rebels. Finally, as stipulated during the nomination of the prize agents, the men were on no account to stop the advance to indulge in plunder.

By some curious twist of fate, 14 September was the anniversary of British troops entering Delhi in 1803 under Lord Lake. If the assault on the walls was successful, British troops would enter the city on the fifty-fourth anniversary of the first capture.

Wilson still harboured doubts, even at this late hour. At 2.15 a.m. he wrote to Baird Smith voicing his concerns:

> From what I can judge on reading this (the reports) I should say the assault on the Water Bastion is hopeless, there is no approach to it apparently. What do you propose? I have received no note from yourself. Must we trust solely to the Cashmere Bastion and Gateway? You are determined I shall not have a moment's sleep to-night. Please reply quick to this, as it may change all our plans.

*****

In the city, it was quite obvious that an attack was imminent. Preparations were duly made, although the British heard about them. Intelligence regarding rebel preparations didn't just come from humble sources, however; one of the informants was Mirza Ilahi Bux, Zafar's father-in-law. He was supplying news to Rajab Ali. The information supplied by the spies largely pointed in the same direction, although perceptions varied when it came to morale.

While the attempt to destroy the British batteries on the 11th had failed, according to Toorab Ali there was certain sense of jubilation among the rebels that something had been achieved:

> To-day the Cavalry have suffered immensely in killed and wounded. But the rebels on the whole are pleased with the ardour now displayed, and declare that if they had fought from the outset with the same spirit the affair would not have been so protracted. All traces of the English would have been swept from the page of history.

Zafar was seemingly disconsolate at the way things were going, however. Some of his personal guard had been asked to accompany the attack.

'The King said that they might do as they pleased,' Toorab Ali reported. 'They had already taken this regiment out once and got many of the men slaughtered. The regiment accordingly went out.'[9]

According to Gowree Shunkur, the cavalry were in much better heart than the infantry. Sowars of the 9th and 13th Irregulars and the 9th Regular Cavalry were particularly buoyant. 'They avow their intention of meeting the assault at the gate. The Infantry who try to escape are brought back by the sowars,' he reported.

The rebels made another attack on 12 September. Several sorties were made, principally from the Ajmer and Lahore Gates. Both infantry and cavalry attacked in concert with a separate body of horsemen crossing the canal in the rear of the British camp. They were chased away by the Guides and Punjabi cavalry, with around thirty rebels killed while the others retreated. This fighting largely ended all initiatives by the rebels to attack the British batteries. From now on, the rebels stayed on the defensive.

With British batteries pounding the northern walls day and night, frantic efforts were being made to strengthen the defences around the Kabul and Kashmir Gates. On 10 September, Gowree Shunkur passed the British a detailed account of the state of the walls and gates. He saw all thirteen gates being strengthened to some extent or another, with the most attention being paid to the Kashmir, Kabul, Lahore and Ajmer Gates, which were closest to the British lines. The Kabul Gate had been strengthened by piling up blocks of masonry behind it. A similar approach had been taken to block the Kela Ghat Gate. Shunkur noticed the rebel guns had been entirely disabled on the Kabul Gate as well as on the Kashmir, Shah and Water Bastions. In addition, the section of wall stretching from the Shah Bastion to St James' Church had been almost entirely levelled by British guns. The rebels were busy transporting more guns to the Kashmir, Kabul and Mori Gates. He also reported the British guns making less of an impact than was thought on other parts of the city walls: 'The fire from the British Batteries carries away the crest of the battlements, but does little damage to the wall itself.'[10] In some places, the rebels had actually broken some of the fringes of the battlements themselves to allow their guns to target British batteries more effectively.

Other informers, such as the *harkaras* Kulloo and Mohun, echoed the general sentiment. They reported that breastworks had been dug on both sides of the Kashmir Gate by 12 September, although they were made only of loose stone. One large breastwork had been dug between the Kabul and Kashmir Gates.[11] A breastwork was also being prepared at the wicket gate at the kutchery leading to the river. Everybody in the city, soldier or civilian, was pressed to help construct these makeshift defences. Mines were being laid as well. Futteh Mahomed reported that the rebels were mulling over laying mines at the Kashmir and Kabul Gates, although he was hearing that there were already mines at the Kabul and

Mori gates. Toorab Ali reported that the officers were contemplating a mine in St James' Church, although no work had been done by the 12th.[12] Gowree Shunkur similarly reported that a mine had been laid under the main guard at the Kashmir Gate. Meanwhile, a trench and breastwork had been constructed at the canal bridge between the Kabul and Mori Gates.[13]

Before work had begun on these defences, Zafar had urged the population of the city to resist the coming British onslaught. One recovered letter described Zafar's instructions to the officers:

> You are directed to have proclaimed throughout the city by beat of drum that this is a religious war, and is being prosecuted on account of the faith, and that it behoves all Hindu and Mussulman residents of the imperial city, or of the villages out in the country, as well as those natives of Hindustan who are arrayed against us on the ridge, or are anywhere employed on the side of the armies of the English, whether they be men of the eastern provinces, or Sikhs, or foreigners, or natives of the Himalaya Hills, or Nepalese, to continue true to their faith and creeds, and to slay the English and their servants: and you are directed to have it further proclaimed, that those who are now present with the English force or the ridge, whether they be people of Hindustan, or foreigners or hillmen, or Sikhs, or whatever country they may be natives of, or whether they be Mahomedans, or Hindus born in Hindustan, they are not to entertain any fears or dread of the enemy. Whenever they come over to this side, kind provision will be made for them, and they will be allowed to continue in their own creed and religions. You are directed to have it proclaimed further, that all who will join in the attacks on the enemy, whether they be or be not servants, will be allowed to keep themselves whatever property they may take from the English in plunder, and that they will beside receive additional rewards from His Majesty, and will be amply provided for.[14]

Estimates varied regarding rebel morale at this time. Shunkur reported on the 10th that the mutineers were in disarray:

> The troops undoubtedly get more and more disheartened every day. Heera Singh, Brigade-Major of the Neemuch Force, is not to be found. The brigade says he has gone to the batteries, and the men at the batteries give out that he is with the brigade. The soldiery are selling off all cumbrous articles of plunder. Many would desert, but the gates of the city are closed and well guarded ... Imdad Allee, Resaldar of Pulwul, with all his men, has left Delhee and is not to be heard of.[15]

This was supported by Toorab Ali, who observed sepoys deserting the city in droves whenever the chance arose. By 13 September, Hodson himself recorded that many of the mutineers were apparently evacuating Delhi in expectation of an attack.

Other informers, however, reported regiments showing much confidence. There were strong rumours of approaching rebel reinforcements. 'The sepoys say that if the assault is delayed for only five days more the English will never win Delhee, for large reinforcements are on the road. The soldiery are ready to fight to the last. None now desert,' one spy reported.[16] Futteh Mahomed had reported high spirits on the 11th: 'The Neemuch Brigade gives out that they will fight to the death. All the troops will fight for their lives. They have all sworn together.' This was confirmed by Gowree Shunkur the next day: 'The sepoys have sworn to each other to die like martyrs on the day of the assault. Those who desert are brought back and disgraced before all their comrades.' Even locals had volunteered for fighting.[17]

As for the civilians, Gowree Shunkur reported on the 12th that those in the Muslim community were likely to fight harder than their Hindu counterparts. 'The city people hear that Mussalmans are killed without mercy by the British, but Hindoos are spared. For this reason the Mussalmans are prepared to fight. This report should be contradicted,' he advised, 'otherwise the rebellion may spread.'[18]

Mirza Mughal appealed to the citizens for help defending the city. 'A proclamation has been issued for every citizen to turn out and join in the fray,' Futteh Mahomed wrote. 'Some of the 3rd Cavalry made the fanatics in the Juma Musjid take part in the fight to-day. Many were killed and wounded. The sepoys inside the city are all ready to meet the assault, but they will not venture out in sorties.'[19] Despite the prince's exhortations, however, it was plain to see that many of the civilians were fleeing, particularly toward the Paharganj area west of the walls.

On 13 September, news of the impending British attack seems to have reached the city for Mirza Mughal sent an order to the *kotwal* of the city informing him that a British attack was expected:

> May you be protected. Intelligence has just been brought that the English intend making a general attack to-night, you are therefore directed to have it proclaimed by beat of drum throughout the city, that it is incumbent on all the inhabitants whether Hindu or Mahomedan, from a due regard to their faith, to assemble directly in the direction of the Cashmere Gate, bringing iron picks and shovels with them. Consider this order imperative…[20]

PART 5

# The Fall of Delhi

# 35

# The Assault

About one third of the city is in our power, and the remainder will shortly follow, but that third has cost us between 600 and 700 killed and wounded, I am most humbly and heartily grateful to a merciful Providence that I was spared, May the God of battles continue His gracious protection to the end...

Capt. Hodson

Between 1 and 2 a.m., the British assault columns began forming in front of the camp without fanfare. Every man was given a double dram of spirits as he marched off. By 3 a.m., the columns had moved in silence to the Flagstaff Tower before advancing down the incline of the ridge to Ludlow Castle, stopping close by No. 2 Battery where scaling ladders were distributed. Here the force was joined by pickets withdrawn from positions close to the city walls, and a brief delay ensued while the guns were employed against some overnight repairs to the walls. 'Our batteries had maintained a tremendous fire up to the moment of the advance of the troops; and not a gun could the enemy bring to bear on the advancing columns,' wrote one artillery officer.[1] Once the order was given, the four columns under Nicholson moved forward, leaving the reserve column behind at Ludlow Castle.

The advance would have been very difficult to see from the city walls in the darkness. The houses, gardens and trees of the Civil Lines also blocked a good view. Wilson's order that the heavy guns continue firing at the defences as usual until the final advance ensured that the defenders had no inkling that this morning was any different. Minutes before sunrise, all columns were ready for the assault. The British guns immediately stopped their firing, and a strange calm fell on the city as had not been experienced for many weeks. Revd Rotton described the scene:

> The siege guns up to this moment had been maintaining a deafening and destructive fire, which the enemy were unable to answer with even a single piece of ordnance. The Moree, Cashmere, and Water Bastions had long been still as death; whereas our batteries had been growing louder and louder, more and more angry than before. Unexpectedly a lull ensued: the raging storm of British artillery was suddenly hushed in silence. In another moment the heads of the columns under Brigadier Nicholson and Jones were distinguishable, peering out, as it were, from their snug hiding places in the neighbourhood of the Khoodsia Bagh.[2]

As Rotton describes, Columns 1 and 2 had by this time made their way to the Qudsia Bagh, just north of the Custom House and the city walls.

The signal was to be an officer stood on a lookout point dropping a white handkerchief. 'We had been watching anxiously for it,' Richard Barter of HM75th, part of Nicholson's column, would recall. 'And now in column of fours right in front we rushed at the double through a high archway into a garden of roses and through this to the foot of the glacis. Small birds were twittering amongst the trees as we rushed on and the perfume of the roses was quite apparent in spite of the sulphury smell of powder.'[3] At the Qudsia Bagh, the 60th Rifles under Col Jones, being light infantry, had been assigned the role of skirmishers and the men immediately spread out left and right, advancing through the low brushwood that lay as close as 50 yards from the ditch. Behind them came the full weight of Columns 1 and 2, the forces crossing a bridge before spreading themselves out in a skirmishing line, two divisions moving left and two right. A short while after this, Column 3 was ordered to advance as well.

As dawn broke on the city walls, some of the lookouts saw the first troops advancing and raised the alarm. Very soon, there were scores of sepoys opening fire on the British from the walls and around the breaches. Some casualties were taken, but protection from the skirmishers of the 60th Rifles allowed others to quickly push on. Richard Barter wrote of the fire that rained down on them, with some men slower and more vulnerable thanks to the scaling ladders.

> Along the walls they swarmed as thick as bees, the sun shone full upon the white turbans and the black faces, sparkling brightly on their swords and bayonets, and our men cheered madly as they rushed towards the breach. The enemy … at first seemed perfectly taken aback at our appearance, but recovering from their surprise they now recommenced in earnest: round shot came screaming from the guns far on our right, while grape and shells whistled from those nearer, and the walls seemed a line of fire along our front. Bullets whistled in the air, and tore up the ground about our feet and men fell fast … Three times the ladder party was swept away, and three times were the ladders

> snatched from the shoulders of the dead and wounded. The only man with them who escaped untouched, as if by miracle, being the officer Lieutenant Faithfull, and he, worn out from all he'd gone through, was dead in little more than a month.[4]

The ditch in front of the walls here was 20 feet deep and 25 feet broad – a considerable obstacle, but the scaling ladders had adjustments that allowed the men to ascend the scarp with little difficulty. Barter continues:

> It was hard work getting up the breach, which was like a sloping bank of sea sand from the pounding of our shot, and behind it were some gabions between which the enemy kept up a smart fire, so close to us that I could feel the flash of each discharge hot on my cheek. To spoil their aim I kept firing my revolver with my right hand while I scrambled up with my left, holding my sword under my arm or as best I could for we carried no scabbards. They kept heaving huge blocks of masonry at us, and tried to roll some down, but they stuck in the bed of the breach, and hurt no one.[5]

Column 1 therefore entered the city with relatively little effort, the element of surprise having been achieved for the most part. Many defenders fled as soon as the attackers reached the top of the walls, although a minority of courageous individuals stayed and sacrificed their lives; most were bayonetted or shot. The 60th Rifles, who had been designated as skirmishers, opted to push on with the column; they were first to top the walls, and waved their caps to the cheering soldiers below.

Column 2, at the Water Bastion, initially faced some difficulty. Of the thirty-nine men assigned to carry the scaling ladders, twenty-nine fell dead or wounded. The ladders were invariably picked up by the men behind them, who carried them to the escarpment. The Water Bastion was soon captured, and the rebel guns were immediately turned on them; in this way the ramparts either side were quickly cleared of defenders.

While Columns 1 and 2 were busy at the breaches in the Kashmir and Water Bastions, Column 3 turned its attention on the Kashmir Gate, which was to be blown in. A small band of men had been assigned the task of laying powder bags and lighting the fuse. This party was led by Duncan, Home and Salkeld of the Engineers. They were accompanied by Sergeants John Smith and Andrew Carmichael of the Bengal Sappers and Miners, and Corporal F. Burgess and Bugler Robert Hawthorne of HM52nd, whose job it was to sound the signal that the gate had been blown. The other eight members of this party were Indians of the Bengal Sappers and Miners: Subedar Toola, Jemadar Bisram, Havildars Madhoo, Tiluk Singh and Ramtaroy and Sepoys Ram Het, Sahib Singh and Ajudhya Park. The Indians were employed to carry the powder bags, each containing 11 kilograms of gunpowder, close to the gate where they were then given to the Europeans. Salkeld meanwhile carried the portfire to light the fuses.

The members of the party were fortunate not to be hit by musket shot from the few men firing from the walls as they approached the damaged drawbridge and crossed to lay the powder bags on the gate. Home went first, and managed to lay his powder bag. Lt Medley, who was attached to Column 1 but heard of the action, describes what happened: 'So utterly paralyzed were the enemy of the audacity of the proceeding, that they only fired a few straggling shots, and made haste to close the wicket with every appearance of alarm, so that Lieut. Home, after laying his bags, jumped into the ditch unhurt.' The second man following him was shot and didn't manage to reach the gate. Sergeant Carmichael was hit, as was Havildar Madhoo. Smith then went and successfully placed his bag along with that dropped by the second man, and prepared the fuses. With a train laid for the lighting of the powder bags, all that was required now was to light the fuses. This was easier said than done:

> Salkeld laid his bags, but was shot through the arm and leg, and fell back on the bridge, handing the portfire to Serjeant [*sic*] Burgess, bidding him light the fuses. Burgess was instantly shot dead in the attempt. Serjeant Carmichael then advanced, took up the portfire and succeeded in the attempt, but immediately fell mortally wounded. Serjeant Smith, seeing him fall, advanced at a run, but finding that the fuse was already burning, threw himself down into the ditch where the bugler had already conveyed poor Salkeld. In another moment, a terrific explosion shattered the massive gate, the bugle sounded the advance, and then with a loud cheer the storming party was in the gateway.

With the gate destroyed, the bugler sounded the call and Column 3 poured through the gate, overpowering the defenders.[6]

Having entered the city, the men of the three columns converged at the Kashmir Bastion to receive orders before advancing. The combined British force now occupied the relatively open space from the Kashmir Gate to St James' Church 250 yards down Lothian Road. The annihilation wrought on the Kashmir Gate vicinity by the British guns over the previous weeks could now be seen plainly by the soldiers, among them Col Bourchier:

> The demon of destruction seemed to have enjoyed a perfect revel. The houses in the neighborhood of the Mooree and Cashmere Bastions were a mass of ruins; the walls near the breaches were cracked in every direction, while the church was completely gutted and riddled by shot and shell: its gilt cross was still untouched, and, as seen of a bright morning from the ridge, glittering in the rising sun, seemed beckoning us onwards, with the full assurance that the religion of the Cross should still, even in that city, soar high over Mahomedan bigotry and

> cruelty the Water Bastion the destruction was still more striking. Huge siege guns, with their carriages, lay about seemingly like playthings in a child's nursery.

Inside the city there was consternation at the ease with which the British had made ingress. Many sepoys rushed to flee the city, leaving the civilians to an uncertain fate. Local accounts say many of the sepoys ran as soon as the British managed to scale the walls at the Kashmir Bastion, abandoning posts from the Kabul Gate all the way to the Kashmir Gate. Zahir Dehlvi recalled the chaotic scenes as some of the rebels lost heart:

> The Indians were going towards the Mithai ka Pul while the British soldiers were heading towards the Kashmiri *Darwaza* [Gate]. The Sawars turned their horses towards the path that ran behind the Lahori Darwaza parapets towards the Kabuli Darwaza. I turned towards my own house. When I reached Bhawani Shankar's Chatta, I saw that there were innumerable *purbias* [easterners, i.e. the mutineers] running out of it. There were many people in the bazaar at this time. They stopped the *purbias* and asked, 'Where are you running after having forced the battle on us?' The *purbias* threw down their weapons and said, 'Brothers, We are done fighting; now you fight yourselves.' And leaving their guns, they ran away. When people saw this state of affairs, they all went back to their houses.[7]

The local citizens had good reason to stay in hiding. Despite the order not to harm civilians, once inside the city the columns gave little quarter in the early stages of the assault. A soldier recorded the attitude of his colleagues as they began combing through the houses near the Kashmir Gate: 'All the city people found within the walls when our troops entered were bayonetted on the spot, and the number was considerable, as you may suppose, when I tell you that in some houses forty and fifty persons were hiding. These were not mutineers, but residents of the city, who trusted to our well-known mild rule for pardon. I am glad to say they were disappointed.'[8]

After the short union at the Kashmir Bastion, the columns went their separate ways as planned. Nicholson initially led a column towards the Jama Masjid, while Columns 1 and 2 led by Brigadier Jones moved northwards, clearing the road behind the walls. The goal was to capture the walls and the Mori, Shah and Burn Bastions, and then to take the Lahore Gate facing the west of the city, which would secure British control of the entire north and north-west of the city. The first defences to be captured were a nearby tower and a rebel battery between the Kashmir and Mori Bastions. After this, the Mori Bastion itself fell along with the Kabul Gate. With most of the rebels disappearing from the ramparts, the walls up to the Kabul Gate had been won rapidly and with few casualties. Jones had been given instructions not to proceed towards the Lahore Gate till word came of the capture of the Jama Masjid, so held back; this was later seen as a mistake, for the Lahore Gate could have been captured quite easily at this point. The delay gave the rebels time to regroup, and the going would get much tougher from here on.

'We might have taken the Lahore Gate without losing another man as the Pandies had all bolted from it,' opined Lt Cadell. 'As soon, however, as they perceived that we did not advance they returned. Before we had been ten minutes at the Cabool Gate they commenced peppering us with grape ... Not content with the Lahore Gate guns playing on us, the enemy brought two field pieces to the end of the street leading to the Cabool Gate.'[9] Cadell, who would be awarded the Victoria Cross for his valour at Delhi, blamed the elderly Jones, suggesting a younger mind would have taken the risk (despite orders) and pushed on. Lt Moffat agreed with Cadell that it was a bad decision to lose the momentum and which caused a panic: 'As long as we rushed on, cheering and never stopping, all went well. But the check was sad: the men, crouching behind corners, and in the archways which support the ramparts, gradually nursed a panic. One by one they tried to get back: we stopped them and staved off the flight for half an hour, but at last out they all came, and, sweeping back the officers, made for the Kabul Gate.'

Then Lahore Gate was only a third of a mile south of the Kabul Gate, but the ramparts as well as the houses facing the walls offered plenty of firing platforms inaccessible to an advancing column. In addition, the rebels had placed a 24-pounder at the gate on high ground ready to fire on any advance coming up the road.

Around this time, Nicholson appeared. He had made his way down the street from the Kashmir Gate and was seen by Brigadier Grant standing on the Mori Bastion a few hundred yards behind the Kabul Gate, surveying the progress. 'He called out to men that the fighting was going on well for us in the town and that he was on his way to attack the Lahore Gate and Bastion, about 500 yards further on,' Grant recalled.[10] When Nicholson reached the position at the Kabul Gate where Brigadier Jones and his men were resting, he expressed some displeasure that the advance had not been continued. Addressing one of the officers, he declared, 'The men are not in hand.' The officer requested orders: 'Tell me and I'll soon show you that they are in hand.' Trying to push towards the Lahore Gate would now be difficult as the rebels had organised themselves, but that was what Nicholson desired and so an attack was made. 'As we rounded the corner, we were greeted by a terrible shower of grape from a 24-pounder gun planted on high ground, and the adjoining houses were full of sepoys, who from such close quarters sent destruction into our ranks,' wrote Major John Angelo.[11] The column hesitated, and Nicholson came forward. In an attempt to rally his men, he advanced down the street with his sword raised. At this point a rebel found his mark. Some say the bullet hit Nicholson in the chest; others said it took him in the back. Capt. Graydon was present:

> It was while again encouraging the men, with his face towards them and his back to the enemy, that a shot, evidently fired from the Burn Bastion, struck him in the back, causing him to reel round. Luckily the recess [in the wall] … was close by. Indeed, he was partly inside it, but not sufficiently sheltered from the enemy's fire. Fortunately, also for him, a sergeant was at hand – probably an orderly – who immediately caught him, and laid him on the ground inside the recess, and tended him.

Graydon gave Nicholson some brandy, which seemed to revive him. Fearing a rebel advance that might sweep up the stricken brigadier, Graydon suggested moving him to the rear. A defiant Nicholson declined, declaring that if he must die he would die where he fell. Despite his protests, he was carried back to the Kabul Gate before being moved further back towards the Kashmir Gate. He lay there till a doolie could be organised to carry him back to the British camp, where he was found by Lt Roberts:

> Just after starting on my errand, while riding through the Kashmir gate, I observed by the side of the road a doolie, without bearers, and with evidently a wounded man inside. I dismounted to see if I could be of any use to the occupant, when I found, to my grief and consternation, that it was John Nicholson, with death written on his face. He told me that the bearers had put the doolie down and gone off to plunder; that he was in great pain, and wished to be taken to the hospital. He was lying on his back, no wound was visible, and but for the pallor of his face, always colourless, there was no sign of the agony he must have been enduring. On my expressing a hope that he was not seriously wounded, he said: 'I am dying; there is no chance for me.'[12]

Roberts attempted to find the doolie bearers, but without luck; already these men and the various camp followers were looting the areas captured by the British force. Nevertheless, Roberts found four men who would be employed to lift the doolie. 'I put them in charge of a sergeant of the 61st Foot. Taking down his name, I told him who the wounded officer was, and ordered him to go direct to the field hospital. This was the last I saw of Nicholson.'[13]

Back in the city, meanwhile, each column had met with stiff resistance. Brigadier Jones' column had already lost eight officers and around fifty men in several assaults on the rebel position, and the decision was taken to pull back towards the Kabul Gate. The Lahore Gate would have to be left for another day.

While Columns 1 and 2 had proceeded northwards to gain control of the city gates to the north and west, Column 3 headed south towards the palace and the Chandni Chowk. This column had enjoyed early success, with Col Campbell sending a party from the Kashmir Gate to help with the capture of the Water Bastion. The kutchery was cleared next, this being next to St James' Church and the *Delhi Gazette* offices. Following this they worked their way south through the bazaar. They came up against a rebel gun, but it was soon captured. From here they advanced towards the Begum Bagh, which connected with the Chandni Chowk. A friendly chaprassy opened the gate for them. Proceeding under fire through the gardens, the column made it to the Jama Masjid, which was found to have its side arches bricked up and its gate closed. No entry could be forced, and there were neither artillery guns nor powder bags to create a new one. The rooftops and adjacent houses, meanwhile, still held rebels who kept up a steady fire. Hopeful of reinforcement, the troops waited a while but were forced back to the Begum Bagh, where they met Column 5, the reserve column, who had fought their way towards the College Gardens through a warren of narrow streets. On their way to meet Column 3, the reserve column had taken Skinner's House and the mansion of Ahmed Ali Khan.

Chronicler Khwaja Hasan Nizami tells a different story of the fighting at the Jama Masjid, writing of an attack by a body of men led by Theophilus Metcalfe. Metcalfe, a resident of the city, knew the backstreets of the metropolis well and led his men down the less frequented alleys that were not marked by sepoys for defence. He therefore reached the Masjid without too much fighting, and he and his men waited for the other columns to join them. In light of the British attack on the city, many Muslims had curiously decided to go to the mosque for their prayers at this time; Nizami described how they drove off Metcalfe's contingent.

> At this time there were thousands of Muslims praying their Juma Prayers at the Jama Masjid. They realized that the British were attempting to blow up the Mosque with gunpowder. They were armed only with swords and did not have any guns or cannon. One of them got up on the Mimbar and told his fellow men, 'The time for your test has arrived. Those who want to fight should go to the North Gate, and those who want to escape should go to the South Gate as there is no enemy there.' Not a single person went to the South Gate. All of them came out shouting Allah O Akbar and drew their swords, and they cut off the scabbards and threw them away in a symbolic gesture of not willing to return their swords to their scabbards. They attacked Metcalfe's forces, but he was ready with guns and the moment they came out his forces fired and about 200 of the attackers died on the steps of the Jama Masjid, however, the rest of them kept attacking and sword fights broke out between the two forces. The attackers fought

> with such valour that Metcalfe and his forces had to retreat towards the Church grounds at the Kashmiri Gate. The Muslims followed them but in view of the large number of troops there they did not go any further.

While Columns 1, 2, 3 and 5 entered the city, Major Reid's Column 4 and the cavalry brigade had waited outside the city on the Grand Trunk Road immediately opposite the Sabzi Mandi picket. By 5 a.m., the column was readied to advance after a delay awaiting the support of three guns; when the guns arrived, it was found they had only come with the gunners to serve one of them. Reid's orders had been to wait for the large explosion signalling the detonation of the Kashmir Gate before an advance. However, the explosion was never heard in their quarter and he had waited for the guns instead. What was heard instead was the sound of musket shots on their right. This was the Jammu contingent prematurely attacking the rebels without waiting for the order. The decision to advance had been taken out Reid's grasp, and in order to assist the Jammu troops he decided to advance the main body of his column towards the Kishanganj. The skirmishers were pushed forwards, but their advance was blocked: the road leading to Kishanganj had a manned breastwork running across it along with another running parallel further back. Observing the British advance, the rebels had held fire until the column was 50 yards away before letting loose a volley. This didn't stop the column, however, and the breastwork was captured by the Rifles and Gurkhas. Since no gun was available at the time, the work was harder than expected. Revd Rotton recalls:

> Up to this time not a gun could be brought to bear against them, for want of gunners; otherwise, at this juncture, the enemy might have been mown down, like wheat beneath the reaper's sickle. Not only were we losing opportunity after opportunity, but the enemy were reinforcing their position at Kissen Gunge. And still more disastrous than all, just as Reid was about to make a feint on the rebel front and a real attack on their flank and rear, he was severely wounded in the head, and obliged to resign his command into the hands of Captain Richard Lawrence.[14]

The second breastwork held by the rebels was very well manned. Reid's plan had been to attack a nearby serai with half the column; having taken it he could assault the breastwork from the rear while a full-frontal attack was launched simultaneously by the other half of the column. The rebels had four heavy guns, which once captured could be turned against them along with the two 8½-inch mortars Reid's column had already captured. Then the column could advance, leaving the Jammu troops in control of the area while they entered the city via the Kabul Gate, which Columns 1 and 2 should have captured.

However, the Kabul Gate had not fallen. Soon the tables began to turn for Reid's column, with the rebels putting up a stiff resistance – much better than elsewhere in the walled city. Soon a stalemate developed. Although the breastwork taken previously was held for some time, the fire was too great and Captain Lawrence eventually signalled a retreat to the column's starting position. Column 4 had lost around a third of its troops. The Jammu troops to the column's right were also outnumbered and outfought, and were pushed back by the rebels in turn. This retreat quickly turned to outright flight, and they managed to lose their four guns as well. The whole column fell into disarray, with fighting raging in the streets and gardens. The Jammu troops, having lost their guns, were in fear of the wrath of the Maharaja of Kashmir. However, fortunately for them, two of their guns were retrieved near the Lahore and Ajmer Gates. Due to their poor performance, the Jammu troops were sent back to guard the camp rather than being engaged in the attack on the city.

The failure of Column 4 and the Jammu troops with so many casualties meant the Kishanganj area remained in rebel hands. Crucially, this meant the British camp was in real danger of being overrun if the rebels chose to advance.

The cavalry brigade, meanwhile, stationed near the No. 1 Battery with the horse artillery under Brigadier Grant, had been earmarked to protect the extreme right of the line. After the various columns had entered the city, the brigade had also been ordered to move through the Kishanganj towards the Mori Bastion and then on to the Kabul Gate. As they advanced they came under fire; the gate was still in enemy hands and their position was exposed. They also received fire from the houses, rooftops and gardens in the area. This continued for nearly three hours, with the guns under Major Tombs firing back, although the men managed to capture and spike two guns stationed in the adjoining gardens. Nevertheless, the column was taking casualties and ended up withdrawing to cover. They were followed by the rebels, who were heartened by the victory.

'The exposed situation caused great losses in the cavalry, and they moved still further to their front, halting amidst some trees,' wrote Revd Rotton. 'The enemy now sallied from the gardens as though with the intention of driving the cavalry in the direction of the Kashmir Gate. The circumstances were most critical, when a body of Guide Infantry, coming up at the time, threw themselves on the rebels, maintaining their place with great resolution till help arrived, with a part of the Belooch Battalion, and the enemy were forced to retire.' Since the rebel cavalry didn't stand for a fight, the advantage was not pressed. Exposed to fire in the narrow streets, the cavalry brigade withdrew. For the next few days, the cavalry brigade was left to guard the British camp.

*****

Wilson had initially stationed himself at Ludlow Castle as the assault on the city walls began. It was impossible to see what was happening in the maze of streets and dead-end alleys within the old walled city, so Wilson had received only confused intelligence on progress during the day. To compound his anxiety, there were reports of many dead and wounded being carried back.

'The long, long line of litters commenced to return to the Field Hospitals from the scene of strife, with their mangled burthens,' recalled Col Bourchier. 'The dead, dying, and wounded in every state were passing by, showing how deadly was the struggle. Though little separated from the scene of action none could tell us what had been doing, or what was the state of affairs. Over and over again the same questions were asked, "Were the columns inside? Were the breaches gained?" None could reply.'[15] Later in the day, as British troops began to fan out inside the city, Wilson entered the city and settled in at St James' Church.

According to Lt Roberts, all the anxiety about capturing the city combined with news of casualties during the assault to play havoc with Wilson's health. It had become clear that the British held all the northern perimeter wall, bastions and gates from the Water Bastion up to the Kabul Gate. Outside the walled city, however, Column 4's failure meant there was a strong danger of rebels attacking the lightly defended British camp.

> He was ill and tired out, and as the day wore on and he received discouraging reports, he became more and more anxious and depressed. He heard of Reid's failure, and of Reid himself having been severely wounded; then came the disastrous news that Nicholson had fallen, and a report (happily false) that Hope Grant and Tombs were both killed. All this greatly agitated and distressed the General, until at last he began seriously to consider the advisability of leaving the city and falling back on the Ridge. I was ordered to go and find out the truth of these reports, and to ascertain exactly what had happened to No. 4 column and the Cavalry on our right.

Roberts found Tombs and Grant alive, and quickly rode back to inform the general that the situations was not as bad as feared.

> The news I was able to give for the moment somewhat cheered the General, but did not altogether dispel his gloomy forebodings; and the failure of Campbell's column, (which just at that juncture returned to the church), the hopelessness of Nicholson's condition, and, above all, the heavy list of casualties he received later, appeared to crush all spirit and energy out of him. His dejection increased, and he became more than ever convinced that his wisest course was to withdraw from the city. He would, I think, have carried out this fatal measure,

> notwithstanding that every officer on his staff was utterly opposed to any retrograde movement, had it not been his good fortune to have beside him a man sufficiently bold and resolute to stimulate his flagging energies.

The man in question was Baird Smith, who despite his wounds was adamant that there should be no retreat. He was supported in this opinion by Brig. Gen. Neville Chamberlain, who was also wounded; Wilson sent two messages to Chamberlain, resting back at the Hindu Rao, to canvas his opinion on whether the force should be pulled back from the city or not. The first note was sent after troops had been pushed back from the Jama Masjid and the Lahore Gate and things looked bleak. He had asked for the Belooch Battalion to enter the city as reinforcements, telling Chamberlain he was hopeful that 'we shall be able to hold what we have got'. The second note was sent at around 4 p.m., when the British troops were exhausted and three of the columns had failed to meet their objectives. By now Wilson sounded desperate. According to Wilson, his question wasn't framed in explicit terms. 'I want your advice,' Wilson had written in the note, asking if Chamberlain 'could do anything from Hindu Rao's house to assist ... Our numbers are frightfully reduced, and we have lost so many senior officers that the men are not under proper control; indeed, I doubt if they could be got to do anything dashing. I want your advice. If the Hindu Rao's picket cannot be moved, I do not think we shall be strong enough to take the city.'

Chamberlain realised that Wilson was really suggesting a full retreat. He could not write himself, due to an injury on his right arm, so he dictated an answer in which he stressed the great advantage that had been gained over the rebels and how the demoralised rebels were already fleeing the city. Holding on was much the better option, he said. Others also chimed in with their support. Major Brind, on being consulted, replied, 'God has favoured us so far, and would not desert us.' Nicholson, dying at that moment, expressed the same view and indeed some anger at the general: 'Thank God I have strength yet to shoot him if necessary,' he is reported to have uttered on hearing of Wilson's indecision. With such strong consensus from his officers, the dithering Wilson felt safe in making the decision to keep the British force in the occupied portion of the city overnight.

By 7 p.m., the line had been stopped for rest. As evening drew on, heavy guns brought into the city began to play on the palace as well as the magazine. The key to the city was the magazine, which was not particularly defensible. Once this was taken, a speedy conclusion was expected to result as the rebels could take little with them due to a lack of carriage. British mortars, meanwhile, were trained on the Salimgarh Fort. Many of the rebel guns on the bastions had also been turned against the remaining rebel positions.

There had been plentiful casualties, as Wilson well knew. Doctors and chaplains had been stationed about half a mile from the city walls, with a building just past the Metcalfe House being used as a hospital. Here, doolies could be seen ferrying the dead and wounded from the various streets of the city. By evening, those killed included Lt Tandy, Engineers; Lt Fitzgerald, 75th Foot; Lt Bradshaw, HM52nd Foot; Capt. McBarnet, 55th Native Infantry; Lt Murray, Guide Corps; and Maj. Jacob, 1st Fusiliers. Among the roughly thirty wounded officers were Brig. Nicholson and engineers Greathed, Maunsell, Chesney, Salkeld, Brownlow, Hovenden and Medley, who had destroyed the Kashmir Gate.

It wasn't just British troops but allies as well. The Jammu contingent had lost around 150 killed and wounded. The Jhind contingent had also lost five or six men. All in all, there had been 1,145 casualties on the first day inside the city, with ten missing. Various estimates were bandied about as to rebel casualties – some suggesting as many as 2,000 killed with another 1,000 wounded.

36

# The Capture

A report has just been brought in that Kishengunje and suburbs have been totally evacuated by the mutineers, leaving their heavy guns in position. The spies report all organization of [rebel] regiments at an end.

Brig. Gen. Chamberlain to John Lawrence,
4 p.m., 16 September 1857[1]

The British force now held a line stretching from St James' Church in the east past Delhi College to the Kabul Gate in the north-east of the city, covering barely 5 percent of the whole. Importantly, the nearby magazine was still held by the rebels. In order to target it, Wilson had ordered the heavy guns and mortars to be brought into the city throughout the evening of the 14th, and Maj. Scott's battery in the college compound had forced a breach. The plan was to assault the magazine complex the very next morning, with the walls reduced further overnight. Meanwhile, British mortars on the captured Water Bastion targeted the Salimgarh Fort while also shelling the palace. Further west, the guns and mortars brought through the Mori and Kabul Bastions began working to reduce the Lahore Gate and Burn Bastion less than half a mile to the south, where the rebels were showing stronger resistance. The rebel guns at Salimgarh Fort were in turn targeting the church; perhaps they had been informed that its gardens were being used to store ordnance brought down from the British camp.

Although the assault on the city the previous day had been successful, little would be achieved on the 15th; British momentum seemed to fail entirely. This was generally considered to be down to the exhaustion of the troops after the exertions of the 14th. There were other reasons as well. Rumours of Wilson's discussions with his officers had got about; there were stories circulating that he thought the troops were insufficient to hold what had already been gained, and that he feared the British camp might fall into enemy hands. It was said he thought it best to return to camp.

However, the foremost reason for the day's failure to advance was the drunken state of many of the soldiers. Copious amounts of alcohol had been discovered near the Kashmir Gate the preceding evening, and many had spent the night indulging. Whether these stocks were deliberately placed near the Kashmir Gate by the rebels, as some suspected, is difficult to say; regardless, it certainly tempted the British soldiers, who became heavily inebriated. More stocks were discovered at shops nearby and were plundered in the darkness. Incapacitated soldiers, staggering about, fell victim to rebel soldiers. Other troops, hoping for a quick profit, left their posts and, despite the vigilance of the prize agents at the gates, spirited bottles of champagne to Ludlow Castle where they were quickly sold on for three pence a bottle.[2] Many voiced surprise that a bigger disaster hadn't occurred overnight; the rebels took almost no advantage of the dark and the state of the British soldiers.

Charles Saunders, Commissioner of Delhi, later wrote of the difficulties encountered in trying to prevent drunken indiscipline over the following critical days:

> Only those on the spot know the difficulties with which our commanders had to deal (i.e. after the assault). The whole Army was utterly and entirely disorganised, and within three or four hours of the assault, discipline was almost at an end. For several days, a majority of our European troops might almost be said to be suffering from delirium tremens. The native troops were almost as, if not equally, disorganised from similar causes, and from the plunder which fell into their hand.[3]

In order to prevent further drunkenness, Wilson ordered all the wine and beer stocks found to be destroyed – much to the chagrin of drinkers and profiteers alike. Even if not consumed, the sale of such a stock would have added a sizeable amount to the prize money. Tens of thousands of bottles were broken up by the guards allocated to the provost-marshal.[4] The Sikh and Punjabi soldiers were given the unpopular task of destroying the supplies. Streams of beer flowed down the streets. Wilson's injunction regarding plundering had also been sorely tested during the night, for there were many shops within the areas occupied by the British.

*****

What undoubtedly helped the British cause was the state of chaos and morale in the rebel camp. Without a guiding mind, the rebels failed to take advantage of the British pause for breath. No attempt was even made to attack the lightly defended British camp on the ridge. Instead, by 9 a.m., rather than making a stand, many of the rebels were melting away. News came in from a *harkara* in Najafgarh to the west of the city that groups of rebel cavalry twenty to fifty strong were passing the village as they fled. Large rebel contingents had even deserted the city during the assault; Rajab Ali passed word that many were now heading south-west in the direction of Rewaree: 'Sowars are out on the various roads endeavouring to stop fugitives, and to persuade them to return, but they will not turn back. There are not many rebels inside the city up to the Delhee Gate.'[5] British officers commented that while they did little themselves there was also far less resistance from the rebels on the morning of the 15th. It was as if a bubble had burst.

During the afternoon, the rebels seemed to recover some poise. The strong contingent at the Lahore Gate, for instance, proved to be resilient. On sensing the British had overstretched themselves, they launched their own counterattacks. Other contingents around the city also took the chance, with the college and its surrounds given particular attention. At the same time, the rebel batteries at Salimgarh Fort continued to pound the Kashmir gate area. 'We are making slow progress in the city,' Hodson complained. 'The fact is the troops are utterly demoralized by hard work and hard drink I grieve to say. For the first time in my life I have had to see English soldiers refuse repeatedly to follow their officers. Greville, Jacob, Nicholson and Speke were all sacrificed to this.'

The church was given over to HM61st, but the whole building was in a sad state – all the pews and ornaments were destroyed, with the pulpit and reading desk torn down. Hardly a pane of glass was intact. It was obvious the rebels had used the church as a sort of canteen because all sorts of utensils and cooking pots lay strewn around the building. The British bombardment had caused damage too, with some of the shot directed at the city walls and the Kashmir Gate having fallen on the church instead. Nonetheless, it was a large building and provided a vast living space preferable to the small buildings around it.

Throughout the day, Wilson allowed locals living in the captured areas to leave the city. This host of refugees could be seen slowly making its way through the Kashmir Gate and past Ludlow Castle. Because of their large numbers, housing them at the British camp was considered impossible; they were instead directed towards a deserted village near the city.

*****

The next day, 16 September, would be more successful for the British force. At 7 a.m., the magazine was stormed. The force assembled for the attack was composed of HM61st, Wilde's 4th Punjab Rifles and a wing of the Belooch Battalion, the whole under Colonel Deacon of the 61st. Curiously, this important building with large stocks of ordinance had few defenders; in all perhaps 100 were found when the force went through the breach. This small force by all accounts put up a good fight, contesting every room they occupied, but the magazine was captured with relative ease. The rebels were bayonetted without mercy, although a few defenders escaped through the rear exit by the river. Around a dozen men were killed and wounded on the British side. Brig. Gen. Chamberlain was happy with what he saw:

> The magazine is full of stores of every description except powder, and notwithstanding the enormous quantity that they have expended during the last three months, no impression appears to have been made on the huge piles still left. The guns have all been brought in from Kishungunj, which has been totally evacuated by the mutineers.[6]

The rumour that the rebels had lacked percussion caps was found to be false; if not, they must have succeeded in manufacturing large quantities themselves, because the magazine held plenty. The only thing lacking, as Chamberlain pointed out, was gunpowder. The magazine and all its stocks laid bare the rebel failure to properly plan or organise; it was imperative above all else to keep possession of the magazine and all it contained, but the defence had been nominal. There had been no serious attempt to remove the valuable guns – no fewer than 125 were inside the magazine. If they could not defend it, they should have tried to blow it up as the British had before them; no such attempt had been made, which was surely proof of the hasty flight of a good bulk of the city's defenders.

The magazine wasn't a safe place after its capture. Rebel guns positioned near the Chandni Chowk and adjacent to the palace continued firing shot into the magazine while rebels near the south walls threw hand-grenades and fired their muskets from nearby houses. A few even climbed nearby trees and threw flaming bamboos into the magazine complex to set fire to the thatched roofs of huts within. Some of the British soldiers defending the magazine opted to return in kind. One Lt Benny of the artillery was seen on the roof of the main building throwing lit shells at the rebels below.

A serious attempt was made to recapture the magazine and adjacent workshops later in the afternoon. Some rebel guns were brought up from the palace gates, and the workshops were at least partly captured by the rebels for a time. Notably, on this day the magazine saw Zafar's only attempt to rally his troops, though his heart wasn't really in it according to Mukand Lal: 'On the 16th September he [Zafar] went in an open litter in the direction of the magazine at the head of the army but had scarcely proceeded 200 yards beyond the palace when he halted for an hour and then returned, the army in the meantime dispersing.'[7]

At the far end of the magazine, work now commenced on the construction of a battery to target the palace itself. The battery that had played on the magazine the previous day was now aimed at the palace as well. The capture of a large mansion to the west around this time was promising as well, the building's height and location making it a useful firing platform over the Lahore Gate, which was still being stubbornly defended by the rebels.

Only one rebel gun had troubled the British columns the previous day. Col Jones had attempted to capture it at the time, but failed. The gun was now targeted by mortars, and its rebel crew were seen retiring. This meant the British column could now advance up the street leading to Skinner's House, although the advance was halted at night and the troops withdrew to their original positions.

Outside the city, the rebels had evacuated the entire Kishanganj suburb by 2 p.m. despite their successes the previous day. They had left all five heavy guns – four 18-pounders and an 8-inch mortar. British guns stationed on the city walls opposite had entirely commanded the area, forcing the rebels to retreat. Wilson was quite relieved at this, for taking the suburb house by house would have been an expensive option; there were barely sufficient troops to take the walled city as it was. The Kishanganj was subsequently put under a detachment of troops formerly stationed at Hindu Rao.

By 3 p.m., the rebels had also abandoned the battery across the river opposite Salimgarh Fort. The only resistance in the heart of the city seemed to be in isolated pockets where rebels fought from the rooftops of houses. By 7 p.m. that evening, the British line stretched south from the Kabul Gate and beyond the magazine. With the rebels having vacated the magazine, the Kishanganj and the rest of the city suburbs, morale was high in the British camp at the end of the day. However, the advance had unforeseen consequences. Despite the strong injunction against the consumption of captured liquor after yesterday's torpor, inquisitive soldiers with a nose for plunder had discovered a new cache near the Kabul Gate and, as before, found it difficult to restrain themselves. Large stocks of cheese and bacon were found in an English-owned shop and predictably seized upon.

Despite the relative success of the day, Wilson was clearly feeling the strain more than ever. 'General Wilson is fairly broken down by fatigue and anxiety,' wrote Hodson. 'He cannot stand on his legs today; fortunately Chamberlain is well enough to go down and keep him straight and Colonel Seaton also; two good men if he will be led by them.'[8]

*****

By 9 a.m. on the morning of the 17th, all British mortars were directed towards the palace walls as a precursor to an assault. It was thought that the capture of the palace would destroy rebel morale entirely, so it was imperative to capture the complex as early as possible. Neville telegrammed John Lawrence around that time outlining the situation:

> The report is that the Royal family and the King's three regiments, one regiment of Native Infantry and some Light Cavalry troopers hold the palace, and intend to fight it out to the last. The mutineers are less active to-day. The Bareilly and Neemuch Troops are said to have come into the town and have started off their baggage under an escort of Infantry and guns down to the Muttra road towards Gwalior. They intend to follow them by forced marches when they have had a fair start. The townspeople continue to fly to the palace, and numberless women have come into our camp.[9]

Chamberlain personally did not think the magazine was a good site from which to mortar the palace; indeed, he didn't think they had any particularly good spots from which to shell it. This hadn't made a difference, he reported: 'The King is reported to be in the palace still; if so, his residence must be a very warm one, for we are pelting shells throughout the length of the palace enclosure from north to south. Great number of women and inhabitants of the city have come in and been passed out of the town by us, and the look-out at Hindoo Rao's house reports streams of people and animals as having issued from the Ajmere Gate.'[10]

The few rebels still inside Salimgarh Fort overlooking the palace now fired only occasionally, and made little impression on the overwhelming British batteries. As many as twenty British mortars had commenced firing on the Salimgarh Fort as well as the palace.

At around 10 a.m., British troops captured the ruins of what had been the Delhi Bank House overlooking the Chandni Chowk. Situated in a large garden full of trees, bushes and other undergrowth, it had been difficult to capture, with hard fighting. Several other buildings along the Chandni Chowk were also temporarily captured, although the British troops had to retreat owing to the fact that rebel guns overlooked these buildings. The bank was held and furnished with mortars, allowing further bombardment of the palace.

The only determined resistance was at the Lahore Gate. This had not fallen despite several determined attempts by the British columns. Part of the position's strength was that it was entirely overlooked by the guns of the Burn Bastion. Capt. Taylor advised Wilson that the bastion should be taken first, which necessitated clearing the nearby. So it was that on the 17th a strong contingent under Taylor comprising fifty Europeans of the 75th Foot and fifty native troops began to work their way through the houses and courtyards near the bastion. They would not be finished for some time yet.

By the end of the 17th, the British line of control was a well-connected series of posts stretching due west from the magazine, passing the bank and on to the Kabul Gate and encompassing all the buildings in between. This was still a small portion of the city, around 10 per cent, but with the rebels in disarray the capture of the rest of the city seemed almost certain. The fading resistance offered by the remaining rebels was unlikely to take a great toll on the assaulting forces. By now, 203 guns had been captured. From intelligence gathered from his spies, Hodson estimated that in total there were no more than 4,000 defenders left in the city, the rest having fled. What was important, he felt, was to capture the palace and Salimgarh Fort before advancing any further into the crowded streets. As the day went on, Wilson received numerous reports of rebels fleeing by the southern gates. 'The enemy are flying in bodies of 100 or 200 men towards Gwalior via Muttra', G. C. Barnes wrote. 'The property of every kind left in the city is immense. All the streets we occupy have been abandoned by the inhabitants. The number of dead sepoys in every quarter is very great.'[11]

* * * * *

The next day, during the morning of the 18th, a partial eclipse of the sun plunged the city into near-darkness for roughly three hours. This heavenly phenomenon led many of the more superstitious rebels remaining to evacuate the city. With the British guns now targeting the bridge of boats more effectively, few rebels tried to cross the river – rather most streamed out from the gates on the south side. It was known that the Bareilly and Neemuch brigades had already decided to leave the city, apparently opting to make their way to Gwalior. They had already despatched some of their baggage and guns south; whether or not they would stay to defend the palace remained uncertain.

What continued to frustrate Wilson from previous days was the continuing failure to capture the Lahore Gate. The British had been repulsed from this position ever since the 14th. There was no success on this day either, with the 75th taking heavy losses, among them Lt Briscoe. The position at the bank had been strengthened, however, and sappers were making progress towards the Burn Bastion as a precursor to another attempt at the gate.

By the end of the day, an advance had been made in the centre of the city and the canal effectively became the front. The banks of the canal were then given over to some light mortars for clearing the vicinity of the Lahore Gate. In addition to this, light guns had been placed at the main road junctions along with sandbag batteries to prevent a counterattack.

On the night of the 18th, heavy rain rendered fighting difficult. By this time, thirty-five more guns had been taken from the rebels and turned on their remaining positions. Hodson received reports that the rebels remaining in the city hoped to negotiate, but was ambivalent: 'I only hope they may find it is too late and that we may pursue and destroy the wretches whom we have to thank for so much barbarity and bloodshed.'[12]

*****

The 19th was a dull and overcast day, but it saw perhaps the biggest success for several days as the British force finally took the Burn Bastion. The rebels had managed to hold it until as late as 7 p.m., when it was taken along with six guns and one mortar. Little or no opposition was met, and the British sustained no losses. Perhaps it was because the city was fast emptying of rebels, and the men at the bastion were no exception. Whatever the case, the capture of Burn Bastion, completely overlooking Lahore Gate, gave hope that the Lahore Gate would shortly be captured too.

Two prominent houses, those of Major Abbott and Khan Mahomed, were also taken. These were just below the palace, and with positions set up here fire could be more easily directed at the palace gate, which was still defended by rebels. Snipers were also placed on the top of these houses to fire up at the defenders. Breastworks were constructed under the command of Col Jones of the Rifles, while four mortars and two guns continued their work on the palace. Wilson ordered a column to form at the magazine with the aim of capturing it. 'The report still is that the King is gone to the old fort, and that the palace is being emptied,' Chamberlain wrote to G. C. Barnes. 'We shall push on a small party during the day to ascertain whether this is the case, and, if so, at once seize the gateway. All our Cavalry sent out this morning under Brigadier Grant to reconnoitre the western and southern faces of the town, and it is hoped that this demonstration will hurry their evacuation of the town.'[13] Meanwhile, a column was sent down the Chandni Chowk to take control of the Jama Masjid.

In less auspicious news, this day saw a prominent casualty in the British camp. The political agent with the force, H. H. Greathed, contracted cholera and died. Charles Saunders took his position as the senior civilian with the force. In the city itself, hardly any casualties were taken by the British on this day. With so many having fled, the rebels didn't incur many losses either. The rebels still had possession of all gates south of the Lahore Gate, so they continued to leave the city at will. Streams of rebels could be seen heading south down the Mathura Road. A number of rebels even risked a crossing at the bridge of boats despite the presence of the British guns. The rebels were also seen to be vacating their camp outside the city.

*****

With almost all the rebels having departed, there was rapid success on the 20th. The Lahore Gate and the Garsten Bastion fell in quick succession, with the advance continuing till the Ajmer Gate was also captured.

Resistance was as almost non-existent, the only thing slowing the British advance being its paucity of numbers and the sheer amount of buildings and streets that had to be combed.

In the early morning, a column of troops led by Capt. Taylor had chanced upon around fifty grain merchants sheltering in a building. Realising that they must know something about the rebels protecting the Lahore Gate, Taylor proceeded to question them and then gave them an ultimatum: 'Your lives shall be spared if you will conduct us safely to some spot from which we may observe how the Lahore gate is guarded.' Two of the men were to guide British officers Lang and Roberts while the other merchants were kept as hostages; they would be executed if the British officers failed to return.

The merchants duly led the two men through the deserted streets of the city to a house which fronted out on the Chandni Chowk close to the Lahore gate. Lang and Roberts peered through the window for a while, noting that the rebels seemed to be in a careless frame of mind, cleaning their muskets, but that they had two guns with them. The merchants also showed the officers a passage and gateway leading from the house directly on to the Lahore Gate. While Lang and Roberts took their time observing the guards on the gate, the British soldiers holding the other merchants hostage were growing anxious. Luckily for them, the officers returned before the other merchants could be shot. Robert and Lang then led the column through the house and into the opening towards the Lahore Gate. Taken by surprise, the rebels were quickly overpowered. Some were killed, while others managed to get away.

Throughout the morning there had been no fire from the Ajmer Gate, suggesting all the rebels had abandoned it as well. Plans were therefore made to advance and capture it. At 10 a.m., the Ajmer Gate was taken with no opposition. Three heavy guns and one 8-inch howitzer were found abandoned there. Wilson also ordered some heavy mortars to the Burn Bastion in order to shell the last remaining pockets of the town still in rebel hands. By noon, the Jama Masjid was also in British hands, taken by Major James Brin. Two hours later, both Salimgarh Fort and the bridge of boats were also in British hands. Only the Turkman and Delhi Gates held out, and even they were expected to fall shortly.

The main success of the day occurred at the palace. Just a few defenders could be seen on the palace walls, directing desultory shots at the British troops below. Col Jones would capture the last of the houses facing the palace, cutting off the possibility of any retreat from the main gate. Reconnaissance of the palace was carried out by Ensign McQueen, who approached the barbican and got the impression that the palace was practically empty. Powder bags were then brought up by Lt Home and some sappers, and the great gate of the palace was blown up. Some moments passed before the smoke covering the opening lifted. Then the men charged in. Inside the palace barbican, seven guns were found.

However, there was a second gate at the end of the entrance. It took time to force this one open, with the Gurkhas and members of the 60th Rifles then storming through into the palace with little opposition. Only twenty to thirty rebel diehards had chosen to stand and fight, and they were bayoneted or shot. Some wounded rebels recuperating in the palace were also mercilessly bayoneted. These palace defenders were apparently not sepoys but ghazis who had promised to be martyred. One of them managed to shoot Ensign McQueen before charging into a hail of shot.

With the palace cleared, Col Jones was seen sitting on the durbar throne of the Mughal emperor, where he proposed and drank to Her Majesty's health to loud cheers from his men. Col Bourchier described the state of the palace at the time:

> The Palace had evidently been hastily abandoned. The tents of Captain De Teissier's battery, stationed at Delhi when the mutiny broke out, were left standing, and contained plunder of all sorts. The apartments inhabited by the royal family combined an incongruous array of tawdry splendour, with the most abject poverty and filth. The apartments over the Palace gate, formerly inhabited by Captain Douglas, who commanded the Palace guards, and Mr Jennings, the clergyman, were denuded of every trace of the unfortunate party which had inhabited its walls; and with whom, not many months before, I had spent a happy week. It was with a sad and heavy heart that I paced its now empty rooms, which could tell such terrible tales of the scenes there enacted.

Meanwhile, a short and terse message was sent to Wilson:

> Blown open the gate and got possession of the Palace.

A delighted Wilson in turn appointed Col Jones the new commandant of the palace. While Jones posed on the inner sanctum, other troops passed through to the north of the palace and entered the Salimgarh Fort unopposed. At the same time, Hodson, with a force of cavalry, circled the palace walls and scoured the tents the rebels had pitched around its perimeter – all wounded and sick rebels were killed without question. British mortars now targeted the Daryaganj area south of the palace to mop up the last of the resistance.

By 5 p.m. that day, Brigadier General Neville Chamberlain was able to telegram the news to John Lawrence:

> Our struggle has ended here. We have possession of the whole city, the Palace, Salimgarh and the bridge. Number of guns taken in the town and Delhi Bastions unknown. Our loss to-day is trifling. The King and Royal family are said to be in a village 4 coss from this towards the Kootub.[14]

The city having effectively fallen, guards were now placed on all the gates to prevent people leaving or entering. In the meantime, parties were sent to patrol up and down the streets and thoroughfares, flushing out any last remaining diehard rebels. At the same time, the entire cavalry was ordered to begin combing through the suburbs outside the city in a southwards sweep towards the Qutb Minar in order to eliminate all resistance outside the city walls.

Hodson witnessed the movements of the last rebels as they departed southwards:

> Well, we all marched out to the top of the hill on which stands the 'Eedgah', and thence, from a safe and respectful distance, overlooked the camp of the Bareilly and Nusseerabad force, under 'General' Bukt Khan, quondam Subadar of artillery. While minutely examining the camp through my glass (I was with Brigadier Hope Grant, to show the way), I perceived by unmistakeable signs that it was being evacuated. Shortly after a loud explosion showed that they were blowing up their ammunition previous to a flight; these signs were on the moment confirmed by the arrival of my *harkaras*.[15]

Hodson immediately requested Wilson's permission to examine the rebel camp. Accompanied by around seventy-five men, Hodson galloped around the city walls, reaching the Delhi Gate without any real difficulty. The camp was quite empty now. Hodson found three more abandoned guns, which were brought away, and plans were made to collect carts to bring back the myriad supplies, tents and other baggage left behind by the rebels. Included in the haul was the mess plate of the 60th NI along with various standards, drums and other accoutrements.

With this done, Hodson and his force continued 3 miles south to the old fort and jail, killing the occasional straggler. At the Ajmer Gate, meanwhile, the British troops found more wounded and sick mutineers who had been left behind with all sorts of clothing, bedding and cooking utensils, along with drums and band instruments.

*****

The day after the capture of the city, at sunrise on 21 September, the silence which had blanketed the city after the end of hostilities was broken by the roar of a royal salute from British guns on the walls of the Salimgarh Fort. A British flag flying from the palace told everybody that the city had fallen. A delighted General Wilson immediately moved his headquarters into the palace. The sanctum sanctorum of the Diwan-i-Khas, the throne room from which the Mughal emperors of old had ruled a vast empire, became a general's office.

Two days later, on 23 September, Brigadier John Nicholson finally expired at the age of thirty-five. He was buried the next day. Revd Rotton attended the ceremony:

> The funeral cortege was comparatively small; very few beside personal friends composed the mournful train. The corpse was brought from the General's own tent, on a gun-carriage; whether covered with a pall or otherwise I cannot say. But no roar of cannon announced the departure of the procession from camp; no volleys of musketry disturbed the silence which prevailed at his grave; no martial music was heard. Thus, without pomp or show, we buried him. He was the second of those commanders who, since the capture of Delhi, was laid beneath the sods of Ludlow Castle graveyard.[16]

Despite the eventual flight of the rebels, British casualties incurred in the capture of the city had been significant. From 15 to 20 September, casualties had been around 200 men killed and wounded, but if one added the casualties on the day of the assault on the 14th, then there were around 1,400, indicating that most rebels had fought back on the first day and then crumbled. Prior to that, from 30 May when the rebels were first defeated at the Hindun River to 13 September, the day before the assault, British casualties had stood at 2,490 men killed and wounded. All in all, the total loss during the Delhi campaign stood at around 4,000 men. A further 1,200 lives had been lost to cholera and other ailments, indicating the considerable toll disease took in warfare at the time.

At 7 a.m. on Sunday 27 September, all troops not on duty were packed into the Diwan-i-Khas. A few days earlier, General Wilson had decided that Sunday would be marked by victory celebrations and a general thanksgiving. A service was duly held, with lessons taken from Isaiah 12 and Luke 17 verses 11 to 19.

On 9 October, the Government of India would issue a proclamation from Governor-General Canning announcing the fall of Delhi. This was to be distributed to the various rulers of North India and further beyond, chief among them the key allies Maharaja Ranbir Singh of Kashmir, Maharaja Narendra Singh of Patiala, Raja Sarup Singh of Jhind and Raja Bharpur Singh of Nabha. However, the news was also to be transmitted to other potentates further off, principally Dost Mohammad of Afghanistan, the Khan of Khiva, the Khan of Kelat and the Khan of Kokand:

> I have the gratification of announcing to Your Highness that Delhi, the focus of the treason and revolt which for four months have harassed Hindostan, and the stronghold in which the mutinous Army of Bengal has sought to concentrate its power, has been wrested from the

rebels. The King is a close prisoner in the palace, the head-quarters of Major-General Wilson are established in the Dewan Khas, and a strong column is in pursuit of the fugitives.

The mutinous soldiery and those who are leagued with them have doubtless found encouragement to commit acts of faithlessness and rebellion in the delusive belief that India was weakly guarded by England, and that before the Government could gather together its strength against them their ends would be gained. They are now undeceived. Before a single soldier of the many thousands who are hastening from England to uphold the supremacy of the British Power has set foot on these shores, the rebel force, where it was strongest and most united and where it had the command of unbounded military appliances, has been destroyed and scattered by an army collected within the limits of the North-Western Provinces and the Punjab alone. The work has been done before the support of those battalions, which have been collected in Bengal from the forces of the Queen in China and in Her Majesty's Eastern Colonies, could reach Major-General Wilson's Army; and it is by the courage and endurance of that gallant army alone, by the skill, sound judgment and steady resolution of its brave Commander, and by the aid of the Chiefs of Putiala, Jheend, Nabha, Jummoo and others, who have been true to their allegiance, that, under the blessing of God, the head of rebellion has been crushed, and the cause of loyalty, humanity and rightful authority vindicated.[17]

37

# The Sack of Delhi

Even the Sabbath brings no rest to either plunderers or plundered.
Col H. P. Burn, Military Governor of Delhi, 18 October 1857

With the city entirely pacified by 20 September, Colonel Burn was chosen to be the military governor of the city and to organize the sack of the city. Burn chose as his residence a wealthy trader's large house on the Chandni Chowk. Much of the population had already fled the city by this time, the British entry through the northern gates and slow progress south allowing easy flight. Many of the residents initially headed towards the Turkman Gate, the Ajmer Gate and the Farash Khana. As the British columns pushed further into the city, many of the residents then streamed out of the gates and began heading south for safety. However, the Gujjars and Mewati villagers, ever ready to loot, had been prepared. Many residents of the city were relieved of the few valuables they had taken with them.

Most of the citizens who remained were now expelled from the city. A plan was formed to eject them in orderly fashion prior to the sack. The men would be directed towards the Kashmir Gate while the women had to exit by the Kabul Gate.[1] Residents carrying possessions were well searched and ordered to surrender anything of value before passing out, meaning the queues at the gates were agonizingly slow over the following days. Few residents had anywhere else to go to, so many simply began to camp in the suburbs outside the city to await permission to return.

Some residents had good reason to stay in the city. The informants and spies the British had managed to recruit had made bargains that their houses would not be ransacked. One such man was Mahasari Parsad, who lived on Nil Ka Katra. Under his assurance, the entire Hindu population of this area stayed in their houses hoping they would be safe from the plundering soldiers, with the residents ransoming their street for 50,000 rupees for certainty. Another such example was a man called Hakim Mahmood Khan, a Muslim living in the Billi Maron area. He had a warm understanding with the Maharaja of Patiala, who was currently supporting the British force with his troops. The maharaja had made an agreement with the British that this particular area would not receive any unwelcome attention from the soldiers. The maharaja was true to his word: as soon as the British force reached the area, his troops were put on guard to prevent looting.

Certain individuals and streets were also promised safety from the ransacking until December if they paid a large ransom or protection money. In return for payment they received a protection ticket from the prize agents. Some wealthy residents had decided to take up this option. The protection tickets supposedly guaranteed that their residence would not be sacked, with a guard being posted at the said property to ensure its safety. Several of the wealthy individuals in the city – men like Sheikh Turab Ali, Rai Sudha Singh and Nihal Chand, diwan of the Maharaja of Patiala – had used this stratagem to protect their properties. Better to pay the large sums than to lose all. However, a problem quickly arose. Wilson did not want too many locals using the ticket system as this might reduce the prize money appreciably. He therefore issued orders that all protection tickets must be countersigned by him. As it was very difficult to get his attention in the days after the capture, few were handed out. 'The consequence was that but few obtained anything like adequate protection,' Saunders later observed. 'No guards could be furnished, and before two or three days had elapsed, there was not a house that had not been ransacked and plundered, friends and foes of the Government suffering to an equal extent.'

There were others who stayed for the wrong reasons, preferring to take their chances in the city. Some of these were Muslim women who were unaccustomed to going out into the open. Fearing defilement by the soldiers, some chose to end their lives. Indeed, so many committed suicide by jumping into wells that a number of faulty wells were found to be clogged with bodies upon investigation. A British soldier described one of these grisly finds: 'We took scores of women out of these wells whose lives had been saved by falling on top of other bodies. When we tried to take them out, they were terrified and begged to be shot, saying they were respectable women and would prefer to die than to be touched by outsiders, some of them were shivering with fear and anger and others fainted.'

In another incident in the area of Farash Khana, two women were found in a well having survived the fall. One was blind while the other was an elderly matriarch. Soldiers, the old woman said, had tried to rape the blind daughter. Knowing her way around the house, the blind woman had quickly made her way to the well and jumped. The older woman had followed her example. Miraculously, they had survived. Some men were caught and hanged; however, it appears to have been a case of mistaken identity. In a letter published in November in *The Times*, a soldier described witnessing a terrible sight. 'I have given up walking about the back streets of Delhi, as yesterday an officer and myself had taken a party of twenty men out patrolling, and we found fourteen women with their throats cut from ear to ear by their own husbands, and laid out in their shawls. We caught a man there who said he saw them killed, for fear they should fall into our hands; and showed us their husbands, who had done the best thing they could do afterwards, and killed themselves.'[2]

Many of the locals had elected to stay in the city, taking shelter in *tykhanas*, or underground chambers, during the fighting. These had provided protection from the fighting raging above them. Capt. Charles Griffiths of the 61st Regiment described such an experience:

> The taikhanas, or underground rooms of houses, scattered all over the city, were found to be filled with human beings—those who, by age or infirmity, had been unable to join in the general exodus which had taken place during the last days of the siege. Hundreds of old men, women and children, were found huddled together, half starved, in these places, the most wretched-looking objects I ever saw. There was no means of feeding them in the city, where their presence also would have raised a plague and many would have died; so, by the orders of the General, they were turned out of the gates of Delhi and escorted into the country. It was a melancholy sight, seeing them trooping out of the town, hundreds passing through the Lahore Gate every day for a whole week. We were told that provisions had been collected for their use at a place some miles distant, and it is to be hoped the poor creatures were saved from starvation; but we had our doubts on the subject, and, knowing how callous with regard to human suffering the authorities had become, I fear that many perished from want and exposure.

Muslims were frequently shown much less sympathy by the British soldiers than their Hindu neighbours. Many saw the Muslims as the driving force behind the rebellion, the more incorrigible element of the population, and they consequently took the brunt of the British anger. 'But, let us pause a moment and consider, was it ever to be expected that Mussulmen, after it suited their interests, would keep faith with those whom they consider infidels; when to be instrumental in their destruction is a meritorious act in the eyes of their accursed religion?' asked Col Bourchier, summing up the mood of the common British soldier. 'The only comfort one of these miscreants possessed was to this effect: "I die happy: I have seen English women polluted in the streets of Delhi."' Soldiers and others took full revenge on the Muslims they encountered. Zaka Ullah in his *History of Hindustan* writes of a British doctor who roamed the streets asking locals whether they were Hindu or Muslim. If they replied they were Hindu, he would let them go; if they were Muslim, he would shoot them dead.

The British capture of the city provided another opportunity for the local gangsters. These underworld figures, who had taken advantage of the chaos after the arrival of the Meerut mutineers, were now seen to side with the British soldiers for the same advantages. 'Once men and women were thrown out of the city, the spies went into action,' wrote Zahir Dehlvi. 'The same ruffians who had joined the ingrate *baghis* [mutineers] now joined the British for the lure of money. They informed the British of the whereabouts of men and money, of the treasure hidden by people, and, as a result, had it plundered. They were paid Rs 2 for every person they helped catch. They helped the British mount many men on the gallows.'[3] Prominent amongst these was a gangster called Ghami Khan. We encountered Ghami Khan earlier in the story, when he sided with the rebels to punish accused traitors. Now he eagerly volunteered his services to the British, falsely accusing many of having been in league with the rebels. Khwaja Hasan Nizami writes of meeting one of the surviving princes, Prince Amir Ul Mulk, also known as Mirza Bulaki. The prince was at the time residing in the Chandni Mahal area of the city. Mirza Bulaki recalled the general uncertainty of that time caused by Ghami Khan:

> People were in great fear of the informant Ghami Khan. When I was with my mother at the Dargah of Hazrat Sultan Ji (Hazrat Khwaja Nizamuddin Awliya (rah), a servant came and told my mother Ghami Khan was saying that this boy (Mirza Bulaki) used to learn calligraphy from Bahadur Shah and I know about him. The moment my mother heard this she was frightened. When she heard that Ghami Khan had arrived at the Dargah she made me lie on the bed and placed the covers in such a way that it appeared that there were only bed covers there. She then took off her golden earrings and gave them to the servant to give to Ghami Khan and requested him not to give reports on me. I stayed in this state until evening.

Although Ghami Khan had the deaths of many men on his hands, his false accusations and his own past were eventually found out by the British. He was hanged for his deeds.

Inevitably, this was also a time to pursue personal vendettas. Locals were seen to report their own family members, neighbours or enemies to the British. These betrayals encompassed humble citizens and royals alike. With the British none too discerning as they sought retribution, innocent people lost their lives. One of those in the royal family who betrayed his relatives, no doubt hoping for reward, was Mirza Kale. He was the son of Mirza Babar, one of Zafar's brothers. One of Mirza Kale's tactics was to encourage other members of the family to approach the British officers and make it known they were members of the royal family; this, he suggested, would safeguard them as they were giving themselves up and would be treated well. He himself declared to the same officers that he had persuaded the princes to hand themselves in owing to their fraternity with the rebels. The officers would then summarily hang the princes. One of the princes to be hanged in this way was Mirza Qaiser. He was a son of Shah Alam, a previous emperor, and was by this time an elderly, senile man. Another unlikely rebel, a grandson of Emperor Akbar Shah, was also hanged due to the machinations of Mirza Kale.

As the vast bulk of the population was expelled, a hush fell on the city. The only sounds to be heard were those of houses being broken into followed by furniture being thrown into the streets as the soldiers rushed to dig into floors in search of treasure. The only other sounds were shouts and the odd musket shot in some place or another as a rebel was caught or a civilian was punished for putting up resistance or failing to point out hidden valuables. There were occasional bursts of fire as locals were executed for having stayed in the city without permission or for seeming belligerent. In the Kocha Cheelan area, for example, where Zaka Ullah lived and where other prominent members of the city resided including Syed Ahmad Khan, the British soldiers exacted a terrible revenge as one of their comrades was hurt entering a property. The house belonged to Nawab Shamsher Jang Khan, whose son had with another man fought a British soldier trying to enter the women's section of the house. All the men in the house were captured and taken to the banks of the river where they were made to stand in a line before being shot dead.

British soldiers walking the streets encountered thousands of corpses littering the city. It's difficult to say how many people were killed or massacred in the capture of the city and its subsequent sacking. Lt Roberts (later to become Field Marshal Lord Roberts) left a graphic account of the city:

> That march through Delhi in the early morning light was a gruesome proceeding. Our way from the Lahore Gate by the Chandni Chauk led through a veritable city of the dead: not a sound was to be heard but the falling of our own footsteps; not a living creature was to be seen. Dead bodies were strewn about in all directions, in every stage of decomposition. We marched in silence, or involuntarily spoke in whispers, as though fearing to disturb these ghastly remains of humanity. The sights we encountered were horrible and sickening to the last degree. Here a dog gnawed at an uncovered limb: there a vulture, disturbed by our approach from its loathsome meal, but too completely gorged to fly, fluttered away to a safer distance. In many instances the positions of the bodies were appallingly life-like. Some lay with their arms uplifted as if beckoning, and, indeed, the whole scene was weird

> and terrible beyond description. Our horses seemed to feel the horror of it as much as we did, for they shook and snorted in evident terror. The atmosphere was unimaginably disgusting, laden as it was with the most noxious and sickening odors.

*****

The prize agents and their teams had been readied for the sack of the city, and it would be carried out in one of the most systematic fashions ever managed. As mentioned earlier, three separate classes of prize agent were made ready: general and field officers, queen's service, and company army. Elected to each post respectively were Capt. Fagan, Capt. Campbell and Capt. Wriford. Each prize agent would have deputies working under him. Each deputy would be assigned a different department, with responsibility for a different portion of the loot to be collected. For instance, one deputy was in charge of more valuable items like jewellery, gold bullion and other precious stones while another was responsible for furniture or artwork. These separate divisions continued into the more mundane and less valuable items like the grinding wheels, while other deputies organised the extensive collection of books. Metal was also collected. In due course, the doors of houses around the city would be set on fire in order to extract brass and iron, which was collected from the ashes the next day.

Below the prize agents and their deputies would be an army of workers responsible for digging up floors and into the walls of buildings in the city to uncover valuables hidden by their owners. Since the work of digging up underground caches of treasure and other valuables secreted inside floors and walls was expected to take many weeks, the whole process was expected to take several months. Once the process had been completed, the goods collected were to be auctioned, with the money realized to be added to the prize money total.

Due to the sheer size and variety of the plunder expected from the city, various large buildings were assigned for the reception of goods, with each building assigned its own kind of item. Books were to be deposited at the *kothee* of Professor Ramchandra. All household goods – silver, copper and bronze plates, spoons and vessels – were ordered to be brought to the mansion of a Mansur Ali Khan. The most valuable items – gold, precious stones, jewellery – were brought into the palace, with one of the inner buildings adjacent to the Diwan-i-Khas utilised for storage. A large tent had also been set up on the roof of the palace for storage of valuable items.

Precautions had been taken to prevent loot being spirited away by the soldiers. Ever since the 14th, the gates of the city had been guarded from the moment of their capture. These measures weren't altogether successful; it proved difficult for the prize agent guards to prevent men hiding valuables in their clothes, for instance. While it did prevent the bulk of the smuggling, more enterprising soldiers began climbing over the city walls with makeshift ladders while others operating with friends would lower loot on ropes to the outside. This was normally done during the night, and due to the extensive length of the city walls it was difficult to prevent. Even on the 14th, various items were brazenly looted. One man was seen with a buggy and two horses, which ordinarily would have fetched a tidy sum; he was willing to exchange this prize for a bottle of rum. An officer who was well known to be short of money was later seen with the same buggy but was noticeably reticent on how he had come by it.

Some former residents were also attempting to re-enter the city. It was difficult to gain entry through the gates, which were manned, so they instead used ropes to climb the city walls and search for valuables in their houses, hoping the soldiers had not looted them already. Several locals had been captured in these activities, so patrols were organised between the gates at regular intervals to watch the walls and to discourage such activities.

A large amount of plunder had already been extracted from residents as they were ushered out of the city gates. An enormous mountain of confiscated items therefore grew up around the gates, and it required combing through for valuables. This meant a huge amount of largely worthless items began blocking the routes out of the city. Clothes of all descriptions along with household goods of all kinds were brought up and collected later from the city as well. The other easy source of loot was the corpses of dead rebels littering the streets; with the rebels having the habit of keeping their valuables on their person, gold mohurs and precious stones were inevitably found by soldiers rifling through their clothes. Other prizes were of the most visible sort: all the horses and carriages in the city were collected. The first target for looting had been the jewellers' shops and warehouses in the Chandni Chowk; these had been thoroughly sacked within minutes of being spotted.

*****

Once the more obvious items had been plundered, more systematic and intense looting was initiated and the diggers got to work. Owners invariably dug holes in floors and walls during the siege to hide valuables. Another supposedly favourite place to hide money and treasure was beneath the staircases of a house. The underside of the staircase, if carefully examined, was found to be thicker than it should be, suggesting cavities in which valuables had been secreted. Courtyards, too, promised buried treasure.

Tapping on the ground and walls of houses was a skill rapidly picked up by the teams let loose on the city; a hollow sound invariably meant a hidden cavity or even a secret room in large residences. Another technique developed by experience was to pour water on the floor and wait to see in which area the water seeped through faster – the water draining faster where there was a cavity. Meanwhile, a careful survey of each house would take place with the roof heights and rooms below. Discrepancies in the heights and depths of ceilings meant hidden cavities either in the ceiling or the floor above.

Soldiers also became very adept at discerning the nature of the people who owned a particular house. Muslim houses had a different atmosphere and feel to Hindu households. Such houses might have Qurans in various rooms strewn around from previous looters searching the place. Furniture, too, was said to be arranged differently. In a Hindu household there might be a profusion of Hindu idols, and the look and feel and clothes in the house suggested Hindu occupants. Who owned the house was of no matter to the looters – rather what was important was the different ways they hid treasure. It was reckoned by many that the Muslims tended to hide valuables below the ground, and freshly cemented floors were immediately torn up to reveal hidden plunder. Hindus, it was rumoured, were adept at hiding loot in cavities in the walls. Soldiers therefore hoping to find quick plunder and without wishing to spend too long in one house would opt for one of the walls or the floors. Many looters swore on the success of this method. Meanwhile, Hindu temples were despoiled of their valuables. Many of the idols had hidden cavities which were soon destroyed by the soldiers' hammers. Experience in various temples taught soldiers that the bases of the idols sometimes held great treasure.

Over the weeks of the sack, a typical day for these teams of plunderers would start with an early breakfast after which they would leave equipped with spades, hammers, crowbars, pickaxes and an assortment of other tools. A house would be picked and the team would begin work. To speed up the task, the prize agents would organise parties of local labourers who were paid a daily wage along with an extra commission for digging up valuables. Houses would be left with the walls barely standing such was the extensive searching. Since the city was large and the residences so numerous, soldiers picking a house had little chance of being disturbed by other parties looking for plunder.

Not all the locals employed by the prize agents were treated well. One of those helping, for example, was Professor Ramchandra, the college professor and convert to Christianity. He had escaped from the city but had made his way back after its capture. Being a Christian, he was trusted more than other citizens and therefore found a job as assistant to a prize agent much more easily than most. Nevertheless, he faced much aggression and suspicion from the British soldiers. As he walked the city, British soldiers would throw missiles as a form of amusement despite his protest that he was a Christian. The professor was employed to gather books under the prize agent Dr James. 'I was attacked as before though I had two Prize Agency chaprassies with me and though I cried to inform the English officers that I had a ticket of the Prize Agents. After that

I found to my great grief that I was not only in danger in deserted streets but in my very house also…'

Violence like this could continue in later days:

> I received a heavy blow on the head from an English Officer passing in Dewani Aum square on horseback with another gentleman in company also on horseback and after inflicting this blow with his stick the officer turned round and required me to make him a salaam. I made many salaam instead of one, and cried I was a Christian Sir, and employed in the Prize Agency and after this he proceed towards the Diwane Khas with abusing me and saying that I was black as jet.

Perhaps feeling he had not inflicted enough punishment, the officer returned once more and hit Ramchandra on the left arm and back with his stick, compelling him to leave.

One of the best narratives on the methods and techniques used to find loot was left by Capt. Griffiths of the 61st Regiment, who acted as an assistant to a British officer. Griffiths had a permit allowing him to search for plunder by the prize agents. Travelling with the officer, he had occasion to witness the search for loot. The officer had said he would have no objection if Griffiths helped himself to some of the loot as long as he showed moderation. Griffiths recorded that locals were of particular help when allowed in to assist in some fashion. They were typically builders or masons who had helped build the houses and so knew the likely placement of hidden cavities, and were happy to divulge information for a cut. In October, Griffiths himself was led to a house by a mason. It had already been plundered, but something had been missed.

> Every article was scattered about in dire confusion; there were piles of clothing and bedding: rich and ornamental stuffs were torn to pieces, and the household furniture, broken up, was strewn about the courtyard. Our guide took us to a small room, about 80 feet square – in fact, it was the closet of the establishment – the walls of which were whitewashed, the floor being covered with a hard cement. Here, we were told, the treasure was concealed under the flooring of the room, and we lost no time in commencing operations, the mason assisting us. Picking through the cement, we came on a large flagstone, which we lifted out of the cavity. Then we dug a hole about 3 feet square, and the same depth in the loose earth, disclosing the mouth of a large earthenware *gharra*, or jar. Loosening the soil all around, we attempted to raise the jar out of the ground, but all our efforts were unavailing-its great weight preventing us from lifting it one inch out of the bed. Then, trembling with excitement, for we felt sure that a rich display would greet our eyes, we began slowly to remove each article from the *gharra*, and place it on the floor of the room. A heavy bag lying at the mouth of the jar was first taken out,

> and on opening it, and afterwards counting its contents, we found that it contained 700 native gold mohurs, worth nearly £1,200. Then came dozens of gold bangles, or anklets, of pure metal, such as those worn by dancing-girls. We were fairly bewildered at the sight, our hands trembling and our eyes ablaze with excitement, for such an amount of pure gold as that already discovered we had never seen before. But the treasure was not yet half exhausted. The jar seemed a perfect mine of wealth – gold chains, plain and of filigree workmanship, each worth from £10 to £30; ornaments of the same metal of every sort of design, and executed in a style for which the Delhi jewelers are celebrated all over India. Then came small silver caskets filled with pearls, together to the number of more than 200, each worth from £3 to £4, pierced for stringing. Others, containing small diamonds, rubies, and emeralds, and the greatest prize of all-reclining in a casket by itself – a large diamond, which was sold afterwards by the prize agents for £1,000. There were many other articles of value besides those I have mentioned – gold rings and tiaras inlaid with precious stones, nose-rings of the kind worn by women through the nostrils, earrings, bracelets, and necklaces of small pearls without number.

There was great temptation to appropriate some of the loot. However, pocketing such a large hoard would hardly have been possible. Although the soldiers allowed themselves a few ornaments, the bulk of it was surrendered to the prize agents, who estimated the value of the hoard at around £7,000 at the very minimum.

Officers enriched themselves as well. 'Often, when wandering through the city in pursuit of plunder, I, in company with others, came across officers engaged in the same quest as ourselves,' wrote Griffiths. 'These rencontres were most amusing, giving rise to mutual interrogations and many jokes, each party affirming that looting was not the object of their perambulations, but that they were only inspecting the houses out of a feeling of curiosity.'

One officer was said to have managed to slip out of the city with a huge hoard of gold and jewellery worth 2 lakh rupees. The value was so great that it was determined a court of enquiry would be held to investigate how the officer had managed to spirit away so much treasure. However, matters were never taken forward and the officer managed to retain the loot.

Colonel Burn in his letter to John Lawrence on 15 January complained of the excessive amount of plunder that had eluded the prize agents, although at the same time he pointed out that stopping soldiers from spiriting away loot was a difficult issue for more than one reason:

> I will not venture to say whether more stringent measures might not have prevented a great deal of the plundering that went on after we occupied Delhie, I did my utmost with the small force placed at my disposal to put it down. I flogged, or fined, every one of the hundreds

> of culprits brought before me without distinction, but I felt that I was treading on dangerous ground. Our troops generally, but those from the Punjab in particular, had been buoyed up with the hope of obtaining as their reward the plunder of Delhie, and I have no hesitation in saying that this was one of the main causes of their struggling on, as they did, against overwhelming odds, and in spite of exposure to heat and rain, at the inevitable cost of mined health.[4]

Because of the privations suffered by the men during the siege, Burn was reluctant to take too strong a stance on the issue. He did, however, stress that effective management by prize agents along with the stringent security at the gates meant many soldiers had retained the confidence to await the prize money rather than securing a fortune for themselves by appropriating plunder. This policy alone had ensured the maintenance of discipline during the attack on the city; if it were not for the prize agents and the promise of equitable division of prize money, many soldiers would have indulged in looting before the city had been captured, endangering the assault.

In the pursuit of plunder, soldiers occasionally exchanged fire. Griffiths recorded the sometimes charged atmosphere present as groups of soldiers searched the houses: 'The shots emanated from these men, who, of course, went about well-armed, and brooked no interference when in the act of securing booty. Altercations of a serious nature had taken place between the Europeans and Sikh soldiers, ending sometimes in blows, and often in bloodshed, when the two parties met in a house or were busy employed in dividing the spoil.'

So extensive would be the digging across the city that several quantities of ancient treasure were found, including gold coins and rupees from bygone eras. An example was a treasure trove worth 60,000 rupees dug up at the residence of Nawab Mir Khan. British soldiers weren't the only people collecting booty, either; it was realised that the local gangsters and petty thieves seemed to be better than the invading soldiers at sniffing out potential valuables. Such cliques would busy themselves during the night when the British soldiers had gone away, quickly extracting what they could from the houses of the wealthy. Some of the residents ejected from the city, meanwhile, were so desperate for money to buy provisions that they disclosed the whereabouts of money hidden in their own homes in order to earn commission on its discovery. The thinking may have been that the valuables would be discovered in any case; at least this way they got something for their trouble.

*****

The extensive excavations in the city and the persistence of the soldiers paid off and the value of the haul brought in to the prize agents every day began to rise dramatically. An account from Capt. Griffiths illustrates this:

> ... in a very short time the rooms of the prize agents were filled with treasures of every kind-jewellery and precious stones, diamonds, rubies, emeralds and pearls without number, from those as large as hen's eggs to the small species used for necklaces; gold ornaments, chains of the most beautiful workmanship, bracelets and bangles all of solid metal. There were heaps, also, of the small, thick, native coin known as gold mohurs, thousands of which were accumulated by the prize agents and helped most materially to swell the amount. I visited one room, the long table in which literally groaned with the riches of "Ormuz and of Ind'—a dazzling sight to the eye, and one calculated to raise the spirit of greed in my breast to possess myself of some of the treasures so temptingly exposed to view.

Among the artistic works collected was a series of miniature paintings, mostly of beautiful women. Being small, these paintings were easy to loot or hide in one's clothes. The frames were usually of gold. They could easily fetch around £20 when sold in London. Many of them had found their way to London by 1858, when they were noted as being in demand. Expensive material like kincob, a cloth of gold usually worn by aristocracy or wealthy individuals, was also in demand. In one house, over a lakh rupees' worth of kincob was discovered in a secret chamber.

The palace was not protected from plunder. Fred Majesty, an army captain, recorded the frenzy of looting inside the palace in the first few days:

> A motley crowd of troops and followers ransacked every hole and corner, turning everything topsy-turvy (themselves included very often) in the search for loot. Muskets were being fired right and left to force the locks off doors. As the men got more and more scattered, the bullets flew more and more avidly, and the risk was considerable. I never saw such confusion. All sort of loot had been brought into the palace by the mutineers and presented to the king and members of the court, and this and the palace furniture, men and women's clothing dancing girls' frippery, vessels of food and drink, rich hangings and trappings, books and manuscripts had all been tumbled higgledy-piggledy in to various rooms about, and were resembled and tossed over and over again by our excited soldiery. Here you saw a group fumbling among mysterious boxes in search of jewels, there others laden with stuff of various kinds – pictures, books, guns, pistols, anything that took their fancy. Some tried the sweetmeats and sherbets; others, less lucky, took long draughts of what seemed some right royal drink – and all turned out to be medicine, and found out too late, that the old King had passion for pharmacy, and kept large supplies close to the royal elbow...

European civilians were allowed to join in the plundering as well. Many, like the soldiers, would seek out local workers who might know where employers had hidden wealth. Mr and Mrs Wagentreiber, who had survived the mutineers' entry into the city, were among those who now took part in the looting, and Florence Wagentreiber described her experience:

> The palace too was searched, beautiful silver (inlaid) boxes, pan dans, hooka stands, silver vessels, small bags filled with money and precious stones and ancient coins. Mrs Tytler, too, was very lucky. She had the palace as her hunting ground, and to her lot fell some beautiful ornaments belonging to the King's family, as also the wonderful silken garment the king wore all through the siege, which had the Koran printed minutely all over. This was said to be a talisman against evil. The old fellow lost faith in its power the day the British entered the city, and cast it aside.[5]

Small items such as the King's cushions in his private pavilions and quarters were seized as trophies, Capt. Majesty himself taking a royal cushion as a memento for his wife.

Some of the more iconic items in the palace were extracted alongside the usual plunder. One of the most remarkable mosaics was to be found on the throne pedestal in the Diwan-i-Aam. This exquisite work had been decorated by Italian artists in the Florentine style of the seventeenth century. The mosaics included various flowers and birds, with the central mosaic depicting Orpheus with his lute playing to animals who sat placidly around him. The large mosaic of Orpheus would be extracted from the wall by an officer of one of the European regiments and taken to England, where it was eventually sold to the India Office in London and later found its way to the South Kensington Museum (now the Victoria & Albert Museum).

The beautiful Pearl Mosque inside the palace, constructed for the females of the royal household, also received rough attention. The construction was said to be very good – the entire mosque, its courtyard and surrounding walls were of highly polished marble. The archways and the inside of the mosque were decorated with gold leaf, and the three outside domes were covered with plates of gold. Soldiers clambered on to its top, and the gold was taken down and added to the other loot.

Other royal residences outside the palace were looted as well, including the personal residence of Zeenat Mahal. This grand mansion was typical of Indian residences, with the house encircling a central courtyard. The front of the house facing the street was three storeys high with the rest being one storey. The house had a remarkable interior courtyard with a garden and water fountains fed by a channel running through it, as in the palace. Mrs Muter described the opulent scene:

> The apartments of the Queen were at the ends of the parallelogram, tastefully decorated. A large portion of the prize had been taken in this house, and in the search the agents had turned it upside down. Broken china strewed the floors, torn drapery and articles of little value covered the court, piles of earth showed where holes had been dug, and walls with great openings dashed through them proved that no difficulties had stood in the way. By a side door I went into a smaller court, and from that into another, no two of them alike. Then I came to a range of outhouses and of stabling. The extent was considerable, though the accommodation was not great.[6]

Meanwhile, Capt. Garstone, one of the officers residing in the palace, had collected his own hoard of items used by Zafar and the other royals. This included antique chairs, 'a beautifully bound and illuminated Koran on vellum',[7] a sandalwood cabinet containing a hidden dagger, a portrait of Zafar himself (or possibly another emperor), a casket of ebony and mother of pearl, a solid silver enamelled flask and numerous gold bangles, rings and numerous other items.

Not all finds were valuable – both in the palaces and outside. In the poverty of the Mughal court, many of the items were found to be imitations. In jewellery, glass was frequently found mixed with precious stones. Pearls were found to be fake, and plunderers became adept at discerning the genuine from the counterfeit. For instance, imitation pearls would crumble when a needle was inserted into them, being paste, while real pearls remained undamaged. 'Often there was something paltry in the richest ornament,' Mrs Muter would record. 'In a crown of pure gold, found by my husband in the palace of the Empress, there were drops of green glass to represent emeralds. Silver vessels were sold for their weight in rupees, and at this rate an officer of the Carabineers purchased a massive tea-pot of spurious metal under the impression that it was silver.'[8]

Some of the booty turned out to be European, or at least had last been in the possession of Europeans who had been massacred or fled the city when the sepoys had arrived. Mrs Muter found a collection of miniatures and portraits of Europeans, for instance. Similarly, Bibles and prayer books with names on them could be identified. Many were found in the palace, the sepoys having transported the loot to the palace for safe keeping.

*****

As proceeds from the city began drying up, another scheme was commenced once the people were allowed to return: ransoming the ransacked houses to their original owners. Houses on streets where hidden treasure was mooted but never found were sold back to their inhabitants for sums between 5,000 and 50,000 rupees depending on opulence. The residents were also allowed to buy the possessions they now needed. Beds, for example, could be purchased (two per house) from the stock taken. Grinding wheels, essential for most households, could be had for the price of 1.5 rupees. All this applied to Hindu residents only; Muslim residents were still banned from entering. All in all, the sums raised in this fashion were said to be between £500,000 and £750,000. Still, there were regrets that the looting could not continue – vast sums were surely still hidden inside the city.

Another form of adding to the prize fund would be given a 'safety of life' certificate to wealthy individuals on the receipt of a large sum; this provided the individual some form of guarantee that they would not be molested or accused in future, unlike other citizens who could still be arrested on suspicion of having been in league with the rebels. Several high-profile individuals like Nawab Hamid Ali Khan, Mufti Sadruddin Khan and Mukand Lal would take up this offer.

The other substantial addition to the prize fund would be the loot extracted from nearby villages and towns that had supported the uprising. The Raja of Ballabgarh, for instance, had all his private property seized. The Raja of Jhajjar had property worth 15 lakh rupees taken from him. Other loot included items belonging to the King and his princes, of whom more later.

*****

Around four weeks after the capture of the city, on 18 October 1857, Burn would write to Major General Penny on the matter of ceasing the plundering.

> I would beg to suggest that the Prize Agents having now had one full month of plunder, they be confined within certain limits. This I believe to have been the practice on former occasions when towns have been taken by assault. I would either put a stop to the collection of prize property altogether, or would restrict the search for plunder to the houses which are the property of rebels. The names of these parties can be learnt from the Officiating Commissioner …
>
> Up to the present time all are treated alike; even the property of our murdered countrymen and of those Englishmen who fled from Delhie on the 11th May last is brought to the hammer, and the proceeds carried to the credit of the Prize Fund.[9]

Burn suggested the residents of Delhi be divided into three types: those who had supported the rebels, those who took no part, and those who helped the British. Those in the first group would have their houses and property sold off. Those in the second should be allowed to ransom their property by paying a tithe of their wealth, maybe 10 per cent. The third class of people should be allowed to occupy their residences immediately and be given protection from any more extortion by the soldiers. 'They have already suffered severely at the hands of the mutineers and by the destruction of their property since the British entered the city,' he wrote. 'The loss of property from plunder by our soldiers, or from its wanton destruction, is estimated at the large sum of two crores of rupees.'[10]

Nevertheless, the search for plunder continued. On 24 November, John Lawrence suggested to Maj. Gen. Penny a definitive end to the process, although the final decision was for the government to make. Allowing the looting to go on would only increase the hatred of Indians towards Europeans and aid in the cause of mutineers in the rest of the country. 'No orders have yet been received,' replied Burn. 'I concur that the city of Delhi should be relieved from the Prize Agents. Their prolonged search by digging is continued to the danger of the houses, but having no share in the captured property I will refer the question.' On 15 December, having received a confirmation from the government, Penny finally ordered an end to all plundering in the city, ending the nearly three-month sack of the city.

*****

Plenty of the loot would turn up in London in later years, with many of the soldiers bringing their gains to England. Many had simply hidden their finds – some for as long as three years – before buying their discharge. Their loot turned up at various jewellers' shops, which suddenly seemed well stocked with items of Indian style and manufacture. Other soldiers would sell up locally, although the loot would have sold for much more in London; the possibility of the illicit loot, jewellery or gold being discovered was simply too great. To quickly turn the private loot into anonymous coin, much was simply sold to the local jewellers.

Fragments of the royal jewel collection, among other items, were being sold in the jewellery shops of Delhi as late as 1872. Emily Metcalfe, daughter of Sir Thomas Metcalfe, recounted walking around the streets of Delhi with the famous Count Waldstein as well as other ladies and gentlemen when the party wandered into the various jewellers' shops to browse:

> But in January 1872, when we were at Delhi at the camp of exercise and Count Waldstein was with us, we made a large party of ladies and gentlemen and went to some of these shops, and those who could afford it got beautiful things, Mrs MacMurdo especially securing some rare specimens of crystal bowls. I had to be spokeswoman on these occasions, being able to speak the language better than most of the party. Once I begged the jeweller to show us any of the valuable jewellery worn by people in the Palace in the King's time, as I felt sure they must have got hold of some of the loot there, and he showed some beautiful articles which I had never before seen – bangles of turquoises,

> pearls, rubies, diamonds and emeralds, a dozen or so for each arm, shaped exactly like the silver bangles that we all possess.
>
> One day while we were sitting at the edge of a shop examining these things a man from the outside crowd that surrounded our party thrust his arm over our heads and handed into the jeweller's shop a beautiful ankus that had belonged to the King of Delhi's mahout, the driver of his state elephant. This was a stick, about two feet long, of beautifully worked gold set with turquoises. The prong with which the mahout goaded the animal's head was made of the finest steel inlaid with gold and set with onyxes, and the knob at the end of the stick was superb cornelian, barred over with gold. Major Edward Burke, who was with us, immediately seized upon it, saying the Viceroy ought to have this regal weapon. He carried it off, telling the owner to come to the Viceroy's tent for payment. Ultimately, however, it became the property of Count Waldstein, who carried it off to Prague.[11]

Books were more vulnerable than other types of loot, and there was a desire that valuable editions be preserved. An order was therefore issued to purchase collections from the prize property and have them transported to Calcutta. However, this seems to have been ignored. In April 1859, the Secretary for the Board of Examination would write that he had not yet received the books. The books that were in the possession of the prize agents included extensive and rare collections from the wealthy class of the city as well as the Mughal Imperial Libraries previously housed in the palace. One of the collections – that of Nawab Ziauddin Ahmad Khan of Loharu – had been used extensively by Sir Henry Elliott in his eight-volume translation of the history of India. The total number of plundered volumes ran into the thousands, with some antique and valuable old books said to be worth at least 300 rupees each.

*****

The reckoning of the total amount of prize money would be a lengthy process. Weeks drifted by after the capture of the city, and then months, with no sign of the expected declaration on the fund. A prize agency committee would be formed in January 1858 to continue the work of selling and realising the profit from plunder.

Complicating the issue was the definition of prize property. The matter arose due to the capture of Zafar's jewellery, arms, items of state and other property in the palace, in Delhi and elsewhere outside Delhi. A ruling was therefore required to clarify matters. There was also the matter of valuables and horses taken from rebels outside Delhi or sent earlier by chiefs sympathetic to the rebels but intercepted before reaching them. Much had originally been government property; was it to be considered loot and added to the prize fund?

On 27 November, a directive was issued by Governor-General Canning clarifying some of the issues on what could be considered rightful plunder. He advised that a 'clear distinction exists, in cases of re-capture, between property of the state originally captured by an enemy in time of war, and similar property seized by rebels or mutineers during an insurrection'. The former could be deemed plunder in normal circumstances, but since the army had in many cases captured property and treasure which had belonged to the British government prior to the insurrection this could not been seen as subject to the laws of prize. Nor could property looted by the rebels and recaptured. Such items must be returned to their lawful owners. Canning also declared that all public property, stores, treasure, etc. captured and belonging to the state be given up to the nearest treasury – in other words, the amount looted from all the treasuries and other public property. Its total value would be taken out of the total prize money collected before distribution occurred. Of course, few possessions were clearly marked or easily identifiable as belonging to someone, so this was entirely moot for most of the plunder collected. Meanwhile, a six-month *batta* was announced for all troops engaged in the siege of Delhi.

The issue of the crown jewels, and whether they were to be added to the prize money, was contentious. Zeenat Mahal had surrendered her jewels on 18 October rather than have them taken in conflict. She had kept them behind her purdah. While Zafar looked on, the jewels had been handed over to Charles Saunders, Commissioner of Delhi, in the presence of other British officers. Saunders would write to the Government of India seeking clarification on 10 February 1858. Precedents had been set during the annexations of territory prior to the mutiny, at Oudh and the Punjab, he suggested, where the crown jewels of these states had been auctioned off to supplement the prize money.

Saunders had ordered a local jeweller to value the crown jewels and other jewellery belonging to the queen. These included head ornaments, necklaces of pearls, diamonds, rubies and emeralds, bracelets, arm pieces, plumes and thirty-two rings. He had estimated their worth to be 66,905 rupees. However, in such uncertain times, and with so much plunder being hawked to jewellers, and with few people having the resources to buy such goods, prices for such valuables were depressed. Selling them at the right time, Saunders estimated, the crown jewels would fetch around 100,000 rupees. Among the items not counted as crown jewels were hereditary or state items which were to be disposed of. Even the King's girdle was valued – it would fetch around 800 rupees.

There was also the property of mutineers and other rebels who had come to Delhi to fight. Were their houses and property in other villages and cities considered part of the Delhi prize money? John Lawrence thought not, although he advised it could all be sold and the money raised be deposited till the government made its decision. While it was usual to hand over all captured booty to the army to be turned into prize money, the government also had the right to place a limit on the extent of this.

The other big question was the plunder raised by the looting of houses belonging to people who had no sympathy or allegiance with the rebels. 'All moveable property which belonged to the mutineers, or to citizens of the town who joined in the insurrection, may fairly be declared prize property. But it seems very questionable if this claim should extend to the goods and chattels of peaceable citizens; of men who, it must be notorious, were in no way implicated, but on the contrary suffered severely in consequence of the outbreak,' wrote Lawrence. He considered 'the property, for instance, of merchants, traders, bankers, artisans, and the like, unless they joined in the war, should not be considered as booty. Unless this be done, the whole of the inhabitants of Delhie, whether guilty or innocent, will be reduced to pauperism, and the trade of the country paralysed. In the analogous case of Multan private property was not, it is believed, so considered, nor in that of Bhurtpoor.'[12] However, discerning the allegiance of each citizen, let alone retrieving their plundered belongings, would be quite a task.

*****

The six-month *batta* promised was finally given in 1858. This would amount to little more than 36 rupees per man, which displeased many of the troops. One of the men of the 60th Rifles then stationed in the palace, showing frustration and no little wit, scribbled on the walls of the palace the following widely publicised ditty:

> For the salvation of India the British soldier gets thirty six rupees ten annas, or one rupee one anna per battle;
> When danger's rife and wars are nigh,
> God and the soldier's all the cry:
> When wars are o'er and matters righted,
> God is forgotten and the soldier slighted.[13]

News of the message reached Calcutta, where it wasn't taken lightly; Governor-General Canning demanded to know who had written the piece. Meanwhile, auctions for the plunder collected would continue during December and January. Col Burn, in a letter to John Lawrence on 15 January, estimated the amount of prize money to be around £1,354,000. This comprised £500,000 by auction sales, £319,000 in cash, around £100,000 from the sale of the royal jewellery, £10,000 in other property and £425,000 in ransom money for those houses that had been protected from plunder. On 20 March 1858, Governor-General Canning finally declared money raised from sale of the Mughal crown jewels valid as prize money. Payment of the prize money would come in two instalments in 1862 and 1865, although no details as to the final total were made public. Capt. Griffiths was not happy:

> The sum had dwindled down to less than one-third of what we expected, and not a few expressed openly their conviction that some tampering had taken place with regard to the distribution. This can hardly be believed, though it has always been a notorious fact that the Government are inclined to treat the claims of those who fight their battles with neglect, and in one particular at least, by repudiating the 5 per cent, promised till the Delhi prize-money was paid, they acted up to their usual unjust policy, and gave occasions for the complaints which were raised at the time.

A private soldier would receive around £17 – much less than hoped for. According to convention, an ensign would receive five shares, a lieutenant six and a half, and a captain eleven and a half. The commander-in-chief would receive one-sixteenth of the total.

# 38

# The Promise of Life

On such a day of excitement I may very probably have made such a mistake.

General Wilson, 28 December 1857

In the British camp, there was considerable confusion as to how the promise of life was ever extended to Zafar – or rather, by whom it was offered. In fact, the controversy would rage for several months after the King gave himself up. The Governor-General's orders early in the proceedings had been quite clear: no conditions or terms were to be offered to rebels offering to surrender, be they high or low.

Zafar had remained in the palace as the British successfully assaulted the city during 14 September, electing to stay as the British advanced through the city. On 16 September, news arrived that the magazine, just a few hundred yards from the palace, had been captured and that only paucity of numbers was slowing the British progress towards the palace, while many of the rebels were deserting the city in large numbers. Zafar must have known the assault on the palace would take place in the next day or two. On the 19th, he made the decision to abandon the palace and left the city by the Ajmer Gate with his retinue and family, heading south and initially taking refuge in the old fort.

One of those who urged Zafar not to surrender was Bakht Khan. The battle at Delhi had been lost, Bakht Khan suggested, because the British force had dug in on the ridge, which was difficult to assault despite the rebels' larger numbers. All the wider mutiny needed was a modicum of success against the British; if this could be achieved then many who had not yet committed themselves would rise up around the country. The British could still be pushed into the sea. Bakht Khan argued that Delhi was of little military significance and that the fight would be continued elsewhere. As the titular leader of the uprising, all eyes in Hindustan were on Zafar. His actions would convince many to move one way or the other. The general recommended that the monarch accompany him to the mountains in the north; he may have been alluding to Nepal.

According to Khwaja Hasan Nizami, Hodson's assistant Rajab Ali had communicated to Mirza Ilahi Bux that Zafar should be discouraged from fleeing with the rebels. If he could persuade the Emperor, there would be a large reward for him. Ilahi Bux, open to the offer, would wait until Bakht Khan had finished before voicing his own advice to the confused monarch. He pointed out to Zafar that the fight had always been between the British and the rebel army. The British, Bux said, were well aware that he had been powerless to influence matters and had merely gone along with their plans out of necessity. They would not hold him responsible for what had happened at Delhi. However, Bux cautioned, if he now decided to leave with the rebel army out of choice, he would be freely committing himself to their cause and would be considered guilty. It was well for Zafar to consider his options carefully. Bux also pointed out the difficulties the ageing Zafar would face in an itinerant existence with the rebels. How could he travel with his queens and family with the British in pursuit? It was better to give himself up. 'I will meet the British and arrange with them to give safe conduct for your life and that of your family against any harm,' he soothed. 'Whatever happens to the country at least your welfare will be looked after.'

Nizami also mentions one of the King's eunuchs warning his master: 'Your Highness, Mirza Ilahi Bux has joined up with the British, you should not listen to him. Please listen to the request of Bakht Khan and do not go with what these others are saying. Death and suffering is linked to everybody.' This, Nizami writes, gave Zafar pause for thought, and he delayed his decision till the next day. In his apathy, however, he decided to forgo accompanying Bakht Khan. Ilahi Bux's offer was taken up. Zafar's cortege would depart for Humayun's Tomb near Delhi, where he would await British terms for his surrender. However, before he departed he had some encouraging words for the Bareilly general:

> Brave, I believe every word you say and I respect all your opinions from my heart, but now my body has no strength, therefore, I have decided to let fate decide things for me. Leave me to my fate, take the name of Allah and go from here and do something. If it is not me, if it is not my family, you or some other Hindustani should keep up our honor, do not worry about me, just go and do your duty.[1]

At Humayun's Tomb, in the large garden enclosure, Zafar and his cortege settled down with many thousands of rebels who, dejected and with no stomach to fight, had also decided to remain close by. Mirza Bulaki spoke with Zafar during this time:

> We had come to the Dargah Sultan before the Badshah [Emperor] came and when the news came that the Badshah had arrived at the Tomb of Humayun my mother asked me to go there and I went there with my servant. The Badshah was sitting resting with a cushion against the grave of Humayun. When he saw me he seemed a bit upset and said, 'Here take this money as a present and go away from here immediately, if we live we will meet again.' I used to get my food from the Badshah, he now gave me Rupees five for my food and parted with me.[2]

*****

On 20 September, Hodson received intelligence that the King had fled no further than Humayun's Tomb, less than 4 miles south of the walled city. On that same day, Ilahi Bux informed Hodson through Rajab Ali that he had successfully dissuaded Zafar from fleeing south with Bakht Khan and the rebel army. It also became apparent that Zeenat Mahal and most if not all the princes had elected to remain with their father and were therefore still in the vicinity. This was the chance for Wilson to apprehend perhaps the whole royal family in one swoop.

Despite Saunders' urging, since the capture of the city Wilson had shown little interest in organising an effective force to pursue the rebels, instead opting to give the bulk of his force an extended rest. Wilson had his reasons for staying put; both his infantry and artillery were exhausted, having had little rest for three weeks. He could not ask them to do more. Although the cavalry were fresh, having had little to do in the capture of the city, he was reluctant to send them without the support of either infantry or artillery. The fact was that the area south of Delhi, covered as it was with dense ruins, walled houses and other structures was hardly fit ground for cavalry. The riders would be easy pickings for any rebels making a stand the ruins, causing unnecessary casualties for little reward. A flying column could only be organised after several days' rest, on the other hand, which would mean the rebels having too much of a head start, so the idea of a pursuit was a non-starter.

More generally, Wilson was not prepared to let part of his force go so soon after the capture of the city. John Lawrence had requested that he send troops north to the Punjab the weak position there; Wilson was not confident he could do so. On 24 September, he would write that he had already detached some of his force towards Bulandshahr to destroy and harry rebel contingents who had been retreating in this direction. He had already lost the Belooch Battalion, which had been sent to Meerut.

The 1st European Regiment had been reduced to 230 men, and the 2nd European Regiment to 300 effective bayonets:

> If you take away another European Regiment before the city is settled, and my camp moved underneath the walls, which is being done as quickly as possible, I shall be seriously crippled. The 52nd, 400 strong, is the only regiment I have here fit to move, and they have 150 sick and wounded. The other three regiments are so reduced by sickness and casualties as to be nearly unfit for any service in the field. If the 52nd is taken away, I shall be unable to send any troops to quell any disturbance in the district.[3]

Wilson was therefore focussed on maintaining a strong hold on the city. He ordered the transport of all the British sick and wounded down from the ridge by 26 September. Many were put up in the Diwan-i-Khas and other open spaces inside the fort, but with the state of the city being what it was, he didn't feel that it was a healthy place in general; discounting the palace, only the Delhi College and St James' Church afforded the open spaces and large interiors required. Tents were therefore pitched on the glacis around the walls of the city.

Wilson's other main concern was to prevent a possible uprising by the population, so maintaining defensible positions inside the city was vital. Simply possessing the palace was insufficient for maintaining a hold on the city, and he was against withdrawing all the troops from the walls and gates. He would communicate this view to the Commissioner on 26 September:

> There is no possibility of maintaining guns on any part of the palace to overawe the city. It is therefore not a defensible position, and by confining ourselves to such position we should be like rats in a trap. The whole vile Mussulman population of the city now turned out would return, and the troops would be shut out from all communication with the country on the right bank of the river, our communications with Kurnaul cut off, and be constantly harassed with sorties and street fighting to protect ourselves from insult. If we wish to hold the palace, we must also hold the city walls, and bastions, and strong positions inside the city.[4]

Wilson also complained of his own health at this time, admitting he could do little after recent efforts: 'I am myself so knocked up in both mind and body, from long continued exertion during the whole of the worst season of the year, that I am incapable of performing to my own satisfaction the duties now entailed upon me, and feel the actual necessity of a short leave of absence to recruit, but I am so situated that there is no one to whom I can entrust the command.'[5] Chasing the rabble of mutineers and the King could come later, after he and his troops had rested for a few days.

When news of Zafar's proximity arrived on the 20th, Saunders, the political agent, was busy attending the funeral of his predecessor H. H. Greathed. Wilson, meanwhile, was busy issuing orders relating to the capture of the palace. Hodson, though, on receiving the intelligence wasted no time gaining permission from Wilson to offer surrender terms to the monarch. Capt. W. M. Stewart, the only person close by at the time, later described the conversation between Hodson and Wilson:

> I did not hear all that passed in the Dewan-i-Khas between the General and Hodson, as I continued writing at my own table for some time after Hodson began talking. Having occasion to speak to the General, I went up to him and found him engaged with Hodson upon the guarantee question. The latter urged him to grant the King's life, and after considerable hesitation the General appeared with reluctance to give his consent, I did not join in the conversation for obvious reasons. There was no one with the General during Hodson's interview. In fact, there was no one in the verandah except myself.[6]

Hodson had asked Wilson if he could lead a detachment of troops to fetch Zafar. Victory would be hollow, he said, if the King and his sons were allowed to escape along with such a large retinue and armed soldiery. Indeed, if the rebels properly regrouped they could force a reversal wherein the British force was besieged by the rebels on the ridge. Mulling it over, Wilson refused to send a European contingent, reiterating that he could spare nobody. Hodson would then volunteer to lead his Irregulars, an idea that he claimed had the support of Brig. Gen. Chamberlain. Quite by chance, while Hodson was busy persuading the general, a messenger arrived from Zeenat Mahal promising to persuade the King to surrender if her conditions were met. Hodson:

> With this purpose I sent for Mirza Elahee Buksh, and through him opened a communication with Zeenut Mahal and her father. Their demands were at first extravagant, the Begum asking that her son should be pronounced heir-apparent, and the succession to the throne guaranteed to him; while on the part of the King it was demanded that his pension should be continued undiminished, and the arrears for the five months subsequent to the outbreak in May paid up at once. It was with considerable difficultly that I succeeded in awakening them to the real position in which the King was placed, and the utter impossibility of either the King or any of his family being ever restored to the throne they had for forfeited.[7]

Negotiations were nevertheless approved, as the King's surrender was preferable if it could be had with token concessions. Foremost in Wilson's mind must have been Greathed's view. The political agent had always been prepared to give the guarantee of life, and had communicated this to the general on previous occasions. In the end, the only offer the general would extend was the promise of life for Zafar, Zeenat Mahal, her son Jawan Bakht and her father Ahmed Kuli Khan. A protection and guard for Zeenat Mahal's house in the city was also extended. Hodson now had something to go on. Zeenat Mahal was asked to provide a 'trustworthy man' to act as messenger for communication with the King.

Wilson therefore gave his clear assent to guaranteeing the King's life in exchange for surrender. It was only when Saunders was making his way back into the city by the Kashmir Gate that he happened to chance upon Hodson heading in the opposite direction. In a short conversation, Hodson informed Saunders that the King could be made to give himself up due to Ilahi Bux's assistance and that Wilson had sanctioned an overture. Saunders later wrote he was a little surprised, being the new political agent, at not being consulted on the issue, although he acknowledged that Greathed had agreed to an overture and had told him so before his death. Greathed in turn had been sanctioned for this by Mr Colvin, Lieutenant Governor the North-West Provinces. However, this had been before Governor-General Canning's recent decrees ordering that no concessions be offered.

Later, on 23 October, when the Government of India asked how the decision to promise Zafar his life had come about, things became much more confused. Wilson, for his part, wrote to the government pushing the responsibility on to Saunders. This was a decision that largely lay with the political officer, he wrote, and he had received a nod to offering life from Saunders himself. It was because of Saunders' recommendation to offer life that he had agreed with Hodson on the evening of 20 September, he explained. It was, Wilson added, also quite in line with Greathed's previous instructions to spare the King's life on the assumption that he was willing to give himself in. 'I allowed Mr Saunders to offer the same guarantee after the city fell into our hands on the condition that the King gave himself up unreservedly,' Wilson wrote. 'The guarantee thus given extended solely to life being spared, and that he was to be disposed of at the discretion of Government.'[8] Later he wrote, 'These instructions were given as it was believed the King was a mere tool of the rebels, and it was considered of great political importance that his person should be in our possession.'[9] The authority for granting the conditional offer rested solely with the political agent, he insisted.

Saunders confessed he was somewhat perplexed at this. He rightly denied being the one who had sanctioned the offer, although he agreed it was the right course. He said he had never been consulted. His explanation of the offer was that since Greathed had previously suggested a promise of life if Zafar gave himself up, then Wilson assumed the situation with the new political agent would remain the same, even though Saunders had not commented or been asked to comment on the issue. Saunders took issue with this, for he had not been consulted, although he saw no subterfuge behind it. 'I do not believe that General Wilson had any intention in writing the above in any way to shift the responsibility for the guarantee upon my shoulders, but on the contrary to imply that he had himself authorised the offer of the guarantee, having previously, as he states, in consultation with my predecessor, Mr Greathed, agreed to do so.'[10] Saunders said that Hodson had never consulted him either, as he had been absent during that vital time. Nor did Wilson after his agreement with Hodson ever signal to Saunders that he had assented to negotiations. Moreover, Hodson had never asserted that Saunders had sanctioned the agreement to begin negotiations.

It was Hodson who then accepted the responsibility for raising the matter of the offer, or at least for urging it and admitting the political agent had never been approached, as he explained on 26 November:

> If any blame is due for sparing the King's life, it is due solely to me, for I begged the General to let me guarantee it on the simple ground that as he had decided *not* to send a column by the direct road in pursuit of Bukht Khan's people, the only chance of seizing the King's person was to bring influence to bear on him and on his love of life so as to induce him to stop and not to go on with the troops. He was within a little of the Kootub when he was persuaded to return. I still think that it was the best course. However much I should have wished to see the King hung or shot, I cannot but think that sparing his life was a less evil than allowing his name to be used as a rallying-point for the disaffected, and as an argument for others to join. We had not, and have not yet, sufficient troops in the country to run the risk of any further insurrection or defection. I have used the words 'personal indignity' in my letter. The words I used were '*be-izzut nahin hone apogee*' in reply to his entreaty that I would protect him from '*be-izzut*' at the hands of the 'gora logue'.[11]

In other words, Hodson had assured Zafar that he would not suffer any humiliation or indignity at European hands. The confusion nonetheless continued, as Hodson had by now left Delhi with Col Seaton's column.

There was also the matter of offering life to other members of the royal family and princes. Saunders would ask Hodson to fully explain the situation leading to Zafar, Zeenat Mahal, Jawan Bakht and Ahmed Kuli Khan being made offers. Also, there was confusion as to why Hodson was given authority to offer protection to the property of the above individuals, and by whom. On 28 December, Wilson clarified his uncertainty as to the day's events:

> I am quite sure that I gave no orders in any political question without the advice of the Political agent with the force. I had Mr Greathed's recommendation to guarantee the King's life, and it struck me when

> writing to Mr Edmonstone on the 23rd October last that I had yours also. I may have been mistaken in supposing I had received your recommendation on the 20th September. On such a day of excitement I may very probably have made such a mistake, but I am quite sure that you approved the measure afterwards, and that when the King was brought in I told you that he was your prisoner, and that you must do what you considered best for his safe custody. I only directed that not more than ten attendants should be allowed for him and his Begum.[12]

He had, he wrote, no wish to suggest that Saunders had taken the decision, especially since all conversations on this topic with Greathed had been verbal.

Saunders himself rather equivocally stated that he was new to the job at the time and had never been given any of the official documents that had been with Greathed bearing instructions on how the King should be treated if he volunteered to surrender. Saunders therefore declared himself entirely ignorant of official policy regarding how to treat the royal family, meaning he could hardly volunteer any advice on the subject in any case. His feelings were that, despite this concession, it was worth it to hold the titular leader of the rebellion. His surrender would be a hammer blow to the morale of the rebels and cause a much quicker extinguishing of the rebellion. The alternative – to refuse to offer life – would mean watching the King lead an insurrection elsewhere. This would only extend the life of the mutiny unnecessarily.

Lengthy to-and-fro communication on the matter continued over the months, but it was more or less brought to a close more than a year later on 4 December 1858. By this time, Capt. Hodson had died and Wilson had departed India, meaning no clear answer could be obtained as to who was responsible for the guarantees to the rest of the royal family. The Government of India would pronounce that 'the Governor-General, without offering to decide the point in question, deems it sufficient to record his opinion that Captain Hodson had no authority from Sir A. Wilson for guaranteeing the life of Zeenut Mahal, of her son Juwan Bukht, and her father, Ahmad Koolee Khan'.[13]

# 39

# Return from Humayun's Tomb

> My dear Hodson, All honour to you (and to your 'Horse') for catching the King and slaying his sons. I hope you will bag many more![1]
>
> Robert Montgomery, 29 September 1857

On the afternoon of 21 September, Hodson rode out of the city with 100 troopers to apprehend the King and escort him back to the city. No shots were fired at Hodson's party as they travelled south despite crowds of disconsolate rebels milling around on the road to Humayun's Tomb. Unsure of the reception he would receive on arrival, Hodson and his party stopped and concealed themselves in some old ruins adjacent to the tomb. Two emissaries were then sent through the gateway of the tomb to meet Zeenat Mahal and to ask her of the King, her son and her father. A long two hours would pass as Hodson's party waited for a reply. Zafar was presumably undecided. The emissaries finally came out with the message that he would only surrender to Hodson and that Hodson should personally repeat the promise of life given by Wilson. Upon hearing the King's decision, Hodson showed his presence, moving to the tomb entrance. A short while later, a procession could be seen approaching Hodson headed by Mirza Ilahi Bux and a moulvi. In a letter to Hodson's brother, a British officer described what happened next:

> Soon a procession began to come slowly out, first Zeenat Mahal, in one of the close native conveyances used for women. Her name was announced as she passed by the moulvi. Then came the King in a *palkee* [palanquin], on which Captain Hodson rode forward and demanded

> his arms. Before giving them up the King asked whether he was 'Hodson Bahadoor' and if he would repeat the promise made by the herald. Captain Hodson answered that he would, and repeated that the Government had been graciously pleased to promise him his life, and that of Zeenat Mahal's son on condition of his yielding himself prisoner quietly, adding very emphatically, that if any attempt was made at a rescue he would shoot the King down on the spot like a dog. The old man then gave up his arms which Captain Hodson handed to his orderly, still keeping his own sword drawn in his hand.[2]

Along with the royal party were a host of other fugitives who followed behind. According to Hodson himself, in a letter to Saunders on 28 November, the crowd seemed threatening, although this seems unlikely given the apathy shown by both Zafar and the rebel soldiers alike:

> I reassured the King and the Begum (both of whom were evidently much agitated and frightened) by the promise that his life would be spared, provided that no attempt was made at a rescue, which at the time I thought very imminent. I then remounted, and in a sufficiently loud tone to be heard by the crowd repeated the words; adding a command to my men to shoot the first person who attempted to move. I then desired Mirza Elahee Buksh and Moulvee Rujjub Alee to proceed with the palanquins, following with my men as soon as they were a sufficient distance from the crowd.[3]

Jawan Bakht was also brought forward, and plans were made to escort king, queen and son back to the city. Zafar was allowed to be attended by a lone servant. The King being carried by palanquin, the pace was naturally slow, and a large crowd followed the party back to the city. Four rebel guns were also found at the tomb and brought back. By the time the party approached the Lahore Gate, much of the assembly had disappeared again. At the gate, a British guard asked Hodson who was on the palanquin, to which he replied, 'Only the King of Delhi.' The guards showed their enthusiasm but were prevented from cheering; it was thought that the King would interpret the cheer as being for himself as he re-entered the city as a monarch, not a prisoner. Passing the gate, the cortege travelled up the deserted road towards the palace.

At the palace entrance, Saunders took charge of the prisoners, exclaiming, 'By Jove! Hodson, they ought to make you Commander-in-Chief for this.'[4] Hodson then visited Wilson's headquarters in the Diwan-i-Khas. 'Well, I'm glad you have got him, but I never expected to see either him or you again!' Wilson commented. As a reward, the general allowed Hodson to select from a set of swords which Zafar had in his possession and which were now surrendered. Hodson wasn't overjoyed at this, however:

> I and most other people considered that I and my party had a right to all we found on the King and princes but the General to whom I referred the question thought otherwise so I gave up all except some of the personal arms of the princes; those of the King were taken by the General. The swords which I secured thanks to the officers assembled when the arms were made over are historically most valuable. One was worn by and bears the name of Jehangire [an earlier Mughal emperor, ruler from 1605 to 1627] and the other is stamped with the seal of Nadir Shah [Persian ruler who sacked Delhi in 1739]. They are singular and interesting trophies or rather relics of the house of Timour the Tartar.[5]

Hodson declared he would present the swords to Queen Victoria. After his death in March 1858, the swords eventually found their way to England as trophies of war and were indeed presented to Queen Victoria.

Once in the city, Zafar was initially incarcerated in the house of Begum Samru, around fifty troops of HM61st selected as his guard. Lost in thought, Zafar quietly rested while various curious Europeans came to gaze at him over the following days. Capt. Griffiths was one of those given the duty to guard the old man:

> Sitting cross-legged on a cushion placed on a common native *charpoy*, or bed, in the verandah of a courtyard, was the last representative of the Great Mogul dynasty. There was nothing imposing in his appearance, save a long white beard which reached to his girdle. About middle height, and upwards of seventy years old, he was dressed in white, with a conical-shaped turban of the same colour and material, while at his back two attendants stood, waving over his head large fans of peacocks feathers, the emblem of sovereignty—a pitiable farce in the case of one who was already shorn of his regal attributes, a prisoner in the hands of his enemies. Not a word came from his lips; in silence he sat day and night, with his eyes cast on the ground, and as though utterly oblivious of the condition in which he was placed. On another bed, three feet from the King, sat the officer on guard, while two stalwart European sentries, with fixed bayonets, stood on either side. The orders given were that on any attempt at a rescue the officer was immediately to shoot the King with his own hand.

*****

Hodson had neglected to bring along the remaining princes still resident at the tomb, who had not been promised life on surrender. The day after Zafar's capture, 22 September, Wilson was still unsure what to do with them. Hodson, however, insisted they too be apprehended before they fled. He was echoed by the ailing Nicholson, who argued that capturing them now would mean far less work later. Prominent among the princes at the tomb was Mirza Mughal, commander-in-chief of the rebel army, as well as Mirza Khizr Sultan and Mirza Abulbakr, son of Mirza Mughal.

'The General at length yielded a reluctant consent, adding, "But don't let me be bothered with them." I assured him it was nothing but his own order which "bothered" him with the King, as I would much rather have brought him into Delhi dead than living,' Hodson wrote in a private letter. With consent given, Hodson promptly organised an arrest party consisting of his second in command Lt MacDowall and around 100 men for the return trip to the tomb. The party left around 8 a.m., riding slowly. Hodson took the precaution of bringing with him one of the lesser members of the royal family, a nephew of the King. In addition to the others discussed, he had been promised life in exchange for acting as an emissary and encouraging the princes to surrender. He was also required to point out the princes and name them, none of whom could be identified by Hodson himself.

When around half a mile away from the tomb, the emissary along with Hodson's principal intelligence assistant, Rajab Ali, went in to see the princes and to give them the uncompromising message that they must give themselves up unconditionally or suffer the consequences. Hodson in his account mentions a considerable delay here, with arguments and discussions taking place between the princes for some time, before the princes decided to surrender. Zaka Ullah described the goings-on in the tomb based on what he later heard.

> On getting this response the Princes turned to their supporters for advice and they said to them, 'Members of the Timur family do not give themselves up in this way, we will take our swords and fight after that it is up to fate. When Aurangzeb tried to get Dara Sikoh murdered when he was in the Jail, he picked up a kitchen knife and fought for a while against his opponents. We should do the brave thing; we can defeat Hudson and his riders in a short time. We have to die today or tomorrow, why not meet death bravely.' The Princes liked this suggestion, but Mirza Ilahi Bux intervened. He opened up with his advice and raised so many objections to this suggestion that the Princes were moved to change their minds in view of the sympathetic attitude and suggestions of Mirza Ilahi Bux. They said their farewells to their sympathizers and came out of the Tomb.

Both Hodson and MacDowall would again make much of the danger from rebel soldiers still milling around. MacDowall related that there were still around 3,000 rebels resting in the tomb while an equal number were hovering around the area. Around half an hour later the princes sent back a message asking whether their lives would be spared. Hodson replied that no promise could be given and reiterated the demand for their unconditional surrender. 'We dared not take them by force, or all would have been lost, and we doubted their coming,' recalled Lt MacDowall. 'We heard the shouts of the fanatics (as we found out afterwards) begging the princes to lead them on against us. And we had only one hundred men, and were six miles from Delhi. At length, I suppose, imagining that sooner or later they must be taken, they resolved to give themselves up unconditionally, fancying, I suppose, as we had spared the King, we would spare them. So the messenger was sent to say they were coming.'[6] Hodson then sent ten men to escort the princes back to his party with instructions to shoot the princes if their rebel supporters initiated any violence. MacDowall continues:

> Soon they appeared in a small 'Ruth' or Hindoostanee cart drawn by bullocks, five troopers on each side. Behind them thronged about 2000 or 3000 (I am not exaggerating) Mussulmans. We met them, and at once Hodson and I rode up, leaving the men a little in the rear. They bowed as we came up, and Hodson, bowing, ordered the driver to move on. This was the minute. The crowd behind made a movement. Hodson waved them back; I beckoned to the troop, which came up, and in an instant formed them up between the crowd and the cart. By Hodson's order I advanced at a walk on the people, who fell back sullenly and slowly at our approach.

Along with the princes were brought various arms belonging to them and their attendants as well as the King's personal elephants, horses and carriages which had not been brought the day before. 'They acknowledged themselves to be the men,' recalled Hodson. 'Their names were Mirza Mogul, the King's nephew and head of the whole business, Mirza Kishere Sultamet who was also one of the principal rebels and had made himself notorious by murdering women and children and Abu Bukt the commander in chief nominally and heir apparent to the throne.' He was asked once more if their lives would be guaranteed. 'I answered, "most certainly not" and sent them away from the tomb towards the city under a guard,'[7] wrote Hodson, reprising them of their crimes and deeds.

The princes were ordered on to the bullock cart to be transported back to the city. Hodson waved the troopers off and the bullock cart escorted by sowars began making its way back to the city, where a large crowd of locals was waiting outside the walls. Hodson asked his sowars to escort the princes up the road to the city while he signalled to the crowd at the tomb to go back inside. Since the princes had surrendered, Hodson decided to investigate the tomb as well. MacDowall would follow him, along with four troopers. In front of him when he entered was the considerable expanse of garden encompassing the tomb. All around him were dejected rebel soldiers, camp followers and other assorted hangers-on of the King and his retinue, resting on the grass and at the tomb itself. How much real danger there was from this mass of people – Hodson records 6,000 to 7,000 gathered – is difficult to say. In any case, Hodson demanded the men before him surrender their arms.

> They immediately obeyed, with an alacrity I scarcely dared to hope for, and in less than two hours they brought forth from innumerable hiding places some 500 swords, and more than that number of fire arms, besides horses, bullocks and covered carts called 'Ruths' used by the women and eunuchs of the palace. I then arranged the arms and animals in the centre, and left an armed guard with them, while I went to look after my prisoners, who with their guard, had moved on towards Delhi.[8]

MacDowall had suggested that the stay at the tomb was fraught with danger. 'Well there we stayed for two hours, collecting their arms, and I assure you I thought every moment they would rush upon us,' he wrote. 'I said nothing, but smoked all the time, to show I was unconcerned; but at last, when it was all done, and all the arms collected, put in a cart, and started, Hodson turned to me and said, "We'll go, now."'[9] The party then rode back out to rejoin the main party escorting the princes.

*****

As they rode back to the city, both Hodson and MacDowall would later claim they sensed danger. Maybe this was true; maybe it was just an attempt to justify what they did next in one of the most controversial incidents of the entire mutiny. MacDowall: 'We came up to the princes, now about five miles from where we had taken them, and close to Delhi. The increasing crowd pressed close on the horses of the sowars, and assumed every moment a more hostile appearance. "What shall we do with them?" said Hodson to me. "I think we had better shoot them here; we shall never get them in," I replied.'[10]

Rather than taking the princes into the city, Hodson ordered that the cart halt outside the city walls. The three princes were then ordered off the cart by Hodson, told to remove their outer clothing and then told to board the cart again. They were also relieved of their jewellery – rings, turquoise armbands and various swords encrusted with jewels. Hodson ordered five troopers on each side of the cart to ward off the crowd, then dismounted, drew his Colt revolver and fired two shots into each of the princes, killing them instantly.

Abulbakr was candid in his last moments, declaring that he died happy because he had seen European women dragged through the streets. 'This was the young fiend who had stripped our women in the open street, and cutting off little children's arms and legs, poured the blood into their mothers' mouths: this is literally the case,' thundered MacDowall.[11] Zaka Ullah heard that the princes confidently alighted from the cart for they thought Hodson could not execute them on his own authority, the decision being Wilson's to make. They had disrobed in the belief that they were to be paraded through the city as a humiliation.

According to MacDowall, the previously belligerent crowd fell silent and moved off. A few moments later, one of the King's eunuchs – his favourite, apparently, and one who was implicated in other murders – was seen running away. MacDowall and a sowar chased after him:

> The sowar cut him down instantly, and we returned, well satisfied that we had rid the world of such a monster. It was now four o'clock: Hodson rode into the city with the cart containing the bodies, and had them placed in the most public street, where all might see them. Side by side they lay where, four months, before on the same spot, they had outraged and murdered our women. I went quietly home with the troop, nearly dead, having had nothing (except water) since six o'clock the previous night.[12]

In a letter to his brother, Hodson himself wrote starkly about the executions:

> I came up just in time, as a large mob had collected, and were turning on the guard. I rode in among them at a gallop, and in a few words, I appealed to the crowd, saying that these were the butchers who had murdered and brutally used helpless women and children, and that the Government had now sent their punishment: seizing a carbine from one of my men, I deliberately shot them one after another. I then ordered the bodies to be taken into the city and thrown out on the 'Chiboutra', in front of the *Kotwalie*, where the blood of their innocent victims still could be distinctly traced …
>
> I am not cruel, but I confess I did rejoice at the opportunity of ridding the earth of these wretches. I intended to have had them hung, but when it came to a question of 'they' or 'us' I had no time for deliberation.[13]

As for the curious order that the princes disrobe, Hodson's brother denied that it was motivated by a desire to take the princes' clothing as spoils. 'He made them strip off their upper garments to render their death and subsequent exposure at the *kotwali* more impressive and terrible,' he argued. As for shooting them himself and not leaving it to his sowars, his answer was that the sowars, being Muslim, might have hesitated or refused and this may have been a signal in that charged moment for the crowd to attack Hodson and his party.

Hodson's actions that day are difficult to understand, and they continue to incite debate today. The true danger faced by Hodson, who had an armed retinue, is hard to discern. Certainly he had had no issue reaching or returning from the tomb that day, or in fact the previous day when he had apprehended the King; nor did he have any issue collecting arms from the rebels in the tomb. His explanation seems flimsy, particularly given his rather boastful confession that he planned to kill them anyway.

Following the action, the bodies of the princes were loaded back on to the bullock cart and transported into the city. The cart was then directed towards the *kotwali* on the Chandni Chowk. Here the three corpses were roughly deposited on the street as an example to the locals. What remained of their clothes was stripped from their bodies apart from rags to cover their loins. The corpses would languish there until 24 September, when they were removed for sanitary reasons. Revd Rotton described the scene:

> Here I saw them that same afternoon; nor can it be said that I or the others who viewed the lifeless remains felt any pity in our hearts for the wretches on whom had fallen a most righteous retribution for their crimes. The eldest was a strong, well-knit man in the prime of life, the next somewhat younger, while the third was quite a youth not more than twenty years of age. Each of the Princes had two small bullet-holes over the region of the heart, the flesh singed by gunpowder, as the shots were fired close; a cloth covered part of the loins, but they were otherwise quite naked. There was a guard, I think, of Coke's Rifles stationed at the *Kotwali*, and there the bodies remained exposed for three days, and were then buried in dishonoured graves.

On the evening of the executions, Hodson betrayed his anger at the princes for having ordered the killing of women and children on 11 May. Since he ordered the bodies be dumped on the Chandni Chowk, the motive seems to have been revenge; European corpses had been similarly displayed in the same spot. Writing to his brother, he wrote, 'I am very tired, but very much satisfied with my day's work, and so seem all hands.'[14]

Hodson was not troubled by the criticism he received for the cold-blooded slayings:

> Strange, that some of those who are loudest against me for sparing the King, are also crying out at my destroying his sons. '*Quousque tandem*?' I may well exclaim. But in point of fact, I am quite indifferent to clamour either way. I made up my mind at the time to be abused. I was convinced I was right, and when I prepared to run the great physical risk of the attempt, I was equally game for the moral risk of praise or blame. These have not been, and are not times when a man who would serve his country dare hesitate as to the personal consequences to himself of what he thinks his duty.

*****

This wasn't the end of the matter. Other prisoners had to be collected from the tomb, and Hodson had left a guard there to protect the arms that had been surrendered. On the morning of the 27th, Brigadier Showers was sent with a strong column towards Humayun's Tomb to apprehend the rest of the royal princes as well as anyone else of high station remaining in the rebel camp. The intention was that they would be tried before a military commission to ascertain their part in the rebellion and for the appropriate punishment to be meted out. 'Their wives, and immediate female relatives of the King and his sons, are to be told that, if they wish to come in, they will receive shelter and protection until the receipt of the orders of Government regarding their ultimate disposal,' Saunders wrote to Lawrence. Any armed men still in the camp were to have their arms taken from them. Disarmament also applied to a large contingent of rebels who had left the city and were encamped at the Kutb Minar around 10 miles to the south of Delhi.

That night, Showers brought in three more princes – Mirza Bakhtawar Shah, Mirza Mendoo and Mirza Jawan Bakht, the latter of whom had not journeyed with Zafar as planned. Two other princes, Mirza Koore Shah and Abdoola, managed to escape. Others remained at the tomb. Another prince, Mirza Kuchak Sultan, was offered refuge by his tutor at the palace, Santa Ullah, but he refused so as not to put the man's family in danger.[15] Instead, Kuchak Sultan made his way to Jaipur where he was apprehended.

At the beginning of October, two more sons of the King were captured and shot; they too had commanded units of the rebel army and were suspected of massacring Europeans. A strange incident took place at their execution when the firing squad, which included men of the 60th Rifles and some Gurkhas, managed to miss or only wound the princes. One could suspect some sympathy for the boys, perhaps. In any case, a provost sergeant finished the job by shooting each prince in the head. They had been dressed in the dirtiest of clothes but apparently met their fate stoically and with dignity.

40

# 'This possessor of mere nominal royalty'

> The execution of such men will strike terror, and produce a salutary fear through the Mahomedan population.
>
> John Lawrence

In the main thoroughfare of the city, the Chandni Chowk, a new wooden structure was added in the days after the fall of the city. This was a gallows opposite the *kotwali* where rebels would be hanged in their hundreds over the coming days. A line of rebels was typically led up to the gallows daily, with each man being escorted forward and hanged while those next in line watched before stepping up themselves. A shop was situated near the gallows, and the enterprising owner, sensing an opportunity, began renting out chairs to European spectators. There they could sit and smoke cigars while watching the queue of people snaking forward to meet their maker. Mrs Coopland, the widow of Revd George Coopland, had occasion to pass by the gallows on a visit:

> The provost-marshal who performed this revolting duty, had put to death between 400 and 500 wretches since the siege, and was now thinking of resigning his office. The soldiers, inured to sights of horror, and inveterate against the sepoys, were said to have bribed the executioner to keep them a long time hanging, as they liked to see the criminals dance a 'Pandie's hornpipe [a naval dance],' as they termed the dying struggles of the wretches.[1]

Many rebels never made it to the gallows. Magistrate Theophilus Metcalfe, who was always an authoritative man, caused much dread in the city with his vengeful manner. During the days after the city's capture he could be seen riding around hunting out rebels and executing those who were caught. One of those apprehended was Mr Frazer's murderer, who was hanged. Metcalfe set up a military court to try hundreds suspected of helping the insurgents. Each day, five would be forwarded for hanging on the Chandni Chowk. As well as these unfortunates, Sir John Kaye, the official chronicler of the mutiny, described eight cartloads of rebels or sympathizer corpses being taken out of the city every day – he estimated a total of 6,000 executions in and around Delhi for actions in favour of the rebels.

The hangings would continue well into the next year, and were not restricted just to the citizens of Delhi. There were seven princely states in close proximity to the city under the jurisdiction of the Delhi Agency; the rulers of these states had been slow to show support for the British Government or for European individuals fleeing Delhi during the early days of the mutiny, and they were called to account. Among them was Nawab Mahomed Hussun Khan, who was hanged along with various minor prisoners. Hussun Khan had been Prince Mirza Khizr Sultan's *mukhtar* or confidential agent as well as doing services for Mirza Mughal. He had fought at the Battle of Hindun River as well as Badli-ki-Serai, where he had been given command of a contingent of troops. Others hanged included Hakeem Mahomed Abdul Huk, who had been the Raja of Ballabgarh's agent. He was an important man, having been given charge of the Gurgaon area. During the mutiny he had functioned as *aide-de-camp* for the King. He was also in command of 400 armed men who had engaged in fighting with the British. As well as being one of the members of the finance committee charged with raising funds, he had also regularly attended court events. He was executed for treason and rebellion.

The Raja of Ballabgarh, Nahar Singh, was brought up on 19 December, found guilty on 2 January and hanged. He had been accused of failing to help a Mr Mandero, a judge in the city. He was also accused of being in league with the rebels and for carrying on secret correspondence with Zafar. His state was annexed. According to Mrs Coopland, the raja presented a stoic exterior at the end:

> Gentle in manner, young and handsome in person, it was the hard fate of this noble to be placed in circumstances wherein every path was fraught with peril and to be tried when death was the award of any act hostile to our rule. There was something touching in the last words he spoke before his judges: 'I was securely seated on a goodly bough of a flourishing tree, and my own act has sawn asunder the branch on which I rested.'[2]

There was also Abdur Rehman, Nawab of Jhajjar, who was implicated in the murder of Mr Fraser. On 8 December 1857, Rehman was up before the military commission. By coincidence, he and a large retinue of his followers had been in Delhi on the day the rebels had arrived from

Meerut. They were charged with refusing to aid Sir Theophilus Metcalfe on the day and failing to assist the Europeans at any point. At his trial, Rehman elucidated what most Europeans would agree with in private: 'that it was England who had armed and trained the ruffians who had brought the calamity on the land; and it was not fair to expect him to compel that obedience in his followers which the rulers of the country and his judges had failed in compelling among their own'. His trial was completed on the 17th, and he was hanged on 23 December. He had apparently been scheduled to hang in the new year, but his hanging was brought forward as there were strong rumours of an uprising against the remaining British garrison in the city on Christmas Day, when the garrison were expected to be most lax. Rehman, recorded Mrs Muter, impressed his accusers with his demeanour during and after the trial. 'This Prince met his fate on the gallows with a calmness, a fortitude, and gentlemanly bearing that inspired my husband, who commanded the escort, with the deepest respect.' Capt. Garstone, who had seen the man hang, recorded that he would take some time to die on the gibbet.[3]

A similar sentence was meted out to Ahmad Ali, Nawab of Farrukhnagar, whose kingdom disappeared into the maw of the East India Company. Ahmad Ali was brought to trial on 12 January and found guilty on 22 January. He was hanged three days later. Two other chiefs, the rulers of Pataudi and Dojana, were released with no punitive action taken.

As far as the princes were concerned, Lawrence had advised quick action: 'I would recommend the trial and on conviction the punishment of the Shahzadas [princes],' he had written on 28 September. 'I do not see that anything is to be gained by delay.' By 7 October, Mirza Bakhtawar Shah and Mirza Mehndoo had been tried and had been found guilty. The princes had defended themselves by stating they were acting under orders from their father and under compulsion, alluding to the ultimate power the rebel officers and sepoys held in the palace, but to no avail. Having been found guilty, the princes were sentenced to death by firing squad. The execution was carried out on the morning of 14 October. 'The execution of such men will strike terror, and produce a salutary fear through the Mahomedan population,' Lawrence wrote. Several other members of the royal family were put to death on 18 October. In all, twenty-six members of the royal family would be executed and thirteen imprisoned in Agra.

*****

Some executions resulting from events at Delhi would happen many years into the future. In 1862 came the trial of Mogul Beg, the palace orderly. He would be charged for the murder of Capt. Douglas and the other assorted Europeans who had taken shelter in their apartments in the palace on 11 May 1857. The trial would be held between 30 January and 1 February 1862. Mogul Beg would plead not guilty to the charge of murder.

Hajee Khan, an accomplice to the murders in Capt. Douglas' apartments, was brought to trial much later than Mogul Beg. His trial was held at Delhi on 10 December 1868, more than eleven years after the events. Hajee Khan was arrested in Delhi having laid low until his discovery. After the fall of the city he had fled to Nizamuddin, a village around 4 miles from Delhi, where he had quickly been apprehended. After his arrest, on the orders of Sir Theophilus Metcalfe, he was transported back to Delhi for trial; however, on his way he encountered Metcalfe, who by sheer coincidence was also travelling into the city at the same time. The vengeful Metcalfe slashed the prisoner with his sword and left him for dead on the roadside. Hajee Khan was lucky. The wound wasn't fatal, and he recovered and slipped away. Sometime later, the Delhi Police were informed that Hajee Khan was alive and well and living in Lahore under the assumed name of Abdullah. He managed to escape another arrest before being traced and successfully arrested in Delhi. This time there was no escape. He pleaded not guilty, just like Mogul Beg. The sessions judge summed up the evidence:

> We need hardly remark that death is the only punishment adequate to the offence committed by the accused; and the only thing which it appears to us it would be possible to urge in mitigation, is his having already suffered in the attack made upon him by Sir T. Metcalfe, who left him on the ground for dead. Considering however the brutality and atrocity of the crime and the leading part in it taken by the accused, we are unable to commute the capital sentence on account of the occurrence to which we have alluded.[4]

The death sentence was passed on 17 December. Six years after his accomplice Mogul Beg, Hajee Khan was launched into eternity in front of the Lahore Gate.

*****

As for the captured king, it was felt that incarcerating him somewhere in the Punjab would be appropriate in the short term. Both Saunders and Barnes had suggested the King be escorted and held there until a final decision could be taken as to his fate. Punjab was a safe place to hold him, for it was supposed he would receive little sympathy from the Punjab population or soldiery, so there would be little chance for intrigue or escape. Ambala and Ferozepore were also suggested. With troops required in the Punjab, as soon as HM52nd had recuperated it was suggested to send them back to Govindgarh Fortress at Amritsar with the King in tow. Wilson suggested he could be held there until a decision was made. There was also the issue of whether he was to be tried by a military commission. Lawrence would advise no hasty action: 'I would not send the King up this way. I would keep him at Delhie and send him to Meerutt when troops move across. His being in our possession would be useful,'[5] he wrote to G. C. Barnes. Seeing the prisoner King in tow as troops moved eastwards to deal with other disturbances would have a powerful impact.

As far as what to do with him in the longer term, since Zafar had been promised life, John Lawrence would, on 23 September, suggest setting up a court of British officers to examine the circumstances behind the mutiny at Delhi and the part played by Zafar and the royal family. The main reason was to extract as much information as possible out of him and as soon as possible. Since he had been guaranteed life, the trial served no other purpose. However, Lawrence believed his final destination should be abroad, perhaps exile to Singapore. If Punjab was to be settled on, then the fort of Kangra would be a most a suitable place; it could easily be defended by a few companies of European troops. Until the military commission was completed, however, it was decided to keep the King at Delhi. For that, Saunders would need to collect all evidence against the King and to clarify the charges against him. The King would in turn be allowed a week to prepare his defence along with selecting a lawyer. If he failed to do this, British officers would be chosen to represent him. 'Should the King be found guilty the sentence is to be carried out without further reference to the Governor-General in Council,' Saunders was advised.

On 13 October, Lt Omanney was placed in charge of Zafar and the other prisoners of high station. This was because the European officers on guard at the time hardly knew the language of the country, being of Her Majesty's Service rather than East India Company regiments. Saunders required someone who could communicate with the prisoners as and when required. Zafar was at this time being kept in a house outside the palace. Mrs Coopland sated her curiosity in seeing the fallen monarch at this time, and she records his melancholy manner:

> Pushing aside the purdah, we entered a small, dirty, low room with whitewashed walls, and there, on a low charpoy, cowered a thin small old man, dressed in a dirty white suit of cotton, and rolled in shabby wraps and rezais, on account of the cold. At our entrance he laid aside the hookah he had been smoking, and he, who had formerly thought it an insult for any one to sit in his presence, began salaaming to us in the most abject manner, and saying he was 'burra kooshee' (very glad) to see us. As we looked at him we thought how strange it was that this frail old man, tottering on the brink of the grave, could harbour such a plot and such deep revengeful feelings against us. His face was pale and wan, and his eyes weak and uncertain, seeming to shun our scrutiny; but an aristocratic expression of face reminded us of his noble descent. He had a venerable-looking white beard, and he swayed about in a frail decrepit way, exciting feelings that were a mixture of contempt,

> abhorrence, and pity: contempt, for the degraded position to which he had brought himself by his wild scheme of reinstating himself on a throne which he could only hope to enjoy for a passing year or two; abhorrence, that he could give up our poor countrymen to be brutally murdered, and even, it is said, feast his eyes and ears on their dying anguish; and pity, that he should have so short a time for repentance, and that the descendant of a line of kings, whose splendour and power were boundless, should be thus degraded.[6]

After meeting the King, the women were allowed to see Zeenat Mahal in another room separated from the King's by a curtain. The queen and her attendants sat in modest circumstances, the room itself being 'bare and shabby'. Zeenat Mahal and the King had been allowed some servant women to cook their dinner. According to Mrs Coopland, both King and Queen retained some element of their earlier airs and graces. Zeenat Mahal, looking at Coopland's black dress, asked what had happened to the woman's husband; Mrs Coopland, suspecting she was being mocked, took great offence. The King, meanwhile, ordered tobacco but rejected what was brought. He also complained that he had to depend on the British allowance of four annas a day (around sixpence of that time) for his sustenance, tobacco and other needs even though he was sure his wife knew of plenty of hidden caches of money and jewels which could easily be used for his comfort.

*****

A question mark still hung over the youngest prince, Jawan Bakht. On 14 November, General Penny recommended to John Lawrence that Zeenat Mahal's seventeen-year-old son also be treated as a prisoner, suggesting the boy could not but have been influenced by his father and family: 'His being kept back from taking a prominent part in the transaction is only attributable to the deep designing character of the mother. I therefore from what I have seen, look on "Jumma Bukht" but little removed from a young viper, who hereafter, if at large, may prove a rallying-point for the disaffected.'[7] John Lawrence agreed, further suggesting keeping the youth under guard along with his father and mother until the Governor-General made judgement on the issue. Certainly there was no chance of him having his liberty.

On 19 November, the *Friend of India* newspaper printed an article criticizing the unnecessary deference shown to the prince by British officers. The behaviour towards the prisoner, it declared, was entirely incompatible with his status as a prisoner. The writer called for 'instant and stern reform' on matters related to the royal prisoners, ending any preferential treatment, although the writer was certain such actions had received no sanction from the Governor-General:

> The youngest son of the King, 18 years of age, has been declared innocent on account of his youth, and rides through Delhi on an elephant with two British officers behind him to do him honor! The statement appears so incredible that it may be set aside as a mere newspaper report. We entreat Government to believe that it is one which we would not publish without such information as produces absolute certainty. The King, also, it is said – but for this we have only the authority of the *Lahore Chronicle* – has a retinue to attend him, and coolly insults British officers who visit him. It is things such as these, the honors paid to our murderers, which exasperates Europeans to frenzy. They are not ordered or sanctioned by this Government, but they should be stopped by court martials, if necessary.[8]

Saunders was rightly critical of the accusations being made. The prince was not eighteen as the article said but seventeen. He was also not the youngest – there was a younger prince, Shah Abbas, albeit from a different mother. Putting this aside, the main issue was that Saunders could find nothing of guilt regarding the prince – he was not mentioned in any documents, nor did he have any position of power. Due to his age, he had not been given charge of any regiment. In fact, after his capture he had helped uncover some of his mother's substantial jewellery to be added to the prize fund. Saunders attributed the special treatment of the prince to this betrayal:

> When I next had occasion to see the King I demanded the surrender of the Crown jewels, which after some hesitation the Begum produced from behind the purdah. On my leaving the King's apartment, Mirza Juma Bukht followed me to the door, and in a low voice told me that, if I would not inform his father and mother, he would point out to me the spot in his mother's house where her jewels, money and other valuables were secreted. I told him I would call for him the next morning, which I accordingly did on the elephant, having in the interim asked the Prize Agents and a few other officers to meet me at the house. On this occasion I again permitted Juma Bukht to climb up on my elephant and seat himself behind me. The search resulted in my securing for the army considerably more than the promised ransom. On no occasion am I aware of his having ridden through Delhi on an elephant with two British officers behind him to do him honor, as stated in the *Friend of India*.[9]

On 31 December, the Governor-General would clarify matters as to the general treatment that Zafar should be given, for it was felt the treatment was inappropriate to his new position. Canning did not desire 'that any hardship or indignity should be put upon the prisoners further than may be unavoidable in securing their safe custody; but he does desire that no honor whatever should be shown to any of them. Whatever may have been the intention of the act, the fact that the King's son is allowed to ride on an elephant with one of the British officers of highest rank at Delhie will be understood, and naturally understood, as at least a proof that the captivity in which the family are held is an honorable one.' Such opinion among the general population was undesirable. 'It will not be difficult to provide air and exercise for the prisoners without placing any of them in such a position as has been given to Jewan Bukht.'[10]

The prince had been allowed to ride on the elephant with Col Hogge, who wrote to the *Lahore Chronicle* advising them the situation had been misunderstood. Hogge explained he was in the habit of taking an airing every evening on an elephant. As Jawan Bakht had asked for an airing himself, the Commissioner had asked Hogge if he could take the young lad with him on the elephant and he had agreed. The reason Hogge put forward for sitting behind the prince, i.e. in an inferior position, was that it was necessary to keep an eye on him in case he attempted to escape.

> As to parading through the streets of the city, the first time I went out through the Cashmere Gate to Ludlow Castle and home when it was quite dusk through the Lahore Gate and Chandnee Chowk; the second time I passed up the Chandnee Chowk, and returned by the Lall Kooa Street, having been induced to go there by Jumma Bukht expressing a wish to show me the house he lived in. Without entering into the question of his guilt or innocence, but presuming that, if guilty, he would never have been allowed to accompany a British officer in public, I can only say that I found him a very intelligent lad; he gave me a good deal of information about the mutineers, their leaders, and their plans, and had I remained longer at Delhi should probably have taken him out oftener, but having returned to Meerut on the 26th October I had no further opportunity.[11]

Saunders replied on 26 January to the Government of India:

> I have in my former letters expressed my regret at having permitted Jawan Bukht to be taken out on the three or four occasions which I have specified either by Colonel Hogge or by myself. Had I known the temper of the public and the newspaper press at the time better, I would not have done so, but I deny that in allowing him to go out either for an airing or for a special purpose I had any intention whatever of showing him honor.

Saunders explained that some of the elder princes who had surrendered at Humayun's Tomb had been put under the guard of Sikh soldiers but that they had allowed the princes to escape. Jawan Bakht had therefore been allowed to go out but only accompanied by a European officer. The elephant was chosen to make escape difficult, not imply honour:

'I remembered that the Seikh [Sikh] Chieftains Chuttur Singh and Sher Singh, Attarewala, the leaders in the last Seikh Campaign, who were sent down in strict confinement as State prisoners to Calcutta, were allowed by the Most Noble the Governor-General to go out daily for an airing in a carriage attended by a European, and I was of opinion that a similar practice in the present instance would not have been forbidden.'[12]

The other reason to treat Jawan Bakht well was to get information. Saunders had received a communique from John Lawrence on 24 September: 'Try and get out of the King, now that he is alarmed, all that you can. Tell him that much will depend upon his making a clean breast.'[13] However, Saunders had managed to get little out of either Zafar or his wife. What they said was designed to minimise their involvement.

> With Jawan Bukht the case was different; in the presence of his parents he was perfectly taciturn on all subjects on which we desired to obtain information. He, however, gave us to understand that if he, were allowed to go out for an airing, he would tell us anything we wished to know. He kept his word, and a great deal of useful and important information was elicited from him on subjects bearing upon the mutiny, the conduct of the war, and the complicity of the Native Chiefs in the rebellion.[14]

*****

The military commission to try Zafar would eventually be organised by order of General Penny in late January. Heading the commission would be Lt Col Dawes of the Artillery, with the other four members being Maj. Palmer (HM6th), Maj. Redmond (HM61st), Maj. Sawyers (HM6th Carabineers) and Capt. Rothney (4th Sikh Infantry). The prosecutor for the Government of India would be Maj. F. J. Harriott, Deputy Judge Advocate General, while Zafar would be given a lawyer by the name of Ghulam Abbas. The military commission would effectively be a court of enquiry. As Lawrence advised Saunders, the trial would simply be 'to place on record the part he [Zafar] played in the insurrection'.[15]

The trial had been delayed as the elderly Zafar had developed a fever. Indeed, it appeared at one point that he was approaching his end. The trial was therefore postponed till he recovered sufficiently. Proceedings eventually began on 27 January in the Diwan-i-Khas, and would last twenty-one days interspersed with intervals imposed due to Zafar's poor health.

On the first day of the trial, Zafar was ushered into the Diwan-i-Khas guarded by a strong detachment of the 60th Rifles. He was carried in on a palanquin with his son Jawan Bakht holding his left hand and an attendant walking on his right side. Also accompanying him was Zeenat Mahal. He was given a place to sit, with a few cushions being thrown on his seat for his comfort. As he settled down, he must have seen figures drawn in chalk very prominently on one of the walls nearby. These were drawn by the British soldiers resident in the palace. Two outlines were drawn of the King; one depicted him with the writing 'The King of Delhi as he is' below. The other showed a figure hanging on a gibbet with the legend 'The King of Delhi as he ought to be'.[16]

After the formalities, the charges against Zafar were read out by the prosecutor. He then reminded the court that regardless of the decision, guilty or not, Zafar could not be given any form of capital punishment, having been promised life by Capt. Hodson under orders from General Wilson. Put simply, the reason for the trial was to record evidence as to the happenings at Delhi and to thereby determine how responsible the King had been, although it was recognised that he was in the hands of the rebels the entire time. Four charges were read out against Zafar: 'Aiding and abetting the mutinies of the troops', 'Encouraging and assisting divers persons in waging war against the British Government', 'Assuming the sovereignty of Hindostan' and 'Causing and being accessory to the murder of Christians'. He was then asked by the prosecutor (through an interpreter) whether he pleaded guilty or not. Zafar seemed a little confused and after a while replied, 'Not Guilty', although he seemed not to understand the nature of the proceedings and questioned the authority of the court.

The trial, which had been postponed from week to week by his illness, was now delayed by frequent adjournments to give him time for repose. Zafar, it was noticed, showed anxiety at the beginning of the trial, but as the days wore on his demeanour became indifferent. It was noticed that he kept his eyes closed for large periods of the proceedings. He seemed tired, looking on passively during the day and sometimes being seen to doze off. Jawan Bakht was quite different, being seen to converse and laugh with the attendant on his father's right – so much so that he was not asked back after a while, his attitude being deemed disrespectful.

Mrs Muter, watching, recalled the respect the various witnesses showed to the King on entering the Diwan-i-Khas to give evidence:

> Amid all the poverty and contempt thrown on the King, I was gratified to observe the demeanour of many of the witnesses when called to give evidence. Bowing to the ground with hands clasped, before the miserable figure on the bed, addressed by them as 'Ruler of the Universe,' though by the Committee as 'tum' [meaning 'you' a term used for inferiors or servants etc rather than a respectful term] they observed to the powerless old man a degree of respect denied to the Court, who had only to nod the signal for their execution.[17]

On the second day, the prosecutor produced a letter from a Nubbee Baksh Khan relating to the European prisoners taken from around the city and brought to the palace. Nubbee Baksh Khan in the document urged Zafar to reject the soldiers' requests to massacre the prisoners. The prosecutor declared this to be the only document or petition that did not bear Zafar's comments in the marginalia. This, he implied, meant that Zafar had no great sympathy for the prisoners himself. Other documents complaining of outrages did have his comments and signatures.

Zafar continued to show indifference towards the proceedings. On some days he would bind his shawl tightly round himself and recline on the cushions provided. But sometimes, apparently listening in, he would interrupt the flow of proceedings and argue against some point or statement a witness made before settling down again with his mind seemingly on other things. Sometimes, to pass the time, he would play with a scarf, tying and untying it on his head. On the issue of his communicating with the Persian court prior to the uprising, he seemed not to understand the complexities of the questions being made, asking, 'Are the Persians and the Russians the same people?' On one issue he was sure: he was innocent, as he proclaimed several times during the proceedings.

On 9 March, the trial came to a close and the judge advocate general addressed the court. This had been, he said, 'a revolt unparalleled in the annals of history, either for the savagery which has been its distinctive feature, or for the suddenness with which elements, hitherto deemed utterly discordant on the score of religion, have united themselves in a common crusade against a faith which, as regards the inhabitants of this country, whether Muhammadan or Hindu, was certainly a most unaggressive one'.[18] The issue, he went on, was complicated and politically charged:

> ... a struggle of the natives for power and place by the expulsion from the country of a people alien in religion in blood in colour in habits in feelings and in everything... Few, I imagine, will peruse these voluminous proceedings without coming to the conclusion that intrigues and conspiracy have long been rife at this fostering Court of Delhi. Insignificant and contemptible as to any outward show of power, it would appear that this possessor of mere nominal royalty has ever been looked upon by Mahomedan fanaticism as the head and culminating star of its faith. In him have still been centred the hopes and aspirations of millions. They have looked up to him as the source of honour and more than this he has proved the rallying point not only to Mahomedans, but to thousands of others with whom it was supposed no bond of fanatical union could possibly be established. To throw the fullest light on a subject like this is not the work of a day, or of a month; time, the great revealer of secrets, will doubtless sooner or later, lay bare the springs from which a stream of so much evil and misery has flowed; but, till then, we must be content with such views as our present investigation affords.[19]

Lawrence largely agreed with the findings of the military commission. His conclusion, upon reading the papers of the trial, was that there never had been a conspiracy involving the King and the sepoys before 10 May. Leaving these matters aside, there was still the matter of Zafar's collusion with the rebels after their arrival:

> I have carefully examined the evidence in the trial of the ex-King of Delhy, and after testing it by all the information which I have obtained since the first outbreak, as well as by my personal knowledge of the prisoner's character and that of the Mahomedan population of the city, I fully concur with the Court in convicting him on the various charges on which he was arraigned.[20]

As far as Zafar's punishment, Lawrence wished to show no mercy. The promise of life had been made, and it would be kept. However, considering after all that had happened, he would recommend exile. On 29 April, Lawrence duly advised the Government of India that exile would be the most sound way of disposing of the ex-king, that 'the said prisoner be transported beyond the Seas as a felon and be kept in some island or settlement where he will be entirely isolated from all other Mahomedans'. His wife Zeenat Mahal and son Jawan Bakht could accompany him into exile if they wished, but if they did not wish to go with him they would be incarcerated as state prisoners somewhere in the lower provinces of the Bengal Presidency.

Others considered it wise never to have exercised capital punishment on the ex-monarch, chief among them the Earl of Dalhousie, erstwhile Governor-General:

> I consider that it is a fortunate thing that the King of Delhi has not been put too death. The execution of an old man of 85, whatever his crimes, would be revolting. No man of candour would maintain that the old man *could* do anything but what the sepoys bade him. To have hanged as a felon an aged man of 85, a throned king, and the head of the Moslem in India, would have disgusted our best friends – and there are still many – among the Mussalmans of the East, and would have produced a revulsion of public feeling against us both in Europe and Asia.[21]

On 22 September 1858, the Government of India ordered Saunders to ready the King for his exile. A wing of HM9th Lancers along with a troop of horse artillery would be passing through Delhi on their way to Allahabad from Ambala around 30 September; the King and his party were to accompany them under the command of Lt Ommaney. With the King would come his wife and son and the few servants still allowed them. From Allahabad the party would eventually be escorted on to Calcutta. The royal persons would be permitted both carriages and palanquins, and security demanded that there be no visitors or outside communication during the journey:

> The few domestic servants who may have been hither-to in attendance on the ex-King may be permitted to accompany him, but they must be kept under surveillance during the journey and prevented from communicating with the people generally. If the ex-King should make enquiries from you as to his destination, you will tell him that he will be conducted in the first instance to Calcutta, and that on arrival there he will be informed of it.

On 27 September, Saunders was advised that another queen, Taj Mahal, and another son, Shah Abbas, would also be travelling into exile with the King. Jawan Bakht's wife would also be coming along.

Several locations had been mooted. The Andaman Islands were rejected since this was the destination for other rebels heading for incarceration; it was felt inappropriate to have the ex-King held in the same location. South Africa was suggested, and the Governor of the Cape of Good Hope began making arrangements. However, due to Zafar's age and the danger of an arduous sea journey it was decided that nearby Burma would do. There the ex-monarch quietly whiled away the days, passing away on 7 November 1862 at the age of eighty-seven.

41

# Raze the City

We shall now have no enemies round Dehlee. No one dare raise his head. All are our devoted servants. We may venture a great deal where circumstances demand our so doing. The effects of the capture of the city and palace of Dehlee and the utter rout of the bulk of the mutineers, in a political and military point of view, are prodigious.[1]

John Lawrence to Maj. Gen. Wilson,
29 September 1857

After Delhi fell, and even while the mutiny elsewhere in India was still being addressed, there were demands for the wholesale destruction of the city, this being the best way of showing British anger. After its sacking, the city was almost wholly vacant, with its population having been ejected from the city and many of the refugees now camped outside the city walls or in neighbouring villages. In this context, razing the city wasn't such a daunting task. Building a large cathedral in place of the walled city was a popular idea, representing as it would the ultimate triumph of Christianity over what was deemed heathenism. The destruction of the city would also effectively destroy its mystique as the seat of the old Mughal rulers, obliterating the symbol of Muslim ascendency in the Subcontinent.

Others felt razing the city was overdoing it. They advocated the destruction of the Jama Masjid and the Red Fort, with British administrative buildings and a church built on the sites. The Jama Masjid, the most prominent manifestation of Islam in the city, came in for particular focus. The general opinion was that it was the heart of the local Muslim community and that destroying it or converting it into a church would be an appropriate act of revenge. Returning it to the Muslims would have been considered madness, according to Mrs Coopland, widow of Revd George Coopland, who summed up the general mood upon visiting the city after its fall:

> If it were destroyed, being their most sacred city, and one that reminds them of their fallen grandeur, it would do more to manifest our abhorrence of their crimes, and our indignation against them, than the hanging of hundreds. Delhi ought to be razed to the ground, and on its ruins a church or monument should be erected, inscribed with a list of all the victims of the mutinies, – if it be possible to gather the names of ALL those who were massacred, – and the funds for its erection should be raised by a fine levied on every native implicated in the mutinies, but not openly accused of murder.[2]

One solution put forward was simpler: convert the Jama Masjid into a church, with crosses somewhat incongruously hoisted on to its four minarets. Towards this end, John Lawrence received various petitions from the British officers in Delhi. A delegation met with him to persuade him of the wisdom of the idea. Their forceful attitude, however, seemed to have had the opposite effect, and Lawrence shared a more irate response than normal: 'I will never agree on this matter, there are many things over which you can argue, but as far as the Jama Masjid is concerned you should not argue with me. It would be better that as far as this matter is concerned you do not bother me any more.' The damaging of the mosque or other religious buildings, he stressed, would not be appropriate as a punishment for enemies and neither would it be to the credit of the British Government of India. With the mutiny still extant elsewhere, razing the mosque would only work to the benefit of the mutineers around the country as they looked for more recruits, jihadis and malcontents willing to fight.

Fortunately, as time went on, anger subsided and the Jama Masjid escaped destruction. The palace was less fortunate. Although several of the more important structures were retained, the vast bulk of the complex changed irrevocably in the coming months, being demolished to make way for practical barracks for a permanent British garrison in the city. Other important changes would permanently alter the balance and nature of the old walled city as well.

On 10 October, Wilson received instructions from the Government of India to maintain a British hold on the city:

> The Governor-General in Council desires that you will at once proceed to demolish the defenses of Delhi, spare places of worship, tombs and all ancient buildings of interest. You will blow up or otherwise destroy all the fortifications, and you will so far destroy the walls and gates of the city as to make them useless for defenses. As you will not be able to do this completely with the force at present available at Delhi, you will select the point at which the work may be commenced with best effect and operate there...

However, it soon became apparent that this would be unwise. Immediately after the city's capture, and with the mutiny still in full swing elsewhere, it was considered imperative to provide a safe, secure place for the remaining British Field Force at Delhi. Demolishing the city walls therefore made little sense. The walls were also convenient for keeping the Delhi population out of the city until its future was decided – a complete razing had not been discounted as yet. During the weeks following the capture, the British authorities would open only three of the eleven city gates: Lahore, Kashmir and Calcutta. Guards checked permits granted to those locals allowed entry. 'This and other regulations of a police nature, whereby the possession of arms was made highly penal, and whereby people were debarred from leaving their houses after a given hour of the night, and before dawn, would render the city even more secure than ever,' Lawrence wrote. 'But should these and similar precautions be considered insufficient, the Mahomedan population might be absolutely prohibited from returning to their habitations inside the walls for the present.'[3]

In the days following the capture of the city, the British camp on the ridge was gradually dissolved, with each regiment moving its camp either inside the city or adjacent to the city walls. This wasn't simply because of the capture of the city but for the fact that the camp on the ridge had become so unsanitary after more than three months of occupation. The decaying remains of thousands of bullocks and camels lay all around. The situation had worsened since the assault on the city, which had occupied every able man. The palace had been fully staffed by European troops and administrators. The barbican of the palace was now patrolled by men of the 60th Rifles as well as the Gurkhas of the Kumaon Battalion, who were given accommodation in the arcade of the palace entrance. Capt. Garstone had taken up residence in Zafar's own mosque along with other officers. Some of the private royal rooms had been occupied by Saunders. Wilson, meanwhile, remained in the Diwan-i-Khas, which doubled as a church, with Revd Rotton leading the service on Sundays. The Salimgarh Fort adjacent was utilized as a hospital, being particularly suited for the purpose given its large rooms and buildings and the fact that it was relatively free of corpses and debris. Meanwhile, the bloodstains in the apartments above the palace entrance where Capt. Douglas and his party met their end could still be seen by curious European officers.

Various plans were mooted to ensure the city never fell to another uprising. Writing to John Lawrence, Wilson expressed doubts that his force, small as it was and with so many soldiers unfit, could defend the city adequately:

> I have 3,300 sick and wounded, immense munitions of war. My own opinion of the best policy to be pursued is to hold the city walls until

> I can transport the whole of my sick and wounded, the recaptured guns and munitions to Meerut, then to blow up the several bastions and portions of the palace, and to take my force to act in the Jungle Doab [meaning the Jumna side]. This will however from want of carriage occupy a long period of time.[4]

However, the main consideration – given much of the country was still in rebel hands – was the care of the sick and wounded in the British force, and the care of the guns and general supplies essential to the war effort. This meant the city had to be fully secure so that a smaller force could peel off and leave the city. Lawrence advised Wilson to use the palace as a defensive compound. The palace walls would allow a force of 3,000 to 4,000 to hold the city, allowing the rest of the Delhi force to pursue rebels in the vicinity. If the palace were to be destroyed, as many desired, it would take years to build another arsenal.

'With very little additions and alterations the palace might also be converted into a strong fort capable of overawing the town, and therefore of preventing any chance of an emeute [riot], such as may at any time occur when large numbers of Mahomedans are brought together,'[5] Lawrence wrote on 23 September. He further suggested that rather than simply holding the fort, the troops should secure the entire middle of the city. He proposed a strong defensive line from the Kashmir Gate to the college and magazine and running past the palace and right up to the Delhi Gate. By this plan the entire east of the city adjacent to the river would be occupied and turned into a defensive compound. This would prevent the British force in the city from being surrounded. In order to satisfy this defensive perimeter, all guns on the city walls would be withdrawn; they were vulnerable to be captured by any enterprising mob since few guards could be arranged for them:

> Each bastion, or redoubt, except that at the Cashmere Gate, is more or less isolated, and open to approach from the city wall. The Chief Commissioner believes that after what they have seen and suffered we have little to fear from the Mahomedan population of Dehlee, with very ordinary precautions. But that whatever does exist, is more to be apprehended from them if we hold the walls in regular military fashion, with inadequate means, than if we withdrew our guns and simply held the gates with policemen. But under such circumstances the Chief Commissioner contemplated that heavy guns and mortars would be placed in a suitable position, near the palace, to overawe the inhabitants.[6]

John Lawrence was also against wholesale demolition of the buildings inside the palace, and suggested only the minimum damage should be inflicted on the palace to make it more practicable for a garrison and an arsenal. Wilson disagreed: 'The Chief Commissioner has, I suspect, very little knowledge of the interior of the palace. With exception to the large courts in the centre and a few gardens, the whole place is a thickly crowded native city, giving little or no cover for troops or stores, and which would take an army of pioneers to knock down and an enormous expenditure for carriage to remove the debris,' he wrote to Lt Taylor, the chief engineer. The fact was that apart from the several open spaces of the palace gardens and other places of assembly, much of the palace was a labyrinth. More importantly, the walls could not hold guns to overlook the city. Wilson was sure drastic alterations would be required inside the palace walls, including the levelling of many of the palace buildings and enclosures, which were obstructions for the British guns and prevented the fort being used as a munitions depot.

Lawrence was likely unaware of Wilson's paucity of able men, too. By 3 October, the Delhi Field Force totalled only 4,918 men at Delhi – out of which only 3,437 were effective, the other men being among the two moveable columns that had been sent out of the city to pursue rebels. HM52nd, meanwhile, was already on its way back to the Punjab.

Nevertheless, in order to investigate a possible defensive line within the city as Lawrence had suggested, Lt Taylor carried out a close inspection of the city walls on 30 September. He came up with the same conclusion as Wilson: the palace walls were too high (48 feet) and too thin at the top (10 feet) to be suitable for British guns. To make bastions at a lower height, meanwhile, would require a great deal of work in destroying the walls at appropriate places:

> It appears to me most clear that the best line to defend is the city wall. That this may be done to advantage, it is, however, most necessary that all inhabitants be turned out of the city and kept out. There can be little doubt that we would find no great difficulty in holding this line against any native force that could be brought to attack us, and as guns mounted in the palace would aid little in defending the city wall, the construction of bastions to carry guns inside the palace enclosure might be dispensed with.

Rather than holding just the palace, then, the entire walled city needed to be held. This would not be difficult, Taylor argued. The only work required would be to repair the breaches made in the northern walls by the British guns. In time the buildings near the city walls could be demolished to make holding the city even easier. However, he recommended the city population be kept out; having potential rebels inside the city would not be wise at this time. The British garrison could then be spread around to guard the city walls and gates with ease.

Wilson, however, was shortly replaced by General Penny. Penny largely agreed with his predecessor and his chief engineer. He recommended bricking up some of the thirteen gateways of the city, making it much easier to control ingress and egress. He also made three recommendations that were much more controversial than the first. One was to clear all buildings and structures close to the palace walls to a certain distance as recommended by engineers. This would allow a clear line of fire for British guns and muskets against any crowds of locals or even a rebel force attempting to reoccupy the city. Secondly, a broad military road could be built inside the palace to allow rapid transfer of troops from one place to another in case of attack; to complement this, another road could be built outside the fort to encircle it. Thirdly, he recommended another broad military road running through the walled city from one end to the other, again allowing for troops to reach areas or defensive positions as quickly as possible. 'If the measures are carried out to the full, it will render Dehli hereafter safe in the keeping of comparatively a much smaller garrison than otherwise will be positively necessary to insure it at all times from revolt,'[7] he explained. Needless to say, this would mean the destruction of large parts of the city. In the palace, too, a military road would mean the elimination of many of the small buildings, particularly in the south of the complex.

John Lawrence once again spoke out against such wholesale changes. While admitting some of these decisions were of a military nature and therefore not a subject of his expertise, he recommended caution. Still heavily against the idea of utilising the city walls, he now suggested earthen ramps and the piercing of the palace walls to allow guns to face the city:

> Guns properly placed on the walls of the latter would effectually overawe the inhabitants of the town. It must be borne in mind that we held Dehli for 50 years and upwards without a single emeute, and with the most ordinary precautions would probably have continued to hold it in like manner. For upwards of 30 years we had removed all our troops from inside the walls, though we allowed both the Imperial family and our munitions of war to remain. But should the people ever again rebel, with the citadel in our hands and strongly fortified, they must be entirely at our mercy. We could bombard the whole town without the loss of a man on our side.[8]

There was also the matter of cost – his suggestion would be much cheaper than reinforcing or altering all of the palace walls to enable them to hold guns. The British government had expended large sums over the previous half century on the walls, magazines and gateways, and if they went through with Penny's plan this money would have been wasted, not to mention the considerably greater amount spent destroying or drastically changing these same areas. Nor could he recommend bricking up the various gateways; this would not increase the security, he thought, and would only inconvenience the locals. Constructing military roads, meanwhile, would prove expensive and highly inconvenient to locals, although he conceded that a broad road around the outside of the fort and the clearing of space might be useful.

Finally, on 17 October, the chief engineer suggested a compromise which incorporated Lawrence's desires. He suggested putting twenty or thirty guns on the palace walls rather than any larger number. This would be sufficient and would save large amounts of money otherwise spent rebuilding. The walls could be widened by roughly 20 feet in those spaces selected for guns.

From a longer perspective, the chief engineer recommended all the city gateways be destroyed. He also opined that the palace was too much encroached by housing and that this gave good cover for musketry fire at the palace walls:

> No cover for a besieger should be left within 700 yards. The palace evidently, no matter to what extent fortified, could not aid very materially in the defence of the city walls. Should we ever be driven from the city works, it would necessarily be by an enemy very superior in point of numbers. Against such an enemy any very prolonged defence of the city would not be practicable. To admit of the fort being held against him even for a limited time, it is necessary … to clear a space all round the place 300 yards wide.

To prevent musketry fire on to the palace walls and bastions, a wall could be built separating the housing from the palace and of sufficient height to prevent anyone on a rooftop aiming at the palace walls. Taylor also recommended constructing a glacis all around the palace walls but with a 50-foot passage in front of the Lahore Gate, which would make it more difficult for any attacking force to reach the gate. Inside the palace, structures needed to be built to store munitions.

Much of this advice never came to anything as focus shifted towards destroying the rebellion elsewhere. However, the palace was converted into barracks, with extensive destruction of the inner buildings, including the entire southern and eastern parts of the complex. Only the important state buildings and the northern gardens were left. The advice to demolish all housing close to the palace walls was also implemented. All structures within a quarter of a mile were destroyed to provide a clear line of fire from the fort walls into the city. In addition to the fort, all structures around the Jama Masjid were razed to open up a clear line of fire against the building. No compensation was given to the owners of the demolished buildings.

On 9 October, despite Wilson's reservations, Lawrence recommended that Hindu civilians be allowed to return. The city returned to normality remarkably quickly after the shock of the siege. Around the end of December, Mrs Coopland travelled into Delhi from Agra via Meerut. She described the uncertain trip and marks of war still apparent everywhere as well as some of the most graphic descriptions of life inside the newly occupied city:

> Passing through one or two deserted looking streets, we entered the 'Chandney Chowk' (the principal street of Delhi), which quite astonished us by its gay appearance; for Delhi was in our minds associated with nothing but gloom and desolation. The natives either mingled in crowds or sat before their shops on pieces of carpet, with raised trays before them, on which were displayed embroidered shawls, skull caps, toys, shells, and sugar cane; here and there brilliant pieces of calico, just dyed, were hung to dry across the street. The natives were all gaily dressed with bright turbans; and they had an impudent, self-satisfied expression on their faces, very irritating to us, when we remembered the merciless and cruel deeds so lately enacted here by their brethren…
>
> … The street was crowded with English soldiers in their bright uniforms, Seiks on their wild looking steeds, funny little Ghoorkahs, European ladies riding on immense elephants, and gentlemen on camels, horses, and ponies. Altogether the gay crowds, the green trees, the bright pieces of calico, and the azure blue sky, formed an enlivening scene; and one might have forgotten the fearful things that had so lately taken place, but for two large gallows in the middle of the street.[9]

There had been rumours of a Christmas Day uprising in the city, but such attacks never materialized:

> We went to service in the Dewan-i-Khas, though we were rather nervous about the threatened rising. In the middle of service we heard a buzzing, chattering noise going on outside, and began to look uneasily at one another; till an officer went out and found the servants quarrelling and making a great noise, which soon ceased, much to our relief. They had a similar panic at Simla on Christmas-day, only of a more serious nature.[10]

*****

In the third week of March 1858, nearly six months after the fall of the city, the Muslim population of the city was finally allowed to return. A deeds register was used ascertain home ownership, and Muslim homeowners were then given certificates allowing them to repossess their property. According to Khwaja Hasan Nizami, the new Muslim population was estimated at just a quarter of its pre-mutiny size. Nizami mentions the larger Muslim properties being retained in British hands until 1859. John Lawrence, who had visited the city by now, had left strict instructions with General Penny to safeguard the lives of the Muslim inhabitants. However, not all had had the capacity to survive. The aristocratic princesses of the palace *salatin* quarters now had to fend for themselves, which was a new experience. 'If you were here ... you would have seen the moon-faced Begums of the Red Fort wandering around in the streets in filthy clothes, ragged pyjamas and broken shoes,' the contemporary poet Ghalib wrote of the fallen aristocrats who could be seen around the city.[11]

Eight months later, in November 1858, the authorities declared an amnesty allowing all to enter the city – although still only through a system of permits. Anyone found in the city without a permit was given five lashes or a 2-rupee fine. Meanwhile, the authorities stamped down on the semi-permanent shelters that the locals had erected outside the city, razing them to the ground. Only in November 1859 were all restrictions lifted and the population allowed to freely enter and leave the city.

From a military standpoint, the focus had already moved elsewhere; the entire north-west of the country was in rebel hands. As early as the morning of 22 September 1857, a column under Lt Greathed, HM8th Foot, was formed under the shadow of the Ajmer Gate. Boasting 2,790 troops and sixteen guns, the force was sent to pursue rebels who had decided to retreat towards Kanpur. The area surrounding Delhi was in a very disturbed state, with looting and plundering raging unchecked, and this column was permitted to dispense 'vindicatory justice' wherever they went, hanging and shooting rebels and anyone felt to have assisted them. Unsurprisingly, the Gujjar tribesmen in the area received particular attention.

This column would take part in the last major fighting in the Delhi area, as Brig. Gen. Chamberlain wrote:

> A remnant of Mohamedan scum with some sepoys, between 200 and 300, who had hitherto concealed themselves in Durreaon Gunje Mohulla [Daryaganj], passed out of the city, cutting up our stragglers who chanced to stray, were this morning destroyed. Relics of our countrywomen were upon them, and in their houses all sorts of European property.

After destroying this party of rebels, the column passed by the village of Ghazi-ud-din Nagar, close to where the first battle of the siege had taken place at the Hindun River. From there, they would move on to Malagarh and Aligarh, and then southwards along the doab to mop up other rebel units that had fled the city. Delhi was now safe, but there was more work to be done.

# Appendix A

## Persian Proclamation found in the Shahzada's (Persian Prince's) tent at Mohumrah during the Anglo-Persian War suggesting a grand alliance of Muslims to wage Jihad against the English. Printed in the *Bombay Telegraph and Courier*, 14 April 1857

Whereas the British Government, through the power acquired by the conquest of India and the advantages thereby gained, has framed its politics, and has pursued a course of aggression, to the end that all the East should be added to its dominion; and for the purpose of accomplishing this, and advancing the performance of it, the British Government attempted the conquest of Afghanistan; and although it was overwhelmed by a complete repulse in this attempt, nevertheless it caused great destruction and mischief in the countries of Affghanistan, and took possession of Lahore, Peshawur, and several other dependencies of that country; and this is the proceeding and politic of this Government to obtain complete dominion in Persia: they try to prohibit the intercourse with the Sirdars of Affghanistan, who are our neighbours and co-religionists, and have always been our allies; and this is with a view to open to themselves a road to Persian soil, so that, whenever they wish, they could advance their troops from every side into Afghanistan and all the countries bordering on Persia; and, even if they found they possessed the power, to reduce the Government of Persia to the state of the Rajahs of Hindostan, and to destroy the religion of Islam in Persia, in like manner as the religion of the Mussulman of India. And in order to carry out this design, the British have commenced invading the kingdom of Persia; they have occupied themselves in deceiving the vulgar, and through deceit and bad faith, and an improper mode of proceeding, whilst our Government have never resented it, and presuming upon our supposed weakness, they have carried their ill practice and bad faith to such an extent that they have tried to seduce persons in the employ of the Persian Government to enter the service of their embassy, and also endeavoured to bring princes and Moonshees of the kingdom under their authority; and they have employed stratagems and artifices, so that, by false pretences and improper proceedings, they have tried to bring to pass that which they desire, and by degrees all their machinations have come to light. Unexpectedly they brought troops to the soil of a power of Islam, and having thus gained a footing, took possession of one of the forts of Islam which was on the sea-shore, and was only held by a small number of troops as its fixed garrison, and thus no army being present they occupied it, and when they saw that if they advanced from the sea-shore they would flounder about like fish on dry land, they have stuck there, for they knew that if they advanced the blows of the sharp swords of the heroes of Islam would not leave breath in the soul of one of them.

But his Majesty the Shah-in-shah has taken advantage of this breach of faith of the British Government to make manifest his royal will and pleasure; and his orders have gone forth that countless armies are to be assembled on the boundaries of every country; and victorious troops have been directed towards the frontiers to drive out the enemies of the faith, and scatter the rubbish and dirt along the shores, for 'God giveth the victory to whom he pleases;' and now, in obedience to the words of the Prophet, 'To him who doeth injury unto you, do ye injury unto him in like manner as he does injury to you.' Let all the people of Heran consider it incumbent upon them to follow the precept, ' Slay, in the name of God, those who wish to slay you and let the old and the young, the small and the great, the wise and the ignorant, the ryot and the sepoy, all without exception, arise in the defence of the orthodox faith of the Prophet, and, having girt up the waist of valour, adorn their persons with arms and weapons; and let the ullema and preachers call upon the people in the mosques and public assemblies, and in the pulpits, to give in a jahâd in the cause of God; and thus shall the Ghazis in the cause of the faith have a just title to the promises contained in the words of the Prophet, 'Verily we are of those who fought in the cause of God.'

But whereas the victorious army of the State have not drawn the sword upon the enemy, we have not permitted the eager multitudes to leave their homes; and in the direction of Fars, wo have appointed the Ameer Ul Umra Mirza Mahomed Khan Kasheekchi Bashi, and Meer Allie Khan Shooja Ool Moolk, and several other generals and commanders, with 20,000 men; and in the direction of Mohumerah, the Prince Nawab Shusham Ool Dowla, with 20,000 fine troops; and in the direction of Kirman, Goolam Hussum Khan, Tipahdar, and Jaffer Koola Khan Meer, Pun-i-jah, with regiments and cavalry of Karache Daghi, and Azerbiyham and Kirmani, to the number of 20,000 men; and in the direction of Cutch and Meekram, towards Scinde, and from the direction of Affghanistan, the Nawab Ahsham Ool Sultanut, with 30,000 men and 40 guns, abundantly supplied and equipped, and the Affghan Sirdars – viz. Sirdar Sultan Ahmed Khan, Sirdar Shah Doolah Khan, Sirdar Sultan Ali Khan, and Sirdar Mahomed Allum Khan, who have been appointed by his Majesty, have been ordered towards India; and they are hopeful that, by the blessing of Divine aid, they may be victorious.

And it is necessary that the Affghan tribes and the inhabitants of that country who are co-religionists of the Persians, and who possess the same kuran and kibla and laws of the Prophet, should also take part in the jahâd, and extend the hand of brotherhood, and, on receiving these glad tidings, act according to the words of the Prophet: 'Verily all true believers are brothers,' and 'also make manifest the decree of God.' 'Verily the Almighty will weigh the wicked in different scales from the pure and for the purpose of settling the quarrel, it is necessary that not only a small number of true believers should stand forth in the defence of the faith, but that the whole should answer our call; and this should also be made known to all the people of Affghanistan, that the Persian Government has no intention of extending its conquests in that direction, except to the Government of Candahar, which should be given over to Sirdar Rahim Dil Khan, and the family of Sirdar Kohun Dil Khan and the governor of Cabool and its dependencies should be vested in its chiefs, and they should join in the jahâd against the enemies of Islam, and be of the number of those to whom the Prophet sayeth, 'The grace of God dwelleth in those who fight in jahâd.' And we are hopeful that, after the publication of this proclamation, Dost Mahomed Khan, Ameer of Cabool, who always was desirous that the Persian armies should extend their conquests to Affghanistan, and who wished to be strengthened by their alliance, should also unite with us against this tribe of wanderers from the path of righteousness, and that he should become one of the leaders of the faithful in this jahâd, and that he should become a Ghazi in Hindostan, for he cannot wish for the friendship of a tribe of whom the Prophet sayeth, 'Verily they do not love you, and neither do ye love them;' nor can he wish to sell his faith for a worldly price. And this proclamation is published for the information of all true believers; and please God the followers of Islam in India and Scinde will also unite with us and take vengeance upon that tribe (the British) for all the injuries which the holy faith has suffered from them, and will not withhold any sacrifices in the holy cause.

# Appendix B

## Translation of a petition from Muhammad Darwesh to his Honour the Lieutenant-Governor, North Western Provinces, warning of communication by the Mughal court with Persia

Nourisher of the poor! May your prosperity continue! Your highness! the arrangements for the despatch of letters from the king of Delhi to the king of Persia, through the Pir-zada Hasan Askari, have been stated in a former petition, and must have come to your knowledge. I, who am a mendicant of itinerant habits, have since learned for a certainty, that two men with letters from the king of Delhi, through the said Hasan Askari, proceeded about three or four months ago towards Constantinople, in company with a caravan going to Mecca. Hasan Askari has now assured the king of Delhi that he has certain information that the prince royal of Persia has fully taken possession of and occupied Bushire, and that he has entirely expelled the Christians, or rather has not left one alive there, and has taken many of them prisoners; and that very soon indeed the Persian army will advance by the way of Candahar and Cabul towards Delhi. He told the king also, that his Majesty was altogether too careless about corresponding with the king of Persia. The king then gave Hasan Askari twenty gold mohurs, and requested him speedily to despatch letters to Persia, and directed him to give the gold mohurs to the man who should take the letters, for the expenses of his journey. Hasan Askari accordingly took the money, and returned to his house, and has prepared four men to carry the letters, making them assume the coloured garments of religious mendicants, and it is reported that they will leave for Persia in a day or two. The petitioner has not been able to ascertain their names. In the palace, but more especially in the portion of it constituting the personal apartments of the king, the subject of conversation, night and day, is the early arrival of the Persians. Hasan Askari has, moreover, impressed the king with the belief that he has learned, through a divine revelation, that the dominion of the king of Persia will, to a certainty, extend to Delhi, or rather over the whole of Hindostan, and that the splendour of the sovereignty of Delhi will again revive, as the sovereign of Persia will bestow the crown on the king. Throughout the palace, but particularly to the king, this belief has been the cause of great rejoicing, so much so that prayers are offered, and vows are made, while, at the same time, Hasan Askari has entered upon the daily performance, at an hour and a half before sun-set, of a course of propitiatory ceremonies, to expedite the arrival of the Persians, and the expulsion of the Christians. It has been arranged that, every Thursday, several trays of victuals, wheat-meal, oil, money in copper coin, and cloth, should be sent by the king in aid of these ceremonies; and they are accordingly brought to Hasan Askari. Some of the higher functionaries of the Government, drawn into a faith in this man by his frauds and deceptions, are in the habit of visiting his house, and consider his words and actions entitled to the greatest reliance. Where would be the use in my naming these traitors! May the Almighty God confound the enemies of the Government! Your petitioner keeps learning these matters from certain of his friends who have admittance to the presence of the king of Delhi, and who are, moreover, in the habit of visiting Hasan Askari also. Actuated by good-will, I have communicated the above particulars. It rests in the province of the ever-enduring Government to make necessary and effectual arrangements.

Petition of the well-wisher Muhammad Darwesh
Dated 24th March 1857
Seal of Fakir Muhammad Darwesh

# Appendix C

## General orders by the Commander-in-Chief, Headquarters, Ambala, 19 May 1857, relating to rumours regarding the new cartridge

The Commander-in-Chief, on May 14, issued a General Order, informing the Native army that it had never been the intention of the Government to force them to use any cartridges which could be objected to, and that they never would be required to do so, either now or hereafter.

His object in publishing that Order was to allay the excitement which had been raised in their minds, although he felt that there was no cause for it.

He hopes that this may have been the case; but he still perceives that the very name of new cartridges causes agitation; and he has been informed that some of those sepoys who entertain the strongest attachment and loyalty to the Government, and are ready at any moment to obey its orders, would still be under the impression that their families would not believe that they were not in some way or other contaminated by its use. The rifle introduced into the British army is an improvement upon the old musket, and much more effective; but it would not be of the same advantage in the hands of the Native army, if it were to be used with reluctance.

Notwithstanding, therefore, that the Government have affirmed that the cartridge is perfectly harmless, the Commander-in-Chief is satisfied that they would not desire to persist in its adoption if the feelings of the sepoys can be thoroughly calmed by its abolition.

His Excellency, therefore, has determined that the new rifle-cartridge, and every new cartridge, shall be discontinued; and that, in future, balled ammunition shall be made up by each regiment for its own use, by a proper establishment entertained for this purpose.

The Commander-in-Chief solemnly assures the army that no interference with their castes or religion was ever contemplated, and as solemnly he pledges his word and honour that none shall ever be exercised.

He announces this to the Native army in the full confidence that all will now perform their duty, free from anxiety or care, and be prepared to stand and shed the last drop of their blood, as they have formerly done, by the side of the British troops, and in defence of their country.

By order,
C. Chester, Colonel,
Adjutant-General of the Army

# Appendix D

## Translation of a Persian notice issued by H.H. the Lieutenant Governor of Bengal attempting to allay fears on the matter of religion

His Honor the Lieutenant Governor of Bengal, having heard that the people of the Country are unnecessarily apprehensive and uneasy on account of certain unreasonable and unfounded stories, fabricated and spread by people equally unreasonable and prejudiced, with regard to the religious rites and ceremonies of the Hindoos and Muhamadans, hereby notifies that Government has no intention of interfering in the matters of religion, rites and ceremonies of the country, nor can it ever have such an intention. His Honor is sorry to find that the people of this country are unnecessarily alarmed at stories invented by seditious persons, and that they do not try to ascertain the truth. He hopes that when the facts are made known to them, all suspicions will be removed from their minds, and that they will rest assured as regards the intentions of the Government towards them. The principal object of the Government is and ever shall be to protect the life, honor, and property of its subjects, to respect their laws and customs and to do what it can to promote their welfare.

Some of the Calcutta Missionaries as is their wont, but without the sanction of the Government, published religious discourses and circulated them amongst the natives who have wrongly understood them to have come indirectly from the Government. The Government has however had no hand in the affair. No attempt was ever made on behalf of Government to persuade the natives to embrace the faith professed by the Government. It is evident that the inhabitants of this country belong to different races and profess different creeds and religions, and are governed by different laws. They have now been long living under the protection of the Government, but the Government, instead of interfering in the religious rites and ceremonies of any class of its subjects, always regards them all as equal in its sight. The proceedings of the Christian Ministers above alluded to are part of their ordinary duties. They are in fact lectures of the same kind as are generally delivered in Muhamadan

Mosques and Hindoo temples on subjects bearing upon faith. A little consideration will shew that there is nothing new in the matter, that discussion on religious subjects are common amongst the votaries of different faiths, and that the Government has no concern with them.

The reports, spread in some Newspapers that all the Muharrum ceremonies, the parda system of the Zenana, the rite of circumcision and other rites and ceremonies practiced under Muhamadan and Hindoos Laws are soon to be done away with by orders of Government must be considered as false and fabricated stories. These reports have no ground whatsoever. The Government cannot possibly meddle with these ceremonies.

To distinguish the Jail from the home, certain Jail Superintendents, ignorant of the customs and creeds of the country, divested prisoners of their necessary utensils used in eating and drinking, and of course without the knowledge and consent of the Government. But no sooner was this brought to notice of Government than orders were telegraphed to put a stop to their proceedings.

His Honor has been further given to understand that the inhabitants of this country regard the establishment of Schools and Colleges for the education of the natives in Arts and Sciences and in the English language as a means to mislead them from their faith, and that for this reason they are disinclined to send their children to School. This is undoubtedly a great mistake of theirs The step has been misunderstood by the people Knowing that the natives of India are generally ignorant and therefore live in want, the Supreme Government has been pleased to establish Schools and Colleges for their education in Sciences and Arts of life, and for the amelioration of their condition in general, and to appoint Inspectors and native subordinates to superintend the work, so that the people may earn their bread more comfortably and live in a better style.

It is a well known fact that the people of England, by their advancement in learning, are able to do every thing properly, whereas the people of India owing to their ignorance can do nothing. If knowledge be generally diffused among them, all would live much more comfortably than they do now. It is a matter of great regret that the people have misunderstood the policy and the good intentions of Government in matters of education. His Honor however believes that the origin of all these evils is a misapprehension on the part of the natives, and that they do not proceed from prejudice or ill-feelings. Be it known that by the spread of English education Government is simply desirous of opening to the people of India a path to all arts and Sciences, and not to mislead them from their religion and time honored customs and habits. It must however be well borne in mind that works relating to all arts and Sciences at present exist only in the English language, and new discoveries and inventions are every day being brought to light. Moreover, English being the language of the rulers of the country it is one of the duties of the subjects to learn it along with Urdu and Bengali, so that they may rise in honor and live in greater ease and comfort. The native tongue of the country has been adopted as the language of the Court with a view that the common people may be able to understand their proceedings.

His Honor the Lieutenant Governor having seen and heard much about the state of the country and the condition of the people is determined to do his best in their behalf, and to raise all classes of Her majesty's subjects in honor and respectability by means of their education, and H.H. therefore notifies the above to H. Majesty's loyal subjects that they may rest well assured of the good intentions of the Government towards them, and take heart and work contentedly praying to God sincerely for the prosperity of their benign Government.

# Appendix E

## Copy of an order from the King, without signature, cypher or seal, but the order was issued under his seal. The letter complains of the behaviour of the mutineers. No date.

To-Our Son, the Illustrious and Valiant Mirza Zohur-ud-Din, otherwise Mirza Moghal Bahadur.

Learn! That when the troops, infantry and cavalry, first came to the royal presence, I told them personally, by word of mouth, that I had no treasures or property with which to assist them, but that I had no reluctance to stake my life if that could help them. They all expressed themselves satisfied with this declaration on my part, and even pledged themselves to sacrifice their lives in subordination and obedience to my commands. On this, they were directed, as the first step, to make proper provisions for the magazine and treasure, so that they might afterwards be profitably used by them and me. After this, they took up their quarters in the Halls of Special and Public Audience, the Mahtab Garden, and other places, and behaved just as they pleased. In consideration of their ignorance, and from a regard to their comforts, the servants of the state were prohibited from preventing them. In the next place, although no promise had been made in the matter, money was borrowed in order that daily allowances might be paid to every man of the cavalry and infantry. Repeated injunctions have been issued prohibiting plunder and. aggression in the city, but all to no purpose; for although ten days have now elapsed, the same evils are prevailing to the present time.

Moreover, the regiments of infantry have certainly left the Halls of Special and Public Audience, but notwithstanding that they were imperatively ordered to encamp outside the city, and the men of the army, whether cavalry or infantry, were prohibited going about armed through the city, and oppressing the inhabitants, yet one regiment of infantry has taken up its quarters at the Delhi, another at the Lahore, and a third at the Ajmir Gate, within the walls of the city, and have thoroughly desolated several of the bazars. Moreover, without reference to night or day. they enter and plunder the houses of the inhabitants on the false plea that they have concealed Europeans. They force locks and shop-doors and openly carry away the property from the shops, and they forcibly loose the horses of the cavalry and take them off. They commit these excesses in the face of the fact that all cities taken without military operations have ever been exempted from sack and slaughter. Even Jangiz Khan and Nadir Shah, kings execrated as tyrants, gave peace and protection to such cities as surrendered without resistance. Moreover, the men of the army go about threatening and intimidating the royal servants and the inhabitants of the city. ... [Illegible] ... Again although repeated orders have been issued to the infantrymen occupying the royal farash-khana, and the regiment of cavalry staying in the garden to vacate these places, they have not yet done so. These are places which not even Nadir Shah nor Ahmad Shah nor any of the British Governor-Generals of India ever entered on horseback.

The troops first requested that the princes royal might be appointed to the different commands in the army, promising they would obey them. This was done. They next urged that it would afford them greater confidence, if dresses of honour should be bestowed on the princes to give a character of stability to their appointments as commandants, and if all the (European) prisoners should be killed at once. This was also complied with: and the same day a notification, under the special seal, was issued publicly, proclaiming that courts of justice had been established in the city, and prohibiting acts of violence on the part of the soldiery. This even had no effect. Setting aside all these points, it may be remarked that whenever the most distinguished officers of the highest ranks in the service of the British Government visited the palace, they dismounted at the door of the Hall of Public Audience, and came from thence on foot. These soldiery, however, used, till recently, to come galloping up to the Hall of Special Audience on their horses, and as a last resort, both the gates were closed a wicket only being left open; but they still ride up to the Hall of Public Audience, and the Jalwa-khana, unsuitably dressed, and without their turbands, in utter disregard to the forms of respect due to royalty. The officers of the army too make a practice of coming into court carelessly dressed, wearing caps instead of turbands and carrying their swords. Never during the British rule did any members of their profession behave in this way. Again, notwithstanding that they have themselves uselessly wasted the whole of the magazine stores, and the money that was in the treasury, they now clamorously demand allowances daily, and above all, daily take allowances for more men than are present.

Besides this, with oppression and violence they forcibly take away the wares of the shop-keepers in the city without paying for them, and commit, moreover, every variety of other excesses and aggressions imaginable. The state of things outside the city also demands notice. In consequence of no military troops going out to keep order, hundreds of people are being murdered, and the property of thousands is being plundered.

As regards the civil administration of the country, in consequence of the insufficiency of the royal troops for the management of the whole of the provinces, revenue cannot be established, and yet none of the military troops, whether cavalry or infantry, can be prevailed on beyond the palace and city. Under these circumstances, it is matter for serious reflection how supplies are to be procured in the country, and how the revenues of the state are to be realized. Accordingly, nothing but the total desolation of the city and country can be expected as the inevitable end of this state of matters.

In addition to all that has been above noticed, the soldiery, accusing the royal servants of entertaining views and feelings opposite to their own, submit them to indignities, and when they come to claim their daily allowances or ammunition enforce their demands with unbecoming assumption of authority, notwithstanding that the royal servants, in consequence orders to them to that effect, nothing but entreaty and every other means of conciliation, and yet the soldiery will not be satisfied. Under these circumstances, how is it to be believed that these people can have the welfare of the state at heart, or that they cherish any desire to yield subjection and obedience to the royal authority? It is further to be considered, that there is no money in the royal treasury, and the city merchants having been plundered and ruined have no longer the ability to provide a loan. How then are the daily allowances to be paid for any length of time? and when they shall, of necessity, have been discontinued, and the supplies from the country shall also have ceased, what will be the state of things then?

The most ridiculously singular part of the proceedings of the soldiery is, that while they themselves commit these acts subversive of all rule, they lay the blame of the misrule on the royal servants. In short, when such is the return made by the soldiery, it is evident that they have no desire to act in any way to the advantage and benefit of the Government, and it is equally evident that the utter ruin of the sovereignty must ensue.

Wearied and helpless, we have now resolved on making a vow to pass the remainder of our days in services acceptable to God, and relinquishing the title of sovereign fraught with cares and troubles, and in our present griefs and sorrows, assuming the garb of a religious mendicant, to proceed first and stay at the shrine of the saint Khwaja Sahib, and, after making necessary arrangements for the journey, to go eventually to Mecca.

It should be considered that when these troops came, the King's servants or the residents of the city did not oppose them in any way, nor did they commit any act of hostility against them, and they are accordingly not liable to the forfeiture of life and property: for if as the representative of the feelings of the people, we had considered the soldiery in the light of enemies, why should we have made common cause with them, and why should we have directly associated our offspring with them in their undertaking? The tyranny and oppression now prevailing are a disgrace to our royal self, as tending to the belief that we, as sovereign, are a party to them, and that we approve of rapine and murder. It is worthy of consideration that when there is amity and good feelings between the King and populace on the one side and the army on the other, is it by acts like these that the soldiery mean to prove their good-will – acts which even an enemy or hostile force would not commit? The more praiseworthy and prudent course for them would have been to protect and cherish the people, to study the approbation of the sovereign, and to preserve unanimity and fellowship with the servants of the state. It was the peace and quiet which would have resulted from this line of conduct that we had expected.

You, our son, will now therefore send for all the officers of the cavalry and infantry, and explain to them that if they are really disposed to serve the state, they ought to execute a written agreement to that effect according to a form which will be furnished: when, for their assurance and satisfaction, we also will give them a written document: and that they should take immediate steps to suppress the evil and unbecoming acts and proceedings now prevailing: that the tents of the infantry regiments be this very day removed to the outside of the city: that every soldier of the army proved guilty of the murder and plunder of any resident of the city be adequately punished, so that others may have no hope of impunity for such acts: and that whenever royal orders directing the movements of regiments, whether singly or in numbers, with the view of their quelling disturbances and keeping order in the country may be issued, they should march without murmur or grumbling, and should make no obstinate demands for provisions and ammunition beyond such as may be reasonable.

Certainly, when authentic information of the near approach of the English army is received, both these regiments will be at liberty to return and then fight and engage in the operations of war as they may themselves arrange and deem expedient, and also determine what amount of forces should be severally kept in different places, and distribute the army accordingly. Then there will be a necessity for the troops being within the city; but there is none just now, seeing the country and city are being alike desolated, and none of the soldiery can be prevailed on to move from his quarters to make the least effort. You will further explain to them that if they are not disposed willingly and unanimously to acquiesce in the above views and wishes, desiring rest and quiet, we shall adopt the profession of a religious mendicant, and shall go to the shrine of the Khwaja Sahib. Let none of them say any thing to prevent this step, but let them quietly remain masters of the palace, the city and the country. For none of the kings of the old antiquity, nor of the warriors who came after them down to modern times, ever subjected any one claiming shelter and quiet to oppression and hardship, but freely allowed him his own way.

You will get the army to embody their answer to the two alternatives presented herein for their selection in a petition which you are directed to have attested with the seals and signatures of the officers, and to forward to the royal presence. You are directed to consider this not as any light or tri vial business, for in consequence of our advanced age and infirmity we are not able to support the burden of such excessive anxiety. The government of a nation, and the control of an army are not to be treated with the same levity as child's play.

# Appendix F

## Proclamation released on 10 July 1857 to be given the widest publicity in local languages

The Governor-General in Council hereby offers, and authorises the payment of the undermentioned rewards by British Civil or Military authorities in every part of India:-

1. For the apprehension of any mutineer or deserter from the Native Army, or of any person guilty of seducing or attempting to seduce any officer or soldier from his allegiance or duty, a reward of fifty rupees if the offender be apprehended with arms belonging to the State, or of thirty rupees if he be apprehended without such arms.

2. For information which shall lead to the apprehension of any such offender, a reward of fifty rupees if he be apprehended with arms belonging to the State or of thirty rupees if he be apprehended without such arms. The rewards will be paid on conviction of the offender.

Whoever delivers to any Civil or Military authority any arms, horses, cattle, or other property belonging to the Government, which shall have been plundered or carried off by force, or gives such information as shall lead to the recovery of any such property, shall be rewarded, due regard being had to the nature of the property, and to its value and condition at the time of delivery or recovery.

Every pensioner of the Government, who conceals or harbours any person whom he knows or has reason to believe to have been guilty of mutiny or desertion, or of waging war against the Government, or of seducing or attempting to seduce any officer or soldier from his allegiance or duty, or who fails to do his utmost to secure the apprehension and conviction of each offender, or who neglects to give immediate notice to the Civil or Military authorities of any mutinous or rebellious designs of which he may become cognizant, will, in addition to the punishment to which he is liable by law, forfeit his pension.

By order of the Right Hon'ble the Governor
General of India in Council,
C. BEADON
Secretary to the Government of India

# Notes

## Preliminary

1. *Mutiny Records Vol. III Part II Correspondence.* Lahore: Punjab Govt. Press, 1911. p. 391

## Prologue

1. Garrett, H. L. O., *The Trial of Muhammad Bahadur Shah.* 1932. pp. 232–4

## Preface

1. *Mutiny Records Vol. III Part II Correspondence*, p. 115. The letter was signed by Bakht Khan and twenty-five colonels of regiments, as well as a Muhammud Shafee Khan of the 8th Irregular Cavalry.

## Introduction

1. Cave-Browne, J., *The Punjab and Delhi in 1857*, Vol. 1. London: William Blackwood and Sons, 1861. p. 93
2. Gubbins, M. R., *An account of the mutinies in Oudh and of the siege of the Lucknow Residency; with some observations on the condition of the Province of Oudh and on the causes of the mutiny of the Bengal Army.* Richard Bentley, 1858. p. 53
3. Napier, C. J., *Defects, Civil and Military, of the Indian Government.* London: Charles Westerton, 1853. p. 3
4. Ibid, p. 12
5. Chick, N. A., *Annals of the Indian Rebellion.* Calcutta: Sanders, Cones & Co., 1859. p. 1

6. Kaye, J. and G. Malleson, *History of the Indian Mutiny* Vol. 2. Cambridge University Press, 1897. Mr J. C. Wilson's Moradabad Narrative (official), 24 Dec. 1858.
7. Chick, *Annals of the Indian Rebellion*, p. 92
8. Ibid.
9. Garrett, *The Trial of Muhammad Bahadur Shah*, p. 264
10. *Mutiny Records Vol III Part II Correspondence*, p. 402
11. Lunt, James (ed.), *From Sepoy to Subedar*. London: Routledge, 1970.
12. *Mutiny Records Vol III Part II Correspondence*, p. 235
13. Ibid, p. 173
14. Ibid, p. 403
15. Muter, E., *My Recollections of the Sepoy Revolt*. London: John Long Ltd, 1911
16. Wigram, Francis Spencer, *Mutiny at Meerut, 1857-58: Being Extracts from Letters from the Joint-Magistrate of that Station*. Southampton: Crabniton Industrial School, 1858. p. 34
17. *Mutiny Records Vol III Part II Correspondence*, p. 384
18. Ibid, p. 158
19. Cave-Browne, *The Punjab and Delhi in 1857*, Vol 2. 1861. p. 290
20. Ibid
21. Wigram, *Mutiny at Meerut*, p. 37
22. Khan, Syed Ahmed, *The Causes of the Indian Revolt*. Benares: Medical Hall Press, 1873. p. 7
23. Gubbins, *An account of the mutinies in Oudh*, p. 50
24. Hodson, W. S. R., *Twelve Years of a Soldier's Life in India: Being Extracts from the Letters of the late Major W.S.R. Hodson*. London: John Parker & Son, 1859. p. 247


## Chapter 1: The Shadow of God


1. St Augustine, *The City of God*. AD 426
2. Kaye and Malleson, *History of the Indian Mutiny Vol. 2*
3. Kaye, J. W., *A History of the Sepoy War in India, 1857-1858*, Vol. 2. London: W. H. Allen & Co, 1870. p. 5
4. Fanshawe, H. C., *Delhi: Past and Present*. London: John Murray, 1902
5. Andrews, C. F., *Zaka Ullah of Delhi*. Cambridge: Heffer & Sons, 1929. p. 13
6. Khan, *The Causes of the Indian Revolt*, p. 4
7. Andrews, p. 13
8. Ibid, p. 15
9. Hayder, Q. and S. Jafri, *Ghalib and His Poetry*. Bombay, 1970. p. 28
10. Ibid, p. 16

11. Kaye, *A History of the Sepoy War in India*, Vol. 2, p. 6
12. *The Universal Review*, Vol. 1. London: W. H. Allen & Co. 1859. p. 418
13. Spear, P., *Twilight of the Mughals: Studies in Late Mughal Delhi*. Oxford University Press, 1973. p. 57
14. *The Universal Review*, Vol. 1, p.418

## Chapter 2: A State of Permanent Penury

1. Napier, C. J., *The Life and Opinions of General Sir Charles James Napier, G.C.B*. London: John Murray, 1857
2. Husain, S. M., *Bahadur Shah Zafar and the War of 1857 in Delhi*. New Delhi: Aakar Books, 2006. p. 108
3. Ibid, p. 129
4. Dehlvi, Z., *Dastan-E-Ghadar*. New Delhi: Penguin, 2017. p. 21
5. Ibid, p. 19
6. Cave-Browne, *The Punjab and Delhi in 1857*, Vol. 1, p. 65
7. Beg, S., *Sair-ul-Manazil*. New Delhi: Tulika, 2017. p. 11
8. Ibid, p. 15
9. Muter, *My Recollections of the Sepoy Revolt*
10. Fanshawe, *Delhi: Past and Present*, p. 24
11. Taylor, Thomas, *Memoirs of the life and writings of Reginald Heber late Lord Bishop of Calcutta*. London: John Hatchard & Son, 1835

## Chapter 3: The Succession

1. Kaye, *A History of the Sepoy War in India*, Vol. 2
2. Coopland, R. M., *A Lady's Escape from Gwalior and Life in the Fort of Agra during the Mutinies of 1857*. London: Smith Elder and Co., 1859. p. 266
3. Mackenzie, H. D., *Life in the Mission, the Camp, and the Zenáná: Or, Six Years in India* Vol. 2. New York, 1853. p. 137
4. Andrews, *Zaka Ullah of Delhi*, p. 15
5. Kaye, p. 16
6. Ibid, p. 190-191
7. Private papers of J. G. Baird, 1 February 1852, p. 189
8. Kaye, p. 32

## Chapter 4: 'The English peace'

1. Muter, *My Recollections of the Sepoy Revolt*, p. 54
2. Forrest, G. (ed.), *The Indian Mutiny 1857–58: Selections from the Despatches and Other State Papers Preserved in the Military Dept. of the Government of India 1857-58* Vol. 1. Calcutta, 1893. pp. 389–90

3. Taylor, B., *A Visit to India, China and Japan in the Year 1853*. New York: G. P. Putnam, 1855. p. 152
4. Powell, A., *Muslims and Missionaries in Pre-Mutiny India*. London: Routledge, 2015. pp 51, 67
5. Majendie, V., *Up Amongst the Pandies, or A Years' Service in India*. London: Routledge, Warne & Routledge, 1859. p. 338
6. Napier, *Defects, Civil and Military, of the Indian Government*, pp. 40–41
7. Ibid
8. Kaye, *A History of the Sepoy War in India*, Vol. 2, p. 17
9. Kaye, M. M. (ed.), *The Golden Calm: An English Lady's life in Moghul Delhi*. London: Webb & Bower, 1980. pp. 126–27
10. Muter, *My Recollections of the Sepoy Revolt*
11. Kaye, *The Golden Calm*, p. 162
12. Andrews, *Zaka ullah of Delhi*, p. 6
13. Kaye, *The Golden Calm*, pp. 142–43
14. Ibid, p. 143
15. Ibid, p. 166

## Chapter 5: Changing Times

1. Regulation III of 1793 in Sutherland, D., *The Regulations of the Bengal Code*. Calcutta, n.d.
2. Lunt, James (ed.), *From Sepoy to Subedar*. London: Routledge, 1970. p. 165–6
3. Powell, *Muslims and Missionaries*, p. 82
4. Ibid
5. Pfander, C. G., *Remarks on the Nature of Muhammadanism: Traditions*. Calcutta: Baptist Missionary Press, 1840. p. 22
6. Ibid, p. 5
7. Ibid, p. 8
8. Ibid, p. 41
9. Pfander, C. G., *The Balance of Truth: Mizan ul-Haqq*. London: The Religious Tract Society, 1910. p. 123
10. Powell, Muslims and Missionaries, pp. 103–4
11. Ibid
12. Ibid, p. 194
13. *Delhi Gazette*, 8 April 1855, O.I.O.C.
14. Chandra, R., *A Treatise on Problems of Maxima and Minima solved by Algebra, with a forward by Augustus D. Morgan*. London: W. H. Allen & Co., 1859
15. Andrews, *Zaka ullah of Delhi*, p. viii
16. Ibid, p. 40
17. Ibid, p. 58
18. Ibid, p. 35

19. Ibid, p. 37
20. Powell, p. 210
21. Andrews, pp. ix–x
22. Powell, p. 193
23. Garrett, *The Trial of Muhammad Bahadur Shah*, p. 261

## Chapter 6: Rumours of a Persian Invasion

1. Chick, *Annals of the Indian Rebellion*, p. 4
2. Allen, C., *God's Terrorists: The Wahhabi Cult and the Hidden Roots of Modern Jihad*. London: Abacus, 2007. p. 115
3. Ibid, p. 92
4. Garrett, *The Trial of Muhammad Bahadur Shah*, pp. 162–4
5. Ibid, p. 257
6. Ibid, p. 162
7. Ibid, p. 229
8. Ibid, p. 207
9. *Authentic News*, No. IV, Vol. III, 26 January 1857
10. *Authentic News* No, II, Vol. III, 16 March 1857; Garrett, p. 208
11. Garrett, pp. 208–09
12. Ibid, p. 141
13. Ibid, pp. 213–15
14. Ibid, p. 196
15. Ibid, p. 110
16. Extract from Urdu newspaper *Compendium of News*, 13 April. The *Compendium of News* also reported of the proclamation on the Jama Masjid. It had a sword and shield drawn on it with a message the substance of which was 'That it was a religious obligation on all true believing Muhammadans to gird their loins resolutely, to assist the King of Persia, and to be faithfully subject and obedient to his authority, and to fight and contend against the English, so that vanquishing and routing them in battle they may receive and enjoy the favours, rewards and titles which the King of Persia will lavishly bestow on them. The proclamation also stated that the Persian king or second Jam would very soon come to India, and annex this country as a dependency, and that great multitudes of people had already assembled, and were constantly repeating the following couplet, as if from some involuntary and irresistible impulse: "Oh God save the very dust of Persia from the winds of misfortune, so long as even dust and wind may exist." The newswriter states that the above is a translation from the Persian, but that it has not yet come to pass. Several petitions without names have been given into the Magistrate's Court on the same subject, and in these it was also mentioned that a month hence from this date, an overwhelming attack will be made on Cashmere, of the

salubrity and beauty of which place a poet has said: "That should a parched and burnt-up soul reach Cashmere, Though he might be a roasted fowl, He would recover his wings and feathers." and that this cool and heavenly country will come into the possession of the writers of the petitions. The writer of this paper considers all this as mere senseless and absurd jesting and levity, for if countries are liable thus to slip out of the hands of Governments, what is the use of armies!' Garrett, p. 212

17. Ibid, p. 132
18. Ibid

## Chapter 7: 'The right arm, the hands and feet of the British government'

1. Alî, H., *A few words relative to the late mutiny of the Bengal army, and the…*, p. 1
2. Ibid
3. Forrest, G., *Sepoy Generals*. Cambridge University Press, 2011. p. 156
4. Gubbins, *An account of the mutinies in Oudh*, p. 89
5. Khan, *The Causes of the Indian Revolt*, p. 51
6. Baird, J. G. (ed.), *Private Letters of the Marquess of Dalhousie*. Shannon: Irish University Press, 1972. 17 Nov. 1849, Camp near River Beas, pp. 101–2
7. *Mutiny Records Vol III Part II Correspondence*, p. 399

## Chapter 8: 'A mine ready for explosion'

1. Chick, *Annals of the Indian Rebellion*, p. 84
2. Ibid, p. 25
3. Forrest, *The Indian Mutiny 1857–58: Selections from the Despatches*
4. Gubbins, *An Account of the Mutinies in Oudh*, p. 86
5. *Mutiny Records Vol III Part II Correspondence*, p. 382
6. Ibid, p. 384
7. Lunt (ed.), *From Sepoy to Subedar*, p. 161
8. Chick, p. 79
9. Gubbins, pp. 12–13
10. Chick, p. 81
11. Ibid
12. Gubbins, pp. 14–15
13. Cave-Browne, *The Punjab and Delhi in 1857*, Vol. 1, p. 44
14. Ibid, p. 45
15. *Mutiny Records Vol III Part II Correspondence*, p. 8

## Chapter 9: Mutiny at Meerut


1. Garrett, *The Trial of Muhammad Bahadur Shah*, p. 117
2. Ibid, p. 169
3. Ibid, p. 128
4. Wagentreiber, F., *Reminiscences of the Sepoy Rebellion*. Lahore: Civil and Military Gazette Press, 1911. p. 4
5. Garrett, p. 133
6. Wagentreiber, p. 4
7. Garrett, p. 170
8. Ibid, p. 173
9. Cave Browne, *The Punjab and Delhi in 1857*, Vol. 1, p. 364
10. Chick, *Annals of the Indian Rebellion*, p. 98
11. Ibid, p. 91
12. Ibid, p. 93
13. Kaye, *A History of the Sepoy War in India*, Vol. 2, p. 45
14. Chick, p. 91
15. Letter from Colonel G. M. C Smyth, Commanding 3rd Regiment, Light Cavalry, p. 223
16. Kaye, *A History of the Sepoy War in India*, Vol. 2, p. 48
17. Ibid
18. Ibid, letter to Vernon Smith
19. Dehlvi, *Dastan-E-Ghadar*, p. 58
20. Rotton, J., *The Chaplain's Narrative of the Siege of Delhi: From the Outbreak at Meerut to the Capture of Delhi*. London: Smith, Elder & Co., 1858.
21. Mackenzie, A. R. D., *Mutiny Memoirs: being personal reminiscences of the great sepoy revolt of 1857*. Allahabad: Pioneer Press, 1891.
22. Ibid
23. Kaye
24. Muter, *My Recollections of the Sepoy Revolt*, pp. 28–9
25. Ibid, p. 33
26. Ibid
27. Kaye
28. Muter, p. 23


## Chapter 10: Paralysis


1. Hodson, *Twelve Years of a Soldier's Life in India*, p. 190
2. Mackenzie, *Mutiny Memoirs*
3. Wigram, *Mutiny at Meerut*, p. 14
4. Ibid, pp. 8–9
5. Mackenzie
6. Ibid

7. Ibid
8. Ibid
9. Muter, *My Recollections of the Sepoy Revolt*
10. Wigram, p. 14
11. 'The foundation of the quarrel was this that thousands of maunds of atta was taken into every resala and regiment; and with this atta was mixed the ground bones of the cow and pig. And the cartridges were also made with the fat of the cow and pig. The shopkeepers in the city were ordered to purchase atta from Government and sell it in all the villages. It was ordered by beat of drum that atta be not ground in any village, and that in every district all the mills be confiscated to Government. It was also ordered that ten maunds of atta be thrown into every well, kucha or pukka, in every village and town. The troops at every station of one accord said that if the troops at Meerutt should receive the atta and cartridges, they would receive them without objection. A few Europeans officers assembled at Meerutt, and having collected the officers of the pultun and ressala ordered them to take the atta from the Government, and to bite the cartridges with the month, A few Sirdars objected to do so, but two, one a Hindoo and the other a Moosulman, bit the cartridge with the mouth. A reward of Rs. 100 was immediately paid to both. The rest said that they would consult each other during the night and intimate the result the next morning. There were about 84 men. They were instantly sent to jail in irons. One among them, Syud, who was fasting, struck his head on the ground and died.' *Mutiny Records Part I Correspondence*, pp. 161–2
12. Kaye, *A History of the Sepoy War in India*, Vol. 2, p. 107
13. Gough, H., *Old Memories (of the Indian Mutiny 1857)*. Normanby Press, 2014.
14. Hodson, p. 190
15. Kaye

## Chapter 11: Arrival at Delhi

1. Cave-Browne, *The Punjab and Delhi in 1857*, Vol 1, p. 64
2. Garrett, *The Trial of Muhammad Bahadur Shah*, pp. 148–9
3. *Selections from the Records of the Government of the Punjab and Its Dependencies*, No. 7. Punjab Printing Company Ltd, 1870
4. Garrett, p. 129
5. Zer Jharokha is literally 'under the lattice' but appears to be a name given generally to the ground immediately under the lattices of the palace.
6. Garrett, p. 149
7. Ibid, p. 136

8. Lieut Forrest writing to Col A. Abbott, Insp. Gen. of Ordnance and Mag., Fort William, on 27 May
9. Garrett, p. 139
10. *Selections from the Records…*, p. 279
11. Ibid, pp. 273–4
12. Ibid
13. Ibid, p. 280
14. Garrett, p. 130
15. Ibid
16. *Selections from the Records…*, p. 276
17. Ibid, p. 279

## Chapter 12: 'We are not seeking loot but life'

1. Wagentreiber, *Reminiscences of the Sepoy Rebellion*, p. 7
2. *Mutiny Records Part I Correspondence*, p. 17
3. Kaye, *A History of the Sepoy War in India*, Vol. 2
4. Garrett, *The Trial of Muhammad Bahadur Shah*, p. 154
5. *Selections from the Records …*, p. 162
6. Wagentreiber, p. 49
7. Hodson, *Twelve Years of a Soldier's Life in India*, pp. 258–9
8. Wagentreiber, p. 50
9. Garrett, pp. 195–6
10. Ibid
11. Dehlvi, *Dastan-E-Ghadar*, p. 60

## Chapter 13: The Magazine

1. Cave-Browne, *The Punjab and Delhi in 1857*, Vol. 1, p. 82
2. Ibid, 76
3. Fanshawe, *Delhi: Past and Present*
4. 'Previous to the Natives deserting us they hid the Priming pouches & one man in particular Kuram Buksh, a durwan appeared to keep up a constant communication with the enemy on the outside & keep them informed of our situation. Lieut. Willoughby was so annoyed at this man's conduct, that he gave me an order to shoot him should he approach the gate.' Forrest in his report to Col. A. Abbott, C. B. Insp. Gen. of Ordnance and Mag., Fort William [dated Meerut, 27 May 1857]
5. Garrett, *The Trial of Muhammad Bahadur Shah*, p. 128
6. Ibid, p. 125
7. Ibid
8. Forrest wrote in his report later to Col. A. Abbott, C. B. Insp. Gen. of Ordnance and Mag., Fort William [dated Meerut, 27 May 1857]

9. Dehlvi, *Dastan-E-Ghadar*, p. 89
10. Wrote Forrest to Col. A. Abbott, C. B. Insp. Gen. of Ordnance and Mag., Fort William [dated Meerut, 27 May 1857]

## Chapter 14: The Flight

1. Garrett, *The Trial of Muhammad Bahadur Shah*, p. 168
2. Wigram, *Mutiny at Meerut*, p. 64. Lieut Gambier's letter, dated 27 and 29 May 1857
3. Ibid, pp. 57–8
4. Wagentreiber, *Reminiscences of the Sepoy Rebellion*, p. 9
5. Ibid, p. 10

## Chapter 15: Empire *ex nihilo*

1. Garrett, *The Trial of Muhammad Bahadur Shah*, p. 150
2. Ibid, pp. 227–8
3. Dehlvi, *Dastan-E-Ghadar*, p. 60
4. Ibid
5. Garrett, p. 175
6. Dehlvi, p. 79
7. Ibid, p. 81
8. Ibid
9. Garrett, p. 163
10. Ibid.
11. Ibid, p. 262
12. Ibid, p. 177
13. Ibid, p. 183
14. Ibid

## Chapter 16: Reign of Terror

1. Garrett, *The Trial of Muhammad Bahadur Shah*, p. 229
2. *Mutiny Records Part I Correspondence*, pp. 74–5
3. Garrett, p. 8
4. Ibid, p. 80
5. *Selections from the Records…*, p. 166
6. Garrett, p. 182
7. Andrews, *Zaka ullah of Delhi*, p. 68
8. Garrett, p. 176
9. Ibid, p. 145
10. *Selections from the Records…*, p. 165
11. Garrett, p. 158
12. *Accounts and Papers, Parliamentary Papers, House of Commons and Command*, Volume 18, 1859, p. 108

13. Khwaja Hasan Nizami.
14. *Accounts and Papers, Parliamentary Papers*, pp. 101–2

## Chapter 17: Puppet Emperor

1. Garrett, *The Trial of Muhammad Bahadur Shah*, p. 81
2. Ibid, p. 184
3. Ibid, p. 179
4. *Selections from the Records …*, p. 163
5. *Accounts and Papers, Parliamentary Papers*, pp. 107–8
6. Joint Petition of Kamdar Khan and others of the Constabulary Force. 'To the King Shelter of the World. WE slaves 50 men of the constabulary force who were stationed over the gaol at Meerut having come thence to your royal presence are now discharging all such duties as are assigned to us by the orders of the commander in chief Bahadur. Your army is now about to leave for Meerut and 16 of our number are anxiously eager to go and fight in its 162 I company We therefore trust that Mirza Moghal may be ordered to direct us to go also that through your Majesty's prestige never to be overthrown we may share in the victory It was necessary and has been submitted Petition of Kamdar Khan and others of the constabulary force Autograph Order by the King in Pencil The officer of the Meerut gaol on duty under the palace lattices will know that he is to go whithersoever our son Mirza Moghal may send him and to forward to him any number of men that he may call for He is to be obedient to all orders of our said son.' Garrett, p. 104
7. *Accounts and Papers, Parliamentary Papers*, pp. 107–8
8. Garrett, pp. 262–3
9. *Delhi Urdu Akhbar*, 24 May 1857
10. Garrett, p. 158
11. Ibid, p. 229
12. Ibid, pp. 228–30
13. Ibid, p. 229

## Chapter 18: Divine Cull of the Unbelievers

1. Garrett, *The Trial of Muhammad Bahadur Shah*, p. 146
2. Ibid, pp. 249–50
3. Ibid, p. 39, petition no. 55. '… it is manifest to Your Majesty, that justice is approved of, and lawless cruelty condemned by the Creator of the Universe. I therefore pray, if in your Majesty's estimation it is proper to do so, that you should tell the Officers of the Army, who request your permission to slay the ladies, children, and other prisoners, that agreeably to their prayers, you placed your hand on their heads, and joined them in the cause of the faith; but that in killing the prisoners in

question, you will abandon the tenets of your religion. That they must first obtain a Fatwa [religious ruling by a recognised muslim authority] and a Bywasta [Vyavastha – ruling by a Hindu pandit] and that, if these shall sanction the slaughter, they can slay the prisoners alluded to; but that your Majesty will not give an order on the subiect, contrary to the laws of the Prophet; and that if they do not approve of this, they may first wreak their rage on your own Royal person. I trust that your Majesty's orders, agreeably to the suggestions above submitted, will be issued to the Officers of the Army in a tone of decision. Considering it necessary I have laid the subject before your Royal presence.' – Nabi Bakhsh Khan

4. Dehlvi, *Dastan-E-Ghadar*, p. 92
5. Garrett, pp. 227–8
6. *Accounts and Papers, Parliamentary Papers*, p. 108
7. Garrett
8. *Selections from the Records ...*, p. 165. 'They further swore by the Koran that the seal on the paper were not theirs, and that the document was a forgery. However the soldiers would not believe their asseverations,' wrote Chuni Lal.
9. Garrett, p. 181
10. Ibid, p. 165
11. According to Chuni Lal.
12. Garrett, p. 157
13. *Selections from the Records ...*, p. 166
14. Chuni also related seeing Prince Mirza Mughal and 'a number of other Mohammedans' watching the events on top of Mirza Mughal's house although he mentioned no names. Whether these were other princes is hard to say.
15. Garrett, p. 157
16. Garrett, p. 146
17. Wagentreiber, *Reminiscences of the Sepoy Rebellion*

## Chapter 19: The Response

1. *Mutiny Records Part I Correspondence*, p. 34
2. Cave-Browne, *The Punjab and Delhi in 1857*, p. 376
3. Kaye, *A History of the Sepoy War in India*
4. Ibid
5. *Mutiny Records Part I Correspondence*, p. 127
6. Ibid, p. 128
7. Hodson, *Twelve Years of a Soldier's Life in India*, p. 183
8. Kaye
9. Ibid
10. Cave-Browne, p. 310
11. *Mutiny Records Part I Correspondence*, p. 49
12. Ibid, p. 54

13. Hodson, p. 192
14. Kaye

## Chapter 20: The Battles of Hindun River

1. Cave-Browne, *The Punjab and Delhi in 1857*, p. 312
2. Ibid, p. 14
3. Dehlvi, *Dastan-E-Ghadar*, pp. 101–2
4. Garrett, *The Trial of Muhammad Bahadur Shah*, 157–8

## Chapter 21: The Battle of Badli-ki-Serai

1. Fanshawe, *Delhi: Past and Present*, p. 114
2. Wigram, *Mutiny at Meerut*, p. 15
3. Fanshawe, p. 121
4. Garrett, *The Trial of Muhammad Bahadur Shah*, p. 197

## Chapter 22: The Possibilities of a *Coup de Main*

1. *Mutiny Records Part I Correspondence*, p. 115
2. Hodson, *Twelve Years of a Soldier's Life in India*, p. 302
3. Ibid, p. 204
4. *Mutiny Records Part I Correspondence*, p. 160
5. Hodson, p. 304
6. Garrett, *The Trial of Muhammad Bahadur Shah*, p. 82
7. *Mutiny Records Part I Correspondence*, pp. 175–6

## Chapter 23: Fighting in the Sabzi Mandi

1. *Mutiny Records Part I Correspondence*, p. 151
2. Rotton, *The Chaplain's Narrative of the Siege of Delhi*, p. 87
3. Cave-Browne, *The Punjab and Delhi in 1857*, p. 388
4. *Mutiny Records Part I Correspondence*, p. 174
5. Ibid, pp. 175–6
6. Ibid, p. 192
7. Vibart, H. M., *Richard Baird Smith, the leader of the Delhi heroes in 1857: private correspondence of the Commanding Engineers during the siege, etc.* London: Constable, 1897. p. 40
8. Hodson, *Twelve Years of a Soldier's Life in India*, p. 205

## Chapter 24: The Imperative of Law and Order

1. Garrett, *The Trial of Muhammad Bahadur Shah*, pp. 15–16
2. Ibid. 'From Your Majesty's goodness, clemency, and justice, equal to Nowsherwan's, we expect that a written order will be addressed to

each of the Royal Princes of illustrious ancestry, namely, His Highness the Lord of the World, Mirza Muhammad Moghal Bahadur, Mirza Khair Muhammad Sultan Bahadur, Mirza Muhammad Abulbakr Bahadur, Mirza Muhammad Abdulla Bahadur, and others, to the effect that for the future, no soldier of the Cavalry or Infantry be permitted to go to your Slave's house and commit acts of aggression there, and that the Military Guard at present stationed there, be removed, because lawless characters of the City take advantage of the Guard being changed to plunder your Slave's property.' Zafr would order Mirza Moghal to organise a Guard for the house.

3. Ibid
4. Ibid, pp. 13–14. Syed Abdulla, priest of the shrine of Hazrat Sheikh Muhammad Chishti, petitioned on 29 June that 'the whole of the autumnal crop of sugarcane, churee, etc ... has been totally devastated, and more than this, the very implements or agriculture such as ploughs, woodwork on wells, have all been carried away in plunder by soldiers.' Similarly, petitions from all types of people. rich and poor, Hindus and Muslims, came in from all quarters of the capital and from towns and rural areas, complaining against the depredations of the mutineers. In his orders to Prince Mughal, the Emperor tells him 'that Troopers of Cavalry come from Jodhpur have piequetted their horses in front of the shops and have taken possession of a number of them', and that the rebel Gujjars of Aliganj. Mallanji, Hasangarh and Alapur are now engaged in highway robbery and in plundering the country.
5. Ibid
6. Ibid, p. 12
7. Ibid, p. 15 no. 21
8. *Mutiny Records Part I Correspondence*, p. 154
9. Hodson, p. 219
10. *Mutiny Records Part I Correspondence*, pp. 150–1
11. Barnes would send the following news to John Lawrence on 22 June, although the news was from 18 June.
12. *Delhi Urdu Akhbar*, 14 June 1857
13. Garrett, pp. 100–1

## Chapter 25: The Arrival of Bakht Khan

1. Vibart, *Richard Baird Smith*
2. *Mutiny Records Part I Correspondence*, p. 194
3. Ibid, pp. 207–8
4. Garrett, *The Trial of Muhammad Bahadur Shah*, p. iv
5. Ibid, p. iv
6. *Mutiny Records Part I Correspondence*, pp. 187–88
7. Ibid, p. 191

8. '... under such circumstances an enterprising and able officer might have prevented the passage of the Rohilkund Force, and at any rate have inflicted on them heavy loss. But no, they were allowed to march in triumph across the Doab, to swell the numbers, and add to the spirit of the Delhy mutineers...'
9. *Mutiny Records Part I Correspondence*, p. 220. Lawrence was passed a letter from an officer stationed at Merutt, who went down to Gurmuktesar Ghaut with a small party, and saw the enemy crossing slowly and gradually in a few boats. '... Our people at Merutt [Meerut] were in an entrenched post, defended by heavy guns. Under such circumstances it must be obvious that a few men might have held the place with perfect safety against large numbers. Indeed, it was so strong that the Rohilkund mutineers would not even approach it ... Such a body under an enterprizing and efficient officer would have prevented the mutineers from ever crossing the Ganges, and even under the supposition that they had crossed previous to his arrival, which was almost impossible, would have harrassed and impeded their march throughout the whole line of their route. So that it is only reasonable to suppose that not half the number would have reached their destination. Encumbered with plunder, rapid movement was impracticable.'
10. Wigram, *Mutiny at Meerut*, pp. 18–19. Wigram also in a private letter of 6 July wrote a damning indictment of Hewitt's inertia. 'I believe that had we had a more efficient, active, and determined General in this division, we might have done some real service, by scouring the district and sweeping the rebellious portion of the community off the face of the earth. ... A couple of guns and one hundred riflemen with what volunteers we could raise, would have been sufficient to hold them in check, but the old General would listen to no one, though civilians as well as every one else were urging him to show a little activity. The consequence was that they passed into Delhi, burning and destroying Government property on their way, and completely losing us the friendship of several influential natives who were disposed to assist us, and who naturally considered themselves neglected when we allowed them to be insulted in any way, for when once the rebels were across the river we could not meet them with the small force at our disposal.'
11. Garrett, p. 187
12. Zaka Ullah, p. 675
13. Ibid
14. Ibid
15. Khan, S. A., *The causes of the Indian revolt*, p. 9
16. Dehlvi, *Dastan-E-Ghadar*, p. 117
17. Hodson, *Twelve Years of a Soldier's Life in India*, p. 259

18. Dehlvi, p. 111
19. Garrett, p. 188
20. *Mutiny Records Vol III Part II Correspondence*, p. 115. The letter was signed by Bakht Khan as well as twenty-five colonels of regiments as well as a Muhammud Shafee Khan of the 8th Irregular Cavalry. The Neemuch rebels, with the Gwalior troops, would not actually arrive until 29 July, having paused to attack the Agra cantonment along the way.
21. Petition of Muhammad Murtaza Khan Risaldar. 'To the King Shelter of the World See Respectfully showeth that agreeably to your royal orders your petitioner and the men of the corps of cavalry have for a month and a half had their quarters in your Majesty's garden generally known as that of Begam Sombre and that having had the bath room under the house cleared of the accumulated filth and rubbish at an expense of one rupee from their own funds they have kept the cavalry appurtenances and accoutrements there. The men of the regular cavalry now come from Gwalior have taken possession of the place and the troopers of my corps are in consequence suffering great inconvenience from exposure to the rain for besides his bath room there is no other place of shelter in the garden in question. I therefore pray that orders may be issued to the men of the regular cavalry directing them not to disturb us in our occupancy but to search out some other quarters for themselves or at least to occupy one half themselves and to leave the other half to us. It was necessary and I have therefore submitted it. Prayers for the prosperity of the reign. Petition of the slave Mir Muhammad Muitaza Khan Risaldar.' 'Mirza Moghal will explain to the Gwalior troopers that they are to occupy half of the place and are to give the other half to the petitioners.' According to orders a written order has been issued dated 9 July 1857. Garrett, pp. 162–3
22. Garrett, p. 206
23. *Mutiny Records Vol III Part II Correspondence*
24. Ibid, pp. 117–9

## Chapter 26: The Heat and Flies of July

1. Vibart, *Richard Baird Smith*, p. 95

## Chapter 27: Wilson's Doubts

1. Baird Smith to a friend, Charles Norton Esq, Professor at Harvard, dated 1 November 1857
2. Vibart, *Richard Baird Smith*, p. 95
3. *Mutiny Records Part I Correspondence*, p. 231

4. 17 July, Wilson. Baird Smith had communicated to Colonel Lefroy who had written to *The Times* a letter published in the newspaper. The letter had been written on 11 May 1858.
5. Vibart, pp. 42–3
6. Ibid
7. Ibid, p. 102
8. Hodson, *Twelve Years of a Soldier's Life in India*, p. 248
9. Vibart
10. Ibid, p. 52
11. Ibid, p. 137

## Chapter 28: War of Attrition

1. Hodson, *Twelve Years of a Soldier's Life in India*, pp. 250–1
2. Ibid, p. 252
3. Ibid, p. 254
4. Ibid, p. 240
5. Rotton, *The Chaplain's Narrative of the Siege of Delhi*, p. 175
6. Vibart, *Richard Baird Smith*, p. 110
7. Greathed, H. H., *Letters written during the siege of Delhi by H.H. Greathed, ed. by his widow [E.F. Greathed]*. Oxford University Press, 1858. p. 191

## Chapter 29: '… no money whatever remains in the Treasury'

1. *Mutiny Records Part 1 Correspondence*, p. 282
2. Garrett, *The Trial of Muhammad Bahadur Shah*, p. 64, appendix 4, no. 1
3. Ibid, pp. 64–5, appendix 4, no. 2
4. 'Petition of Mirza Muhammad Azim. That the servants of Your Majesty who came from Hansi and Hissar, and who have been placed under your slave, have not received their pay for two months and twenty days. As the treasuries of Sirsa, Hissar, Hansi, and other places, were, with great care and zeal, brought by them, and lodged in the Royal Treasury, and here too, accompanying your slave in every engagement, three or four of these servants daily certify their fidelity with their lives, they therefore now demand their pay. Your slave, actuated by zeal, has arranged that Your Majesty will now grant one month's pay out of the two months and twenty days' arrears which are due, he will satisfy the men. If, on the other hand, no pay whatever is granted, the force will have cause to be disheartened. It is strange that all the rest of the Army should have been paid. I transit enclosed in this petition, an abstract for one month's pay for all the men of the force in expectation that orders may be issued. It was necessary

and has been represented. (Prayers for the prosperity of the reign.)' 'Petition of the special slave, Muhammad Azim, door-keeper (may his sins be forgiven). *Autograph order by the King, Mirza Moghal will give one month's pay.*'

5. No. 6. 'Petition of Mirza Moghal, dated 13th July 1857. To The KING ! Shelter of the World ! Hitherto, Karim Bakhsh, Risaldar of the 1st Lucknow Irregular Cavalry, and the men of his Corps, have been paid monthly. He has now presented a petition, dated the 12th July 1857, soliciting payment of daily allowances, in the same Way that they are paid to others, and demanding arrears for nineteen days. The real state of the matter is, that these people have learned that there is very little money in the Treasury, and it is on this account they now apply for daily allowances. Such orders as may be issued, will be complied with. (Prayers for the prosperity of the reign.)' 'Petition of the slave Zohur-ud-din. *Autograph order by the King, in pencil. Zafar – Those who are paid monthly will not get daily allowances.*'
6. Garrett, p. 66
7. Ibid, appendix 4, no. 4. 'A very small balance of cash remains in our Treasury.'
8. Ibid, p. 67, no. 5
9. Ibid, p. 69
10. *Mutiny Records Part I Correspondence*, p. 315
11. Garrett, p. 34, petition 44
12. Ibid, pp. 108–9
13. Ibid, p. 37, petition 50
14. *Mutiny Records Vol III Part II Correspondence*, p. 2
15. Ibid, pp. 17–18
16. Ibid
17. Ibid, pp. 17–18, 34
18. Ibid, p. 18
19. Ibid, p. 7

## Chapter 30: A Shortage of Gunpowder

1. *Mutiny Records Part I Correspondence*, p. 408
2. 'To Mirza Moghal the illustrious and valiant Mirza Zohur ud din oitherwise Mirza Moghal Bahadur Learn That owing to the large daily expenditure of powder none is now left in the magazine and orders have in consequence been issued that materials required in its manufacture should be purchased and that though large numbers of powder makers are employed it cannot be produced as expeditiously as is necessary while the daily demand for it is very emergent ... You are directed to collect it from the men named in the subjoined list as well as all that you may find after search in places where barrels of

it are likely to be forthcoming and to have all you may thus collect conveyed to the magazine by tomorrow. Consider this business as taking precedence in importance above all others and see,' he wrote to Mirza Moghal.

3. *Mutiny Records Part I Correspondence*, p. 192
4. Dehlvi, *Dastan-E-Ghadar*, pp. 118–9
5. 14 August, from a correspondent of one Colonel Becher. Following the explosion, the powder was now being manufactured at a house belonging to Hussun Allee Khan. The correspondent wrote that this property would be in the range of British guns if stationed at Qudsia Bagh.
6. *Mutiny Records Part I Correspondence*, p. 352
7. Ibid
8. Ibid, p. 5
9. *Mutiny Records Part I Correspondence*, p. 217
10. Ibid, p. 224
11. 'At a council held yesterday a Moulvee had the courage to tell them they knew they had mutinied for their own aggrandisement and not for religion and that as they could not hope for victory they had better endeavour to get terms. But they have not even that hope to trust to and nothing but death stares them in the face. It is a good satire on the Mahomedans fighting for their faith that at this Eed under the Mahomedan king no one was permitted to sacrifice a cow and that the King did not venture to go as formerly in state to the Jumma Musjid and was obliged to perform the ceremonies within the palace walls. Altogether they must feel that the ruin in which they wished to involve us is recoiling on their own heads.'
12. *Mutiny Records Part I Correspondence*, p. 353
13. Ibid
14. Husain, *Bahadur Shah Zafar and the War of 1857 in Delhi*, p. 183.
15. Garrett, *The Trial of Muhammad Bahadur Shah*, p. 225
16. Ibid
17. Ibid, p. 187
18. *Mutiny Records Part I Correspondence*, pp. 193–4
19. Ibid, p. 384
20. Ibid, p. 408
21. 'In round numbers the mutineers may be estimated at 4,000 cavalry and 12,000 infantry. The rest, say 1,000 cavalry and 3,000 infantry are undisciplined levies of no account whatever. It is impossible to give an exact amount of their fluctuating numbers, but this is a fair approximation, perhaps rather over-stated,' G. C. Barnes, the Commissioner of the Cis-Sutlej states would send to John Lawrence. 18 August.

## Chapter 31: The Battle of Najafgarh

1. Rotton, *The Chaplain's Narrative of the Siege of Delhi*, p. 206
2. Ibid, p. 207
3. *Mutiny Records Part I Correspondence*, p. 443
4. *Mutiny Records Vol III Part II Correspondence*, p. 5

## Chapter 32: Overtures from the King

1. *Mutiny Records Vol III Part II Correspondence*, p. 6
2. Ibid, pp. 6–9
3. Translation of *Delhee News*, 1 September 1857
4. *Mutiny Records Vol III Part II Correspondence*, p. 17
5. *Mutiny Records Part I Correspondence*, p. 443
6. Garrett, *The Trial of Muhammad Bahadur Shah*, pp. 34–5, petition 46
7. *Mutiny Records Part I Correspondence*, p. 193
8. *Mutiny Records Vol III Part II Correspondence*, p. 21
9. Ibid, pp. 12–13
10. Greathed, *Letters written during the siege of Delhi*, p. 251

## Chapter 33: The Demons of Destruction

1. *Mutiny Records Vol III Part II Correspondence*, p. 14
2. Ibid, p. 2
3. Hodson, *Twelve Years of a Soldier's Life in India*, p. 280
4. Mutiny Records Part I Correspondence, pp. 422–3
5. Ibid, pp. 424–25
6. Forty heavy guns and howitzers; ten heavy mortars; twelve light mortars; two Light Field Batteries; four Troops of Horse Artillery (thirty-four 24- and 18-pdrs or 8-inch howitzers, ten 10-inch and 8-inch mortars and 12 coehorns.
7. Greathed, *Letters written during the siege of Delhi*, p. 251
8. Bourchier, G., *Eight Months' Campaign Against the Bengal Sepoy Army During the Mutiny of 1857*. London: Smith, Elder & Co., 1858. p. 50
9. Ibid, p. 53
10. Fremont-Barnes, G., *The Osprey Guide to the Indian Mutiny 1857–58*. London: Osprey, 2014.
11. Greathed, p. 259
12. Hodson, p. 282
13. *Mutiny Records Vol III Part II Correspondence*, p. 56

## Chapter 34: The Plan of Attack

1. Vibart, *Richard Baird Smith*, letter no. 69
2. Flinders, S., *Cult of a Dark Hero*. London: I. B. Tauris, 2018. p. 134

3. Ibid, p. 135
4. Vibart, p. 129
5. Ibid, appendix 2
6. Ibid, p. 142
7. Ibid, pp. 129–30, letter no. 67
8. Flinders, p. 135
9. *Mutiny Records Vol III Part II Correspondence*, p. 54
10. Ibid, pp. 33–4
11. Ibid, p. 56
12. Ibid, pp. 53–4
13. Ibid, pp. 33–4
14. Garrett, *The Trial of Muhammad Bahadur Shah*, pp. 248–9
15. Mutiny Records Vol III Part II, pp. 53–4
16. Ibid, p. 56
17. Ibid, pp. 33–4
18. Ibid
19. Ibid, p. 56
20. Garrett, p. 219

## Chapter 35: The Assault

1. Named as Felix in Bourchier's book.
2. Rotton, *The Chaplain's Narrative of the Siege of Delhi*, p. 269
3. Flinders, *Cult of a Dark Hero*, p. 145
4. Ibid
5. Ibid, pp. 145–6
6. Lt Salkeld, Lt Home and Sgt Smith would receive the Victoria Cross for this dangerous action, as would a soldier of HM52nd who assisted Salkeld and bound his wounds despite heavy fire.
7. Dehlvi, *Dastan-E-Ghadar*, p. 125
8. Thompson, E., *The Other Side of the Medal*. London: The Hogarth Press, 1925. p. 75
9. Flinders, p. 147
10. Ibid
11. Ibid, p. 148
12. Ibid, pp. 149–50
13. Ibid
14. Rotton, p. 282
15. Flinders, p. 146

## Chapter 36: The Capture

1. *Mutiny Records Vol III Part II Correspondence*, p. 49
2. 'At the very entrance [Kashmir gate] were large stores filled with wine, beer, and spirits, in the greatest abundance; and for a time,

our tenure of the position we had gained was deeply imperilled. Our guard fell victims to their vice, and were all murdered at their posts; while champagne was taken by the followers outside the city to the Ludlow Castle and sold for about 3d. a bottle,' Bourchier wrote of the temptations of this particular loot.

3. C. B. Saunders, the Commissioner at Delhi, to W. Muir (afterwards Sir W. Muir), at Agra.
4. 'The most vigorous efforts were at once made to destroy all the liquor in the town. Thousands of dozens were broken up by guards placed at the disposal of the Provost-Marshal, and order was once more restored. Yet although the passions of the troops were, by drink and revenge, worked up to burning heat, not a case, it is believed, was heard of a woman or child having been intentionally hurt – all credit to them.' – Bourchier
5. *Mutiny Records Vol III Part II Correspondence*, p. 48
6. Ibid, pp. 60–61
7. Garrett, *The Trial of Muhammad Bahadur Shah*, p. 167
8. Hodson, *Twelve Years of a Soldier's Life in India*, p. 294
9. *Mutiny Records Vol III Part II Correspondence*, pp. 60–1
10. Ibid, pp. 62–3; telegram from Brigadier General Neville Chamberlain, Skinner's house, Delhi, to the Chief Commissioner, Punjab, dated 17 September 1857, 6 p.m.
11. *Mutiny Records Vol III Part II Correspondence*, pp. 61–2; telegram from the Assistant Adjutant* General of the Army, Belli, to Mr Barnes, Umballa; Colonel Macpherson and General Gowan, Lahore, 17 September 1857.
12. Hodson, p. 295
13. *Mutiny Records Vol III Part II Correspondence*, pp. 65–6
14. Ibid, p. 68
15. Hodson, p. 299
16. Rotton, *The Chaplain's Narrative of the Siege of Delhi*, p. 321
17. *Mutiny Records Vol III Part II Correspondence*, p. 136

## Chapter 37: The Sack of Delhi

1. 'As far as the rest of the city was concerned, men and women were pushed outside the walls,' Dehlvi wrote. 'The men were thrown out of the Kashmiri Darwaza [Kashmir Gate] and the women out of Kabuli Darwaza [Kabul Gate], which resulted in everyone being separated. They ran around wildly, searching for each other.' Dehlvi, *Dastan-E-Ghadar*, p. 143
2. Thompson, *The Other Side of the Medal*, p. 76; letter in *The Times*, 19 November 1857 (Montgomery Martin)
3. Dehlvi, p. 143
4. *Mutiny Records Vol III Part II Correspondence*, pp. 290–1

5. Wagentreiber, *Reminiscences of the Sepoy Rebellion*, p. 45
6. Muter, *My Recollections of the Sepoy Revolt*, p. 153
7. Coopland, *A Lady's Escape from Gwalior*, pp. 258–9
8. Muter, p. 142
9. *Mutiny Records Vol III Part II Correspondence*, p. 274
10. Ibid, p. 275
11. Kaye, *The Golden Calm*, p. 211
12. *Mutiny Records Vol III Part II Correspondence*, p. 270
13. Hodson, *Twelve Years of a Soldier's Life in India*, p. 375

## Chapter 38: The Promise of Life

1. Nizami, S. K. H., *The Agony of Delhi*. Delhi: Ibn Arbi, 1922
2. Ibid
3. *Mutiny Records Vol III Part II Correspondence*, pp. 99–100
4. Ibid
5. Ibid
6. Ibid, p. 344
7. Ibid, pp. 323–25
8. Ibid, p. 329
9. Ibid, p. 332
10. Ibid, p. 329
11. Ibid, p. 327
12. Ibid, p. 343
13. Ibid, p. 356

## Chapter 39: Return from Humayun's Tomb

1. Hodson, *Twelve Years of a Soldier's Life in India*, p. 316
2. Ibid, pp. 306–7
3. *Mutiny Records Vol III, Part II*, pp. 323–25
4. Hodson, p. 307
5. Ibid, p. 327
6. Ibid, pp. 310–314
7. Ibid
8. Ibid, p. 301
9. Ibid, pp. 310–14
10. Ibid
11. Ibid
12. Ibid
13. Ibid, pp. 301–2
14. Ibid, p. 297
15. Andrews, *Zaka Ullah of Delhi*, p. 50

## Chapter 40: 'This possessor of mere nominal royalty'

1. Coopland, *A Lady's Escape from Gwalior*, pp. 268–9
2. Muter, *My Recollections of the Sepoy Revolt*, p. 146
3. Coopland, pp. 268–9
4. Selections from the Records ..., p. 298
5. *Mutiny Records Vol III Part II Correspondence*, p. 73
6. Coopland, p. 266
7. *Mutiny Records Vol III Part II Correspondence*, pp. 299–300
8. Ibid, p. 304
9. Ibid, p. 318
10. Ibid, p. 346
11. Ibid, p. 348
12. Ibid, p. 352
13. Ibid
14. Ibid, p. 353
15. Ibid, p. 366
16. Muter, p. 147
17. Muter, p. 151
18. Garrett, *The Trial of Muhammad Bahadur Shah*, pp.232–4
19. Ibid, p. 232
20. *Mutiny Records Vol III Part II Correspondence*, p. 381
21. Baird, *Private Letters of the Marquess of Dalhousie*, p. 397

## Chapter 41: Raze the City

1. *Mutiny Records Vol III Part II Correspondence*, pp. 101–3
2. Coopland, *A Lady's Escape from Gwalior*, pp. 278–80
3. *Mutiny Records Vol III Part II Correspondence*, pp. 101–3
4. Ibid, p. 74
5. Ibid, p. 72
6. Ibid, pp. 101–3
7. Ibid, p. 162
8. Ibid, p. 163
9. Coopland, pp. 253–4
10. Coopland, pp. 273–4
11. To Tufta in April 1861. Varma, P. K., *Ghalib: The Man, The Times*. Delhi: Penguin, 1989. p. 170

# Bibliography


## Records and Documents

*Accounts and Papers of the House of Commons relating to the East India Mutiny*, Volume 18 (House of Commons, 1859)

*Papers relative to the mutinies in the East Indies presented to the Houses of Parliament by Command of her Majesty* (London: Harrison and Sons, 1857)

*Mutiny Records Reports*, Vol. 7 part 2 (Lahore: Punjab Govt Press, 1911)

*Mutiny Records Reports*, Vol. 8 part 1 (Lahore: Punjab Govt Press, 1911)

*Mutiny Records Reports*, Vol. 8 part 2 (Lahore: Punjab Govt Press, 1911)

*Mutiny Records Correspondence in two parts*, part 1 (Lahore: Punjab Government Press, 1911)

*Mutiny Records Correspondence in two parts*, part 2 (Lahore: Punjab Govt Press, 1911)

*Mutiny Report by the Government of Punjab* (Lahore: Punjab Govt Press, 1911)

Montgomery, R., *Punjab Mutiny Report* (Lahore Chronicle Press, 1859)

*Selections from the Public Correspondence of the Administration for the Affairs of the Punjab: Punjab Mutiny Report* (Sang-e-meel, 2005)

*Selections from the Records of the Government of the Punjab and Its Dependencies*, No. 7 (Punjab Printing Company, 1870)

## Published Works

Anderson, Clare, The Indian uprising of 1857-8: Prisons, prisoners and Rebellion (London: Anthem, 2007)

Andrews, C. F., *Zaka Ullah of Delhi* (Cambridge: W. Heffer & Sons Ltd, 1929)

Anon., *Allen's Indian Mail and Register of Intelligence for British*, Vol. 15 (London: Wm. H. Allen and Co., 1857)

Anon., 'The Last of the Moguls', *The Universal Review*, Vol. 1 (London: Wm. H. Allen & Co., 1859), pp. 416–431

Anson, O. H. S. G., *With HM9th lancers during the Indian mutiny* (Normanby Press, 2014)

Baird, J. G. (ed.), *Private letters of the marquess of Dalhousie* (London: W. Blackwood and Sons, 1910)

Ball, Charles, *The History of the Indian Mutiny: Giving a Detailed Account of the sepoy insurrection in India*, Vol. 1 (London: The London Printing and Publishing Company Ltd, 1858)

Barter, Richard, The Siege of Delhi: Mutiny Memories of an Old Officer (London: The Folio Society, 1984)

Bartlett, D. W., *The heroes of the Indian rebellion* (Columbus, Ohio: Follett, Foster &Co, 1859)

Bates, Crispin (ed.), *Mutiny at the margins: New perspectives on the Indian uprising 1857*, Vol. 1 (Delhi: Sage Publications, 2013)

Bird, Major R. Wilberforce, *The Indian Mutiny: Two lectures delivered at the Southampton Athenaeum* (London: Bosworth & Harrison, 1858)

Bourchier, Colonel George, *Eight months' campaign against the Bengal sepoy army, during the mutiny of 1857* (London: Smith Elder & Co., 1858)

Browne, John Cave, *The Punjab and Delhi in 1857: Being a Narrative of the Measures by which the Punjab was saved and Delhi recovered during the Indian mutiny* (Edinburgh: William Blackwood and Sons, 1861)

Chenoy, Shama Mitra (ed.), *Delhi in Transition, 1821 and beyond* (Mirza Sangin Beg's *Said-ul-Manazil*) (Oxford University Press, 2017)

Chick, Noah Alfred, *Annals of the Indian Rebellion 1857-58* (Calcutta: Sanders, Cones & Co, 1859)

Cooper, Frederick, *The crisis in the Punjab from the 10th of May until the fall of Delhi* (London: Smith, Elder and Co. 1858)

Coopland, R. M., *A Lady's escape from Gwalior and life in the fort of Agra during the Mutinies of 1857* (London: Smith Elder and Co., 1859)

Daly, Hugh, *Memoirs of General Sir Henry Dermot Daly* (J. Murray, 1905)

Dodd, George, *The history of the Indian revolt, and of the expeditions to Persia, China and Japan 1856-7-8* (London: W. and R. Chambers, 1859)

D'Oyly, Sir Charles, *Eight months' experience of the Sepoy revolt in 1857* (Blandford: Henry Shipp, 1891)

Dunlop, Robert Henry Wallace, *Service and adventure with the Khakee Ressalah or, Meerut Volunteer Horse during the mutinies of 1857-8* (London: Richard Bentley, 1858)

Fanshawe, H. C., *Shah Jahans' Delhi - past & present* (Delhi: Sumit Publications, 1902)

Fanshawe, H. C., *Delhi, Past and Present* (Delhi: John Murray, 1902)

Flinders, Stuart, *Cult of a Dark Hero* (London: IB Tauris, 2018)

Forrest, George W. (ed.), *The Indian Mutiny 1857-8: Selections from the letters despatches and other state papers preserved in The Military Department of The Government of India 1857-58* (Calcutta: Military Department Press, 1893)

Forrest, George W., *Sepoy Generals: Wellington to Roberts* (Cambridge University Press, 1901)

Garrett, H. L. O., *The trial of Muhammad Bahadur Shah* (National College of Arts, reprinted 2003)

Grant, Sir James Hope, *Incidents in the Sepoy War, 1857–8, Compiled from the Private Journals of General Sir Hope Grant* (London: W. Blackwood, 1873)

Greathed, H. H., *Letters written during the siege of Delhi* (London: Longman, Brown, Green, Longmans & Roberts, 1858)

Griffiths, Charles John, *A narrative of the siege of Delhi with an account of the mutiny at Ferozepore in 1857* (London: John Murray, 1910)

Gubbins, Martin Richard, *An account of the mutinies in Oudh and of the siege of the Lucknow Residency; with some observations on the condition of the Province of Oudh and on the causes of the mutiny of the Bengal Army* (London: Richard Bentley, 1858)

Harcourt, Capt. A., *The New Guide to Delhi* (Meerut: A. David & Co., 1870)

Hodson Revd George H. (ed.), *Twelve years of a soldier's life in India being extracts from the letters of the late Major W.S.R.Hodson* (London: John Parker and Son, 1859)

Holmes, Thomas Rice, *A history of the Indian mutiny: and of the disturbances which accompanied it among the civil population* (London: WH Allen & Co., 1891)

Hunter, Sir William, *The Indian Musalmans* (London: Trubner and Company, 1872)

Husain, Iqbal, 'Bakht Khan - A leading sepoy general of 1857', *Proceedings of the Indian History Congress*, Vol. 46 (Indian History Congress, 1985), pp. 373–386

Husain, Iqbal, 'Fazle Haq of Khairabad - a scholarly rebel of 1857', *Proceedings of the Indian History Congress*, Vol. 48 (Indian History Congress, 1987), pp. 355–365

Ireland, William Wotherspoon, *History of the siege of Delhi by an officer who served there* (Edinburgh: Adam and Charles Black, 1861)

Islamuddin, Shaheen, 'Legalizing the plunder in the aftermath of the uprising of 1857: The city of Delhi and the Prize agents', *Proceedings of the Indian History Congress*, Vol. 72 Part 1 (Indian History Congress, 2011), pp. 670–682

Jones, Kenneth W. (ed.), *Religious Controversy in British India: Dialogues in South Asian Languages* (New York: State University of New York, 1992)

Kaye, Sir John & George Bruce Malleson, *The History of the Indian Mutiny of 1857-58*, Vol. 2 (London: Longmans, Green and Co., 1896)

Kaye, M. M. (ed.), *The Golden Calm: An English lady's life in Mogul Delhi* (New York: Viking Press, 1980)

Khan, Sir Syed Ahmad, *The causes of the Indian revolt* (Benares: Medical Hall Press, 1873)

Knollys, Henry (ed.), *Life of General Sir Hope Grant: With selections from his correspondence* (Edinburgh: W. Blackwood and Sons, 1894)

Laird, M. A. (ed.), *Bishop Heber in Northern India: Selections from Heber's journal* (Cambridge University Press, 1971)

Leckey, Edward, *Fictions connected with the Indian Outbreak of 1857 exposed* (Bombay: Chesson & Woodhall 1859)

Lumsden, General Sir Peter S. & George R. Elsmie, *Lumsden of the Guides* (London: John Murray, 1899)

Lunt, James (ed.), *From Sepoy to Subedar: Being the Life and Adventures of Subedar Sita Ram, A Native Officer* (Macmillan, 1988)

Mackenzie, Col. A. R. D., *Mutiny Memoirs: Being personal reminiscences of the Great Sepoy revolt of 1857* (Allahabad: Pioneer Press, 1891)

Mackenzie, Mrs Colin, *Life in the mission, the camp, and the zenana or six years in India*, Vol. 2 (New York: Redfield, 1853)

Majendie, Lt Vivian Dering, *Up among the pandies, or, a year's service in India* (London: Routledge, Warne and Routledge, 1859)

Malleson, George Bruce, *The mutiny of the Bengal Army: An historical narrative* (London: Bosworth and Harrison, 1857)

Marshman, John Clark, *The history of India from the earliest period to the close of Lord Dalhousie's administration*, Vol. 2 (London: Longmans Green Reader & Dyer, 1867)

Masselos, Jim & Narayani Gupta, *Beato's Delhi 1857 and beyond* (Penguin, 2011)

Metcalfe, Charles Theophilus, *Two native narratives of the Mutiny in Delhi* (London: Archibald Constable & Co, 1898)

Murray, John, *A handbook for travellers in India, Burma, and Ceylon* (Calcutta: John Murray, 1911)

Muter, Mrs, *My recollections of the sepoy revolt (1857-58)* (London: John Long Ltd, 1911)

Napier, Lieutenant-General Sir Charles James, *Defects, civil and military of the Indian Government* (London: Charles Westerton, 1853)

Nizami, Syed Khwaja Hasan, *The agony of Delhi (Delhi ki Jan Kuni)* (Delhi: Lanand Thakur & Sons, 1922)

Norman, Sir Henry Wylie & Mrs Keith Young, *Delhi-1857, The siege, assault and capture as given in the diary and correspondence of the late colonel Keith Young* (London: W. & R. Chambers, 1902)

O'Callaghan, Daniel, *Scattered Chapters of the Indian Mutiny: The Fatal Falter at Meerut* (Meerut: Army and Navy Co-operative Society, 1897)

Osborne, A. E., *Some recollections of a Sepoy officer between 1844 to 1858* (Calcutta, 1872)

Owen, Sidney, *India on the eve of the British conquest* (London: Wm. H. Allen, 1872)

Palmer, J. A. B., *The Mutiny outbreak at Meerut in 1857* (Cambridge: Cambridge University Press, 1966)

Pearson, Hesketh, *The hero of Delhi* (London: Penguin, 1948)

Pfander, Revd C. G., *Remarks on the nature of Muhammadanism* (Calcutta Baptist Missionary Press, 1840)

Pfander, Revd C. G., *The Mizan Ul Haqq* (London: Church Missionary House, 1866)

Pollock, Arthur William Alsager, *Colburn's The United service Magazine and Naval and Military Journal 1857*, Part 2 (London: Hurst and Blackett, 1857)

Reid, Sir Charles, *Extracts from letters and notes written during the siege of Delhi in 1857* (Henry S. King & Co., 1951)

Roberts, Earl Frederick Sleigh Roberts, *Forty-one years in India from subaltern to Commander-in-Chief* (New Delhi: Asian Educational Services, 2005)

Rotton, John Edward Wharton, *The chaplain's narrative of the siege of Delhi from the outbreak at Meerut to the capture of Delhi* (London: Smith, Elder and Co., 1858)

Sachdeva, Krishan Lal & Krishna Lal Sachdeva, 'A study of Europeans' inscriptions in Delhi (1782-1857)', *Proceedings of the Indian History Congress*, Vol. 19 (Indian History Congress, 1956), pp. 355–367

Savarkar, Vinayak Damodar, *The Indian War of Independence of 1857 by an Indian nationalist* (London, 1909)

Seaton, Major-Gen. Sir Thomas, *From Cadet to Colonel: The record of a life in active service*, Vol. 2 (India: Hurst and Blackett, 1866)

Singh, Ajit, 'Jind State and the sepoy mutiny of 1857', *Proceedings of the Indian History Congress*, Vol. 46 (Indian History Congress, 1985), pp. 387–392

Singh, Dr Ganda, *The Indian Mutiny of 1857 and the Sikhs* (Delhi: Gurdwara Parbandhak Committee, 1969)

Smith, R. B., *Life of John Lawrence* (London, 1883)

Stewart, Col. Charles E., *Through Persia in disguise with reminiscences of the Indian Mutiny* (London: George Routledge & Sons, 1911)

Taylor, Bayard, *A visit to India in the year 1853* (London: G. P. Putnam & Co., Sampson Low, Son & Co., 1855)

Taylor, Thomas, *Memoirs of the life and writings of the Right Reverend Reginald Heber, D.D. Late Lord Bishop of Calcutta* (London: John Hatchard and Son, 1836)

Thompson, Edward, *The other side of the medal* (London: The Hogarth Press, 1925)

Thornhill, Mark, *The personal adventures and experiences of a magistrate during the rise, progress and suppression of the Indian Mutiny* (Cambridge University Press, 1884)

Trotter, L. J., *The Life of John Nicholson, Soldier and Administrator* (London, 1898)

Varma, Pavan K., *Ghalib the man the times* (New Delhi: Penguin, 1989)

Vibart, Col H. M., *Richard Baird Smith, The leader of the Delhi Heroes in 1857* (Westminster: Archibald Constable & Co., 1897)

Wagentreiber, Florence, *Reminiscences of the sepoy rebellion of 1857* (Lahore: Civil and Military Gazette Press, 1911)

Wagentreiber, Elizabeth Florence, *The Story of Our Escape from Delhi in May, 1857, from personal narrations by the late George Wagentreiber and Miss Haldane* (Delhi, 1894)

Wigram, Francis Spencer, *Mutiny at Meerut 1857-58* (Southampton: Crabniton Industrial School, 1858)

Wilberforce, Reginald G., *An unrecorded chapter of the Indian Mutiny, being the personal reminiscences of Reginald G. Wilberforce* (London: John Murray, 1894)

Dehlvi, Zahir, *Dastan-e-ghadar (The tale of the mutiny)* (Gurgaon: Penguin Books, 2017)

# Index